ROUTLEDGE HANDBOOK OF POLITICS AND TECHNOLOGY

This handbook provides a comprehensive global survey of the politics of technology. Written by an outstanding line-up of distinguished scholars in the field, the handbook covers all aspects of the relationship between politics and technology including:

- demand and support for new technologies and innovation by the state;
- the effects of technology policies;
- technology development and innovation difference between various countries and regions;
- policy instruments and techno-industrial innovation;
- dynamism and change as outcomes of government policies;
- driving forces for science and innovative development;
- skills, education and human capital.

Forming the basis of this handbook are examples of regional development, country studies and a rich variety of technologies, as well as topical issues such as divergent political interests in relation to technology and the economic exploitation of technologies. Employing a comparative and interdisciplinary approach in order to analyse the interplay between government activities and the development of new technologies, this handbook will be an invaluable resource for all students, scholars and practitioners working in the politics of technology, public policy and policy analysis.

Ulrich Hilpert is Professor of Comparative Government at Friedrich Schiller University Jena, Germany. He is also Fellow of the Academy of Social Sciences (AcSS), visiting professor at a dozen universities in Europe and the US, Chairman of the IPSA Research Council on Science and Politics, and consultant to the EU and a number of national and regional governments, labour unions and business organisations.

ROUTLEDGE HANDBOOK OF POLITICS AND TECHNOLOGY

Edited by
Ulrich Hilpert

Routledge
Taylor & Francis Group
LONDON AND NEW YORK

First published in paperback 2018
by Routledge

First published 2016
by Routledge
2 Park Square, Milton Park, Abingdon, Oxon OX14 4RN

and by Routledge
711 Third Avenue, New York, NY 10017

Routledge is an imprint of the Taylor & Francis Group, an informa business

British Library Cataloguing in Publication Data
A catalogue record for this book is available from the British Library
Library of Congress Cataloging in Publication Data
Routledge handbook of politics and technology/edited by Ulrich Hilpert.
pages cm
1. Technology and state – Case studies. 2. Technological innovations – Political aspects – Case studies. I. Hilpert, Ulrich, 1951–
T49.5.R68 2015
303.48′3–dc23
2015009768

ISBN: 978-0-415-69201-4 (hbk)
ISBN: 978-1-138-60901-3 (pbk)
ISBN: 978-1-315-72523-9 (ebk)

Typeset in Bembo
by Florence Production Limited, Stoodleigh, Devon, UK

CONTENTS

FIGURES

TABLES

CONTRIBUTORS

Sharmistha Bagchi-Sen is Professor of Geography at the State University of New York-Buffalo. Her research has focused on innovation in bio-pharmaceuticals and biofuels. She is also interested in industrial shifts and urban-regional development.

Paul M.A. Baker, PhD, is Senior Director, Research and Strategic Innovation, with the Center for Advanced Communications Policy (CACP) at Georgia Institute of Technology. He is also a Principal Research Scientist and holds an Appointment by Courtesy with the School of Public Policy, at Georgia Tech. He is Adjunct Professor at the Centre for Disability Law & Policy at the National University of Ireland, Galway. He is currently researching institutional change and innovation in higher education, the role of policy in advancing technology and universal accessibility goals for people with disabilities; the operation of communities of practice and online communities in virtual environments, and state and local government use of information and communication technologies (ICTs). He has served as chair of the Rehabilitation Engineering Society of North America's (RESNA) Government Affairs Committee, and as a member of the executive committee of NARRTC (National Association of RRTCs). He has published in a number of journals, and serves on the editorial boards of ten journals.

Nicola Bellini is Professor of Economics and Management at the Institute of Management of the Scuola Superiore Sant'Anna (Pisa, Italy – currently on leave), and Director of the La Rochelle Tourism Management Institute at the Groupe Sup de Co, La Rochelle (France). He is author and editor of books and articles on industrial policy, local and regional development, business support services and place branding.

Saradindu Bhaduri teaches at the Centre for Studies in Science Policy, Jawaharlal Nehru University, New Delhi, India. His research interests include unorthodox economic analyses of technology, innovative behaviour, regulatory institutions and technology policies.

Alberto Bramanti is Associate Professor of Applied Economics at Bocconi University, Milan. He works in the Department of Policy Analysis and Public Management (PAM) and CERTeT – Centre of Research on Regional Economics, Transport and Tourism.

Shiri M. Breznitz, an economic geographer, specializes in innovation, technology, and regional economic development. Her research is at the critical intersection of theory and policy to fit the new realities of globalization. Professor Breznitz's work has informed policy making at the local, national, and international levels. She has advised on the role of universities in the larger story of innovation, on the economic impact of biotechnology, and on the role of clusters in driving innovation. Professor Breznitz's latest book, *The Fountain of Knowledge* with Stanford University Press (July 2014), analyses universities' relationships with government and industry, focusing on the biotechnology industry as a case study. Additional work by Professor Breznitz has been published in *Regional Studies*, *Canadian Journal of Regional Science*, *Economic Development Quarterly*, *Journal of Product Innovation Management*, and *The Journal of Technology Transfer*.

Christopher Briem is a research specialist in the program for Urban and Regional Analysis at the University Center for Social and Urban Research (UCSUR) at the University of Pittsburgh. His research focus is on economic development policy, regional economic competitiveness and the processes of post-industrial transformation including the interaction of population migration and industrial change.

Keith R. Bujak is a Senior User Experience Engineer at the John Deere Technology Innovation Center. His current research includes advanced training simulators, mobile and wearable apps, and human-robot systems. He also has research and design experience with massive open online courses, instructional design, and mobile learning. Keith received a PhD from the Georgia Institute of Technology in engineering psychology and a BS from Rensselaer Polytechnic Institute in mechanical engineering and psychology.

Xiangdong Chen has been a full professor at Beihang University since 2000, in the fields of international technology transfer and innovation studies, in particular, patent based technology competition in the Chinese market. He used to be a visiting scholar at Manchester Business School in the early 1990s while he was conducting an international technology transfer survey of 58 British companies in the UK, and later on he did similar studies of German companies in Germany in the early 2000s. He and his research team have concentrated on evaluation of intellectual property and patented technology in particular; in these fields he has conducted four NSFC (Nature Science Foundation of China) projects, one key research project supported by China Social Science Foundation, and an IDRC project from Canada, all related to patent studies. He has published more than 80 research papers in international journals, book chapters, international conferences, and Chinese academic journals. He has been invited to present research works in a number of important international conferences and workshops on innovation and IP systems, and has also been invited for collaborative research projects with overseas scholars and lectures in training programs for graduate students on technology management and programs related to IPRs, in the US, Germany, Netherlands, Sweden, Finland, Japan, Korea, Brazil, and other countries and districts.

Anica Liu Chang has recently published short stories and novels based on Singapore's history. She won two literary awards by National Arts Council of Singapore, with Green Mango Romance for the 2nd Prize, Short Story (Chinese), Golden Point Award 2015, and Photography for the 3rd Prize, Short Story (Chinese), Golden Point Award 2017.

Sherwin Ignatius Chia is Head of Programme (Human Resource Management) and Senior Lecturer, Singapore University of Social Sciences.

Sunyang Chung received his PhD from the University of Stuttgart in Germany. After this, he worked at a Korean governmental research institute, Science and Technology Policy Institute (STEPI) for several years. He also worked at the Fraunhofer Institute for Systems and Innovation Research (ISI) in Karlsruhe, Germany. He was a distinguished visiting professor at the Haas School of Business, University of California at Berkeley and also at the Graduate School of Business, Stanford University. In March 2009, he established the William F. Miller School of MOT (Management of Technology), Konkuk University in Seoul, Korea and has been serving as Dean of the Miller MOT School. He is also a Professor of Technology Management and Policy at the Department of Technology Management of the William F. Miller School of MOT. In November 2002, based on his excellent research and education performance in technology management and policy, he was selected as a permanent fellow of the Korean Academy of Science and Technology (KAST), and since September 2008 he has been serving KAST as director of its Policy Research Center. His main research areas are technology management, S&T policy, regional innovation, innovation theory and sustainable development.

Willie Donnelly is President of Waterford Institute of Technology (WIT). He was previously Vice-President for Research, Development & Innovation at WIT. With a PhD in Experimental Physics from University College Dublin, he is Director of the Telecommunications Software and Systems Group (TSSG), a world class research mobile service and communications management research centre. Prior to entering academia he worked for 15 years in the telecommunications and utilities industries. He founded the Telecommunications Software & Systems Group (TSSG) at WIT in 1996, which has grown from three to 120 people and has received over €80M in competitive funding. He has positioned the TSSG as one of Europe's leading research centres in the Future Internet program. The TSSG has established a cluster of High Potential Start-up companies in mobile services at its research centre at Arclabs. He is a founding member of spin-out companies FeedHenry and Zolk C.

Alexander Ebner is Professor of Political Economy and Economic Sociology at Goethe-Universität Frankfurt, Germany. His research interests include industrial and technology policy, comparative economic systems, and regional economic development.

Cornelia Fraune is working as a postdoctoral researcher at the Institute of Political Science at the Technische Universität Darmstadt, Germany. Her research interests include Energy Policy, Political Participation, and Gender Relations.

Robert Hassink is Professor of Economic Geography at Kiel University in Germany and Visiting Professor in the School of Geography, Politics & Sociology at Newcastle University, UK. After receiving his PhD in 1992 from the University of Utrecht, the Netherlands, he worked at several research institutes and universities in the Netherlands, Germany, Norway and South Korea. He has considerable research experience in regional innovation policies, industrial restructuring and regional economic development in countries in Western Europe and East Asia.

Simon Hegelich, PhD, is managing director of the interdisciplinary research centre 'Shaping the Future' (FoKoS) at the University of Siegen, Germany. His main field of research is political data science. He has published in (among others) *Policy Studies Journal*, *German Politics*, and *Der Moderne Staat*.

Stephan Heinrich studied political science, law and geography at the University of Marburg and received his PhD at the University of Duisburg. Until 2008, he was a member of the research group polikon at the Rhine-Ruhr Institute for Social Research and Policy Consulting at the University of Duisburg. Since 2008 he has been working for Prognos AG Basel/Berlin. As project manager at Prognos, he currently works on topics at the intersection of innovation policy, research and technology promotion.

Desmond Hickie has researched and published about public policy and high technology industries, in particular aerospace, for many years. He is an Emeritus Professor of the University of Chester, where he was the founding Dean of the Faculty of Business, Management and Law. He is a researcher and management consultant.

Ulrich Hilpert is Professor of Comparative Government at the University of Jena. His main areas of research are comparative studies in technology, innovation, regional development, global networking and skilled and university trained labour. He is Fellow of the Academy of Social Sciences (AcSS) and chairman of the IPSA Research Council on Science and Politics. He has been visiting professor at a dozen universities in Europe and the US, and consultant to the EU and a number of national and regional governments, labour unions and business organisations.

Xiaohui Hu is a PhD candidate in economic geography at the Department of Geography, University of Kiel, Germany. His doctoral project is sponsored by China Scholarship Council (CSC). His research interests lie in the fields of evolutionary and institutional economic geography with a particular focus on the restructuring of old industrial areas in transitional China.

Peter Kedron is a Professor of Geography at Ryerson University, Ontario. His research has focused on the landscapes of renewable energy. He is also interested in spatial statistics, environmental justice, and urban-regional change.

Iryna Kristensen, MSc, is a Doctoral Researcher at SCEUS – Salzburg Centre for European Union Studies, University of Salzburg, Austria.

Helen Lawton Smith is Professor of Entrepreneurship, Department of Management, Birkbeck, University of London. Her research career has focused on the links between entrepreneurship, innovation, public policy and regional development in national and international contexts. She is the Founder and Research Director of the Oxfordshire Economic Observatory, School of Geography and the Environment, Oxford University (http://oeo.geog.ox.ac.uk) and is Director of the Birkbeck Centre for Innovation Management Research (http://bbk.ac.uk/innovation). She is the author of nine books and of over 90 journal articles and book chapters and is Associate Editor, *Strategic Change: Briefings in Entrepreneurial Finance*.

Xiaming Liu is Professor of International Business at the Department of Management, Birkbeck College, University of London. He received his BA and MPhil from Anhui and Fudan Universities respectively in China and his PhD from Strathclyde University in the UK. Before joining Birkbeck in January 2006, he had held various academic and management positions in Shanghai and Hang-Zhou (now Zhe-Jiang) Universities in China, and Abertay Dundee, Aston and Surrey Universities in the UK. Prior to becoming an academic, he had many years' agricultural and industrial experience in China. His research interests include foreign direct investment, technology transfer and spillover, innovation and economic development.

Connie L. McNeely, PhD, is Professor of Public Policy at the School of Public Policy, George Mason University (USA), where she is also Co-Director of the Center for Science and Technology Policy.

Ronald W. McQuaid is Professor of Work and Employment at the Management, Work and Organisation Division, Stirling Management School, University of Stirling, UK.

Sami Mahroum, Director of INSEAD Innovation and Policy Initiative, has a PhD in the Social Studies of Innovation from the German Armed Forces University in Hamburg, an MSc in Science and Technology Dynamics from the University of Amsterdam, and an interfaculty BSC degree in Political Science and Development from the University of Oslo, Norway. He is the Director of IIPI, a post he has held since March 2010. Prior to that he was a Senior Analyst with the OECD in Paris and a Visiting Reader at Birkbeck College, University of London. He was also Research Director at the UK leading and only innovation oriented agency NESTA. He is also a member of the WEF Global Agenda Councils on Education and Skills. Over the course of his career, he has worked as a researcher and advisor on innovation policy in Austria (at the Austrian Institute of Technology), Canada (Ontario Government), France (OECD), Holland (TNO and RAND), Spain (European Commission think tank), Switzerland (University of Neuchatel), and the UK (University of Manchester and NESTA). As a result he has published widely in this area and on various policy-related themes ranging from innovation governance, measurement and policy at the national level to brain-drain and skills and learning issues. His writings and publications appeared in peer-reviewed journals as well as in broadsheets such as the *Financial Times* and *Business Week*.

Pedro Marques is a Research Associate at Cardiff University, working on smart specialisation and EU innovation policy. He has done research in Portugal, the UK and Germany, on various topics related to regional development, innovation and the role of institutions in enabling or hindering economic growth. He has worked previously at the University of Kiel in Germany and at Newcastle University in the UK, where he also got his PhD in Economic Geography.

Emanuela Marrocu is Associate Professor of Econometrics at the Department of Economics and Business, University of Cagliari and Crenos, Italy. Her main research interests are spatial econometrics and productivity analysis at regional and firm level; tourism determinants and the growth effects of the tourism industry; time series econometrics and forecasting evaluation.

Xin Niu graduated from the School of Economics and Management, Beihang University. While she was studying for her PhD degree in technology innovation and regional innovation management, she was doing research and published three important papers in Chinese journals on regional innovation. She is now working at Beijing Aeronautical Science and Technology Research Institute of Commercial Aircraft Corporation of China. Her current areas of research are in strategic management on technologies in enterprises.

Bill O'Gorman is Director of Research at Waterford Institute of Technology's (WIT) Centre for Enterprise Development and Regional Economy (CEDRE). His research focuses on entrepreneurship, enterprise policy, developing entrepreneurial regions, and examining linkages between multinational corporations and indigenous enterprises. Prior to joining University College Cork, in 2000, where he taught entrepreneurship, he qualified as an engineer in industrial electronics, and accrued over 27 years of industrial experience working in several multinational corporations and as managing director of his own electronics sub-contract company. Bill retains links with the business community, through research and mentoring entrepreneurs; he is a director of the South Eastern Business Innovation Centre

(SEBIC), and the Dungarvan Enterprise Centre, a member of the Enterprise Development Team of the South Tipperary Chambers of Commerce, co-founder of the Irish Network for Teachers and Researchers in Entrepreneurship (INTRE), non-executive board member of a number of SMEs, and serves on a number of government round-tables for enterprise policy, development and education.

James M. Ohi worked at the National Renewable Energy Laboratory (NREL) in Golden, Colorado, from 1978 to 2008 in technical, analytic, and management capacities for a number of technology development programs, including those for amorphous silicon photovoltaic materials, wind energy, buildings technologies, transportation systems, and hydrogen energy. At NREL, he also served as a project team leader for advanced fuel cell R&D and as a principal investigator on renewable energy technology deployment to mitigate global climate change. Before joining NREL, he worked for the Governor of Colorado's Land Use Commission on energy and environmental regulation and for county and city agencies in Colorado and California on environmental and land-use planning and regulation. He earned a BS in chemistry and a MA in English at the University of California, Los Angeles, and a MA and PhD in International Studies at the University of Denver, Graduate School of International Studies, with a focus on environmental and energy science and technology policy.

Raffaele Paci is full Professor of Applied Economics at the Department of Economics and Business, University of Cagliari and Crenos (Italy) and Jean Monnet Chair of 'Regional Economic Integration in the European Union'. His main research interests are tourism economics, innovative activity and externalities, spatial spillovers, and regional growth.

Cecilia Pasquinelli is a post-doctoral fellow at the Gran Sasso Science Institute, L'Aquila (Italy). She previously worked in the Dept. Social and Economic Geography at Uppsala University, Sweden. She received her Ph.D. in Management, Competitiveness & Development from Scuola Sant'Anna (Italy). Her research interests include place branding, local and regional development, and urban tourism.

Oliver Pfirrmann, PhD, studied political science and economics in Bonn and Berlin; in 1991 followed his dissertation and 2007 respectively his habilitation at the Free University of Berlin. After graduation he was researcher at the Fraunhofer Institute for Systems and Innovation Research (ISI), Karlsruhe, from 1990 project manager at VDI/VDE-Information Technology GmbH, Berlin in the field of technology analysis, from 1995 coordinator of a research and consulting group at the Free University of Berlin; with research in the US and Austria. From 2006 to 2012, he was head of unit at Prognos AG Basel/Berlin. Currently he is head of department at the National Academy of Science and Engineering in Germany. He has published a series of essays and monographs on new technologies, innovation policy and funding and teaches regularly at the Free University of Berlin.

Ainurul Rosli is a lecturer in Entrepreneurship, Creativity and Innovation at University of Wolverhampton Business School, UK. She worked for several years with the R&D arm of a telecommunication company in Malaysia as well as a consultant for two London based firms. Her research interests focus on university–industry relationship, knowledge transfer strategies, innovation activities of firms and entrepreneurship.

Federica Rossi is lecturer at Birkbeck (School of Business, Economics and Informatics), University of London, UK. She has worked as a consultant for the OECD, the UK's Strategic Advisory Board for Intellectual Property, the EC/Eurostat and regional and local development agencies. Her research interests focus on the economics and management of intellectual property rights, innovation activities of firms and networks of firms, the economics and governance of the higher education sector, science and technology policy.

Walter Scherrer is Associate Professor at the Department of Economics and Social Science, University of Salzburg, and Salzburg Centre for European Union Studies, University of Salzburg, Austria.

Eva Schindler studied political science and economics (BA European Studies, MPA Public and Economic Policy) at the University of Passau, the Pontificia Universidad Católica del Ecuador, the London School of Economics and the Institut d'Études Politiques in Paris. During and after graduation, she worked as a freelance consultant for the French energy company Electricité de France, carrying out two studies on nuclear safety regulation in Europe and the USA. Since November 2009, she has been working as a consultant at Prognos AG Basel/Berlin. Her work focuses on innovation policy studies, particularly the evaluation of public support programs for innovation and technology policies.

Laurie A. Schintler, PhD, is Associate Professor of Public Policy at the School of Public Policy, George Mason University (USA), where she is also Associate Director of the Centre for the Study of International Medical Practices and Policies.

Art Seavey is a Program Officer with the Bill and Melinda Gates Foundation. He focuses on investing in traditional and startup higher education institutions, pursuing new business models to dramatically improve access and success for at-risk learners.

Vijai Singh is Professor of Sociology and Associate Chancellor at the University of Pittsburgh. His PhD is from the University of Wisconsin, Madison. His current research interests include social stratification and mobility and the study of sociology of science, specifically the comparative study of the processes of production of scientific knowledge in the US and Western Europe.

Li-si Song graduated from the School of Economics and Management, BeiHang University. Her major area of research while she was reading for her PhD degree was science and technology innovation and urban innovation systems. She is now working as an assistant researcher at FangDi Institute of Economic Development in Beijing. She is also working at China Association of Invention (CAI), mainly engaged in technology transfer and commercial adoption and transformation of emerging technologies, and related issues on intellectual property protections, and training programs on technology innovation.

Joseph S. Szyliowicz is a Professor at the Josef Korbel School of International Studies, University of Denver. He is the recipient of various awards including the University's Distinguished Service Award and the Burlington Northern Foundation award for outstanding scholarship. He has served as a consultant and reviewer to many US governmental agencies including the National Science Foundation and the Office of Technology Assessment and as Chair of the International Political Science Association's Science, Technology and Public Policy Research Committee. He has published extensively on various aspects of technology policy, sustainable development, political change, and transportation security.

Lai Si Tsui-Auch is an Associate Professor of strategic management in the Nanyang Business School at the Nanyang Technological University, Singapore. She obtained her PhD degree in Sociology–Urban Studies from Michigan State University, USA. Prior to her appointment in NTU, she worked as a research scientist at the Social Science Research Center (WZB), Technological University of Berlin, Germany. Her research interests include the state–capital relations, innovation in Asia, corporate governance reforms and institutional change.

Stefano Usai is Professor of Applied Economics at the Department of Economics and Business, University of Cagliari, and the Director of CRENoS (Center for North-South Economic Research), Italy. His main research interests concern regional and development Economics and the Economics of technological change.

Rupert Waters is Research Fellow at the Centre for Innovation Management Research at Birkbeck, University of London, Research Associate at the Oxfordshire Economic Observatory and a local government officer in Buckinghamshire, UK. His research focuses on the role of labour market in high productivity local economies.

PREFACE

The subject of new technologies is fairly new to political science and also to other social sciences or economics. It is still a very young area of research. The increasing importance of new technologies for both problem solving (e.g. energy supply, environmental problems or better pharmaceuticals) and socio-economic development (e.g. new industries and enterprises, modernization of traditional industries, new areas of employment) meets a key societal expectation of modern governments – i.e. to foster development through government policies. Thus, policies are discussed and there is an impression that these are no longer questions of interests and ideologies but a technocratic competition to find the best solutions. Indeed, looking at technologies divergent interests are not always immediately apparent. But, when we are aware of the different political positions taken towards global warming, environmental protection or employment opportunities, it becomes obvious that there are different interests, and that there are different ideological positions that favour one or the other policy.

Policies are based on political decisions and, thus, they are related to majorities and interests. It is particularly interesting to see both that such interests are hiding behind technocratic arguments and that these particular interests are associated with government policies. Once such decisions are made and certain policies are realized, processes of development become politicized – although they may appear as regional rationalities, matters of collaboration or the availability of skilled and university trained labour etc. These few indications may already make the reader alert to a situation where political science demands close correspondence and the exchange of findings with other academic disciplines. Thus, the research on new technologies and innovation will transcend the traditional orientation of political science and will have to enter new areas of research using findings from other disciplines – and it will provide for an interdisciplinary approach that makes the contribution of political science to research on new technologies significant. Because of the relationship with other disciplines this handbook includes quite a number of contributions from scholars with a background in economics, sociology or geography. This may help to better understand this area of research and while deepening this understanding it allows the interdisciplinary area of exchange of ideas, findings and interpretation to be entered.

This particular understanding of political science, as a contribution to scientific research in collaboration with other disciplines, also includes different traditions in research and different styles in presenting research findings and analysis. It is among the aims of this book to indicate that there are many opportunities to both link with cross-disciplinary research and contribute useful findings. The recognition of valuable research findings from an audience across different disciplines may encourage researchers to present their findings in the tradition of their individual disciplines, in the confidence that they will receive wider attention. Because there are different areas of research, disciplines and traditions included in this volume, this fosters a fresh understanding of certain new phenomena in a new and different context – and it will lead to new research questions, answers and understandings. This is also an intention of this book. It may be pointed out here that this is an intermediate state that shall be followed by further research and a deeper understanding of political science concerning the subjects of new technologies and innovation.

The reader may use this handbook in different ways.

1 It may be used in the way it is presented. The handbook may allow readers to have both (i) a systematic understanding on the role of government science, innovation and technology policies, and (ii) a comparative view on such policies. While realizing these aims, it covers a number of fundamental issues where there is a scientific analysis focused on how science, technology and innovation correspond and integrate; but it also takes into account *where* this may be achieved and what opportunities exist for locations where top-research is not based. Highly skilled and university trained labour, processes of continentalization and reference to a globalizing world, up-and-coming new countries and locations, are all discussed.

 Additional information indicates where particular, individual processes of development are involved; including individual technologies, as well as individual countries, continents or up-and-coming new locations and countries. These chapters of the handbook will help to provide further information that complements the above mentioned, more systematic, overview, as well as helping the understanding of the particular countries or locations, in the light of the framework and overviews discussed earlier. Chapters on methods and methodology are meant to draw attention to this point as it is fundamental to research and will demand further engagement as the research may become more complex in future.

 The handbook may serve for researchers, as well as for MA- or PhD-seminars. A wide selection of contributors helps to intensify discussion with the scientific community in this area of research, as well as allowing the readers to contact scholars in the area of research in which they may have a particular interest.

2 The book is broadly oriented towards comparative research. Although technologies may be understood under a particular common label, activities in different countries and regions, or by different researchers, academics or enterprises, may vary widely and may refer to particular areas of expertise. New technologies differ a lot according to the capital or the human labour required and they also differ according to research structures and the available industrial opportunities to apply such new technologies. A comparison between technologies allows the identification of divergences between technologies, and may help the reader to understand that the specificities of individual technologies need to be taken into consideration.

 Since the development of new technologies has to be understood as a collaborative process, where the participants contribute and exchange their competences and opportunities, a comparison between technologies helps one to identify and analyse similarities and systematic relationships, despite the divergences between technologies (e.g. concerning capital demanded and opportunities to build Islands of Innovation). This indicates the situation of individual technologies, and, using the chapters of this book, may provide some ideas to understand how contributors to collaborative networks may benefit from such processes although they themselves are rather small and they may lack the support of strong industrial structures.

3 The development of new technologies and high-technology based socio-economic development demands a wide selection of variables. Industrial structures, research capabilities and human capital are important elements to induce such processes. But, there are, in addition, other indicators that obviously matter. Regional concentration tends to be important for both a participation in continental or transcontinental networks and for synergy across different technologies or for merging competences. Using the wide range of information presented here about individual technologies and processes of regionalization and continentalization, there is an opportunity to identify certain general conditions for innovation and development.

   Thus, regional concentration, networking and development build an understanding of how different elements help to introduce the innovative processes that induce the development of new technologies. This indicates the contribution of labour, capital and locational factors, and also indicates the windows of opportunity that clearly point out both what scientific and technological processes are under investigation and that time matters a lot to understand the development process. It also helps an understanding of why there are divergences among apparently similar innovative situations, and why they may differ over time.

   Here, again, the different chapters can help to provide information to begin developing a more systematic view on processes of innovation.

No matter which way this book, or the individual chapters, are used by the reader, it will refer to the role and the opportunities of political decisions, interests and government policies in the development of new technologies and their innovative exploitation. The individual chapters will indicate the demand for such political support and the systematic relevance of such support to achieve effective participation in new technologies – although the precise circumstances of participation may vary widely. Hence, this diversity may become noticeable to the reader and can be understood in a systematic way, and so may also be used as a basis for further investigation. Certainly, more research is needed and clearly, political science with an interdisciplinary orientation can collaborate with other disciplines and can make substantial contributions.

This is also the place to thank the authors for their contributions which emerged through a rather unusual procedure. During seven workshops in Berlin, Pisa, Oxford, Atlanta and Pittsburgh a process of constant exchange of ideas, suggestions and revisions was the basis of this book. The intensive discussion provided the basis for both fresh contributions and further research and workshops. Due to the close collaboration among the participants additional research and publications are already under preparation under the umbrella of the International Political Science Association (IPSA), Research Council 11 on Science and Politics, and the Standing Group on Politics and Technology associated with the European Consortium of Political Research (ECPR). Finally, indeed the important and enabling grant by the Hans-Böckler-Foundation, Düsseldorf, covering the costs of the workshops, travel expenses and organization, needs to be recognized. This generous funding of the workshops allowed for a highly productive and constructive discussion, and for collaboration among the authors and, of course, with the editor. This generous grant enabled the personal exchange of ideas and learning from different disciplines and contributions, as well as informal contact. Hence, it provided for the basis of future joint research.

Ulrich Hilpert, Berlin 2014

1

CHANGING OPPORTUNITIES IN GLOBAL AND REGIONAL CONTEXTS

The relationship between politics and technology

Ulrich Hilpert

Technologies are related to everyday life, and to the future of socio-economic development, as well as to urgent or pressing problems. Electronics help to make life easier. Biotechnology or genetic engineering may help to overcome diseases. New energy technologies provide for the efficient use of resources and climate protection. Environmental technologies may help to reduce the contamination of soil, air and water. New materials may help to improve existing products, or new transportation systems may allow for cheaper, more efficient and environmentally 'greener' travelling. Many technologies or technological improvements also help to modernize industries and products and keep these industries innovative. Since modern nation states are expected to provide policies that allow for economic growth, prosperity, employment, and a sound environment, government policy makers are confronted with changing policy needs of increasing complexity. Still, political parties and different social interests are put into competition during elections, and they aim to convince the electorate with their political programmes and their demands of policy makers.

Thus, government policies aim both to meet the interests of the electorate and to induce processes of development that satisfy the expectations of important interest groups. While the interests of the different groups are divergent, and even contradictory, implemented government policies are not simply responses only to the actual situation, but also indicate whose interests are provided for best. Nevertheless, among different interest groups in highly industrialized Western countries there is a strong interest in such new technologies that allow for new products and markets and provide higher value added, as well as for higher incomes and wages. Since global warming has become a major issue, in particular in Europe, technologies that help to solve this problem are experiencing active political attention. New energy technologies, fuel efficient cars or alternative engines, changes in metropolitan transportation, and new materials that reduce weight are being developed.

While these situations differ between countries, and even within countries between regions and locations, policies vary a lot. But still a strong focus is oriented on technologies and their innovative application. Government policies are strongly debated and disputed – concerning their effects and their effectiveness in achieving the aims set for them. Often, of course, such policies are discussed as if countries, regions or large and dynamic metropolises are in a position both to control such processes and to address the existing situation. Nevertheless, such processes of innovative development and new technologies are decreasingly addressed to a single country but instead there are collaborative processes that emerge. Even the dominant position of the US in leading edge research and new technologies does not put the country into a situation to achieve such processes independently. They are embedded in networks across countries and continents, and the country as well as its Islands of Innovation finds itself in a position that privileges it for the participation and exploitation of new findings, new knowledge and new processes. European countries are even more closely related to collaborative networks and the exchange of knowledge and competences – and all these countries participate as long as they can and are prepared to contribute. Thus, technology policies and the fostering of scientific research and university education becomes an important policy field (Chapter 16) and it clearly refers to both localization and worldwide collaboration with partners who can provide leading edge capabilities, findings, competences and labour force.

New technologies and processes of techno-industrial innovation clearly cover a variety of spatial dimensions and require particular situations to be developed and to flourish. It requires government action if such policies are needed, but they will not be successfully implemented everywhere in a national territory. Consequently, such policies are related to the locations that can provide appropriate opportunities for leading edge research, highly creative personnel and industries that can apply new findings for economic exploitation. Such policies are inhibited by a particular geography of both innovation and scientific research because such new technologies follow from new findings and new knowledge (Chapter 6 and 12). Consequently, national research and technology policies are related to regional processes and policies, which are effective on a regional or even metropolitan level. Thus, it is the generation of leading edge research that underpins a particular policy related geography, as well as the application or exploitation of such research results that create a policy related geography (Chapter 20).

On the other hand, scientific breakthroughs are generated by small research groups that possess the necessary competences, and search for collaborators to exchange knowledge and to engage in joint research projects. Such research is frequently uncertain until it reaches the point where the breakthroughs are realized, published and widely accepted. The more successful such research strategies are, the more research opportunities and research projects will follow from this situation, demanding more researchers and the exchange of knowledge. These situations clearly cannot be established in a single region, and even large nation states in Europe or even the US are not equipped to undertake such research and innovation strategies on their own (Trippl 2012). Thus, based on individual local or regional situations the exchange of knowledge and findings reaches out across borders building continuous networks of collaboration in research and even in economic exploitation (Chapter 19). While the concentration of leading edge research indicates territorial divergences that emerge as Islands of Innovation, simultaneously, these Islands of Innovation provide the basis for collaboration across borders. International or even global networks of innovation are built and continue collaboration among locations with outstanding competences. As a consequence, new technologies based on such leading edge research is de-nationalized and based on global networks of Islands of Innovation (Chapter 2). Such locations are prepared to contribute appropriately to these outstanding networks; and it is this regional or metropolitan participation in the global body of knowledge that helps to build the national capabilities for high technology industries.

This outstanding importance of Islands of Innovation provides for a relationship between national R&T policies, regional participation and societal opportunities, and global networks of collaboration. In addition, national and global networks provide for a globally growing body of knowledge that is also applied nationally or locally. This aim can be realized on the basis of policies that facilitate engagement in techno-scientific research and the building of such Islands of Innovation. Thus, techno-scientific competences and processes of innovation are based on previous political decisions (Chapter 3). In general, societies have different opportunities and the divergent profiles of their political programmes indicate the priorities they have chosen. Decisions taken in favour of solar technologies or environmental technologies clearly relate to political majorities that were present in particular societies (Chapter 23). This is particularly visible in Western democracies. In addition, such democratic decisions again vary between governmental systems. This is particularly obvious, when it comes to centralist vs. federalist countries. Sub-national governments of federalist countries (e.g. Germany or the USA) can design and realize their individual strategies that suit the situation and the existing interests of social and political groups from their region. Nevertheless, even in non-federalist countries and outside of Western democracies such processes of regionalization can be identified. This refers to small countries (e.g. Singapore, Ireland or Denmark) and regions in newly emerging innovative locations (e.g. China) (Chapter 12, 13 and 18). Since processes of technology development, leading edge research and innovation demand a concentration of competences and capabilities, regional patterns emerge – and recognition of such concentrations is related to such patterns. Branding becomes an important issue (Chapter 5) and it clearly refers to existing innovative clusters, highly skilled labour and science–industry relationships (Chapter 6, 19 and 22). Such constellations need to be arranged but they also need to be identified and brought to global attention.

When taking these phenomena into account there is a strong relationship with innovative labour and its habits of research, engineering and migration (Criscuolo 2005: 1352; Breschi and Lissoni 2009: 442). Since such kinds of highly trained labour provide the basis for techno-industrial innovation, a concentration in particular regions or metropolises, and their orientation towards centres of scientific excellence (Mahroum 1999: 382, 2000b: 374; Williams *et al.* 2004: 39) puts Islands of Innovation and countries that contain such locations into a privileged position. Thus, regions and metropolises are of particular analytical interest as phenomena of innovative processes since almost all innovative processes and technology developments are related to leading metropolises. It is their particular situation and the opportunities they provide that enable them to participate in new technologies and innovation. Focusing on existing and newly emerging Islands of Innovation or innovative metropolises in different countries or located on different continents provides methods to indicate similar processes and to get closer to the generalization of processes and variables that are necessary to participate in continental networks of collaboration and innovation. Again, the empirical findings vary systematically along with different technologies and rationalities of innovation. While biotechnology and new pharmaceuticals demand high amounts of capital and access to markets, new software may be developed based on less capital and virtual market access through internet opportunities. Consequently, the general process of both innovation and the development of new technologies may be identified in divergent expressions, but it demonstrates the role of government, divergent political interests and spatial patterns of regionalization and continentalization.

Taking these processes and the spatial variations into consideration indicates the interplay of different polities with different interests in particular policies (Chapters 8 and 20). In addition, regional or local situations, and their embeddedness into continental or global networks of collaborative innovation, provide highly divergent opportunities concerning different technologies. Thus, the analysis of the relationship between politics and government policies on the one hand and new technologies and innovation on the other hand, demands complex analysis that takes these multiple interplays into account (Chapters 28, 29, 30 and 31). A better understanding of processes of innovation helps to identify the role of government; and a deeper look into the situations when governments launch policies helps a better understanding of the particular interests underpinning particular policies (Chapter 23). Politics rarely come along as direct influence taken but become obvious when the situations and opportunities on different levels of government or governmental systems are taken into account (Chapter 20). A comparative view helps to identify the role of interests and ideologies. Such an analysis clearly takes advantage of other disciplines and indicates the contribution of an interdisciplinary approach when the role of modern governments in advanced socio-economic development is under investigation. Since capable governments that find themselves in proximity to leading edge research institutions, creative academics and knowledge workers, innovation oriented enterprises and industries, and globally or continentally oriented locations can launch highly divergent programmes in different policy fields. The variety of perspectives is related to systems, cultures and aims, and it disseminates before being identified as complementary contributions to a process that relates closely to government activities – or even relies on them. The fact that governments regard new technologies and processes of innovation as means to fulfil their role in a changing situation and to solve emerging problems makes them become major players concerning a process that is of fundamental importance for the future of the society and economy.

Strategies and politics: the role of government

Role of government – emerging technological powers

New technological opportunities are inseparably tied with modern capitalism and industrialization. Technological breakthroughs in shipbuilding and sailing allowed overseas trade and in relation with modern weapons it provided for the expansion of European colonialism. Steam engines and railroad systems allowed for highly efficient manufacturing and transportation. Systematic scientific research provided the basis for growing both a country's wealth and individual incomes; governments played an important role in supporting such changes by improving transportation systems and expanding universities and polytechnics (Kuhn 1996). There were, of course, also problems associated with such changes as energy supply, environmental impacts, diseases and the supply of highly trained or university educated labour. Still, today one can identify more efficient or new energy technologies, green technologies that protect from pollution of air, water and soil. There are more efficient transportation systems, new pharmaceuticals etc. Thus, there was a growing demand for new technologies in manufacturing and for problem solving. A better knowledge of such problems and how to avoid them led to increased interest in new technologies, and simultaneously political interests and regulation created markets for new technologies that were considered to help in overcoming such problems (e.g. catalysts in automobiles or filter systems to avoid pollution). Clearly, public policies had an opportunity to achieve both problem solving and socio-economic development.

The history of modern shipbuilding or steam engines, of course, also indicate that such modernization may become mature, and may become firmly established at locations that were not industrialized before. Electronics industries are a much more recent example which also points out that time is an important factor when it comes to socio-economic development (Chapter 3). People at other locations learn how to make use of technologies and there may emerge cheaper places to manufacture products (Chapter 15 and 26). While the transformation of former Third World countries into Newly Industrialized Countries (NICs) has introduced a fundamental change in structures of world trade (Chapter 25), it also indicates that new technologies that meet a need and their markets will provide the basis for both new industries and modernization of existing industries when merging traditional competences with new technologies (Chapter 11; Sable *et al.* 1991). Advanced mechanical engineering, precision engineering, medical instruments, plant construction etc. was made possible due to new technologies, new materials and new scientific findings. New products provide opportunities for higher value added and allow for both higher profits and higher incomes. Government policies thus find themselves in a situation, where policies become more closely related with technologies, innovation and universities – public support of research, technologies and education became an important issue to continue economic growth, employment and the growth of high incomes (Chapter 9, 14 and 16). As governments in leading Western countries engaged increasingly in support of scientific research and the development of new technologies, processes of innovation became closely related with political decisions.

The continuing transfer of mature technologies from Western industrialized countries to countries that were not manufacturing industrial goods before, simultaneously transferred competences and know-how to these countries (Chapter 12, 13, 15 and 26). Multinational enterprises, in addition, were greatly interested in exploiting cheap labour forces and weak regulation to increase their profits when transferring both equipment and competences to such countries; and, of course, they continue to be interested in these newly emerging markets and opportunities to manufacture high end products at low cost (e.g. Apple products manufactured in China). A growing stock of capital from low cost manufacturing and the idea of the developmental state has put these countries into a position both to design and to follow a path of improvement of the quality of their products and to strengthen their capabilities in scientific research. The role that government played during the rise of Japan (Johnson 1982) to become a major player in industrial goods and high tech products providing showed that there are opportunities for fast socio-economic development and to link up with the most developed countries. High tech products need not be a reserved market for some European Countries and North America. There are obviously opportunities for additional countries to participate in such attractive markets and sectors.

While the processes are different, there is again an involvement of government policies and of particular interests that aim at a continuing modernization of economy, industry and society (Chapter 25). The model referenced is generally the Japanese Ministry of International Trade and Industry (MITI) which has strongly coordinated the strategies of industrial development and technological innovation (Johnson 1982). This outstanding role has diminished as Japan has reached a similar economic level to the leading industrialized countries. In addition, Japan was strong in some technologies and industries; the country showed a clear pattern of specialization and still does. Similarly, strategies of industrialization of the other Newly Industrialised Countries of East Asia indicate clear patterns of specialization. Since these countries do not exploit natural resources they aim at higher value added products. After the early periods of industrial development and economic growth, the national capabilities and capital available was concentrated on selected sectors. This allowed a small country such as Singapore, which simultaneously is a metropolis, to invest substantial amounts into modern technologies and technological research such as solar energy, micro-electronics or biotechnology (Chapter 13). Faced with a limited territory, Singapore also had to focus on industries and sectors that do not demand a lot of space but are high values added. Strong investments in education and research, and international recruitment of personnel for the national university, helped the location to become a strong and innovative place in Southeast Asia. Recognized expertise and excellence helped it to link with partners from the established centres of leading edge research in Europe and North America. Government policies induced the change and served the interests of the local industry and capital supported by strong activities for place branding to spread the information about the changes in and the capabilities of Singapore.

Similarly, Korea, a former poor Third World country, found its path to industrialization, knowledge intensive products and a major place of micro-electronics challenging the leader in international markets (Chapter 15). Strong positions in shipbuilding and automobile industries paved the way towards a modern industrial structure. In addition, national investments in education built a labour force based on a high percentage of university educated young personnel, as a basis for new technology oriented industries. There was a growing population, as in Asia in general, and simultaneously an increasing proportion of highly skilled personnel, and a fundamental improvement in the capability of the labour force in just a few decades. As industrial centres were developed, and competences were concentrated on competitive sectors, technologies and places, both contributions to and participation in networks of new technologies have emerged during the recent decade.

Political strategies were important to create a path towards more innovative industries applying opportunities of research and new technologies. Universities became instruments for sustainable development and put the location on the map of new technologies. The concentration of research and university teaching is identifiable in these countries as an opportunity for both building a strong location based on a recognizable body of knowledge and expertise, and participating in networks of collaboration (Chapters 12, 13, 15, 19 and 26). While in a country such as Korea key enterprises such as Samsung play an important role in the realization of such aims, in China these are state owned companies and joint ventures that perform as the main economic actors in innovation. Again similarly to capitalist newly emerging economies, in China also the level of education, the available skilled labour force and the innovative competence of both the region and the company play an important role for future development and Foreign Direct Investment (FDI) (Chapter 12). Thus, divergent patterns of regional development that have emerged in Western industrialized countries and that continue through innovation, can be identified clearly in these countries and relate to the government policies of an entrepreneurial state (Chapter 25). Central governments' policies are fundamental both to successful processes that build new and major technological actors (e.g. Samsung) and to regional disparities. Thus, although government policies might have an effect on the interests of business and, in addition, also provide higher incomes and better standards of living, they cause problems for regions lagging behind (Chapter 8), which can neither engage in technological research or innovative industries nor develop appropriately skilled and educated labour. Clearly, such policies are oriented in the interests of locations that meet these necessary conditions, and are based on the expectation that this focus might serve the development of the entire country.

Role of government – leading Western countries

Although the process of politics and policy making in leading Western democracies might be fundamentally different from East Asian countries – no matter whether these are representative democracies or non-democratic, authoritarian systems – nevertheless, in Europe and the US, governments and their political strategies play an important role for innovation and new technologies. While in centralist countries such as the United Kingdom or France central governments play the key role, even in federal countries such as the US or Germany (where regional governments of individual states or Länder are responsible for local universities), national programmes on technologies and scientific research indicate the outstanding role of politics and policies. Research universities or public research institutes receive strong funding once they have managed to compete successfully for the funding provided (Chapter 9 and 16). While continuing success in acquiring such funding will strengthen these institutions, they simultaneously provide the new knowledge, important findings and university trained labour that are demanded by new technologies and modern industries.

National technology programmes – complemented by those of the European Union for member countries – provide the funding required and enable participation in innovative development and new technologies; in federal countries this is complemented by the interplay between different levels of government (Hilpert 1992, 1998). This highlights a changing role of universities that emerged during recent decades, transforming universities and public research institutes into instruments of government policies. Capable regional governments also were placed in a situation to apply these instruments and to take advantage of the commercialization of scientific findings on their territories. Such opportunities are particularly strong where regions can also provide the personnel required. While university trained labour is frequently taken into consideration, one needs to be alert to the fact that manufacturing rather complex technological products does also demand highly skilled blue collar labour (Chapter 24), which allows for a rich variety of strategies concerning the application of new technologies for both new and traditional products (e.g. mechanical engineering, medical instruments, precision engineering, measurement apparatus). Regional governments that have the capability to design and establish appropriate educational systems are prepared to facilitate the creation of situations that suit the needs of highly dynamic enterprises and act as high technology locations.

Based on such regional government opportunities, there are situations that allow regional interests to organize and these regional interest groups influence technology development and participation in such processes. According to the directions of socio-economic change and cultural divergences such interests might be highly divergent although the technology in question might be identical (Chapter 20 and 24). Thus, technology policies may refer to different strategies because of influential and effective politics, interests and ideologies. Understanding technology policies in Western democracies indeed includes taking into account such processes as well as divergent polities and political structures. Nevertheless, policies play an important role in all Western democracies when it comes to new technologies. Public policies and capable programmes for particular technologies or areas of research are fundamental to the leading position of countries. The US, Germany, the UK or France as well as the EU, spend substantial funds and support new technologies,[1] whereas Italy as another highly industrialized Western democracy clearly lags behind concerning both public policies and new technologies (Morano-Foadi and Foadi 2003: 2–3; Marginson 2006: 26). Public spending strengthens innovative activities or even provides the basis for such processes, which in return helps to increase patenting records (Chapter 7). In addition, strong areas of research benefit from networking and the available global body of knowledge (Chapter 19) and Foreign Direct investment (FDI) which help to transform knowledge into socio-economic development and to strengthen economic capabilities (Chapter 12).

Despite the differences between Western democracies and authoritarian countries, similar patterns and phenomena can be identified. Government policies are fundamental for regions to appear on the map of innovative locations and as locations that relate to outstanding competences in particular technologies. This allows for branding to make regional competences known to potential customers or partners in technology development (Chapter 5). Regional concentration of public funding thus changes the technology map due both to the appropriate structure established and the regional opportunities, which can give particular advantage to metropolises but also may provide opportunities to rural regions (Chapter 20). Consequently, the international geography, as well as the regional geography, of the emergence of a new industry clearly relates to government policies and the governmental system existing in different countries. Such highly divergent technological opportunities and different areas of expertise at different locations in a country demand highly specific policies and the most appropriate implementation. For a long period in innovation research, it was suggested that partners in innovation would be clustered and concentrated at a particular location. In science based development it became clear that the development of new technologies is different and often based on collaboration among partners who are intellectually close but geographically far apart. This was the debate about the importance of proximity. Thus, today it has become clear that there may not be sufficient competence in the scientific research and the development of new technologies at any one particular location. This means that in the development of new technologies proximity is not common nor is it achievable.[2] However, in leading edge research the feeling of working closely on joint research projects is widely achieved virtually by electronic means, international travel and knowledge exchange (Chapter 19 and 28). So, physical proximity is replaced by the internet and air travel. As a consequence, policies cannot simply be spatially focused. They must support participation in these almost virtual communities, which are linked through networks but are based in well informed and capable public research institutions. Federalized countries such as the US or Germany are placed in a situation where national programmes can be both applied to an existing situation and complemented by sub-national policies (Chapter 17). Federal countries, as a consequence, develop a richer variety of Islands of Innovation than centralized countries such as France or Britain, and, in addition, clearly indicate that the political impact on the regional geography of innovation can become highly influenced by the governmental system (Chapter 9 and 20) even when the technology and the product in question are converging.

In Western democracies it is clear that government policies are fundamentally important to new technologies and innovation. In addition, the implementation of such policies matters widely and indicates the opportunities and the effectiveness of political decisions and funding with regard to such modern roles of government. National and regional, or local, interests concerned with new technologies meet when regional centres of excellence are prepared both to contribute to a global body of knowledge and to participate in it, so that these resources can be exploited for economic development. A strategy of specialization can help even small countries to participate in expensive processes of techno-industrial innovation (Chapter 13 and 18) despite different political systems. The aim of emerging as an important knot in the global network, and the search for partners in such processes, allows a transfer of knowledge, an exchange of expertise and a joint exploitation of such opportunities regardless of the political system of a country. Similarly to large countries[3] (Chapter 22), small countries can adopt distant capabilities (Chapter 7) and provide opportunities in the need to create a synergy across different regions and despite their non-proximity.

While aiming at such processes, particular situations and opportunities are important and can be arranged through government policies. When building Islands of Innovation, a concentration of public and university research provides attractive labour markets for young scholars as well as star scientists (Avveduto 2001: 1; Khadira 2001: 45; Meyer *et al.* 2001: 309; Williams *et al.* 2004; Ackers 2005: 105; Laudel 2005; Regets 2007: 15; Trippl 2012). Attractive jobs and opportunities for top research are instruments both to link with networks of knowledge and to exchange findings in collaborative research projects that help to recruit the creative labour. This builds technological and scientific competences as a basis for technological synergy and allows divergent applications and specialized technologies (Hilpert 2012). Thus countries can take advantage of new scientific findings that suit the opportunities of existing industries. Such a complementarity of industries, new enterprises and leading edge research takes advantage of existing market positions for the economic exploitation of new technologies. Government policies are important to arrange for such complementary situations, as can be learned from the relationship between nano-technology research and opportunities of industrial application in the US, Germany and Korea (Chapter 19 and 22). Such regionalized innovative labour markets allow for the accumulation, distribution and exchange of personnel and embodied knowledge which indicates that such magnets of science (Mahroum 1999: 382; 2000b: 374; Williams *et al.* 2004: 39) and Islands of Innovation are providing both appropriate policy instruments and opportunities for branding (Chapter 5) to make a global audience alert to these capabilities.

Universities act as an instrument for the realization of both top research and the production of graduates and postgraduates as future knowledge workers. Such opportunities are in the interests of national governments as well as regional or metropolitan development. At locations of top research the most innovative findings are generated, and are available to the regional or local economies as well as contributing to national innovation. Strong participation in networks of collaboration and the exchange of highly innovative labour (Chapter 19) provides for a continuation of such competitiveness, or they help new locations to emerge. Some Asian metropolises are examples of such changes and are new contributors to a global body of knowledge. National and sub-national policies both become particularly effective when they provide for a participation in continental processes of innovation and technology development (Chapter 2). In relation to internet opportunities universities are also changing their role, becoming global providers of education and competences. Internet programmes make available competences and degrees from top universities although the internet students are geographically far away (Chapter 16). Such distribution of knowledge may also make universities an even more interesting instrument for national policies addressed towards university trained labour. It may even allow for skill improvement at locations or regions outside of countries and regions that participate in innovative networks of institutions of top education. Nevertheless, the unavailability of internet and computer equipment or of a reliable supply of electricity, again, can exclude some regions from participation.

Concerning the interplay between research universities, excellent university trained labour and some state of the art communication technology clearly indicate that participation in new technological and innovative development will continue a clear concentration on countries and locations where sufficient capital exists that can be invested into brains, infrastructure and research projects. Once governments control appropriate budgets, research universities can be established as linkages and contributors to technological development, new research-based enterprises will emerge and their socio-economic effects will be based on exploitation of patents and findings related to previous government policies. Appropriate government policies that take into consideration the wide range of divergent policies are also fundamental in leading Western countries and continue to be required to meet the processes of both new technologies and techno-industrial innovation. Although democratic processes and decision-taking play a fundamental role for providing such funding and institutional support, which make such processes possible, it is interesting that these decisions are made and that these countries are still the leading countries in new technologies and the most dynamic innovation.

Policy travelling and politicization of policies

While there is the focus on the development of new technologies and their linkages with public research institutions, universities, higher education and the application of new findings and technological opportunities with new or improved products, it needs to be borne in mind that such new technologies are meant to be applied for particular purposes and situations (Chapter 14, 19, 20, 21 and 22). Energy technologies, biotechnologies, genetic engineering or communication technologies are meant to help find a solution concerning energy demand and supply, to follow a path in plant and animal breeding, to provide for new or better pharmaceuticals, or to allow more efficient transfer of data and improved collaboration. New technologies are not the purpose of such policies rather technologies are expected to provide appropriate technological solutions in different policy fields. The cases of federal environmental and energy policies in the USA clearly indicate the role of both new technologies and areas of innovation (Chapter 23). Due to the demand for new energy sources and the aim to have a better environment, there was both the introduction of new regulations and support for solar energy technologies.

Sometimes scientific findings were applied and new technologies would be developed and were then applied to solve policy problems that were not directly technology policy issues (e.g. environmental policies or the demand for new energy resources or the modernization of traditional industries). While new technologies were developed and more policy fields became involved in the entire process, governments and political decisions became fundamental for many areas of society and economy. Enterprises started to produce such technologies and contribute to technology-based economic development and new areas of employment for skilled and university trained labour emerged (Hilpert and Lawton Smith 2012; Singh and Briem 2012). Similarly the development of nano-technology was based on fundamentally new research findings that introduced new applications in a variety of industries (Chapter 22). This relationship of technology policies with industrial policies is clearly seen in the different policy aims of industrial modernization in Korea, the USA or Germany. It indicates that technologies and technology policies become related when technologies and techno-scientific research are considered to contribute fundamentally to achieving an aim defined from other policy areas. But, even more than this, there are other interrelated policy fields that make sure that the skilled labour and university degree holders are available. Thus, high level education policies and university teaching in the fields of high-technology industries' needs become important issues of government policies and build particular relationships of policies with new technologies. In addition, the constantly increasing demand for top-scientists leads to policies that aim at the immigration of such personnel to the country and so contribute to its technological development. Government policies are important when such highly specific labour markets are created based on research and technology policies, public funding and research institutes. Attracting scientific and high-technology labour to a country's research institutes and universities will strengthen capabilities to develop new technologies or to participate in a global body of knowledge (Chapter 19). Thus, technology policy is clearly related with such particular labour market initiatives, which allow participation in leading edge research and development.

It clearly indicates that new technologies and techno-industrial innovation cannot be understood without taking the process of innovation in different areas of economy, industry, society or environment into consideration. While taking into consideration such expectations of technological solutions and influences from other policy fields, it becomes clear that neither new technologies nor processes of innovation can be understood exclusively in the light of techno-scientific rationality. There are clear links between health services and new pharmaceuticals based on genetic engineering or biotechnology research in developed welfare states. There is a clear link between government, environment and industry when it comes to renewable energy (Chapter 20). Also in the case of solar energy, a relationship between technology policy and policies towards climate change and environmental problems of fossil energy consumption, the interplay is clear (Chapter 23). While there is the search for technological solutions to problems emerging from a variety of different situations, it is also clear that in Western market economies such demand for new technologies creates new markets. Government regulations and research and technology policies, consequently, serve socio-economic development and thus achieve the aims of modern governments' policies in Western democracies. While this provides the impression of purely rational departmental policies, a decision to support solar energy and to improve photovoltaic cells is based on particular interests that manage to organize majorities in democratic decision making institutions (Chapter 23). The emergence of a new industry highlights the role of government in socio-economic development but it also indicates that there are opportunities to choose from. New technologies, thus, are also to be considered in relation to particular decisions taken that exclude other techno-industrial paths of development. When a presidential administration in the US launches such a programme that supports a new industry, it clearly refers to particular goals that may be part of a political controversy.

Thus, what appears as rational public policy concerning both environmentally sound energy generation and a contribution to fight climate change, illustrates the particular role of the presidential administration in the US and such programmes clearly relate to particular interests and ideologies and indicate how politics are transformed into individual policies. Similarly, there are policies on technologies that indicate the interplay between ideologies, interests and socio-economic opportunities (Chapter 14) but they provide the impression of a rational public policy rather than interest driven decisions – although there are clearly such interests involved and served.

Public recognition of such situations and policies is used for branding (Chapter 5) which indicates particular opportunities but hides the interests that they are based on. In a global context, where innovation is built upon collaboration, exchange of knowledge and synergy of divergent competences, such orientations of public policies and the competences based on them will find both attention and eager collaborators to help advancing technologies that are based originally on political decisions and ideologies. Diverging interests and ideologies may foster different technologies that are suitable to meet the opportunities within the current global situations. When merging across regions, countries and continents branding, driven by interests, helps to disseminate an impression of rational processes and political decisions. When understanding the role of politics with regard to new technologies, it is important to understand the strategic role of technologies in achieving certain policy aims that, in the end, are the products of particular ideologies, interests and politics.

Such differences in politics and ideologies can be identified when national government policies are implemented regionally. Divergent opportunities for application and the divergent paths of new technologies allow choices that may suit particular interests. The example of biofuel production and refineries in the US demonstrates the full picture of problems in energy supply that requires a technological solution and divergent technological opportunities to achieve such aims (Chapter 20). New technologies and technology policies respectively are expected to help solving a problem that emerges in energy supply policies and climate change. Since it takes place in agricultural locations and involves refining crops, the federal structure of the US also allows for divergent policies in different US states. There are large enterprises and refineries, and there are also smaller producers and cooperatives refining the crops. Influenced by different ideas, ideologies and interests, both technological paths, of course, indicate new opportunities that have clear consequences for research, education, industry, training etc. When paying attention to such differences within a common national government programme and the budget for individual technologies, it becomes clear that such decisions may relate to particular rationalities and technological opportunities, but the basis of the decisions and the consequences that follow from them characterize future development (Chapter 31). Although it is not visible from the technology or the socio-economic development based on such new opportunities, it clearly relates to underlying politics or ideologies. Thus, research on the impact of technologies always indicates the role of government policies for future development by preparing a suitable structure. Neither technologies, nor socio-economic development, nor impact on climate is independent of politics and ideologies. Divergent paths taken within a system and even within the same programme indicate political opportunities and the ideological content of policy outcomes – and show how intensively these impacts condition the structure of future developments.

Understanding technology and innovation policies, and the broad impact of government clearly necessitates taking such impacts into consideration. Since ideology and politics often play an important role these need to put into any account of mission oriented innovation policy and investigations what the aims of policies are (Chapter 9). Thus, the desire to solve problems in different policy areas on the basis of new technologies, and setting policy goals aimed at socio-economic development, employment, clean environment or climate protection, often become fundamental drivers for technology policies, in particular, when politicians want to be re-elected. As the examples of national programmes and divergent regional applications indicate, such orientations can be effective *on all levels of government and in all policy fields* when technology or innovation policies are concerned. The more a macro level of both policy design and goal setting are linked to appropriate micro level policy implementation, then the more will divergent interests impact upon these processes. Such collaborative political activities reflect intergovernmental relations within the different governmental systems, and put emphasis on the polity, and what opportunities such polities allow for sub-national governments to adjust national programmes according to their local situations, or to launch regional programmes that suit their particular situations. Flexible polities, which provide wide opportunities to sub-national governments, will be put into a situation that allows for divergent politics, but, in addition, they can both reflect and take advantage of regional, local and metropolitan levels. These, of course, are regionally influenced by variations in culture, society or governmental structures (Chapter 6 and 10) and can mutually take advantage of their situations while contributing to the national development aims.

Thus, technology policies as well as innovation policies indicate the role of politics as well as polities. In a situation where opportunities, cultures and societies vary within a national territory, it becomes obvious that the interplay between the different governmental levels and the relationship with different policy fields provides a systematic analysis. The national potential for problem solving through new technologies allows for increased opportunities of political activities, and capable sub-national governments can help to draw on divergent areas of synergy for development and create a richer variety of solutions. A discussion about technologies, innovation and appropriate policies, of course, shapes the reference to politics, ideologies and cultures; but it also indicates the far reaching impact of these policies for current problems and future opportunities. Since new technologies and divergent processes of innovation become apparent it also points to the richness of different contributions, which may suit individual regional, local or metropolitan situations. The relationship between national and sub-national governments may become a vital element of technology development, application and innovation, which is to be understood in the light of such political, governmental and sociocultural situations.

Regionalization of techno-industrial innovation and changing government opportunities

Embedded innovation and an emerging landscape of technologies

Processes of scientific research and techno-industrial innovation are necessarily bound to particular territories or locations. New findings are generated by researches in particular institutes at certain locations. In addition, the more such research is characterized by the collaboration of research teams, the more there is a demand for a sufficient number of personnel working on projects. International recognition for particular competences and a branding as an outstanding location (Chapter 5), in general, requires a certain agglomeration of competences and expertise. Traditions in outstanding research and a long-lasting reputation as a leading center of expertise helps to create such findings and helps them to be well publicized, and so reinforces the location's position as a place requiring attention, and as one in which to search for partners of collaboration, because they will contribute expertise and reputation. While having gained such international notice as a magnet for science, governments can make use of such locations and Islands of Innovation, because the institutions located there on the basis of collaborative networks will have access to a continental and global expertise that contributes to the existing body of knowledge and assists the country's processes of innovation.

While taking advantage of such reputation and branding technology policies consequently refer to such patterns of regionalization, no matter whether these are countries that are traditionally leaders in science and technology or whether these are NICs. Funds will be directed towards the researchers at leading institutes based at particular locations, and government policies will aim at continuing or building such centres, because this provides an instrument for participation in both a global body of knowledge and most advanced processes of innovation and development. What can be recognized as patterns of regionalization and regional participation is the expression of successful processes of innovation in a country, which take into account that this is a highly collaborative process that allows a wide range of opportunities to contribute and participate in new findings and developments. Regionalization becomes an instrument of technology and innovation policies and refers to the rationality that is evident in collaborative processes of leading edge research and techno-industrial innovation. Thus, it is obvious that governments aim at such centres, and it is even particularly clear that regional governments and small countries aim to benefit from such tendencies for regionalization (Chapter 6). Locations or regions that have such highly recognized expertise in particular areas of leading edge research or new technologies will provide the basis for both regional and national participation, although the available budgets for funding are clearly limited. Collaborative research networks integrate a rich variety of competences contributing to the final process and technology and expressing specific opportunities and areas of technological and industrial strength. Thus, patterns of specialization and reference industries become noticeable that can transform knowledge into individual and outstanding products and, based on this, they will allow for advanced socio-economic development, despite a lack of scale. A concentration on certain technologies, or on selected areas of leading edge research, indicates the territorial dimension of innovation and technology development, which enables these locations to play their role in transcontinental networks as well as in national processes and for the benefit of the region by becoming important contributors and participators in such processes.

Open economies and global or continental networks of collaboration (Chapter 2 and 19) allow both a contribution to and participation in a global body of knowledge that expands permanently through new research findings. These findings are predominantly generated at these locations and re-emphasize and continue their role and position, as can be seen in the importance of Islands of Innovation for both the developments within the networks, where the global body of leading edge knowledge is widely concentrated, and in the national processes of innovation, which uses the Islands of Innovation to take advantage of knowledge shared among the network contributors. Thus, building such strong research locations allows a visible contribution and indicates the important and instrumentality of regions for processes of innovation and for participation in it. It also provides the evidence of branding (Chapter 5) that makes leading institutes, academics and enterprises alert to positive opportunities for collaboration. During such collaborative projects there is more than synergy to achieve new findings, because there is also an exchange of knowledge, expertise and research strategies, which mutually widens competences at participating locations and continues to make them different from locations without such capabilities or on a lower level of technological innovation. While this demands sufficient budgets and the regional concentration of funding, it also allows for smaller countries, emerging industrial countries or NICs to link up with the most attractive processes of socio-economic development through techno-scientific specialization (Chapter 13 and 18). Although small countries are incapable of providing large budgets for new technologies and expensive research programmes, they can concentrate their funding while specializing in particular areas to make certain locations recognizable as knots in a global network of collaboration (Chapter 15).

While small countries demonstrate similarities with regions in larger countries, there are still important differences to be identified when paying attention to the regional or metropolitan level. In larger countries, Islands of Innovation play an intermediate role to transfer the global body of knowledge to the national situation. This is particularly the case in strongly federalized countries (e.g. the US or Germany). They also benefit from the country's concentrated, large budgets and thus indicate clearly the opportunities that emerge when different governmental levels are involved while they relate to the effective budgets of each. The national programmes of leading industrialized countries provide funding for many different areas of research and technologies, and allow regions to specialize based on their own opportunities and policies. They can also prepare opportunities for particular locations and may make use of regional government budgets to prepare for successful regional competition for national funding (Hilpert 1992, 2003; Hickie 2006). Such divergent regional profiles add up to a full national profile in scientific research and technology development. While small countries have to decide on specialization, large countries can launch wide programmes which will be complemented and adjusted by regional government policies. This allows for a variety of regional strategies and even the politics and the ideologies, that are fundamental to regional strategies might be different from those prevailing at the national level, which supplies the funding. There is a rich diversity of regional policies derived from different interests, politics and ideologies (Chapter 6 and 20) that contribute to the general national policy goal.

Such divergent technology applications and different processes of technology based regional development form a national picture that includes plenty of opportunities for future development. Regional policies and strategies, thus, are more than just processes of regionalization. The variations both contribute to national policies and suggest a wide variety of technological opportunities. Even a single federal policy can generate divergent effects within different regional situations when applying a single technology. This also helps to create a better and deeper understanding of the role of EU technology policies, and funding of regional participation in technological innovation even for locations in a small country or for a region in a large country. Such funding can help to integrate locations and regions into a continental context (Chapter 2). This clearly indicates that regions are not only locations where such processes take place, but they are also places where new knowledge is produced that contributes to an inter-regional body of knowledge. Regions that belong to such continental networks of course benefit from knowledge and competence based at other locations (Chapter 7). Variations also form divergent patterns of continental constellations (Chapter 24). Regions are both elements of networks and locations where processes of development can be identified.

These diversities also reflect both divergent situations and divergent interests. Highly innovative small- and medium-sized enterprises, and leading edge universities, have different interests from those large enterprises, which are not strongly engaged in research based products; interests of multinational enterprises differ from those oriented in national markets; and market driven processes are clearly different from those that are driven by government procurement. Technological solutions, applications of existing technologies, and new technologies that refer to the socio-economic opportunities, clearly vary and they clearly receive public support to serve different strategies and to achieve technological targets. When there are alternative opportunities to choose from, one can find politics is influential on decision making which then takes particular interests into account (Chapter 20 and 23). As the examples indicate, national government policies can generate divergent regional processes of innovation and technology development – and a large country or a continent that has a rich variety of regional situations will benefit from a large number of technological opportunities and innovative processes that also reflect the relationship between its politics and the policies chosen.

Thus, the technology and innovation policies of regions clearly must vary because they are designed for particular situations and constellations of interests and opportunities. A match of public policies and private interests helps to address public funding to make private enterprises become effective multipliers when it comes to the economic exploitation of new technologies and new applications. This orientation converges with ideas to vitalize private capital to initiate new development when applying the policy instrument of public–private partnership (PPP) (Chapter 17). In particular on a smaller sub-national level PPP tends to provide an appropriate instrument for regional innovation and research and development policies, because both sides of the funding equation reflect the existing political and economic situation, and draw support to possible regional opportunities. Such concepts allow for strategies that again contribute to a rich variety of technological diversity among the regions and locations in question and help to make any particular development rather unique and highly visible to consumers or partners elsewhere.

Such variations emerge from the generation and application of new technologies based on divergences of both socio-economic situations and political orientations. Consequently such divergent opportunities and policies make new regional patterns emerge and indicate the enabling effect of government policies that are widely facilitatory for innovation processes (Chapters 8 and 20). Such a geographic picture based on regional technological patterns can relate to new technologies, but they can also draw attention to industrial modernization and restructuring when new technologies are applied as in the case of nano-technologies in Germany to provide new and sustainable techno-industrial opportunities (Chapter 22). Simultaneously, spin-off firms from public research contribute to changing a region's industrial and technological structure. They provide additional opportunities based on new knowledge (Chapter 16). Consequently, this allows intra-regional transfer of knowledge and increased synergy based on new technologies, and trans-regionally it widens the scope of a region's opportunities to collaborate with others on areas that were not available before.

The regionalization of techno-industrial innovation indicates a particular landscape of new technologies that is changing constantly, either because of the continuous strengthening of outstanding regions or because regions disappear from the map because they do not participate in next generation technologies. In addition some new regions may emerge and will both contribute and participate in the existing and constantly growing global body of knowledge. Regions and metropolises that continue and increase their role in collaborative networks and are outstanding centres of expertise and creativity emerge as Islands of Innovation (Hilpert 1992, 2012). These patterns, including the outstanding position of Islands of Innovation, indicate the role of regions or locations as centres that contribute to new technologies and to the realization of national technology policies. Simultaneously, they refer to political processes that provide the basis of technology development, as well as the divergences of new technologies and their applications. There is clearly a correspondence between the existing structures and opportunities on the one hand and decisions on policies taken in conjunction with interests and ideologies on the other hand. Thus, the landscape of techno-industrial innovation indicates more than just new technologies. It clearly indicates the fundamental role of political decisions and decisions about alternative opportunities that are made at different locations. Islands of Innovation and the ways regions, metropolises or countries participate in opportunities of networking, and in their shared bodies of knowledge, refer to a number of non-economic or non-technological conditions that are made fruitful through political decisions.

The role of universities and highly trained labour for regionalized contributions to a global body of techno-scientific knowledge

There is a constantly enhancing role for knowledge and knowledge workers, and academics and scientific researchers in particular. New technologies, as the basis for advanced socio-economic development and as means to solve problems from other policy areas, increasingly indicate the importance of new and additional skills (Khadira 2001; Rolfe 2001; Ackers 2005; Millar and Salt 2008; Abel and Deitz 2009). Such highly skilled labour provides the basis of both a continuation of modernization of regional industrial structures and the establishment of new and modern industries at locations in NICs. Initiatives and public investment in the labour force accompanied by well recognized expertise helps to build new linkages and a new body of knowledge addressing (Chapter 16) a wide range of new opportunities. Continuing leading edge research can provide the basis for both new spin-off enterprises from universities or public institutions, and the supply of a strong demand for highly skilled and educated labour (Florida 2002; Power and Lundmark 2004; Berry and Glaeser 2005; Lawton Smith and Waters 2005). Thus, opportunities for structural change and industrial modernization are based on appropriate labour to generate or apply new technologies, manufacture new products, or to supply the high-tech services required.

In the way that new technologies and research-based innovation will consequently change the landscape of innovation, they induce a geographically different demand that makes such processes also relate to, and depend on, a changing landscape of highly skilled labour and higher education. While universities and research institutions are bound to the places where they are located, knowledge and teaching increasingly can be transferred across distances and requires little physical presence. The availability of the internet allows a transfer of such knowledge and competences to distant places (Chapter 16) and helps to create some opportunities at places where such opportunities are physically not present. Although much knowledge that is not bound to laboratory experiments or other such practices can be introduced into distance learning, some traditional roles of universities continue and thus are bound to particular places. Consequently, this divergence based on the opportunities of the regional labour force will continue, despite the effects of internet teaching. Since top universities are centres of research and collaboration they are also institutions where many star scientists (Trippl 2012) prefer to work or to spend some time because of the presence of other star scientists. Thus, Islands of Innovation are places where top universities are concentrated and they act as magnets of science (Mahroum 1999: 382; Williams *et al.* 2004: 39). There centres of internationally outstanding competence exist in different areas of scientific research and form a situation where divergent knowledge may merge to facilitate synergies (e.g. the Boston area or the San Francisco Bay Area). As centres of top research and synergy these locations act as major knots in science-based technology development.

Academics, researchers and knowledge workers become particularly important when it comes to synergy and new technologies. Although there are some locations that are particularly outstanding, they are still part of larger systems of collaboration and are likely to have access to leading edge knowledge and research. Thus, at such locations, which are knots in continental or global networks, the synergy across different areas of technology clearly includes knowledge that has its origin at other places and is transferred through collaboration to the places where they merge. This provides opportunities to participate in geographically distant bodies of knowledge and technology development. The number of scientific researchers or those developing new technologies in high-tech enterprises plays an important role in producing such knowledge and in collaboration. The size of regional innovative labour markets provides an important instrument to take advantage of the knowledge produced through university research and research-based enterprises in the region. Although there are new opportunities provided on the basis of internet access and temporary collaboration, universities still act as policy instruments for the regionalization of innovation, knowledge creation and transfer and a participation in continental development (Chapter 16).

Based on the importance of universities and academically trained labour, countries and locations that are not part of the highly industrialized countries in Europe or the US aim to build such competences. Human capital becomes the main resource to foster research and innovation based on new technologies and needs to be enabled to demonstrate its creativity in findings and products. Korea managed to become a major player in electronics and they also continue with a strong basis in university trained personnel (Chapter 15). In new high tech areas and new technologies, in addition to the role of Seoul and the Korean Institute of Science and Technology (KIST), the country established a centre in the south (Daedock Science Park) where international recognition of research is achieved. Seoul already has become prominent in collaborative scientific research and provides an example of newly emerging locations based on regionalized innovative labour markets and the role of university trained labour. Similarly, the Chinese locations of Beijing, Shanghai and Hong Kong become apparent when the co-publications of partners from different locations is investigated. In addition, Singapore, which performs as a nation state but in fact is rather a big city, manages to become strongly interlinked in networks of scientific collaboration and co-publication (Chapter 19). This indicates that the resources of a large country may help to build such centres, but, again, even small countries or locations can participate or emerge *ab initio* when development is based on academic research and creative labour.

There is a close relationship between techno-scientific competences and economic opportunities. While in Western democracies such situations have emerged over the history of universities,[4] a similar relationship can be identified in newly emerging locations. This is also indicated by China's strongly politically directed development, and the rapid emergence of new locations with rapidly growing research infrastructures and research personnel at a level that is in the interest of foreign investors (Chapter 12). Here, similarly to Singapore (Chapter 13), one can notice that the activities of multinational enterprises and the growth of attractive FDI is predominantly directed to locations that have a strong research capability. Locations of leading research institutes that are known for particular competences benefit most from such foreign capital. Knowledge is brought to the region and a socio-economic development based on products of higher values added takes place. The linkage with such investment by enterprises that are globally active allows participation in technologies and application that was not available before.

The strategy of Singapore also indicates more than a pattern of specialization and concentration of highly creative academic labour (Chapter 13). It is a location where policy makers want to take advantage of the fact that it is regionally and culturally close to emerging markets (e.g. China and other Southeast Asian countries). While Western locations have inhibitory cultural differences, Singapore has become the home of many academics with an East Asian background, which may help to foster collaboration, the transfer of knowledge and an orientation towards application between it and culturally similar emerging economies. Since technologies are not neutral to the cultural and societal situations of their application, a design that takes these divergences into account can provide a competitive advantage. Similarly, research processes are embedded in cultural situations and may embody the tacit knowledge of laboratories and managements. The large cultural space of East Asia and the existing attitude towards research and technology there creates new situations and opportunities. While Singapore is benefitting from similar cultures it also points to a relationship between high values added and social and cultural contexts. Since such social and cultural spaces have their own geography that is close to such newly emerging locations in East Asia, these can emerge as a link between Western technologies and application in East Asia and research strategies. Technologies and academic knowledge refer to the cultural situations where they are generated and need to be implemented in a variety of situations. Multicultural metropolises of excellence in research may be ready to provide for such transformation. Thus, there is a specific geographic situation in Singapore related to its natural environment – which predominantly is related with manufacturing plants – and climate and a specific sociocultural situation that is close to other emerging places in East Asia and may help to provide culturally sound technological solutions.

It is such cultural knowledge-based relationships that allow socio-economic development in situations where sufficient territory for space hungry economic activities is not available. Both strong socio-economic development and increasing energy demand in East Asia creates a market for advanced technologies that clearly relate to opportunities provided by Western technologies, but the vast area of socioculturally compatible applications creates a particular demand for focused applications. While this situation is impressive in a case such as Singapore, the situation is similar in other emerging metropolises in East Asia. China, as an example, is establishing strong research locations that are already well connected in international networks of collaboration, but they continue to have a close relationship with the culture of their customers. The close collaborations with partners in Europe and the US reflect a strategy to participate in and contribute both to such networks of collaborative scientific research and the global body of knowledge. Risks of 'locked-in' provincial strategies can be avoided and specific paths of technology development become possible. Singapore's efforts in biotechnology and solar energy (Chapter 13) reflect explicitly the location's situation. Korea's orientation in continuingly improving its existing strong technological base, or its attempts to establish new internationally competitive competences in nano-technology or biotechnology (Chapter 15 and 22) are impressive examples of strategies designed to match newly emerging opportunities.

Knowledge, scientific research and universities play an important role for technology development and networking. Thus, there is codified knowledge, which can be transferred across long distances, but the way research is conducted successfully in divergent sociocultural environments, of course, varies. Thus, highly trained and university educated labour is fundamental for regional participation in such networks, but, in addition, it also means that specific opportunities may be feasible in only a few regions and they may make a region both rather unique and particularly suitable for some markets. Regional or metropolitan cultures may encourage particular social attitudes that can alter contributions to networks, have an impact on research and development, and can alter strategies in new technologies. Although this might be based on shared research and knowledge, there will be diversities of innovation. Universities and spin-off enterprises indicate that regional participation in new technologies relates also to a particular relationship with existing industrial competences and traditions. The variations between regions and the specific contributions to a continentally or globally collaborative technology development and application are widely based on a correlation with the qualities of available labour force.

Social structures and politically induced change: labour and culture for new technologies

Societies as conditions of political opportunities

Opportunities for technological innovation are clearly determined by locational factors. Universities and appropriate industries, which allow for the transfer of research findings; a highly skilled labour force consisting of a sufficient number of knowledge workers and scientific researchers; innovative labour markets that attract such personnel to come and that are of a size that provides further jobs at the locality; and an attitude of openness towards people who enter the country, region or metropolis, are important factors that are fundamental for advanced socio-economic development. These are rather social dimensions that characterize conditions for techno-industrial innovation. Knowledge, education and a strong orientation in high level research are important orientations of societies and indicate their distinct cultures and regional development (Bercovitz and Feldman 2006: 177; Dickinson *et al.* 2008). Thus, leading edge techno-scientific research and highly creative knowledge workers vary across national, regional or metropolitan societies and provide highly divergent situations. While technologies formally might be similar, the contexts within which they emerge are clearly divergent and so are the areas of application.

Thus countries pass through constant periods of social change. They face particularly strong and fast change in the case of NICs, where they need to develop structures similar to those in traditional industrialised countries in Europe or North America, but within a very short time. Such fundamental changes can be identified in countries such as Taiwan or Korea, where to become a strong and innovative industrialized country based on its previous phases of development, is closely related to a constantly growing share of university trained labour. This caused a fundamental change from a poor Third World country into a knowledge-based economy (Chapter 15). The transformation of the society beyond industrialization towards a clearly knowledge-based economy, which fundamentally effects wide social classes with higher levels of education, indicates that education and the orientation towards research plays an important role in such economic development. Similarly, Singapore faced a fast change to become a location of both knowledge workers and new industries, which are competitive because of the highly educated work force (Chapter 13). Thus, these examples are not different from the situations in European countries or in North America. This contrasts that the change towards such a society – which is capable of innovation and new technologies – was significantly faster and clearly indicates the role of knowledge, science and research. Since modern technology development involves both Islands of Innovation and networks of collaboration, which exchange knowledge and personnel (Hilpert and Lawton Smith 2012) there needs to be particular attention paid to a society's labour force and providing for its ability to participate and contribute to such networks.

The fundamental importance of highly skilled and university trained labour refers to sociocultures that are open and ready to exploit such new opportunities, and it indicates the outstanding role of language in exchanging such new findings and knowledge (Bellini and Hilpert 2013). Processes of innovation that are concentrated at a few outstanding locations on the one hand, but on the other hand demand collaboration and an exchange of ideas and findings globally as well point to non-economic or proto-economic conditions that enable participation in such processes (Chapter 10 and 27). The USA clearly presents an example of how to take advantage of both. English as the *lingua franca* of science provides a highly advantageous situation to attract highly creative scientists and the local culture of internationally oriented metropolises and university locations inhibits a culture that is open for people from abroad (Ackers 2005: 13;

Criscuolo 2005: 1360; Breschi and Lissoni 2009: 442; Hilpert 2012; Trippl 2012). Thus, countries such as the USA or the United Kingdom, of course, are in a particularly advantageous situation and emerge as countries where knowledge workers aim to migrate (Ackers 2005: 13; Laudel 2005: 388).

Social structures of such locations will change over time and attitudes towards the world abroad will vary as the local or regional society at Islands of Innovations changes. The innovative capability of such situations as well as their socio-economic development is visibly linked with the changing sociocultural situation there and provides more opportunities in future. Because of the demand for new technologies and their economic opportunities, such innovative labour and knowledge workers in particular are of increasing importance. This helps to place open societies into a beneficial situation as these will attract more knowledge workers (Power and Lundmark 2004; Berry and Glaeser 2005). When it comes to migrant knowledge workers, government regulations are important, because these can either support or hinder contributing to the development of the innovative labour force needed (Mahroum 2001; Williams *et al.* 2004). As these regulations relate to already existing social attitudes towards immigration, it suggests more than just government policies but points directly to regional and metropolitan societies (Herzog *et al.* 1986; Angel 1989; Florida 2002; Favell *et al.* 2006; Abel and Deitz 2009). Political decisions about such regulations clearly are bound to politics and political representation.

International recruitment is of course much easier in English speaking countries. Academics and scientific researchers are familiar with the language and often also with the sociocultural situations. In places such as Silicon Valley a particularly high share of migrant workers and entrepreneurs can be found (Saxenian 2002: 20–22). The United States has a lot of highly skilled immigrants at university locations. In addition, the countries that are most frequently chosen by highly educated knowledge workers and academics also provide the opportunity to use the same language in everyday life. The global situation of university trained labour indicates a situation that may weaken some countries that may face the emigration of such labour as Italy or India, which is the world's largest exporter of academic labour (Khadira 2001; Morano-Foadi and Foadi 2003). A recruitment from other countries that is not an exchange of labour among the networked innovative regional labour markets (Hilpert and Lawton Smith 2012) will replace the engineers or researchers in quantity, but not on an equal level of creativity and education (Bernard *et al.* 2012). A country's system of education and research plays an important role in developing the capabilities of knowledge workers and their contribution to innovation and new technologies.

Facing a shortage of highly educated labour also requires additional labour beyond those attracted from abroad. Since university trained labour is considered of increasing importance in many fields, particular attention is now paid to women's labour (Chapter 4). While this has been considered a matter of equal rights, it is now changed into an important issue for innovation and the development of new technologies. While populations in Western industrial countries are widely decreasing, the demand for knowledge workers is constantly growing, along with the importance of highly innovative and technology-based industrial development. Societies that encourage female education to the highest levels can create a larger university trained labour force. This is a fundamental change in most societies, because still it is only recently that women have gained widespread access to higher education and attractive jobs. Nevertheless, this does not mean that more female knowledge workers necessarily mean more top positions for women where they could contribute their full creativity (Chapter 4). Thus, even more socially advanced societies and political programmes are needed to support women in their professional careers and achieve important positions to exploit their potential, and thus contribute to innovation and new technologies.

Education forms an important basis for knowledge workers and a highly innovative labour force. Universities act as producers of graduates (Rolfe 2001; Bélanger 2002; Berry and Glaeser 2005). The more students that pass through university education, the more knowledge workers will be available. Consequently, a substantial number of young people must pass through schools to prepare for universities to deliver an increasing number of students and so finally contribute to a highly skilled labour force. Minorities that are underprivileged thus are potentially a source of skilled or university trained labour. The wider the access to higher education provided in societies, the better are the opportunities to provide the labour and the knowledge workers that the economy and enterprises need. Innovative industries are based on innovative societies that provide the basis for new technologies and innovation. It is more than population. It requires education available to everyone as capable as possible. Nevertheless, an increase in the number of knowledge workers will make the most efficient use of such opportunities only if the additional labour force has career opportunities to contribute their creative competences in positions that are critical for such processes.

New technologies become important to understand fully both the situation and the opportunities available. The growing demand for such labour relates to the development of new technologies as well as the application of new technologies in traditional industries and products. The changing role of universities in supplying knowledge through the internet to distant places allows building of the labour force, which provides opportunities at places where such education cannot be acquired (Chapter 16). It is the interplay between internet opportunities, online courses of universities and the job opportunities through changing labour markets that indicate such constant changes and the modernization of regional labour forces. Even in less central regions higher value can be added and higher incomes can be realized, and a regional pattern of social exclusion potentially can be avoided. Although such knowledge transfer can be realized, universities continue to contribute new knowledge and findings based on the established culture (Chapter 16; Laudel 2005; Lawton Smith and Waters 2005; Gottlieb and Joseph 2006; Hilpert and Bastian 2007; Abel and Deitz 2009). Nevertheless, the most modern and most advanced labour forces remain at central knots and concentrate, in general, at metropolises. Distance learning may help to modernize the labour force at distant places, but there is clearly a changing landscape of skilled labour and university education at its highest level. This demands public funding and again relates to the fact that some national or even regional societies are ready to fund such searches for new opportunities. Some even involve a wide number of disciplines and include those that are currently not of economic relevance – but might be in future (e.g. the relationship between linguistics and computer sciences).

As innovation and new technologies are associated with a particular geography, accordingly, societies and political decisions vary a lot following such patterns. Variations within a country – and particularly when focusing on federal countries – indicate divergent situations and interests. Regional societies might be oriented in research and education, as might newly emerging industrial countries, innovative regions or metropolises, participating in innovative networks and paying particular attention to state of the art knowledge, leading edge research and university trained personnel. Such social situations are based on particular interests in technology-based development and appropriate areas of employment. Accordingly, political interests address strategies that match such expectations.

Thus, it is noticeable that knowledge societies are clearly characterized by frequent access to leading edge knowledge, the existence of highly prestigious universities, and the high level of education in the labour force. This situation also indicates that these societies exhibit attitudes of intellectual curiosity and openness towards new ideas and technologies, which make their economies particularly innovative. This is widely identifiable with new technologies, findings in natural sciences and its application with new and marketable products. This means also that the regional pattern of Islands of Innovation, dynamic metropolises, highly skilled and university trained labour, and participation in innovative networks and collaborative development of new technologies, all indicate a relationship with the regional societies. Such regional societies are characterised by a large proportion of knowledge workers and personnel, recruited from other innovative regions and from abroad (Avveduto 2001; Saxenian 2002; Finn 2003; Williams *et al.* 2004; Marginson 2006). Clearly, interests that exist in such regions or metropolises, and the politics that take place relate to the social structure to be found at these locations. Consequently, these complement the situation and further contribute to the decision to pursue policies that continue the development of new technologies and innovation. At these locations a socioculture has emerged that is supportive of such processes.

Research and education/knowledge as a change of the sociocultural situation: new players in new technologies

A society's willingness to invest in research and university education is both an important contribution to establishing a knowledge-based economy and a preparation for participation in a global body of knowledge. Once there are innovative labour markets such locations can attract knowledge workers and even star scientists (Hilpert and Lawton Smith 2012; Singh and Briem 2012; Trippl 2012). The importance of the attraction of such labour is more than just the availability of additional labour. Associated with knowledge workers from abroad or other locations is a transfer of knowledge that helps to create new and additional competences (Meyer *et al.* 2001; Regets 2007; Mason and Nohara 2008). Different attitudes towards research and tacit knowledge when research work is conducted (Criscuolo 2005; Millar and Salt 2008; Breschi and Lissoni 2009) help the improvement of innovative processes and the application of new technologies in traditional industries (Chapter 11; Hilpert 2003). The fact that both universities and technology programmes are government funded provides an opportunity to link regional societies with the knowledge embodied in knowledge workers. Although knowledge, increasingly, can be acquired through new internet learning, still universities provide an important institutional context for research and higher education at especially advanced levels. A society's orientation towards research and university education is fundamental in producing new and creative degree holders (Chapter 4). The political willingness to fund universities provides a basis for excellence in research that allows locations to act as Islands of Innovation (Hilpert 1992) and magnets of science (Mahroum 1999, 2000b; Williams *et al.* 2004), and strongly supports the quality of teaching (Chapter 16). Thus, academic labour markets and the attraction of knowledge workers provide important policy instruments that help for a regionalization of innovation, knowledge and development through the participation in networks. Such labour is of fundamental importance to such processes.

The more universities play a fundamental role in relation with innovative labour, the more will such societies pass through a sociocultural development towards a situation that is fundamental for innovation and new technologies. Universities are outcomes of such policies and help to attract innovative labour to further contribute to a culturally important milieu (Hilpert 2012). Again, political majorities, which take decisions about such policies, provide for this important and constant improvement of human capital that is available in a region or a territory. This indicates that there is a close relationship between policies for innovation and human capital, providing the necessary labour on the one hand, and the politics of immigrant labour and production of graduate labour on the other hand (Berry and Glaeser 2005; Gottlieb and Joseph 2006; Regets 2007; Dickinson *et al.* 2008). This, of course, also includes the reintegration of expatriates. Once expatriates are well established in their new home countries, they can take advantage of a continuing relationship with their native countries. This is obvious with Indian and Chinese entrepreneurs in Silicon Valley (Mahroum 2000a; Saxenian 2002; Williams *et al.* 2004), who collaborate with partners in their home countries. But there are also examples (e.g. Italy, Czech Republic) of engineers and academics who hardly continue such contacts and frequently continue to stay abroad (Morano-Foadi and Foadi 2003; Bernard *et al.* 2012).

Consequently, continuing contacts and collaboration with partners from the emigrants' countries, the return of expatriates (Bernard *et al.* 2012; Trippl 2012) and government policies that strongly support research and education, together help to develop innovative situations that allow participation in both leading edge research and new technologies – and it contributes to a continued participation in collaborative networks of research and technology development. While this is advantageous for existing Islands of Innovation, which are located in technologically leading, highly industrialized countries, this also provides opportunities for new locations even in countries that were not previously recognized as significant contributors to a global body of techno-scientific knowledge. A large number of students and PhDs acquired abroad allows a concentration of such a labour force using well equipped laboratories after they return to their home countries. Accordingly, new players emerge, when there are new locations of excellence established and if these locations are increasingly included in networks of collaborative innovation. Such new contributors and participants that become participants in such networks are built upon newly emerging situations. These were widely induced through government policies and a strong improvement in education, skills and the sociocultural orientation of knowledge-based development.

While government policies play an important role in new technologies and innovation, they tend to focus on both a continuation of existing industrial development and so can inhibit future innovative potential and access to new technologies that are at the forefront of new technological development. This has already been experienced in traditional industrial countries and regions characterized by old industries (Chapter 11; Sable *et al.* 1991; Girratani *et al.* 2003). There, public research and technology programmes clearly focused on those new technological opportunities that best fit with existing industrial structures. In addition, of course, such research allows new areas of economic activity based on the competences and knowledge acquired. Nevertheless, newly emerging industrialized countries take advantage of currently available industrial opportunities that are based on traditional industries, or that are not oriented in leading edge research. While incomes increase and exchange rates vary they are also exposed to the global division of labour and need to improve their technological opportunities. Consequently they aim at a continuation of their path of industrialization based on both new technological opportunities and intensified research. Again, the pattern of publicly funded research and technology programmes can be identified and there is also a clear regional concentration that allows for collaboration at a particular locality and across borders with partners abroad. For half a century, increasing technological and scientific education at universities has built a strong and large labour force that provides an opportunity for participation in the forefront of the development of new technologies. Thus, Korea aims to become established as a part of the leading networks in nano-technology, is building a strong position in biotechnology, and is continuing to be a major player in information and communication technologies. Singapore aims at a participation in biotechnology, solar energy and micro-electronics (Chapter 13, 15 and 22).

Thus, a time consuming attempt to build a highly skilled and university educated labour force provides the basis of future innovative processes. Since private capital is not available sufficiently to fund large leading universities that include a strong research orientation, government policies play a particularly fundamental role. Universities clearly are important instruments for building the labour force which is needed by innovative industries, and provide the knowledge required for transfer to enterprises to exploit commercially. But even more important is the participation of countries in state of the art knowledge through collaboration and exchange of academic personnel, which can be achieved through universities and research personnel. A research-based contribution to a global body of knowledge allows collaboration and exchange. Research at a location with other interesting institutions and researchers reflects a particular brand (Chapter 5) and improves opportunities for the exchange of leading edge knowledge based on collaboration. Focusing on particular areas of scientific research and concentration of the strongest intellectual capabilities at a location helps to make these places well recognized (Chapter 16).

Consequently, locations that provide particularly good opportunities to become both internationally recognized, and included in global networks of collaboration and innovation, are of particular political interest. There, leading institutions emerge and the funding of research is concentrated, which again creates additional employment of creative academics and researchers, and attracts more knowledge workers. The expansion of such academic labour markets creates very specific situations and the basis for new research-based enterprises providing additional highly attractive jobs (Power and Lundmark 2004; Berry and Glaeser 2005; Hilpert and Lawton Smith 2012). This is particularly the case when innovative clusters are formed. Consequently, participation is uneven and metropolises have particular positions within these collaborative processes of innovation, as locations where new technologies are introduced or developed. This is particularly challenging for small countries that aim to build such innovative capabilities or to maintain their position globally.

Political actors and institutions need to take an interest in new technologies and in innovation, to create demand for such policies, and industrial structures. In addition they need to recognize a society's interest in higher value added and in higher standards of living, which need to be shared across divergent social groups and competing interests. Consequently, such policies are evidence of shared views and help to establish a capable publicly funded research system for techno-industrial innovation (Chapter 22). While democratic systems need to arrange majorities to launch such policies, and to cope with both the demand for new technologies and the technological change, it is interesting that non-democratic or authoritarian systems aim for similar processes and try to take part in collaborative networks (Chapter 12, 13, 15 and 26). When launching such processes of technology oriented research there are new countries and locations emerging as participants and contributors to a global body of knowledge, and as potential partners in new projects.

While advanced research and technologies have, for a long time, been carried out and developed in Western industrialized countries, especially during the recent decade following the turn of the millennium, such competences are increasingly identified outside these global regions. Korea alone has gained a similar level of development, and at least in some areas has a market leading level of competence (e.g. in micro-electronics). Nevertheless, these societies have already passed through fundamental changes and still continue to do so. Thus, it needs to be borne in mind that the number of countries and new players in world markets has increased. Korea has a fairly broad expertise in a number of industries and technologies, and is on its way to participating effectively in energy technologies, nano-technology or biotechnology (Chapter 15 and 22). Singapore tries to take advantage of its location as a hub in Southeast Asia, hosting institutes and competences in a number of areas, concentrating on biotechnology and energy technologies (Chapter 13). China has some technologies that are maturing quite quickly, for example there solar technologies are manufactured at extremely low costs organized as mass-production (Chapter 23). These technologies were developed in Western industrialized countries and were considered modern with a promising future identified about one or two decades ago. Nevertheless, China is not yet regarded as likely to become a major player in high-technology soon, but may have to develop infrastructure, institutions and capabilities for a further one or two decades (Chapter 26). During such periods of catching up with the leading countries, newly emerging countries can take advantage of existing knowledge, competences and the geographical dislocation of manufacturing and research. A transfer of competences may take place and help to advance future processes.

While catching up with the leading countries, taking increasing advantage of mature and modernizing industries, and building strong research competences, traditional situations in the NICs change according to the demands for modern and innovative developments in capitalist countries. This can be identified particularly at locations where these countries support the collaboration and industrialization through foreign investors and multinationals. Consequently, the process of industrial modernization and the governments' orientations in research and technology-based socio-economic development causes a concentration at particular locations (Chapter 12, 15 and 26). Thus, new metropolises, which can be identified in collaborative processes of research and technology development, are emerging both due to countries' policies and because of the regional concentration, which makes such processes more recognized and successful and attracts the labour they need. While there are many locations in newly industrialized countries that show such tendencies, they are particularly strongly indicated by Singapore, which is also intensively oriented towards attracting highly creative and innovative academics from Western countries and knowledge workers from around the world (Chapter 13). This also indicates the role of social and cultural change and the capacity to adopt new opportunities that provide a global and diverse academic labour force. A consistently increasing exchange of innovative labour with other highly innovative metropolises and Islands of Innovation, and the constant immigration of knowledge workers contribute to a change that is appropriate to attract labour and to realize knowledge transfer. Thus it can be used for the development of such locations elsewhere. A certain change of attitudes and cultures (Chapter 10 and 27) at these locations indicates that there are opportunities for participation in networks of collaboration and technology development, but it also indicates the role of culture in such highly innovative processes.

Consequently, uneven regional participation in new technologies (Chapter 12 and 15) and collaborative networks are conditions for both participation in and contributions to developments that can link a country to innovative processes. Thus, a longer lasting process of education and the building of universities with a high potential for scientific research can make government policies successful. It is important to see that building a location that provides interesting opportunities for research and suggests a culturally rather internationalized situation in a society (e.g. Singapore), will allow the attraction of personnel from abroad and the reintegration of returning expatriates (Chapter 13; Bernard *et al.* 2012; Trippl 2012). It is clear that participation in new technologies and leading edge research and innovation, requires policies that will deliver a well regarded research milieu and a sociocultural situation that suits highly mobile academics, researchers and knowledge workers. Participation in current networks of research (e.g. biotechnology), and the individual success of some countries (e.g. Korea) in certain technological products, indicate both that these changes take time and that they are possible.

Taking these constellations into consideration, national processes of innovation and the building of Islands of Innovation are essential conditions for both the emergence of new locations and players, and for the continued participation of those countries and Islands that already exist and have already participated in networks. Government policies and political interests reflect cultures and their adaptability towards collaboration with other institutions, individuals and strategies at other locations. Islands of Innovation are not just regional phenomena and concentrations, these are elements of national, continental and trans-continental networks and constellations. At such locations and their societies there is found a concentration of particular cultural arrangements and an adaptability of competences. Understanding the role of politics and governments for technology and innovation, it is fundamental to take into consideration the variety of variables that influence innovation. Consequently, technologies, application of new technological opportunities, and the role of government policies, as well as political interests in certain strategies and technologies, will vary according to national, regional and even continental contexts. The interrelationship between technologies, situations and political activities form highly divergent situations that also indicate the significance of politics and government policies.

Technology and innovation: the role of government and its relationship with politics and society

Political impact on technology development and technology-based innovation in different countries faces highly divergent situations. The size of a country and its budget available obviously indicate divergent opportunities. In addition, regional divergences and disparities, skilled labour and university trained personnel, structures of enterprises and research capabilities, attitudes towards new technologies and innovation, regulation, and the timeframe of technology cycles, all play fundamental roles in creating opportunities for political impacts, and how they are utilised to induce both socio-economic development and new solutions for emerging problems. Since these indicators vary greatly between countries and form divergent situations, clearly there are divergent political interests to be identified, and the policies conducted are often different – or conversely similar political decisions and policies generate divergent processes. Finally, a country's situation in international markets, or its access to energy and natural resources, may influence the interest in particular technologies.

This may also help one to understand why certain countries participate in certain types of technologies, whereas other countries do not – or they may develop other technologies or strategies of innovation. It also indicates that leading edge technologies are developed only at particular locations in particular countries, based on existing networks of collaboration and recruitment from other countries. There may either be a contribution to such processes or they may apply new technologies in existing traditional industries and products (Chapter 11). Processes of maturation also help one to understand why countries are newly emerging in global markets and networks and may become new players in technologies and innovation. They may use available technologies and advantageous production costs and cost efficient arrangements of manufacturing (e.g. environmental regulations, labour markets, organization of capital and labour). New technologies (e.g. biotechnology or nano-technology) clearly demand outstanding research and creative labour, the application of new technological opportunities (e.g. electronics or new materials in mechanical engineering or transportation technologies), demand for products from appropriate industries, skilled labour. In addition they may draw on maturing (e.g. consumer electronics) or less complex technologies (e.g. solar panels). Technologies and innovation will confront governments with constantly changing situations. In addition, the roles governments play in such situations change during the lifetime of technologies (Chapter 3). A political impact on technologies and innovation needs to be identified and understood in divergent and changing situations fully to understand the role of politics and government policies more generally and even theoretically.

Thus, technologies relate to particular situations and the opportunities of divergent countries. While certain processes, such as continental or transcontinental networking, regionalization, skilled labour development, and certain enterprises, can be identified in many countries, in contrast, the technologies in question are not developed in all countries. In the case of nuclear energy, large programmes are required to fund research and development and large markets are needed to repay the public and private money invested (Chapter 14; Hilpert 1991). Countries such as the United States, France, Germany, Britain and Japan are the leading countries in this highly disputed technology. Governments use this technology to supply energy and they provide a demand that allows large, high-technology enterprises to make private investments. In addition, regulations are under the control of governments. While the German, French or British internal markets are too small on their own and nuclear enterprises must look additionally to export markets, smaller countries are not in a situation even to engage in such expensive large scale technologies. It is remarkable that even NICs such as India or China are ready to engage in such a technology, which is particularly complicated when it comes to safety regulations and design.

Small countries' and regions' technology policies obviously lack the scale to take part in such nuclear technologies, but they may make use of other energy technologies. In solar technology or wind technology there are both large and small scale technologies, but in particular small scale technologies (or those that can be applied in divergent contexts) have found their way into markets. This allows opportunities for smaller countries such as Denmark in wind technology or Singapore in solar technology (Chapter 13). This requires smaller amounts to be invested, and international production networks can be utilized, because the final technology is manufactured using different parts and components. Such locations or small countries are also embedded in international networks of collaboration that allow for specialization and the development of highly complex and advanced elements to be incorporated into the final technology. Thus, even larger technological innovations – or even technological revolutions that need large budgets and appropriate research and industrial structures – create opportunities to contribute complex elements to a final large scale technology. Such elements match patterns of techno-industrial specialization and provide opportunities for small countries and locations to participate in new technologies and to contribute to new developments. In a similar way, small countries and locations participate in biotechnology, which in general is a fundamental innovation and is funded through large programmes by the leading industrialized countries of Europe and the United States (Chapter 13, 14 and 19; Norus 2006).

Smaller industrialized countries, such as the Scandinavian countries or the Netherlands, benefit from the programmes of the European Union and can find positions in the global division of labour, while participating in industries that can take advantage of the innovative opportunities provided by biotechnology. Again, the existing situations of industries that apply such technologies have an important impact on the design of public policies and on the areas of technology development. Enzymes have been important for breweries in Copenhagen and they are again important for modern biotechnology in Denmark. Measurement instruments or medical instruments are important industrial products in Jena, Germany; and again biotechnology is applied to develop modern medical instruments and measurement instruments today (Norus 2006; Hilpert and Bastian 2007). This indicates divergent situations and dispersed participation even in fundamental new technologies. Opportunities for technology development vary according to the size of countries and existing patterns of specialization. But, in addition, strong research, which applies to new products and can provide the basis for innovative development and new enterprises, indicates that new locations can emerge that do not relate to existing industries that may apply the new technology or to findings in this new area of research. Building strong research capabilities can link countries and new locations with emerging science-based technologies (e.g. Munich in Germany or Seattle, WA) and provide attractive socio-economic development. Even small locations such as Singapore (Chapter 13 and 19) can take advantage of internationally recognized research capabilities and link themselves to the global networks of collaboration and exchange of knowledge.

Technologies that can be applied in aircraft present a similar situation. While it is a rather old industry that has existed for a century, its products change constantly based on new technologies, materials and changes in design and manufacturing. As the aircraft is assembled with many different parts from a large number of enterprises, again, a number of opportunities are provided for large technologies and small enterprises to contribute (Chapter 21; Hickie 2006). Regional patterns of specialization and even national competences based in small countries can find an opportunity to participate in such processes and to contribute to technology development (e.g. aeroengines in Singapore). Large technologies clearly demand large programmes and appropriate budgets but the size of such technologies also indicates contributions from different sources of research and development. Thus, large technologies allow for niches that can be used by small countries with smaller budgets, or even by regions. Automobile industries and high technology suppliers provide a similar example. Although the product and the general idea of this technology is already much older than a century it is still a subject of technological change. New technologies such as the application of lasers, electronics or new materials are constantly applied for the advancement of automobiles and the continuing modernization of a mature industry (Chapter 21).

Such cross-fertilization of a product, when applying technologies from other sectors, changes automobile technology fundamentally and allows for many niches and regional or small country opportunities as high technology suppliers. Technology programmes and policies can be tailored appropriately, and participation in the constant advancement of the technology can be realized without necessarily being a major player in automobiles. The supplier networks, that characterize a highly globalized industry, allow specific policies and contributions. Thus, even cases of large scale technologies and public programmes with big budgets allow for a wide variety of participation and contribution. Taking such opportunities into consideration, of course, demands for specific strategies. Technologies clearly refer to industries, or potential industries, that might emerge or become established within a foreseeable future. Nano-technology provides an interesting example, as it is heavily based on leading edge research and relates to a variety of large industries that can apply such technologies. In addition, it indicates that NICs (e.g. Korea) can both contribute to and participate in a new technology (Chapter 22). The rich variety of applications of nano-technology, of course, allows for specialized programmes, products and policies to take advantage of these opportunities. Similarly to consumer electronics, or particular software (e.g. computer games), industries spread out to countries and locations that provide the situations required and contribute to a growing body of knowledge available at such places, which are linked to technology networks. Such changes can become the basis for further development and new contributors to networks of collaborative technology development and innovation.

Processes of maturing technologies allow for both new locations and participation in a technology during the life cycle (Chapter 3). Government policies of leading countries in scientific research and technology development may provide the basis for new technologies, but the process of technological maturation and the modernization of manufacturing opportunities in other places indicates different forms of participation in countries and regions during the life technological cycle. While during the early stages when a new technology emerges from research, it will provide for science-based development; the new technologies can be applied in existing industries, and it may help to keep industries and products innovative (e.g. mechanical engineering or measurement instruments, or personal computers or mobile phones). Government programmes become increasingly important for leading countries to continue at their position in the global race in new technologies, and to retain their place in collaborative networks. However, such programmes are equally important for countries that aim to enter during the process of technology maturation. While the latter are latecomers in the life cycle of these maturing technologies they benefit from this process and can design policies that may establish them as future leading players in some technologies and industries (e.g. Korea). In understanding the divergent opportunities of countries and the role of government policies for technology development and innovation, time becomes a fundamental dimension; its significance defined by the technology itself and by political attempts to reduce the time to market. Strong technology programmes may shorten this period and may also influence both the life time of a technology (until it is replaced by another technology) and the continuation of a national or regional competitive position based on a continuous process of technological innovation in mature products and industries (e.g. automobile, aircraft, mechanical engineering, precision engineering, pharmaceutical products, energy generation).

Public policy programmes supporting new technologies are clearly decisive for technology development and the kind of technology that might be developed in a particular country. It is obvious that large countries with big budgets that have a competitive position in innovative industries and research structures can support different technologies compared to small countries or those that are less advanced. Equally, it is obvious that the particular situation of a country or region is fundamental to the opportunities that it can reasonably consider. Existing situations, the structure of industries, and the workforce available, have a critical influence on the individual decisions taken. The interests of these groups will have influence through the political process. The individual situation in a country or region will be transmitted to policy making in two ways: by the opportunities that exist as a result of the technology development; and, in addition, through the political interests expressed by the groups that are involved with such opportunities. Their interest in particular technologies, or to supply particular facilitating and contributory technologies influences the design of public technology programmes. While large countries with big markets such as the USA or multinational institutions such as the European Union can influence through regulation, markets and public investments, small countries cannot make use of such broad scale policies to contribute particular parts and complex elements to a final new technology. Also, large enterprises that are globally active and hold a dominant position in markets are in fundamentally different situations when compared with markets where small and medium sized enterprises aim to enter market niches, or become a supplier for large technologies and industries. Situations also vary fundamentally according to the national and local availability of skills, education, and attitudes towards modernization and new enterprises.

When taking these divergences into account clearly, at the empirical level, public programmes and opportunities to develop new technologies vary widely and will suggest very divergent outcomes. Technologies need particular political support in a wide area of initiatives, and so they help to produce divergent technological solutions that may be applied in different economic, social and political circumstances. The situation created by industries, enterprises, research capabilities, workforce, position in international trade and government opportunities, can be identified very clearly, while identifying a wide variation in national and regional contexts. In addition, the opportunities that are used in different countries also relate to governmental systems and policies that take into account different societies including their divergent political interests and cultural attitudes. Clearly, ostensibly similar situations vary according to the political systems and societies; and they perform differently in technology and innovation. Finally, the life cycles of particular technologies demonstrate specific contexts that exist and that need to be appreciated in order to understand the relationships between political decisions and technologies. There are different, often transient, opportunities, and there are changing contexts that arise as different countries (with all their national complexities) pass through the process of development. The rich variety of empirical situations is not, however, confusing. Rather, because they vary systematically, their variety helps to identify situations ripe for comparison. Thereby such comparisons aid understanding of the variations found in the relationships between technologies and the political systems in which they are embedded. In addition, there are context variables, such as international trade, the exchange of academic knowledge, and the demand for collaboration that help to integrate different findings and contribute to a general understanding of this global process.

Methods of analysis clearly are fundamental to gain this deeper understanding of the relationship between the political system and technology. It is important to define appropriate indicators that measure the situation and relate to the process of innovation (Chapter 28). The European situation clearly varies from the North American one, and by being different it indicates that there is also a divergent situation that requires analysis. Industrial change, research strategies, societies and industries create specific situations that need to be matched with the knowledge that is available or that needs to be generated. While in North America the scientific system is quite unified all over the continent, in Europe each country has established its own system according to its history, its society's attitude towards science and technology, its budgets and the government's relationships with the enterprises that will apply such new knowledge and new technological opportunities. Thus, public policies vary across Europe, and the efficacy of particular policies and policy instruments varies between countries, because of their divergent political and governmental systems. This diversity may increase globally as the different newly emerging Asian countries emerge. These are now a subject of research that reveals the emergence of their own innovative systems. Certain indicators may become more, or less, important and – due to cultural divergences – additional indicators may have to be identified and applied appropriately.

The relationship between academic knowledge and innovative technologies indicates the particular importance of knowledge transfer (Chapter 30) to develop a better understanding of the role of government policies. Again, variations between particular university systems, and particular industries, in the context of different countries matter. They point to the variations that are fundamental for public policies that serve the interests of certain industries, labour and interest groups. Learning more about such relationships and their variations may help us to understand why countries and regions may have an expertise in particular technologies, and why they pursue different strategies that lead to the development of divergent niche technological specialisms and applications within a broad technology. The indicators and models provided will refer to the broader, underlying relationships and help integrate empirical information. As the situations investigated may vary between technologies and countries, the overall picture that can be identified will indicate divergences and similarities. Newly emerging technological players that use their universities and science systems in processes of innovation may require additional indicators and some re-modelling. Thus they will help to generate key knowledge to understand the process of technological development and innovation and its relationship with political decisions and public policies.

The development of new technologies and its variations is closely related with the political system and the governmental system. It also indicates that it demands more than just technologies, because it always refers to particular situations or problems to be solved on the basis of new technologies or new applications of technologies. Thus, in addition to divergent opportunities, the effects of policies that are in the political interest of social groups or parties vary according to the underlying ideas, aims and contributors, but they also vary with regard to the situation that should be met (Chapter 20). Methods of evaluation and analytic frameworks (Chapter 29) help to integrate such different indicators and relationships (e.g. university–industry knowledge transfer) and to learn about the effects and outcomes of certain policies. While this is of high relevance for governments to estimate their impact on such processes, in addition, such research based on indicators, models and individual relationship will also help to develop a deeper understanding of the divergences of the political impact on processes of technology development and innovation.

Since technologies and their effects differ, and situations of countries and regions vary, the impact of these indicators' divergent contexts will induce processes that lead to empirically different outcomes. Appreciating these empirical differences will help to understand this complex inter-relationship that includes the political system and the governmental system, and that influences political decisions. Methods of simulation (Chapter 31) help to identify the empirical variations and how they emerge. Applying the method to different technologies will lead to a better understanding of the general impact of political decisions on technology development, for example why certain technologies might be more responsive to political decision making than others; while applying the method to different countries or regions will help to better understand the impact of particular interests and governmental systems on technology development. Developing the methodology, again, is a contribution to learning about the relationship between political decisions and technologies, and how they vary systematically.

Such methods help develop a deeper understanding, and draw particular attention to the socio-economic effects of new technologies and public policies. A comparison between countries and regions may help us to understand the opportunities for intervention either in similar situations (the most similar cases) or in different situations (the most different cases). In addition, different social and industrial structures, and different positions in global networks suggest varieties of strategies that can be designed and realized by employing different policy instruments. The changes that take place in societies and industries also point to changing interests in particular technologies and the kinds of technologies developed. There are the divergent roles of national and regional governments, and there are the similarities and divergences among democratic and authoritarian political systems. The demand for appropriately skilled and university trained labour, again, changes the context over time, and allows policies that either aim at shorter periods of development or at participation in the benefits of a technology that already exists. The long development time periods of a technology will always embrace changing situations within countries and societies and between countries and societies. They will also indicate changing relationships between the public policies conducted and the technologies developed. Particular technologies are pursued according to the situations, opportunities or political aims that exist in a society. Thus, there is a question about how these relationships emerge, change and mutually influence one another.

Notes

1 E.g. 'Star Wars' of the US, information technologies, biotechnologies, new materials, nano technologies or environmental technologies.

2 It is important to remember, however, that proximity is likely to remain important in the application of new technology which draws on the competences of traditional industries. For example a local university or research facility might assist an established local industrial cluster to apply a new technology and so enhance its competitiveness.

3 See the strong specialization of the US in nano-technology to support and modernize the automobile industry.
4 I.e. research institutes and public funding that have led to both current Islands of Innovation and vital spin-off enterprises.

References

Abel, J. and Deitz, R., 2009: *Do Colleges and Universities Increase their Region's Human Capital?* Federal Reserve Bank of New York: Staff Reports No. 401.

Ackers, L., 2005: Moving people and knowledge: scientific mobility in the European Union. *International Migration* 43(5), pp. 99–131.

Angel, D.P., 1989: The labour market for engineers in the U.S. semiconductor industry. *Economic Geography* 65(2), pp. 99–112.

Avveduto, S., 2001: International mobility of PhDs. In: Organisation of Economic Co-operation and Development (OECD) (eds).

Bélanger, J., 2002: From human capital to organisational learning. *Canadian Public Policy/Analyse de Politiques* 28(1), pp. 143–148.

Bellini, N. and Hilpert, U. (eds), 2013: *Europe's Changing Geography*. London and New York: Routledge.

Bercovitz, J. and Feldman, M., 2006: Entrepreneurial universities and technology transfer: a conceptual framework for understanding knowledge-based economic development. *Journal of Technology Transfer* 31, pp. 175–188.

Bernard, J., Patocková, V. and Kostelechý, T., 2012: Islands of Innovation in the Czech Republic. In: Hilpert, U. and Lawton Smith, H. (eds): *Networking Regionalised Innovative Labour Markets*. London and New York: Routledge, pp. 136–159.

Berry, C.R. and Glaeser, E.L., 2005: The Divergence of Human Capital Levels across Cities. Harvard University, Taubman Center Research, Working Papers, WP 05-03, Cambridge, MA.

Breschi, S. and Lissoni, F., 2009: Mobility of skilled workers and co-invention networks: an autonomy of localized knowledge flows. *Journal of Economic Geography* 9, pp. 439–468.

Criscuolo, P., 2005: On the road again: researcher mobility inside the R&D network. *Research Policy* 34, pp. 1350–1365.

Dickinson, S., Thompson, G., Rabhakar, M., Hurstfield, J. and Doel, C., 2008: Migrant workers: economic issues and opportunities. *Viewpointseries* 2.

Favell, A., Feldbaaum, M. and Smith, M.P., 2006: Mobility, migration, and technology workers: an introduction. *Knowledge, Technology and Policy* 19(3), pp 3–6.

Finn, M.G., 2003: Stay Rates of Foreign Doctorate Recipients from U.S. Universities. Oak Ridge Institute for Science and Education.

Florida, R., 2002: The economic geography of talent. *Annals of the Association of American Geographers* 92(4), pp. 743–755.

Girratani, F., Singh, V.P. and Briem, C., 2003: Dynamics of growth and restructuring in the Pittsburgh metropolitan region. In: Hilpert, U. (ed.): *Regionalisation of Globalised Innovation: Locations for advanced industrial development and disparities in participation*. London and New York: Routledge, pp. 136–152.

Gottlieb, P.D. and Joseph, G., 2006: College-to-work migration of technology graduates and holders of doctorates within the United States. *Journal of regional Science* 46(4), pp. 627–659.

Herzog, H.W., Schlottmann, A.M. and Johnson, D.L., 1986: High-technology jobs and worker mobility. *Journal of Regional Science* 26, pp. 445–459.

Hickie, D., 2006: Knowledge and competitiveness in the aerospace industry: the cases of Toulouse, Seattle and north-west England. *European Planning Studies* 14(5), pp. 697–716.

Hilpert, U. (ed.), 1991: *State policies and techno-industrial innovation*, London and New York: Routledge.

Hilpert, U., 1992: *Archipelago Europe – Islands of Innovation*, Synthesis Report. Prospective Dossier No. 1: Science, Technology and Social and Economic Cohesion in the Community, Brussels: Commission of the European Communities.

Hilpert, U., 1998: Regieren und intergouvernementale Beziehungen. In: Hilpert, U. and Holtmann, E. (eds): *Regieren und intergouvernementale Beziehungen*. Opladen: Leske und Budrich, pp. 23–48.

Hilpert, U. (ed.), 2003: *Regionalisation of Globalised Innovation: Locations for advanced industrial development and disparities in participation*. London and New York: Routledge.

Hilpert, U., 2012: Networking regionalized innovative labour markets: towards spatial concentration and mutual exchange of competence, knowledge and synergy. In: Hilpert, U. and Lawton Smith, H. (eds): *Networking Regionalised Innovative Labour Markets*. London and New York: Routledge, pp. 35–57.
Hilpert, U. and Bastian, D., 2007: *Innovation und Beschäftigung*, Unpublished research report, Jena.
Hilpert, U. and Holtmann, E. (eds), 1998: *Regieren und intergouvernementale Beziehungen*. Opladen: Leske und Budrich.
Hilpert, U. and Lawton Smith, H. (eds), 2012: *Networking Regionalised Innovative Labour Markets*. London and New York: Routledge.
Johnson, C., 1982: *MITI and the Japanese Miracle: The growth of industrial policy: 1925–1975*. Stanford, CA: Stanford University Press.
Khadira, B., 2001: Shifting paradigms of globalization: the twenty-first century transition towards generics in skilled migration from India. *International Migration* 39(5), pp. 45–71.
Kuhn, T.S., 1996: *The Structure of Scientific Revolutions*. Chicago, IL and London: University of Chicago Press.
Laudel, G., 2005: Migrant currents among scientific elite. *Minerva* 43, pp. 377–395.
Lawton Smith, H. and Waters, R., 2005: Rates of turnover in high-technology agglomerations: knowledge transfer in Oxfordshire and Cambridgeshire. *Area* 37(2), 189–198.
Mahroum, S., 1999: Global Magnets: science and technology disciplines and departments in the United Kingdom. *Minerva* 37, pp. 379–390.
Mahroum, S., 2000a: Scientists and global spaces. *Technology and Society* 22, pp. 513–523.
Mahroum, S., 2000b: Scientific mobility: an agent of scientific expansion and institutional empowerment. *Science Communication* 21, pp. 367–378.
Mahroum, S., 2001: Highly Skilled Globetrotters: The international migration of human capital, presented at the OECD Workshop on Science and Technology Labour Markets, May 17, 1999, *Proceedings*, Paris.
Marginson, S., 2006: Dynamics of national and global competition in higher education. *Higher Education* 52, pp. 1–39.
Mason, G. and Nohara, H., 2008: What's left of internal labour markets for scientists and engineers? New evidence from the UK and France. Paper prepared for IWPLMS Conference at Porto, 8–10 September 2008. Available online at: www.fep.up.pt/conferences/iwplms/documentos/WP_Papers/Paper_GMason_HNohara.pdf (accessed 19 May 2015).
Meyer, J.-B., Kaplan, D. and Charum, J., 2001: Scientific nomadism and the new geopolitics of knowledge. *International Social Science Review*, pp. 309–321.
Millar, J. and Salt, J., 2008: Portfolios of mobility: the movement of expertise in transnational corporations in two sectors – aerospace and extractive industries. *Global Networks* 8(1), pp. 25–30.
Morano-Foadi, S. and Foadi, J., 2003: Italian Scientific Migration: from Brain Exchange to Brain Drain. Paper presented on the Symposium on Science Policy, Mobility and Brain Drain in the EU and Candidate Countries at the Centre for Studies of Law and Policy in Europe, University of Leeds, July 27–28, 2003.
Norus, J., 2006: Building sustainable competitive advantage from knowledge in the region: the industrial enzymes industry. *European Planning Studies* 14(5), pp. 681–696.
Power, D. and Lundmark, M., 2004: Working through knowledge pools: market dynamics, the transference of knowledge and ideas, and industrial clusters. *Urban Studies* 41 (5/6), pp. 1025–1044.
Regets, M., 2007: Research Issues in the International Migration of Highly Skilled Workers: A Perspective with Data from the United States. Working Paper, SRS 07-203, Arlington, VA: Division of Science Resources Statistics, National Science Foundation.
Rolfe, H., 2001: Qualifications and international mobility: a case study of the European chemicals industry. *National Institute Economic Review* 175, pp. 85–94.
Sable, C.F., Herrigel, G., Kazis, R. and Deeg, R., 1991: Regional prosperities compared: Massachusetts and Baden-Württemberg. In: Hilpert, U. (ed.): *Regional Innovation and Decentralization: High tech industry and government policy*. London and New York: Routledge, pp. 177–195.
Saxenian, A., 2002: Silicon Valley's new immigrant high-growth entrepreneurs, *Economic Quarterly* 16(1), pp. 20–31.
Singh, V.P. and Briem, C., 2012: Metropolitan area migration patterns of the scientific and engineering workforce within the United States. In: Hilpert, U. and Lawton Smith, H. (eds): *Networking Regionalised Innovative Labour Markets*. London and New York: Routledge, pp. 78–95.

Trippl, M., 2012: Star Scientists, Islands of Innovation and internationally networked labour markets. In: Hilpert, U. and Lawton Smith, H. (eds): *Networking Regionalised Innovative Labour Markets*. London and New York: Routledge, pp. 58–77.

Williams, A.M., Baláz, V. and Wallace, C., 2004: International labour mobility and uneven regional development in Europe: human capital, knowledge and entrepreneurship. *European Urban and Regional Studies* 11(1), pp. 27–46.

PART 1

Dynamic development and the role of the state

Demand and support for new technologies and innovation

2

TRANSATLANTIC COMPARISON OF CONTINENTAL INNOVATION MODELS

A differentiation of regionalised processes of innovation in Europe and the US

Desmond Hickie and Ulrich Hilpert

Introduction

Over recent decades, processes of scientific discovery and technological innovation create the impression of an intensifying globalisation. Both are generated at many different locations, and participation in them, as well as the demand for the products that eventually result from them, is geographically dispersed. However, what has been experienced is a globalisation of markets for the commercialisable findings of scientific research and the products of technological innovation, rather than a globalisation of processes of innovation.

For many years nation states have been key actors in technological innovations that have had profound economic consequences (Ó Riain 2004; Breznitz 2008; Block and Keller 2009), such as the jet engine (Hickie 1991) and more recently the iPhone (Mazzucato 2013). Much state intervention was in military technologies, but there has also been strong demand for new scientific findings that could be both applied and exploited for non-military purposes (Hurt 2011). Advances in biotechnology (Collins 2004) and microprocessors have amply demonstrated that scientific research is not just a cultural activity driven by intellectual curiosity. It is also fundamental to advanced socio-economic development. This has created an intense economic interest in scientific research, in particular when its findings can enhance the competitiveness of existing industries or help generate new ones (Auerswald and Branscomb 2003; Geiger and Sa 2008).

The demand for scientific findings has increased greatly because of the changing international division of labour. The processes of industrialisation in developing economies, particularly in Asia, have been and still are characterised by the relocation of much of manufacturing to former Third World Countries, and a growing concentration on both research and knowledge intensive industries in Western countries. Clearly, knowledge intensive industries were focused largely on the introduction of new products and the creation of new industries and markets, but scientific advances and technological innovation also generated new products and processes in some established industries (e.g. biotechnology in pharmaceuticals; robotics in the automotive industry). While such industrial impacts were, arguably, felt most intensively in the developed economies, they also clearly often had a strong impact in newly industrialising countries.

Processes of innovation were related to national research infrastructures and scientific capabilities wherever these may be. Even before the intensive globalisation of markets of the last two decades, national scientific communities were integrating, to enhance the exchange of new knowledge and scientific findings. Growing international trade, and the development of lucrative markets for technology based products in Japan, Western Europe and North America, increased the potential benefits available for technological first movers in such markets. The increased competitive intensity in these high technology industries had two structural consequences both for the scientific community and the industries that used its findings: (i) dynamic industrial change and rapid economic development were concentrated in regions characterised by their scientific and techno-industrial potential and, (ii) the competitive pressure to innovate, and apply new technological advances intensified inter-organisational collaboration with partners wherever they might be located. While the regional concentration of collaboration and networking within and between science and industry was not new (Hilpert 1992) the competitive pressure for rapid techno-scientific progress intensified the search for suitable partners in other regions – both nationally and internationally.

The internationalisation of scientific research and formation of joint projects provided the basis for the networks of collaboration that facilitated the creation of competitive innovations. Hence, regions with strong research structures were able to engage in international research networks and had opportunities to participate in research-based and technology intensive economic development (Hilpert 1992; Mahroum 2000b, 1999; Williams *et al.* 2004; Trippl 2012). These regions were in a position to concentrate research and to form centres of collaboration in such international networks. The growing concentration of scientific and technological activities in particular regions, and their dominance in international collaborative networks, meant that only a limited number of regions was equipped to participate effectively in these processes of scientific advance and technological innovation. These are Islands of Innovation where the most advanced scientific research and high technology innovation are primarily located. On average, about two thirds of the research projects funded by governments in Europe or the US are carried out at these locations and even more important is their position as the locations of preferred collaborative partners and both situations have continued for over a quarter of a century (Hilpert 2012, 1992). Of course, national research funds could be used most effectively in these Islands, and so were spent overwhelmingly within them, thereby intensifying the disparity between them and less fortunate regions. The networks of collaboration between Islands of Innovation served the aims of public policies, both identifying and generating synergies between regions and by spreading new scientific findings and technological advances between competent research facilities, nationally and internationally. Additionally, in Europe, the European Union aimed to 'Europeanise' research and fostered collaborative research among European research institutions. Needless to say, such support was focused primarily on regions that were already scientifically strong and in receipt of national research funding.

Building Islands of Innovation – creating concentrations of internationally competitive research institutions and projects – was a clear outcome of the global race in innovation among the leading industrialised countries. National policies, as well as European policies, supported such concentrations as a means to participate in the socio-economic benefits of techno-industrial innovation. The more such policies are successful, the more they strengthen regional participation in international or global networks, and the intensification of national and/or European collaboration. Such participation is not widely diffused, but is focused on the Islands of Innovation.

Locations and regional development

Given the networks that are formed by collaborative research and the support that is provided by nation states and the European Union, regions have become increasingly important to economic growth in highly developed countries. This raises questions about what enables regions to act as centres of scientific research and technological innovation, and how does a region become an Island of Innovation? Once they are immersed in networks of innovation where they participate in developments that are mutually beneficial to all participating locations, regions and locations are no mere sub-national entities, they are almost semi-autonomous actors in an international process that is characterised by supra-national processes and that has already passed beyond the control of nation states – at least beyond that of European nation states.

Advanced socio-economic development, when it is characterised by science-based innovation, is linked to geographically dispersed processes. It is important to see that such partnerships, or established collaborations, are usually built upon existing networks in scientific research. It is not simply that such regions, with their strong scientific research capabilities, are better placed to participate in research-based innovation (Hickie 2003; Hilpert 2003). It is also because such regions have larger numbers of high technology enterprises founded on the basis of earlier scientific research at universities or public research institutes. Such enterprises usually retain, and may even enhance, their links with the scientific community both inside and outside their 'home' region. In principle, the more intensively they interact with researchers and high technology businesses in other regions, the more access they will have to new knowledge (Powell *et al.* 2005). Variations in the economic development of different regions can be induced by their varied positions and roles in research networks, by the extent of transfers of knowledge from universities to neighbouring businesses, and the extent to which national research policies allow the spin-out of new research-based businesses from universities.

In Islands of Innovation, regional development and regional universities are closely linked, so the more regional authorities have the financial, legal and cognitive capacities to enhance local universities' research strengths, the more they can leverage their universities' network positions, and facilitate the creation of innovation opportunities. So, it is not just the pure competence in research that matters. It is also the access to others' research findings, probably discovered elsewhere, and the capacity to transform such knowledge into the creation of new enterprises within the region. This requires a variety of conditions:

- the opportunities of universities to participate in new enterprises;
- the recruitment of personnel to form larger research departments and to generate synergies; and
- the ability to retain researchers in the region, where they can contribute to both university research and to enterprises that apply the new knowledge.

In the US the relationship between scientific research and economic application is much closer than in Europe (Lerner 2005; Berman 2012). In particular, frequently universities in the US are especially closely related to enterprises in their home region, sometimes because these enterprises are start-ups based on university research, or set up by former students. In addition, researchers can easily be recruited from across the continent, and in larger metropolises with large labour markets for university trained personnel they may stay in the same region throughout their academic lives (Mahroum 2000a; Bélanger 2002; Morano-Foadi and Foadi 2003; Williams *et al.* 2004; Coulombe and Tremblay 2009). This contrasts with the European situation, where universities do not generally participate in the founding of new research-based enterprises (except in the UK), and where the relationship between universities and the innovative local enterprises is generally far less developed than in North America. In addition, the different European cultures and languages still form barriers to recruitment from other European countries. Furthermore, some European countries (e.g. Germany) force researchers to leave the university and in general the region where they completed their postgraduate studies to continue their academic career at a different university. Hence, in Europe, it is not common for researchers to be recruited from across the continent, nor are they generally helped to build advantageous regional networks with enterprises. Hence, even though technologically advanced regions in Europe and North America may each have infrastructures of universities, public research institutes and high technology enterprises, their opportunities to innovate and create opportunities for economic growth are not the same.

The close relationship between research and start-up enterprises in research-based areas and the role of universities when recruiting personnel both play an important role for the networks that the enterprises are involved in and the regions they are participating in. So, although regions have to meet similar conditions to perform as appropriate locations, the opportunities for development are different between North America and Europe. The relationship between university research and the founding of research-based enterprises, the recruitment of scientific personnel at the universities, and the relationship between research-based enterprises located in the region and the strengths of the university research are forming different situations for development.

North America is an area that is rather similar in culture, language and regulation, whereas, Europe is widely characterised by a multinational, multicultural situation and a multilingual culture that cannot recreate the homogeneity of the US. In Europe while research is embedded in particular national and regional contexts, it may also be linked with scientific research elsewhere. However, due to regulations and different traditions that may become difficult to handle when changing positions across countries, recruiting outstanding scientific personnel from abroad can create a significant problem. It needs to be borne in mind that the vast divergences throughout leading European countries and academic communities also provide many opportunities for merging different research traditions and research strategies for new findings and applications. However, regulations and tradition in some situations are a barrier to potential synergies that might be generated by the fusion of knowledge from across Europe. Although the Islands of Innovation are linked with a global body of knowledge, an international network of collaboration, European regions are still bound into their national contexts and national scientific systems. This does not hinder the development of scientific research excellence, but European and American regions face different situations if they try to develop as an Island of Innovation. While in North America they can take advantage of a shared scientific system that allows for a frequent exchange of personnel and for advantage to be taken of vast government programmes, in Europe they first relate to smaller national government programmes, and even complementary EU-programmes do not provide a situation that compares with the US. The problem arises in the economic application and exploitation of scientific findings within a region and when trying to take advantage of high levels of the European scientific competence to form an Island of Innovation. University research, or research carried out at public scientific research institutes, is more frequently used for regional development in North America than in Europe. As explained above, there are differences in European and North American universities' recruitment patterns and the opportunities to keep experienced research personnel in a region. National situations in Europe limit the opportunities for regions to become Islands of Innovation, be it because of the smaller size of the countries and their regions, or because of the inappropriate constraints placed on regional innovation policies by national governments. So, in the end, some regions are better placed than others to participate in international high-technology-based economic development, with US regions being frequently somewhat better placed than those in Europe when it comes to leading edge research technologies, while it might be different when merging such competences with traditional industries for modernisation (e.g. the application of biotechnology with medical instruments or measurement instruments or the application of electronics or new materials in mechanical engineering).

Trans-regional collaboration as a tendency towards continentalisation

Regions are linked to one another in various ways (e.g. universities may collaborate with one another, with government research institutes, or with enterprises across regional boundaries). Trans-regional collaboration can generate beneficial effects at all locations that are involved. The stronger a region is both in scientific research and in technological innovation, the more likely it is to attract trans-regional collaborative partners, whether it seeks them proactively or waits for potential partners to seek it out.

The European Union is particularly interested in fostering collaboration among partners from different member countries *inter alia*, encouraging the development of networks and the potential for synergies. European programmes on research and technology give particular priority to participation by a variety of EU-member countries. In contrast, programmes and funding provided by individual European countries focus on the national strengths and networking among national participants. Hence national technology funding focuses primarily on the country's technologically and economically strongest regions. In doing so it enhances the opportunity for such regions to participate in European networks, thereby creating a reciprocally supportive process enhancing the competitiveness of existing Islands of Innovation. Participating regions benefit mutually from their collaboration, not least learning from each other. In the spirit of European integration several EU programmes (e.g. ENABLE, INTERREG and EUREGIO) foster inter-governmental collaboration that may help regions to form relationships that contribute to their collective and individual development and enable regions to design their own path of development. In the US, as in European states, national science and technology programmes are oriented towards American participants.

However, European regions do not only engage in trans-regional collaboration because of funding from EU programmes. They also see such relationships as being in their longer term economic and social interests. This recognition has evolved very rapidly, from an early exploratory approach to trans-regional collaboration into a more mature awareness of the opportunities that international cooperation offers for regional development policies. For example, international networks can assist regions to manage the challenges of international outsourcing, the delocalisation of production, the attraction of inward investment, and migration flows. This is indicated most impressively in Silicon Valley when referring to the immigration of labour and even more so when foreigners act as new entrepreneurs in high technology (Saxenian 2002). Similar economic and social situations exist in various European regions. This creates both an interest in the exchange of knowledge, and an opportunity for institutional learning, as well as for joint activities mutually to foster regional development. Clearly, all European regions are characterised by their nation states, and by the opportunities created by the European Union. However, they vary markedly, because of the heterogeneity of their national governmental systems (e.g. federalist, centralist, regionalist systems), which have a profound impact upon the legal autonomy, budgets and cognitive capacity that regional governments can mobilise to develop their own regional policies. For example, the larger and more economically successful German Länder that often have the capability of smaller industrialised countries[1] have far more opportunities to draw upon EU-programmes than smaller and poorer regions in the new member states (Medve-Bálint 2013). Hence, although EU regional programmes are common to all member states, they have to be taken up and applied in a wide variety of regional contexts, and this contextual heterogeneity impacts directly upon take up rates, the quality of implementation, and ultimately on policy impacts and effectiveness. In some areas of science European regional governments, universities and research institutes are involved in trans-Atlantic collaborations. These collaborations occur only in those regions that already have a strong science base (that makes them internationally significant) and access to the funding necessary to participate effectively. So, trans-regional collaboration can be economically significant and mutually beneficial, and public policy at both national and regional levels can play a crucial role in developing innovative international networks.

Different levels of government play a key role in these innovatory international networks, because strong regional governments (as with the large German Länder of Baden-Württemberg, Bavaria or North Rhine-Westphalia) provide budgets that widely define both which networks regions participate in, and the choice of regions with which they collaborate (Bellini and Hilpert 2013). Hence, network participation and the benefits derived from it depend upon both the intrinsic scientific, technological and economic strength of the region, and upon the policy decisions of the public authorities that govern it. Stronger regions, characterised by dynamic scientific and technological development are both more likely to participate in international collaborative networks, and to occupy a key role within them. Thus, it is not a surprise that leading regions are well placed in international networks such as Greater Paris, Rhône-Alpes with Grenoble as the centre, the regions of Milan or Turin in Italy, Greater London, the Øresund or the strong German Länder, which also have significant budgets. Conversely, regions that are less innovatory and economically dynamic are both less likely to participate and to be key players in such networks. Among those regions that were characterised by old industrial structures only one third were successful in transforming into an Island of Innovation (Hilpert 1992). There is also a correspondence between inter-regional networks of innovation and other broader inter-regional networks of governmental collaboration among the more economically dynamic regions of the EU, which was already indicated by the Four Motors of Europe in the 1990s and again in the development of cross-border regions in the upper Rhine Valley including regions from France, Germany and Switzerland (which also share a cultural history) and the emerging strong European macro-regions (Bellini and Hilpert 2013). It may also be the case that such strong regions are more frequently engaged in activities without EU-funding, than might be the case for less advantaged and less dynamic regions. In forming such a complex situation based on national opportunities in academic research and capable industries, different national governmental systems and traditions that are complemented by the European Union as a supra-national organisation provide for a specific constellation that is clearly different from the US which characterises the North American situation but it characterises the European situation also as a continental system.

The preceding analysis raises two questions: to what extent, and why, do regions deliberately aim to participate in the continentalised innovation system that is emerging from their inter-regional collaborations? Economically strong regions in federalised countries, and small countries with strong research capabilities, may be in a position to choose their partners for trans-regional collaboration more freely than less favoured regions and small countries. They may also be in a position autonomously to support both continental and trans-Atlantic collaboration in scientific research. So, although the overall tendency may indicate a process of continentalisation, there may be some regions that have more freedom to decide for themselves. This, in turn, may also suggest the possibility that less favoured regions may be more bound into the process of continentalisation, even though they benefit less from it, because their lack of autonomy makes them dependent upon EU funded projects whose focus is continental. In the end, continentalisation might be a tendency that is not just identifiable with regard to the activities of the innovative actors, but it might also be induced politically, a consequence of the policies introduced by the various levels of government and of inter-governmental relationships (Bellini and Hilpert 2013).

Regional labour markets and innovative networking

Highly skilled and university trained labour are both essential for regional participation in the processes of innovation that are generated within trans-regional networks among Islands of Innovation. New findings need to be produced by researchers, and the collaborative objectives set out in formal agreements between regions can only be achieved by the workers in research-based enterprises or universities. The regional labour supply of such personnel is clearly a necessary condition for taking part in such processes. Since the recruitment of the right personnel plays a critical role in enabling effective networking, the exchange of knowledge and the creation of synergy, the existence of a labour market for such personnel is fundamental to participation in inter-regional high technology networks. Businesses predominantly recruit their staff regionally, within the Islands of Innovation where they are located. Universities are strategically important when forging links with top researchers from other regions. So if the Islands of Innovation are able to retain and attract new highly skilled labour, this raises a question about what impact their competitive advantage in the markets for highly skilled labour has on less favoured regions.

The demand for university trained labour is particularly strong at the Islands of Innovation and creates career opportunities for those from other regions or countries. Few job opportunities exist for the most highly trained scientists and technologists outside these favoured locations and the migration of such labour into them can be identified in several ways (Hilpert and Lawton Smith 2012; Trippl 2012). So, the creation of innovative labour markets plays an important role both for advanced regional development and the migration of researchers and engineers to the strongest regions. Because the supply of this labour is limited, these regionalised labour markets in the Islands of Innovation are also linked to broader global or continental labour markets. This raises the issues: to what extent such innovative labour is recruited by firms and universities in the US from Europe (and vice versa), and to what extent US and European Islands of Innovation recruit from other continents?

Significant differences are evident in the migration patterns of highly skilled scientists and technologists. Only a small percentage of recruitment takes place across the continents. To a certain extent, this indicates that European integration is taking place in these regionalised innovative labour markets. However, it also means that countries from Eastern Central Europe and from the European periphery (e.g. Portugal, Spain and Greece) can neither provide attractive working conditions and incomes, nor provide a research environment as attractive as those in the established Islands of Innovation. Even though the number of researchers and personnel emigrating may not be very high, outward migration weakens these countries and reduces their ability to build a critical mass of highly qualified scientists and technologists. Conversely, the established Islands of Innovation are highly attractive to, and benefit from the inward migration of university trained labour. Those emigrating into the Islands are frequently among the best qualified scientists and technologists in their home countries. They need to be, to find suitable work in the highly competitive skilled labour markets in the Islands of Innovation. Migration contributes to a pattern of continental innovation (Bernard *et al.* 2012; Waters and Lawton Smith 2012) that is achieved through a defined network of outstanding locations.

Similarly, migration to North America has a particular pattern. Immigrants from Asia to North America have a higher education level than the average American and, not surprisingly, they are strongly attracted to regions with a strong demand for university trained personnel. Regions with research universities have proved to be especially attractive locations for highly trained Asian migrants and here they contribute positively to regional labour markets. It is interesting that such university trained personnel are more strongly oriented towards North American locations rather than to European Islands of Innovation. Even the former colonial powers, Britain and France, with close traditional contacts and a significant impact on academic and cultural life in many of these Asian countries, cannot attract academic migrants in such numbers. Fewer than 10 per cent of the star scientists are based in these countries. In contrast, they generally aim for jobs at the 'magnets of science' and finally there are a number who start enterprises in the US as is demonstrated by the Indian or Chinese immigrants in Silicon Valley (Mahroum 2000b, 1999; Saxenian 2002; Williams *et al.* 2004; Trippl 2012). While this may not have a profound impact on the regional labour markets in North America, particularly in the US, it nevertheless contributes positively to these Islands of Innovation.

There are significant differences between migration patterns for highly trained migrants in Europe and the US Islands of Innovation. European Islands are more likely to recruit other Europeans, whereas in North America the migrants come from other continents. In addition, the migrants tend to come from different university cultures. The Asian migrants tend to come from systems heavily influenced by Western educational practice (especially the British and US systems), East European migrants come from universities that are still restructuring, following the abandonment of Communism, and whose educational systems were not easily compatible with Western university cultures. So, such migrants have to adjust not only to the broader sociocultural environment, but also to a radically different organisational environment and scientific tradition.

Although there are these divergent pictures of academic migration, the innovative centres exchange such labour predominantly among each other or else retain it in their own region. Since there is rather limited trans-Atlantic exchange, most migration between Islands of Innovation is therefore intra-continental. For Europe this means most migration is national, between centres in the same country. Different languages and cultures form barriers that are the more effective because of various national regulations (e.g. about the employment of university staff) and differences in everyday life (e.g. schools, jobs for partners, social security and pension funds). Such differences are far fewer and less intrusive in North America. Innovative regional labour markets, as a consequence, in Europe are identified primarily with national contexts, and migrants who may consider a change of country attractive. Age also plays a part, in that junior personnel can often change country more easily, having invested less in their national university system's career structure than their more senior colleagues. So, regional innovative labour markets exist to serve a small, highly educated labour force, and in Europe are essentially multinational, reflecting the diversity of European regions, not least their Islands of Innovation.

Despite strong attempts for European integration, both national regulations and national policies remain highly influential, and the stronger the individual European countries or regions are, the more their policies counterbalance processes of Europeanisation, enabling regions and nations to retain their highly skilled workers. So, while there is a process of continentalisation in both Europe and North America, it materialises differently in each continent.

The roles of nation states and the EU for continentalisation of innovation

While the scientific community is interested in partnership and collaboration to advance scientific knowledge, nation states (and the EU) have a profound interest in ensuring that these processes take place in their own territories where potentially they can have beneficial economic effects (Breznitz 2008). Hence, the individual countries in North America and Europe wish to intensify the exchange of knowledge among scientific research institutes and research-based enterprises within their own territory, and launch programmes to achieve this. The European Union, in addition, supports research that involves different partners within Europe, in particular from the European periphery, and forms the basis for a European network.

This political interest, in maximising the effects of innovation and socio-economic development within the countries of Europe and North America, provides research funding. As scientists spend this money it has two identifiable, and mutually reinforcing effects. First, it is the strongest regions, the Islands of Innovation, that are most successful in gaining this funding, and they spend it on staff and capital equipment that both enhances their competitiveness, and makes them more attractive to potential partners for inter-regional partnerships. Second, the largest and economically strongest European countries can afford to spend more on research in their Islands of Innovation, further enhancing their competitiveness, not least when competing for EU funding. Hence the flows of research funding serve to enhance the disparity between the stronger and weaker regions. A somewhat similar position exists in the US, where national programmes prioritise participation by American research institutions, and permit foreign participation only when necessary for the success of the project. A case in point is the US Strategic Defense initiative (Star Wars), which was not only a defence project, but one that was seen as enhancing the commercial competitiveness of the US microelectronics industry, among others. In both the US and Europe, scientific research is seen as having the potential to catalyse technological innovation, as new scientific findings are taken up by both new and established businesses, primarily in Islands of Innovation, where researchers and businesses are often co-located.

National scientific communities continue to exist, and they also broadly retain their standings within the international scientific community, provided there are no drastic changes in the governance and economy of their home country (as for example in the former Soviet Union). Nation states or the European Union continue to encourage the exchange of basic research findings, providing mutual access to new discoveries and advanced scientific findings and helping to avoid national scientific isolation. However, there are clear differences between Europe and the US. Europe will retain its variety of national scientific communities, although it will continue to be dominated by the science systems of its leading and most technologically advanced economies. This may create some problems of efficiency when compared with the unitary system that exists in North America, but the divergent traditions of individually strong research cultures, and their cross-European fertilisation achieved through collaboration, may be a basis for finding heterogeneous research methodologies and varied solutions to technological problems. So, the heterogeneity of Europe's nation states, their structures and their public policies, can lead to a diversity of Islands of Innovation, research cultures and science-based enterprises that enhance their collective competitiveness. There is also, of course, scientific and technological collaboration between Europe and the US and joint research projects. But the intensity of this trans-Atlantic activity is much lower (e.g. in biotechnology, where collaboration on one's own continent counts for about 75 per cent of all contracted joint activities whereas trans-Atlantic collaboration amounts to only 18 per cent) (Hilpert 2012).

The policies of the nation states in Europe and North America, and those of the European Union, are fundamental to the continentalisation of innovation, in particular the ways in which they fund research and innovation. The existing Islands of Innovation provide a vehicle for successfully achieving national policy objectives, and they are fundamental for the processes of continentalisation. Their varied profiles and their heterogeneous regional agglomerations of research competence allow both different patterns of specialisation and divergent paths of innovative development (Schrank 2011). This variation in policy impacts can be identified both in the varied profiles and performances of individual regions, and in the differences in the innovatory profiles and performances of the larger nation states, which are, of course, agglomerations of Islands. This heterogeneous archipelago of regions, which is linked by inter-regional research programmes, is fundamental to the processes of continentalisation that are the outcome of the public policies pursued by nation states and the EU. A diverse picture emerges when Europe and North America are compared: the rather unified and homogeneous North American science system reflects the dominance of a single political system, the United States, whereas Europe shows a wide variety of science systems, political systems, cultures and while the EU is yet another distinctive actor in these processes that together enable different and divergent processes of innovation. A more Europeanised science system in the future still will not overcome the national interests and will be characterised by the heterogeneous public policies of national governments applied to their national territories. Hence, continental differences can be expected to continue, and the processes of continentalisation in the US and Europe will remain divergent.

How to participate in innovative networks: emerging Islands of Innovation and their structures of collaboration

While the two continental systems of the Archipelago Europe and the North American system of Islands of Innovation (which are predominantly located at both coasts) characterise the predominant global processes of innovation and advanced socio-economic development, there are other regional concentrations of high quality research that are growing to add a more global dimension to the existing system of innovation. For a long time, new technologies and processes of industrial innovation were related to the research capabilities of Europe and the US. During the 1970s and 1980s new industrial plants were established in Third World countries that increasingly supplied the older industrialised countries with mass produced goods. Simultaneously these older industrialised countries took advantage of lower production costs and the supply of cheaper goods for consumers. The relocation of mass production industries that relied on cheap labour, away from Europe and the US, induced a permanent structural change in Western economies, which are now characterised by an orientation towards knowledge-based and research intensive products. Microelectronics, aviation industries, new energy technologies or – more recently – biotechnology, exemplify this change. But the maturing of such products, allied to the industrial development of the newly industrialised countries (NICs), has led to a situation where products, previously regarded as complex and technology intensive, can now be manufactured competitively in these NICs (e.g. aircraft designed and manufactured in Brazil). Continuing industrial development and advanced manufacturing in these countries has allowed an accumulation of capital, which has been accompanied by attempts first to establish and then strengthen their domestic research capabilities. So, the global picture has already changed and is still changing, allowing new locations to develop strong research capabilities and contribute significantly to the international scientific community.

As part of its industrial and technological development, Korea established the Korean Institute of Science and Technology (KIST) in 1966 to help develop its capabilities in advanced manufacturing and innovation. It contributed to Korean industrial development, particularly during the 1970s and 1980s. Currently it focuses on areas of research suited to Korea's industrial structure and that are similar to those pursued in the US and Europe (e.g. energy technologies, nano technology, new materials, life sciences). Equally, in the late 1990s Taiwan was able to develop its mechanical engineering industry so that it could challenge global market leaders in Germany, Switzerland and Italy, which continued their leading position based on developing technologically more advanced and well equipped products. Singapore continues to invest strongly in its research capacity as a means to develop itself into a global centre for advanced manufacturing. In India, Bangalore has become a globally competitive centre for software design and production (especially in computer gaming) since the 1980s, building on its investment in research and education. More recently attempts have been made to repeat this success in biotechnology and aerospace. However, it is important to add that each of these Indian developments is characterised by market entry in subsectors that are not at the leading edge of global innovation in these three industries.

These different examples of innovative activities outside of Europe or North America indicate two tendencies: there is a high level of engagement in various areas of research and technology that are not part of the two continental modes of innovation; and that participation in such networks is related to quite specialised contributions within a global division of research work. However, it also indicates that the continentalisation of innovation need not be exclusive. There are opportunities for global participation from locations that are neither European nor North American Islands of Innovation. It may be that a new situation is emerging regarding leading edge science-based innovation. Given both the capabilities of countries such as India or China and their numbers of researchers, one has to ask whether their emerging Islands of Innovation will continue to seek research and industrial partners in Western industrialised countries. It might well be that national policies aimed at creating a substantial number of strong research and innovation centres in the large emerging economies (e.g. India, China and possibly Brazil) may place priority on creating collaborative links between them, so building first Islands of Innovation and then networks of Islands within a single national system – creating a kind of sub-continentalisation.

Conclusions

Although economic development is increasingly related to consumer markets and producers that need not be geographically close, thereby rendering space increasingly virtual, regional concentrations of research and innovative activity remain hugely significant. Yet, although the concentration of these activities is essential to the creation of Islands of Innovation, the resulting Islands provide the concentration of resources and capabilities that equip a region to innovate in collaboration with other regions and locations. Equally, it is the region's concentration of scientific and technological resources that attracts potential collaborators from other regions and countries. Simultaneously, Islands of Innovation represent geographical concentrations of innovatory activity, while facilitating the building of much more geographically dispersed inter-regional research and innovation networks – thus forming continentalised patterns of collaboration in Europe and the US.

Continentalisation consequently is based on Islands of Innovation that are interrelated by systems of networking. In addition, the regional concentration of both innovative activities and research capabilities is a process that takes place because of the cumulative agglomeration of universities, public research institutes, innovative and research driven enterprises, and of innovative labour markets. So, only a limited number of regions can both contribute to and participate in the systems of innovation. This means that understanding regionalised innovation must be understood in the context of a region's position in one or more networks of collaboration. It is also an important condition for understanding both innovation in general and why it adopts a continentalised pattern of development. Furthermore, since research and technology policies, and funding provide the basis for scientific research, the location of these activities and the networks of collaboration that form around them are clearly significantly dependent upon the aims and implementation of public policies.

Building strong Islands of Innovation is thus an important policy instrument to achieve processes of innovation, nationally or continentally. The stronger these locations are, and the more attractive they appear for potential collaborators, the more critically they are placed within their continental networks of innovation. Indeed they even participate significantly in trans-Atlantic structures of collaboration. It would also be reasonable to assume that in future intercontinental collaboration that spreads to locations outside North America or the European Union, will be strongly oriented towards key Islands of Innovation. So, understanding the dynamics that form the networks of Islands of Innovation helps in understanding the process of innovation in general – regionally, nationally, internationally and even intercontinentally. More specifically, it helps in understanding the individual national, regional or continental positions of particular regions, universities and enterprises and how they can participate in innovatory networks. Hence, science-based innovation is always subject to scientific advances that may be generated globally. Public policies and traditions in science play an important role supporting existing patterns of participation in innovation and the exploitation of new technologies to achieve industrial and socio-economic development. Understanding the regionalised processes of innovation in Europe and North America can provide scope for identifying more clearly the different models of the continentalisation of innovation.

Note

1 E.g. Baden-Württemberg is similar to Sweden, Bavaria similar to Austria, and North Rhine-Westphalia on its own would count as one of the ten strongest industrialised countries in the world.

References

Auerswald, P. and Branscomb, L., 2003: Valleys of Death and Darwinian Seas: financing the invention to innovation transition in the United States. *Journal of Technology Transfer* 28, pp. 227–239.

Bélanger, J., 2002: From human capital to organisational learning. *Canadian Public Policy/Analyse de Politiques* 28(1), pp. 143–148.

Bellini, N. and Hilpert, U. (eds), 2013: *Europe's Changing Geography*. London and New York: Routledge.

Berman, E., 2012: *Creating the Market University: How academic science became an economic engine*. Princeton, NJ: Princeton University Press.

Bernard, J., Patocková, V. and Kostelechý, T., 2012: Islands of Innovation in the Czech Republic. In: Hilpert, U. and Lawton Smith, H. (eds): *Networking Regionalised Innovative Labour Markets*. London and New York: Routledge, pp. 136–159.

Block, F. and Keller, M., 2009: Where do innovations come from? Transformations in the US economy, 1970–2006. *Socio-Economic Review* 7(3), pp. 459–483.

Breznitz, D., 2008: *Innovation and the State: Political choice and strategies for growth in Israel, Taiwan and Ireland*. New Haven, CT: Yale University Press.

Collins, S., 2004: *The Race to Commercialize Biotechnology*. New York: Routledge-Curzon.

Coulombe, S. and Tremblay, J.-F., 2009: Migration and skills disparities across Canadian provinces. *Regional Studies* 43(1), pp. 5–18.

Geiger, R. and Sa, C., 2008: *Tapping the Riches of Science Universities and the Promise of Economic Growth*. Cambridge, MA: Harvard University Press.

Hickie, D., 1991: *Archipelago Europe – Islands of Innovation: The case of the United Kingdom*. Brussels: Commission of the European Communities.

Hickie, D., 2003: Islands of Innovation in the UK Economy: high technology, networking and public policy. In: Hilpert, U. (ed.): *Regionalisation of Globalised Innovation*. London and New York: Routledge.

Hilpert, U., 1992: *Archipelago Europe – Islands of Innovation, Synthesis Report. Prospective Dossier No. 1: Science, Technology and Social and Economic Cohesion in the Community*. Brussels: Commission of the European Communities.

Hilpert, U. (ed.), 2003: *Regionalisation of Globalised Innovation: Locations for advanced industrial development and disparities in participation*. London and New York: Routledge.

Hilpert, U., 2012: Networking regionalized innovative labour markets: towards spatial concentration and mutual exchange of competence, knowledge and synergy. In: Hilpert, U. and Lawton Smith, H. (eds): *Networking Regionalised Innovative Labour Markets*. London and New York: Routledge, pp. 3–31.

Hilpert, U. and Lawton Smith, H. (Eds.), 2012: *Networking Regionalised Innovative Labour Markets*. London and New York: Routledge.

Hurt, S., 2011: The military hidden hand: examining the dual-use origins of biotechnology in the American context. In: Block, F. and Keller, M. (eds): *State of Innovation: The US government's role in technology development*. Columbia: Paradigm.

Lerner, J., 2005: The university and the start-up: lessons from the last two decades. *Journal of Technology Transfer* 30(1–2), pp. 49–56.

Mahroum, S., 1999: Global magnets: science and technology disciplines and departments in the United Kingdom. *Minerva* 37, pp. 379–390.

Mahroum, S., 2000a: Scientific mobility: an agent of scientific expansion and institutional empowerment. *Science Communication* 21, pp. 367–378.

Mahroum, S., 2000b: Scientists and global spaces. *Technology and Society* 22, pp. 513–523.

Mazzucato, M., 2013: *The Entrepreneurial State: Debunking public vs. private sector myths*. London: Anthem Press.

Medve-Bálint, G., 2013: Incentives and obstacles to cross-border cooperation in post-communist central Europe. In: Bellini, N. and Hilpert, U. (eds): *Europe's Changing Geography*. London and New York: Routledge, pp. 145–170.

Morano-Foadi, S. and Foadi, J., 2003: Italian scientific migration: from brain exchange to brain drain, Research report No. 8, University of Leeds: Centre for the Study of Law and Policy in Europe. Available online at: www.leeds.ac.uk/law/cslpe/phare/No.8.pdf (accessed 21 May 2015).

Ó Riain, S., 2004: *The Politics of High-Tech Growth: Developmental network states in the global economy*. Cambridge: Cambridge University Press.

Powell, W., White, D., Koput, K. and Owen-Smith, J., 2005: Network dynamics and field evolution: the growth of inter-organizational collaboration in the life sciences. *American Journal of Sociology* 110(4), pp. 1132–1205.

Saxenian, A., 2002: Silicon Valley's new immigrant high-growth entrepreneurs. *Economic Quarterly* 16(1), pp. 20–31.

Schrank, A., 2011: Green capitalists in a purple state: Sandia National Laboratories and the renewable energy industry in New Mexico. In: Block, F. and Keller, M. (eds): *State of Innovation: The US government's role in technology development*. Columbia: Paradigm.

Trippl, M., 2012: Star Scientists, Islands of Innovation and internationally networked labour markets. In: Hilpert, U. and Lawton Smith, H. (eds): *Networking Regionalised Innovative Labour Markets*. London and New York: Routledge, pp. 58–77.

Waters, R. and Lawton Smith, H., 2012: High-technology local economies: geographical mobility of the highly skilled. In: Hilpert, U. and Lawton Smith, H. (eds): *Networking Regionalised Innovative Labour Markets*. London and New York: Routledge, pp. 96–116.

Williams, A.M., Baláz, V. and Wallace, C., 2004: International labour mobility and uneven regional development in Europe: human capital, knowledge and entrepreneurship. *European Urban and Regional Studies* 11(1), pp. 27–46.

3

TECHNOLOGY AND SOCIO-ECONOMIC DEVELOPMENT IN THE LONG RUN

A 'long wave' perspective

Walter Scherrer

Introduction

The dynamics of economic life is not of a simple and linear but of a complex nature, Nikolai Kondratieff noted when he detected that economic development in capitalist economies is characterized by 'long waves' of approximately fifty years' length. His suggestion that these waves are likely to be linked to technological change was taken up by Joseph Schumpeter who endogenized technical change in a theory of economic development. Neo-Schumpeterian economists refined this idea, many of them emphasizing the key role of institutional change for innovation and diffusion of new technologies that drive the dynamics of the long wave. Each wave is historically unique and driven by the diffusion of specific clusters of technologies, and the related political and institutional change has shaped socio-economic development in each individual historical epoch differently. The dynamics of long waves, however, is characterized by patterns and regularities of how technologies are diffused, and how and under what conditions this process brings about fundamental change in the economy. Thus, there is the question of how this relates with government policies – be it to induce techno-scientific progress as a basis for new technologies or be it how to adapt to the newly emerging technologies and the related organizational change.

Technological change and economic development: Early long-wave contributions

In econometric analyses of long time series Kondratieff (1926, 1935) and van Gelderen (1913, 1996) independently claimed to having detected wave-like movements of an average length of approximately fifty years. Each 'long wave' marks a distinct historical epoch comprising a long-term upswing and a long-term downswing of economic activity (Kondratieff) or a 'spring tide' and an 'ebb tide' (van Gelderen). Both authors suggest a close link between technological change and the long wave. Kondratieff claimed to merely describe the phenomenon of long waves;

the direction and intensity of technical change would be determined by 'the necessities of real life', and by the preceding development of science and technique (Kondratieff 1935: 112). An exceptionally large number of important discoveries and inventions in the technique of production and communication would emerge in recessions, which would be applied on a large scale only in the following long upswing (Kondratieff 1935). In Kondratieff's understanding the introduction and diffusion of new technologies are not drivers *of* the long wave but are driven *by* the long wave. By contrast, van Gelderen notes that 'the sudden emergence of a new production branch which, in a more powerful way than before, satisfies a certain human need', or 'the cultivation of previously largely uninhibited areas' (van Gelderen 1996: 40) establish the conditions for the emergence of a period of springtime. Innovation is considered a driver *of* the long wave, but it is not explained why and how new branches or new markets emerge in order to create the conditions for an expansion of the long wave.

Taking up Kondratieff's idea of long waves – and actually naming them 'Kondratieff cycles' – Schumpeter (1939)[1] developed a framework in which profit-driven entrepreneurs who compare perceived risk and expected returns of new ventures make innovation and technical change endogenous to the economic process. Technological innovation is the driver of at least three types of cyclical economic fluctuations, the forty-month Kitchin cycle, the ten-year Juglar cycle, and the Kondratieff cycle. Radical innovations give way to the formation of new industrial sectors, and incremental innovations based on the initial innovation and imitation lead to a swarming of innovations and trigger the upswing of a long wave. But improvement innovations are subject to the law of diminishing returns and profits are competed-away so that the innovating impulse will dissipate over time.

A brief historical record of long waves

The diffusion of the new technologies that trigger the long wave dynamics is complemented by the build-up of related transport and communication infrastructures and by innovations in the organization of the economy and the management of production.[2] The first Kondratieff or early mechanisation wave occurred during the Industrial Revolution at the turn of the eighteenth to the nineteenth century. Limitations of scale and of process control were inherent to the pre-industrial mode of production and were overcome by mechanization based on the use of water power and factory organization as a major innovation in organizing the production process.

In the second Kondratieff wave the organization of production in terms of location and scale became more flexible through the use of steam power and railways. Limited liability and joint stock companies were major organizational innovations allowing new forms of finance, risk taking and ownership. The first wave was not much felt outside Britain, and the second wave was observed only in a few economically advanced countries (Table 3.1).

The third Kondratieff wave saw the electrification of industry, transport and the home. Steel as a key new input substituted iron as it provided better performance in terms of strength, durability and precision, thus opening new possibilities for metal working industries. Electrification allowed more flexibility in the location of industries and more flexible production organisation at the factory floor. Large firms emerged and management as a profession was established, government policy supported the founding of technical schools in many countries and thus contributed to the development of the required skill base.

The fourth Kondratieff wave was characterized by the large-scale diffusion of mass production to manufacturing industries and later to other economic sectors. Economies of scale could be reaped in firms that operated under oligopolistic competition and became increasingly multinational. The widespread use of automobiles and the adaption of government policies

Table 3.1 Major characteristics of Kondratieff waves

Kondratieff waves and their approximate timing of upswing and downswing	*Leading countries*	*Leading branches of the economy*	*Transport and communication infrastructure*	*Managerial and organizational characteristics*
Early mechanisation Kondratieff				
up: end of 1780s to 1810–1817 down: 1810–1817 to 1844–1851	Britain; France, Belgium	Cotton spinning, iron products, water wheels	Canals, turnpike roads, sailing ship	Factory system, entrepreneurs, partnership
Steam power and railway Kondratieff				
up: 1844–1851 to 1870–1875 down: 1870–1875 to 1890–1896	Britain; France, Belgium, Germany, USA	Railways, railway equipment, steam engines, machine tools	Railways, steam ship, telegraph	Joint stock company, subcontracting to craft workers
Electrical and heavy engineering Kondratieff				
up: 1890–1896 to 1914–1920 down: 1914–1920 to end of 1930s/early 1940s	Germany, USA; Britain, France, Belgium, Switzerland, Netherlands	Electrical equipment, heavy engineering, heavy chemicals, steel	Steel railways, steel ship, telephone	Specialized professional management, giant firms
Fordist mass production Kondratieff				
up: end of 1930s/early 1940s to 1968–1973 down: 1968–1973 to 1987–1992	USA, Germany; Other EEC, Japan, Sweden Switzerland, USSR, other EFTA, Canada, Australia	Automobiles, planes, oil, gas, synthetic materials	Motorways, airports, radio, television	Mass production and consumption, hierarchical organization, oligopolistic competition, multinational firms
Information and communication Kondratieff				
up: 1987–1992 to 2008 (?) down: 2008 (?) to ???	USA, Japan, Germany, Sweden; most other OECD countries	Computers, chips, electronic capital goods, software, information services	Information highways (internet)	Networks (internal, local, global), production on demand, individualized mass production

Sources: Perez (2009); Reati and Toporowski (2009); Freeman and Perez (1988); Goldstein (1988); Kondratieff (1926, 1935).

particularly in the fields of land use, transport and infrastructure changed the location patterns of production, consumption and housing.

The fifth Kondratieff wave, finally, has been triggered by modern information and communication technologies (ICT). The inflexibility of the mass production model to satisfy a diversified demand was overcome by new ICT that allowed the formation of flexible networks within and across firms at a local and global level, production on demand, and finally individualized mass production. The fifth Kondratieff wave also provides an example of the impact of government policies – mostly in the field of research, telecommunications and defence – on the development and diffusion of a new technology triggering the upswing of a long wave. Which technologies will be the drivers of the next long wave remains to be seen; candidates include nanotechnology (see Heinrich and Pfirrmann 2014), biotechnology, new materials, and new energy technologies.

Do long waves exist at all?

The mostly narrative historical account of long waves highlights crucial structural changes and has enriched the understanding of the conditions under which the long wave dynamics unfold. But the 'obvious inadequacy of these procedures to demonstrate this scheme of historical succession of periods with distinctive social, political, and economic features consequently created strong doubts about the justification for the research itself' (Freeman and Louçã 2001: 95). Trying to detect the existence of long waves of approximately fifty years' length in economic time series by using traditional statistical methods or simulation techniques has proved to be a complex undertaking that is still a topic of controversy. Kondratieff already eliminated the trend that is present in some of his time series because of its non-stationary character. But without a convincing assumption about the particular trend form almost any long-period cycle can be produced by using higher-order polynomial trends (Silverberg 2007). A considerable part of research on long waves was devoted to refining econometric techniques. Taking first differences has become a standard method of trend elimination, and structural time series models have been used for testing the existence and synchronization of long waves in GDP series (e.g. Goldstein 1999). Spectral analysis has been frequently used for investigating the existence of long waves in the economy (Ewijk 1982; Haustein and Neuwirth 1982; Metz 1992); recently Korotayev and Tsirel (2010) found waves of fifty-two to fifty-three years' length in the world GDP for the 1870 to 2007 period, though, possibly, with a shortening of the waves' length to approximately forty-five years at the end of the period. There is also evidence that upswings of the long waves usually might be somewhat longer than downswings (Coccia 2010).

A shortcoming of econometric methods in the analysis of very long time series is the implicit assumption that no major structural economic changes that could have a disruptive effect on the causality and time structure occur over one or even several cycles stretching over a period of fifty or a hundred or even more years. But as long as wave research postulates such structural changes and tries to explain the drivers of such changes an empirical method that is based on such an assumption seems to be inadequate to the research topic. Further, smoothing or de-trending procedures require trend and cycle to be independent which is unlikely if long time series are considered; they may create artefacts with respect to the cycle (Freeman and Louçã 2001: 99). An alternative route to analyse the existence of long waves in economic time series is based on formal models without a direct empirical claim (Forrester 1971) by trying to achieve a good fit of a model's simulation results with empirically observed time series through tuning model parameters properly. While such models can be useful for the creation of hypotheses in order to analyse the historical record 'they are not the reality itself, nor can they reproduce it' (Freeman and Louçã 2001: 117).

The apparent difficulties of statistical treatment of long waves have led to rather different conclusions for the direction of further research. Silverberg (2007: 814) considers it:

> essential that we continue to seek the connection between such models [of long waves] and their expression at the level of statistically testable aggregate time series effects . . . To turn one's back to this issue is to retreat into metaphysics or relegate long-wave analysis to a sophistic form of . . . historical analysis.

Freeman and Louçã (2001: 116ff), however, suggest an 'approach of reasoned history' that combines historical, analytical and descriptive methods. Their approach includes 'the rejection of the claim for a complete quantitative description of the universe', giving priority to 'identification of features of the real time series, instead of the fabrication and simulation from an abstract model', and to 'the acceptance of complex determination and the importance of social, institutional, and political factors, represented by semi-autonomous or "hybrid" variables'. Such an approach does not suggest giving up quantitative analysis altogether but recognizing its limitations and supplementing it with qualitative, historical analysis.

Conceptual requirements of technology-driven long waves

Even if the existence of long waves in time series of economic indicators could be empirically shown, this could be the result of a regularity observed in the past that need not necessarily be continued into the future or it could be of random causation. Therefore a theoretical foundation is needed to explain the dynamics of economic change in a way that it generates long waves in the economy.

Concerning technological innovation as a causing factor of long waves most authors would accept either implicitly or explicitly the following ideas (Thompson 1990: 203f): major technological innovations are discontinuous in time and space, and the pace of growth differs across economic sectors. They propel economic growth because new leading sectors and new ways of doing things emerge that require considerable investment and extensive infrastructures. The new industrial sectors and new ways to do things are subject to variable mixes of diffusion and imitation, increasing competition and protectionism, market saturation and overcapacity, increasing costs, diminishing marginal returns and institutional rigidities that constrain further growth and innovation.

While acknowledging the role of new technology, some strands of long wave research emphasize other aspects than innovation including the reinvestment process (e.g. Kondratieff 1928; Forrester 1981), fluctuations in the prices of primary commodities (e.g. Rostow 1978; Modelski 1982), war as a driver of long waves (e.g. Kondratieff 1926, 1935; Thompson and Zuk 1982; Goldstein 1988), or the generational cycle (e.g. Neumann 1990; Tylecote 1990; Devezas and Corredine 2001; Papenhausen 2008). Analyses in the Marxian tradition emphasize the rate of profit as the main source of long waves (e.g. Mandel 1980; Wallerstein 1984a) or the 'social structure of accumulation' (Gordon *et al.* 1983), the regulation school refers to the 'regime of accumulation' (Boyer 1988).

The emergence and diffusion of new technologies and complementary institutional change that shape socio-economic development is at the core of research on long waves in the tradition of Schumpeter. His work was harshly criticized by Kuznets (1940) for its meagre empirical foundation and for conceptual weaknesses, and the debate about long wave models and the role of innovation in it regained momentum only in the 1970s and early 1980s (e.g. Mensch 1975; Kleinknecht 1981; Freeman *et al.* 1982; van Duijn 1983) when most economies entered a downswing phase of a Kondratieff wave. Rosenberg and Frischtak (1983, 1984) formulated four interrelated conceptual requirements (causality, timing, economy-wide repercussions, and recurrence) for technological change to generate long cycles of approximately fifty years length that are still important criteria for validating theories of technology-driven long waves.

The first requirement ('causality') states that a 'precise knowledge of what are the necessary and sufficient changes in the environment which . . . can bring out a bandwagon-like diffusion of some number of basic innovations' (Rosenberg and Frischtak 1984: 276) is required. By implication, Kondratieff's idea that the long wave mechanism is the driver of innovation does not meet this requirement. Schumpeter, however, has already developed the major theoretical elements, and many Neo-Schumpeterian analysts (e.g. van Duijn 1983; Freeman and Louçã 2001; Perez 2002) provide detailed explanations for why innovation is the core variable that brings about economic change as a driver of the long wave via investment decisions of innovative entrepreneurs.

The second requirement ('timing') calls for an explanation for why technological innovation leads to long periods of economic expansion followed by similarly long periods of stagnation spanning two to three decades, each. The diffusion of new technologies depends on the actual and expected trajectory of their performance and cost reduction potential. Timing within this process is complex as gestation periods may be long, new technology may lead to improvements in the old technology, new technologies may depend upon the availability of complementary inputs or supporting infrastructures, and lock-in effects can render further improvements within the existing technological framework more promising than the search for new technologies (Rosenberg and Frischtak 1983: 147ff). While radical inventions are randomly distributed over time, major innovations could cluster because in good (macro-) economic conditions exploiting existing technologies is profitable and therefore firms will abstain from radical innovations. Only when profit rates fall (because of an exhaustion of the potential of existing technologies) is there no alternative to innovation (Mensch 1975, 1979). But during the downswing of the long wave implementing radical innovations seems particularly risky, and therefore firms could prefer cost saving process innovations that are less of a radical than of an incremental nature (Clark *et al.* 1981). Perez (2002) argues that a clustering of innovations takes place in the downswing of a long wave because of the interplay between financial markets and the diffusion of a 'technological revolution' consisting of a bundle of interrelated new technologies that give way to a new 'techno-economic paradigm'. Patent activity increases during upswings and decreases during downswings as the vast majority of patents are granted for incremental innovations that tend to become more important during upswings (Korotayev *et al.* 2011). Methodological problems complicate the empirical research on clustering of innovations (Kleinknecht *et al.* 2002) because there is no objective way of identifying the proper timing of innovations (e.g. its first appearance need not have a major impact) and their impact on the intensity of innovation activity (Silverberg 2003).

The third requirement ('repercussions') is that the impact of innovations or clusters of innovations must be strong enough to cause a sizeable macroeconomic impact (Rosenberg and Frischtak 1983, 1984). Such an impact can result from investment expenditures (buildings, machinery, equipment and raw materials), a second wave of innovations focusing on process innovations, and from new inputs that open the possibility for bringing new products to the market. Leading sectors trigger the upswing of a long wave because their key technologies have a huge economic potential and decrease the cost of production (Perez 2002). Within an economic mainstream context (and without explicit reference to the long wave debate) the concept of general purpose technologies (Bresnahan and Trajtenberg 1995; Helpman 1998) also emphasizes the property of universal use of such technologies and their overall impact on the economy.

The fourth requirement ('recurrence') is to explain mechanisms that are endogenous to the economic process and that make the waves repeat themselves. As recurrence must be more than a theoretical possibility or the result of historical accidents explanations of the availability of inventions at the proper time and of the forces causing the lower and upper turning points of the long wave are required (Rosenberg and Frischtak 1983, 1984). Perez (2002) demonstrates that a long wave theory with endogenous innovation can explain innovation clustering and the recurrent nature of long waves as a result of the interplay between financial capital and production capital in a slowly changing socio-institutional framework. Technology and innovation policies of governments, systematic research and development effort of firms, and the use of ICT as a powerful means of information processing and as a tool of innovation have accelerated the development and dissemination of new technologies. Whether long waves will actually tend to become shorter depends on the characteristics and perceived risks of the new technologies, and on the scope and willingness of society to adapt to technology-driven change.

The requirements formulated by Rosenberg and Frischtak are rather stringent for explaining such a complex phenomenon that is characterized by multi-causality, autonomous political and social influences, and numerous feedback effects (Freeman 1996). Two more conceptual questions were raised later (Goldstein 1988; Mandel 1992; de Groot 2006): Is there an influence of wars and international relations on long waves, and are they internationally synchronized? Both questions are disputed and need further research: while some authors argue – last but not least for reasons of statistical treatment – to leave wars out from long wave analysis (van Duijn 1983), others include wars because structural changes in economic history could not be explained in ignorance of the concrete historic ruptures (Freeman and Louçã 2001). Interestingly, in a spectral analysis long waves are found both in the original time series that include the war periods and in time series using interpolated values for the war periods (Korotayev and Tsirel 2010).

Finally, Kondratieff (1935) claims that long waves occur almost simultaneously worldwide, while Hirooka (2003) considers long waves as a technology leadership phenomenon with the possibility for lagging countries to catch up, and Goldstein (1988) holds that synchronization occurs among countries of similar stage of development. While global 'Islands of Innovation' remain stable over a period of at least thirty years (Hilpert 2003), innovation- and imitation-based catching up is possible as the recent economic performance of some (mostly Asian) nations has shown. ICT have accelerated the international dissemination of knowledge and have facilitated joint research and innovation effort across countries in the current long wave (e.g. through international cooperation networks, co-publication, co-patenting) that allows for a more synchronized innovation activity across nations and for catching-up processes.

The dynamics and phases of technology-driven long waves

A theory of technology-driven long waves that apparently meets the Rosenberg-Frischtak criteria developed by Perez (2002, 2010) has its focus on the transformative power of technological revolutions on the economy and on the entire structure of society. This explains 'why economists have such a difficult time proving or disproving the existence of long waves, although historical memory and the people of each period clearly distinguish the "good times" from the "bad times"' (Perez 2004: 218). Therefore the notion 'long wave', which is more suggestive of cyclical fluctuations around a growth path (Escudier 1990), is replaced by 'long surge of development' (Perez 2002).

The dynamics of a long surge starts with a set of interrelated radical breakthroughs (a 'technological revolution') that are strongly interconnected and that have the capacity to profoundly transform the rest of the economy by establishing a new '*techno-economic paradigm*'. This is a best practice model for the most effective use of the new technologies within and beyond the new industries, which breaks the existing organizational habits in technology, the economy, management and social institutions (Perez 1983, 2002). When markets get increasingly saturated and the potential for improvements within this paradigm get exhausted, the speed of change and diffusion slows down and profitability of investment within the techno-economic paradigm decreases. Consequently, both real-economy entrepreneurs and financial investors start searching for opportunities outside the prevailing paradigm, thereby giving way to a new techno-economic paradigm.

The diffusion of a technological paradigm (see Figure 3.1)[3] starts with the first appearance of a new technology (a 'big bang' like Intel's first microprocessor in 1971) that is characterized by rapidly falling relative cost, almost unlimited availability over long periods,[4] and a strong potential for use or incorporation in products and processes all over the economy. After having started from a small industrial base, in the *frenzy period* the wealth creating potential of the new paradigm and the exhaustion of the still prevailing old paradigm become apparent. Entrepreneurs try to find out the most profitable business opportunities created by the new technology; deregulation of the economy and financial innovations – both typically occurring in the frenzy periods – support this process. While science-based innovation supported by government policies has triggered development in the early phases of the current development surge, technology-based innovation has become more important later as new technologies have been increasingly applied in traditional products and industries.

Examples of innovative firms that have successfully adapted to the new technologies cause profit expectations and demand for similar investment opportunities to rise. Stock markets are booming in the frenzy period, even people with modest salaries turn into 'hopeful "investors"' (Perez 2002: 3), until 'irrational exuberance' (former chairman of the Federal Reserve Board, Alan Greenspan) and wild financial speculation come to an end. The build-up of a speculative bubble (and its burst) is endogenous to long surges of development: It is driven by *opportunity pull* caused by technological innovation such as the dot-com bubble and subsequent NASDAQ collapse in 2001 or by *easy liquidity push* caused by financial innovation such as the financial bubble emerging due to lack of financial market regulation which burst in 2008 (Perez 2009). Both bubbles at the beginning of the twenty-first century are related to the unfolding of the techno-economic paradigm, both types of bubbles can occur either simultaneously or sequentially, and are followed by a recession or even depression.

At the '*turning point*' of the development surge the mismatch between the new paradigm and the still prevalent old paradigm gets most apparent. Because change in technology is discontinuous and fast but change in the socio-institutional framework is slow and lagging behind technological change, various types of mismatch between these systems arise (Tylecote 1994): microeconomic (firm organization does not suit to the paradigm), macroeconomic (macro-economic factors prevent demand to grow sufficiently), and socio-political mismatch (socio-political tensions arise from the diffusion of the new paradigm), each type having a national and an international dimension. The existing regulatory and institutional framework restrains the exploitation of the new paradigm's full economic potential, and the build-up of a financial bubble is the expression of an increasingly dysfunctional relationship between production capital and financial capital. Possible social benefits from the implementation of the new paradigm notwithstanding, many individuals and groups have strong vested interests in the old paradigm and will be reluctant to change. The transition from the prevailing old paradigm to the new

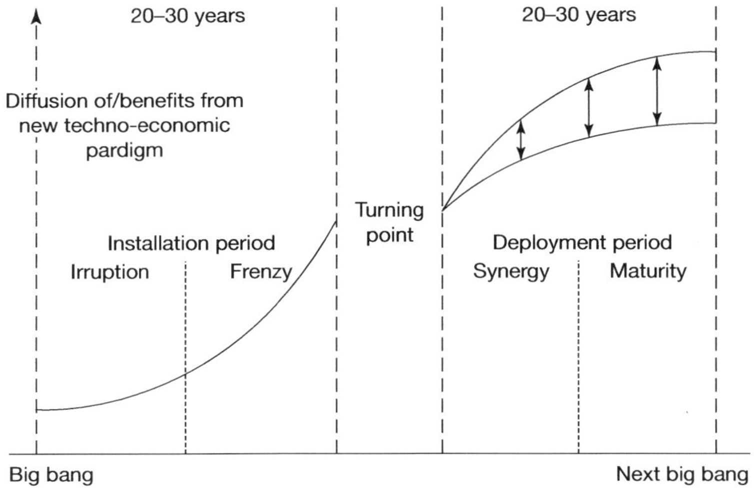

Figure 3.1 Phases of a surge of development.
Source: based on Perez (2002) and Scherrer (2011).

paradigm is a time of social conflict as the structural changes coming along with the change of paradigms do not only produce winners but also losers.

In the *deployment period* large parts of the population have access to the new infrastructure, have the appropriate physical equipment, and accept new technologies as the advantages of the new economic paradigm have become apparent. While during the frenzy period financial capital had been geared towards short-term gains from financial speculation, the deployment of the new paradigm would need now a more stable financial system, which is to be achieved by more rigorous government control (Kregel 2009: 203). Investors could turn now from the financial economy to the real economy thus rendering possible a 'golden age' of the diffusion of a techno-economic paradigm like mass production did during the post-World War II boom. Whether such a golden age will eventually be reached depends on establishing a socio-institutional framework that is conducive to the exploitation of the benefits of the already established techno-economic paradigm. In particular, a new balance between individual and social interests has to be found. Ultimately, every paradigm will reach the stage when its potential to further increase wealth and productivity is exhausted in the *maturity period*. Modernization and restructuring return to the political agenda as the prevailing paradigm becomes less attractive for parts of the population while others still benefit from it; political and ideological confrontation is likely to arise. Real-economy entrepreneurs and financial investors will start searching for opportunities outside the prevailing paradigm, thereby giving way to the next technological revolution and to the upcoming of the next techno-economic paradigm.

Policy-related aspects of technology-driven long wave theories

Policy can have an impact on long-term socio-economic development

As theories of long waves or long surges of economic development stipulate the recurrence of economic phenomena the question arises whether these theories would be sufficiently *non-deterministic* in order to allow for a potential impact of economic policy on the course of economic development. Kondratieff (1926, 1935) already emphasized that the repetition of certain processes is not subject to the same degree of determinism as, for example, in astronomy. Based on an analysis of the changing uses and meanings of the concept of long waves in the economy over time, across cultural and language borders, and across disciplines Escudier (1990) suggested that long waves be considered transformations rather than repetitions of previous stages, and thus the concept is distinctly non-deterministic. Therefore the dimension of time in the analysis of socio-economic development cannot be captured by a time index given to variables but time is historical time and thus an important dimension of analysis by itself. Technology-driven long waves evoke social processes that can decelerate or accelerate the diffusion of a techno-economic paradigm in historic time. Long wave theories that stipulate the recurrence of economic phenomena have a heuristic value through providing a structure with which regularity can be assessed and uniqueness of historical development can be fully valued (Perez 2002: 161).

With respect to economic policy relevance the long wave literature is divided into '*two camps*' (Dator 1999: 369): one camp seeks 'to find in the long waves the forces which will finally bring down capitalism and usher socialism', although apparently without success so far. The other camp searches for 'a set of economic measures . . . that will either speed up the recovery or allow given states to emerge [from the downswing of the Kondratieff wave] in a good relative position' (Wallerstein 1984b: 579). This paper is clearly sympathizing with the latter camp as it holds that the descending phase of the long wave (in Kondratieff-Schumpeter-type theories) or a golden age of deployment of a new techno-economic-paradigm (in Perez' theory) do not occur automatically but the diffusion of a paradigm, the related benefits, and the distribution of these benefits across social groups are influenced by policies. In Figure 3.1 the space between the two upward sloping curves in the deployment period schematically symbolizes the possible implications of two institutional designs on the diffusion of the new techno-economic paradigm and the related benefits to be drawn from it. While it is likely that the policy impact is not sufficient to cause a downswing or upswing when considered alone (Tylecote 1990), the arrows in the diagram symbolically mark the potential impact of policies on establishing a set of institutions in the turning point phase that accommodate either better or worse to the paradigm.

Having entered the decade after a 'turning point'

There is no full agreement among long-wave researchers about the phase in which the economies of (at least) the developed nations currently are. On the one hand the financial crisis and global recession could constitute a deflationary depression like the crash of 1929, which would be typical for the ending of a Kondratieff wave (Gore 2010: 722ff). On the other hand the decade 2011–2020 could be 'probably one of worldwide economic expansion corresponding to the second half of the expansion phase of the fifth Kondratieff wave' (Devezas 2010: 739). Based on a long wave approach, Synnott (2012) finds that long-term real interest rates in the United States will remain low for an extended period which would be a good basis for investment and growth as in previous long waves. The fifth Kondratieff wave having emerged, 'the information and communications sector will replace energy, transport and material as the central sector in the economy' (Göransson and Söderberg 2005: 210). Thus it seems likely that the developed nations have entered the deployment period of the ICT-based techno-economic paradigm (Perez 2009; Reati and Toporowski 2009) after the 'double bubbles' of 2001 and 2008 which have marked the 'turning point' of the paradigm.

Different modes of regulation over a long wave's lifetime

In the installation period individual interests govern the mode of regulation and pro-business governments tend to dominate politics (Perez 2002). Deregulation or – in the case of newly emerging technologies – non-regulation is considered conducive to innovation and economic growth because the incentives to experiment with new technologies and to innovate would be strengthened if successful entrepreneurs are rewarded with extremely fast growth of their business and huge profits.

In the synergy phase a re-coupling of the real economy and the financial economy requires:

> the elimination of the excessive financial layering through a financial collapse, and increased regulation of the financial system through more rigorous government control in a way that does not prevent the full deployment of the new technology led by production capital reaping the full economic and social potential of the now prevailing paradigm.
>
> *(Kregel 2009: 203)*

'Concerted open market operations to regulate liquidity in the financial markets . . . would eliminate the excess liquidity in the markets that are the origin of financial speculations and bubbles' (Reati and Toporowski 2009: 186).

Inequality and income policy changes over the long wave's lifetime

The frenzy period is not only the high time of individualism but also one of creating enormous individual wealth that is characterized by 'a huge process of income redistribution in favour of those directly or indirectly involved in the casino, which funds the massive process of creative destruction in the economy' (Perez 2002: 116). In this period the process of income concentration is fostered by unemployment and stagnating or even decreasing income in those industries and jobs that do not benefit from the roll-out of the new techno-economic paradigm. Historical analysis (Berry *et al.* 1995) suggests a parallel movement of technology-driven long waves and long political swings: four long surges in inequality in the history of the United States occurred in the aftermath of major stagflation crises, and each surge was followed by an 'egalitarian backlash in which a political agenda dominated by technological innovation, efficiency and growth was replaced by one concerned with social innovation, equality and redistribution' (Berry *et al.* 1995: abstract).

Periods of increased inequality occur in the early stages of the development of a new techno-economic paradigm (the installation period) and are followed by periods of less inequality when paradigms mature (the deployment period). This does not necessarily mean that new technologies and innovation require social inequality to emerge or widen, but in a market-dominated environment that was typical for the installation period of the ICT-based techno-economic paradigm values such as solidarity are not 'fashionable' in such times. Therefore it is difficult to get topics that are in a social-democratic tradition (such as reducing inequality or redistributing income) onto the political agenda.

The deployment period might see a tendency to reverse income concentration because the increased inequality constrains the purchasing power of significant parts of the population and the state which, in turn, constrains the demand for goods and services related to the new techno-economic paradigm. As consumers forego potential benefits and firms forego profit opportunities 'the case for a Keynesian policy of demand' (Reati and Toporowski 2009: 164ff) is suggested for the turning point period. In order to prevent countries falling into deflationary recessions 'the IMF and the World Bank should be brought closer to the original Keynesian ideal' (Freeman 2011: 23), and in order to reduce inequality social policies should get priority and taxation should return to the principle of redistribution (Freeman 2011: 23f). It is important to recognize that the argument for policies that reduce inequality and foster demand at the beginning of the deployment period does not resort to social policy considerations but can be based on purely economic grounds.

The new socio-institutional framework can either establish 'institutions for increasing social cohesiveness, improving income distribution and general wellbeing or it can try to reinstate the "*selfish prosperity*" of the frenzy period, though more closely connected with real production and finding some means to expand demand' (Perez 2002: 53). Currently it seems doubtful whether political decisions have been adequate to provide a better fit between the techno-economic system and the socio-institutional framework to warrant another 'golden age' of economic development (e.g. Castellacci 2006; Tylecote and Ramirez 2008; Perez 2009; Reati and Toporowski 2009; Gore 2010; Freeman 2011).

An active role for technology policy

Theories of technology driven long waves suggest an active role of government in supporting technological development. In the installation period the risk that a nation misses out on taking up the technological developments that are the key elements of a new paradigm should be reduced. Such a policy requires a long time horizon and could include supporting major infrastructure investments in the new technology even if profitability is not yet warranted, and creating a research and policy climate that tolerates mistakes, particularly in basic research, and building competences in the public sector to enable government to implement technology policies appropriately (Drechsler *et al.* 2009). Both in the installation and in the deployment period the design of sectorial, national and regional systems of innovation is important for a country's adaptability to the requirements of the new techno-economic paradigm and its capability to benefit from it.

The process of adjusting to a new techno-economic paradigm in general and to successfully approach the emerging key technologies in particular is critical for a nation's ability to keep its relative position of economic welfare or even to start a catch-up process. While changes in the techno-economic paradigm create new opportunities particularly for newly industrializing countries and increase the potential for national public policies to support catching-up processes, institutional change at the international level seems to reduce the scope for state intervention (Castellacchi 2005: 32f). This paradox suggests a mismatch between the techno-economic and the socio-institutional system that makes catching up difficult. The situation is complicated further because institutions that work in one social-political-economic context cannot necessarily be transferred and adapted to the conditions of another (Nelson 2009: 283). While this clearly indicates that there is no 'one best way' of policy it also highlights the importance of policies and understanding policy environments for a society to benefit from the dissemination of a new techno-economic paradigm.

Notes

1 Neither Kondratieff nor Schumpeter knew about van Gelderen's work which was published in Dutch; it was translated to English only in 1996. Kondratieff's work had been translated from Russian to German in 1926 and to English in 1935.

2 See Table 3.1. The dating of the first two and a half waves is equal to Kondratieff (1926, 1935), the dating of the latter waves are influenced by Goldstein (1988), Freeman and Perez (1988), and Perez (2009). Waves are named according to Freeman and Perez (1988). Leading countries are mostly taken from Freeman and Perez (1988), leading branches of the economy, transport and communication infrastructure, and managerial and organisational characteristics are based on Freeman and Perez (1988) and Reati and Toporovski (2009).

3 The dating of Perez' surges of development differs from the dating of traditional long waves.

4 In the case of the ICT surge this is best reflected in the steady and long-term decrease of computing power cost which is described by Moore's law.

Bibliography

Berry, B.J., Edward, L., Harpham, J. and Euel, E., 1995: Long swings in American inequality: the Kuznets conjecture revisited. *Papers in Regional Science* 74(2), pp. 153–174.

Boyer, R., 1988: Technical change and the theory of regulation. In: Dosi, G., Freeman, C., Nelson, R. R., Silverberg, G. and Soete, L. (eds): *Technical Change and Economic Theory*. London: Pinter, pp. 67–94.

Bresnahan, T.F. and Trajtenberg, M., 1995: General purpose technologies: 'Engines of growth'?, *Journal of Econometrics* LXV, pp. 83–108.

Castellacci, F., 2006: Innovation, diffusion and catching up in the fifth long wave. *Futures* 38(7), pp. 841–863.

Clark, J., Freeman, C. and Soete, L., 1981: Long waves, inventions and innovations. *Futures* 13(4), pp. 308–322.

Coccia, M., 2010: The asymmetric path of economic long waves. *Technological Forecasting and Social Change* 77(5), pp. 730–728.

Dator, J., 1999: Trajectories: return to long waves. *Futures* 31(4), pp. 361–372.

De Groot, B., 2006: *Essays on Economic Cycles*. Erasmus Management Research Institute 2006, Erasmus University Rotterdam.

Devezas, T., 2010: Crises, depressions, and expansions: global analysis and secular trends. *Technological Forecasting and Social Change* 77(5), pp. 739–761.

Devezas, T. and Corredine, J., 2001: The biological determinants of long wave behavior in socioeconomic growth and development. *Technological Forecasting and Social Change* 68(1), pp. 1–57.

Drechsler, W., Kattel, R. and Reinert, E.S., 2009: *Techno-Economic Paradigms*. London: Anthem Press.

Escudier, J.-L., 1990: Long-term movement of the economy: terminology and theoretical options. In: Tibor, V., Ayres, R. and Fontvieille, L. (eds): *Life Cycles and Long Waves: Lecture notes in economics and mathematical systems 340*, Berlin: Springer, pp. 239–260.

Ewijk, C. van, 1982: A spectral analysis of the Kondratieff cycle. *Kyklos* 35, pp. 324–372.

Forrester, J.W., 1971: *World Dynamics*. Cambridge, MA: Wright-Allen.

Forrester, J.W., 1981: Innovation and economic change. *Futures* 13(4), pp. 323–331.

Freeman, C., 1996: Introduction. In: Freeman, C. (ed.): *Long Wave Theory: The international library of critical writings in economics*. Cheltenham: Edward Elgar, pp. xiii–xxxvi.

Freeman, C., 2011: Technology, inequality and economic growth. *Innovation and Development* 1(1), 11–24.

Freeman, C. and Louçã, F., 2001: *As Time Goes By: From the industrial revolutions to the information revolution*. Oxford: Oxford University Press.

Freeman, C., Clark, J. and Soete, L., 1982: *Unemployment and Technical Innovation: A study of long waves and economic development*. London: Pinter.

Goldstein, J.S., 1988: *Long Cycles: Prosperity and war in the modern age*. New Haven, CT and London: Yale University Press.

Goldstein, J.P., 1999: The existence, endogeneity, and synchronization of long waves: structural time series model estimates. *Review of Radical Political Economics* 31, pp. 61–101.

Göransson, B. and Söderberg, J., 2005: Long waves and information technologies: on the transition towards the information society. *Technovation* 25(3), pp. 203–211.

Gordon, D.M., Weisskopf, T.D. and Bowles, S., 1983: Long swings and the nonreproductive cycle. *American Economic Review* 73(2), 152–157.

Gore, C., 2010: The global recession of 2009 in a long-term development perspective. *Journal of International Development* 22, pp. 714–738.

Haustein, H.D. and Neuwirth, E., 1982: Long waves in world industrial production, energy consumption, innovations, inventions, and patents and their identification by spectral analysis. *Technological Forecasting and Social Change* 22, pp. 53–89.

Heinrich, S. and Pfirrmann, O., 2014: Nanotechnology for green and sustainable growth: a recent example on the social construction of technology. In: Hilpert, U. (ed.): *Handbook on Politics and Technology*. London: Routledge.

Helpman, Elhanan (ed.), 1998: *General Purpose Technologies and Economic Growth*. London: MIT Press.

Hilpert, U. (ed.), 2003: *Regionalisation of Globalised Innovation: Locations for advanced industrial development and disparities in participation*. London: Routledge.

Hirooka, M., 2003: Nonlinear dynamism of innovations and business cycles. *Journal of Evolutionary Economics* 13(5), pp. 549–576.

Kleinknecht, A., 1981: *Innovation, Accumulation, and Crisis: Waves in economic development*, Review (Fernand Braudel Center) IV, spring, pp. 687–711.

Kleinknecht, A., van Montfort, K. and Brouwer, E., 2002: The non-trivial choice between innovation indicators. *Economics of Innovation and New Technology* 11(2), pp. 109–121.

Kondratieff, N.D., 1926/1935: Die langen Wellen der Konjunktur. *Archiv für Sozialwissenschaft und Sozialpolitik* 56(3), pp. 573–609; English: The long waves in economic life. *The Review of Economic Statistics* XVII (6), 1935.

Korotayev, A. and Tsirel, S. V., 2010: A spectral analysis of world GDP dynamics: Kondratieff Waves, Kuznets Swings, Juglar and Kitchin Cycles in global economic development, and the 2008–2009 economic crisis. *Structure and Dynamics eJournal* 4(1).

Korotayev, A., Zinkina, J. and Bogevolnov J., 2011: Kondratieff waves in global invention activity (1900–2008). *Technological Forecasting & Social Change* 78, 1280–1284.

Kregel, J., 2009: Financial experimentation, technological paradigm revolutions and financial crisis. In: Drechsler, W., Kattel, R. and Reinert, E.S. (eds): *Techno-Economic Paradigms*. London: Anthem Press, pp. 203–220.

Kuznets, S.S., 1940: Schumpeter's Business Cycles. *American Economic Review* 30(2), pp. 257–271.

Mandel, E., 1980: *Long Waves of Capitalist Development: The Marxist interpretation*. Cambridge: Cambridge University Press.

Mandel, E., 1992: The international debate on long waves of capitalist development: an intermediary balance sheet. In: Kleinknecht, A., Mandel, E. and Wallerstein, I. (eds): *New Findings in Long-Wave Research*. New York, St Martin's Press, pp. 316–338.

Mensch, G., 1975/1979: *Das Technologische Patt*. Frankfurt: Umschau Verlag. English translation, 1979: *Stalemate in Technology*. Cambridge, Ballinger.

Metz, R., 1992: A re-examination of long waves in aggregate production series. In: Kleinknecht, A., Mandel, E. and Wallerstein, I. (eds): *New Findings in Long-Wave Research*. London: Macmillan.

Metz, R., 2011: Do Kondratieff waves exist? How time series techniques can help to solve the problem. *Cliometrica* 5(3), pp. 205–238.

Modelski, G., 1982: Long cycles and the strategy of United States international political economy. In: Avery, W. and Rapkin, D.P. (eds): *America in a Changing World Political Economy*. New York: Longman, pp. 97–118.

Nelson, R.R., 2009: Technology, institutions and economic development. In: Drechsler, W., Kattel, R. and Reinert, E.S. (eds): *Techno-Economic Paradigms*. London: Anthem Press, pp. 269–286.

Neumann, M., 1990: *Zukunftsperspektiven im Wandel. Lange Wellen in Wirtschaft und Politik*. Tübingen: Mohr.

Papenhausen, C., 2008: Causal mechanisms of long waves. *Futures* 40(9), pp. 788–794.

Perez, C., 1983: Structural change and the assimilation of new technologies in the economic and social system. *Futures* 15, pp. 357–375.

Perez, C., 2002: *Technological Revolutions and Financial Capital: The dynamics of bubbles and golden ages*. Cheltenham: Edward Elgar.

Perez, C., 2004: Technological revolutions, paradigm shifts and socio-institutional change. In: Reinert, E.S. (ed.): *Globalization, Economic Development and Inequality: An alternative perspective*. Edward Elgar: Cheltenham, pp. 217–242.

Perez, C., 2009: The double bubble at the turn of the century: technological roots and structural implications. *Cambridge Journal of Economics* 33, pp. 779–805.

Reati, A. and Toporowski, J., 2009: An economic policy for the fifth long wave. *PSL Quarterly Review* 62(248–251), pp. 147–190.

Rosenberg, N. and Frischtak, C.R., 1983: Long waves and economic growth: a critical appraisal. *American Economic Review* 73(2), pp. 146–151.

Rosenberg, N. and Frischtak, C.R., 1984: Technological innovation and long waves. *Cambridge Journal of Economics* 8(1), pp. 7–24.

Rostow, W.W., 1978: *The World Economy: History and prospect.* Austin, TX: University of Texas Press.
Scherrer, W., 2011: Surges of development and techno-economic paradigms: a review essay of the Festschrift for Carlota Perez. *uprava* IX(1), pp. 189–201.
Schumpeter, J.A., 1939: *Business Cycles: A theoretical, historical and statistical analysis of the capitalist process.* New York: McGraw-Hill.
Silverberg, G., 2003: Long waves: conceptual, empirical and modelling issues. In: Hanusch, H. and Pyker, A. (eds): *The Elgar Companion to Neo-Schumpeterian Economics*, Cheltenham: Edward Elgar, 800–819.
Silverberg, G., 2007: Long waves: conceptual, empirical and modelling issues. In: Hanusch, H. and Pyker, A. (eds): *The Elgar Companion to Neo-Schumpeterian Economics.* Cheltenham: Edward Elgar, pp. 800–819.
Synnott, T.W., 2012: The long wave revisited. *Business Economics* 47, pp. 119–125.
Thompson, W.R., 1990: Long waves, technological innovation, and relative decline. *International Organization* 4(2), pp. 201–233.
Thompson, W.R. and Zuk, G., 1982: War, inflation and Kondratieff's long waves. *Journal of Conflict Resolution* 26, pp. 621–644.
Tylecote, A., 1990: Generational factors in an evolutionary theory of the long wave. In: Vasko, T., Ayres, R. and Fontvieille, L. (eds): *Life Cycles and Long Waves: Lecture Notes in Economics and Mathematical Systems 340.* Berlin: Springer, pp. 261–274.
Tylecote, A., 1992: *The Long Wave in the World Economy: The present crisis in historical perspective.* London: Routledge.
Tylecote, A., 1994: Long waves, long cycles, and long swings. *Journal of Economic Issues* 28(2), pp. 477–488.
Tylecote, A. and Ramirez, P., 2008: Finance, corporate governance and the new techno-economic paradigm. *Recherches économiques de Louvain* 74(4), pp. 583–613.
Van Duijn, J.J., 1983: *The Long Wave in Economic Life.* London: George Allen & Unwin, pp. 147–172.
Van Gelderen, J. [J. Fedder, pseudo], 1913/1996: Springvloed Baschouwingen over industrielle Outwikkalieng en prijsbeweging. In: De Nieuwe Tijd, 184/5 and 6; English translation: Springtide: Reflections on industrial development and price movements. In: Freeman, C.(Ed.): *Long Wave Theory: The international library of critical writings in economics.* Cheltenham: Edward Elgar, pp. 1–56.
Wallerstein, I., 1984a: *Long Waves as Capitalist Process.* Review (Fernand Braudel Center) VII(4), pp. 559–575.
Wallerstein, I., 1984b: Economic cycles and socialist policies. *Futures* 16(6), pp. 579–585.

4

RECOGNIZING OPPORTUNITIES FOR S&T WORKFORCE DEVELOPMENT AND PRODUCTIVITY

The gendered resource

Connie L. McNeely and Laurie A. Schintler

Introduction

In countries around the world, concerns about deficits in the science and technology (S&T) workforce have come to occupy places of prominence on policy agendas. Indeed, human capital development in fields associated with science, technology, engineering, and mathematics generally has been recognized as crucial to progress and growth in today's innovation-driven knowledge economy. Human capital is at the centre of innovative activity and can be addressed either as a constraint or as an opportunity for innovation policy (Zimmerman 2012). Persons with S&T training and skills play an important role in channelling investments in knowledge into productivity and growth and, accordingly, achieving technological advancement requires human capital development as an investment in research and innovation. This situation has brought increasing attention to questions about educational access and workforce opportunities for populations who have been especially underrepresented in S&T fields, referring particularly to women (and, also, to some underprivileged minorities). Indeed, their underrepresentation has emerged as a major political, economic, and social issue for workforce development and growth. Recognizing women as a rich, yet under-utilized and often untapped resource in the S&T research enterprise (Pearson *et al.* 2015), gender dynamics and relations are a critical consideration in matters associated with politics and technology and the development of the future S&T workforce.

Arguably, *depressing the potential, participation, and contribution of women and other groups in society is actually harmful to efforts for S&T supported economic advancement.* While some progress has been made, female participation and, more, female professional advancement in S&T fields have, at best, been uneven (Hill *et al.* 2010; Ceci and Williams 2011; EC 2013; OECD 2013a). This situation speaks particularly to the demand for university-trained labour across academic, public, and private sectors and to the need for a more realistic and fully informed assessment of S&T education and workforce conditions. Academia is a crucial consideration in this regard given that it is, in fact, the training ground for the S&T workforce. This point is especially relevant to the issue at hand since expanded and increased networks constituted by various (academic, public, and private sectors) researchers suggest a greater demand for academic labour – a demand that could be met by females if more favourable conditions existed for their recruitment, retention and general participation (McNeely and Vlaicu 2010).

To that end, gender mainstreamed and inclusive analytical perspectives and metrics are needed as policy inputs and determinants for related investments in human capital (Leggon *et al.* 2015). While there is a rich and burgeoning literature addressing women in S&T fields, a great deal of work remains to be done in delineating related processes and linking key indicators of scientific productivity and workforce development to broader contexts and concrete outcomes (Pearson *et al.* 2015). Thus, major theoretical and methodological issues are identified and examined here to provide insights for furthering research on scientific and technological knowledge creation, diffusion, and application relative to gender relations and dynamics. The principal aim is to consider the situation of women in S&T, particularly as reflected in their relatively low participation and status in related careers.

The underpinning notion for this work is pragmatically straightforward: *a broader pool of academics and researchers will provide a better means to S&T productivity and innovation.* Thus, increased numbers and inclusion of qualified women will strengthen the potential for S&T workforce and expand possibilities for advancement and growth. As such, gender is a central analytical point for addressing resources for S&T workforce development across sectors at individual, national, and international levels of analysis.

Background

Although there have been gains in advanced degree attainment by women in S&T fields, they still tend to be underrepresented and to occupy less than favourable positions in general (Bell 2010; Hill *et al.* 2010). Also, various studies have pointed to women in S&T as having lower levels of productivity than men,[1] referring to the tendency for women to publish at lesser rates (Duch *et al.* 2012; West *et al.* 2013). This 'productivity puzzle', as it was framed by Cole and Zuckerman back in 1984, has been a fundamental concern for S&T workforce capacity and development.

- *These interrelated gender issues – underrepresentation and lower productivity – signify important analytical and policy considerations in the face of calls for building the S&T workforce.*

However, the conventional operationalization of scientific productivity principally as publication levels neglects the dynamic and interactive ways in which research is conducted, disseminated, and evaluated. Indeed, scientific productivity might be more aptly framed as a *process* rather than an outcome (McNeely and Schintler 2010a, 2010b). Moreover, 'given the complexity attending the conduct of science and innovation today, the life of an idea – from its "eureka" moment through its growth, development, and diffusion – is rarely the product of a single individual' (Schintler and McNeely 2012: 125). Rather, innovation results from the influence of collections of people, i.e. of networks and collaborations (cf. Rycroft and Kash 1999; Gladwell 2002). As such, the underrepresentation and lower productivity of women also must be considered largely in terms of collaboration and participation in scientific networks as gendered aspects of the creation and transfer of scientific knowledge and of innovation.

Still, in practice, publications again are used to indicate networks and collaborations among scientists. Co-authored publications have been the chief means for measuring scientific collaboration and productivity. Indeed, co-authorship has been treated as synonymous with collaboration and network positioning.[2] However, accounting for less than 30 per cent of co-authored publications globally, women are less likely to participate in collaborations that lead to publication and, when they do, are much less likely to be listed as lead author in national and international contexts (Larivière *et al.* 2013; West *et al.* 2013). As suggested by recent studies showing that gender differences in spatial and other outcomes can be largely attributed to nurture and education (Hoffman *et al.* 2011), the process from which the puzzling outcomes result must be taken seriously relative to productivity levels. Accordingly, the productivity puzzle is examined here in terms of collaboration and networks as a policy concern and central issue for understanding female contributions, participation, and roles in S&T workforce and innovation processes.

Collaborative networks

Fostering the development of both formal and informal networks of women with other researchers, including partnerships within and across academia, government and industry, has been identified not only as an important step for advancing women in S&T careers, as it is for men, but also as crucial for technological progress (OECD 2006, 2012a). Increased productivity can be explained relative to participation and status in the S&T community, and increased participation in research networks and collaborative relationships can enhance the scientific intellectual, social, and cultural capital that support human capital development.

Networks are central to the generation and dissemination of research, thus contributing to innovation and technological developments. Related connections arguably can contribute to interpersonal influence (Brass 1984) and career opportunities (Burt 1992), and the structure of collaborative networks and relative positions within them influence access to resources (Lin 2002). Also, network composition is a crucial feature relative to the range of colleagues and collaborators and the density of their connections. Accordingly, sensitivity to network boundaries and awareness of bias incorporated in network positions might reflect gender as a differentiating factor. While network structure, role, and position are key determinants of collaboration possibilities (Hill 2008; Welch and Melkers 2008; Lin 2002), moving beyond or expanding such boundaries and overcoming bias could mean creating opportunities for participation and research for technological advancement.

Related workforce development largely depends on such networks that, in the literature, have been identified and operationalized through analyses of collaboration patterns and participation. These networks are defined through spatial, cultural, and political links, affecting participation and the size, specialization, centrality, reach, and autarky of broader networks that enable or constrain collaboration and productivity (cf. Schott 1993; Centola 2010). Also, collaborative relationships can be marked, to varying degrees, by a division of labour and hierarchical positions, often evincing considerable difference between women and men in co-authorship tendencies (Cronin *et al.* 2004; Newman 2004). While S&T research embodies a culture that encourages collaboration, it is not necessarily equal collaboration; collaborative partners may not receive equal recognition and value for their role and contributions in the relationship (Wray 2006; Zucker *et al.* 2007; Heinze and Kuhlmann 2008). That is, co-authorship as a measure of scientific interaction can be an incomplete and inaccurate characterization of collaboration and network participation. For example, it does not reflect the degree or way in which an individual author might actually contribute to a publication. In fact, authors may be listed on an article, not for their contribution to the research, but rather for social or political reasons (Katz and Martin 1997), which also can reflect preferential attachment considerations.

Moreover, listed authors (or even acknowledgements) do not necessarily reflect all of the individuals involved at various steps in the research process (Sonnenwald *et al.* 2009).

Collaboration and network construction are iterative processes reflecting various activities, stages, and contextual conditions (Sargent and Waters 2004; Sonnenwald 2007). They are dependent on the ways in which research is organized, conducted, and located, i.e., on the culture and organization of S&T and on the contexts in which research is conducted, whether academic, public, or private. The social and organizational features of work influence research performance and, as such, represent important areas for investigating scientists' productivity (Drori *et al.* 2003; Fox and Mohapatra 2007; Wagner 2008). Thus, for example, several studies reveal that the pervasive culture of high-technology organizations reflects a decided gender gap in which women typically are excluded from professional networks and leadership positions (Tai and Sims 2005; Cross and Linehan 2006; NRC 2012).

Cross-sector dimensions

Female educational attainment is a fundamental consideration in framing workforce capacity issues, and recognizing disparities in higher education is critical to understanding related challenges to innovation. Generally speaking, while women lag behind men in advanced research degree attainment, they have reached parity in some countries and fields. As an example, general and female doctoral degree attainment in mathematics and in statistics can be quite variable across countries, as illustrated in Figure 4.1 showing selected countries that reported gender disaggregated data on degree awards in 2011. (These are arrayed by a relative number of the advanced research degrees and then, within the size groupings, percentage of women earning advanced research degrees in mathematics and statistics. Following OECD reporting conventions, advanced research degrees refer to doctoral or the highest level degree awarded in a country.)

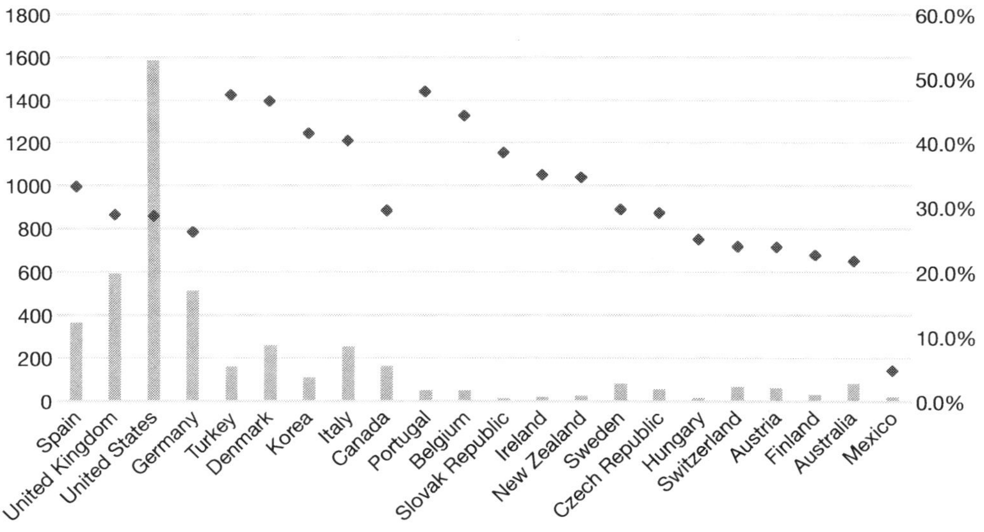

Figure 4.1 Example: Mathematics and statistics advanced research degrees (bars) and per cent women (diamonds) among recipients, 2011.

Source: Frehill (2014).

For the most part, although not across the board, the number of women earning advanced research degrees has grown, as illustrated in Figure 4.2 again using mathematics and statistics as examples showing change in female degree attainment in selected countries between 1998 and 2011. Overall, such changes indicate expanded opportunities for S&T workforce development.

Increased educational attainment arguably has accounted for half of the economic growth in 'developed' countries in the past 50 years, owing in large part to females reaching higher levels of education and making gains in gender equality in number of years spent in education (OECD 2012a). However, this situation has not necessarily translated into workplace equality and, even with expanded degree attainment, gaps in workforce representation remain significant. Even in the developed world, the overall number of women attaining degrees in S&T fields is much higher than the number of women actually employed in research and related positions (OECD 2006, 2013a; NRC 2010; EC 2013). In other words,

- *In terms of S&T workforce needs, a large part of the societal and individual investment in human capital is lost.*

For example, on average in European countries, 1.75 per cent of the total workforce are women scientists or engineers, compared to 3.65 per cent of men. This, then, is an unexplored workforce resource and basis of creativity that undergirds technology and innovative activity. Of course, this representation varies by country, as observed in the United Kingdom with 1.22 per cent women, compared to 4.48 per cent men, scientists in the total workforce, ranking behind such countries as Iceland, Belgium, and Ireland that report parity in representation.[3]

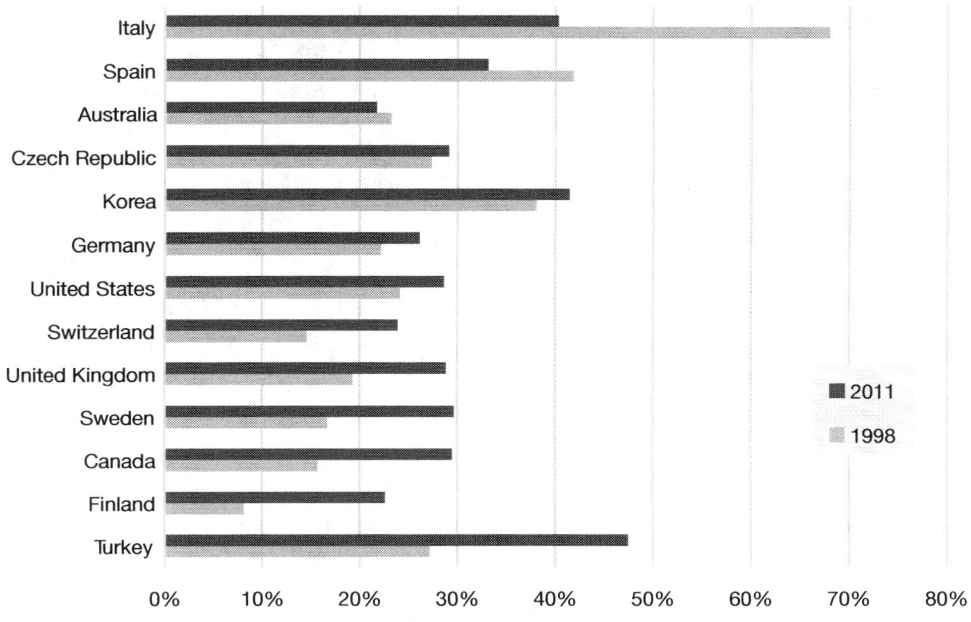

Figure 4.2 Example: Per cent women among recipients of mathematics and statistics advanced research degrees, 1998 and 2011.

Source: Frehill (2014).

Looking more specifically at female researchers across sectors, the European average is 33 per cent (EC 2013). Similar to educational attainment patterns, the largest regional differences in female employment overall have been found in Italy, Spain, Turkey, the United States (US), and the Slovak Republic (OECD 2013a). Generally speaking, regions with relatively low gross domestic product and income levels reflect the largest differences in female and male labour force participation rates overall.[4]

Both internal and external social, economic, and political factors influence decision makers regarding mobilizing and supporting S&T research (Callon *et al.* 1986; Latour and Woolgar 1986; Katz and Martin 1997). Such factors include, among others, societal, organizational, and disciplinary cultures, funding, research team size, institutional support and structure, and location (Bukvova 2010). Thus, national and institutional politics can affect researcher behaviour, and S&T productivity often results from collaboration among researchers in different organizations and countries. Network participation and collaboration among researchers from both developed and developing countries provide access to knowledge and expertise, to the extent that international collaboration has been framed as a means for capacity building, as reflected in increased international co-authorships that have characterized globalization processes (Chung 2002; Glänzel and Schubert 2004; Oldham 2005; Wagner and Leydesdorff 2005).[5] These co-authorships have been enabled by technological and communications advances (Stokols *et al.* 2008). The internet and email have lowered communication costs, thereby facilitating collaboration and network participation, with recent evidence suggesting disproportionately positive effects on female co-authorship rates relative to those of males (cf. Butler and Butler 2011). Accordingly,

- *A gender dimension is indicated in the extent to which productivity is reliant upon spatial correspondence and the potential for workforce development.*

Growing involvement in collaborative relationships and S&T networks across sectors, organizations, or countries demands a continually increasing workforce. The more prevalent such involvement, the more possibilities and opportunities exist for innovation and research activities. Thus, particularly pertaining to highly-skilled S&T trained women, the development of collaborative researcher capabilities is critical for innovation and for network building and participation.

Also, various factors, such as policy motivations, including government fostering and support of research, historical considerations, and S&T globalization, compel not only individual researchers but broader scientific networks and communities to respond to social and political mobilizations for collaborative relationships (cf. Drori *et al.* 2003; Hwang 2008), with cultural differences in gender relations and participation providing relative advantages and disadvantages for S&T workforce development and productivity.

Unexplored potential

Female publication productivity is also strongly influenced by both structural and individual factors (cf. Prpić 2002). Of these, situational issues, such as *female underrepresentation* itself in some S&T fields, are arguably crucial considerations for understanding the observed unequal outcomes. Furthermore, broader *disciplinary cultures* represent another factor that must be considered, given that some fields have been referenced as relatively more 'female friendly'. Accordingly, some research suggests that the male-dominated disciplinary cultures and organization of some fields contribute largely to low expectations and performance by women (Murphy *et al.* 2007), explaining productivity differences. Women tend to be concentrated in fields and industries such as the biological sciences, agriculture, and pharmaceuticals, but to have little presence in physics, computing, and engineering (which typically are considered higher remunerative fields), thus contributing to disciplinary and occupational segregation and stereotypes and providing a clear example of uneven participation (OECD 2006, 2012a, 2013a; Roos and Gatta 2009). Also, reflecting the growing complexity of S&T disciplines, *research specialization* may be an important intervening variable that negatively affects productivity. Evidence suggests that women specialize more often than men, but the most productive scholars tend to be those with more broadly diversified research programs (cf. Leahey 2005).

Additionally, scientific research typically involves working with others to pool resources, and collaborative projects can provide researchers with expertise in associated disciplines, collegial vetting and support networks, a sense of community, and opportunities to relate to others (Rhoten and Pfirman 2007). This combining of resources is an especially relevant issue for female researchers given the explicit and implicit challenges and barriers to professional advancement and productivity that they often face – e.g., exclusion from information networks, exclusion from grant writing opportunities, marginalization of their research areas, smaller and less well-equipped offices and laboratories, and general denial of voice in institutional decision making (Roos and Gatta 2006 ; Hwang 2008; Ceci and Williams 2011; Duch *et al.* 2012). Such gender imbalances constitute a circular pattern in which *gender disparities lead to gender disparities.* More to the point,

- *Gender disparities are detrimental to S&T capacity; they hinder creativity and innovation.*

Women also tend to be concentrated in lower-level positions in their professional lives (Cross and Linehan 2006; Symonds 2007; Ceci and Williams 2011); female career trajectories generally are somewhat hampered compared to those of males. Even in academia in fields in which women have reached parity in advanced degree attainment, they are still grossly underrepresented in full time senior faculty positions (e.g., 30 per cent in the life sciences). For example, in Europe, men advance at three times the rate of women; women rarely reach more than 20 per cent of the top ranks in academia (OECD 2006). In both the US and European countries, large declines in female representation occur at each rung of the professional ladder, indicating a bottleneck in human capital development and, thus, lost opportunities and resources for ideas and creativity. These outcomes reflect various determinant conditions. In particular,

- *Lower rates of female advancement are linked to gaps and differences in employment conditions, career management, evaluation standards, and research and productivity incentives and opportunities.*

Women tend to have fewer opportunities for attaining positions at research universities where the availability of related resources and support facilitates increased faculty productivity (OECD 2006; Murphy *et al.* 2007; Hill *et al.* 2010; Moss-Racusin 2012).

Gender differences in publishing productivity have been attributed to the greater likelihood for women to work in non-tenure track and contingent positions, to work at teaching (rather than research) institutions; to lack access to institutional support, resources, and time; to participate in service activities that detract from research; to be excluded from broader professional networks; and to have family responsibilities that encroach on time for research (Bentley 2003; Xie and Schaumann 2003; Francl 2005; Robinson 2006; Fox and Mohapatra 2007; NAS 2007; Symonds 2007; Ceci and Williams 2011).[6] In general, lower female productivity reflects the increased unpredictability of their careers (Symonds 2007).

Given technology and innovation defined workforce needs, related organizational and cultural determinants must be addressed to determine means for exploring opportunities represented by the participation of women in support of the S&T endeavour. In this sense, inclusion, along with credible and improved conditions for productivity and advancement, will allow women to contribute (through, e.g., findings, patents, products, etc.) to a more dynamic economy. Of course, related factors can vary dramatically, especially in the face of divergent sociocultural and political conditions, with fundamental implications for technology and innovation. Societies in which female educational attainment is more highly accepted and supported will ultimately benefit from greater S&T productivity and development; i.e., higher female productivity means greater contributions to knowledge, technology, and innovation.

As Susan Windham-Bannister once remarked, 'What is the story of women in science? It is the story of the few and the fewer'.[7] Facing discriminatory practices from the very start of their careers, women have held only 27 per cent of S&T jobs (NRC 2012). Even with progress in educational attainment in some countries, 'the glass is still only half full: women continue to earn less than men and are less likely to make it to the top of the career ladder' (OECD 2012a: 13). That is, while females outnumber males in degree attainment in many countries (OECD 2012b), gender disparities remain rife in, for example, hiring, earnings, funding, patents, advancement, and satisfaction (Holden 2001; Ding *et al.* 2006; Ley and Hamilton 2008; Moss-Racusin *et al.* 2012; Shen 2013). Having said that, increased demands for qualified S&T researchers have raised questions regarding policies and interventions that might better provide access and advancement opportunities for women and other underrepresented groups in related fields, which could result in improved network positioning and collaborations and, thus, in technology development and innovation.

The analytical nexus of representation and productivity processes

Network and collaborative relations in general are highly complex processes and, when gender is explicitly recognized and engaged as a critical influence on observed outcomes, it adds another layer of complexity to those processes to the extent that further study is needed in order to gain insight and understanding of the interrelated institutional, cultural, political, and economic dynamics and structures that shape today's S&T workforce. In other words, gender identity alone hardly explains or is responsible for S&T pipeline issues or related disparities in productivity and workforce development. Rather, as shown in Figure 4.3,

- *Gender must be recognized as a critical determinant at each step within a complex web of relational dynamics and processes.*

Only by capturing related interactive dynamics can the kind of understanding be developed on which to formulate effective policies and interventions for building an inclusive and diversified – and ultimately world-class and strengthened – S&T workforce. The issue here is how to effectively introduce gender into a model as either a contextual factor or, perhaps more importantly, as an intervening factor affecting productivity and workforce development.

Also, although, as discussed above, the operationalization of productivity as publications and of collaboration as number of co-authored publications is widely accepted, publication counts do not indicate quality or relevance. Indeed, using publication counts to study knowledge creation and dissemination does not require that they effectively convey knowledge; it is enough that the processes that transfer knowledge also tend to produce the publication (Hicks and Narin 2001). This type of measure says little about actual quality or whether they encompass new

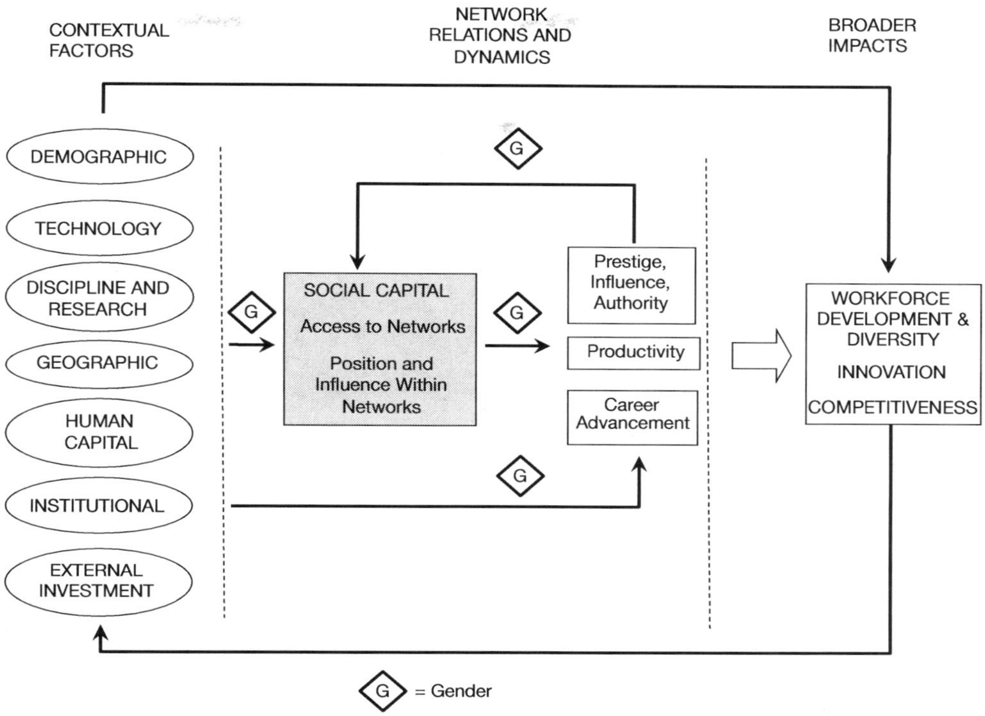

Figure 4.3 Collaborative processes for productivity and workforce development.
Source: author.

insights, applications, or significant discoveries. To some extent, attempts to address such issues have been made by considering number of citations. Employing citation rates to examine co-authorship relative to productivity, some research considers the value of collaborations for further productivity in national and international contexts, using citations to indicate collaboration importance (e.g., Moed 2005; Leydesdorff and Wagner 2008). This concern is especially notable given another side of the productivity puzzle: the 'impact enigma' in which, in some fields (e.g., biochemistry and biology), women's publications, although fewer, have been found to be more frequently cited than those of their male counterparts – even when the women occupy more 'marginal' professional positions (Long 1992; Symonds 2007; Duch *et al.* 2012).

However, other recent work suggests that articles with women as lead authors in general receive fewer citations (Larivière *et al.* 2013). 'Given that citations now play a central part in the evaluation of researchers, this situation can only worsen gender disparities' (Larivière *et al.* 2013: 212), constituting a circular process that operates to retrench existing imbalances, as previously mentioned. Citations are the conventional metric for determining impact, but they too might occur for a variety of (positive or negative) reasons and still do not necessarily indicate substantive quality or relevance. The 'citation disadvantage' accentuates the fact that there is a problem and, while conflicting findings have yet to be explained, they lead to challenges and questions about analytical reliance on numbers of publications as the primary indicator of productivity (Francl 2005). In general, there are potential contributions and human capital that are essentially wasted; opportunities are left unexplored due to systemic disadvantages incurred by females in S&T. By redressing such disadvantages that result in underrepresentation and lower productivity, gains could be made for societal and innovative progress and development. Accordingly, in this regard, *innovation is fundamentally a gender issue.*

Conclusion

Opportunities for growing the S&T workforce – based on increasing the participation and status of women – means more university trained labour comprising a larger pool of academic, government, and private researchers. However, related problems will not take care of themselves; policy action is needed to address the issue of women's participation in S&T careers across sectors (OECD 2006). Moreover, positive outcomes rely on the existence of credible opportunities and conditions for their effective participation and position in S&T professional networks and communities, which are further dependent upon political, economic, and cultural contexts.

As a policy issue, effecting change means meeting the challenge of mobilizing political will and resources for developing and implementing commitments to gender equality and equity across levels of analysis. Policies for prioritizing gender equity must be integrated as central concerns in broader political agendas. Especially given pressures for higher value-added technologies and products in academia, government, and industry (NRC 2012), innovation as a goal demands increasing the university trained S&T workforce rather than increasing competition for already existing positions. To that end, the issue of gender mainstreaming is critical for addressing related needs. Effecting gender mainstreaming requires a wide variety of actions (cf. OECD 2013b): strengthening analytical tools and frameworks to incorporate gender considerations and ensure appropriate skills for related analysis; building evidence-based gender sensitive policy and programmatic approaches; enhancing support and accountability and monitoring mechanisms for gender equity activities; using international platforms and networks to support national and local change; identifying and addressing gaps in organizational capacities and skills to ensure access and influence in policy decisions; and fostering local and national organizational linkages and networks to ensure access to support and decision-making resources.

Overall, a range of policies and programmes have been proposed in many countries to attract and retain women in S&T careers in different sectors (Leggon *et al.* 2015). In addition to gender mainstreaming research initiatives and data collection and evaluation programmes, awareness raising measures, efforts aimed at promoting female S&T workforce participation and advancement in academic, public, and private sectors have included, for example, coaching and mentoring activities, work returnee support, targeted awards, and comprehensive multi-dimensional policy strategies (OECD 2006, 2012a).

The discussion here has been an initiating step in noting important issues that remain to be explored as analytical approaches, calling for a more politically and culturally informed approach to engaging gender as a dynamic and vital issue in the pursuit of innovation and technological advancement. This task will require a multidimensional approach (cf. OECD 2013b):

- developing a highly nuanced and contextualized understanding of related conditions;
- employing diverse strategies to seize short and long term opportunities and direct and indirect approaches;
- supporting female empowerment across sectors and purposes;
- engaging a wide range of institutions and actors to facilitate identification of common interests and collaborative relationships to promote gender equality; and
- developing and using political opportunities and leadership influence and commitment to related goals.

Taking these points together means framing gender inequality as an integral concern in the complex causal relations reflected in network and collaboration processes. Doing so is a crucial step in delineating the gendered dynamics attending S&T workforce participation, development, and productivity.

Gender is one of those issues that so permeates social interaction that its effects cannot be rightly captured by characterizing it simply as a separate factor in related analyses. Growing attention to research on networks and collaboration as key aspects of S&T productivity – not only as outcome, but as process – reveals that it must be understood within the context of larger social, cultural, political, and economic conditions that have determined the underrepresentation of women, and of other disadvantaged groups as well, which ultimately translates into lost opportunities for future progress. The complex character of the embedded gender dynamics requires the explicit recognition of its critical interactive nature and influence. Moreover, in-depth analyses of societal relations and changing network patterns over time and place are needed in order to better understand the role of gender relative to other determinant factors affecting the development of the S&T workforce and to meet the needs and challenges of today's innovation-driven knowledge society.

Notes

1 E.g., see references in Larivière (2013); Hill *et al.* (2010); NAS (2007); Turner and Mairesse (2003).
2 Smith (1958) was one of the first advocates for the use of co-authored papers to measure scientific collaborations, and de Solla Price (1963) was one of the first to produce and establish direct bibliometrics measurement as the standard for that purpose.
3 http://ec.europa.eu/unitedkingdom/press/frontpage/2013/13_32_en.htm (accessed 21 May 2015).
4 Note that, worldwide, approximately 17 per cent of countries have relatively equal numbers of men and women scientists (UNESCO 2007).
5 However, some analysts argue that political gains of formal collaborations may have been lessened by globalization dynamics that have made international collaboration more commonplace (Skolnikoff 2001).
6 Regarding arguments crediting increased family responsibilities for women as the cause of lower publication rates, this is the general perception, but empirical evidence is mixed (Sax *et al.* 2002). It is also the case that this situation may be due to specification issues.
7 Cited in NRC (2012).

References

Bell, N., 2010: *Graduate Enrollment and Degrees: 1999 to 2009*. Washington, DC: Council of Graduate Schools.

Bentley, J.T., 2003: *Gender Differences in the Careers of Academic Scientists and Engineers: A literature review*. Arlington, VA: National Science Foundation.

Brass, D.J., 1984: Being in the right place: a structural analysis of individual influence in organization. *Administrative Science Quarterly* 29, pp. 518–539.

Bukvova, H., 2010: Studying Research Collaboration: A Literature Review. *All Sprouts Content*, Paper 326. Available online at: http://aisel.aisnet.org/sprouts_all/326 (accessed 21 May 2015).

Burt, R., 1992: *Structural Holes*. Cambridge, MA: Harvard University Press.

Butler, D.M, and Butler, R.J., 2011: Is the internet bridging the gender gap? The case of political science. *Economics of Education Review* 30(4), pp. 665–672.

Callon, M., Law, J. and Rip, A., 1986: *Mapping the Dynamics of Science and Technology: Sociology of science in the real world*. Houndmills, UK: Macmillan.

Ceci, S.J. and Williams, W.M., 2011: Understanding current causes of women's underrepresentation in science. *Proceedings of the National Academy of Sciences of the United States of America* 108(8), pp. 3157–3162.

Centola, D., 2010: The spread of behavior in an online social network experiment. *Science* 329(5996), pp. 1194–1197.

Chung, S., 2002: Catching up through international linkages: science, technology, and the Korean experience. *Science and Public Policy* 29(6), pp. 431–437.

Cole, J.R. and Zuckerman, H., 1984: The productivity puzzle: persistence and change in patterns of publication of men and women scientists. In: Steinkamp, M.W. and Maehr, M.L. (eds): *Advances in Motivation and Achievement*, vol. 2. Greenwich, CO: JAI Press.

Cronin, B., Shaw, D. and La Barre, K., 2004: Visible, less visible, and invisible work: patterns of collaboration in 20th century chemistry. *Journal of the American Society for Information Science and Technology* 55(2), pp. 160–168.

Cross, C. and Linehan, M., 2006: Barriers to advancing female careers in the high-tech sector: empirical evidence from Ireland. *Women in Management Review* 21(1), pp. 28–39.

de Solla Price, D.J., 1963: *Little Science, Big Science*. New York: Columbia University Press.

Ding, W.W., Murray, F. and Stuart, T.E., 2006: Gender differences in patenting in the academic life sciences. *Science* 313(5787), pp. 665–667.

Drori, G.S., Meyer, J.W., Ramirez, F.O. and Schofer, E., 2003: *Science in the Modern World Polity: Institutionalization and globalization*. Stanford, CA: Stanford University Press.

Duch, J., Zeng, X.H.T., Sales-Pardo, M., Radicchi, F., Otis, S., Woodruff, T.K. and Nunes Amaral, L.A., 2012: The possible role of resource requirements and academic career-choice risk on gender differences in publication rate and impact. *PLOS ONE* 7: e51332/DOI: 10.1371.

European Commission (EC), 2013: *She Figures 2012: Gender in research and innovation*. Brussels: European Union.

Fox, M.F. and Mohapatra, S., 2007: Social-organizational characteristics of work and publication productivity among academic scientists in doctoral-granting departments. *Journal of Higher Education* 78(5), pp. 543–571.

Francl, M.M., 2005: The 'Productivity Puzzle' and the 'Impact Enigma', The Culture of Chemistry. Available online at: http://cultureofchemistry.blogspot.com/2005/06/productivity-puzzle-and-impact-enigma.html (accessed 21 May 2015)

Frehill, L.M., 2014: An Analysis of Organization for Economic Cooperation and Development Data (accessed via OECD.stat Extracts).

Gladwell, M., 2002: *The Tipping Point: How little things can make a big difference*. New York: Back Bay Books.

Glänzel, W. and Schubert, A., 2004: Analyzing scientific networks through co-authorship. In: Moed, H.F., Glänzel, W. and Schmoch, U. (eds): *Handbook of Quantitative Science and Technology Research*. London: Kluwer.

Heinze, T. and Kuhlmann, S., 2008: Across institutional boundaries? Research collaboration in German public sector nanoscience. *Research Policy* 37(5), pp. 888–899.

Hicks, D. and Narin, F., 2001: Strategic research alliances and 360 degree bibliometrics indicators. *Proceedings of NSF Workshop: Strategic Research Partnerships*. Available online at: www.nsf.gov/statistics/nsf01336/p1s6.htm (accessed 21 May 2015).

Hill, C., Corbett, C. and St Rose, A., 2010: *Why So Few? Women in science, technology, engineering, and mathematics*. Washington, DC: American Association of University Women.

Hill, V., 2008: Collaboration in an Academic Setting: Does the Network Structure Matter? CMU-ISR-08–128. Technical report.

Hoffman, M., Gneezy, U. and List, J.A., 2011: Nurture affects gender differences in spatial abilities. *Proceedings of the National Academy of Sciences of the USA* 108(36). pp. 14786–14788.

Holden, C., 2001: General contentment masks gender gap in first AAAS salary and job survey. *Science* 294(5541), pp. 396–411.

Hwang, K., 2008: International collaboration in multilayered center-periphery in the globalization of science and technology. *Science, Technology, Human Values* 33(1), pp. 101–133.

Katz, J.S. and Martin, B.R., 1997: What is research collaboration? *Research Policy* 26(1), pp. 1–18.

Larivière, V., Ni, C., Gingras, Y., Cronin, B. and Sugimoto, C.R., 2013: Global gender disparities in science. *Nature* 504, pp. 211–213.

Latour, B. and Woolgar, S., 1986: *Laboratory Life: The construction of social facts*. Princeton, NJ: Princeton University Press.

Leahey, E., 2005: Solving the productivity puzzle: Research specialization as a missing link. Presented at the annual meeting of the American Sociological Association, Philadelphia.

Leggon, C., McNeely, C.L. and Yoon, J., 2015: Advancing women in science: policies for progress. In: Pearson, W., Jr., Frehill, L. and McNeely, C.L. (eds): *Advancing Women in Science: An international perspective*. New York: Springer, pp. 307–327.

Ley, T.J. and Hamilton, B.H., 2008: The gender gap in NIH grant applications. *Science* 322(5907), pp. 1472–1474.

Leydesdorff, L., and Wagner, C., 2008: International collaboration in science and the formation of a core group. *Journal of Informetrics* 2(4), pp. 317–325.

Lin, N., 2002: *Social Capital: A theory of social capital and action*. Cambridge: Cambridge University Press.

Long, J.S., 1992: Measures of sex differences in scientific productivity. *Social Forces* 7(1), pp. 159–178.

McNeely, C.L. and Schintler, L., 2010a: Exploring Epistemic Communities: A Gendered Perspective on Scientific Collaboration. *ERN Public Policy Institutes Research Paper Series* 2(3). Available online at: http://ssrn.com/abstract=1596134 (accessed 21 May 2015).

McNeely, C.L. and Schintler, L., 2010b: Gender Issues in Scientific Collaboration and Workforce Development: Implications for a Federal Policy Research Agenda. *Science of Science Measurement*, U.S. Office of Science and Technology Policy, Washington, DC. Available online at: www.nsf.gov/sbe/sosp/workforce/mcneely.pdf (accessed 21 May 2015).

McNeely, C.L. and Vlaicu, S., 2010: Exploring institutional hiring trends of women in the U.S. STEM Professoriate. *Review of Policy Research* 27(6), pp. 781–793.

Moed, H.F., 2005: *Citation Analysis in Research Evaluation*. Dordrecht, Netherlands: Springer.

Moss-Racusin, C.A., Dovidio, J.F., Brescoll, V.L., Graham, M.J. and Handelsman, J., 2012: Science faculty's subtle gender biases favor male students. *Proceedings of the National Academy of Sciences of the United States of America* 109(41): pp. 16474–16479.

Murphy, M.C., Steele, C.M. and Gross, J.J., 2007: Signaling threat: how situational cues affect women in math, science, and engineering settings. *Psychological Science* 18(10), pp. 879–885.

National Academy of Sciences (NAS), 2007: *Beyond Bias and Barriers: Fulfilling the potential of women in academic science and engineering*. Washington, DC: National Academies Press.

National Research Council (NRC), 2010: *Gender Differences at Critical Transitions in the Careers of Science, Engineering, and Mathematics Faculty*. Washington, DC: National Academies Press.

National Research Council (NRC), 2012: *From Science to Business: Preparing Female Scientists and Engineers for Successful Transitions into Entrepreneurship, Workshop Summary*. Washington, DC: National Academies Press.

Newman, M.E.J., 2004: Co-authorship networks and patterns of scientific collaboration. *Proceedings of the National Sciences of the United States of America* 101(Supplement 1), pp. 5200–5205.

Oldham, G., 2005: International Scientific Collaboration: A quick guide, science and development network policy brief. Available online at: www.scidev.net/en/policy-briefs/international-scientific-collaboration-a-quick-gui.html (accessed 21 May 2015).

Organization for Economic Cooperation and Development (OECD), 2006: *Women in Scientific Careers: Unleashing the Potential*. Paris: OECD.

Organization for Economic Cooperation and Development (OECD), 2012a: *Closing the Gender Gap: Act Now*. Paris: OECD.

Organization for Economic Cooperation and Development (OECD), 2012b: *Education at a Glance 2012*. Paris: OECD.

Organization for Economic Cooperation and Development (OECD), 2013a: Gender differences in employment opportunities. In: *OECD Regions at a Glance 2013*. Paris: OECD.

Organization for Economic Cooperation and Development (OECD), 2013b: *Gender and Statebuilding in Fragile and Conflict-Affected States*. Paris: OECD.

Pearson, W., Jr., Frehill, L. and McNeely, C.L. (eds), 2015: *Advancing Women in Science: An International Perspective*. London: Springer.

Prpić, K., 2002: Gender and productivity differentials in science. *Scientometrics* 55(1): pp. 27–58.

Rhoten, D. and Pfirman, S., 2007: Women in interdisciplinary science: exploring preferences and consequences. *Research Policy* 36: 56–75.

Robinson, D., 2006: *The Status of Higher Education Teaching Personnel in Australia, Canada, New Zealand, the United Kingdom, and the United States*. Education International Report.

Roos, P. and Gatta, M., 2009: Gender (in)equity in the academy: subtle mechanisms and the production of inequality. *Research in Social Stratification and Mobility* 27(3), pp. 177–200.

Rycroft, R. and Kash, D.E., 1999: *The Complexity Challenge: Technological innovation for the 21st century*. New York: Pinter.

Sargent, L. and Waters, L.E., 2004: Centers and academic research collaborations: an inductive process framework for understanding successful collaborations. *Journal of Vocational Behavior* 64(2), pp. 308–319.

Sax, L.J., Hagedorn, S., Arredondo, M. and Dicrisi, F.A., 2002: Faculty research productivity: exploring the role of gender and family-related factors. *Research in Higher Education* 43(4), 423–446.

Schintler, L. and McNeely, C.L., 2012: Gendered science in the 21st century: productivity puzzle 2.0? *International Journal of Gender, Science, and Technology* 4(1), pp. 123–128.

Schott, T., 1993: World science: globalization of institutions and participation. *Science, Technology, and Human Values* 18, pp. 196–208.

Shen, H., 2013: Inequality quantified: mind the gender gap. *Nature* 495, pp. 22–24.

Skolnikoff, E.B., 2001: The political role of scientific cooperation. *Technology in Society* 23, pp. 461–471.

Smith, M., 1958: The trend toward multiple authorship in psychology. *American Psychologist* 13, pp. 596–599.

Sonnenwald, D.H., 2007: Scientific collaboration. *Annual Review of Information Science and Technology* 41, pp. 643–681.

Sonnenwald, D.H., Lassi, M., Olson, N., Ponti, M. and Axelsson, A., 2009: Exploring new ways of working using virtual research environments in library and information science. *Library Hi Tech* 27(2), 191–204.

Stokols, D., Misra, S., Moser, R.P., Hall, K.L. and Taylor, B.K., 2008: The ecology of team science. *American Journal of Preventive Medicine* 35(2S), pp. 96–115.

Symonds, M., 2007: Quantity, quality, and equality. *New Scientist* 194(2611), pp. 48–49.

Tai, A.R. and Sims, R.L., 2005: The perception of the glass ceiling in high-technology companies. *Journal of Leadership and Organizational Studies* 12(1), pp. 16–23.

Turner, L. and Mairesse., J., 2003: Individual Productivity Differences in Scientific Research: An Econometric Study of the Publication of French Physicists. Paper presented at the Zvi Griliches Memorial Conference, Paris.

United Nations Educational, Scientific and Cultural Organization (UNESCO), 2007: *Science, Technology, and Gender: An International Report*. Paris: UNESCO.

Wagner, C.S., 2008: *The New Invisible College: Science for development*. Washington, DC: Brookings Institution Press.

Wagner C.S. and Leydesdorff, L., 2005: Network structure, self-organization, and the growth of international collaboration in science. *Research Policy* 34(10), pp. 1608–1618.

Welch, E. and Melkers, J., 2008: Effects of Network Size and Gender on Research Grant Awards to Scientists and Engineers: An Analysis from a National Survey of Six Fields. Paper presented at the 2008 Meeting of PRIME, Mexico City, Mexico.

West, J.D., Jacquet, J., King, M., Correll, S.J. and Bergstrom, C.T., 2013: The role of gender in scholarly authorship. *PLOS ONE* 8: e66212/DOI: 10.1371.

Wray, K.B., 2006: Scientific authorship in the age of collaborative research. *Studies in History and Philosophy of Science, Part A* 37(3), pp. 505–514.

Xie, Y. and Schaumann, K.A., 2003: *Women in Science: Career processes and outcomes*. Cambridge: Harvard University Press.

Zimmerman, K.F., 2012: The human resource challenge. In: *Meeting Global Challenges: U.S.-German Innovation Policy*. National Research Council. Washington, DC: National Academies Press, pp. 79–84.

Zucker, L.G., Darby, M.R., Furner, J., Liu, R.C. and Ma, H., 2007: Minerva unbound: knowledge stocks, knowledge flows, and new knowledge production. *Research Policy* 36(6), pp. 850–863.

5

BRANDING THE INNOVATION PLACE

Managing the soft infrastructure of innovation

Nicola Bellini and Cecilia Pasquinelli

Introduction

Cities, regions and countries are increasingly engaged with the management of their image and, in many cases, this coincides with an attempt to build their reputation as innovation hubs. In place branding the reference to innovation is, indeed, crucial: places are branded as 'the' location where innovative activities can flourish, either because of previous performance or because of emerging favourable conditions. Nonetheless, we know very little about the actual linkage between branding initiatives and innovative developments. It seems quite safe to say that there is no straightforward connection of such a kind that we may dare (or hope to dare in the future) some econometric regression.

As often happens in policy analysis, it is the causal relationship between the two phenomena that is unclear and needs to be investigated, by looking into the set of values, attitudes and mentalities that shape, constrain and trigger innovative behaviour at both individual and institutional level. Such is the objective of this chapter.

In the next paragraph we recall and discuss the main features of the place branding phenomenon, in particular in relation to innovation. The following paragraph suggests that the linkage between place branding and innovation as the engine of economic development may be better defined in relation with the 'soft infrastructure', a concept that we also try to analyse in its dynamics. This chapter discusses innovation policy dimensions by arguing that place branding is one possible way to influence the soft infrastructure and its evolution, and that the soft infrastructure may either support or pose barriers to innovation.

Place branding and innovation

Place branding is an emerging topic in economic development research, especially at regional and local level. For some time place branding issues have been dealt with mostly within practice; it has been an opportunity for many consultancy firms e.g. Future Brand, Saffron and GfK Roper, selling place branding 'solutions' to local and national governments worldwide. From a theoretical point of view, the field has been mostly considered as instrumental to 'place marketing' and therefore has been dominated by the 'market analogy', which has underpinned the equally dominating reference to the marketing literature.

In many cases place branding has made reference to the innovative character of local industries, to the role of education and research institutions and more generally to the propensity to innovation within the local society. The innovation brand often coincides with the branding of an 'intelligent island' where intensive investments in the structuring of a national innovation system and education capabilities are coupled with a local buzz about the meaning and value of 'innovation' for the local economy; these were the elements assumed to make Singapore an 'intelligent island' attractive to foreign investors (Wong *et al.* 2006).

A sort of rhetoric of innovation has been entangled and shows a global reach. Such rhetoric, however, has been changing over time by adopting different perspectives on innovation and, above all, showing different expectations about what the innovation place should be. Different waves of innovation branding were identified (Pasquinelli and Teräs 2011); during the 1990s, the spatial focus on the high-tech cluster prevailed and innovation brands used to communicate the will of becoming the new or the next Silicon Valley, thus representing local economic systems as rapidly growing and capable of reshaping local socio-economic reality. There has been a tendency towards the creation of 'Silicon Somewhere' (Hospers 2006b) brands: Silicon Glen (Scotland), Silicon Seaside (South Norway) and Silicon Kashba (Istanbul) are only a few examples giving evidence of the (perceived) power of the 'Silicon' and/or 'Valley' imagery. The 'valley' evokes a physical agglomeration of firms depicted as 'naturally' inclined to network knowledge and expertise, as well as the 'two-guys-in-a-garage' story, sometime even suggesting an unsolvable conflict between the upcoming high-tech phenomenon and traditional local economy (Pasquinelli 2010).

The second wave of innovation branding started at the beginning of the 2000s, when the concepts of creativity and 'creative city' were fully endorsed by public governments worldwide. The human being and the living urban contest have been at the core of innovation brands, thus putting young highly educated professionals – their personal and professional aspirations – at the core of the brand message. The innovation brand has been conceived as in charge of delivering an 'inspiring message' so that a series of 'inspiring capitals' emerged (e.g. Edinburgh Inspiring Capital, Oulu Inspires), inviting talents to move into the place and turn their aspirations into reality (e.g. Pittsburgh. Imagine what you can do here). The case of Singapore highlights a path towards a notion of innovation as a capacity to attract and nurture knowledge-intensive companies forming a dynamic creative and cultural hub, even in a context where opportunities for creativity and experimentation conflict with the state propensity towards control on society (Wong *et al.* 2006; Ooi 2008).

The creative city brand script has progressively transformed into the 'smart city' one, being unanimously endorsed in a multilevel policy arena. The rhetoric of smartness is based on the immanent role of technology (and especially ICT) in every manifestation of people's daily life, involving the entire local community and affecting urban life (Caragliu *et al.* 2011).

Branding the smart city has become an arena for competition among cities (Peacock 2011). Cities participate in contests, such as the Smarter Cities Challenge by IBM, that are launched by TNCs willing to enter the market of urban technologies and technological services. City governments make efforts to create the conditions to become urban innovation laboratories for global firms, which thus have the opportunity to test and sell their technology to relevant public clients. This was, for instance, the case of San Francisco whose Mayor agreed in 2009 with CISCO for the implementation of Cisco Smart+Connected Communities in the city, i.e. a 'solution using intelligent networking capabilities to bring together people, services, community assets, and information to help community leaders address world challenges'.[1] Since then, Cisco solutions have been implemented in several 'smart' cities all around the globe.

In China the 'smart city' discourse is being looked at as a necessary answer to the challenges faced by Chinese mega-cities (Wei and Li 2012). For similar reasons, South Korea has been collaborating with Samsung and other global players to build the U-City brand (Peacock 2011). Being a strategy for urban regeneration and economic development, the 'smart city' is an opportunity for co-branding that involves a city and a technological partner: strong technological corporate brands, e.g. Cisco, Siemens, Samsung and IBM, enrich the city brand with innovation values by means of a collaborative association.

Overall brand uniqueness has tended to decrease, notwithstanding the apparent quest for differentiation (Turok 2009). Based on 'credo of creativity' (Peck 2005: 740), all cities willing to follow the 'high roads' of economic development in the age of the knowledge economy, shape an urban narrative around symbols and values that fit with the assumed preferences of the global creative class. In contrast, place-based innovation strategies, as in the case of Pittsburgh, US, tend to allow an urban collective process of adaptive reinterpretation of local identity, i.e. symbols and values that are linked to the old industry (the steel industry in Pittsburgh), so that the innovation place is not represented as antithetical to traditional local vocation (Treado 2010).

In regional policies homogenization and standardization of innovation brands went in parallel with the diffusion of 'best practices' (Hospers 2006a), encouraged by EU cohesion policy and structural funds programmes that have boosted a pan-European competition played on an ideal-type of innovation. In the next years a potential counter-trend to differentiation may emerge as the result of the reorientation of regional innovation strategies along the paradigm of smart specialization (Foray and Goenaga 2013). We may expect that the search for policies linking innovation to specific regional vocation and assets to be mirrored by a new wave of innovation place brands where the vocational specialization of a territory needs to be made visible and generally understood.

Identity and images

Place branding interacts with crucial and complex variables of local polities. In particular branding tries to manipulate the place identity that is 'constructed through historical, political, religious and cultural discourses . . . and . . . influenced by power struggle' (Govers and Go 2009: 17). To do so, branding attempts to shape place images, i.e. the perceptions of the place in people's minds (Anholt 2007), which tend to result in a 'simplification' of a large number of associations and information about the place (Warnaby and Medway 2008). As a practice of brand image management, branding has to deal with two relevant mechanisms. A branding input determines multiple (and uncontrollable) images in relation to diverse brand associations triggered in audience minds (Jevons *et al.* 2005). The image is also influenced by forces that are exogenous to the branding process and are unpredictable and out of control, e.g. dramatic economic crisis, global cultural turns or diplomatic issues (van Ham 2008).

Place image is self-reinforcing since actors' behaviours tend to conform to their expectations which are highly influenced by perceptions. When consolidated, the image is likely to become a self-fulfilling prophecy (Bellini 2004) so that perceptions are made a reality and become an integral part of the place identity according to a perception–expectation–action circuit. In a context of change re-branding actions may (or may not) trigger innovative images about the place, thus communicating change and encouraging a positive attitude towards innovation. This is especially true for the *internal image* (the perceptions of insiders, i.e. residents, local entrepreneurs etc.), where 'evaluative' components reflecting actual experiences mix with 'preferential' components reflecting desires, visions and projects about the area (Ashworth and Voogd 1988; Bellini *et al.* 2010).

On the other hand, external images (the perceptions of outsiders, i.e. individuals not living in the city or region but still having a perception about the place) contribute to positioning the region/city within the competitive arena of global innovation hubs, global value chains and collaborative innovation networks, both as such (like in the case of the Øresund region aggregating even German universities: Berg 2000) and through the association with products (like in the case of the iconic Apple devices labelled as 'Designed by Apple in California': Pike 2010).

Greater complexity originates from the interaction between external and internal images as well as between images as perceived by different audiences (e.g. tourists vs. inhabitants or tourists vs. investors). Typically tourists may require for some kind of timeless authenticity in contrast with the need for modernity and innovation by the residents (Lazzeroni *et al.* 2013). The mismatch between internal and external images is also clear in the case of the Øresund region that, branded as 'The Human Capital of Scandinavia', has been celebrated in Europe as 'best practice' in establishing a knowledge economy (Pasquinelli 2013), whereas it determined a lack of enthusiasm among inhabitants who did not visualize the region in their daily life (Hospers 2006a), and even a sort of 'irritation' for an 'artificial region'.

The politics of branding

In a context of change, where socio-economic discontinuities may be necessary or even unavoidable, one should expect that different social groups translate their (possibly diverging) expectations into potentially conflicting visions for regional/local development. As a consequence, multiple place images may coexist and compete.

A process of interaction and negotiation leads a community to select the values that compose the brand identity, revealing power relations and conflicts among territorial agents (Ooi 2004; Hospers 2006a; Jensen 2007) and often rewarding local hegemonic narratives (Ward 2000; Therkelsen and Halkier 2008). In other words, branding processes are far from being fully inclusive (Kavaratzis and Ashworth 2005). On the contrary, they can be purposely exclusive, allowing specific social groups to own the brand and to use it as a symbolic source of legitimization. In some cases the dynamics may favour 'progressive coalitions' that support substantial change, the emergence of new social groups and/or new paradigms in the economic structure. In other cases conservative groups prevail and place branding can be instrumental to lock in the present power structure.

Local and regional governments usually play a key role in building the place brand as they contribute to building 'spaces' and artefacts that, symbolizing innovation and change in the urban context, improve place perceptions. However, their role is very controversial: progressive coalitions may not have the consensus of citizens' majority, thus creating democratic dilemmas; on the other hand, political elites may drive the system to maintain the status quo regardless of a collective interest in innovation and change.

Multiple narratives merged into a 'story of urban transformation' in the case of Aalborg, Denmark. Tensions, due to the multiple perceptions of the urban context and diverse expectations on the regeneration process, emerged during the transformation of Aalborg from industrial and peripheral city to cultural centre of the knowledge economy. The urban vision of culture-led development lacked public validation and a huge part of the local community considered the urban transformation as an 'elitist' project (Jensen 2007).

The case of Tuscany, Italy, shows 'how different images and visions are built upon a very selective narration of the region's history and shared values' (Bellini *et al.* 2010: 109). The emphasis on the romantic, anti-modern, timeless image of Tuscany shows an inability to articulate multiple discourses on the region. Cultural heritage is interpreted in relation to the 'preservation of the past' and, when an attempt was made to brand regional high tech industries as 'Arnovalley' at the end of the 1990s, the narrative of the Silicon Valley of Tuscany was preferred to the mobilization of symbols rooted in regional heritage, leading to a failure (Pasquinelli 2010).

Beyond competition

Along with increasing awareness about the role of territorial complementarities for constructing a competitive advantage (Gordon 2011), a co-opetitive approach – i.e. mixing a competitive attitude with a cooperative one – has also been adopted in place branding. The collaborative network of territories is the framework for boosting a process of transformation and change that needs a regeneration of symbols, values and images (Pasquinelli 2012; Bellini and Hilpert 2013). The reputation of individual territories and their actors can favour inter-territorial networking and 'brand alliances', which can be seen as ways to improve the regional profile of innovative place.

The case of the Ruhr in North Rhine Westphalia, Germany is an example of a network of towns and cities collaborating for the mobilization of resources – including symbolic resources – for change (Pasquinelli 2012). By capitalizing on regional culture and its economic potential, the Ruhr region 'has undergone a major transformation and has changed from a grey industrial area into a modern and trendy culture metropolis',[2] a 'conglomeration' of creative businesses, leisure facilities and technological innovation (Krajewsky 2008).

A network of territories helps local communities to visualize and imagine change and innovation. In the case of Val di Cornia, Italy, the network of five municipalities gave local communities the opportunity to build a heavily renewed perception of their area, based on symbols and values, such as environmental sustainability and the preservation of cultural heritage, that, contrasting with the imagery of the old steel industry, embody the local way to interpret innovation and change (Bellini and Pasquinelli 2011; Pasquinelli 2011).

The 'soft infrastructure'

The growing literature on place branding is providing an impressive wealth of case studies and an increasingly deep knowledge of its technicalities. Yet a more fundamental issue seems to be untouched and unresolved. Does place branding really matter? Besides all evaluations about the appropriateness, the communicative effectiveness, the market response etc., are we able to give evidence that place branding makes a difference in local/regional development, in the same way as we can give evidence of and measure the effects of other policies?

At the present stage this 'final' evidence of the relevance of place branding is still missing, marking a strong contrast with the diffusion of the branding practice. In our opinion, however, this is due to the still unclear causal connection between place branding and development that requires a more careful consideration of some preconditions of innovation that are partially overlooked in the literature. These preconditions are summarized in the concept of 'soft infrastructures' and we suggest that place branding is one way to impact on it. In other words, the aim is to emphasise the linkage between place branding and innovation as an engine of local and regional economic development, a linkage that, in our opinion, is framed by the 'soft infrastructure' of innovation.

Definition and characters

The infrastructural endowment of regions plays a significant role in boosting their innovative capacity. From an economic perspective, both hard and soft infrastructures affect firms' transactions and the marginal rate of return on investments (Lin 2011). If hard infrastructure is composed of highways, port facilities, airports and telecommunications, soft infrastructure coincides with institutions, regulations, social capital and with the so-called cultural value system.

According to Cooke (2001), infrastructural and suprastructural characteristics are 'ideal-type conditions for systemic innovation'. That is, key elements of a systemic innovation are the quantity and quality of the infrastructures that the region can control and manage, including regionalized credit facilities, administrative and taxation capacity, as well as the hard infrastructure, e.g. transport and telecommunications. On the other hand, 'softer or knowledge infrastructures' play a role, such as universities, research institutes, science parks and technology transfer centres. 'Soft' identifies knowledge as cognitively accumulated infrastructure within the region. In Cooke's words, the cultural dimension contributes to systemic innovation and is defined as the 'suprastructure'; this refers to the 'mentalities' of regional actors and, in particular, to the institutional and organizational culture characterizing the region (2001).

In fact 'culture' is mainly understood as industrial culture, entrepreneurial culture or systemic/institutional culture, in relation to the interactions among different economic and institutional actors that are bound by an economic (development) purpose. However, as soon as one suggests the existence of something such as a 'culture of innovation', the above-mentioned dimensions seem insufficient. In our opinion, it is therefore wiser to expand the notion of culture to include the whole cultural value system (Lin 2011) and a wider range of 'mentalities' (Cooke 2001), thus considering the broader soft infrastructure as generated and embedded within the whole regional community – including social, political, economic actors, i.e. a multifaceted collectivity – in multiple contexts, beyond the mere industrial and productive context. In turn, this view is consistent with an understanding of innovation as an interactive and iterative process within a multi-actor ecosystem.

Thus, the soft infrastructure is here defined as the set of values, beliefs and attitudes that, narrated through the area's cultural heritage and reflected into images, influence innovative decisions at individual and collective levels. This occurs because innovation needs to be legitimized. Beyond contemporary common places, it is sometimes overlooked that innovation implies attitudes and behavioural patterns that are not necessarily accepted in our societies: innovators are often unconventional, anarchical, visionary, 'different' and 'weird' individuals.

The soft infrastructure can also be understood as symbolic infrastructure. The importance of this can be explained in light of Bourdieu's notion of symbolic power (1989): the mobilization of symbols has the power to make groups by imposing a vision that, looking at the past or defining future trajectories, emerges from forms of social authority or credit accumulated in history. A crucial source of symbolic power is history, as the evidence of a long-term persistence of symbols strengthens the credibility of their meanings to 'heritage', in which 'very selective material artefacts, mythologies, memories and traditions become resources for the present' (Ashworth and Graham 2005: 4).

As recently argued (Manniche 2012), territorial innovation research has overlooked the symbolic and creative category of 'knowing' as epistemological practice, while emphasizing the use of analytical and synthetic knowledge. The symbolic dimension of regional systems was conceptualized as 'symbolic knowledge', which is part of the 'differentiated knowledge bases' contributing to regional innovation (Asheim *et al.* 2007). Symbolic knowledge refers to the creation and communication of cultural meanings, symbols and aesthetic values, a form of tacit knowledge that is rooted within specific sociocultural contexts with little or no opportunity of transfer. The symbolic knowledge in combination with synthetic and analytical knowledge is at the basis of regional systems and their innovative capacity (Manniche 2012). The dynamics of symbolic knowledge accumulation occurs outside of the spatial circuits of economic production. In fact, symbolic knowledge accumulation occurs informally in non-commercial and daily life contexts, e.g. streets and public events (Asheim *et al.* 2007), where interactions among people and interactions between individuals and (urban) artefacts create a symbolic buzz. Informality, however, does not mean absence of guidance by the State and/or by other entities (such as churches, political organizations etc.).

In the literature on regional innovation the role of symbols has been only marginally analysed. Some scholars argued the relevance of symbolic capital for regional innovation and competitiveness; it was said that three intangible assets rule value creation in the knowledge economy, i.e. informational, social and symbolic capital, this last coinciding with the aggregation of myths, meanings and identities. Cultural identit(ies) work as 'system activators' since they facilitate local communities in interiorizing and reacting to the challenge of 'radical innovation', while 'weak identities' are considered evidence of structural fragility and weak innovative capacity. This was argued in the case of Vancouver, Canada, where booming high-tech industries have not been mirrored by consistent cultural identity, so that the 'high-tech' remains peripheral in the city's self-perception (Sacco *et al.* 2007). On the contrary, the Silicon Valley is the example of a place where 'technology' became a socialized symbol per se, the main component of local and individual identities that are both reinforced by people's loyal commitment to 'advancing technologies, rather than to individual firms or even industries' (Saxenian 1994, cited in Benner 2003: 28). In other words, the soft infrastructure plays a role in regional innovation since it produces symbols endorsing innovators within a regional network.

Innovation policies and the soft infrastructure are therefore deeply intertwined. On the one hand, the design and implementation of innovation policies depend upon the quality of the regional soft infrastructure and the latter can be fine-tuned with innovation by a variety of means, including place branding, aiming at symbolizing, socializing and legitimizing change. In discussing the concept of resilience in a regional economic context, Pike *et al.* (2010) stated that 'the political construction of adaptation and adaptability narratives' is fundamental for those regions in need of shaping stories of recovery and 'meaningful narratives of change', e.g. for old industrial regions. This seems to suggest that, under the impact of forces propelling change, there is not only an issue of adaptation and adaptability of the 'material' and economic dimension of the regional system (for instance, number of firms and their performance and profitability, jobs, etc.), but also an issue of adaptation and adaptability of the 'immaterial' and symbolic dimension, which might be impacted by 'transformative interventions' and, in our analysis, by innovation (branding) policies. That is, 'in the politics of adaptation and adaptability integral to resilience, nation states are centrally important agents in framing and narrating development paths in places' (Pike *et al.* 2010: 66). In the history of modern industrialization powerful contributions to the establishment of functional 'soft infrastructures' have been provided by economic nationalism (from Friedrich List to its most contemporary variations), by the progressive rhetoric of positivism during the nineteenth century and by the autarchic propaganda of twentieth-century totalitarianisms. Place branding (whose internal dimension shows several analogies with older kinds of 'propaganda') is just the latest version of the repeated attempts to sustain the symbolic infrastructure of innovation as the basis for competitiveness and economic growth.

On the other hand, innovation policies may impact on the soft infrastructure, by fostering an accumulation of values and a projection of images that enrich or impoverish, more generally change, the soft infrastructure. In other words, innovation policies may (or may not) trigger a virtuous circuit fuelling entrepreneurial spirit and risk propensity of regional actors (both entrepreneurs and policymakers), as well as the innovative behaviours and their acceptance within the regional community.

The evolution of the soft infrastructure

To frame the evolution of the soft infrastructure, an 'ecological' interpretation referring to two interrelated concepts, i.e. resilience[3] and variety,[4] is here proposed. Based on the notion of variety we may suggest that the richness and even redundancy of symbols, values and identities are considered as signals of a potentially resilient soft infrastructure. A resilient[5] soft infrastructure is capable of timely reacting to opportunities for innovative transformation and adaptation, and opens to alternative infrastructural configuration, thus supporting the regional process of innovation. While a higher variety of symbols and values is likely to support diverse routes of innovation, as enabling multiple creative approaches to the interpretation and socialization of change, a limited range of symbols and values is likely to limit the capacity of regional community to reinterpret its identity in an adaptive/transformative way.

The variety of symbols and values composing the soft infrastructure impacts on the type and degree of resilience characterizing it; at the same time, variety is arguably influenced by innovation branding policies that, as said earlier, in some cases may favour the emergence of 'progressive coalitions' including new social groups and their values (increasing variety), while in some other cases may further strengthen conservative coalitions, promoting a limited set of traditional values and symbols.

In reaction to a process of territorial change and (necessary or unavoidable) innovation, soft infrastructures show different resilient behaviours. The soft infrastructure may return to a steady equilibrium by absorbing any innovative or evolutionary shock that thus disappears without leaving any trace. This was the case of the Arnovalley brand promoting the high-tech economy of Tuscany, which promptly dissolved and was absorbed by the strongly perceived brand of the romantic, timeless and anti-modern region. The branding process was not able to favour a process of reinterpretation of local identity and did not favour an adaptive behaviour of the soft infrastructure. As a matter of fact, innovation branding had no effects. A process of reinterpretation did not occur since innovation branding did not succeed in promoting a process of socialization of the symbols of innovation. This may be due to technical and operative mistakes, but strategic flaws were decisive: e.g., the narrative of the Silicon Valley of Tuscany was preferred to the mobilization of strong symbols rooted in regional heritage which – in fact disconnected from innovation and change – easily prevailed in people's perceptions (Pasquinelli 2010).

Then, if the innovative push is very strong, the soft infrastructure may abandon the equilibrium and, as not being able to adapt, end up collapsing and dissolving, thus provoking a serious cultural loss. Aalborg branding initiatives played a role in the transformation from industrial and peripheral city to cultural centre of knowledge economy but arguably contributed to the erosion of the local soft infrastructure in the direction of an elitist urban transformation. This left behind values and symbols that were relevant to the part of the local community excluded from urban developments (Jensen 2007). The branding process lowered variety, marking a process of impoverishment of the soft infrastructure. Similarly, in the case of NewcastleGateshead (UK), innovation branding seems to have swept away the old industrial heritage in order to support culture-led regeneration. Old symbols of the industrial region were completely replaced by the new values of the cultural capital, thus avoiding any cross-fertilization or synergy between past and present values (Pasquinelli 2014).

In contrast, there are also cases in which the soft infrastructure regenerates by accumulating new symbols and values that are not necessarily in contrast with the 'old' ones, since an adaptive evolution determines a constant creative reinterpretation of the whole set of values. These are the cases in which branding has arguably played a positive role. In Pittsburgh, where the 'creative' and 'inspiring' city brand coexisted in synergy with local steel legacy, branding did not delete the symbols of the old industry and, instead, made them instrumental to the promotion of a new technological vision for the area.

A similar trajectory was undertaken by the Ruhr region (Germany) where branding the network of several towns and cities favoured an increase in the variety of symbols and values to rely on. Especially in the case of the Ruhr, a symbolic redundancy enabled a smooth transformation of the regional system and its soft infrastructure through a collective mobilization and socialization of change that succeeded in recreating an innovation ecosystem.

Final remarks and future research

This chapter discussed the potential contribution of place branding to regional innovation processes and regional development, by conceptualizing the 'soft infrastructure' of innovation. In so doing, we emphasized the two-way character of the relationship between soft infrastructure and regional innovation processes, and we tried to suggest that this is a field where conscious manipulation interacts with long-term trends in our economies and societies. In this perspective, place branding (and especially its use in promoting 'innovation places') deserves to be considered as much more than a new fashion in territorial policies.

The analysis of the soft infrastructure highlighted a bundle of dynamics: place branding represents only one mechanism of the process of socialization of those symbols and values that marks the evolution of the soft infrastructure. In the absence of innovation policies, no branding initiatives can properly 'manage' the soft infrastructure. That is, the socialization of change, even though involving symbols, values and images, is necessarily grounded in the materiality of spaces and artefacts that turn the abstract notion of innovation into reality. At the same time, however, innovation branding may play a facilitating and legitimizing role, thus contributing to making innovation (and a place-based notion of innovation) understood and endorsed by the regional community. Thus, in the absence of branding, innovation policies may result in socially and politically weaker policies, since they are unable to strategically promote the engagement of the regional community in the process of change.

Future research should further explore this perspective. The proposed framework utilized case studies available in the literature to discuss the potential role of place branding (especially in the sense of adding or removing values and symbols to/from the soft infrastructure), by adopting an ex post perspective. Further research, including dedicated empirical efforts, could devise and test analytical frameworks able to predict the potential effects of place branding on the soft infrastructure, in the direction of innovative developments.

This chapter suggested the notion of variety as systemic property influencing an adaptive evolution of the soft infrastructure, but it is evident how variety is one of the multiple factors playing a role and deserving attention. We highlighted the emergence of multiple resilient behaviours of the soft infrastructure, which need further explanation. If, from our perspective, place branding is only one of the mechanisms influencing the evolution of the soft infrastructure, historical, cultural and sociological studies should contribute to the analysis of soft infrastructure dynamics, thus opening to more interdisciplinary scholarship in the field.

Notes

1 www.cisco.com/web/strategy/smart_connected_communities.html (accessed 20 January 2013).
2 www.ruhrmetropolis.com/ (accessed April 2011), cited in Pasquinelli 2012.
3 There are two different definitions of resilience. First, the engineering resilience (or ecological resilience according to Simmie and Martin 2010), is the 'ability of a system to return to an equilibrium or steady state after a disturbance' or the 'magnitude of the disturbance that can be absorbed before the system changes its structure' (Holling 1996, cited in Davoudi 2012: 300). Second, the evolutionary resilience challenges the idea of equilibrium as it describes a process of adaptation and adaptability of the system. It implies that a system may change over time smoothly, with or without a clear and evident stress at a specific point in time (Scheffer 2009, cited in Davoudi 2012: 302). In other words, the evolutionary resilience is the 'ability of complex socio-ecological systems to change, adapt and transform . . . in a dynamic interplay of persistence, adaptability and transformability across multiple scales and timeframes' (Davoudi 2012: 302, 304).
4 From an ecological perspective, the principle of variety says that redundant species, meaning diverse species carrying out same functions, are deemed necessary to maintain the ecosystem resilient, so that the higher the number of species present in an ecosystem, the higher the capacity of response to shocks (Peterson *et al.* 1998).
5 In this case we refer to the notion of *evolutionary resilience*.

References

Anholt, S., 2007: *Competitive Identity: The new brand management for nations, cities and regions*. Basingstoke: Palgrave.

Asheim, B., Coenen, L. and Vang-Lauridsen, J., 2007: Face-to-face, buzz and knowledge bases: socio-spatial implications for learning, innovation and innovation policy. *Environment and Planning C* 25(5), pp. 655–670.

Ashworth, G.J. and Graham, B., 2005: Senses of place, senses of time and heritage. In: Ashworth, G.J. and Graham, B. (eds): *Senses of Place: Senses of Time*. Ashgate: Burlington, pp. 3–14.

Ashworth, G. and Voogd, H., 1988: Marketing the city. *Town Planning Review* 59, pp. 65–79.

Bellini, N., 2004: Territorial governance and area image, *Symphonya* 1, pp. 1–14.

Bellini, N. and Pasquinelli, C., 2011: Il brand reticolare: strumenti di analisi per la costruzione di un marchio di luogo. *Mercati e Competitività* 3, pp. 65–84.

Bellini, N. and Hilpert, U. (eds), 2013: *Europe's Changing Economic Geography. The impact of inter-regional networks*. London: Routledge.

Bellini, N., Loffredo, A. and Pasquinelli, C., 2010: Managing otherness: the political economy of place images in the case of Tuscany. In: Ashworth, G. and Kavaratzis, M. (eds): *Towards Effective Place Brand Management: Branding European cities and regions*. Cheltenham: Edward Elgar, pp. 89–116.

Benner, C., 2003: Learning communities in a learning region: the soft infrastructure of cross-firm learning networks in Silicon Valley. *Environment and Planning* A, 35: pp. 1809–1830.

Berg, O., 2000: Dreaming up a region? Strategic management as invocation. In: Berg, O., Linde-Larsen, A. and Lofgren, O. (eds): *Invoking a Transnational Metropolis: The making of the Øresund region*. Lund: Studentlitteratur, pp. 55–94.

Bourdieu, P., 1989: Social Space and Symbolic Power. *Sociological Theory* 7(1), pp. 14–25.

Caragliu, A., del Bo, C. and Mijkamp, P., 2011: Smart cities in Europe. *Journal of Urban Technology* 18(2), 65–82.

Cooke, P., 2001: Regional innovation systems, clusters and the knowledge economy. *Industrial and Corporate Change* 10(4), pp. 945–974.

Davoudi, S., 2012: Resilience: a bridging concept or a dead end? *Planning Theory & Practice* 13(2), pp. 299–333.

Foray, D. and Goenaga, X., 2013: The Goals of Smart Specialisation. S3 Policy Brief series, no. 01/2013. Seville: European Commission, Joint Research Centre, Institute for Prospective Technological Studies.

Gordon, I., 2011: Territorial competition. In: Pike, A., Rodriguez-Pose, A. and Tomaney, J. (eds): *Handbook of Local and Regional Development*. Oxon: Routledge.

Govers, R. and Go, F.M., 2009: *Place Branding: Glocal, virtual and physical identities, constructed, imagined and experienced*. London: Palgrave.

Hospers, G.-J., 2006a: Borders, bridges and branding: the transformation of the Øresund region into an imagined space. *European Planning Studies* 14(8), pp. 1015–1019.
Hospers, G.-J., 2006b: Silicon somewhere? *Policy Studies* 27(1), pp. 1–15.
Jensen, O.B., 2007: Culture stories: Understanding cultural urban branding. *Planning Theory* 6(3), pp. 211–236.
Jevons, C., Gabbott, M. and Chernatony, L.D., 2005: Customer and brand manager perspective on brand relationships: a conceptual framework. *Journal of Product and Brand Management* 14(5), 300–309.
Kavaratzis, M. and Ashworth, G.J., 2005: City branding: an effective assertion of identity or a transitory marketing trick? *Tijdschrift voor Economische en Sociale Geografie* 96(5), pp. 506–514.
Krajewski, C., 2008: Postmodern Tourism and Experience Economies in the Ruhr Valley as a Strategy for Structural Change. Regions: The Dilemmas of Integration and Competition? Regional Studies Association Annual Conference, Praha.
Lazzeroni, M., Bellini, N., Cortesi, G. and Loffredo, A., 2013: The territorial approach to cultural economy: new opportunities for the development of small towns. *European Planning Studies* 21(4): 452–472.
Lin, J.Y., 2011: New structural economics: a framework for rethinking development. *The World Bank Research Observer* 26(2), pp. 193–221.
Manniche, J., 2012: Combinatorial knowledge dynamics: on the usefulness of the differentiated knowledge bases model. *European Planning Studies* 20(11), pp. 1823–1841.
Ooi, C.-S., 2004: Poetics and politics of destination branding: Denmark. *Scandinavian Journal of Hospitality and Tourism* 4(2), pp. 107–121.
Ooi, C.-S., 2008: Reimagining Singapore as a creative nation: the politics of place branding. *Place Branding and Public Diplomacy* 4(4), pp. 287–302.
Pasquinelli, C., 2010: The limits of place branding for local development: the case of Tuscany and the Arnovalley brand. *Local Economy* 25(7), pp. 558–572.
Pasquinelli, C., 2011: Place branding and cooperation: can a network of places be a brand? In: Pike, A. (Ed.): *Brands and Branding Geographies*. Cheltenham: Edward Elgar, pp. 230–247.
Pasquinelli, C., 2012: Competition, cooperation, co-opetition. Widening the perspective on place branding, PhD Thesis, Scuola Superiore Sant'Anna. Available online at: www.phdmanagement.sssup.it/documenti/awarded/pasquinelli_thesis.pdf (accessed 19 May 2015).
Pasquinelli, C., 2013: Competition, cooperation, co-opetition: unfolding the process of inter-territorial branding. *Urban Research and Practice* 6(1), pp. 1–18.
Pasquinelli, C., 2014: Branding as urban collective strategy-making: the formation of NewcastleGateshead's organisational identity. *Urban Studies* 51(4), pp. 727–743.
Pasquinelli, C. and Teras, J., 2011: Branding peripheral knowledge-intensive regions: an insight into international innovation brands. *Regional Insights* 2(2), pp. 9–11.
Peacock, H., 2011: Cities in competition: branding the smart city, www.tedxamsterdam.com/2012/cities-in-competition-branding-the-smart-city/ (accessed 14 November 2012).
Peck, J., 2005: Struggling with the creative class. *International Journal of Urban and Regional Research* 29(4), pp. 740–770.
Peterson, G., Allen, C.R. and Holling, C.S., 1998: Ecological resilience, biodiversity, and scale. *Ecosystems* 1(1), pp. 6–18.
Pike, A., 2010: Origination: How brands are capturing the power of pace and why it matters. Inaugural Lecture, Wednesday 10 November 2010, Great North Museum, Newcastle upon Tyne. Available online at: www.ncl.ac.uk/curds/assets/documents/FinalInauguralLectureBooklet-Origination.pdf (accessed 19 May 2015).
Pike, A., Dawley, S. and Tomaney, J., 2010: Resilience, adaptation and adaptability. *Cambridge Journal of Regions, Economy and Society* 3, pp. 59–70.
Sacco, P.L., Williams, B. and Del Bianco, E., 2007: *The Power of Arts in Vancouver: Creating a great city*. Vancouver: Vancity.
Simmie, J. and Martin, R., 2010: The economic resilience of regions: towards an evolutionary approach. *Cambridge Journal of Regions, Economy and Society* 3, pp. 27–43.
Therkelsen A. and Halkier H., 2008: Contemplating place branding umbrellas. The case of coordinated national tourism and business promotion in Denmark, *Scandinavian Journal of Hospitality and Tourism* 8(2), pp. 159–179.
Treado, C.D., 2010: Pittsburgh's evolving steel legacy and the steel technology cluster. *Cambridge Journal of Regions, Economy and Society* 3, pp. 105–120.

Turok, I., 2009: The distinctive city: pitfalls in the pursuit of differential advantage. *Environment and Planning A* 41, pp. 13–30.

van Ham, P., 2008: Place branding: the state of the art. *The Annals of the American Academy of Political and Social Science* 616(1), 126–149.

Ward, K., 2000: Front rentiers to rantiers: 'active entrepreneurs', 'structural speculators' and the politics of marketing the city. *Urban Studies* 37(7), pp. 1093–1107.

Warnaby, G. and Medway, D., 2008: Bridges, place representation and place creation. *Area* 40(4), 510–519.

Wei, W. and Li, R., 2012: A primary investigation into revolution and way to reform under the background of smart city construction. *Advanced Materials Research* 368–373, pp. 3593–3597.

Wong, C., Millar, C. and Choi, C. J., 2006: Singapore in transition: from technology to culture hub. *Journal of Knowledge Management* 10(5), pp. 79–91.

PART 2

Effects of technology policies: regional situations and how they form innovative networks

6

UNIVERSITIES, REVOLUTIONS AND CONTINUITY IN REGIONAL INNOVATION POLICIES IN EUROPE

Rupert Waters and Helen Lawton Smith

Introduction

While universities are important actors in local economic development, their impact on the design and implementation of innovation policy is shaped by national and regional administrative structures. By focusing on the role of universities in regional innovation policies in different countries, this chapter examines the underlying logic and the intended outcomes of science and technologically focused policies, and addresses issues both about the relationship between the national and regional level in policy formation and implementation, as well as the extent to which different levels reinforce existing Islands of Innovation (Hilpert 1992, 2003) or enable the formation of an Island of Innovation in its field of techno-specific expertise effects.

Whether universities are actively or passively engaged in science policy at the regional level is examined within a regional innovation systems (RIS) framework (Asheim *et al.* 2011). Illustrative case study countries are two centralist countries (the UK and France) and a federalist country (Germany), and a region in each: Oxfordshire in the UK, Bremen in Germany and Grenoble in France.

The UK and France have recently undergone revolutions in policy and administrative systems while Germany provides an example of continuity. We show, while historically there are important differences in the role of universities within each national system, there is some convergence in the direction of policy towards a more active regional role. In France and in Germany in a few places universities are regional stakeholders and part of the decision making process in the design of regional science and innovation policies (Crespy *et al.* 2007). In the UK, incentives had been put in place to create such regional connections, but following the change of national government in 2010, regional structures were removed with policy delivery instead at the local level, albeit with some local structures being larger than the regional ones they replaced.

The context to these discussions are major changes enacted by the EU towards regional policies in 2011, following a general shift in the 1990s towards entrepreneurship, innovative regions and milieux with a focus on the role of science and technology in providing the raw material for innovation (Toedtling and Trippl 2005). Underpinning regional policy has been the RIS approach reflected in the shift in focus of EU regional policy (Landabaso *et al.* 2003). This has included an increasing proportion of structural funds under the European Regional Development Fund (ERDF) assigned to regional innovation measures, and more recently within Europe 2020 the EU's growth strategy for the coming decade brings the aims of the EDRF alongside other innovation-based strategies.[1] Within Europe 2020 are the goals of 'smart specialisation', which emphasises good institutions and strong policy capabilities at the regional level (Foray and Goenega 2013). Universities are seen as having a pivotal role in the social and economic development of their regions and in developing smart specialisation strategies.[2] Access to European funding works within country specific administrative structures, those related to both regional policy and research institutions (universities, research laboratories) that apply for research funding independently of bodies responsible for regional policy.

We begin by discussing why universities might be expected to play important roles in regional economic development and then position them within how regional innovation policies operate in theory and then in practice. We differentiate between different types of policy, and where universities are positioned within them. These themes are then illustrated by the case study countries and regions.

Universities and regional innovation policies in theory

Policy towards universities as actors in regional policy has taken an 'instrumentalist position' – of getting things done (Charles 2003) – since at least the 1980s. The extended role which goes beyond teaching and research encompasses an entrepreneurial and innovation role (universities as knowledge exploiters (Asheim and Gertler 2005)), as well as a role in the local community that relates to social equity, sustainability and culture. Universities are expected to plan strategically for their regional role in contributing to improving the local economy, for example through cluster development and responsiveness to the needs of industry (Glasson 2003).

Conceptually, this role is developed in the RIS approach which offers a heuristic for examining the kinds of possibilities of the ways in which universities are positioned with systems of governance, as well as identifying possible systems of governance per se. Perry and May (2007) take this line of analysis further by providing a typology of regional dimensions to science policy with universities as potential regional actors. Together the RIS approach and Perry and May's typology form the framework used here for examining polity structures in the UK, Germany and France, and the extent to which they reinforce existing Islands of Innovation.

The RIS approach (Cooke 1992) comprises three dimensions: regional structure – administrative, legal, constitutional and institutional arrangements; the long-term evolution and development of regional industry specialisation; and additional core/periphery differences in industrial structure and innovative performance (Howells 1999). In each dimension universities are regional change agents through their position in local policy institutional arrangements and through knowledge exchange with business as the principal actors in the regional learning process (Asheim *et al.* 2011). This takes into account a wide set of knowledge transfer mechanisms including contract research, consulting, and formal R&D cooperations as well as forms of knowledge transmission that do not involve financial compensations for universities such as knowledge spillovers (through the provision of graduates to the local labour market) and informal collaboration with industry. The third concerns the match of universities with their regional industrial structures, hence their potential contribution to innovation performance.

Many factors mediate possible relationships. They include the strength of the science base (nationally and locally), the institutional setting; the financial system; education and training; the availability and mobility of skilled labour; and public policy measures designed to promote innovation and growth. The situation is further complicated because of different context specific types of RIS structures where universities play a role (Asheim 1998). These indicate the degree of embeddedness of universities into local or national and international networks: whether a 'territorially embedded RIS' characterised by localised learning processes and local university–industry interactions, a 'networked RIS' that relies on a specific network of universities, firms and supporting institutions that underpin learning, or a 'regionalised RIS', universities are more important in sustaining regional specialisation and global–local links. How policy intervention as suggested by 'smart specialisation' could in practice help improve the functioning of RIS is contingent on regionally specific RIS structures, resources and dynamics (Cooke *et al.* 2004; Tödtling and Trippl 2005) and their relationship with national policymaking processes, particularly with respect to science policy.

Defining science policy 'as the justification, management, prioritisation and funding of basic research and development', Perry and May (2007: 1040) offer the framework for analysing the regional dimensions to science policy. This distinguishes between those regions that are passive as actors, with either 'regions as stages' or as 'implementers', or as active players.

As passive actors, regions are appropriate scales of action but regional authorities and agencies are not part of the decision making process. Regional authorities and agencies can also have a role in the implementation of nationally defined and funded policy initiatives.

As active players regions can be either partners with an agency for shaping national priorities or are participants in national policy processes. They can also be independent policy makers. This is where regional authorities and bodies increasingly devote own finance and resources to funding regionally significant scientific investments and projects. As a consequence regional science policies emerge.

Similarly, Crespy *et al.* (2007) identify three prerequisites for the development of a multilevel polity: a national framework that envisages, or even depends on, regional action for the successful implementation of its policies; arenas for negotiation of national and regional 'priorities' and the capacities and capabilities of regional actors to develop clear strategies from the bottom up.

Beyond a multilevel polity within countries, the ability of the EU to influence what happens at the regional level is not clear. In the early 1990s, Hooghe and Keating (1994) found that there had been a great deal of regional mobilization but that its effectiveness was questionable. Member states had been able to maintain and recently reinforce their primacy in defining the modalities of intervention. Moreover, within Perry and May's (2007) framework, EU spend on innovation goes directly to institutions such as universities, creating additional dimensions to autonomy within regions. These include the circumvention of all of those possibilities by the reinforcement of national patterns of regionalisation or support for emerging strengths as in the vertical logic of smart specialisation (Foray and Goenega 2013). Next we examine major national and sub-national level policies in the case study countries.

Universities and regional policies in the UK, Germany and France

UK regional innovation policy

In the UK 1979 is the date from which both entrepreneurship and universities' contribution to economic development entered mainstream regional policy formulation. Under the

Conservative Governments 1979–1997 the underlying policy had shifted from Keynesianism intervention to Friedman free market economics. For the universities and other parts of the science base such as the national laboratories this meant cuts in funding and other 'incentives' to become more entrepreneurial and commercial in their dealings with industry adopting a more market approach to commercialising their intellectual property. Indeed, the UK was the first country to develop a national university commercialisation policy (Geuna and Muscio 2009). In 1985, the British Technology Board lost its monopoly access to intellectual property arising from universities and public sector research institutions from Research Council-funded projects. Responsibility was transferred to those institutions giving them autonomy to decide on their commercialisation strategies.

Following the election of successive Labour Governments (1997–2010), the regional scale through the formation of regional development agencies (RDAs) in 1999 was introduced which included active roles for universities and various funding streams for 'third leg' activities (i.e. civic responsibilities as well as active economic activities many of which have a regional focus or have a local impact). In effect this saw the introduction of regional innovation policies that included national priorities of cluster creation. Within the government's policy framework, Perry and May (2007: 1041) noted a 'policy blurring between science, innovation, higher education and regional policy'. The spatial dimension to regional policy was couched as either passive (regions as stages and regions as implementers) or as active (regions as partners and regions as independent policymakers), with an increasing role for the RDAs (Perry 2007) as well as Regional Science and Industry Councils, which were given a role of 'encouraging universities to develop their 'third mission or third leg' role.

Perry (2007) argued that the centralised policy process in the UK thus had been subtly transformed in the generation of linkages between the research base and industry. She suggests that the novelty of the English case (Scotland and Wales having their own regional (national) development agencies) is not the changing dynamics of national science policy but extensive sub-national mobilisation and institutional creation.

During that period, sub-national university engagement with central government funding was also introduced at the level of the city. In 2005, the 'science city' initiative was launched. Six cities (Newcastle, Birmingham, Bristol, Manchester, Nottingham and York) were designated as 'Science Cities'. Their objectives are to harness 'the research power of academic institutions, the world-class quality of their scientists, engineers and technologists and the entrepreneurial skills of the business sector, as well as promoting public engagement in science'.[3] However, as Perry (2007) points out, what actually occurred was a greater concentration of scientific resources. By the late 1990s over 40 per cent of GERD was concentrated in the Golden Triangle (London, Oxford and Cambridge).

The RDAs were abolished by the Coalition government (Conservatives and Liberal Democrats) in 2010. Their abolition removed a layer of sub-national mobilisation, and an incentive for universities to be active local players. They were replaced by Local Enterprise Partnerships (LEPs), led by business, that were established to oversee coordination of local growth strategies that emphasise entrepreneurship and innovation as well as infrastructure as key components. LEPs, which have much less funding and leverage than the RDAs, are incentivised to develop more integrated strategies with the introduction of such funding streams as the Growing Places Fund, the Regional Growth Fund, Enterprise Zones and City Deals – many of which explicitly involve universities in policy formulation.

Alongside those measures include third-leg funding streams for which universities compete in for third-leg activities (Table 4.1). These comprise (i) non-spatial research grants with conditions relating to projections of impact, for example those funded under the seven UK research councils,[4]

Table 6.1 HEI innovation programmes in the UK

Department	*Initiative*
OST/HEFCE	Joint Infrastructure Fund (JIF) (1998) Science Research Investment Fund (SRIF) (2001)
DfEE, DTI, HefCE	1999 Higher Education Reach-Out to Business and the Community (HEROBC) • special funding for activities to increase universities' capability to respond to the needs of business and the wider community, where this will lead to wealth creation • includes the promotion of spin-out companies
DTI/OST/ Engineering and the Engineering Physical Sciences Council (EPSRC)	1999 Science Enterprise Challenge (SEC) Fund • financed Science Enterprise Centres and the Foresight Directorate • encourages regional-level activity • Faraday Partnerships • joint university–industry initiatives • Biotechnology Challenge Fund
OST/Treasury/Wellcome Trust and Gatsby Foundation	1999 University Challenge Fund (UCF) • seed funding to help selected universities make the most of research funding through support for early stages of commercial exploitation of new products and processes
HEFCE	2001–2004 Higher Education Innovation Fund (HEIF) • £140 million to knowledge transfer • 2004–6 HEIF 2 • £187m 2006–2008 HEIF 3 £238 million HEIF 4 2009–2011 HEIF 5 2011–2015 – £150m pa.
Innovate UK (formerly Technology Strategy Board) (focus on innovative businesses)	Knowledge Transfer Networks • *Collaborative research and development* • *Knowledge Transfer Partnerships* • *Micro and Nanotechnology Centres* • Small Business Research Initiative • *International programmes* • Technology specific programmes

(ii) funding programmes specifically designed to have commercial outcomes (e.g. spin-offs), for example those of the Higher Education Funding Council for England (HEFCE), and (iii) funding that has regional/local engagement or governance built in. In 2009, the Labour government launched the framework for the future success of higher education, setting out the important role universities will play in securing the country's economic recovery and long term prosperity, in *Higher Ambitions: the Future of Universities in a Knowledge Economy*.[5] This emphasized the importance of research, high level skills and widening access in economic development.

HEFCE covers 130 HEIs. Its HEIF programme provides funding for universities to support them in developing third function activities such as knowledge transfer to firms and interactions with the wider community. The SEC and the UCF were set up as separate funds under HEIF 1. The science enterprise centres provide a focus for commercialisation and entrepreneurship, aimed at both staff and students. In 2001 University Innovation Centres were launched – large, regionally based research and innovation centres often focused on a collaboration between HEIs (Charles 2003). As the HEIF programme has expanded, it has become more commercially orientated and has sought to be more inclusive. In line with the Sainsbury Review recommendations that more funding be directed towards business-facing institutions, HEIF 4 rose to £150 million in 2010–11 with the intention of redistributing funding from the richer to poorer universities. Its approach to the regions recognises the diversity of HEIs and of regions, and supports the relationships that are already being developed between regional and local bodies and HEIs.

Recently the emphasis has shifted back towards science policy in regions rather than regional innovation policy per se. In January 2013 £600 million funding for science and research in 'eight great technologies' identified as strategic by the national government was announced. The eight are big data, space, robotics and autonomous systems, synthetic biology, regenerative medicine, agri-science, advanced materials and energy. The funding is for research into cutting-edge technology and designed to help make the UK one of the best places in the world to do science. It is likely that these will reinforce existing 'science regions' (Perry and May 2007). This policy sits alongside the Witty Review (2013)[6] which explored how universities can support growth by working with organisations such as LEPs in building on sectoral strengths and clusters. Moreover, the key sectors agreed at national level will also have an impact on policy choices at the local level with respect to 'smart specialisation'.

Regional level – the Oxfordshire example

In the late 1990s, Oxfordshire had made a transition from a traditional economy to a dynamic high tech economy, one with a very strong research base in the form of Oxford University, Oxford Brookes and some ten research laboratories (for example in nuclear energy, space, biomedical science). Alongside its high tech firms was a network of support activities including science parks and incubators, networks and specialist financial support organisations. Recognition of the strength of the county's high tech economy and its innovation support system came when in 2002 Oxfordshire received its second *Award of Excellence* as one of Europe's most innovative regions.

Oxford University is a major component of the regional science infrastructure. It was ranked fourth in the world on the 2012 THES rankings and has engaged in an extensive range of technology transfer activities through its technology transfer organisation Isis Innovation, established in 1988. The local, national and international impact of Isis Innovation, Oxford University's commercialisation organisation has grown broader and stronger as it has captured more of the wealth creating and outreach roles within the university. It successfully commercialises its research through robust spin-offs, patents and licenses, thereby increasing the value realised to the university of its intellectual property (IP) (Lawton Smith and Bagchi-Sen 2012). With respect to reinforcing regional specialisations, in 2010 the University was ranked seventh participant organisation in the EU Framework 7 programmes.

The Oxford and Oxfordshire LEP was set up in 2011 with in principle an active regional role for Oxford's two universities: the University of Oxford and Oxford Brookes. Both are members of the LEP board at vice-chancellor level, 'reflecting their role in supporting and promoting enterprise in the local economy'.[7] The Business Plan for Growth in 2013[8] prioritises seven key issues: improving access to finance, improving access to business support services, investment for infrastructure, improved broadband, skills, inward investment and lastly innovation. In its 'smart specialisation' agenda it highlights four of the national eight great sectors as having the greatest potential for growth: life sciences, high performance technologies, space, energy, all of which reflect the strengths of the universities and research laboratories, plus digital, publishing and media.

The Oxford and Oxfordshire City Deal bid, awarded in January 2013:

> has brought together all six Oxfordshire councils, the two universities, the big science facilities at Culham and Harwell to the south of the county, and the Oxfordshire Local Enterprise Partnership in a unique joint proposal that seeks to boost the knowledge economy and create a new partnership for growth.[9]

The Science Vale Enterprise Zone[10] which covers two district councils encompasses sites at Harwell Oxford (the location of the county's big science laboratories) and MEPC Milton Park, a large scale business park, is an example of a region as implementers, but at the same time being active as independent policy makers (Perry and May 2007).

While Oxford University and the Rutherford Appleton Laboratory (space research) have long been in receipt of major EU funding, there is some evidence that the local authorities have begun to be more active in innovation policy building on those strengths. In 2012, Oxford City Council led a bid for funding in partnership with Oxfordshire County Council and was awarded a £930,000 European grant funding towards a £1.24m programme to develop local renewable energy and energy efficiency projects.[11]

In sum, Oxfordshire is a regionalised RIS in that Oxford University is important in sustaining regional specialisations (and diversification), through its international research and industrial contacts and the mobility of its staff (Waters and Lawton Smith 2012). Its technology system, characterised as a passive regional system (Perry and May 2007) is underpinned by the dirigiste national government and to some extent by the EU. The science base is reinforced by national and EU research awards to Oxford University and to the county's research laboratories.

Germany

In Germany the division between the national government and the federal states (*Länder*) for example on science and technology policy is enshrined in Germany's basic law (*Grundgesetz*) in Article 30 (Koschatsky and Kroll 2007). This means that the national government should not interfere with policies in the sixteen federal states, a very different situation to that which exists in the UK. Each federal state has its own school and higher education laws, as well as ministries for cultural affairs or science. A crucial element of the science policy of the Länder is the financing and organisation of higher education (Heraud and Koschatzky 2006). In 2003, around 60 per cent of total German expenditures for science were borne by the *Länder* with a third from the federal government and 5.2 per cent by scientific non-profit organizations (Koschatsky and Kroll 2007). Universities are public corporations funded from *Länder* budgets (Hartwig 2006). Overall, Germany has various types of research locations: universities, universities of applied sciences, non-university institutes, companies and federal as well as *Länder* institutions, some 750 in all.[12]

The standing conference of the ministers of education and cultural affairs (KMK) is an important coordination, rather than a dirigiste, body with regard to education, science and research policy.[13] Its responsibilities include universities and promotion of cooperation between education and scientific organisations. Although the federal states are involved in science, technology and innovation policy, drivers also come from the federal government level, especially from the ministries of education and research (BMBF), of economics and technology (BMWI) and defence.

The BMBF and BMWI budgets for institutional promotion and promotional programmes are much greater than those of the single *Länder* (Koschatzky and Kroll 2007).

Some national programmes are designed to strengthen the science base. For example the national Excellence Initiative potentially has regional outcomes. The objective is to promote top-level research and to improve the quality of German universities and research institutions in general. The idea is that this will make Germany a more attractive research location and internationally competitive. After the Excellence Initiative was passed by the German federal and state governments in 2005, the DFG was given responsibility for running the initiative together with the German Science Council.[14]

Science policy should be seen within the core problem in Germany of ongoing structural socio-economic disparities between old and new *Länder* (OECD 2012).[15] This is despite some positive developments in recent years that have facilitated closing the gap in major urban areas in the east. The new *Länder* not only continue to lag behind the rest of the country on key indicators such as GDP per capita and unemployment, but have also experienced significant demographic decline in recent years, partially due to the out-migration of younger, educated people. Some areas in the old *Länder* also face specific structural problems, for example, due to long term industrial or agricultural restructuring. Convergence in economic conditions operates through the *Finanzausgleich* or fiscal equalization payment, which is an instrument to redistribute financial means from financially strong to financially weak federal states in order to achieve the balance objective (Doring 2005 in Koschatzky and Kroll 2007).

The influence of the EU on German policy was noted by Audretsch (2005) and later by Grimm (2011) who agues that EU entrepreneurship policymaking has contributed to a shift from hierarchical government to a more horizontal and interactive form of governance in the new German *Länder* which were highly exposed to Structural Funds and the Lisbon Agenda of 2000. The new approach which involves universities as in the UK is illustrated by Koschatzky and Kroll (2007). They identify two aspects between science policy and regional development relating to two interfaces between the federal and *Länder* governments. The first is joint task university building – extension and new university building. The second is the joint task of the regional economic structure. Both are active roles as regions as partners with the national government. We next explore how this works in the case of Bremen.

Bremen

Bremen is the smallest *Land* in Germany. It lacks the resources of the four big *Länder*: NRW, Baden-Wurttemberg, Baveria and Lower Saxony, especially those of Baden-Wurttemberg and Baveria which also have greater concentrations of research institutions and research funding. For example, Baden-Wurttemberg is home to eighty HEIs including nine research universities and has a strong record of research commercialisation.[16] Bremen has a much smaller science base and does not have a leading university, and therefore lacks the associated international networks as are found in the bigger *Länder*.

However, like all *Länder*, it is an autonomous federal state and has a high level of autonomy in policy design and responsibility for research and education. Although Bremen possesses its own research budget, crucial cash flow stems from the federal government (Koschatzky and Kroll 2007). Its history of policymaking makes an interesting comparator to Oxfordshire and Grenoble which are much larger and have stronger universities, but which also rely on national funding. However, major R&D and innovation policies are decided at *Länder* level, rather than nationally as in the UK and France, with the *Land*'s Ministry of Education and science and ministry of economic affairs being key actors.

Research and education are the responsibility of the Bremen state government: the University of Bremen (UoB), the Private International University of Bremen (IUB) (now state run following bankruptcy), University of the Arts and universities of applied science in Bremen and Bremenhaven. Other national public research organisations such as Max-Planck, Frauhofer Institutes as well as other regional research institutes are also located in Bremen.

UoB, founded in 1971, although not a leading university, being ranked 367 by QS World University Rankings (2011), has been selected as an Excellence University and has recently been attracting considerable research funding. In 2010 the University's scholars and scientists acquired some 91 million euros of research funding. These included the award in 2009 of funding under the Excellence programme which was extended for three years for the Ocean in the Earth System. Since June 2012, the University of Bremen has been entitled 'University of Excellence'. Some of the ground-breaking educational concepts implemented in those early days, which became known as the 'Bremer Modell', have since become established features of modern university education all over Germany; for example, interdisciplinary study and research, research-based teaching projects, orientation to practice, and responsibility towards society. This infrastructure is attracting more and more enterprises to the adjacent Technology Park, making it one of the leading high-tech locations in Germany, hosting close to 320 companies.[17]

Science and technology policies reflect transformations in the economy. Although it has less R&D intensive manufacturing than the German average, it has specialisations in science and engineering, particularly in aerospace and aeronautics as well as high-end car manufacture. As in other countries, the local economy has been transformed; from one dominated by traditional industries including ship building and car manufacturing, it has become 'a pronounced service economy' (Koschatzky and Kroll 2007: 1121).

One of the most important examples of an active independent regional dimension to science policy was InnoVision 2010. The objective was to make Bremen one of the top ten German technology regions by 2010. To do this it invested in science infrastructure, focusing on selected technology fields and regional networking. However, Koschatzky and Kroll (2007) found that the Bremen STI policy has had a tendency towards setting overambitious and unfocused goals due to independent policy agenda-setting, oriented towards regional development. One of the problems seemed to be that the chosen sectors were not likely to become internationally successful. The InnoVision 2010 policy has since been revised to build on state excellence in areas of science and technology.

EU as well as national funding is important for reinforcing areas of excellence in the science base.[18] Researchers at the University of Bremen in 2013 were involved in fifty projects within the European Commission's Seventh Framework Programme for Research and Technological Development, for example in health, food, ICT, nanosciences and the environment. This may reflect a shift towards concentrating resources in a small number of scientific and technological areas rather than a broader regional development strategy as was the case in the past (Koschatzky and Kroll 2007). The co-ordination of scientific and economic interests in Bremen provides good practice for regions as implementers, partners and independent policy makers (Perry and May 2007). Mistakes have been made but the *Land* is using its science base to help transform its economic base.

France

The key to understanding France's new forms of state intervention in science policy at the regional level is the country's productivity gap in research and innovation (Crespy *et al.* 2007). The blame for inefficiencies has been attached to a 'vast and ossified public science and research system', matched by an absence of a culture of exploitation.

Budgetary constraints on funding for science and the European Research Area project have led to the incorporation of sub-national actors by both accident and design (Perry and May 2007). Crespy *et al.* (2007) find evidence of a more 'regionalised' national science policy emerging and creation of spaces for the negotiation of science policy. Regions are now allowed to play a role, which in effect means a 'dirigiste' regionalised innovation system with some elements of a bottom up approach. Moreover, regionalisation is seen as a corollary to European developments and as 'a stepping stone to international visibility' (Crespy *et al.* 2007: 1074). Consequently, new forms of state intervention have emerged to manage a more spatially distributed science policy in which, 'decentralisation actors . . . must respond to proposals and initiatives within a centrally defined framework' (1073 in Perry and May 2007: 1043). While policy is formulated between top-down and bottom-up procedures, albeit with diluted capacity for central control over science, research and higher education with regional actors such as regional authorities having to respond to proposals and initiatives with a centrally designed framework – regional co-financing is necessary. Recent examples of policy are shown in Table 6.2.

Crespy *et al.* (2007: 1073) note that these and a raft of other measures, 'represent varying attempts to bring combinations of academic, industry and local economic actors together within geographically proximate spaces. The emphasis on clusters and networks as tools for economic and scientific development builds on existing regional science and innovation infrastructures.' Regions are also now welcomed as partners in basic science and research as much as exploitation and universities are seen as key actors in regional policy with regional authorities as active partners and actors (territorially embedded RIS combined with networked RIS, Asheim 1998). Crespy *et al.* (2007) find that financing higher education has been a key area in which regional authorities have developed substantial roles, despite having no official competence in this area. Through the programme Université 2000 (U2000), the state put in place a negotiation procedure in order to involve regions in addressing the huge and rapid investment necessary in university infrastructures. In exchange for regional money, the state conceded a role to sub-national authorities as partners in the policymaking process. Cities and other sub-national authorities, as well as regional councils, have taken a lead in science and technology policy, driven by the desire to host university or higher education training on their territory. Université du Troisième Millenaire (U3M) was the second large planning operation involving national and sub-national authorities in higher education.

Table 6.2 Recent French entrepreneurship and innovation initiatives

Poles de Competitivité (Competitiveness Clusters) 2005 to promote the development of world class high technology clusters across France. 3 year budget of E1.5 billion committed with Ministries encouraged to allocate around 25 per cent of their funds to collaborative projects. 66 clusters initially approved.
Reseaux Thématique de Recherche Avancée – RTRA (Thematic Advanced Research Networks) 2005 designed to carry out research projects in order to create clusters of internationally excellent science, networks will receive substantial funding for new infrastructures and to attract top scientists.
Poles de Recherche et d'Enseignement Supérieur – PRES (Research and Higher Education Poles) Mechanism for the coordination of research and HE activities within a particular geographic area, to increase efficiency, visibility and the attractiveness of French HE.

Source: adapted from Crespy *et al.* 2007: 1073.

However, universities remain relatively autonomous and while they have the capacity to engage with regional actors, they do not always have the willingness to do so. Moreover, sub-national authorities have no constitutional rights to intervene in research and higher education (Crespy *et al.* 2007). While the potential exists for regional authorities to adopt greater roles in relation to French science and higher education policy, not all regions are currently in a position to fulfil these functions. Differences exist in regional capacities in relation to science-based economic development, hence in the capacity and intent to engage in RIS. In absolute value, the most important regions are Ile-de-France and Rhône-Alpes (which includes Grenoble), together accounting for 55 per cent of French R&D, which also have the largest regional budgets devoted to Science and Technology. Both have emerged in terms of participation within a multilevel science polity.

Crespy *et al.* (2007) identifies a shift in policy with (at least partial) bottom-up and competitive procedures being encouraged at the national level. New instruments such as 'competitiveness clusters' or PRES are designed at the initiative of decentralized actors (universities, territorial communities, firms) and only subsequently 'labelled' by the central administration. In so doing, the French government is creating frameworks that have to be shaped by territorial configurations, leading to more selective action and resource concentration. Within the new national frameworks, regions are emerging as intermediate actors within complex governance structures. However, the authors argue that as a result of such changes, relations between the national and the sub-national level are becoming less hierarchical and more interdependent but it remains the case that central government remains the key driver of policy. We next turn to examining how these changes operate in Grenoble.

Grenoble

Grenoble is the first pole of innovation after Paris, and is a major 'science region'. This in part is possible because of the local share of the national budget devoted to science (Crespy *et al.* 2007). The city-region has more than 62,000 students, with 9,000 coming from abroad. It has six engineering schools, important universities, a business school, more than 20,000 researchers both in the public and private sector, four international laboratories, European exceptional facilities (European Synchrotron Radiation Facility, Laüe Langevin Institute, European Molecular Biology Laboratory and so on). Its expertise in innovative technologies is mainly organised around three poles: the Information technology pole (microelectronics, telecommunications and software development), biotechnology pole and new technologies of energy.

It also implicitly identifies itself as having a strong active regional innovation system (regions as partners and as independent policymakers) engaging in a multilevel science polity with much of the leverage from within relationships between key local research organisations and the regional authorities.

> Anchored in a strong regional dynamic of technological innovation, the Grenoble research centre relies on the regional development and technology transfer structures to support its technology transfer actions and has developed strategic partnerships with large regional companies, such as Schneider, ST Microelectronics and CEA, in particular.[19]

The competitiveness pole TENERRDIS cluster (industrial and research cluster for renewable energies in the Rhône-Alpes region and for the development of new energy technologies) is designed to promote research and business spin-offs in new energy technology.[20] The cluster includes the CEA, Grenoble Institute of Technology, the University of Savoy and many other public sector research and teaching bodies.

A strength of Grenoble's science policy is its focus on clustering involving local authorities, universities and research institutes. Several initiatives date back to the late 1990s, including the creation of the incubator GRAIN (Grenoble Alpes Incubator) at the end of 1999 and the first French seed-fund: EMERTEC. Grenoble is one of eighteen regions that have received a label of excellence for its innovation support policy by the EU. Its research strengths underpinned by the French state have enabled the city region to win major EU research and innovation grants, such as in 2013 under the SEMI (semiconductor) Europe programme, strengthening national patterns of regional specialisation and as a regional partner with national government. It is also a member of the five country European Molecular Biology Laboratory, Europe's flagship laboratory for the life sciences.[21]

In sum the Grenoble experience matches the account of regional development told by Crespy *et al.* (2007) about the location of research spending and changes in the French Innovation system, and a multilevel science polity. EU monies have also been important in the design of and support for innovation policies. Grenoble should, however, be seen as a special case comparable only to other regions where innovation is linked to big spending, for example Toulouse (Aerospace). In the Perry and May (2007) quadrant it is both a passive and active independent policymaker and an implementer of nationally defined science policy initiatives.

Conclusions

This chapter asks, what impact do national and regional administrative structures have on the design and implementation of innovation policies involving universities operating at the regional level? In answer, the chapter shows that administrative structures operate in a variety of ways. Taking the national level first, a major feature is the extent to which science funding is concentrated in particular disciplines, which inevitably means that some regions have disproportionate shares of the budget. The consequence is that these 'Islands of Innovation' accumulate further assets such as skills and have leverage to acquire further funding on the basis of excellence. This process coexists with regional policies designed to overcome regional economic and social disparities. Possible outcomes are regionalised RIS in which universities play a key role in sustaining regional specialisations. With an increasing investment in science comes the likelihood of a globalised RIS coexisting with a region actively working as a partner with the national government as in France and Germany.

At the regional level, it is also possible for universities to be part of regionalised RIS but not to be engaged as in the UK. Thus, Oxfordshire might be characterised as not even being a 'region as stages' because neither Oxford University nor the local authorities play more than a token part in decision making processes (Perry and May 2007). Local outcomes arise from the attraction of national and international funding that underpins commercialisation activities in the science base. Bremen is shown to be an active partner in regional science policy formulation and practice, but has also received national funding and EU funding for research. Although it is a much smaller German example than the big four *Länder* it is an interesting case study of a region in transition working towards being a more fully developed 'Island of Innovation'.

France has moved more closely to the German model, whereby regions are welcomed as partners in basic science and research as much as exploitation (Crespy *et al.* 2007), as for example Grenoble. Grenoble is also a striking example of multilevel governance with EU funding and policy a very strong component of policy formulation and practice. Thus, the state as an enabler of Islands of Innovation or science regions, through high levels of national spend can be seen in France and the UK. Germany is increasingly going that way.

The chapter also shows that RIS structures and regional dimensions to science policy change over time. Revolution has taken place at the level of the EU, in France and the UK, but with continuity in Germany. The EU Smart Specialisation agenda firmly places universities at the heart of science-innovation regional policy. However, despite theoretically informed policy advances, universities are powerful institutions, especially in the UK, and may frustrate the practical realisation of regional policies – except where it is in their interests to become involved.

Notes

1 http://ec.europa.eu/europe2020/index_en.htm (accessed 29 August 2013).
2 http://s3platform.jrc.ec.europa.eu/documents/10157/80310/Report%20on%20Seville%20Joint%20EUA-JRC%20Workshop%20on%20RIS3%20%20Feb%202013%20FINAL.pdf (accessed 29 August 2013).
3 www.timeshighereducation.co.uk/story.asp?storyCode=198532&sectioncode=26 (accessed 9 February 2011).
4 www.rcuk.ac.uk/Pages/Home.aspx (accessed 21 February 2011).
5 http://webarchive.nationalarchives.gov.uk/+/www.bis.gov.uk/wp-content/uploads/publications/Higher-Ambitions-Summary.pdf (accessed 29 August 2013).
6 www.gov.uk/government/uploads/system/uploads/attachment_data/file/225442/bis-13-1048-independent-review-universities-and-growth.pdf (accessed 29 August 2013).
7 http://portal.oxfordshire.gov.uk/content/publicnet/other_sites/LEP/meetings/executive/GovernanceandWorkingArrangementsAgreedMarch2012.pdf (accessed 26 May 2015).
8 www.oxfordshirelep.org.uk/cms/sites/lep/files/folders/documents/meetings/LEP%20Exec%20Board%20Meeting%2024/Item_6_%20Oxfordshire_LEP_Business_Plan_for_Growth_2013.pdf (accessed 28 August 2013).
9 www.oxford.gov.uk/PageRender/decN/newsarticle.htm?newsarticle_itemid=51419 (accessed 5 June 2013).
10 www.oxfordshirelep.org.uk/cms/content/science-vale-uk-enterprise-zone (accessed 5 August 2013).
11 www.oxford.gov.uk/PageRender/decN/newsarticle.htm?newsarticle_itemid=51072 (accessed 26 May 2015).
12 www.germaninnovation.org/research-and-innovation/german-research-landscape (accessed 26 May 2015).
13 www.european-agency.org/country-information/germany/general-information (accessed 26 May 2015).
14 www.dfg.de/en/research_funding/programmes/excellence_initiative/index.html (accessed 26 May 2015).
15 www.oecd.org/eco/49616833.pdf (accessed 29 August 2013).
16 www.google.co.uk/url?sa=t&rct=j&q=&esrc=s&frm=1&source=web&cd=2&ved=0CEsQFjAB&url=http%3A%2F%2Fwww.bw-studyguide.de%2Fdownload.php%2FKIuAL%2Fa%2F1352.pdf&ei=KPkAUtCvN8yo0wWgjoCQBA&usg=AFQjCNFhgUYj0PEITja6SL04MuCbJma0w (accessed 26 May 2015).
17 www.bw-studyguide.de/en/home.html
18 www.uni-bremen.de/en/research/external-funding-of-research.html (accessed 26 May 2015).
19 www.inria.fr/en/centre/grenoble/innovation/our-partners (accessed 22 January 2012).
20 www.grenoble-inp.fr/presentation/tenerrdis-industrial-cluster-27471.kjsp (accessed 5 April 2013).
21 www.embl.fr/aboutus/general_information/index.html (accessed 26 May 2015).

References

Asheim, B., 1998: Learning regions: a condition for prosperity. *European Planning Studies* 4(4), pp. 379–400.
Asheim, B. and Gertler, M., 2005: The geography of innovation. In: Fagerberg, J., Mowery, D. and Nelson, R. (eds): *The Oxford Handbook of Innovation*. Oxford: Oxford University Press, pp. 291–317.

Asheim, B., Lawton Smith, H. and Oughton, C., 2011: Regional innovations systems: theory, empirics and policy. *Regional Studies* 45(7), pp. 875–892.

Audretsch, D., 2005: University Spillovers and Entrepreneurship in Germany. Paper presented at Global Perspectives on Entrepreneurship Policy, A Pre-Conference Session of the International Council for Small Business Annual Meeting. Available online at: http://angelnetwork.com/images/docs/tools_rprtst_proc05.pdf (accessed 26 May 2015).

Charles, D., 2003: Universities and territorial development: reshaping the regional role of UK universities. *Local Economy* 18(1), pp. 7–20.

Cooke, P., 1992: Regional innovation systems: competitive regulation in the New Europe. *Geoforum*, 23(3), pp. 365–382.

Cooke, P., Heidenreich, M. and Braczyk, H.-J. (eds), 2004: *Regional Innovation Systems* (2nd edn). London and New York: Routledge.

Crespy, C., Heraud, J.-A. and Perry, B., 2007: Multi-level governance, regions and science in France: between competition and equality. *Regional Studies* 41(8), pp. 1069–1084.

Foray, D. and Goenega, X., 2013: The goals of smart specialisation. S3 Policy Brief Series No. 01/2013. Available online at: http://ftp.jrc.es/EURdoc/JRC82213.pdf (accessed 28 August 2013).

Geuna, A. and Muscio, A., 2009: The governance of university knowledge transfer. *Minerva* 47(1), pp. 93–114.

Glasson, J., 2003: The widening local and regional development impacts of modern universities: a tale of two cities (and north–south perspectives). *Local Economy* 18(1), pp. 21–37.

Grimm, H., 2011: The Lisbon Agenda and Entrepreneurship policy: Governance implications from a German perspective. Available online at: www.brandtschool.de-/fileadmin/downloads/Publications/grimm_lisbon_agenda.pdf?PHPSESSID=52ec209eab7be7cdc9d655bdbf003c1e (accessed 26 May 2015).

Hartwig, L., 2006: Funding Systems and Their Effects on Higher Education Systems: country study – Germany. Available online at: www.oecd.org/germany/38308008.pdf (accessed 29 May 2015).

Héraud, J.A. and Koschatzky, K., 2006: Governance II: regions, universities, and excellence in Europe. *Regions* 263, pp. 8–9.

Hilpert, U., 1992: Archipelago Europe – Islands of Innovation, Synthesis Report. Prospective Dossier No 1: Science, Technology and Social and Economic Cohesion in the Community, Commission of the European Communities, Brussels.

Hilpert, U. (ed.), 2003: *Regionalisation of Globalised Innovation: Locations for advanced industrial development and disparities in participation*. London: Routledge.

Hooghe, L. and Keating, M., 1994: The politics of European union regional policy. *Journal of European Public Policy* 1(3), pp. 367–393.

Howells, J., 1999: Regional systems of innovation. In: Archibugi, D., Howells, J. and Michie, J. (eds): *Innovation Policy in a Global Economy*. Cambridge: Cambridge University Press, pp. 67–93.

Koschatzky, K. and Kroll, H., 2007: Which side of the coin? The regional governance of science and innovation. *Regional Studies* 41(8), pp. 115–128.

Landabaso, M., Oughton, C. and Morgan, K., 2003: Learning regions in Europe: theory, policy and practice through the RIS experience. In: Gibson, D., Stolp, C., Conceição, P. and Heitor, H. (eds): *Systems and Policies for the Global Learning Economy*. Connecticut and London: Praeger.

Lawton Smith, H. and Bagchi-Sen, S., 2012: The research university, entrepreneurship and regional development: research propositions and current evidence. *Entrepreneurship & Regional Development* 24(5–6), pp. 383–404.

Perry, B., 2007: The multi-level governance of science policy in England. *Regional Studies* 41(8), pp. 1051–1068.

Perry, B. and May, T., 2007: Governance, science policy and regions: an introduction. *Regional Studies* 41(8), pp. 1039–1050.

Toedtling, F., and Trippl, M., 2005: One size fits all? Towards a differentiated regional innovation policy approach. *Research Policy* 34, pp. 1203–1219.

Waters, R. and Lawton Smith, H., 2012: High-technology local economies: geographical mobility of the highly skilled. In: Hilpert, U. and Lawton Smith, H. (eds): *Networking Regionalised Innovative Labour Markets*. London: Routledge.

7

LOCAL CLUSTERS AND GLOBAL NETWORKS

The role of different dimensions of proximity

Stefano Usai, Emanuela Marrocu and Raffaele Paci

Introduction

Countries and regions worldwide are forced by the current economic crisis and a tighter budget constraint to design policies able to balance efficiently the short run downturn with the long run perspectives. The European Union (EU) is trying to achieve such goals with a complex set of interventions where the European innovation strategy, as set out in the Innovation Union initiative, is the crucial instrument to achieve sustainable and inclusive growth in the long run. This strategy, essentially, targets the ability of each region to improve both its internal innovative capacity and, most importantly, its external connective networks with other territories, clusters and innovation players.

It is widely recognized that the capacity of a region to generate, transmit and acquire knowledge and innovation depends on a multifaceted set of factors: investment in R&D, work force experience, education and training, collaboration networks, joint research ventures, researchers' and workers' mobility and many other technology transfer mechanisms. In particular, the literature has distinguished between the creation of new ideas and inventions and the absorption of innovations generated in other regions. The ability to adopt technologies developed in other contexts has long been recognized as a crucial mechanism for knowledge accumulation and economic growth (Romer 1986; Lucas 1988). As far as knowledge has a public nature, the diffusion of ideas produces increasing returns that are at the root of growth dynamics (Grossman and Helpman 1990; Rallet and Torre 1999; Antonelli 2008). Such diffusion can be enhanced when knowledge barriers, either tangible or intangible, are reduced, or even abated, thanks to proximity among economic agents. Usually this proximity has been translated as geographical closeness since face-to-face contacts are believed to facilitate the transmission of tacit knowledge and to lessen transaction costs (Von Hippel 1994). Consequently, the spatial proximity has been the most thoroughly investigated dimension (Jaffe *et al.* 1993; Anselin *et al.* 1997; Bottazzi and Peri 2003). However, local relations often go together with wider links and networks, thanks to trade relationships for example (Coe and Helpman 1995; Keller 1998) or to foreign direct investments (Cantwell and Iammarino 2003; Di Guardo *et al.* 2015). In this respect, the spatial dimension may be just a counterpart of other forms of a-spatial proximity. Boschma (2005), along the research avenue set up by the pioneering work of the French School of Proximity (Kirat and Lung 1999; Torre and Gilly 2000), proposes five proximity dimensions: institutional, cognitive or technological, social or relational, organizational and obviously geographical.

This implies that, no matter whether the knowledge flow is due to collaborations, imitation or workers' mobility, there is a global perspective in the processes of knowledge diffusion that goes beyond the local systems of innovation.

In this perspective, the general object of this chapter is to analyse how internal and external factors interact in determining the technological performance of the European territories. More specifically, we investigate to what extent the regional inventive activity depends on intra-regional characteristics (mainly R&D expenditure and human capital) and on regions' ability to operate within inter-regional networks in order to absorb knowledge. These aspects are investigated by applying spatial econometric techniques to a Knowledge Production Function (KPF) model augmented with extra-regional factors, mediated by different kinds of proximity and networks (institutional, geographical, technological, social and organizational).

Our analysis is based on an ample dataset referring to almost 300 regions in Europe over the last decade.[1] Results show that geography is not the only dimension that may favour knowledge diffusion and not even the most important one. Complementary industrial structures of either near or distant regions may contribute to the creation of networks based on technological proximity that is the most relevant dimension in knowledge transmission. At the same time, social and organizational networks are also significant although their role is modest. The existence of external effects that move along different channels implies that policy interventions have to be coordinated along diverse dimensions to be effective in reaching the overall targets concerning innovation and economic growth.

The chapter is structured as follows. In the next section we present the concepts, definitions and measures of the different channels of technological externalities that correspond to the five proximity dimensions. In the third section we briefly describe the empirical model of the Knowledge Production Function and the specific and original estimation strategy applied. The fourth section discusses synthetically the set of empirical results. The last section is devoted to a thorough discussion of the main conclusions and of some potentially relevant policy implication that may apply to the European and also to a broader context.

Proximity dimensions

Technological progress is a complex process that may result from the combination of the internal direct production of innovation together with the absorption of the knowledge produced in proximate contexts. Different schools of thoughts provide theoretical backing to this idea, based on the presence of local spillovers both within and across regions and countries (see Castellacci 2007; Christ 2009 for recent surveys). Such spillovers are first of all due to geographical proximity since close-by agents can exploit pecuniary and pure technological externalities bounded in space. More specifically, they have less costly access to information and they can share tacit knowledge (a local public good) through face-to-face contacts. Nonetheless, the French School of Proximity has argued that geographical proximity is neither necessary nor sufficient and that a separate role for a-spatial links among economic entities has to be recognized (see Carrincazeau and Coris 2011 for a recent review).[2] Such recognition has been achieved thanks to the contribution by Boschma (2005) who discusses and classifies five dimensions of proximity across agents: geographical, institutional, technological (or cognitive), social (or relational) and organizational. The proximity dimensions proposed above have so far been implemented at different aggregation levels: agents, firms, regions and countries.

Nonetheless, there have been no attempts that manage to operationalize all the five concepts of proximities at the regional level. This is the main contribution of our research thanks to an ample dataset referring to European regions. The data sources and definitions are reported in Table 7.1, while Table 7.2 summarizes the main descriptive statistics of the proximity measures, which refer to each couple of regions in our dataset. The correlation among each proximity matrix is also reported in Table 7.2.

Geographical proximity. We implement the standard and widely used indicator of proximity that is the distance between the centroids of any two regions. This measure is preferred to the

Table 7.1 Data sources and definition for proximity matrices and variables

Proximity matrix/Variable	*Primary Source*	*Years*	*Definition*
Geographical matrix	own calculation		inverse of distance in Km
Institutional matrix	own calculation		binary matrix: value 1 if the two regions belong to the same country and 0 otherwise
Technological matrix	OCSE Pat-Reg	average 2002–2004	similarity index based on 44 sectoral shares of patenting activity
Social matrix	OCSE Pat-Reg	average 2002–2004	co-inventorship relation among multiple inventors of the same patent by inventors' region (intra-regions relationships are not considered)
Organisational matrix	OCSE Pat-Reg	average 2002–2004	applicant-inventors relation of the same patent by region of residence (intra-regions relationships are not considered)
Patent	EPO	average 2005–2007	total patents published at EPO, per million population
Research & Development	Eurostat	average 2002–2004	total intramural R&D expenditure, over GDP
Human Capital	Eurostat	average 2002–2004	population aged 15 and over with tertiary education (ISCED 5–6), over total population
Population density	Eurostat	average 2002–2004	population per km^2, thousands
Manufacture specialization	Eurostat	average 2002–2004	manufacturing employment over total employment
Settlement Structure Typology	ESPON project 3.1 BBR	1999	1=less densely populated without centres, 2=less densely populated with centres, 3=densely populated without large centres, 4=less densely populated with large centres, 5= densely populated with large centres, 6=very densely populated with large centres

Source: own elaborations.

contiguity matrix since it allows to consider all the potential interactions among regions so that spillovers are not limited to those regions that share a border. Table 7.2 shows that the median spatial distance across regions in Europe is 1270 km, ranging from a lowest value of 18 km among Belgium's regions to the maximum distance that is 4574 km, between Cyprus and Ireland.

Institutional proximity. The effective transmission of knowledge is facilitated by the presence of a common institutional framework, such as laws and norms. This can provide a set of standard procedures and mechanisms that form a shared background for all agents. This mutual endowment proves relevant in reducing uncertainty and in lowering transaction costs and, thus, favours cooperative behaviours among agents in different regional environments (Maskell and Malmberg 1999; Gertler 2003). Consequently, two regions belonging to the same national institution are expected to have more knowledge exchanges. A simple, and widely used, way to account for these time invariant common factors is to include a full set of country dummies.[3]

Technological (or cognitive) proximity. Knowledge transfer often requires specific and appropriate absorptive capacity[4] (Cohen and Levinthal 1990), which entails, among others, a homogenous cognitive base with respect to the original knowledge. Without this common knowledge base it is difficult or impossible to understand and process effectively the new incoming knowledge. In practical terms, we expect that territories that have in common a similar specialization structure can exchange information more easily and less costly, and this may favour innovation. To measure the technological, or cognitive, proximity across regions we compute a similarity index (with interval going from zero to one) between region i and region j, based on the distribution of patenting activity among forty-four sectors. Table 7.2 shows that the two most technologically distant regions (Ionia Nisia/Notio Aigaio in Greece) exhibit an index of 0.05. Interestingly, the higher degree of technological similarity (0.94) is found for two non-adjacent regions, located in different countries: Piedmont in Italy and Niederbayern in Germany.

Social (or relational) proximity. Economic relationships, according to·Granovetter (1985) may reflect social ties and vice versa. In the context of innovation processes, this implies that social closeness facilitates firms' capacity to absorb external knowledge since social nearness breeds trust that, in turn, lowers transaction costs and facilitates collaboration. In this chapter we measure social proximity by means of co-inventorship relations among multiple inventors of the same patent in case they are resident in different regions. The rationale is that the number and the intensity of links among inventors located in different regions are able to catch the existence

Table 7.2 Summary statistics for proximity matrices

Proximity matrices	Units of measurement	Min	Max	Mean	Var. coeff.	Links % ★
Geographical	km	17.86	4574.57	1370.15	0.56	–
Technological	index [0, 1]	0.05	0.94	0.70	0.18	–
Social	num links	0.00	137.84	0.16	10.68	18.18
Organisational	num links	0.00	480.13	0.58	10.52	17.11

★ % of total cells, excluding the principal diagonal

	Sample correlation coefficients		
	Geographical	Technological	Social
Technological	0.200		
Social	0.120	0.070	
Organisational	0.113	0.069	0.740

Source: own elaborations.

of a social network between regions, which facilitates the exchange of knowledge. The last column in Table 7.2 shows that the number of non-zero links (co-inventorships) in the matrix represents only a small fraction (18 per cent) of all potential relationships. The highest social interaction (137) is reached by the two contiguous German regions of Düsseldorf and Köln, followed by other couples of contiguous German regions located in the industrialized area of Baden-Wurttemberg: Karlsruhe with Rheinhessen-Pfalz and Stuttgart with Karlsruhe. As expected, spatial proximity favours social interactions among inventors although from the bottom part of Table 7.2 we can see that the correlation coefficient between the geographical and social proximity matrices is quite small (0.12).[5]

Organizational proximity. When agents operate within the same group or organization, this influences the individual capacity to acquire new knowledge coming from different agents, because this reduces uncertainty and incentives to opportunistic behaviour (Kirat and Lung 1999). The agents may therefore share an area of definition of practices and strategies within a set of rules based on organizational arrangements that goes from informal relations among companies to formally organized firms. As for the measurement, we follow Picci (2010) and Maggioni *et al.* (2011) who use the affiliation to the same organization of the applicant and the inventors of a patent. Given this definition, we are not considering the case in which the applicant and the inventor are the same as much as the case in which they are different but located in the same region.[6] Table 7.2 shows that the number of non-zero links in the organizational matrix amounts to 17 per cent of total possible relationships among European regions. Interestingly, the highest value (480) is reached by two distant regions within France: Île de France and Rhône Alpes. The former hosts the capital, Paris, where most French companies locate their headquarters, while the latter is renowned for its scientific parks and research laboratories which are apparently linked to parent companies.

Being proximate along the different dimensions discussed above can be seen as a crucial condition for firms' interaction and cooperation, the evolution of networks among agents, and the resulting innovation (Boschma and Frenken 2010). The interconnected role of proximity and networks on local innovation performance can be analysed thanks to the KPF approach, introduced by Griliches (1979) to study the relationship between knowledge inputs and outputs at the firm level. Since then it has been extensively used to analyse how this relationship works both at the firm and at the territorial level. In particular, regional KPFs have been estimated to assess the role of both internal and external factors on regional innovation systems. The seminal paper by Jaffe (1989) proves the existence of geographically mediated spillovers from university research to commercial innovation in US metropolitan areas. Successive studies (Anselin *et al.* 1997; Acs *et al.* 2002; O'hUallacha'in and Leslie 2007), based on US regions and states, introduced the concept of geographical proximity and test its importance by means of spatial econometric techniques. Along the same vein, several studies have been proposed for the EU regions. In particular, Bottazzi and Peri (2003), Greunz (2003) and Moreno *et al.* (2005) investigate inter-regional knowledge spillovers across European regions by adding technological to geographical proximity. Results show that inter-regional knowledge spillovers exist both between close-by regions and between distant regions with similar technological profiles. Furthermore, all these studies consider institutional proximity (measured by means of country dummies) and find it relevant in identifying the more and less innovative regions. Only a few contributions examine the role of social or relational networks[7] together with geographical proximity within a KPF.[8] Maggioni *et al.* (2007), Kroll (2009) and Ponds *et al.* (2010) find that both the local neighbourhood and the connections with other regions based on cooperation matter for the local process of knowledge generation. However, none of these studies operationalizes this concept to measure the degree proximity for each couple of regions, rather they use it as a regional indicator that measures the region's degree of connectivity and openness. Finally, to the best of our knowledge, there are no contributions that focus directly on the role of organizational proximity on regional innovation performance. The only partial exception is the article by Sorensen *et al.* (2006), where organizational proximity is considered as a determinant of knowledge flows proxied by citations.

The KPF model with different proximities and main results

This section presents the econometric models used to investigate the determinants of the process of knowledge creation and diffusion in Europe, followed by the description of the dependent variable and of the main internal production inputs. Finally, we discuss the main results.

The literature on the determinants of innovative activity at firms' and regional level has been traditionally based on the estimation of the KPF model, where the output is measured by the patenting activity and the input by the R&D expenditure and by human capital. Indeed, in the case of traditional sectors and small enterprises, the creation of innovation is not only the result of a formal investment in research but it is often derived either from an informal process of learning by doing (Nelson and Winter 1982) or from the absorption of external knowledge (Abreu *et al.* 2008). Firms' and regions' ability to understand, interpret and exploit internal and external knowledge relies on prior experiences embodied in individual skills and, more generally, in a well-educated labour force (Engelbrecht 2002; Archibugi and Filippetti 2011). In light of the discussion on the role of proximity presented in the previous sections, we also explicitly consider the presence of external factors coming from 'proximate' regions that may enhance the impact of the internal ones thanks to spillover effects.

The standard indicator for innovative activity is the number of patent applications. We consider patent intensity, i.e. the absolute value divided by population. Data are retrieved from the European Patent Office (EPO) classified by priority year and by inventor's region.[9] Since patenting activity, especially at the regional level, is quite irregular over time we smooth the variable by computing a three-year average. Thus, our dependent variable is measured as the yearly average of patents per million inhabitants in 2005–2007. The summary statistics, reported in Table 7.3, show substantial differences in patenting activity among European regions, ranging from near zero in the Romanian region of Sud-Vest Oltenia, to 627 in the German region of Stuttgart. The high value (1.2) of the coefficient of variation (CV) confirms the great degree of spatial concentration of innovative activity that is clustered in the north-centre of Europe while little patenting activity is performed by the eastern and southern regions.

Investments in R&D are the most common way to measure the principal input of the KPF. We use expenditure in R&D rescaled for the value of regional production, that is GDP. This indicator has an average value of 1.4, but the spatial distribution in Europe is quite concentrated

Table 7.3 Summary statistics for dependent and exogenous variables

Variable	*Unit of measurement*	*Min*	*Max*	*Mean*	*Var. coeff.*
Patent	per million pop	0.20	627.6	105.4	1.20
Research & Development	over GDP, %	0.07	7.6	1.4	0.85
Human Capital	over total population, %	3.51	23.3	10.5	0.39
Population density	thousands per km^2	3.08	9049.6	331.3	2.47
Manufacture specialisation	over total empl., %	3.67	36.2	17.3	0.37

Source: own elaborations.

(CV=0.85) in Scandinavia, Central Europe (Germany, Switzerland, France) and in Southern England. As an additional input, expected to influence the process of knowledge production at the local level, we consider the availability of human capital, which is proxied by the share of population with tertiary education (ISCED 5–6). The spatial distribution of this variable across European regions appears more uniform (CV=0.39) and with a clearly identifiable national pattern. A high endowment of human capital characterizes the Scandinavian countries, UK, Germany and Spain while lower values are generally detected in the eastern countries, France and Italy.

Moreover, some controls are introduced: population density in order to account for possible agglomeration effects; the regional share of manufacturing activities to take into account the fact that the location of manufacturing activity is one of the most relevant factors that explain the spatial distribution of innovative activity (Audretsch and Feldman 1996); and, following Usai (2011), a GDP dummy (which takes value 1 for regions with a GDP per capita level above the European average and zero otherwise) to consider the different levels of access to market across European regions.

The final crucial aspect in our KPF model pertains to the inclusion of the five proximity dimensions (geographical, institutional, technological, social and organizational) in order to assess the potential role of spillover effects channelled along them, as explained in detail in Marrocu *et al.* (2013) and Paci *et al.* (2014). This is accomplished by estimating spatial autoregressive models,[10] where the proximity is included first one at a time and then two at a time. Their overall effect is then obtained by combining the model's evidence on the basis of the Akaike information criterion.[11]

The spatial autoregressive specification is chosen because it permits to distinguish between the *direct* effect, which measures the change in region *i*'s dependent variable caused by a change in one of its own regressors plus a series of feedback effects (region *i* is neighbour to its neighbours so affecting them will receive in turn a feedback influence), and the *indirect* or *spillover* effect, due to a change in another region's regressor. The *total* effect is obtained as their sum. It is worth noting that feedback and spillover effects occur over time through the simultaneous system of interdependence among regions, so that the effects have to be considered as the result of a new steady state equilibrium. In this study, on the basis of the direct effect, we assess the role played on patenting activity by regional internal R&D and human capital endowments, while the indirect effects provide the extent such internal factors are amplified by positive externalities acquired from proximate territories. It is worth remarking that, conditional on the amount of productive factors, the strength of such effects is related to the intensity of the cross-regional dependence/interconnectivity, measured along the different proximity dimensions, and to the absorptive capacity of each region.

Results are summarised in Table 7.4, where we report the direct, indirect and total effects computed by deriving an all-proximities multiplier for both R&D and human capital on the basis of the weighted averages of the relevant parameters. In the bottom part of the table we report the estimated coefficients of the proximity dependence for all combinations of matrices.

A remarkable result is that human capital is more effective than formal research expenditure in determining knowledge production at the regional level. We find that the total impact of human capital is always higher with respect to R&D in all models, ranging from a multiple of around five in the model with technological similarity to above eight in the model with social networks. As the creation of new knowledge is often based on informal learning processes and on the ability to exploit external knowledge, a well-educated labour force plays a key role in these processes. It is also worth noting that indirect effects are almost always significant and sizeable for human capital, accounting for up to one third of the total effects in the case of the

Table 7.4 Combined effects of the KPF inputs

Dependent variable: Patents, 2005–2007 average per capita values	
R&D	Effect
direct	0.211
indirect	0.119
total	0.329
Human capital	
direct	1.298
indirect	0.730
total	2.028
Proximity matrix	Proximity dependence
geographical	0.067
technological	0.319
social	0.025
organizational	0.016

Effects are computed on the basis of the weighted averages for the inputs coefficients and the spatial autocorrelation coefficients. Weights are given by model probabilities obtained on the basis of AIC values.

Source: own elaborations.

technology based connectivity. As for the controls, the GDP per capita indicator and the manufacture specialization structure exhibit positive and significant coefficients across the four models indicating that knowledge creation exhibits a significant correlation with both high income levels and manufacturing productions. It is worth highlighting that indirect effects are significant in all the specifications that we have estimated but only in the case of human capital. This result is consistent with the claim that R&D expenditure per se is not sufficient to activate knowledge externalities[12] and this, in turn, calls for policies and production devices capable of increasing the absorptive capacity of the regional systems of innovation.

Turning to external effects, the first interesting outcome is that they are always positive, signalling that each of the different proximity measures captures the cross-regional dependence arising from the knowledge transmission mechanisms described in previous sections. In other words, we find that, according to the analytical literature, the different types of proximity are complements rather than substitutes, as they may represent knowledge transmission channels that reinforce each other over time and across space (Mattes 2012). More specifically, the strongest association (the spatial dependence proximity is equal to 0.32) is found for the technological proximity, which turns out to be the most important channel of knowledge spillovers, while geographical proximity ranks second (0.07). As far as the network dimensions are concerned, they have a relatively more modest role: the spatially lagged dependent variable exhibits a coefficient of 0.025 when it is computed using the social proximity and 0.016 in the case of the organizational one.

Concluding remarks and policy implications

The availability of knowledge and its diffusion is universally considered a fundamental determinant of economic development both for regions and nations. In particular, it is widely accepted that the diffusion of innovation depends on the relative position of agents and therefore regions within different dimensions that go beyond the geographical space. These dimensions include the institutional, technological, social and organizational ones. In this chapter, we address the issue of the role of these diverse dimensions within the research line of the KPF model and we propose some interesting and original findings on the role of internal and external factors in promoting knowledge creation at the regional level.

The main result confirms our analytical expectations and a few previous empirical findings: R&D and human capital are essential components of technological progress. Most importantly, we find that they have a very distinct impact: investing in human capital is six times more effective than in research and development. This outcome is a clear indication of the relative importance of a skilful and qualified labour force in order to ensure an incremental technological path based on pervasive and continuous learning, ideas circulation and experience accumulation. Such a learning process is more and more essential since new technological trajectories continue to emerge, nowadays, with a much higher frequency with respect to the past. This change, consequently, requires that agents operate with a specific ability to process and manage more or less radically new ideas.

The second important result is more novel in this setting: all dimensions of inter-regional proximity and connectivity are significantly related to innovative performance. Most importantly, we find that their relative strength differs significantly: cognitive or technological proximity has an effect 1.5 times higher than the one due to geographical proximity and up to three-four times higher than that of social and organizational networking. The existence of a common knowledge and productive base is more relevant with respect to unintended interactions due to spatial proximity. Moreover, we find that intended interactions, which are behind social and organizational networks, are important but with quite a modest impact. Consequently, a substantial part of the impact of R&D and human capital on regional knowledge creation derives from spillover coming from other regions. Such spillovers move along a complex set of inter-regional channels, which make the intensity of these effects dependent on the proximity dimension.

It is worth underlining that the current study opens a potentially very fruitful avenue of further researches. Social and organizational proximities can be specified in different ways in order to provide more robustness tests on our outcomes. Moreover, further research is necessary to unveil the underlying links between the aggregate regional macro level and the micro level, where individual behaviour and relations are shaped along each dimension of proximity. An interesting attempt in this direction is provided in Usai *et al.* (2015) who assess knowledge flows, thanks to joint ventures and strategic alliance, at the micro level and manage to test for complementarity with an encompassing model. Interestingly enough, all dimensions are relevant and the prominent role of the technological/cognitive one is strongly confirmed.

All in all, we believe that our work offers some relevant and original empirical findings that allow for a better understanding of the processes of knowledge creation and diffusion within the current global scenario – a scenario that is more and more characterized by complex interconnection and networks that shape the relationships among agents, regions and countries. In the following we put forward some general comments on regional strategies for technological advance and economic growth.

The first general implication is that regions in Europe, but also in other global contexts, need to concentrate their policies on actions aimed at increasing the endowments of well-educated labour force. This part of the labour force is proved to have a strong and pervasive role in making regions ready to contribute to innovation and to take benefit from others through external networking. The impact of human capital on inventive activity and innovation production is stronger than formal R&D expenditures. New ideas, inventions, product and process innovations come mainly from the inventive capacity of well-educated people and thus education in general and universities in particular have to be central in any innovation policy. This is a clear indication of our contribution and points to further research in this area in order to understand better the mechanisms through which policies may be more effective in obtaining this crucial goal.

The second general implication derives from the existence of several channels of inter-regional spillovers and externalities. This complex setting asks for a policy able to envisage a coordinated strategy in order to find the right balance among an array of diverse interventions. We support the idea that there is no single path to innovation, but there are several variations and each region needs to identify its own opportunities, its own targets, and as a result its specific instruments and actions.

In general, policies should aim directly at investments in knowledge diffusion and absorption together with those in research and development – an idea that is now perfectly embedded in the so-called Smart Specialisation Strategy of Europe 2020 which promotes place-based policies. According to such strategy, each region is asked to strengthen its competitive advantages by acquiring as much as possible from ongoing knowledge flows and, at the same time, spreading the benefits of innovation throughout the entire regional economy (Asheim *et al.* 2011).

Other more specific policy recommendations are implied by the presence of diverse complementary spillovers transmission channels. The presence of flows of knowledge, which move along the technological space, for instance, implies that regions should try to develop a balanced policy to create a common wide knowledge base and specific industrial platforms to maximize the absorptive capacity and its effective application. Regions need wide ranging schemes that encourage the formation of dense specialised networks among territorial innovation systems even when they are not contiguous or even very far away. The fact that technological proximity matters even more than the geographical one in transmitting spillovers means that knowledge diffusion is facilitated within a-spatial technological clusters. This suggests the implementation of specific industrial policies to support the functioning throughout Europe of such non contiguous industrial clusters; policies that aim at fostering not only regional competitiveness but also the complementarities among potentials and relative specialization patterns of different regions in a very wide geographical scenery.

Furthermore, the relevance of institutional closeness implies that agents need some form of public coordination in the form of common procedures and standards. As a matter of fact this common institutional framework may prove crucial for avoiding opportunistic, or merely inefficient, behaviours due to lack of trust among agents in different regions. Thus, a process of effective homogenization of norms and procedures for the whole of Europe, and even beyond Europe, is required to favour institutional proximity; a process that should not entail an increase of the bureaucratic burden, which on the contrary is a strong delaying factor in the integration process of different institutional and cultural settings.

Finally, externalities arising from relational interconnectivity among agents in different regions require interventions that target those areas where there is either a lack or a shortage of social and/or organizational capital which may hamper the creation of such networks. Most importantly, such actions have to provide a balanced set of incentives to motivate more cooperative attitudes without, nonetheless, impeding market relations and competitive behaviours.

Acknowledgements

We would like to thank Barbara Dettori and Marta Foddi for excellent research assistance. This chapter is based on materials developed in Marrocu *et al.* (2013) and Paci *et al.* (2014).

Notes

1 For twenty-three countries we use the NUTS 2 level (Nomenclature des Unités Territoriales Statistiques) defined by Eurostat. For six small countries (Cyprus, Estonia, Lithuania, Luxembourg, Latvia, Malta) the regional breakdown is not available so they are considered at the country (NUTS0) level.

2 Another relevant concept for the analysis of knowledge flows is the distinction between unintended and intended spillovers (Maggioni *et al.* 2007). In the latter case, knowledge may flow among agents on a voluntary basis thanks to formal or informal agreements that may also have an a-spatial nature (for instance, technological connections). Such exchanges can be either market or non-market mediated (Breschi and Lissoni 2001).

3 Alternatively, one can model institutional proximity by means of a weight matrix, whose elements take value 1 if two regions belong to the same country and zero otherwise. However, in our case the empirical specification based on such a proximity matrix is outperformed by the estimation that includes country dummies.

4 The concept of absorptive capacity does not depend only on cognitive proximity and has a wider application at the level of firms, sectors, regions and nations.

5 It is interesting to notice that the correlation coefficient with the contiguity matrix is much higher (0.39), signalling that strong social relationships are more likely to develop among contiguous regions.

6 A characteristic of the applicant–inventor matrix is that it is not symmetric. Since we are interested in the total number of organizational relationships between the two regions, we sum up mirror cells so that the generic element o_{ij} of the organizational matrix O is defined as the total number of bilateral relationships between applicants and inventors located in the regions i and j.

7 Social proximity has also been included in studies of R&D cooperation networks, such as that of Autant-Bernard *et al.* (2007), who find that the probability of collaboration is influenced by each individual's position within the network and also that social distance seems to matter more than geographical distance. In the same vein, Hoekman *et al.* (2009) find negative effects of both geographical and institutional distance on research collaboration, using data on inter-regional research collaboration measured by scientific publications and patents in Europe.

8 An interesting parallel study that has tried to provide a measure of different proximities, namely relational, social and technological, to assess their role in affecting productivity growth, rather than innovative activity, has been recently proposed by Basile *et al.* (2012).

9 In case of multiple inventors, we assign a proportional fraction of each patent to the different inventors' regions of residence.

10 For a comprehensive discussion on the spatial autoregressive models refer to LeSage and Pace (2009).

11 Methodological aspects and detailed results are presented in Paci *et al.* (2014). It is worth noting that the current state of the art in spatial econometrics (Elhorst 2010) does not allow to estimate a single model comprising all the different proximity dimensions at the same time. The workable alternative adopted in this study was to estimate standard spatial autoregressive specification with one proximity at a time (four models) and spatial autoregressive models that include two proximity measures (Lacombe 2004) at a time (six models) and then work out the overall effects by means of post-estimation techniques. Note that in the estimation stage we refer to four, rather than five proximities, because the institutional proximity is also accounted for in our models via the inclusion of the complete set of country dummies.

12 This is likely due to the fact that a large part of R&D expenditure is represented by researchers' wages, whose effect is evidently captured by the human capital variable. Moreover, it is often the case that expenditures classified as R&D are not directly related to research activities, but rather to infrastructures and logistics, so they have basically no effect on proximate regions. A similar result has been found by Crescenzi and Rodriguez Pose (2012) for the case of the US.

Bibliography

Abreu, M., Grinevich, V., Kitson, M. and Savona, M., 2008: Absorptive capacity and regional patterns of innovation. *DIUS Research Report* 08–11.

Acs, Z.J., Anselin, L. and Varga, A., 2002: Patents and innovation counts as measures of regional production of new knowledge. *Research Policy* 31, pp. 1069–1085.

Anselin, L., Acs, Z.J. and Varga, A., 1997: Local geographic spillovers between university research and high technology innovations. *Journal of Urban Economics* 42, pp. 422–448.
Antonelli, A., 2008: *Localised Technological Change: Towards the economics of complexity*. London: Routledge.
Archibugi, D. and Filippetti, A., 2011: Is the economic crisis impairing convergence in innovation performance across Europe? *Journal of Common Market Studies* 49, pp. 1153–1182.
Asheim, B.T., Boschma, R. and Cooke, P., 2011: Constructing regional advantage: platform policies based on related variety and differentiated knowledge bases. *Regional Studies* 45, pp. 893–904.
Audretsch, D.B. and Feldman, M.P., 1996: R&D spillovers and the geography of innovation and production. *American Economic Review* 86, pp. 630–640.
Autant-Bernard, C., Billand, P., Frachisse, D. and Massard, N., 2007: Social distance versus spatial distance in R&D cooperation: empirical evidence from European collaboration choices in micro and nanotechnologies. *Papers in Regional Science* 86, pp. 495–519.
Basile, R., Capello, R. and Caragliu, A., 2012: Technological interdependence and regional growth in Europe. *Papers in Regional Science* 91, pp. 697–722.
Boschma, R.A., 2005: Proximity and innovation: a critical assessment. *Regional Studies* 39, pp. 61–74.
Boschma, R. and Frenken, K., 2010: The spatial evolution of innovation networks: a proximity perspective. In: Boschma, R. and Martin, R. (eds): *Handbook of Evolutionary Economic Geography*. Cheltenham: Edward Elgar, pp. 120–135.
Bottazzi, L. and Peri, G., 2003: Innovation and spillovers in regions: evidence from European patent data. *European Economic Review*, 47, pp. 687–710.
Breschi, S. and Lissoni, F., 2001: Knowledge spillovers and local innovation systems: a critical survey. *Industrial and Corporate Change* 10, pp. 975–1005.
Cantwell, J. and Iammarino, S., 2003: *Multinational Corporations and European Regional Systems of Innovation*. London: Routledge.
Carrincazeaux, C. and Coris, M., 2011: Proximity and innovation. In: Cooke, P., Asheim, B.T. and Boschma, R. (eds): *Handbook of Regional Innovation and Growth*. Cheltenham: Edward Elgar, pp. 269–281.
Castellacci, F., 2007: Innovation and the competitiveness of industries: comparing the mainstream and the evolutionary approaches. *Technological Forecasting and Social Change* 75, pp. 1–23.
Christ, J.P., 2009: New Economic Geography reloaded: localized knowledge spillovers and the geography of innovation. *FZID Discussion Papers 01–2009*, University of Hohenheim.
Coe, D.T. and Helpman, E., 1995: International R&D spillovers. *European Economic Review* 39, pp. 859–887.
Cohen, W.M. and Levinthal, D.A., 1990: Absorptive capacity: a new perspective on learning an innovation. *Administrative Science Quarterly* 35, pp. 128–152.
Crescenzi, R. and Rodríguez-Pose, A., 2012: R&D, Socio-Economic Conditions and the territorial dynamics of Innovation in the United States. *Growth and Change*, 44(2), pp. 290–323.
Di Guardo, M.C., Marrocu, E. and Paci, R., 2015: The concurrent impact of cultural, political and spatial distances on international Mergers and Acquisitions. *The World Economy*, published on line, DOI: 10.1111/twec.12275 working papers 13/08.
Elhorst, J.P., 2010: Applied spatial econometrics: raising the bar. *Spatial Economic Analysis* 5, pp. 10–28.
Engelbrecht, H.J., 2002: Human capital and international knowledge spillovers in TFP growth of a sample of developing countries: an exploration of alternative approaches. *Applied Economics* 34, pp. 831–841.
Gertler, M.S., 2003: Tacit knowledge and the economic geography of context, or the undefinable tacitness of being (there). *Journal of Economic Geography* 3, pp. 75–99.
Granovetter, M., 1985: Economic action and social structure: the problem of embeddedness. *American Journal of Sociology*, 91, pp. 481–510.
Greunz, L., 2003: Geographically and technologically mediated knowledge spillovers between European regions. *Annals of Regional Science* 37, pp. 657–680.
Griliches, Z., 1979: Issues in assessing the contribution of research and development to productivity growth. *Bell Journal of Economics* 10, pp. 92–116.
Grossman, G.M. and Helpman, E., 1990: Trade, innovation, and growth. *American Economic Review* 80, pp. 86–91.
Hoekman, J., Frenken, K. and van Oort, F., 2009: The geography of collaborative knowledge production in Europe. *Annals of Regional Science* 43, pp. 721–738.
Jaffe, A.B., 1989: Real effects of academic research. *American Economic Review* 79, pp. 957–970.
Jaffe, A.B., Trajtenberg, M. and Henderson, R., 1993: Geographic Localization of knowledge spillovers as evidenced by patent citations. *The Quarterly Journal of Economics* 108(3), pp. 577–98.

Keller, W., 1998: Are international R&D spillovers trade-related?: Analyzing spillovers among randomly matched trade partners. *European Economic Review* 42(8), pp. 1469–1481.
Kirat, T. and Lung, Y., 1999: Innovation and proximity: territories as loci of collective learning processes. *European Urban and Regional Studies* 6, pp. 27–38.
Kroll, H., 2009: Spillovers and Proximity in Perspective. A Network Approach to Improving the Operationalisation of Proximity. *Fraunhofer Working Papers Firms and Region*, N. R2/2009.
Lacombe, D.J., 2004: Does econometric methodology matter? An analysis of public policy using spatial econometric techniques. *Geographical Analysis* 36, pp. 105–118.
LeSage, J.P. and Pace, R.K., 2009: *Introduction to Spatial Econometrics*. Boca Raton, FL: CRC.
Lucas, R. Jr., 1988: On the mechanics of economic development. *Journal of Monetary Economics* 22(1), pp. 3–42.
Maggioni, M.A., Nosvelli, M. and Uberti, T.E., 2007: Space versus networks in the geography of innovation: a European analysis. *Papers in Regional Science*, 86, pp. 471–493.
Maggioni, M.A., Uberti, T.E. and Usai, S., 2011: Treating patents as relational data: knowledge transfers and spillovers across Italian provinces. *Industry & Innovation*, 18, pp. 39–67.
Marrocu, E., Paci, R. and Usai, S., 2013: Proximity, Networking and Knowledge Production in Europe: what lessons for innovation policy? *Technological Forecasting and Social Change* 80, pp. 1484–1498.
Maskell, P. and Malmberg, A., 1999: The competitiveness of firms and regions. 'Ubiquitification' and the importance of localized learning. *European Urban and Regional Studies* 6, pp. 9–25.
Mattes, J., 2012: Dimensions of proximity and knowledge bases: innovation between spatial and non-spatial factors. *Regional Studies* 46, pp 1085–1099.
Moreno, R., Paci, R. and Usai, S., 2005: Spatial spillovers and innovation activity in European regions. *Environment and Planning A* 37, pp. 1793–1812.
Nelson, R.R. and Winter, S.G., 1982: *An Evolutionary Theory of Economic Change*. Cambridge, MA: Harvard University Press.
O'hUallacha'in, B. and Leslie, T., 2007: Rethinking the regional knowledge production function. *Journal of Economic Geography* 7, pp. 737–752.
Paci, R., Marrocu, E. and Usai, S., 2014: The complementary effects of proximity dimensions on knowledge spillovers. *Spatial Economic Analysis* 9, pp. 9–30.
Picci, L., 2010: The internationalization of inventive activity: a gravity model using patent data. *Research Policy* 39, pp. 1070–1081.
Ponds, R., van Oort, F. and Frenken, K., 2010: Innovation, spillovers and university–industry collaboration: an extended knowledge production function approach. *Journal of Economic Geography* 10, pp. 231–255.
Rallet, A. and Torre, A., 1999: Is geographical proximity necessary in the innovation networks in the era of the global economy?, *GeoJournal* 49, pp. 373–380.
Romer, P.M., 1986: Increasing returns and long-run growth. *Journal of Political Economy* 94, pp. 1002–1037.
Sorensen, O., Rivkin, J.W. and Fleming, L., 2006: Complexity, networks and knowledge flow. *Research Policy*, 35, pp. 994–1017.
Torre, A. and Gilly, J.P., 2000: On the analytical dimension of proximity dynamics. *Regional Studies* 34, pp. 169–180.
Usai, S., 2011: The geography of inventive activity in OECD regions. *Regional Studies* 45, pp. 711–731.
Usai, S., Paci, R. and Marrocu, E., 2015: Networks, proximities and inter-firm knowledge exchanges. *International Regional Science Review*, published online, doi: 10.1177/0160017615576079.
von Hippel, E., 1994: 'Sticky information' and the locus of problem solving: implications for innovation. *Management Science* 40(4), pp. 429–439.

8

THE REGIONAL INNOVATION PARADOX REVISITED

Robert Hassink and Pedro Marques

Introduction

Regional innovation policies have developed strongly in Europe since the mid 1980s. This surge is mainly due to the increasing importance of the regional level with regard to diffusion-oriented innovation support policies (Cooke and Morgan 1998; Asheim *et al.* 2003; Fritsch and Stephan 2005). Partly supported by national and supranational support programmes and encouraged by strong institutional set-ups found in successful regional economies such as Baden-Württemberg in Germany and Emilia-Romagna in Italy, many regions in Europe have been setting up science parks, technopoles, technological financial aid schemes, innovation support agencies, community colleges and initiatives to support clustering of industries since the second half of the 1980s. The central aim of these policies is to support regional endogenous potential by encouraging the diffusion of new technologies both from universities and public research establishments to small and medium-sized enterprises (SMEs), between SMEs and large enterprises (vertical cooperation) and between SMEs themselves (horizontal cooperation). Over the years these policies have however been the target of strong criticism for a variety of reasons: for example Lovering (1999) claimed that the theory behind them was poorly developed and was in fact being led by a few policymakers' desire to make claims about nonexistent regional economic transformation; Tödtling and Trippl (2005) criticized one-size-fits-all approaches, on the basis that different regions suffer from different shortcomings, and that innovation policy should be designed with that in mind.

In this chapter we will focus on one particular shortcoming of regional innovation policies that has received relatively little attention: the innovation paradox, as defined by Oughton *et al.* (2002). It refers to the observed fact that lagging regions are often the ones with less capacity to make effective use of the policy instruments created to increase innovation potential. Therefore, innovation policies are likely to reinforce current regional inequalities, by allowing those firms in core regions to develop even further their potential. We will however argue that in line with recent work in Economic Geography we need to avoid looking at the region as a bounded, relatively closed entity (Hassink and Klaerding 2012). As a way to build on this concept we will suggest a multi-scalar approach that considers not only the regional dimension, but also the organizational (below the region) and the national (above the region) scales. We will suggest that the effectiveness of innovation policy, particularly in poorer regions, results from the interaction between these three scales of activity.

In the following section we will describe the general trends in innovation policy and its theoretical foundations. We will then discuss its main shortcomings, in particular those related to the innovation paradox. We will then use the case study of the moulds industry in Portugal, which is based on PhD research by one of the authors (Marques 2011), to illustrate our argument. We will conclude with some brief remarks and policy suggestions.

Regional innovation policies: general trends and theoretical foundations

Regional innovation policies consist of four groups of measures. First, a large range of financial aid schemes, such as support for R&D, is devised both at national but in some countries also at regional level to boost innovativeness of SMEs. Second, technology transfer and consultancy agencies, which includes all agencies found in a region operating at three different stages of support: the provision of general information, the provision of technological advice and support for joint R&D projects, between firms (of which technology-following SMEs are the main group) and universities and public research establishments (Hassink 1996). Agencies that belong to this group try to help to solve innovation problems mainly of technology-following SMEs by either giving them advice themselves or by referring them to other agencies in a further stage of support. Third, in the 1990s, technology parks, a land and property-led technology policy concept, aimed at encouraging the spatial clustering of high-tech firms and R&D organizations. They were very popular among local, regional and national policymakers as a tool to boost regional economic growth (Hassink and Berg 2014). They often adopted different denominations, such as science parks, high-tech centres, incubator centres, technology parks, technoparks or science cities, but their final aim was similar, namely, to boost regional technology transfer, innovativeness and hence competitiveness. Fourth, in addition to the three more traditional policy measures, the most recent measures focus on the 'smart specialization' of regions (McCann and Ortega-Argilés 2015). The objective of this new wave of innovation policies is twofold: first it aims to build on the complementarities that exist in a region and encourage processes of path creation through related variety and cross-sectoral collaboration. Second it aims to go beyond a narrow emphasis on stimulating the production of codified knowledge (R&D, patenting), to consider both other types of knowledge (synthetic, symbolic) but also other elements such as good governance, and human capital that are seen as essential to ensure good policymaking. For an extensive description of innovation policies in different contexts see McCann and Ortega-Argilés (2013).

Regional innovation policies: why did they surge?

The increasing importance of regions for innovation policy can be considered as the outcome of a convergence of regional and technology policy since the early 1980s (Fritsch and Stephan 2005). These two policy fields converged into regional innovation policies since their aim became partly the same, namely supporting the innovative capabilities and thus competitiveness of SMEs. Moreover, there have been decentralization and regionalization trends in innovation policy not only in Europe, but also in the USA and East Asia (Dodgson and Bessant 1996; Cooke and Morgan 1998). These trends fit into what Asheim *et al.* (2003) observed as a shift from a firm oriented, static allocation of resources for innovation to a trans-sectoral, dynamic and system oriented, learning-to-innovate policy based on proactive, multi-actor partnership. Although we can speak of a general phenomenon, there are of course large differences between individual regions and countries concerning the extent to which these trends take place (see also Prange 2008). Generally, contributing factors to regional innovation policies are a federal political system, decentralization, strong regional institutions and governance, a strong industrial specialization in the region, sociocultural homogeneity and thus relationships of trust, large economic restructuring problems and a strong commitment of regional political leaders (Hassink 1996).

One of the main arguments supporting the use of the regional level for innovation support has been called the 'garden argument' (Paquet 1998): if the economy is regarded as a garden with all kinds of trees and plants, for the gardener (government) there is no simple rule likely to apply to all plants. Growth is therefore best orchestrated from its sources at the level of cities and regions. At this level, rather than at the national level, policymakers can better tailor policy in relation to demand (Nauwelaers and Wintjes 2003). Regionalization, therefore, allows for differentiation in policies, which is necessary because of differing regional economic conditions and thus different support needs of industries and firms. Regionalization also raises the enthusiasm and motivation of regional policymakers, as they are now able to devise 'their own' policies. Moreover, because of the large variety of institutional set-ups and initiatives in Europe and North America, these laboratories of experimentation offer both national and regional policymakers plenty of institutional learning opportunities (Hassink and Lagendijk 2001). The arguments in favor of regionalization and unfolding endogenous potential in regions have been recently taken up again by scholars in favour of a place-based approach towards regional development policy (OECD 2011; Barca *et al.* 2012).

Standardization and the innovation paradox

Despite the above-mentioned garden argument and the plea for tailored regional innovation policy, the use of benchmarking, the creation of partnerships and the search for best practices has led to the standardization of regional innovation policies in Europe (Martin and Sunley 2003; Tödtling and Trippl 2005). Partnerships and benchmarking between cities and regions are strongly supported in Europe by the European Commission in the framework of several programmes (see for instance the IRE-Network and the Mutual Learning Platform on www.innovating-regions.org). Moreover, an increasing number of consultancies, such as McKinsey, earn their living with benchmarking exercises and advices to regional governments all over the world with lessons learned in successful regions. There is also a rich literature describing policy initiatives in full detail and trying to come to some kind of comparison in the concluding sections (Cooke *et al.* 2004; OECD 2007, 2010, 2011). Learning from best-practice initiatives is the main credo of many of these studies. Particularly in Europe one of the main arguments in favour of inter-regional learning processes has been the institutional diversity in that continent: one should benefit from the strengths of the diversity of innovation policies in regions and nations (Dodgson and Bessant 1996: 11).

In this chapter we will focus specifically on the regional innovation paradox (Oughton *et al.* 2002) which is another important, yet relatively ignored argument against standardization and in favour of differentiated, fine-tuned policies. Oughton *et al.* (2002) identified more than a decade ago an important paradox in this field: due to the lack of absorptive capacity, less-favoured regions cannot benefit to the same extent from innovation policies in comparison with structurally strong regions, which leads to stronger territorial disparities and hence to eroding cohesion. Their argument is fairly simple yet powerful and based on several indicators that show that richer regions make a better use of policy instruments to stimulate further innovative capacity. For example, they demonstrate that in the European Union (EU) 'almost 70 per cent of the total variation in R&D expenditure across regions is accounted for by variation across regions *within* states, while variation across nation states accounts for around 30 per cent' (Oughton *et al.* 2002: 99 – emphasis in the original). What this means in practice is that the richer regions in the EU have relatively similar performances, while the poorest regions lag behind significantly in their national contexts. Theoretically, they draw on the concept of regional innovation systems (RIS) to argue that explanations for poor performance result from the lack of complementarities between business, education and government policy in the poorest regions. Therefore the problem is not specific to a single element within each region, but rather due to systemic failures.

We will build on this concept to argue that in order to understand better the problem of the regional innovation paradox it is necessary to complement the analysis of systemic failures at regional scale with both the organizational ('below' the region) and the national ('above' the region) level. There are different arguments for including these two extra scales. Regarding the organizational level, research on absorptive capacity (Cohen and Levinthal 1990; Abreu 2011) has shown that there can be important variations between firms regarding their capacity to innovate. According to Cohen and Levinthal (1990) 'prior related knowledge confers an ability to recognize the value of new information, assimilate it, and apply it to commercial ends. These abilities collectively constitute what we call a firm's "absorptive capacity"' (Cohen and Levinthal 1990: 128). While we do not want to deny that the RIS is crucial to have region-wide effects on innovation and development, it is important to emphasize that lagging regions are not homogeneous entities. For example Lorentzen (2006) and Vale and Caldeira (2007), using two very different case studies, showed that in a lagging region the most dynamic firms can connect with key agents in other places to have access to the knowledge that they would probably acquire locally, if they were located in more dynamic territories. Based on our own research, there is evidence that in lagging regions some firms are efficient in using policy instruments to increase innovation capacity. Usually this implies having both the deep technological knowledge that allows firms to engage in R&D projects, but also the extensive knowledge necessary to fulfil policy requirements and manage the expectations of policymakers. Both types of knowledge are important to generate absorptive capacity (Abreu 2011).

The presence of a small number of firms with higher levels of absorptive capacity could be seen as a potential source of change for the whole RIS, since they could be the trigger that unleashes a wave of knowledge accumulation through systemic interaction with other co-located organizations. However, as identified by Tödtling and Trippl (2005), poorer regions often manifest systemic failures in their RIS which is likely to hinder this process. Variation in absorptive capacity among firms in poorer regions therefore poses two important questions: the first is whether those firms that have the capacity to make effective use of policy instruments are well connected with their environment to generate positive knowledge externalities. The second is whether these firms, probably operating in fragmented or less well developed institutional settings, monopolize the use of policy instruments and therefore reinforce their distance to other firms in the same region.

The second level identified above (the national) is equally important, though for a different set of reasons. It might be contradictory to identify the national level as relevant, when as discussed before the main differences in innovation performance are *within* countries and not *between* countries. However, there are both positive and normative arguments that support the inclusion of this level of analysis. The first derives from the central role played by national governments in devising policy, not only for innovation but also in many other areas of government intervention. It is true that in some countries regions have more autonomy to devise policy; however recent research has been unable to find conclusive evidence that strong regional decentralization leads to higher levels of growth in the OECD countries (Ezcurra and Rodríguez-Pose 2013). In practice this means that national institutional variation is likely the most important element explaining different growth rates. On a different study, Percoco (2013) suggested that the main factor explaining different levels of efficiency in regional development are national institutional settings. Both sets of studies point to the continuing relevance of national policies in explaining different rates of economic growth and should lead us to incorporate this level of analysis when explaining dysfunctions at the regional or local levels. The normative arguments in favour of using this scale of analysis are to a great extent a product of these research results. For example at the EU level Barca (2009) suggested a 'place-based' approach to regional development, that is both strongly supportive of incorporating local knowledge in the design of the policy itself, but that also seeks to integrate the different scale of government to ensure good coordination and effectiveness. In what concerns our particular focus, the innovation paradox at the regional level, we argue that to understand systemic failures in some regions it is necessary to analyse them in relation to their national setting. Many key policies, such as those covering education (including higher education), science and technology, industrial development, labour markets and others are primarily devised at the national level, with regions only having a certain amount of input. As a consequence, if we observe deficiencies at the regional level for example in terms of skills, it would be a mistake to take into consideration only the endogenous features of that region.

Summarizing, we have argued that variation in the quality of regional innovation systems is indeed important in explaining the innovation paradox. However, we have also argued that in order to fully understand this phenomenon we have to integrate in our model both the level below the region (organizations) and above the region (the nation). We will now use the case study of the moulds industry in Portugal to illustrate the main points in our theoretical framework.

The innovation paradox revisited: the case of the mould industry in Portuguese regions

In order to develop our argument we will start by presenting a brief contextualization of our case study. We will then proceed with the discussion of empirical results by focusing first on differences between firms in terms of their access to innovation policy, second on how they are partly explained and influenced by broader systemic problems at the regional level, and third discuss the importance of the national institutional environment.

The Portuguese moulds industry for plastic injection has existed in Portugal since the 1940s, as a spin-off from the glass industry, which had been established by royal decree in the eighteenth century. After 1986, when Portugal joined the European Union, its growth rate accelerated exponentially. Currently the sector comprises about 450 SMEs, employing over 7500 workers, and is mostly located around two cities: Marinha Grande and Oliveira de Azemeis (CEFAMOL 2012). Around 90 per cent of its total production is exported, mostly to EU countries. Its main clients are firms in the automobile sector. Annual turnover for the whole sector has remained relatively stable for most of the twenty-first century, with a significant increase in 2012 (CEFAMOL 2012). The same cannot be said, however, for the regions where it is located. Table 8.1 gives us the GDP (measured in power purchasing parities) for different regions in Portugal as a percentage of the GDP in the twenty-seven countries of the EU. Portuguese GDP in 2010 was 80 per cent of the EU average, down from 81 per cent in 2000. The highest concentration of mould firms is in the NUTS 3 region of Pinhal Litoral and the NUTS 2 region of Centro. A smaller concentration of firms is in the NUTS 3 region of Entre Douro e Vouga, part of NUTS 2 region Norte. What this table shows is that despite the stability in the Portuguese moulds industry both regions (at the NUTS 3 level) have seen their relative GDP decline substantially. This discrepancy between the evolution of an important local industry and its

Table 8.1 Gross domestic product at current market prices by NUTS 2 regions measured in power purchasing parities in per cent of EU average, 2000 and 2010

Region NUTS2	*2000*	*2010*
Norte	65	65
Entre Douro e Vouga (NUTS 3)	69	64
Algarve	88	83
Centro	69	67
Pinhal Litoral (NUTS 3)	85	79
Lisboa	114	112
Alentejo	75	74
Região Autónoma dos Açores	68	75
Região Autónoma da Madeira	91	104

Source: EUROSTAT (2013).

surrounding region lends support to the idea that an exclusive emphasis on the regional scale might be misleading.

Regarding the innovation support system for the Portuguese moulds industry, it includes a variety of organizations. At the sectoral level we have CEFAMOL, the association of Portuguese mould makers; CENTIMFE, a technological centre funded by a combination of public and private funds, that supports firms through consultancy and the management of collaborative R&D projects. It is similar to other technological centres working for other sectors in Portugal, both in its funding scheme (public and private) and in its aims (CENTIMFE 2012). And finally CENFIM, a training school offering technical qualification to people who want to work in this sector. At the regional level we find the regional development agency CCDR-C, which has responsibility for implementing central government policy, and several higher education institutions, though some firms have relationships with higher education institutions located outside their region. At the national level we find government agencies such as AICEP and IAPMEI, which are responsible for specific programs directed at firms in the whole country.

Firms and innovation policy

In some of the academic literature about the Portuguese moulds industry, we find a narrative about a dynamic sector, where knowledge and ideas are shared freely through informal contacts (Beira *et al.* 2003; Mota and Castro 2004). However, we found in our research that even among this relatively small group of SMEs there are significant differences in the way they use the RIS support system and policy instruments in general. One relevant example is the participation rates of firms in R&D projects either managed by the technological centre (CENTIMFE) or the ones where the technological centre is a partner. These projects are usually funded by a mixture of private and public funds, including EU funds, and often involve partners in several countries. Table 8.2 shows some data collected by the authors based on information available at CENTIMFE's website. In total there were twenty-one R&D projects listed on the website, and a total of thirty-two companies listed as partners. As Table 8.2 illustrates, only eight of them have participated in more than one project. Iberomoldes, the second biggest mould firm in Portugal (the biggest is Simoldes), clearly dominates with eleven participations – probably relevant is the fact that one of the owners of this firm was the president of the board for CENTIMFE, plus the former president of the association of mould makers (CEFAMOL), of the Forum ManuFuture Portugal and of the International Special Tooling and Machining International.

Table 8.2 Partners in more than one of the projects listed by CENTIMFE

Name of firm	*Number of projects involved*
Iberomoldes	11
Intermolde	5
LN Moldes	4
Vangest	3
F. Ramada	2
Famolde	2
Ferespe	2
Somoltec	2

Source: Author's calculation based on CENTIMFE (2009).

This dominance of a small number of firms is not unique to the moulds industry, as confirmed in an interview with a high-level policymaker:

> The technological centres, created many years ago, have had many difficulties to find clients and in reality they often have three or four big clients in the region where they're located, or sometimes out of it, with whom they work intensively and then there are many other firms that don't use them or use them only sporadically.
>
> *(Advisor to the National Coordinator of the Lisbon Strategy and the Technological Plan; Central Government Body; Author's interview; 01/09/2008)*

What our research demonstrated is that the main reason why there is such a significant difference between firms is variation in absorptive capacity. According to our empirical results and anecdotal evidence about the development of the sector (Beira and Gomes 2007), most firm owners tend to have quite strong technical skills about mould making, but very limited management training. Additionally most of their learning was tacit and on-the-job, with very little incorporation of engineering skills. Therefore there is both a lack of the deep technical knowledge that would allow them to participate in R&D development, and the lack of the extensive knowledge about management that would encourage them to think strategically and invest more in long-term firm development. It is therefore no surprise that among those interviewees whose firms were actively engaged in technological development we found two groups: 1) older owner-managers who had learned tacit skills working for other firms, but who later engaged in formal training, for example at university; 2) younger owner-managers, usually with higher education or at least technical training, who had either created firms recently or inherited them from the original owners (normally the parents). These two groups are not, however, the majority within the sector.

Variation in absorptive capacity between firms also had an impact on the use of other policy instruments, such as those managed by the regional development agency (CCDR-C) or by central government agencies. In interviews with firm owners it was widely mentioned that a small number of companies tended to have privileged access to public innovation funds. This fact was accepted by the policymakers themselves in interviews. However, despite a general perception that these differences were a result of nepotism (which we are not denying could play some role in this process) the main reason was as before explained by absorptive capacity. Those firms that had both the knowledge resources to understand and participate in R&D programmes, together with the knowledge and resources to deal with the administrative issues involved in managing public funds, were more likely to access them. The more often they accessed these funds the more experience they gained, therefore generating a cycle of knowledge accumulation that gave them an advantage in subsequent rounds of public support. From the perspective of policymakers, engaging with these privileged firms was seen as preferable, because they were more likely to deliver results that could be presented to the organisations that scrutinise the use of public money. This point was acknowledged by policymakers at both the regional and the national level who complained about the general lack of skills in Portuguese small firms and their lack of capacity to manage complex projects.

The regional level

Differences in absorptive capacity among firms translate into a combination of fragmentation and institutional weakness at the regional level. What we mean by the region can have multiple meanings in this context. If we refer to the functional regions where these firms are located, then the RIS would be constituted mainly by the sectoral support system, together with the informal (or cultural) setting that frames its functioning. Institutional weakness was mostly the result of very little engagement from a significant number of economic agents, which makes institutions such as CENTIMFE both financially weaker and also less capable of having a significant impact on the sector as a whole. At the more informal level, the fact that some firms are more effective in taking advantage of CENTIMFE or other organizations reinforces the lack of trust that is present in the sector. It is true that the Portuguese moulds industry is known for having strong informal networks, between owners and also between workers that support the exchange of knowledge and ideas. But as most interviewees admitted, these very rarely translated into active collaboration. On the contrary, interviewees would only work closely with a small number of people with whom they had developed strong personal relationships over the years.

At the level of administrative regions, it is slightly more difficult to draw conclusions. As Markusen (1994) warned two decades ago, it is important to be very cautious when moving between different levels of analysis, since what is true for a firm or group of firms is not necessarily true for the whole region where they are located. This is definitely the case in the Portuguese context. Regional development agencies are for example organized at the NUTS 2 level, but at this scale we find highly heterogeneous regions, with many different industries and localities with different development paths. Below that level there are no public authorities with capacity to participate actively in economic development policies, even if some municipalities may sometimes collaborate with the private sector in specific projects. Nonetheless, what we found in our research is that the general issue of variation in absorptive capacity has a significant impact at this level also. Both for regional development agencies, and for other relevant institutions such as universities, there is a certain difficulty in involving large numbers of economic agents. There tends to be a small number of firms with whom these institutions actively engage, making the system highly biased towards them. This fragmentation is then combined with a high level of informality, which is partly a result of institutional deficiencies at the national level (as will be discussed in the next section) but also of the lack of competencies in private (and public) organizations. This lack of competencies encourages policymakers to work with a small number of trusted people rather than trying to engage with different ones. The following statement neatly summarizes many of the points we are making here:

> Generally speaking there is a good regional innovation system, but it works on an informal basis. And I have doubts that it would work better if we formalized it. The

problem is that formality is an obligation and because it's an obligation it's frustrating, because you're often working for the photograph. Besides, its informal character gives us a lot of flexibility, a lot of immediate responses. Because more than an institutional connection there is a personal connection, which makes things happen faster. On the other hand if there was more formalization, the rights, duties and obligations would be clearer. So we have actually tried to make it more formal. Regarding the companies there are those that are usually interested and tend to participate and those that don't pay much attention to what we do. It's normal to see in the private sector the same lack of competencies that we see in the rest of the country.

(Assistant Manager in the Commission for the Coordination and Regional Development of the Centro Region; Regional Development Agency; Author's Interview; 22/10/2008)

In this case study we argued that variation in firms' absorptive capacity had an impact on the functioning of the RIS. But crucially, we must not forget that a fragmented and weak RIS means that this lack of capacity at firm level was not addressed systemically. It also meant that the benefits enjoyed by the small number of firms who actively participated in these projects did not spillover as swiftly as if there were stronger mechanisms for sharing results. Therefore, more than privileging the firm level of analysis, we emphasize that there are multiple feedback mechanisms that must exist in order to have a strong regional innovation system. The lack of these mechanisms is both created by variation among firms, and is also responsible for the fact that this variation is not addressed. We are as a result arguing that both scales of analysis are important, and must be understood as complementary and mutually reinforcing. They are also ultimately influenced by the wider institutional environment, particularly the rules and norms set by the nation state.

The national level

The financing of policy is a key strategic dimension, because those who have the money have the capacity to influence public policy tremendously

(Coordinator of the Quadro de Referência Estratégico Nacional (QREN);1 Public Policy organisation; Author's interview; 09/07/2008).

The continuing relevance of the nation state in policy design and resource allocation must be taken into consideration to explain some of the underlying characteristics shaping this RIS and the Portuguese moulds industry. As the previous quote illustrates, the control of financial resources is crucial in policymaking, and in Portugal the government remains highly concentrated at the national level. We would in particular emphasize two areas of national policy that are relevant to our case study: the first, not directly related to innovation policy, is the persistent lack of skills in the Portuguese society. This affects everyone, including business owners, and can only be explained as a result of long-term educational policy (or its absence), which is mostly defined by the central government. Failure at this level helps to explain why so many SMEs in the moulds industry, and in Portugal in general, are led by individuals with only basic qualifications. The educational level of the owners or managers is particularly important for small firms, because these organizations are less likely to have specialized departments that could for example participate in R&D development.

The second area of national policy relevant for our article is the combination of industrial policy and innovation policy, which as mentioned at the beginning of this chapter has been converging in many countries, including Portugal. For example between 2005 and 2011 one of the national government's flagship policies was the Technological Plan, whose objective was to reconvert the Portuguese economy through an investment in knowledge and innovation. According to senior level policymakers interviewed for this case study, firm support in Portugal has changed significantly over the last ten to fifteen years. Whereas in the 1990s policy actions were often dispersed through many small investments, which both limited their impact and created some cases of rent-seeking behavior, more recently the objective has been to concentrate investment in the high growth sector and firms. This story was corroborated by firm owners, who in their interviews confirmed that policy support had indeed changed in this direction, a move that was generally appreciated.

The downside to this process is that the demands made on firms in terms of managing the application and use of these funds has become too onerous for most, except for the bigger ones. This tendency reinforces the differentiation between firms, but also the fragmentation at the RIS level, since as mentioned previously it is a source of distrust and resentment for those who feel that the attribution of these funds is not fair. Another potential problem is that as described in much research on economic geography, a local economic agglomeration is similar to an ecosystem, with each component playing a role in the aggregate performance. The concentration of resources on a few key firms may make sense from a policy point of view, especially in order to ensure that public funds are used with maximum impact. However, in the long-term it may contribute to an erosion of competitiveness among smaller firms, whose existence is important to sustain the sector as a whole.

Conclusions

In this chapter we have first described the surge of regional innovation policy and then focused on one particular shortcoming of these policies that has received relatively little attention: the innovation paradox (Oughton *et al.* 2002). It refers to the observed fact that lagging regions have least capacities to make effective use of the policy instruments created to increase innovation potential. We have used the case study of the Portuguese moulds industry not only to analyse in detail how the innovation paradox can be observed empirically, but also to show that it is time to revisit it. On the basis of that case study and in line with what Lagendijk (2011) has recently suggested, we see three ways out of the innovation paradox. First, we need to develop a realistic approach to opportunities in structurally weak regions, which means that in these kind of regions we cannot expect highly innovative high-tech industries to emerge. Instead, the focus should be on realistic opportunities and in that sense smart specialization might be a good strategy to follow. Second, we need to avoid looking at the region as a bounded, relatively closed economic entity (Hassink and Klaerding 2012). By having a relational, unbounded view of the regional economy, which includes analyses of the integration of the regional economy in both national and international research networks, as well as its position in global production networks, we disclose development opportunities that lie outside of the region. Third, from a governance perspective, a vertical, multilevel governance model is necessary, in addition to a horizontal (regional) model of coordination and collaboration. Regional innovation policy should be an integral part of the multilevel governance approach to innovation. The effectiveness of innovation policy, particularly in structurally weak regions, results from the interaction between these scales of activity. We would caution against reifying one of these levels, and instead emphasize their interdependence (Lagendijk 2011).

Notes

1 In English: National Strategic Reference Framework – determines the national strategy for the distribution of EU Strategic and Cohesion funds.

Bibliography

Abreu, M., 2011: Absorptive capacity in a regional context. In: P. Cooke (Ed.): *Handbook of Regional Innovation and Growth*. Cheltenham: Edward Elgar, pp. 211–221.

Asheim, B.T., Isaksen, A., Nauwelaers, C. and Tödtling, F. (eds), 2003: *Regional Innovation Policy for Small–Medium Enterprises*. Cheltenham: Edward Elgar.

Barca, F., 2009: An agenda for a reformed cohesion policy. A place-based approach to meeting European Union challenges and expectations. Commission, European. Brussels. Available online at www.europarl.europa.eu/meetdocs/2009_2014/documents/regi/dv/barca_report_/barca_report_en.pdf (accessed 24 April 2014).

Barca, F., McCann, P. and Rodriguez-Pose, A., 2012: The case for regional development intervention: place-based versus place-neutral approaches. *Journal of Regional Science* 52, pp. 134–152.

Beira, E. and Gomes, N., 2007: Indústria de moldes no Norte de Portugal. PROTAGONISTAS uma colecção de testemunhos. CENTIMFE. Oliveira dos Azeméis.

Beira, E., Crespo, C., Gomes, N. and Menezes, J., 2003: Dos moldes à engenharia do produto, a trajectória de um cluster. In: Working papers 'Mercados e Negócios' TSI WP 34.

CEFAMOL, 2012: Situação actual da indústria portuguesa de moldes. CEFAMOL. Marinha Grande. Available online at www.cefamol.pt/cefamol/pt/Cefamol_IndustriaMoldes/Situacao_Actual/(accessed 28 April 2014).

CENTIMFE, 2012: Technological Center for the Mouldmaking, Special Tooling and Plastics Industries. Available online at www.centimfe.com/centimfe/index_html_en (accessed 28 April 2014).

Cohen, W.M. and Levinthal, D.A., 1990: Absorptive capacity: a new perspective on learning and innovation. *Administrative Science Quarterly* 35(1), pp. 128–152.

Cooke, P. and Morgan, K., 1998: *The Associational Economy: Firms, regions, and innovation*. Oxford: Oxford University Press.

Cooke, P., Heidenreich, M. and Braczyk, H.-J. (eds), 2004: *Regional Innovation Systems: The role of governances in a globalized world*. London, New York: Routledge.

Dodgson, M. and Bessant, J., 1996: *Effective Innovation Policy: A New Approach*. London, Boston, MA: International Thomson Business Press.

Ezcurra, R. and Rodríguez-Pose, A., 2013: Political Decentralization, Economic Growth and Regional Disparities in the OECD. *Regional Studies* 47(3), pp. 388–401.

Fritsch, M. and Stephan, A., 2005: Regionalization of innovation policy – Introduction to the special issue. *Research Policy* 34, pp. 1123–1127.

Hassink, R., 1996: Technology transfer agencies and regional economic development. *European Planning Studies* 4(2), pp. 167–184.

Hassink, R. and Berg, S.-H., 2014: Regional innovation support systems and technopoles. In: Oh, D.S. and Phillips, F.Y. (eds): *Technopolis: Best practices for science & technology cities*. Heidelberg: Springer, pp. 43–65.

Hassink, R. and Klaerding, C., 2012: The end of the learning region as we knew it; towards learning in space. *Regional Studies* 46, 1055–1066.

Hassink, R. and Lagendijk, A., 2001: The dilemmas of interregional institutional learning. *Environment and Planning C: Government and Policy* 19, pp. 65–84.

Lagendijk, A., 2011: Regional innovation policy between theory and practice. In P. Cooke (ed.): *Handbook of Regional Innovation and Growth*. Cheltenham: Edward Elgar, pp. 597–608.

Lorentzen, A., 2006: The geography of knowledge sourcing: a case study of Polish manufacturing enterprises. *European Planning Studies* 15(4), pp. 467–486.

Lovering, J., 1999: Theory led by policy: the inadequacies of the 'new regionalism' (illustrated from the case of Wales). *International Journal of Urban and Regional Research* 23, pp. 379–395.

McCann, P. and Ortega-Argilés, R., 2013: Modern regional innovation policy. *Cambridge Journal of Regions, Economy and Society* 6, pp. 187–216.

McCann, P. and Ortega-Argilés, R., 2015: Smart specialization, regional growth and applications to European Union cohesion policy. *Regional Studies* 49:8, 129–1302.

Markusen, A., 1994: Studying regions by studying firms. *The Professional Geographer* 46(4), pp. 477–490.
Marques, P. M. F., 2011: Power in territorial innovation systems: a case study of the Portuguese moulds industry (Doctoral dissertation, University of Newcastle upon Tyne).
Martin, R. and Sunley, P., 2003: Deconstructing clusters: chaotic concept or policy panacea? *Journal of Economic Geography* 3, pp. 5–36.
Mota, João Q. and Castro, L.M.D., 2004: Industrial agglomerations as localised networks: the case of the Portuguese mould industry. *Environment and Planning A* 36, pp. 263–278.
Nauwelaers, C. and Wintjes, R., 2003: Towards a new paradigm for innovation policy? In: Asheim, B., Isaksen, A., Nauwelaers, C., Tödtling, F. (Eds.) *Regional Innovation Policy for Small-Medium Enterprises*, pp. 193–220. Cheltenham: Edward Elgar.
Organisation for Economic Cooperation and Development (OECD), 2007: *Competitive Regional Clusters*. Paris: OECD.
Organisation for Economic Cooperation and Development (OECD), 2010: *Regional Development Policies in OECD Countries*. Paris: OECD.
Organisation for Economic Cooperation and Development (OECD), 2011: *Regions and Innovation Policy, OECD Reviews of Regional Innovation*. Paris: OECD.
Oughton, C., Landabaso, M. and Morgan, K., 2002: The regional innovation paradox: innovation policy and industrial policy. *Journal of Technology Transfer* 27, pp. 97–110.
Paquet, G., 1998: Techno-nationalism and meso innovation systems. In: Anderson, R. *et al.* (eds): *Innovation Systems in a Global Context: The North American experience*. Montreal: McGill-Queen's University Press, pp. 58–75.
Percoco, M., 2013: Strategies of regional development in European regions: are they efficient? *Cambridge Journal of Regions, Economy and Society* 6, pp. 303–318.
Prange, H., 2008: Explaining varieties of regional innovation policies in Europe. *European Urban and Regional Studies*, 15, pp. 39–52.
Tödtling, F. and Trippl, M., 2005: One size fits all? Towards a differentiated regional innovation policy. *Research Policy* 34(1), pp. 203–1219.
Vale, M. and Caldeira, J., 2007: Proximity and knowledge governance in localized production systems: the footwear industry in the north region of Portugal. *European Planning Studies* 15(4), pp. 531–548.

9

THE ROLE OF UNIVERSITIES IN THE EVOLUTION OF TECHNOLOGY-BASED ECONOMIC DEVELOPMENT POLICIES IN THE UNITED STATES

Christopher Briem and Vijai Singh

Introduction

By the end of the twentieth century, technology-based economic development (TBED) programs had become a nearly ubiquitous tool for public sector economic development policies in the United States. TBED programs are not limited to federal policies but have become the key element of most state level economic development efforts. In addition, innumerable local public initiatives across the nation are based on promoting technology to foster regional economic competitiveness and growth. Publicly financed TBED programs focus on the attraction, retention, and growth of advanced technology-based firms and industries. Expanded technology-focused policy efforts have fostered growing partnerships between the public sector and institutions of higher education, especially those with expertise in research. Some reports go so far as to say that regional research centers and institutes are "undisputedly the most important factor in incubating high-tech industries" (DeVol 1999; State Science and Technology Institute 2006, p. 13). Unlike anytime in the past, American research universities have developed extensive and formal collaborations with both state and local governments, making them primary partners in local economic development policy in regions across the nation.

Today, virtually all U.S. research universities attempt to build successful technology transfer programs aimed at commercialization of university developed intellectual property, with a goal of generating licensing fees and revenues based on equity appreciation. These efforts are complementary to public efforts broadly geared toward the promotion of entrepreneurship and firm creation. As a result, many university programs are more closely integrated with public efforts promoting regional economic growth than they ever were in the past. This paper traces the evolution of government policies that have facilitated the new and growing role of research universities in public sector economic development policies. This expanded role of universities results not only from changing priorities within academic institutions, but from deliberate shifts in economic development priorities at both state and federal government levels.

Changing fiscal conditions in higher education have significantly altered the way universities view technology commercialization. The potential for generating private revenue from university generated research is a relatively recent phenomenon in American higher education. These efforts were catalyzed by the passage of federal Bayh-Dole legislation in 1980 which dramatically shifted the incentives for universities to promote technology transfer of publicly financed research. The new legislation allowed institutions of higher education to benefit financially from the commercialization of publicly funded research in ways they were mostly precluded from previously. Accelerated university-based technology transfer efforts have coincided with a dramatic shift in the focus of economic development programs promoted by all levels of government in the U.S. State governments and, in particular, have moved beyond older 'smokestack chasing' programs almost exclusively devoted to attracting manufacturing enterprises. Many of these efforts have been supplanted by a vast expansion of public programs targeting smaller and technology intensive industries.

Research universities are almost always a partner of public TBED programs. Research universities are typically often the largest regional concentrations of research and development, but they play a crucial role in both workforce development and new company formation. TBED programs emphasize the creation of new companies based on advanced technologies, precisely the goal of many university-based programs. After a broad description of what constitutes TBED policies, the paper will describe the independent histories of science and technology policy at the federal and state government levels in the U.S. The paper will then review the impact of Bayh-Dole legislation and the changing role of technology transfer within research universities and how it has changed university attitudes toward commercialization. In conclusion, the paper covers more recent trends in TBED policies and the expansion of local government efforts focusing on technology-based programs.

Defining technology-based economic development

What differentiates TBED programs from broader economic development policies of state and local governments? TBED initiatives exist as a subgroup of policy efforts aimed at promoting economic growth. The goals of economic development programs vary but usually concentrate on the promotion of employment and income growth and bolstering public sector tax revenues. TBED efforts are typically implemented by public or nonprofit sectors organizations, or hybrid organizations that incorporate both public and nonprofit characteristics, with the intent of influencing private sector investment.

How TBED policies promote investment varies from program to program. The current focus of TBED efforts has been characterized as 'influencing, either directly or indirectly, private sector activity specifically in high-tech or technology intensive companies and industries' (Phillips and Pittman 2002). A myriad of tools has been developed to promote the ultimate goal of increasing investment and economic outcomes: direct marketing can be used to recruit new technology companies into a region; subsidies for technology incubators facilitating firm creation; direct financial support such as loan guarantees can be provided to existing technology companies for expansion; indirectly, local governments can finance specific infrastructure that encourages growth of technology industries.

The specific tools used do not distinguish TBED programs as much as the specific industries targeted. TBED efforts attempt to foster growth in technology intensive industries. The actual definition of what constitutes "high technology" industries lacks consistent definition. Many programs focus on firms engaged in early stage research and development, regardless of industry. Because this research often starts as university-based research, governments attempt to partner with academic institutions to facilitate the movement of academic research into commercial products and services. These collaborative efforts are almost always characterized as a public–private partnerships (PPP). Typical TBED effort brings together business, government, foundation, and not-for-profit sectors toward the goal of building fast-growing industry clusters.

U.S. federal government's role in technology policy

The interaction between universities and the U.S. federal government changed dramatically over the twentieth century. Through the nineteenth century, federal government support for institutions of higher education was limited or indirect, such as support for the creation of land grant colleges via the passage of the Morrill Land-Grant Act of 1862. Over the same period, the federal government played little role in funding research activity at academic institutions. Prior to World War II, the bulk of research in the U.S. was directly financed by the private sector. Federal impact on university-based research expanded rapidly during World War II. A National Defense Research Committee (NDRC) was formed in 1940 to organize civilian scientists working on problems of national defense (Bush 1941). From that emerged the Office of Science, Research and Development (OSRD) under the direction of Vannevar Bush, which became the primary mechanism for federal support of university-based research funding. By 1945 over 83 per cent of all support for research in the natural sciences was coming from the federal government (Douglass 1999). After WWII, the federal government continued its role as the dominant sponsor of university-based research, surpassing the private sector as the largest sponsor of research at academic institutions.

The federal government's new role was by design. Vannevar Bush's 1945 report, *Science: The Endless Frontier*, called for a permanent centralized role of federal government in science funding. The report, even only partially implemented, was considered a seminal document shaping postwar federal science and technology policy, which led to the creation of the U.S. National Science Foundation in 1950. Federal science policy as envisioned by Bush and others did not emphasize the commercialization of new technologies to promote economic development. During the war, scientific advancement was a tool deemed essential to furthering military efforts that were increasingly technology-intensive.

Greater federal funding of scientific research followed from the expansion of Cold War tensions between the United States and the Soviet Union in the 1950s. Federal efforts to support university research and education accelerated further following the Soviet Union's launching of the Sputnik satellite in October 1957. The public perception that the United States was losing technological competitiveness with its Cold War rival led directly to several significant new initiatives to improve not only scientific education but research production in the U.S. The National Defense Education Act (NDEA), passed in 1958, was premised with a 'Declaration of Policy' that stated: 'an educational emergency exists and requires action by the federal government. Assistance will come from Washington to help develop as rapidly as possible those skills essential to the national security' (Forest 2002). The NDEA included support for loans to college students, the improvement of science, mathematics, and foreign language instruction in elementary and secondary schools, graduate fellowships, foreign language and area studies, and vocational–technical training.

Particular regions experienced significant economic impacts as a result of these defense focused expenditures. The concentration of defense and aerospace firms in Los Angeles benefited the regional economy of Southern California. Massachusetts, and in particular the Massachusetts Institute of Technology (MIT), garnered sizable concentrations of federal research grants, later catalyzing technology driven economic growth along Massachusetts' Route 128. Sizable federal expenditures in research and development benefited Stanford University and the Silicon Valley area of California.

Nonetheless, the Cold War goals of federal expenditures were focused on scientific outcomes, not regional economic impacts. Where regional economies grew as a result of concentrated federal research expenditures, the result was more incidental than intentional. In the U.S., intentional federal involvement in regional economic development has generally been limited to support of the Tennessee Valley Authority (TVA) and to a lesser extent the Appalachian Regional Commission (ARC). Both of these programs focused on historically underdeveloped areas. Both regions remained minimally impacted by federal science and technology expenditures in the decades after World War II.

Because the primary motivation for increased federal support of academic research was not economic development, it is not surprising that policies did not encourage the efficient transfer of new technology to the private sector. In addition to university-based research, a core of federal labs expanded during the Cold War. These organizations were not charged with facilitating technology transfer into the private sector. As a result, federal labs placed virtually no emphasis on encouraging regional economic growth. Before 1980, it was generally considered illegitimate for federal labs to even try and provide economic support for the regions where they were located (Hill 1994).

Inconsistent federal policies for intellectual property inhibited efforts to move new innovations out of the laboratory. Existing federal law in the decades following World War II required that the federal government retain licensing rights to all research developed with federal funding, whether or not those developments were made in federal labs, universities, or private companies. Partner institutions lacked incentives to pursue the commercialization of research they were producing. As a result, the level of new innovations directly transferred into the commercial sector was minimal. Before 1980 only 5 per cent of government patents were eventually licensed (Schacht 2009).

State and local economic development policies

Regional economic development policies in the U.S. have developed independently from federal policy from the very birth of the nation. For much of the nation's history, state level economic development policies were dedicated primarily to the promotion of manufacturing industries and were often in direct competition with each other. Federalism as the defining construct of the American political system has inspired economic competition between states dating back at least to 1791. That year, the U.S. Secretary of the Treasury Alexander Hamilton began efforts to locate a new manufacturing corporation in what would later be named Patterson, New Jersey. The new quasi-public entity, named the Society for Establishing Useful Manufactures (SUM), was chartered as a state-favored enterprise, exempted from certain state taxes by the New Jersey legislature. Arguably, SUM was the first public–private partnership in U.S. history. That early tax incentive soon generated complaints from legislators in neighboring Pennsylvania who observed that the "powers, rights and privileges, given to this company would be, in their operation, very injurious to this state as well as other states" (Seneca et al. 2004, p. 2). State economic development programs remained mostly independent of federal policies, and often fiercely in competition with each other, through the next two centuries.

The state of Mississippi accelerated publicly financed competition for commercial investment when it passed the Mississippi Industrial Act in 1936. The act permitted communities in the state to issue Industrial Revenue Bonds (IRBs) to support private sector investment. IRBs were generally offered to firms relocating establishments into targeted regions. The use of public bonds lowered borrowing costs for investors. The use of IRBs and similar publicly funded financial incentives expanded after World War II, but the targets of these industry attraction efforts were almost always existing manufacturing enterprises (Mead 2005).

Major shifts in state level economic development efforts began in the 1980s. Plosila (2004) traces the development of state level economic development policies in the United States. Through the late 1970s, state policies continued to be concentrated on "brick-and-mortar issues," including: infrastructure development; subsidies for land acquisition and building costs; and property tax abatement and support through regulatory processes. These efforts focused almost exclusively on influencing the site selection or relocation for large industrial facilities. States directly competed against each other for the highest priority projects. The epitome of these practices arguably came in 1975 when the Volkswagen Corporation of Germany announced its intention to build a new automobile manufacturing plant in the U.S. Multiple states engaged in a fierce competition to attract the new automobile manufacturing facility. The Commonwealth of Pennsylvania "won" the site selection decision in 1976. A new plant was built and production began in 1978. The decision was facilitated by a then unprecedented $78 million in tax abatements and publicly funded incentives provided directly and indirectly to the corporation.

Where there was state level science policy during the 1970s, it was generally not focused on economic development efforts. The U.S. Department of Commerce and the U.S. National Science Foundation (NSF) had encouraged states to establish high level science advisor positions in the early 1960s. Again Plosila, who himself served as a senior policy advisor to Pennsylvania Governor Richard Thornburg in the early 1980s, notes that these advisors and foundations were primarily interested in broader scientific issues with little focus on economic development:[1]

> Issues about talent, the role of higher education, the building of entrepreneurial cultures and related issues deemed more important today were rarely considered components of state economic development policy and programs through the post-World War II period until the early 1980s.
>
> *(Plosila 2004, p. 114)*

Through the 1980s state economic development programs moved away from what was considered "first wave" economic development policies that emphasized the relocation of manufacturing facilities—policies characterized as "smokestack chasing." Much of the shift was precipitated by the slow economic growth of the period. Severe national recessions between January and July of 1980 and between July 1981 and November 1982 had concentrated impacts on traditional industrial areas. Older economic development practices focused almost exclusively on attracting manufacturing enterprises were seen as ineffective, given the contraction of the manufacturing sector concentrated in specific regions.

To understand the independence of state and federal economic development efforts it is important to note that the United States broadly lacks structural adjustment policies to deal with major regional economic shifts. Addressing regional economic downturns is mostly left to state and local governments. To deal with the multiple recessions of the 1980s, states developed new programs to promote economic competitiveness. Instead of focusing on attracting large industrial plants in traditional industries, new policies began to focus on smaller firms in emerging growth sectors. States were most interested in attracting firms in emerging technology-based industries. New emphasis was also placed on growing new firms and encouraging entrepreneurial activity. These new policies broadly constituted what has been called the "second wave" of economic development policies (Eisinger 1988).

Despite little experience in leveraging technology, states rapidly shifted economic development efforts. In January 1981, the state of California proposed a $23 million program focused on small innovative companies. That same year the Ben Franklin Partnership program was authorized by the state of Pennsylvania. In February 1982, the new Ben Franklin program evaluated applications from seven proposed consortiums to establish regional Advanced Technology Centers. At its inception, the program had four major project thrusts: Research and Development, Entrepreneurial Development, Workforce Training, and University-based Centers of Excellence. Research and Development projects focused on new product/process development or the improvement of existing products and processes. The majority of these projects had a university partner that performed the actual research and then transferred the knowledge or prototype to the private sector for application (Ben Franklin Technology Partnership 2013). Other states soon followed with similar programs, including the New Jersey Advanced Technology Centers and the Thomas Edison Program in Ohio. Most of these emerging programs emphasized product development from applied research taking place within existing research institutions, typically universities.

A fundamental difference between emerging state-level TBED efforts and older economic development programs was an emphasis on smaller firms, including those at the earliest stages of formation. To encourage new company formation, states engaged for the first time in direct financial support for seed, venture, and working capital programs supporting private sector enterprises. These efforts were aimed directly at encouraging the commercialization of research likely to be generated at existing research institutions. This directly translated into greater cooperation between local governments and research focused universities.

By 1983 there were at least 153 state-level technology programs that were intended to stimulate the growth of existing technology-dependent businesses and new businesses (United States Office of Technology Assessment 1984). The attraction of technology-based initiatives stemmed from the perception of continuing growth and potential for employment and job creation. These policy efforts focused on investments in applied research and development, venture capital, science parks, and business incubators (Rosenfeld 2002). New state policies evolved including expanded use of research and development tax credits. The state of Minnesota adopted what is considered the first state level Research and Development tax credit in 1982. The new program was enabled by the federal Research and Experimentation Tax Credit authorized in the Economic Recovery Act of 1981. Over forty states offered similar tax credits over the subsequent thirty years (Miller and Richard 2010).

State interest in TBED programs accelerated just as the federal government shifted the legal framework for commercialization of publicly financed research. Almost all of these new programs were focused on taking advantage of university-based research originally funded in large part by federal research initiatives. The dramatic shift in state and local policies could not have taken place without the enactment of new federal legislation which encouraged the commercialization of publicly financed research for the first time.

Universities and Bayh-Dole legislation

The lack of effective federal policies promoting technology development became a growing political issue by the end of the 1970s. Through the 1970s critics found limited cohesion to federal technology policies and a general disinclination to support the commercialization of technology (Feller 1992). Some of the largest roadblocks to technology commercialization were federal rules constraining the ownership of virtually all intellectual property resulting from federal funding. Slowing national economic growth through the 1970s motivated new legislative efforts to facilitate faster commercialization of technologies being developed at U.S. federal labs, or at universities with federal funding (Stevens 2004).

U.S. Senators Robert Dole and Birch Bayh led legislative efforts to redefine the federal government's role in technology transfer. Their efforts resulted in the passage of the Bayh–Dole Patent and Trademark Act of 1980. The act gave institutions receiving federal grants the right to retain title to the inventions that resulted. The new legislation had pronounced impacts on how academic institutions managed research activities. This reassignment of intellectual property rights fundamentally changed the role of universities in the process of commercialization of new technologies. The new legislation enabled universities, industries, and individual researchers working on publicly funded projects to benefit financially from their inventions. The Bayh–Dole Act hastened the entry of many American universities into patenting and licensing activities that most formerly avoided as a matter of policy (Mowery and Ziedonis 2000). The bill may have assisted the geographic spread of university–industry knowledge transfers and contributed to commercialization of research products and establishment of new start-up firms (Balasubramanian and Sakakibara 2005).

In addition to the passage of the Bayh–Dole Act, other legislative efforts attempted to further open federally funded research, including research generated within federal labs. In 1983, a federal Laboratory Review Panel chaired by David Packard, Chairman and Co-founder of the Hewlett Packard Corporation, concluded:

> The United States can no longer afford the luxury of isolating its government laboratories from university and industry laboratories. Already endowed with the best research institutions in the world, this country is increasingly challenged in its military and economic competitiveness. The national interest demands that the federal laboratories collaborate with universities and industry to ensure continued advances in scientific knowledge and its translation into useful technology. The federal laboratories must be more responsive to national needs.
>
> *(Gross and Allen 2003, p. 23)*

Through the decade, federal policy promoting technology transfer was dramatically altered by a series of new legislation. The 1980 Stevenson–Wydler Technology Innovation Act mandated the creation of a technology transfer office in federal agencies and required federal laboratories to facilitate the transfer of federally owned and originated technology to state and local governments and the private sector. In 1982, the Small Business Innovation Research (SBIR) program was established. The National Cooperative Research Act of 1984 encouraged U.S. firms to collaborate on generic, precompetitive research by establishing a rule of reason for evaluating the antitrust implications of research joint ventures. The 1986 Federal Technology Transfer Act amended the earlier Stevenson–Wydler Act authorizing cooperative research and development agreements between federal laboratories and other entities, including state agencies. The 1988 Omnibus Trade and Competitiveness Act established the Competitiveness Policy Council to develop recommendations for national strategies and specific policies to enhance industrial competitiveness. The act also created the Advanced Technology Program and the Manufacturing Technology Centers within the National Institute for Standards and Technology to help U.S. companies become more competitive. The 1989 National Competitiveness Technology Transfer Act further amended the Stevenson–Wydler Act to allow government-owned, contractor-operated laboratories to enter into Cooperative Research and Development Agreements (CRADA) with the private sector (Heisey et al. 2006).

Collectively the broad set of new legislation shifted the relationship between the federal government and educational institutions. While the Bayh–Dole Act itself has been called "one of the most enlightened pieces of economic legislation of the 20th century" (*Economist* 2002), its adoption in 1980 was not without critics. Early criticism centered around the perception that publicly funded assets were being "given away" to the private sector. Those criticisms have quieted over time, but arguments continue over the impact of commercial ventures within academic institutions. The emphasis on protecting intellectual property is considered by some antithetical to the norms of open science.[2] And while some consider any commercial focus inappropriate for academic institutions, others actively seek to expand the role of universities in creating economic relevance for the communities they serve, to the point of calling economic development a "fourth mission" for universities after teaching, research, and outreach (Geiger and Sá 2009).

University attitudes toward technology transfer

Spurred by the Bayh–Dole Act and other factors, the attitude within American universities toward commercialization of research has shifted dramatically since World War II when participation in federally funded projects was seen as a wartime exigency. Even some of the most significant inventions resulting directly from university-based research were rarely patented. For example, when Jonas Salk developed an effective vaccine for polio in 1946, the new medicine was not patented.[3]

Even when university researchers wanted to commercialize their research, opposition within academic institutions often prevented collaboration with the private sector. At one extreme, university attitudes bordered on disdain for commercial efforts, even those spawned from academic research. One early example comes from the history of the ENIAC project at the University of Pennsylvania. The project was responsible for the development of the first digital computer during World War II. Following the war, the two engineers most responsible for the ENIAC, electrical engineers J. Presper Eckert and John Mauchly, saw the commercial potential for digital computing and sought to extend their research within the university. Senior academics argued at the time not only against the commercialization of computers, but against the continuation of the digital computing project at the university (Lasar 2011). That rejection prompted Eckert and Mauchly to independently found the Eckert-Mauchly Computer Corporation (EMCC) in 1947, which after being acquired by the Remmington Rand Corporation, went on to produce the first UNIVAC, the world's first successfully marketed commercial computer in 1951 (Ceruzzi 1999).

Despite a vast expansion of federal research expenditures after World War II, the linkage between universities and regional economic development efforts remained limited. Berman (2012) has traced the broad history of academic science and its interaction with economic development policies. Most telling is the experience of Otto Kerner, the Governor of Illinois in 1961, who asked the University of Illinois that year to study its impact on economic development within the state in 1961. The university was mostly confused by the request, replying that "certain basic factors are far more important in attracting industry and in plant location decisions, and therefore in stimulating regional economic growth, than the advantages offered by universities."

University–industry partnerships began to evolve in the late 1970s. An experimental National Science Foundation effort incentivized the collaboration of engineering focused universities with specific industries. Programs at the California Institute of Technology, Carnegie Mellon

University, Rensselaer Polytechnic Institute, and the University of Delaware started and met with varying levels of success[4] (Berman 2012). State governments soon became partners in the growing collaboration between universities and industry. One of the earlier efforts came in 1978 in Arizona. That year advanced technology firms based in the state approached then Governor Bruce Babbitt with a plan to collaboratively strengthen engineering education at Arizona State University. The impetus for the plan was a need for more technology workers. The effort reflected an early shift toward workforce development in economic development policies.

University–industry collaboration produced a new revenue stream for universities. Many universities were receiving millions of dollars in licensing fees based on university research by the end of the 1980s (Dill 1995). Revenue generation from university-based technology transfer programs are increasing and have the potential to become much more significant in the future. Revenues accrued to universities result from research performed years earlier. In December 2012, a lawsuit brought by Carnegie Mellon University (CMU) against the Marvell Technology Group resulted in a $1.17 billion verdict in favor of the university. The litigation alleged infringement of integrated-circuit patents derived from research at the university completed in 1996.[5] The potential award could reach beyond $3 billion.

Continuing evolution of TBED policies

From 1980 forward the expansion of public TBED programs has been unabated. At the state level, aggressive strategies continue to be pursued to attract technology ventures by offering various types of incentives including financial support. One particular focus has been efforts to grow clusters of biotechnology or life science-based industry clusters. By 2001 it was estimated that forty-one of fifty U.S. states had state-level policies focused on the promotion of biotechnology and life sciences alone (Biotechnology Industry Organization 2001).

One of the most noteworthy aspects of state level TBED programs in the United States remains how independent state efforts remain from both federal programs and each other. The absence of federal leadership in early TBED efforts was not seen as a disadvantage at the state and local level. By the 1990s, a consensus among state policy makers was that the federal government should not take a lead in emerging technology-based economic development efforts and instead should play a supporting role to state, local, and regional efforts (Thornburgh 1998). In 1992, the Carnegie Commission on Science, Technology, and Government reaffirmed the decentralized role of states in promoting a national innovation system. The commission did not encourage any greater federal role, instead encouraging states to work together to establish an interstate compact identifying the "policies [that] work best in a decentralized and variegated nation" (United States President's Council of Advisors on Science and Technology 2004).

Into the twenty-first century, the federal role in local economic development efforts remains minimal and legacy efforts have diminished. One of the first federal agencies focused on regional economic development, the Economic Development Administration (EDA) formed in 1965 has been described as a "shell of its former self" (Markusen and Glasmeier 2008; Singerman 2008). That criticism may reflect a transition period for federal involvement in local economic development. Ongoing programs at the federal level focus increasingly on entrepreneurial programs including greater incentives for collaboration with research universities. The Small Business Administration's Small Business Innovation Research (SBIR) program, first authorized in 1982, continues with an allocation of over $1 billion in federal funds in 2010. A complementary Small Business Technology Transfer (SBTP) program coordinates with eleven different federal departments and agencies. The National Science Foundation's Partnerships for Innovation competitive grant program fosters collaboration between academia, government, and the private sector. The EDA also supports an Advanced Technology Education program and the Industry–University Cooperative Research Partnership program promoting collaboration with technical colleges. The Department of Commerce runs federal innovation programs such as the Manufacturing Extension Program (MEP) designed to leverage existing resources from government, business, or academic institutions. Other ongoing cooperative efforts between federal and state agencies include the National Association of State Development Agencies, the State Science and Technology Institute (SSTI), the National Association of Manufacturers, and various universities and community colleges (Schacht 2011).

American federalism was once described by U.S. Supreme Court Justice Louis Brandeis as implementing "laboratories of democracy." The phrase has come to epitomize the execution of state and local economic development policies in the United States (Osborne 1988). This independence has fostered continuous change in the types of programs used to promote economic growth. Similarly, state TBED programs continue to evolve new tools for advancing their goals. One of the more creative funding mechanisms for state TBED programs resulted from the 1998 Tobacco Master Settlement Agreement (MSA), a consent decree between forty-six state attorney generals and the four largest tobacco companies operating in the United States. The agreement provided funding as redress for tobacco related illnesses and health care costs incurred by the states. While the uses of tobacco revenues varied across the states, many dedicated the new funding directly into TBED initiatives. The state of Pennsylvania, in particular, used the money to create several dedicated "Life Science Greenhouses" promoting biotechnology focused research and development in collaboration with local universities and corporations.

TBED efforts are not limited to any one technology and have adapted both their industry and geographic focus. In Pennsylvania, new TBED efforts include the Pennsylvania Initiative for Nanotechnology, which began in 2005 (Sá et al. 2008). TBED efforts have also expanded into local programs. Through the 1990s, TBED efforts devolved further, becoming central to programs limited to specific metropolitan areas or even smaller areas. These efforts put even greater emphasis on the role of research-based universities in regional economies. Universities in particular are key to hiring "stars" in targeted research fields that have been shown to be critical to attracting federal research funding, increasing corporate sponsored research and promoting state initiatives that leverage both corporate and federal funds (Innovation Associates 2005). As a result, these efforts took on new priorities including the attraction and retention of the professional workforce seen as crucial to technology development.

Local public sector TBED programs continue to expand (State Science and Technology Institute 2012). TBED efforts have been more and more devolving to local efforts as cities and counties also attempt to implement TBED programs focused on more specific geographic areas, some programs even designed to benefit specific neighborhoods within municipalities. Examples of programs being implemented at the local level include direct grants offered by the St. Louis Arch Grants program to promote startup companies in the St. Louis metropolitan area. In the Wake County/Research Triangle Park region of North Carolina, $1 million set-aside for attracting workers into key advanced technology industry clusters was ongoing in 2013.

Older tools of economic development policy are being repurposed to support TBED efforts at the local level. Tax Increment Financing (TIF), a widely used tool to provide public financing of local development efforts, use anticipated tax revenue to subsidize investment in specific projects. Typically, development bonds are issued by a public entity to raise money for these projects. The bonds themselves are guaranteed by the higher property tax revenues anticipated to be generated once the project is completed. Typically used to finance construction projects, recent use of TIFs have been more focused on TBED focused projects.[6] In Chicago a 2012 TIF provided $3.7 million to support a biotech lab for a company that tests pharmaceutical products. A new innovation for the Chicago project is a formal profit-sharing arrangement between the company and the City of Chicago, once certain profit thresholds are met. In effect, the TIF investment has been described as venture capital financing, with the City of Chicago as the investor (Wang 2012).

Conclusions

Public efforts targeting technology-based industries to foster regional economic development have not been limited to the U.S. However, U.S. TBED efforts are distinguished by the scale of sub-national competition that defines them. Much like what was happening in the U.S., Japan's Ministry of International Trade and Industry (MITI) proposed a "technopolis" program in the early 1980s designating fourteen cities for focused investment (Glasmeier 1988). The efforts were intended to spark economic growth in less developed regions. Also like efforts in the U.S., the program was designed to take advantage of existing concentrations of university-based research and development. While the program was designed to have a larger degree of local autonomy than was typical of other economic policies in Japan, it still was far more centralized than the emerging TBED efforts across the U.S. (Bass 1998). In the U.S., state and local economic development efforts are definitively not driven by top-down mandates, and have broad independence from federal efforts, often operating in direct competition with each other.

Competition and change will undoubtedly continue to be core characteristics of economic development policies at the state and local level in the United States. Factors impacting regional economic competitiveness are less and less tied to particular regions. The result has been a magnified interest in promoting industry clusters based on advanced technology firms. The public sector continues to search for new mechanisms to incentivize technology investment. Often the most innovative approaches have evolved first at the state and local level, only to be adopted by federal programs.[7]

TBED policy has also expanded with greater emphasis on human capital formation, attraction, and retention. The earliest TBED programs at the University of Arizona and in North Carolina both were spurred by shortages of workers needed by advanced technology industries. These shortages are likely to be exacerbated into the future. This will likely force further evolution of TBED efforts to promote workforce skills and expanded worker attraction policies. These new priorities are consistent with increasing research documenting the important role of "star scientists" in catalyzing research activities (Zucker and Darby 2006; Tripple and Maier 2011). Where competition once focused more on bringing financial capital into regions, those goals are now often secondary to strengthening human capital, particularly when the goal is attracting advanced technology industries.

Early TBED efforts in the United States were catalyzed in part by state efforts to respond to rapid declines in the manufacturing sector. The legacy of those early TBED efforts in the American "Rust Belt" continues. In many ways TBED programs have come full circle with new efforts again focused on promoting manufacturing industries in formerly manufacturing-centric regions. Often the focus remains on manufacturing industries, though most successful manufacturing firms have been forced to adopt technology on par with the most advanced technology firms. In 2012 a $30 million grant was made to promote manufacturing-based enterprise development at the National Additive Manufacturing Innovation Institute. The institute was located in the TechBelt Initiative region spanning Cleveland, Ohio; Youngstown, Ohio; and Pittsburgh, Pennsylvania, regions once considered the core of the American Rust Belt (Bagley 2012). Additive manufacturing includes the growing application of three dimensional printing in the production process for rapid prototyping and other applications. The one project brought to together federal funding with state and economic development agencies to work with universities in promoting an emerging technology. Where such technology-focused public–private partnerships were once considered novel, they have long since become routine.

Notes

1 Plosila himself spent eight years working in the administration of Richard Thornburg, governor of Pennsylvania 1979–1987, serving first as a policy advisor and later as the state's Secretary of Commerce and Industry. Osborne (1987) has described Plosila's seminal role in changing the economic development paradigm: "Plosila dreamed up 90 percent of Thornburg's economic development initiatives."

2 For a compilation of the interdisciplinary debates surrounding the impact of Bayh-Dole legislation see McManis and Noh (2011).

3 Whether Salk and his sponsors, the University of Pittsburgh and the National Foundation for Infantile Paralysis, wanted to patent the vaccine remains a matter of debate. Smith (1990) notes that the institutions at least analyzed the potential for patenting the vaccine and concluded it could not be patented.

4 Berman provides a longer list of UIRCs that came into existence in both the 1970s and 1980s.

5 The final disposition of the case was ongoing in early 2013, but the initial jury verdict recommended the $1.17 amount which was affirmed by the judge early in 2013. Appeals of the case were expected. For more see Bloomberg News: "Marvell to Seek to Void $1.17 Billion Patent Verdict," December 27, 2012.

6 The use of TIFs in TBED efforts is not entirely new. In 1983 the City of Pittsburgh began a multi-decade effort to redevelop the former LTV steel works on 48 acres near downtown Pittsburgh. A $7.5 million TIF was used to supplement state and local funding to redevelop the site into the Pittsburgh Technology Center, intended to be an incubator of technology-based firms. Funding for the site brought together private sector investment and at least four different public funders, including the local water and sewer authority (Urban Redevelopment Authority, Western Pennsylvania Brownfields Center).

7 See Bloomberg News: "Incentives Watch: States Are Laboratories of Democracy for Biotech Credits," September 19, 2012.

References

Bagley, R., 2012: Are Public–Private Partnerships the "Secret Sauce" to a Resurgence in American Manufacturing? Forbes.com, September 4. Available online at: www.forbes.com/sites/rebeccabagley/2012/09/04/are-public-private-partnerships-the-secret-sauce-to-a-resurgence-in-american-manufacturing/(accessed July 1, 2015).

Balasubramanian, N. and Sakakibara M., 2005: Importance of University Research to Corporate Patenting: The Impact of the Bayh-Dole Act. Working paper. Anderson School of Management at University of California at Los Angeles.

Bass, S., 1998: Japanese research parks: national policy and local development. *Regional Studies* 32(5), pp. 391–403.

Ben Franklin Technology Partners, undated: History of BFTP/CNP. Available online at: http://cnp.benfranklin.org/about/history-of-bftpcnp (accessed January 10, 2013).

Berman, E., 2012: *Creating the Market University: How academic science became an economic engine*. Princeton, NJ: Princeton University Press.

Biotechnology Industry Organization, 2001: *State Government Initiatives in Biotechnology*. Washington, D.C.

Bush, V., 1941: Science and national defense. *Science* 94(2451), pp. 571–574.

Bush, V., 1945: *Science, the Endless Frontier. A Report to the President of the United States*. Washington, DC: United States Office of Scientific Research and Development.

Ceruzzi, P., 1999: *A History Of Modern Computing*. 2nd ed. Cambridge, MA: MIT Press.

DeVol, R. and Wong, P., 1999: *America's High Tech Economy: Growth, development and risks for metro areas*. Santa Monica, CA: The Milken Institute, July.

Dill, D., 1995: University–industry entrepreneurship: the organization and management of American university technology transfer. *Higher Education* 29(4), pp. 369–384.

Douglass, J., 1999: The Cold War, Technology and the American University. University of California and Berkeley, *Research and Occasional Paper Series*: CSHE.2.99, July.

Economist, 2002: "Innovation's Golden Goose," December 12.

Eisinger, P., 1988: *The Rise of the Entrepreneurial State: State and local economic development policy in the United States*. Madison, WI: University of Wisconsin Press.

Feller, I., 1992: American state governments as models for national science policy. *Journal of Policy Analysis and Management* 11(2), pp. 288–309.

Forest, J., 2002: *Higher Education in the United States: An encyclopedia*. Santa Barbara, CA: ABC-CLIO.

Geiger, R. and Sá, C., 2009: *Tapping the Riches of Science: Universities and the promise of economic growth*. Cambridge, MA: Harvard University Press.

Glasmeier, A., 1988: The Japanese Technopolis programme: high-tech development strategy or industrial policy in disguise? *International Journal of Urban & Regional Research* 12(2), pp. 268–284.

Gross, C. and Allen, J., 2003: *Technology Transfer for Entrepreneurs: A guide to commercializing federal laboratory innovations*. Westport, CT: Praeger.

Heisey, P., King. J., Day-Rubenstein, K. and Shoemaker, R., 2006: Government patenting and technology transfer. *Economic Research Service Report No. 15 (ERR-15)*, Washington, DC: United States Government Printing Office (March).

Hill, C., 1994: *Outlook for the Federal Labs, Report P-7871*. Santa Monica, CA: RAND Corporation.

Innovation Associates, 2005: Accelerating Economic Development through University Technology Transfer, Report to the Connecticut Transfer Technology and Commercialization Advisory Board of the Governor's Competitiveness Council, February.

Lasar, M., 2011: UNIVAC: the troubled life of America's first computer,' *ARSTechnica* (online), September 18.

McManis, C. and Noh, S., 2011: The impact of the Bayh–Dole Act on genetic research and development. In: Keiff, F. (Ed.) *Perspectives on Commercializing Innovation*. Cambridge: Cambridge University Press, pp. 435–488.

Markusen, A. and Glasmeier, A., 2008: Overhauling and revitalizing federal economic development programs. *Economic Development Quarterly* 22, pp. 83–91.

Mead, C., 2005: A tale of two approaches. *Chamber Executive*, November/December, pp. 18–21.

Miller, C. and Richard, B., 2010: The policy diffusion of the state R&D investment tax credit. *State and Local Government Review* 42, pp. 22–35.

Mowery, D. and Ziedonis, A., 2000: Numbers, quality, and entry: how has the Bayh-Dole Act affected U.S. university patenting and licensing? *Innovation Policy and the Economy* 1, pp. 187–220.

Osborne, D., 1987: *Economic Competitiveness: The states take the lead*. Washington, DC: Economic Policy Institute.

Osborne, D., 1988: *Laboratories of Democracy*. Cambridge, MA: Harvard Business School Press.

Phillips, R. and Pittman, R., 2002: Technology-Based Economic Development. *IQ Report*, International City/County Management Association, 34: 5, May.

Plosilla, W., 2004: State science- and technology-based economic development policy: history, trends and developments, and future directions. *Economic Development Quarterly* 18(2), pp. 113–126.

Rosenfeld, S., 2002: Regional technology and innovation strategies in the United States: small steps, high expectations. In: Morgan, K. and Nauwelaers, C. (Eds.): *Regional Innovation Strategies: The challenge for less favoured regions*, London: Routledge, pp. 172–193.

Sá, C., Geiger, R. and Hallacher, P., 2008: Universities and state policy formation: rationalizing a nanotechnology strategy in Pennsylvania. *Review of Policy Research* 25(1), pp. 3–19.

Schacht, W., 2009: The Bayh-Dole Act: Selected Issues in Patent Policy and the Commercialization of Technology. Washington, DC: Congressional Research Service, February 3.

Schacht, W., 2011: *Manufacturing Extension Partnership Program: An overview*. Washington, DC: Congressional Research Service, Washington, April 25.

Seneca, J., Hughes, J. and Nagle, G., 2004: An Assessment of the New Jersey Business Employment Incentive Program. Report submitted to New Jersey Treasurer John E. McCormac, July 27.

Singerman, P., 2008: Repurposed federal economic development programs: a practitioner's perspective. *Economic Development Quarterly* 22(2), pp. 99–106.

Smith, J., 1990: *Patenting the Sun: Polio and the Salk vaccine*. New York: William Morrow & Co.

State Science and Technology Institute, 2006: A Resource Guide for Technology-based Economic Development Positioning Universities as Drivers Fostering Entrepreneurship Increasing Access to Capital.

State Science and Technology Institute, 2012: Trends in Technology-Based Economic Development: Local, State and Federal Action in 2012. A report prepared for The Economic Development Administration U.S. Department of Commerce, August.

Stevens, A., 2004: The enactment of Bayh–Dole. *Journal of Technology Transfer* 29, pp. 93–99.

Thornburgh, R., 1998: A path to smarter federal leadership in economic development: learning, leveraging, and linking. *Economic Development Quarterly* 12, pp. 291–298.

Tripple, M. and Maier, G., 2011: Star scientists as drivers of the development of regions. In: P. Nikamp and Siedschlag, I. (Eds.): *Innovation Growth and Competitiveness, Dynamic Regions in the Knowledge –Based World Economy*. Berlin: Springer, pp. 113–134.

United States Office of Technology Assessment, 1984: *Technology, Innovation and Regional Economic Development*, NTIS Order #PB85–150894, Washington, DC: Government Printing Office, July.

United States President's Council of Advisors on Science and Technology, 2004: Federal-State R&D Cooperation – Improving the Likelihood of Success. Summary of a Workshop convened by the President's council of Advisors on Science and Technology. Cleveland, Ohio, June 29.

Urban Redevelopment Authority of the City of Pittsburgh, undated: Pittsburgh Technology Center Brownfield Site Redevelopment. Available online at: www.ura.org/working_with_us/brownfield Projects/PTC_BrownfieldBrief.pdf (accessed July 1, 2015).

Wang, A., 2012: Emanuel used TIF as VC fund for testing firm. Crain's Chicago Business, January 18. Available online at: www.chicagobusiness.com-/article/20120118/NEWS02/120119766 (accessed July 1, 2015).

Western Pennsylvania Brownfields Center, undated: Pittsburgh Technology Center (LTV). Available online at: www.cmu.edu/steinbrenner/brownfields-/Case%20Studies/pdf/pittsburgh%20technology%20center %20-%20LTV.pdf (accessed July 1, 2015).

Zucker, L. and Darby, M., 2006: Movement of Star Scientists and Engineers and High-Tech Firm Entry. NBER Working Paper No. 12172, April 2006.

PART 3

Enabling government policies

Technology development and innovation difference between innovative countries and regions

10

THE CULTURE–TECHNOLOGY NEXUS

Innovation, policy and the successful metropolis

Ulrich Hilpert

Introduction

There are many ideas about innovation and the ways to promote such attractive socio-economic developments. There is also a clear tendency for innovation to take on regional patterns and to be addressed towards the most technologically and industrially advanced locations. Nevertheless, discussions about best practice (such as the discussions some years ago about introducing Japanese methods of management and manufacturing) have shown the problems of transferring such concepts from one area in the world to another. Statistically, regions differ; and processes of change are complex, requiring advice and expertise if they are to be effective (Doner and Hershberg 1999).

Given the fact that there are many different sociocultural arrangements within which successful economic developments take place, consequently there are many cultural settings that can lead to dynamic economic development processes. Traditions, values and attitudes towards change play an important role. Industrial systems, research systems and governmental systems, form social arrangements that vary greatly by history, orientation and capability. So, even when considering enabling policies questions arise concerning the relationship between culture and innovation, in particular the question: what cultural attitudes and settings allow regions to participate and contribute towards innovative processes?

The different elements of culture create a set of opportunities that can be added to social structures such as industries, research units, markets and political programmes: attitudes, orientations and the eagerness that generates a specific kind of creativity. In that way, culture is perceived not as 'high culture', but as something that can be identified in the systems of manufacturing, research, and politico-administrative processes. It adds an additional dimension for understanding diversities and disparities – and it may also help to identify pathways that advance socio-economic development from a regional perspective, as well as from national or European ones.

Divergences in settings and cultures

There are major differences that can be identified, particularly between the US and central and Northern Europe, but there are also significant variations within Europe. Such arrangements are decisive in determining the products that can be manufactured at such locations today and in future. Thus, they are fundamental conditions for political initiatives. For a long time industrial development was considered in terms of a reduction of production costs (Brülhart and Torstensson 1996). Since the mid 1980s, and particularly since the 1990s, it is competence in advanced and consumer oriented products that provides the basis for most modern industries. Such changes are related with an almost fundamental reorganisation of manufacturing (Doner and Hershberg 1999). Today the advancement that can be identified in the leading industrial sectors and locations is closely related to anthropocentric production systems (Lehner 1991). This gives a particular significance to craftsmanship, quality circles, etc. But not all locations in industrialised countries have the conditions necessary to achieve the changes required.

European countries have a wide variety both of research systems (Fritsch and Schwirten 1999; Morano-Foadi and Foadi 2003), and of their socio-economic linkages. They are different with regard to their orientation towards application and the role of universities. While in the Scandinavian countries, as well as in Britain, Germany and the US, universities form important elements of the research systems, in France or Italy most universities are predominantly oriented towards teaching (Eberlein 1997; Morano-Foadi and Foadi 2003). In Eastern Europe, in addition, there is a change towards new social and economic requirements (Bernard *et al.* 2012). It is important to identify in the research system whether there is an orientation towards generating economically or socially desirable progress (Bercovitz and Feldman 2006: 180); and it is also important to identify whether or not the areas of scientific expertise match the existing industrial structures.

The importance of such attitudes that provide the basis for different research cultures can be identified very clearly: in engineering facilities at German technical universities; and, a rather similar situation exists in Sweden concerning the role of advanced engineering for making use of new technologies or of knowledge generated elsewhere. Socio-economic development is related increasingly to appropriate and enabling government policies; but governments are generally not organised to foster economic advance. The organisation of states and administrations is strongly influenced by historical and cultural differences, or by the desire for national homogeneity. It is understanding of the role of bureaucracies and political systems in social and economic development that highlights different attitudes and variations in policy outputs. Hence, they are a visible expression of cultural circumstances.

In addition to such attitudes regarding government's role in enabling economic development, there is also the importance of being physically close to the problems, and developing an understanding of problem solving. It is interesting that federally organised countries, such as the US and Germany, demonstrate the significance of such variations in approach (Ciemniewski 1993; Bellini and Hilpert 2013). Capable regional entities (e.g. states or *Länder*) are ready to foster regional potential for research and industry. Centralised countries, in contrast, conduct both industrial policy and regional policy centrally; so they are rather distant from the problems they deal with (Ostrom 1973; Hilpert 1998). Finally, there is also the bureaucratic rationality when dealing with socio-economic problems (Bruns 1998), that provides a basis for dealing with questions of development and advancement in either an active or a merely bureaucratic way.

Opportunities for innovation and development

The development of new communication and information technologies has taken place significantly to meet specific demands from particular industries and markets (e.g. defence). In a more direct way this is the case in biotechnology or new materials. Established industries with a potential for innovative products provide the sociocultural context for the advancement of new industries and technologies. When industries are oriented towards large markets that are characterised by strong demand, they are ready to move onto the next stage of development. Plants and facilities that participate in such developments, because of their traditional capabilities, are thus strengthening their industrial region on the basis of their historical development and competences.

The orientation towards high tech, as a consequence, provides a continuity of sectoral development. There are few tendencies to take advantage of opportunities for cross-sectoral application and use. Traditional sectoral structures still predominate even in science-based innovation. That also leads to a reduction in the number of industries ready to proceed to the next stage of industrial development. Those with the innovative potential necessary are selected for participation by such processes (Hassink 1992). Since this relies on structures that already exist, this will also reinforce existing regional disparities rather than provide a broad basis for development in other regions.

Advanced industries in Europe are characterised by their potential for innovation. Southern and Eastern European (Glasmeier and Conroy 1999), or American locations to a significant extent, are not yet prepared to restructure with an orientation towards innovative manufacturing. When discussing consumer oriented products, this is related closely to the design and manufacture of products (Giarratani *et al.* 2003). Changing consumer demand can provide the basis for new products, but can do so only given that there already exists both an appropriate expertise in manufacturing and a highly skilled labour force. Traditional, or even old, industries often have the potential to catch up with such changes, provided that their organisational structure is sufficiently flexible. It is particularly interesting that the OECD refers to such capabilities when discussing the knowledge-based economy (KBE) (OECD 1996). Here it is the stock of knowledge, capabilities, attitudes and organisations that point to the future and the direction of innovative manufacturing (Criscuolo 2005: 1352; Breschi and Lissoni 2009: 442). Such resources can provide for development at the traditional locations of industries, as long as, in sum, they provide an infrastructure for advanced manufacturing.

Quite frequently, new products are developed on the basis of new applications of industrial capability rather than breakthroughs in science and technology. Such fertilisation of traditional and old industries is not necessarily based on high tech, but it demands creativity. This can merge existing capabilities and knowledge to develop new products or new solutions to problems. Of course, such developments can also take advantage of new technologies. Success is based on existing knowledge that is merged with new ideas, or those from other industries and experiences (e.g. modern textile industries, engineering industries, precision engineering, medical instruments, plant construction, ceramics, etc. in France, Germany, Scandinavia, Switzerland or Italy). Consequently, regions that are traditionally characterised by the exchange of ideas, and by a variety of different industries, are in a better position to take advantage of collaborative networking (Grabher 1993) that links different capabilities and competences. Their industrial cultures have a capacity to generate more creativity. There is innovative potential when new technologies merge with attitudes to industrial manufacturing that are ready to modernise such processes. This situation requires policies that provide for existing social and economic interests.

Diversity as a basis for economic development

Socio-economic development oriented towards different products, services and technologies will have an uneven effect on regional development, even when the industrial and research structures are richly diverse. Since such development requires an existing configuration of industries, research facilities, personnel, government activities and budgets, it is extremely demanding for firms and regions to participate. Regions that do not already possess appropriate structures, can participate only in very particular circumstances; and after going through a development period of perhaps two to three decades (Hilpert 1992).[1]

Such tendencies, as a consequence, provide valuable opportunities for particular existing locations of techno-industrial innovation, because they had participated in such advantageous processes previously (Barnes and Gertler 1999). But these tendencies are highly selective, so that peripheral regions are rarely prepared for participation. In addition, the variety of industries at the locations in question plays an important role. It is not just the continuation of a particular industrial history. It is also the clustering of industries with a potential for collaboration and cross-sectoral fertilisation that provides for a further advancement of existing innovative capability. There is also an agglomeration of individuals with attitudes of openness and towards collaborative activities since high tech-based development is strongly oriented towards Islands of Innovation within particular technologies (Hilpert 2012). Such locations may be complementary with each other, but will hardly relate at all technologically to those regions not participating in the network system of the Archipelago Europe or in other continental network systems.

When analysing different innovative locations, it is the case that new technologies are not only generated outside traditional industrial centres. Innovatory developments are based on a broad variety of opportunities that, of course, take advantage of science and new technological advances, but that are also related to existing knowledge and industrial creativity. So, in contrast to the concept of footloose industries in high technology sectors, in the US and in Europe about 90 per cent of the Islands of Innovation known today have a tradition in related, precursor industries. So, new technologies can provide a variety of processes of innovative restructuring. Old industries have a stock of knowledge that can provide for new products that meet consumer needs. Very clearly, the cultural arrangements encountered at different locations or regions provide a basis of creativity and product advancement.

When referring to economic development and benefitting from the sociocultural arrangements mentioned above, there are at least three factors that are to be considered:

Governments for Development. Public policies need to design a path for development that can enable regions to benefit from their sociocultural heritage. This requires a market oriented discussion on industrial opportunities for regional industries, and their opportunities for networking within their regional setting (Simmie 1997). The role of government policies is well demonstrated by the developments that took place at Bavaria, Sophia Antipolis, Edinburgh, Dublin and the Øresund.

A Tradition of Innovation. The stock of knowledge and the creativity of the personnel that are employed in the enterprises within traditional industries at the locations in question provide the basis for innovation. This must be related to a focus on the particular products that might be manufactured in such regions. The tradition in innovation is well demonstrated by developments that took place in electronics industries, precision engineering and pharmaceutical industries.

A Culture Fostering Higher Value Added. Since there are few opportunities to compete on the basis of lower production costs with Southeast Asia etc., a development that is expected to provide a basis for employment and economic growth needs to be oriented towards high value added. Traditional industrial locations are quite often in an almost unique position in the world to meet demand. So, it is important to make use of the fundamental cultural arrangements that underpin such production systems and to advance them in a way that enables them to meet the requirements for modern, innovative and high value added products (Peck and Tickell 1997). The development of regions such as Terza Italia, Baden-Württemberg or Grenoble clearly relate to such cultural arrangements.

The metropolitanisation of the technology–culture nexus

Metros agglomerating cultural attitudes and orientations: social change following with the attraction of innovative labour

It is interesting that most innovative activities are located in metropolises. Leading universities and research institutes are to be found in such areas and innovative enterprises or technology-based firms also predominantly agglomerate in such areas. Attitudes towards collaboration and openness concerning new ideas, opportunities and applications are fundamental for research and innovation in small high-tech enterprises, and consequently characterise such locations. While traditional industries or services require particular competences and improve their products using new technologies and innovation, metropolises that have a strong research basis need to be open to take advantage of ideas and influences from outside. The gateway functions of metropolises that are the home of public and private centres of decision making, innovative and research-based enterprises, and are the locations of research universities and institutes (Blotevogel and Danielzyk 2009) and thus meet the necessary conditions for innovation and technology development, international networks, close relationships with other metropolises and innovative locations, and the exchange of labour, create a particular and most advantageous situation. Such a situation matches the collaborative mode of innovation, which is based on contributions to a shared global body of academic knowledge. Existing research competences and enterprise headquarters have easy access to international airports and help to exploit attitudes that permit meetings and the exchange of ideas.

The existing socioculture in metropolises is characterised by particular individuals and their creativity, which further contribute to make these locations even stronger magnets of science (Mahroum 2000: 374; Williams et al. 2004: 39) and create a context for spin-off enterprises (Franco and Filson 2000: 19; Berry and Glaeser 2005: 29; Bercovitz and Feldman 2006: 177) that are based on leading edge academic research. Although such knowledge might be accessible at many locations around the world, such metropolises agglomerate individuals with such attitudes, and thus do not just agglomerate a rich variety of competences, but create a situation where such a culture can generate new paths of research, innovation and development. The collaborative process of the transformation of knowledge into technology is a global process, but it clearly demonstrates the existence of such metropolitan situations that are prepared to produce both new findings and new technologies. In contributing to, and taking advantage of, this situation, they perform outstandingly well. But they are highly divergent, because their individual competences are characterised throughout a rich variety of areas of specialisation across the different metropolises. The different areas of technological subfields of specialisation, and the simultaneity of different technologies, provide situations where divergencies of cultures (which make a metropolis different from old industrial areas or centres of finance and realty) link with different technologies and build highly individual, even sometimes unique, constellations.

Thus, innovative metropolises provide attractive job markets that make knowledge workers, researchers and academics move to these locations. In fact, they are fundamental for an agglomeration of such attitudes and ideas about development. This creates a situation that is both characterised by, and supportive of, attitudes that are oriented towards international collaboration and, in addition, is beneficial for the industrial structure at an innovative metropolis. Such research oriented metropolitan situations are also fundamental to a dynamic situation where entrepreneurial attitudes of researchers are achieved by the continuous founding of innovative, new enterprises. A mix of industries, enterprises and research facilities needs creative individuals many of whom are potential founders of technology-based enterprises, which can build mutually supportive metropolitan collaborations. The positive correlation between income and talent in metropolises (Florida 2002: 752) is an expression of the agglomeration of university trained personal who form a metropolitan socioculture that is fundamental for additional innovative synergy.

Such tendencies towards a divergent agglomeration of individual orientations and talents, associated with university education and creativity based on academic research, can be identified as a clearly emerging geographical pattern. Such metropolises, of course, find a sociocultural basis to maintain their position in innovative networks and become especially different from those regions that do not perform as these metropolises do. A rich diversity of attitudes can be found that is based on the agglomeration, which allows for divergent talents to be developed. Islands of Innovation converge strongly with the magnets of science where the leading universities and research institutes are located. Consequently, these metropolitan locations require a particular population that is highly trained, but they also provide an attraction for highly innovative migrant labour. Thus, there is a highly diverse and multicultural situation associated with processes of leading edge innovation. Cities, in general, and metropolises in particular, are becoming even more special because of their educated population and workforce. In addition, they are increasingly characterised by the changing sociocultural situations and opportunities based on these situations.

This can be seen clearly in the changing structures of cities that are characterised by a growing percentage of college graduates correlated with an initial share of population with sixteen years of schooling (Berry and Glaeser 2005: 9–12; Abel and Deitz 2009: 18). In addition, the cities demonstrate rather heterogeneous tendencies that also reflect the differences in both their innovative potential and the labour force needed. There is an increasing differentiation between Islands of Innovation and metropolises in general. Innovative metropolises are built on existing and previous competences, and allow the research based future development of a selected number of locations. In 1970 an average metropolitan area in the US had 11.2 per cent college graduates and they were relatively homogeneous, because in 50 per cent of the metros there were between 8.7 per cent and 13.1 per cent college degrees. But by 1990 in the average metropolitan area the share of college graduates rose to 16.4 per cent and the decreasing homogeneity is indicated by the increasing gap of 6.3 per cent from the 25th percentile to the 75th percentile. This development was intensified further by 2000, when sixty-two metropolitan areas had a labour force with less than 7 per cent holding a college degree, but thirty-two metropolitan areas had a share of more than 30 per cent. It is important to notice that already in 2000 there were forty-nine metropolitan areas that had a labour force of more than 30.8 per cent, while in 1970 that could not be identified in a single case.

The situation of innovative metropolises maintains their position as Islands of Innovation that already made them different during the 1980s (Hilpert 1992) and they still differ due to their labour markets. Thus, while in 1970 in a metropolitan area where about one eighth of the population held such degrees, by 2000 more than a quarter of the employed personnel had the same amount of schooling (Berry and Glaeser 2005: 9–12). This indicates a fundamental change in the metropolitan population, their attitudes and the sociocultural situation that allows for further innovative technology development. Islands of Innovation are even more characterised by such change and also attract star scientists to contribute to both the innovative strength of the metropolis and its acquisition of sociocultural advantages. Clearly, the changing population of innovative metropolises agglomerate particular attitudes and orientations as compared with other locations or regions. Thus, they are different from surrounding regions but also from metropolises that are characterised by finance and realty services. It is important to see that in such metropolises there is a high probability of meeting a person with similar interests and attitudes and collaborating with them to create new findings and new technologies or applications.

In innovative metropolises these cultures clearly vary from those that are centres of finance and realty services, because research and the requirement for specific motivations that clearly differ from creating a financial surplus by investment banking, disregards the specific areas of investments. Different types of metropolises with the highest levels of modernization and of research and development (Abel and Deitz 2009: 18) are also the home of different labour forces and individuals. In addition, such metropolises, which act as Islands of Innovation, are involved in manufacturing and, consequently, provide jobs for both 'high' and 'low' human capital occupations. This again contributes to a specific situation that is not just different but also the basis of new technologies, as the individuals provide skills, attitudes and knowledge. The cultural orientation in research and collaboration allows a rich variety of opportunities that cannot exist even in other agglomerations, as the orientation of the actors is neither so frequent nor is it oriented towards a particular high-technology development.

Attitudes and culture permit leading edge research: policies concentrate at certain locations

While such persons concentrate at particular locations, they provide a situation that is characterised by highly receptive attitudes towards research and the development of new technologies. The concentration of research institutes, universities and science-based industries consequently provides jobs. These help to concentrate those with attitudes that help to take advantage of government support or opportunities for local collaboration. An agglomeration of skills and university degrees (Florida 2002: 743), thus, is more than just a knowledge base, and allows for the exchange of ideas and talents. Such a concentration of talents is associated with orientations in the diversity of opportunities and openness towards new areas of innovative activities. Consequently, large innovative metropolises that provide an attractive labour market (Lawton Smith and Waters 2005: 2–3) indicate situations where both the concentration and the exchange of labour among such metropolises (Hilpert and Lawton Smith 2012) provides a continuing change of attitudes and highly divergent metropolitan culture that is characterised by the continuing dynamic development.

While labour markets or enterprises demonstrate the demand for such personnel, it is important to see that the momentum for further accumulation of skills, the development of a local pool of specialised labour, is always related to attitudes and orientations that allow for further development and exchange across distances. In addition, the exchange of such attitudes based on distant recruitment provides new areas of creative synergy. The fact that metropolises offer large labour markets maximises the matching opportunities and can relate to both a continuation of existing sociocultural situations of innovation and their matching with additional or new attitudes and ideas from outside, frequently from other metropolises. An agglomeration of science-based firms at such locations clearly allows for economic exploitation of these sociocultural situations because it helps to transform such creative attitudes into fundamental academic research and technology development. While this indicates the generation of new ideas and technologies, existing manufacturing industries provide opportunities to continuously innovate and improve manufacturing technologies.

Although there is a close relationship between innovative industries and high-tech enterprises, the impact of science-based and research intensive enterprises and new firms has continued for a long time (Herzog *et al.* 1986: 446). Due to their increasing percentage of engineers, technicians and scientists, the success of such enterprises and industries is clearly labour intensive and is related with the agglomeration of such individuals. The relationship with highly innovative universities requires intensive research and thrives on the application of advances in sciences. In the end, to continue successful paths of economic development, high-tech manufacturing firms and locations depend on R&D and the personalities of the individuals employed. A regional concentration of academics and scientists consequently had already been identified during the 1990s (Williams *et al.* 2004: 39) when Oxford and Cambridge alone employed 15 per cent of all foreign academics, with about 58 per cent in London and the South-East of England, and even more in fields such as biosciences (Hilpert and Bastian 2007).

This clearly indicates a metropolitan situation that is socioculturally basically different from peripheral or old industrial regions (Berry and Glaeser 2005: 20). Islands of Innovation are not simply built predominantly in metropolises, they need more than just a clustering or agglomeration of innovative capabilities, university trained labour and research competences. The phenomenon of an increasing number of innovative enterprises, an agglomeration of research and funding, and the growing number of jobs for highly skilled and specialised personnel, is based on the openness of academics and researchers who continuously pursue research projects or start new and innovative enterprises. Thus, it is not merely the agglomeration or clustering of enterprises, but the synergy across different areas that is created because of the eagerness to seek new findings, and the opportunities for the people who are attracted to come to these locations. Their attitudes allow the development that is found in new technologies, innovation and innovative labour markets.

Thus a polycentric collaboration among metropolises, and the networking among such locations, is not merely a process of matching competences nor of balancing deficits. The networks among such outstanding locations allow for particular sociocultural arrangements that make their situation particularly different. Leading universities are magnets of science (Mahroum 2000) but even more they can act as a home for both such creative individuals and the generation of new findings. Consequently, metropolises benefit from high-skilled national migration and additional foreign born competences. While international migration can affect the distribution of human capital (Coulombe and Tremblay 2009: 6) this provides access to a great variety of knowledge and competences that come together at the places that attract such highly creative individuals most. The openness towards divergent understandings and new opportunities makes those metropolises specific and makes them also different from other agglomerations of a similar size. Thus, widely based on the important role of outstanding research universities, they act as innovative clusters or Islands of Innovation that are ready to generate spin-off enterprises from university research (Simonen and McCann 2008: 147). The large number of such small firms reflects an agglomeration of enterprises that produce new and innovative technologies, which again indicates the vital contribution of divergencies of metropolitan sociocultural situations. Such additional innovative enterprises contribute to a sociocultural situation, expanding the local labour market for such individuals and as a result of the networking of regionalised innovative labour markets (Hilpert and Lawton Smith 2012) they attract and even support the exchange of such labour among the specific metropolises.

Complementarity and exchange vs competition

Since innovation and technology development are widely related with the merging of knowledge and competences from different areas that are embodied in individuals, consequently there is an increasing probability of generating such opportunities when the agglomeration of such individuals allow for more collaboration. While attitudes of openness and eagerness to explore opportunities provide an important basis, it is the rich variety that exists in metropolises that allows for a wider area of application. Clearly, different places with divergent traditions in research and scientific expertise can make such knowledge innovative in a larger number of areas. That makes both the expansion of knowledge and the trans-continental networks of knowledge production important instruments of innovation. They merge particular scientific structures and education across the world. Since innovative metropolises provide labour markets that attract individuals with creative attitudes (Florida 2002: 744), the emerging metropolitan cultures help create a continuity of leading positions despite the changing structure of the network.

But, such metropolises are still embedded in their national systems (Williams *et al.* 2004: 29) and academic research and related technology development depends strongly on public funding and the existing areas of expertise. In addition, national systems of regulation continue and are widely fundamental for the dynamism of such processes and for opportunities of economic exploitation. Again, one needs to see that the existing situations may allow for further and even increased migration of innovative labour, following earlier creative migrants. Frequently there is a continued strengthening of Islands of Innovation that maintain their positions over decades. Given the importance of tacit knowledge even in research and technology development (Criscuolo 2005: 1358; Breschi and Lissoni 2009: 44) and the increasing opportunities of innovative ideas based on frequent academic interaction, innovative metropolises benefit greatly from their cultural situations, which help to exchange such personnel. Such metropolises concentrate high quality innovation and widely monopolise both the exchange of innovative knowledge and participation in collaborative technology development. Language and culture are important to allow those from outside to become integrated into the work and life situations; thus they are important for building innovative creativity among knowledge workers coming from different locations and different research backgrounds (Power and Lundmark 2004: 1040).

The innovative US metropolises are clearly in an advantageous position because they generally have the same language, college culture and scientific system, while Europe is characterised by many different national situations that limit both the exchange of such individuals and the building of the culture necessary to make creative locations more open. This demonstrates both the importance of national exchange among different metropolises, and international exchange in addition. The wider the range of academic backgrounds in a particular field of research, or in contiguous fields, the wider the potential for innovation. The individual researchers, academics or knowledge workers act as pipelines of knowledge (Power and Lundmark 2004: 1029) drawn to cultural situations that are absorptive to such attitudes and personnel. Dynamic labour markets are clearly more than just opportunities to work or attract embodied knowledge and competences. Such labour markets are an expression of the existing metropolitan culture that allows such multinational situations to perform and to become innovative. Networks of such regional innovative labour markets (Hilpert and Lawton Smith 2012) demonstrate their complementary cultural situations, which are fundamental for the migration and exchange of labour as observed above. The more metropolises build such situations they will become embedded in the situation. In addition, the more they become different to other regions. In particular they attract creative individuals from peripheral regions either to experience education at such metropolises or to seek their professional career.

Consequently, metropolises develop the situation that exhibits the sociocultural opportunity to attract and agglomerate creative and innovative individuals. During the long time periods over which they enjoy their outstanding position as innovative metropolises and Islands of Innovation, they foster university education by building and continuing to support leading edge universities and research milieux. Thus, leading researchers and creative personnel are predominantly reproduced at such locations (Straubhaar 2000: 16; Williams *et al.* 2004: 39; Trippl 2012). Over time there still remains a continuing attraction to these favoured metropolises which creates a 'core–periphery' division, but when personnel are attracted by job opportunities, they bring additional attitudes and orientations to these open and dynamic locations. While this was often considered a problem for peripheral development, it in fact indicates the specific situation and sociocultural arrangement in the metropolises in question. Such an arrangement further contributes to the development of regional diversities that reinforce divergent opportunities of innovation and economic development, and are reflected in certain path dependencies in more peripheral regions.

It is the sociocultural situation that is characterised by openness, fewer hierarchies and integration that allows frequent exchange of ideas and personnel, and acts as a rather open and liberal metropolitan society. This makes them the home of new enterprises based on outstanding competences and leading edge research that contribute to metropolitan economic growth (Florida 2002: 744; Abel and Deitz 2009: 18–19). Although these metropolises may increasingly differ from other and surrounding regions, they are still bound to the national systems from where they receive governmental research funding and to which they contribute innovation and socio-economic development. But during such contributions the culture-based industrial structures and network participation are re-strengthened. While metropolises function to collect and organise human capital they continue to provide for the specificities of their socio-economic development that reflects their metropolitan societies.

A continuation of the momentum towards further accumulation of skills in metropolises (Lawton Smith and Waters 2005: 3) creates a situation where such locations provide rather similar work and life situations. The attraction of talent and creative individuals makes them mutually become nodal locations for collaboration and change of jobs. Nevertheless, within this common tendency there are variations that relate to divergences among the metropolitan situations and cultures (Williams *et al.* 2004: 38). This causes divergencies in the intensity of their capability to attract such individuals. Thus, although they are linked by different networks, and although there is a general tendency to develop a specific culture of innovative metropolises, they still vary in their opportunities and tendencies. Such metropolises inhibit a tendency towards sociocultural modernisation, and provide the link for countries towards future innovative development and technology development. They continue to be based nationally, but they need to have openness towards new and divergent influences while collaboration and exchange allows advantageous socio-economic opportunities.

Conclusions: culture allows for advanced participation and creativity

When innovation and new technologies are investigated, it is frequent that Islands of Innovation are identified and these are predominantly located at metropolises. It is important that such metropolises are not just large agglomerations of people but they act as centres of expertise, decision-making and provide appropriate labour markets drawing on research institutions and enterprises. The particular attitudes of academics, researchers, knowledge workers and innovative entrepreneurs create situations that are socioculturally very open and creative. Agglomeration supports larger, innovative, regional labour markets and provides for a metropolitan sociocultural situation – and thus indicates a culture–technology nexus of local, national and transnational interest. Taking these situations into account means identifying metropolises and Islands of Innovation not just as geographic locations and clusters of expertise and opportunities. They need to be understood as open and liberal metropolitan societies that attract highly educated individuals. Consequently, star scientists and the entrepreneurs of new high-technology firms are attracted to live and work there.

When political decisions are taken to support research there are jobs created for university-educated personnel that exhibit the attitudes that are fundamental for collaborative processes of innovation and technology development. Thus, there are policy instruments available that provide for the attraction of the individuals required. The fact that such agglomerations of individuals are also the basis for new research-based enterprises also provides additional jobs for university educated personnel and contributes to further concentration. Labour markets and policies aimed at attracting such labour help the technology–culture nexus that is to be found at innovative metropolises.

Knowing about this correspondence between society, culture and new technology, it is important to understand that neither the location nor a phenomenon such as a cluster or university alone can be the basis of innovation and new technologies. Neither capital, nor institutions, nor research funding generates new technologies. Although labour markets or migration flows of highly trained personnel relate to the role of creative and innovative individuals, this is still addressed to the phenomena identified. The generation of new breakthroughs in science and technology, today, is a highly collaborative research process and is based on a situation where those individuals meet who are open and eager to provide both new and better understandings and applications. This privileges locations that match the criteria of metropolises (vs metropolitan agglomerations). There is a rich variety of opportunities for such individuals to integrate in the socioculturally inclusive situation by contributing and participating in both academic research and technology development. These attitudes, and the collaboration with partners who help to advance understandings and applications, make the location an Island of Innovation or an innovative metropolis – and are fundamental for the culture–technology nexus that is made clear through a variety of phenomena.

Understanding the role of sociocultural situations, for the matching of competences and opportunities, will also help us to better understand the continuing position of such metropolises and Islands of Innovation in networks of collaboration and the exchange of innovative labour. The culture–technology nexus can be identified geographically and indicates the synergy that builds locations of networks. Transfer and exchange in various areas also indicates the readiness to merge the different capabilities of a continent, or more widely from around the world. The high percentage of foreign born populations in innovative metropolises also indicates the wide and divergent cultural resources of which innovative metropolises can take advantage, and this becomes possible because of the sociocultural embeddedness of innovative development. Political decisions and government policies provide opportunities to arrange for such a culture–technology nexus located in metropolises, through research funding and the creation of innovative labour markets, which are complemented by the potentials of spin-off research enterprises.

Notes

1 E.g. with regard to biotechnology this took place at Seattle, RTP in North Carolina, and Munich.

2 Nevertheless, locations not contributing to these networks may, of course, have the opportunity to contribute to the production of other goods and services, and so participate in other, lower technology sectors.

3 These situations and locations also provide the basis for individual careers and influence which attitudes are successful for individual opportunities in academia.

References

Abel, J. and Deitz, R.R., 2009: *Do colleges and universities increase their region's human capital?* New York: Federal Reserve Bank of New York.

Barnes, T.J. and Gertler, M.S., 1999: *The New Industrial Geography: Regions, regulation and institutions.* London: Routledge Studies in the Modern World Economy.

Bellini, N. and Hilpert, U. (eds), 2013: *Europe's Changing Geography: The impact of inter-regional networks.* London: Routledge.

Bercovitz, J. and Feldman, M., 2006: Entrepreneurial universities and technology transfer: a conceptual framework for understanding knowledge-based economic development. *Journal of Technology Transfer* 31, pp. 175–188.

Bernard, J., Kostelecký, T. and Patočková, V., 2012: Islands of Innovation in the Czech Republic: the international labour market of highly skilled workers and brain gain policies. In: Hilpert, U. and Lawton Smith, H. (eds): *Networking Regionalised Innovative Labour Markets.* London and New York: Routledge, pp. 136–159.

Berry, C. and Glaeser, E., 2005: The divergence of human capital levels across cities. NBER (National Bureau of Economic Research) working paper series. Cambridge, MA: Cambridge Press.

Blotevogel, H.H. and Danielzyk, R., 2009: Leistungen und Funktionen von Metropolregionen. In: Knieling, J. (ed.): *Metropolregionen und Raumentwicklung.* Hannover: Verlag der ARL, pp. 22–29.

Breschi, S. and Lissoni, F., 2009: Mobility of skilled workers and co-invention networks: an anatomy of localized knowledge flows. *Journal of Economic Geography* 9, pp. 439–468.

Brülhart, M. and Torstensson, J., 1996: Regional integration, scale economies and industry location, CEPR Discussion Paper No. 1435. London: Centre for Economic Policy Research.

Bruns, J., 1998: Standortentwicklung durch intergouvernementale Arbeitsteilung. Das Beispiel Umwelttechnik. In: Hilpert, U. and Holtmann, E. (eds): *Regieren und intergouvernementale Beziehungen.* Opladen: Leske und Budrich, pp. 215–238.

Ciemniewski, S., 1993: Between unity and separation. In: Kramer, J. (ed.): *Föderalismus zwischen Integration und Sezession. Chancen und Risiken bundesstaatlicher Ordnung,* Baden-Baden, pp. 59–63.

Coulombe, S. and Tremblay, J.-F., 2009: Migration and skills disparities across the Canadian provinces. *Regional Studies* 43(1), pp. 5–18.

Criscuolo, P., 2005: On the road again: researcher mobility inside the R&D network. *Research Policy* 35, pp. 1350–1365.

Doner, R.F. and Hershberg, E., 1999: Flexible production and political decentralization in the developing world: elective affinities in the pursuit of competitiveness? *Studies in Comparative International Development* 34(1), pp. 45–82.

Eberlein, B., 1997: Abschied vom Etatismus in Frankreich: das Beispiel der Forschungs- und Technologiepolitik. *Politische Vierteljahresschrift* 38, pp. 441–474.

Florida, R., 2002: The economic geography of talent. *Annals of the Association of American Geographers* 92(4), pp. 743–755.

Franco, A. and Filson, D., 2000: Knowledge Diffusion Through Employee Mobility, Claremont Colleges Working Papers 2000–61, Claremont Colleges.

Fritsch, M. and Schwirten, C., 1999: Enterprise–university co-operation and the role of public research institutions in regional innovation systems. *Industry and Innovation* 6(1), pp. 69–83.

Giarratani, F., Singh, V. and Briem, C., 2003: Dynamics of growth and restructuring in the Pittsburgh metropolitan region. In: Hilpert, U. (ed.): *Regionalisation of Globalised Innovation: Locations for advanced industrial development and disparities in participation.* London: Routledge, pp. 136–154.

Glasmeier, A.K. and Conroy, M.E., 1999: Left in or Left out? Peripheral Regions in the Age of Globalization. *Options Politiques Montréal* 20(9), pp. 48–53.

Grabher, G. (Ed.), 1993: *The embedded firm: On the socioeconomics of industrial networks.* London and New York: Routledge.

Hassink, R., 1992: *Regional innovation policy: Case studies from the Ruhr Area, Baden–Württemberg and the North east of England.* Utrecht: Koninklijk Nederlands Aardrijkskundig Genootschap.

Herzog, H.W., Schlottmann, A.M. and Johnson, D.L., 1986: High-technology jobs and worker mobility. *Journal of Regional Science* 26, pp. 445–459.
Hilpert, U., 1992: *Archipelago Europe – Islands of Innovation*, Synthesis Report, Brussels: Commission of the European Communities.
Hilpert, U., 1998: Regieren zwischen Problemnähe und Regierungsrationalität. Die EU-Politik im Geflecht veränderter intergouvernmentaler Arbeitsteilung. In: Hilpert, U. and Holtmann, E. (eds): *Regieren und intergouvernementale Beziehungen*. Opladen: Leske und Budrich, pp. 193–214.
Hilpert, U., 2012: Networking innovative regional labour markets: towards spatial concentration and mutual exchange of competence, knowledge and synergy. In: Hilpert, U. and Lawton Smith, H. (eds): *Networking Regionalised Innovative Labour Markets*. London and New York: Routledge, pp. 3–31.
Hilpert, U. and Bastian, D., 2007: Innovation und Beschäftigung, Jena: Unpublished research report.
Hilpert, U. and Lawton Smith, H., 2012 (eds): *Networking Regionalised Innovative Labour Markets*. London and New York: Routledge.
Lawton Smith, H. and Waters, R., 2005: Employment mobility in high-technology agglomerations: the cases of Oxfordshire and Cambridgeshire. *Area* 37(2), pp. 189–198.
Lehner, F., 1991: Anthropocentric Production Systems: The European Response to Advanced Manufacturing and Globalization. Synthesis Report. Gelsenkirchen.
Mahroum, S., 2000: Scientific mobility: an agent of scientific expansion and institutional empowerment. *Science Communication* 21, pp. 367–378.
Morano-Foadi, S. and Foadi, J., 2003: Italian Scientific Migration: From brain exchange to brain drain. CSLPE Research Report No 8.
OECD, 1996: Employment and growth in the knowledge-based economy. Paris: OECD.
Ostrom, V., 1973: Can federalism make a difference? *Publius* 3(2), pp. 197–237.
Peck, J. and Tickell, A., 1997: Searching for a new institutional fix: the after-Fordist crisis and the global–local disorder. In: Amin, A. (ed.): *Post-Fordism: A reader*. Oxford: Blackwell, pp. 281–315.
Power, D. and Lundmark, M., 2004: Working through knowledge pools: labour market dynamics, the transfer of knowledge and ideas, and industrial clusters. *Urban Studies* 41(5–6), pp. 1040.
Simmie, J., 1997: *Innovation, Networks and Learning Regions?* London: Kingsley.
Simonen, J. and McCann, P., 2008: Firm innovation: the influence of R&D cooperation and the geography of human capital inputs. *Journal of Urban Economics* 64, pp. 146–154.
Straubhaar, T., 2000: International mobility of the highly skilled: brain gain, brain drain or brain exchange. HWWA Discussion Paper 88/2000, Hamburg: Hamburg Institute of International Economics.
Trippl, M., 2012: Star scientists, Islands of Innovation and internationally networked labour markets. In: Hilpert, U. and Lawton Smith, H. (eds): *Networking Regionalised Innovative Labour Markets*. London and New York: Routledge, pp. 58–77.
Williams, A.M., Baláz, V. and Wallace, C.D., 2004: International labour mobility and uneven regional development in Europe: human capital, knowledge and entrepreneurship. *European Urban and Regional Studies* 11(1), pp. 27–46.

11

EXPLAINING DIFFERENCES IN THE ADAPTABILITY OF OLD INDUSTRIAL AREAS

Xiaohui Hu and Robert Hassink

Introduction

Explaining the causes and consequences of uneven economic development within and between regions is a core theme in economic geography. The research focus and conceptual frameworks related to this theme have been affected by several meta-theoretical paradigm turns in the discipline, shifting from a material-centric and equilibrium way of thinking to a non-material cultural and institutional–evolutionary perspective (Scott 2000). In recent years, one of the most frequently asked questions in the discipline is why it is that some regional economies are able to adapt more positively and move onto new developmental trajectories, whereas others remain locked in decline over time. This question simultaneously mirrors the reality of increasing cross-region/border interactions and unpredictable crises in a globalizing economy, which raises a new topic of conceptualizing the nature of geographically uneven economic adaptability (Martin and Sunley 2006; MacKinnon et al. 2009; Hassink 2010a; Martin 2010; Cooke 2012). It has been shown that not only many modern theoretical concepts, such as path dependence and lock-in, are applied to help to understand long-term regional evolution, but also several newly imported notions (e.g. regional resilience) are adopted to assess short-lived mutation and adaptation (Pike *et al.* 2010). This body of work tries to provide a much broader view by combining useful concepts from evolutionary economic geography and other related social sciences, in which not only the micro-level norms, routines and practices within firms and organizations are closely focused, but also multi-actors interactively involved in networks, systems, institutions, power and politics beyond the narrow firm-based scale are taken into account in contributing to a better understanding of the spatial patterns of economic landscape evolution.

Old industrial areas that are blighted by prolonged downturns of traditional industries (e.g. steel, textile, coal mining and shipbuilding etc.) and the lack of sufficient capital, advanced technologies and know-how, face greater challenges in adapting than other regions do. Many formerly prosperous old industrial areas in Western Europe and North America experienced painful processes of de-industrialization in the 1970s and 1980s. Similar industrial restructuring occurred in the first generation of newly industrializing countries in East Asia during the 1990s, and then in the second generation economies after the 2000s. However, one of the most intriguing phenomena is that the outcomes of industrial restructuring vary remarkably from region to region. Pittsburgh, for instance, is regarded as a successful model of a transformative shift from a steel-producing region to a steel related technology and service centre (Treado 2010), while Northeast England is still suffering from cyclical downturn due to the inflexibility of traditional and structured institutions, as well as the tensions of local-central power relations (Hudson 2005; Shaw and Robinson 2012). This spatially uneven phenomenon, in which old industrial regions evolve and adapt following divergent processes and with varying consequences, raises important questions: how can we explain the differences in the adaptability of old industrial areas? What are the inherent mechanisms driving the rise and fall of old industrial areas? What sort of evolutionary paths do different old industrial areas follow and how can we distinguish them? So far, economic geographers working on this topic have been busy in empirically investigating the various processes and causes mainly on the basis of individual cases with place-specific evolutionary features. Much less attention has been paid to the types, mechanisms and patterns of evolutionary trajectories observable in the adaptability of old industrial areas. Furthermore, it still remains unclear how many factors/elements are involved in regional renewal and how to distinguish the features and roles of different factors in shaping the uneven trajectories in a broader context. Drawing upon these points, this chapter will attempt to critically assess impact factors on regional economic adaptability in old industrial areas aiming to promote further multidimensional thinking and disciplinary cross-fertilization in doing evolution in economic geography.

The remainder of this chapter is structured as follows. Section 2 distinguishes two main types of factors affecting the strengths and weaknesses of regional renewal based on a critical review of the literature on the restructuring of old industrial areas across various industries and nations. Section 3 seeks to synthesize positive and negative factors by employing notions from evolutionary economic geography and other sociopolitical sciences to cast greater light on the uneven dynamics of old industrial areas. In section 4 research gaps are identified and several hypotheses as well as research questions for future studies on this topic are proposed. Finally, conclusions are drawn.

What factors are affecting the restructuring of old industrial areas? A literature review

Based on a series of cross-border comparative studies of industrial dynamics and regional restructuring, Hassink (2010b) initially proposed two types of impact factors (economic-structural impact factors and political–institutional impact factors) as an analytical framework for analysing the differences in the ability of old industrial areas to restructure and reshape. Inspired by this work, we start with a critical review of the literature on the restructuring of old industrial areas with a particular focus on two main impact factors, namely industrial–sectoral impact factors and institutional–political impact factors.

Industrial–sectoral impact factors

Prior to the 2000s, the decline of old industrial areas was often linked to economic over-specialization and the maturity of the product life-cycle, emphasizing the inflexible economic structure and rigid supply–demand linkages that incrementally generate obstacles for further regional growth (Steiner 1985). Grabher (1993) defines those structural obstacles as a 'functional lock-in', which refers to strict inter-firm relations, close trade interdependences and mature infrastructures that may lead to a 'rigid specialization trap' and the absence of adaptation.

A region with one specific dominating industry may have a strong potential for functional lock-in. Hassink's (2010b) study of the shipbuilding region of Gyeongnam in South Korea, for example, demonstrates how the '*chaebol*' (close-knit family corporations), coupled with strong ties to the central government contribute to high exit and entry barriers that impede industrial diversity. Similar examples can be captured in Northeast China, where state owned enterprises (SOEs) and their subsidiaries are firmly embedded in the local economic system. In this sense, little space is left for the formation of new industries (paths), as SOEs dominate market, labour and financial resources (Hu and Lin 2013). In addition, the spatial unevenness in restructuring may also be associated with different types or characteristics of industries, such as firm ownership, size and number. For instance, large and capital intensive SOEs (such as the steel industry) tend to be committed to high sunk costs that make it hard for them to exit and change, while labour intensive and private SMEs (such as the textile industry) seem to be affected rather less due to the low entry barriers, flexible firm relations, and low sunk costs (Chapman 2005).

Additionally, the regional innovation system (RIS) approach, which highlights the power of cross-sector interactions for innovation, has been extensively regarded as a policy priority to foster or revitalize regional economies. Tödtling and Trippl (2005) reveal that the 'lock-in' effect in old industrial areas is highly relevant to their performance of RIS (links within industries and with other sectors). Several comparative studies on old industrial areas in Austria (Styria and Upper Austria) and Germany (Saarland) illustrate that regions with thick and networked RIS exhibit stronger dynamism for regional renewal than those with thin and fragmented RIS (Tödtling and Trippl 2004; Trippl and Otto 2009). Since regions differ in their preconditions in terms of university–industry relations, inter-industry networks and the density of supporting agencies, differentiated topologies of RIS as well as the quality of subsystems in old industrial areas influence the nature and geography of adaptation. In addition to the RIS approach, which very much emphasizes the endogenous industrial systemness for regional innovation and economic change, exogenous economic factors such as the national innovation system, international industrial relocations and cross-border economic cooperation play an increasingly important role in helping old firms/industries absorb new technologies and complementary knowledge and, in turn, escape from the lock-in situation (Kaufmann and Tödtling 2000; Hudson and Swanton 2012; Bathelt *et al.* 2013).

More recently, the concept of path creation has contributed to a historical dialectic perspective for explaining where the sources support for creating new industries/paths, and how contingency and place dependence co-evolve and are geared to a certain path over time (Martin and Sunley 2006; Martin 2010). This concept indicates that the emergence of new industries and paths in old industrial areas is by no means without foundation, but is usually (pre)conditioned by the previous localized legacies and pre-existing paths. For instance, the environmental technology industry is built upon the pollution reduction activities of the coal mining industry in the Ruhr area of Germany, and the fashion design industry in 'Third Italy' districts developed from the established close relations between the global market and local specific assets of textile production (Hospers 2004; Belussi and Sammarra 2006). However, it is not to say that all old industrial areas are able to renew themselves like a 'phoenix from the ashes'. The new path creation seems more likely to benefit from neighbouring or technologically related sectors. Recently, related variety and regional branching have been seen as useful notions to understand endogenous processes of new firm formation and industrial transformation, as Boschma and Frenken (2011: 191) articulated 'the higher the number of related industries in a region, the higher the number of possible recombinations, and thus the higher the probability that regions will diversify successfully into related products'. As for old industrial areas, Fornahl *et al.* (2012) examined the causality between the declining shipbuilding industry and the emerging offshore wind energy in Northern Germany, and concluded that the offshore wind energy industry primarily benefits from related onshore wind firms and other branched sectors rather than from the shipbuilding industry. In contrast, new findings from several Scandinavian industrial regions reveal that new path creation may emerge from the process of interaction or combination based on different or unrelated people, firms and sectors (Cooke 2012). Therefore, industrial relatedness, variety and proximity can be seen as very important explanatory factors for regional path creation. Meanwhile, however, this has raised difficult questions about the extent to which industrial proximity in a region can really facilitate invention and innovation, and why regions still act in different ways when restructuring even though they have similar or the same conditions of industrial relatedness.

Institutional–political impact factors

With the theoretical paradigms changing from 'neoclassicism' to 'new regionalism', attention is increasingly being paid to the role of noneconomic factors in shaping the uneven landscapes of regional economies (Amin and Thrift 1994; Saxenian 1994; Cooke and Morgan 1998). One of the most cited references on the restructuring of old industrial areas shows that thick institutional tissues, together with a common worldview or mindset may lead to a political and cognitive lock-in that incrementally erodes the renewing processes of regional economies (Grabher 1993). This work opens up an alternative perspective for rethinking the continuity and change of old industrial areas by highlighting the role of local culture, institutions, politics and policies. For instance, there is wide agreement in the literature that the slow restructuring process in Northeast England is due to its localized industrial culture (e.g. strong labour unionism and the continuing legacy of recruitment traditions) and strong regional protectionism, which lead to the short-sightedness of local actors and the inability to move on to new activities (Sadler and Thompson 2001). Although the political and cognitive lock-in concept has been used extensively to explain the failure or continuity of old industrial areas, this does not mean that lock-in is a cul-de-sac for the further development of old industrial areas. Hassink (2007) demonstrated how local actors in Westmünsterland in Germany took advantage of weak institutional lock-in to encourage diversification into new activities among textile complexes. Daegu, on the other hand, a textile city-region in South Korea, is regarded as an unsuccessful lesson in restructuring because of the strong regional protectionism of vested interests in textile production, and high institutional resistance to change (Cho and Hassink 2009). In this sense, regional political and cognitive lock-in actually provides varied possibilities for regional further evolution instead of only setting hindrances to stability. Old industrial areas may move beyond the lock-in situation and pave the way to regional renewal if the lock-in effect is relatively weak. In other words, the different paths of restructuring followed in old industrial areas are strongly associated with the degree of regional institutional resistance for restructuring, namely the strength and weakness of political–cognitive lock-ins.

Several concrete political–institutional factors have been examined in an attempt to answer more detailed questions about the type of factor that plays the dominant role in shaping the leeway for regional renewal. Cao and Xi's (2007) study of China's coal-mining heartland, Shanxi province, articulates the pessimistic role of regional identity since the long-term coal-driven economy plays an important role in damaging the motivation and aspirations of local actors to attack existing old institutions protected by vested interests and initiate new ones. Likewise, a widely shared cultural (institutional) ideology of collectivism in *danwei* inherited from the centrally planned economy in the Mao era can be well observed in Northeast China, leading to a severe lack of commercialism and entrepreneurship (Zhang 2008). In the US, a comparative study of two *Rustbelt* regions indicates that social capital of the civic networking plays a pivotal role in accessing external resources for coping with external shocks, and encouraging collective action to form adaptive social orders for regional revitalization (Safford 2009). Moreover, there is much evidence presenting political impulses such as institutional reforms, industrial policies and renewal initiatives that provide tailor-made vehicles for enhancing the strength of regional restructuring. But more importantly, the formulation and implementation of those political impulses cannot be inseparable from the efforts of place-specific human actors. Especially, political leaders who have power to develop new institutions, initiate effective policies and nurture new visions can directly facilitate regional renewal of old industrial areas. Taking the examples of the mechanical industry of Prato (Italy) and the automotive industry of the West Midlands (UK), Bailey *et al.* (2010) explained how forms of leadership vary from region to region in very different ways to influence the processes of decision making, which led to divergent trajectories for industrial renewal.

The impact factors we discussed above tend to overemphasize the role of localized factors in hindering or enabling the restructuring of old industrial areas, which, indeed, remains problematic. Hassink (2010b) pointed out that regional adaptability is a multi-scaled evolutionary process and it is important to take into account the institutional context at all spatial levels. Evidence has also shown that extra-local political–institutional factors such as national political change, cross-state strategies, and international regulations affect or even determine the capacity for regional adaptation. Goodwin *et al.* (2002) reviewed four British industrial regions and found that devolution altered the institutional architecture and exacerbated the uneven capacities of regional economic development within the UK. Birch *et al.* (2010) analysed the different patterns of adaptation of old industrial areas across Western Europe and concluded that the varieties of capitalism among different nations play a salient role in shaping different favoured 'paths' of regional adaptation. In addition, since several global agreements have been achieved on climate change, such as the Kyoto Protocol, many energy-intensive and manufacturing regions are required to reduce carbon emissions and speed up the processes of deindustrialization and transformation towards a low-carbon economy. Thus, the emergence of endogenous factors may be caused by exogenous triggers and vice versa. This means that political–institutional factors coming from all different spatial levels coexist and co-evolve with each other and jointly affect regional restructuring.

As the above discussions have shown, it is obvious that factors affecting the restructuring of old industrial areas tend to be exceedingly complex. By drawing upon single spatial perspectives or applying one specific concept it may be possible to some extent to understand the evolutionary characteristics of some specialized industries or regions; however, it is hard to generate full and reliable insights into this question within the evolving context of a globalized economy. Therefore, we contend that it is crucial to rethink the restructuring of old industrial areas using an evolutionary, multi-scalar and complex perspective to regard the relationship between adaptation, adaptability and evolution in old industrial areas. This perspective needs to be oriented toward exploring some less well understood questions, such as: how do locally embedded institutional architectures, interacting with regional, national and international institutions, local political dynamics, and the differentiated agency of individuals and organizations, help to shape particular evolutionary paths over time and how are they shaped by them? What is the role of the state in responding to all kinds of external shocks and internal crises, how does it coordinate local agents, power and institutions to create an adaptive environment for regional restructuring and transformation? In general, how many factors are there and what are their roles in shaping distinctive developmental trajectories over time and space that help us to understand the uneven adaptability of economic landscapes in old industrial areas?

Synthesizing the impact factors of regional adaptability

The notion of adaptability, originally derived from biology, has been recently employed to explain the evolutionary reaction and response of old industrial areas in a rapidly changing world. It principally refers to the systemic capability to cope with unforeseen events in the future and also the dynamic ability to overcome long-term lock-ins for socio-economic evolution (Hassink 2010b; Dawley *et al.* 2014). This section, therefore, will not only assess the features of varied impact factors on regional adaptability in old industrial areas, but also introduce related insights in evolutionary economic geography and other social sciences about the interpretation of these features. In particular, we attempt to shed light on two main unsolved issues: study on multidimensioned impact factors that are closely associated with the nature of adaptability in old industrial areas; research on properties and features of the main factors that could give a direction of how to assess the strengths and weaknesses of regional adaptability. Informed by the existing impact factors discussed above, all sorts of factors (e.g. logical and non-logical, local and trans-local, economic and institutional, etc.) interact together in shaping out different degrees of regional adaptability and, in turn, divergent paths of old industrial areas (Figure 11.1). These main impact factors also include the characteristics of sub-factors in different spatial levels as follows.

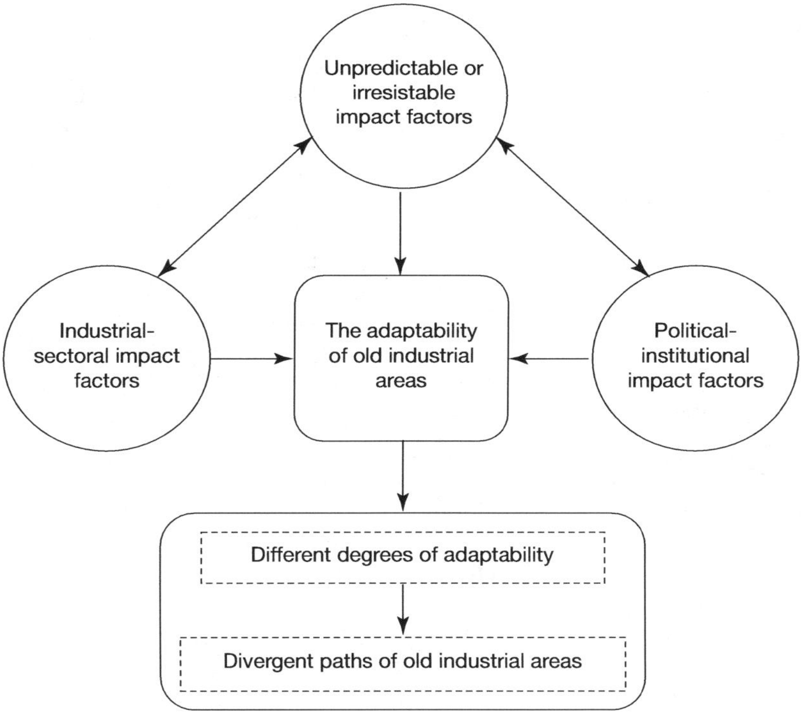

Figure 11.1 The process of multidimensioned impact factors affecting the adaptability in old industrial areas.

Source: authors' own compilation.

Industrial-sectoral impact factors

1 Regional economic structure
   (a) The extent of industrial specialization: whether there is an industrial mono-structure or not (indicators include the percentage of the total manufacturing employment made up by the dominant industry in a region; its share of total GDP growth; the extent of other sectors and subsidiaries supporting and serving the dominant industry).
   (b) The characteristics of the dominant industry: ownership (State owned or private or hybrid?), types of capital (labour-intensive or capital-intensive), forms of organization and size (oligopoly companies or SMEs).
2 The industrial–sectorial proximity
   (a) The quality of regional innovation system: the systemic relations among the different industries, agencies and actors, such as, university–industry linkages, the role of intermediates in bridging the gap between knowledge base and application sectors.
   (b) Technologically industrial relatedness and unrelatedness: technologically related industries tend to foster new path creation and diversification as related variety, but unrelated variety can promote industrial portfolio that benefits from regional adaptability against external shocks.
3 International economic influences, consisting of international industrial relocation, labour mobility and circulation, mergers and acquisitions, and project-based technology transfers and science cooperation, which help local traditional industries integrating into global production networks and restructuring economic structures, technological bases, and institutions of regions.

Political-institutional impact factors

1 Regional political–institutional conditions
   (a) Differentiated political status of regions (or the differences of central-local relations): politically decentralized regions have more autonomy than others as they are legally able to formulate institutions such as laws, policies, regulations and other arrangements served for regional needs, which is a fundamental factor in leading to regionally uneven adaptability.
   (b) The degree of regional cognitive and political lock-in: this factor is related to a number of concrete elements such as place-specific cultural traditions, written and unwritten rules of communities, regional identity of individuals and groups, social capital and trust, often place-based and different in degrees across regions, that contribute to the regionally different extent of institutional lock-ins.
   (c) The role of political leaders and their actions: particularly, the functions, aims and incentives of political leadership in regions, namely, the different forms of regional political leadership, that play a key role in initiating and implementing policies, strategies and visionary plans for regional restructuring.
2 A national political system and state strategies
   (a) National varieties of capitalism: the notion of 'varieties of capitalism' provides a promising analytical framework to interpret why and how regions with different versions of institutional and political settings influence the degree of adaptive capacity (Peck and Theodore 2007).
   (b) The asymmetric state strategies: many state strategies aiming at spatially bounded regions or specific industries without considering inter-regional coordination that may enhance geographical differences of regional adaptation.

3 Supra-national institutional influences that strongly affect the conditions of industrial policy related to the dominant industry and main old industrial regions.

Unpredictable and irresistible impact factors

1 Irresistible slow crises such as resource exhaustion, climate warming and environmental degradation that influence the results of decision making in dealing with regional development in the future.
2 Unpredictable shocks such as financial crises, natural disasters, terrorism and man-made emergencies have been regarded as important indicators to evaluate and test regional adaptability.

In the light of the listed impact factors above, we try to distinguish the key 'positive' and 'negative' factors for regional adaptability by identifying the different characters of the main generalized impact factors from multiple spatial levels (Table 11.1). In this section, we emphasize the positive impact factors of regional adaptability, as they can provide the potential avenues for regional renewal and show significant implications to policy makers. As we have discussed, the evolutionary school and some related social sciences seem to be useful for understanding the evolving regional adaptability and its geographical nature of old industrial areas. On the one side, there are industrial–sectoral factors that foster regional adaptability. First, the recently developed theoretical concepts in evolutionary economic geography (EEG), such as related variety (Frenken *et al.* 2007), regional branching (Boschma and Frenken 2011), regional innovation platforms (Harmaakorpi *et al.* 2011) and transversality (Cooke 2012) pointing into the direction of industrial diversification show effective ways to break the functional lock-in and strengthen the extent of regional adaptability. In contrast to industrial specialization and mono-structure, a region with a diversified industrial structure can positively affect the renewal process. Second, the notion of path creation and positive path dependence conceptualizes how new developmental paths can emerge out of old ones via recombining (pre)existing competences, knowledge, technologies and institutions. A higher degree of industrial relatedness in a region is more likely to develop positive feedback mechanisms of knowledge interaction and recombination that promote the potential of learning and innovation. Third, a thick and well-networked RIS is endowed by regional multi-agent interactions, in which both codified and tacit knowledge can be effectively transferred and embedded into new technologies and products that foster regional transformation. According to the 'local buzz' and 'global pipelines' concept (Bathelt *et al.* 2004), too much local buzz in RIS may generate an inward-looking perspective that leads to regional industrial rigidity. In this case, developing an appropriate number of extra-regional linkages or global pipelines may help a local economic system to absorb new resources in order to avoid regional stagnation.

On the other hand, political–institutional factors can facilitate the process of regional adaptation. First, the use of evolutionary perspective within a geographical political economy approach seems to be a useful method to rethink spatially uneven evolution by emphasizing the role of the state, social agency and capital accumulation (Mackinnon *et al.* 2009). A region that, situating a higher political status in a country or having a close power relation with the central state, is likely to gain more institutional advantages in driving regional economy. We also recognize the specific role of political leaders in affecting regional policy-making processes and planning, supervising and practising the ways, modes and speed of regional economic adaptation. For example, active leaders with transformative leadership can be seen as 'initiators' or 'triggers' who not only build up new regional images and concrete visions of regional growth

Table 11.1 Placing the key positive and negative factors of adaptability of old industrial areas

Positive factors facilitating regional adaptability	*Negative factors constraining regional adaptability*
Industrial–sectoral impact factors	
A regional diversified industrial structure; An absence of monopoly enterprises; Technologically related firms and industries; A good performance of RIS; Adequate external economic linkages.	A strong industrial mono-structure; A presence of large monopoly enterprises; A poor performance of RIS; A lack of external economic linkages.
Political–institutional impact factors	
A high regional political status; Active leaders and strong transformative leadership; A weak cognitive and political lock-in; Supporting national and international institutions.	A low regional political status; A weak or lack of transformative leaders and leadership; A strong cognitive and political lock-in; An absence of national and international institutions.

Source: Adapted from Hassink (2010b).

and change, but also connect with varied actors to participate and take actions in reframing new organizations and widely shared institutions toward regional transformation. Second, the cognitive and political lock-in represents comprehensive institutional conditions that incorporate social relations, cultural norms, political ideologies, and all sorts of formal and informal institutions. A weak cognitive and political lock-in situation has been testified as a positive factor because it implies more room and possibilities for regional renewal than a strong one. Third, a regional economy that is involved in national and international institutions such as national industrial strategies, international laws and policies, among others, might be more capable of strengthening regional economic adaptability.

Conclusions

The idea of regional adaptability has rightly attracted increasing attention from economic geography as part of their growing interest in the evolution and geography of regional and local economies in a complex environment. The question, however, is what impact factors affect the adaptability and how they evolve to shape the adaptive path in differences among old industrial areas. To address this question more clearly, the chapter contributes to a conceptual inspiration by synthesizing multi-scaled impact factors and their characters on regional adaptability. It has shown that, first, impact factors affecting the adaptability are derived from all spatial levels (including local, regional, national and international) with varied features (e.g. economic and non-economic; positive and negative; unpredictable and foreseeable, etc.). Second, although EEG and other social sciences have provided several useful concepts such as lock-in, path dependence, relatedness and transversality in helping to conceptualize how impact factors enable or constrain regional economic adaptability over time, several issues still remain unsolved. More empirical research is needed to deal with those issues and a future research agenda should be centred on four broad themes: (1) conceptualizing the term of adaptation, adaptability and evolution in old industrial areas; (2) continuing to conceptualize the role of regional lock-in, path dependence, relatedness and complexity, and other concepts in affecting the strengths or weaknesses of regional adaptability; (3) searching for complementary theoretical perspectives (e.g. relational and institutional perspective, global production networks, geographical political economy approach, etc.) and encouraging 'engaged pluralism', which is beneficial for further conceptualizing regional adaptability and evolutionary economic geography (Barnes and Sheppard 2010); and (4) conducting more studies on regional adaptability in new contexts, and more cross-sector and intra-regional comparative research between the Western world and emerging economies; by carefully examining the role of 'varieties of capitalism', power relations, and international labour divisions in different countries to advance the understanding of uneven economic adaptation and adaptability of old industrial areas.

References

Amin, A. and Thrift, N., 1994: Living in the global. In: Amin, A. and Thrift, N. (Ed.): *Globalisation, Institutions and Regional Development in Europe*. Oxford: Oxford University Press, pp. 1–22.

Bailey, D., Bellandi, M., Caloffi, A. and Propris, L.D., 2010: Place-renewing leadership: trajectories of change for mature manufacturing regions in Europe. *Policy Studies* 31(4), pp. 457–474.

Barnes, T. and Sheppard, E., 2010: Nothing includes everything: towards engaged pluralism in Anglophone economic geography. *Progress in Human Geography* 34(2), pp. 193–214.

Bathelt, H., Malmberg, A. and Maskell, P., 2004: Cluster and knowledge: local buzz, global pipelines and process of knowledge creation. *Progress in Human Geography* 28(1), pp. 31–56.

Bathelt, H., Munro, A.K. and Spigel, B., 2013: Challenges of transformation: innovation, re-bundling and traditional manufacturing in Canada's Technology Triangle. *Regional Studies* 47(7), pp. 1111–1130.

Belussi, F. and Sammarra, A., 2006: Evolution and relocation in fashion-led industrial districts: evidence from two case studies. *Entrepreneurship and Regional Development* 18(6), pp. 543–562.

Birch, K., MacKinnon, D. and Cumbers, A., 2010: Old industrial regions in Europe: a comparative assessment of economic performance. *Regional Studies* 44(1), pp. 35–53.

Boschma, R. and Frenken, K., 2011: The emerging empirics of evolutionary economic geography. *Journal of Economic Geography* 11(2), pp. 295–307.

Cao, X.W. and Xi, Y.M., 2007: A social psychological perspective on the forming of path dependence in old industrial regions: the case of Shanxi Province in China. *Canadian Social Science* 3(1), pp. 21–28.

Chapman, K., 2005: From growth centre to cluster: restructuring, regional development, and the Teesside chemical industry. *Environment and Planning A* 37(4), pp. 597–615.

Cho, M. and Hassink, R., 2009: Limits to locking-out through restructuring: the textile industry in Daegu, South Korea. *Regional Studies* 43(9), pp. 1183–1198.

Cooke, P., 2012: Transversality and transition: green innovation and new regional path creation. *European Planning Studies* 20(5), pp. 817–834.

Cooke, P. and Morgan, K., 1998: *The Associational Economy: Firms, regions, and innovation*. Oxford: Oxford University Press.

Dawley, S., Marshall, N., Pike, A., Pollard, J. and Tomaney, J., 2014: Continuity and evolution in an old industrial region: the labour market dynamics of the rise and fall of Northern Rock. *Regional Studies*, 48(1): 154–172.

Fornahl, D., Hassink, R., Klaerding, C., Mossig, I. and Schröder, H., 2012: From the old path of shipbuilding onto the new path of offshore wind energy? The case of Northern Germany. *European Planning Studies* 20(5), pp. 835–855.

Frenken, K., Van Oort, F.G. and Verburg, T., 2007: Related variety, unrelated variety and regional economic growth. *Regional Studies* 41(5), pp. 685–697.

Goodwin, M., Jones, M., Jones, R., Pett, K. and Simpson, G., 2002: Devolution and economic governance in the UK: uneven geographies, uneven capacities? *Local Economy* 17 (3), pp. 200–215.

Grabher, G., 1993: The weakness of strong ties: the lock-in of regional development in the Ruhr area. In: Grabher, G. (ed.): *The Embedded Firm: On the socioeconomics of industrial networks*. London and New York: Routledge, pp. 255–277.

Harmaakorpi, V., Tura, T. and Melkas, H., 2011: Regional innovation platforms. In: Cooke, P., Asheim, B., Boschma, R., Martin, R., Schwartz, D. and Tödtling, F. (eds): *The Handbook of Regional Innovation and Growth*. Cheltenham: Edward Elgar, pp. 556–572.

Hassink, R., 2007: The strength of weak lock-ins: the renewal of the Westmünsterland textile industry. *Environment and Planning A* 39(5), pp. 1147–1165.
Hassink, R., 2010a: Regional resilience: a promising concept to explain differences in regional economic adaptability? *Cambridge Journal of Regions, Economy and Society* 3(1), pp. 45–58.
Hassink, R., 2010b: Locked in decline? On the role of regional lock-ins in old industrial areas. In: Boschma, R. and Martin, R. (ed.): *The Handbook of Evolutionary Economic Geography*. Cheltenham: Edward Elgar, pp. 450–468.
Hassink, R. and Shin, D.H., 2005: Guest editorial: the restructuring of old industrial areas in Europe and Asia. *Environment and Planning A* 37(4), pp. 571–580.
Hospers, G.J., 2004: Restructuring Europe's rustbelt: the case of the German Ruhrgebiet. *Intereconomics: Review of European Economic Policy* 39(3), pp. 147–156.
Hu, F.Z.Y. and Lin, G.C.S., 2013: Placing the transformation of state-owned enterprises in North-east China: the state, region and firm in a transitional economy. *Regional Studies* 47(4), pp. 563–579.
Hudson, R., 2005: Rethinking change in old industrial regions: reflecting on the experiences of North East England. *Environment and Planning A* 37(4), pp. 581–596.
Hudson, R. and Swanton, D., 2012: Global shifts in contemporary times: the changing trajectories of steel towns in China, Germany and the United Kingdom. *European Urban and Regional Studies* 19(6), pp. 16–29.
Kaufmann, A. and Tödtling, F., 2000: Systems of innovation in traditional industrial regions: the case of Styria in a comparative perspective. *Regional Studies* 34(1), pp. 29–40.
MacKinnon, D., Cumbers, A., Pike, A., Birch, K. and McMaster, R., 2009: Evolution in economic geography: institutions, political economy, and adaptation. *Economic Geography* 85(2), pp. 129–150.
Martin, R., 2010: Roepke lecture in economic geography-rethinking regional path dependence: beyond lock-in to evolution. *Economic Geography* 86(1), pp. 1–27.
Martin, R. and Sunley, P., 2006: Path dependence and regional economic evolution. *Journal of Economic Geography* 6(4), pp. 395–437.
Peck, J. and Theodore, N., 2007: Variegated capitalism. *Progress in Human Geography* 31(6), pp. 731–772.
Pike, A., Dawley, S. and Tomaney, J., 2010: Resilience, adaptation and adaptability. *Cambridge Journal of Regions, Economy and Society* 3(1), pp. 59–70.
Sadler, D. and Thompson, J., 2001: In search of regional industrial culture: the role of labour organizations in old industrial regions. *Antipode* 33(4), pp. 660–686.
Safford, S., 2009: *Why the Garden Club Couldn't Save Youngstown: The transformation of the Rust Belt*. Cambridge, MA: Harvard University Press.
Saxenian, A., 1994: *Regional Advantage: Culture and competition in Silicon Valley and Route 128*. Cambridge, MA: Harvard University Press.
Scott, A.J., 2000: Economic geography: the great half-century. *Cambridge Journal of Economics* 24(4), pp. 483–504.
Shaw, K. and Robinson, F., 2012: From 'regionalism' to 'localism': opportunities and challenges for North East England. *Local Economy* 27(3), pp. 232–250.
Steiner, M., 1985: Old industrial areas: a theoretical approach. *Urban Studies* 22(5), pp. 397–398.
Tödtling, F. and Trippl, M., 2004: Like phoenix from the ashes? The renewal of clusters in old industrial regions. *Urban Studies* 41(5/6), pp. 1159–1179.
Tödtling, F. and Trippl, M., 2005: One size fits all? Towards a differentiated regional innovation policy. *Research Policy* 34(8), pp. 1203–1219.
Treado, C.D., 2010: Pittsburgh's evolving steel legacy and the steel technology cluster. *Cambridge Journal of Regions, Economy and Society* 3(1), 105–120.
Trippl, M. and Otto, A., 2009: How to turn the fate of old industrial areas: a comparison of cluster-based renewal processes in Styria and the Saarland. *Environment and Planning A* 41(5), pp. 1217–1233.
Zhang, P.Y., 2008: Revitalizing old industrial base of Northeast China: process, policy and challenge. *Chinese Geographical Science* 18(2), pp. 109–118.

12

CHINESE GEOGRAPHICAL BASED INNOVATION CLUSTERING

Major driving forces and their functions

Xiangdong Chen, Xin Niu and Li-Si Song

Introduction

China's geographical landscape covers a wide range of economic regions with significant differences in economic and industrial development. The interesting points in Chinese economies are that there are diversified driving forces, such as local or regional companies, local and central government, and overseas invested firms in relevant regions, to jointly develop local economies, with heavier geographical agglomerations over different industries. Among them, concentration and distribution of innovation capacities in China may be one of the most dynamic parts in this fast growing economy. Questions in this regard are often raised on the driving forces in different regions in China on geographically bounded innovation activities, and the potentiality of economic development in the region. This chapter will deal with related topics to those possible driving forces and the geographical pattern of economic development and innovation activities in China.

Regional innovation clustering in China: FDI development as a major driving force

Research background

Geographical concentration of foreign direct investment (FDI) development has been discussed on numerous occasions. FDI is generally defined as investment that provides the investor with effective control and is accompanied by managerial participation and widely considered as an amalgamation of capital, technology, marketing, and management. These contents would definitely stimulate production knowledge transfer through collaborations and competitions between FDI firms and local suppliers/industrial customers in local markets.

China, as one of the largest FDI host countries in the world since 2002, is transferring rapidly from a rather closed economy in the late 1970s, through partially opening up to the more commercial and business world in the 1980s (represented by the dominant part of investment from close overseas connecting regions such as Hong Kong, Taiwan, Macao, and other regions and countries in Asia), towards becoming largely international in the mid 1990s and early 2000s, when almost all larger MNEs (typically most Fortune 500 companies) in Europe and North America came to China for their fortune. Profound facts that indicate important changes are twofold. First, investment by MNEs from Western countries has been rapidly growing in terms of both numbers of projects and investment volume size since the mid 1990s, showing stronger commitment to China's market for their longer term strategies. Second, heavier R&D investment has been developed in China since the late 1990s from technology intensive MNEs, implying that clustering of FDI in China is gradually transferring from labor intensive to capital intensive as well as technology intensive in nature, while this also proves that competition in the Chinese market among those MNEs is increasingly keen with more comprehensive technology content. These changes, particularly changes in geographical concentration of FDI-based technology resources, are becoming an important issue for analysis of FDI development in China. This section, under a conceptual research framework on FDI-based technology competition, or quality of FDI, focuses on performances in terms of technological innovation indicators by FDI firms in China, through a picture of the overall geographical pattern of FDI-based technology competition in China, and also a picture contrasting with the local industrial innovation in different regions.

It is commonly understood that along with an unevenly distributed pattern of economic output in China, FDI also develops in a rather unbalanced volume in terms of geographical distributions. There is a significant difference between eastern regions (87.8 percent of accumulated FDI inflows into China from 1983 to 1998) and the other two regions (FDI inflows in central China regions: 8.9 percent; and western China regions: 3.3 percent); and this situation did not change much even during the 2000s (86.9 percent in eastern and coastal regions, and less than 15 percent in inner and western regions in China, 2007). It is reported that some 70 percent of FDI flows into only limited numbers of provinces and cities in China (for example, Guangdong Prov., Jiangsu Prov., Zhejiang Prov., Shandong Prov., and Shanghai city, in 2007). However, on the other hand, overseas investment in mid and western regions sometimes can be significantly huge in size, implying that investment from larger MNEs abroad can be motivated for special capital intensive projects, such as natural resource oriented investment. It can be expected that mid and western regions in China would absorb more investment in the coming years since a more opening up policy has been implemented since the late 1990s onward.

Data selection on geographical distribution of FDI development

In order to reveal the nature of technological innovation capacity in FDI companies, a set of indicators regarding FDI quality is selected in this study. Also, technically, in order to show a clearer picture for overseas readers on the direction of the Chinese geographical landscape with economic and innovation performances, the following code system (see Table 12.1) is used in the relevant data analysis. Particularly, this code system can be used to identify different regions in certain directions, either inner land or coastline, northern or southern, etc. In this way, the study is trying to provide a clearer picture of geographical distribution of FDI quality during recent years.

In fact, FDI related innovation and technology capacity has been discussed ever since FDI projects first appeared in China, and the related concept changes from time to time. For example, major concerns in FDI studies in China in the 1980s were simply the investment volume of newly established FDI firms, when labor intensive projects were more frequent, represented by

Table 12.1 Geographical code system for typical Chinese regions

Code	*Description*	*Region name in Chinese Pinyin system (pronunciation)*
BJ	The Capital City	Beijing City
SHcst	The 1st biggest coast City	Shanghai City
TJcst	The 2nd biggest coast City	TianJin City
NE1	North East region 1	Hi Long Jiang Prov.
NE2	North East region 2	Ji Lin Prov.
NE3	North East region 3	Liao Ning Prov.
CN1	Central North region 1	NeiMengGu Meng Nationality Autonomous Region
CN2	Central North region 2	Shanxi Prov.
CN3	Central North region 3	He Bei Prov.
CN4	Central North region 4	He Nan Prov.
Ecst1	East coast region 1	Shan Dong Prov.
Ecst2	East coast region 2	Jiang Su Prov.
Ecst3	East coast region 3	Zhe Jiang Prov.
MS1	Middle South region 1	AnHui Prov.
MS2	Middle South region 2	Hu Bei Prov.
MS3	Middle South region 3	Hu Nan Prov.
MS4	Middle South region 4	Jiang Xi Prov.
Scst 1	South coast region 1	Fu Jian Prov.
Scst 2	Southern coast region 2	Guang Dong Prov.
Scst 3	Southern coast region 3	Hai Nan Prov.
SW1	South West region 1	Si Chuan Prov.
SW11	South West region 11	Chong Qing City
SW2	South West region 2	Gui Zhou Prov.
SW3	South West region 3	Yun Nan Prov.
SW4	South West region 4	Guang Xi Zhuang Nationality Autonomous Region
NW1	North West region 1	Xin Jiang Wei Wu Er Nationality Autonomous Region
NW2	North West region 2	Gan Su Prov.
NW3	North West region 3	Qing Hai Prov.
NW4	North West region 4	Ning Xia Hui Nationality Autonomous Region
NW5	North West region 5	Xizang (Tibet) Zang Nationality Autonomous Region
NW6	North West region 6	Shannxi Prov.

Note: The letters are used to indicate geographical regions, e.g., east, west, or central regions, and the numbers are used to indicate south–north directions: the smaller numbers are more northern-bounded and the larger numbers are more southern bounded. "cst" means the coastline regions. Here south–north, as well as coast regions are more emphasized because these regions are generally shown significantly in differences in economic development terms.

smaller average investment size for each project, and by investors primarily from Chinese Taiwan, Hong Kong, and Marco districts. Immediate and short-term return was naturally the major motivation for the investment. Capital and technical contents of FDI have gradually come to dominate since the late 1990s, along with the development of an active market in China, and larger MNEs' participation with more capital supplies from North American and European companies. With such change in mind, some meaningful measures can be selected as more appropriate indicators for the quality of the investment, such as average investment size per project (with a presumption that larger average size of capital inflows, or more condensed investment project, would bring more capital intensive and possibly technology intensive productions).

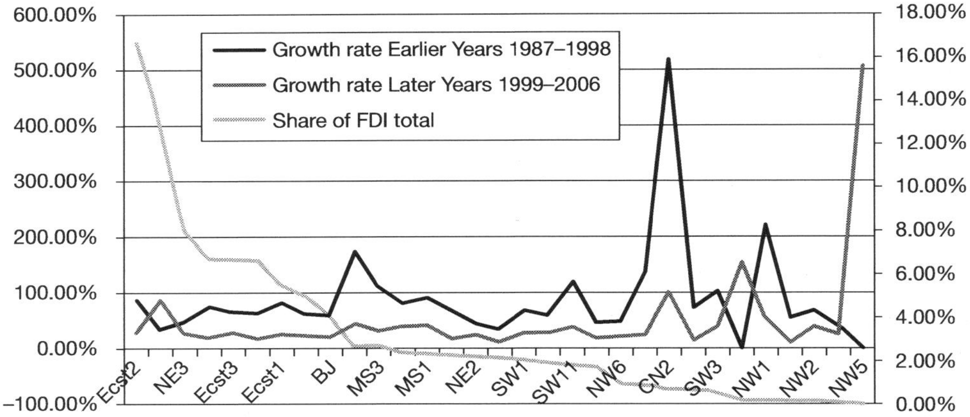

Figure 12.1 Comparison of regional FDI in China: growth rate vs FDI volume shares.

Notes:

1) Shares of FDI in the region to total FDI in the country (right scale is used)

2) Regional FDI growth rate in the two time periods (left scale is used).

Source: *China Statistical Yearbook* (1999 through 2008).

It is worth noting that although FDI volume may change over time in certain regions, the technology and innovation based quality contents should be rather steady, especially when the manufacturing sector based infrastructure is heavily implemented in the region. In this case, the size of the capital flows can be considered as one of the stable indicators, as this is usually related to long term relevant measures. For example, a larger average size of FDI inflows in certain regions may reflect investors' consensus not only in a higher level of capital or more technology intensive in nature, but also in confidence in that region in the longer term vision for future development.

In this study, the growth rate of FDI is also used in different time periods (refer to Figure 12.1), in order to contrast differences in relevant regions and dynamic changes in overseas capital inflows. In Figure 12.1, the sample regions are ranked by FDI volume, with a contrast of average growth rate of FDI inflow in two time periods. It is interesting to note that for those condensed FDI volume areas in China, investment growth has been rather steady, and for those geographical regions with fewer FDI inflows, investment growth rate can fluctuate highly, which implies that FDI in China can be versatile with different motivations, on different regional markets in China.

Figure 12.2 is produced with an accumulated volume of FDI in related regions in the late 1990s, contrasted with overall innovation capacity measures by sample regions in China. It is interesting that regions with higher FDI volume may not necessarily be regions with larger average investment size, such as cases in Guangdong province. Considering strong possibilities of embedded technologies in larger sized investment, size difference in FDI inflow across regions can imply FDI quality in many cases. Further, it is also necessary to compare regions in more precise terms on regional innovation over FDI and in local companies.

FDI quality measures and empirical results

Based on these discussions, more detailed measurement on FDI quality is applied to the study and compared among sample regions. Generally speaking, three groups of indicators would be

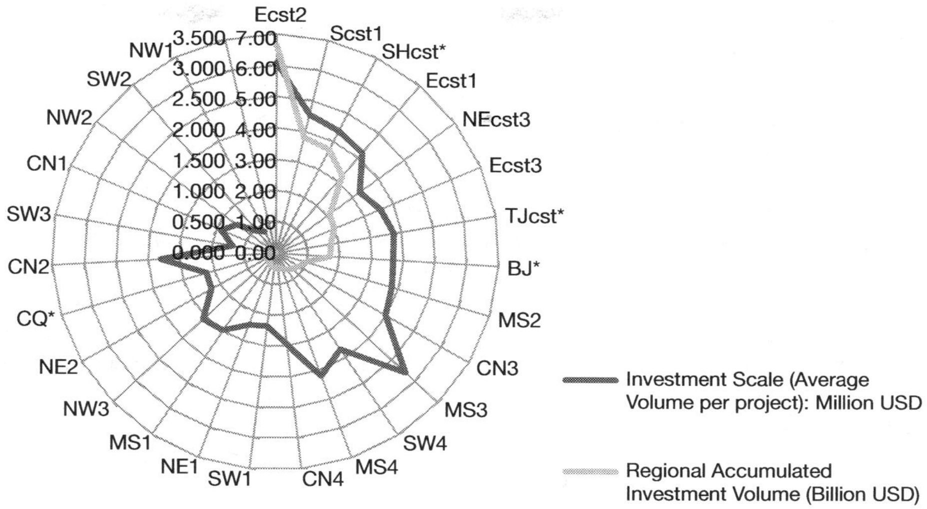

Figure 12.2 FDI size in terms of relative measures on FDI movement in China.
Source: authors' own calculation based on data from the *China Statistical Yearbook* (1996 through 2000).

applied, usually over innovation input, output, and together with investment quality (e.g., size, volume, and growth rate). In a more detailed description, the following 18 indicators have finally been chosen according to the characteristics of the indicators and availability of the corresponding data set. They are:

1 Technological innovation input (in total 11 indicators):
   a) R&D labor input (2): numbers of Science & Technology (S&T) personnel, numbers of companies with R&D organization;
   b) R&D fund input (6): S&T investment total, internal investment total, new product development total, technology renovation investment, investment on imported technology, investment size (scale measure) of S&T institution, etc.;
   c) technology resource (3): S&T project, technology import, domestic technology acquisition;
2 Technical innovation capability output (in total four indicators):
   a) R&D and innovation output (2): patenting numbers, granted patents;
   b) innovation output in market (2): profit margin in new product, industrial value-added from new product;
3 FDI indicators (in total three indicators):
   a) FDI strength (1): average size of FDI projects in the region;
   b) FDI volume (1): absolute value of the investment and growth rate of FDI.

In order to compare the competitiveness of FDI firms, contrasted with local industrial firms, regional referential measures on industrial technology activities are necessary. In this regard, a parameter of Relative Innovation Competitive Index (RICI) is designed, in order to contrast the relative power of the FDI quality measure to local companies, especially state-owned enterprises in the region. The following formula is provided to indicate the relative differences between FDI firms and local state owned companies on each of the typical relevant indicators. It should be noted that RICI is an abstracted parameter from more detailed indicator C_{ij}:

where: FDI_{ij} is indicator j of FDI firms in region i; SO_{ij} is indicator j of state-owned companies' in region i. In this way, if $C_{ij}>0$, then FDI firms will be stronger than local companies on quality indicator j in region i (value of C_{ij} can thus be achieved between −1 and +1). RICI is further abstracted from Principle Factor Analysis based on those sample C_{ij}s, in order to summarize effectively overall information from the original 18 parameters. The following chart (Figure 12.3) shows the relationship between the compound innovation factor (RICI), or in other words, FDI quality, and volume of FDI.

According to this chart, it is highly implacable that in terms of major innovation capability, correlations between FDI volume and FDI quality is not always matched in parallel; FDI quality in general is higher in those high FDI volume backed regions and in coastline regions in China. Exceptions occur in two interesting regions where FDI quality is lower: 1) heavier FDI volume regions such as in Ecst2 (Jiangsu Prov.), Ecst1 (Shan Dong Prov.), and especially NE3 region (Liao Ning Prov.) where local companies are more competitive; 2) lower FDI volume regions. It is also noticeable that in some lower FDI volume regions, average size of the FDI can be big, which indicates larger investment projects with heavier equipment in those regions (such as CN1, SW11, NW4 regions during those particular years), usually for capital intensive projects on upper stream sectors, where FDI firms are stronger than local companies in those quality measures.

Further, by contrasting FDI Size (in terms of project scales) and FDI quality (RICI), a two dimension map is produced (Figure 12.4) according to values of each sample region in China.

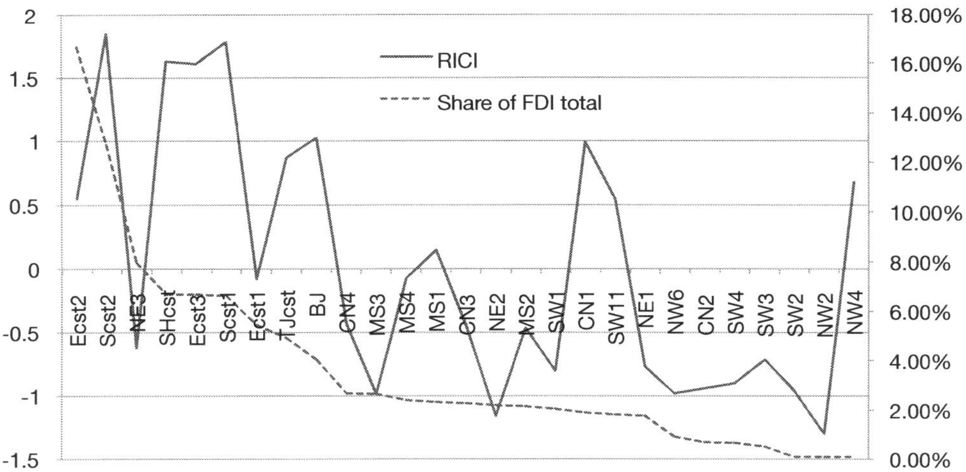

Figure 12.3 FDI quality distribution in different geographical regions in China.

Note: the value of RICI here in this chart is the abstract value from the PFA analysis.

Source: based on 18 indicators collected from the China Statistical Yearbook on Science and Technology and other related publications on the science and technology movement in China, covering a time period between 1990 and 2005.

It is obvious that three groups of regions (with corresponding circles) can be derived based on distributions of FDI quality:

The Dominative Position (Group I) represents related geographical regions where FDI firms are in a strong position in technology and innovation capacity (represented by overall RICI), with both larger volume of the investment and higher level of innovation capabilities against local firms, i.e. highly dominative in industrial technology resources.

The Competitive Position (Group II) represents those geographical areas where overseas investment is comparatively diversified in its average size, and at the same time, only manages to stay in the medium and lower level of innovation capacity, compared with local companies, which may indicate that in these regions, foreign capital firms' innovation and technology competitiveness are comparable with or even lower than the level of domestic firms.

Less-Technical Competitive Position (Group III) represents those geographical areas where overseas investment brings much diversified average size and at the same time stays in a lower position in terms of technology and innovation capacity, compared with local firms, i.e. foreign capital firms are clearly less competitive in terms of industrial technology and innovation capabilities.

Naturally, there has been larger accumulative volume of overseas investment in coastal provinces and cities, where the invested firms and projects are significantly characterized in higher investment scale, intensive technology contents, and higher innovation capabilities, typically in Group I, while in other regions, overseas capital firms are rather diversified in terms of investment scales, ranging from larger capital intensive to smaller labor intensive in nature, and generally less intensive in technology and innovation capacity.

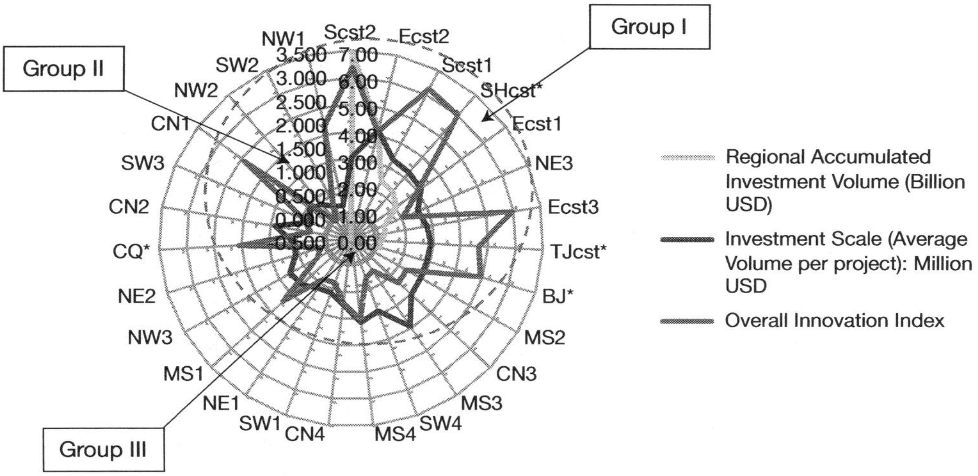

Figure 12.4 FDI quality: innovation-based dimension vs FDI strength dimension (Ranked by accumulated FDI volume in the region, % of average).

Note: only partial regions are selected in this chart, NW3 then is Shaanxi, instead of Qinghai Prov.

Source: calculated based on data from *China Statistical Yearbook*, 2003–2005.

In summary of this section, under a conceptual framework of FDI quality, two facts matter in this distribution. First, FDI quality is generally higher against local Chinese companies in most coastal regions, but this situation holds only after total FDI volume reaches a certain level in that region (around 2 billion USD), which implies that the large multinational enterprises' (MNE) investment, especially larger sized projects, are decisive. Second, there are exceptions in diversified regions where local Chinese companies appear stronger than overseas companies in technology content and innovation capacities; however, it should be noted that this change has only occurred in recent years.

Regional innovation clustering in China: market and policy combined driving force and diversification of innovation performances

Geography related international business studies tend to be concentrated on two streams, the first one deals with geographical clustering of FDI movement, in particular, production clusters generated by capital flows, as mentioned in the previous section, the second one concerns location character of innovation activities by local economic institutions, new knowledge or emerging technology generation, and related production clustering in certain geographical regions, such as geographical concentration of R&D. Both concentrations may bring positive economic return and social welfare; however, there are conditions and limits. Based on current research literature, it is generally believed that both innovation activities and FDI movement need certain economic conditions, though the practical nature in the relevant environment might be different. De Bresson *et al.* (1994)[1] mentioned that the nature of clustering of research based innovation is in some way connected to existing economic development and this relationship determines ways by which firms or research agents could learn and create knowledge. On the other hand, at company level, research shows that technology activities in local firms are dependent on both existing technology competence (such as the gap between the old and the new technology, by Nelson and Winter 1982[2]) and overall industrial activities in certain sectors, with special influence from dominant firms (Patel and Pavitt 1996[3]). These dominating firms may be technology leading companies or MNEs in developing country cases. The central point here is that the diffusion of new technological processes may occur faster in geographical areas where the density of knowledge source about such technologies is higher. Similarly in developing country cases, diffusion of new technology can be locally innovative, rather than globally new, and faster diffusion can be realized in regions where the density of production and engineering based knowledge resource about such technologies are higher. These innovation studies prove that, apart from influence by international companies, local economic innovation clustering in a specific regional context might be crucial, and this more endogenous resource would be further strengthened by the knowledge creation process itself.

This section will focus on regional innovation performance in China, with different resources taken into account. The nature of geographical dispersion and convergence will be especially considered.

Geographical division on eastern-middle-western regions in China and regional performance on technological innovation

The study in this chapter applies the most commonly accepted indicators for measuring and contrasting the dispersion–convergence level on innovation, with economic parameter dimension as a reference in typical regions in China, for example, GDP, or regional GRP and import and export volume are included. At the same time, typical innovation indicators, primarily R&D

investment (or local research expenditure on science and technology, as reported in the annual statistic yearbook on science and technology in China), S&T personnel, are used as input measures and patent numbers, as well as other relevant indicators being used as output measures.

In terms of geographical divisions, this research will use traditional classification of economic zones in China, e.g., Eastern, Mid, and Western regions. However, in order to compare regional difference in convergence and dispersion, more detailed division of ten typical sub-regions under these three geographic groups is also designed and defined as follows, according to their economic performance and geographical closeness:

1 Eastern China regions:
   - Jing-Jin (Capital region) including Beijing, Tianjin, and Hebei Province;
   - Su-Zhe-Hu region (primarily Yangtize River Delta, or YRD region) including JiangSu and Zhejiang provinces, and Shanghai City;
   - Shandong and Liaoning provinces around Huanghai sea;
   - Southern coastal regions including Fujian, Guangdong, and Hainan Provinces;
2 Mid China regions:
   - Northeastern regions, including Jilin and Heilongjiang Provinces;
   - Mid East regions, including Shanxi, Niemenggu, and Henan Provinces;
   - Mid Southern regions, including Jiangxi, Hubei, Hunan, and Anhui Provinces;
3 Western China regions:
   - Southwestern regions, including Sichuan, Guangxi, Guizhou, and Yunnan Provinces, and Chongqing City;
   - Northwestern I regions, including Shaanxi, Gansu, Qinghai, and Ningxia Provinces;
   - Northwestern II regions, including Xinjiang and Xizang Provinces.

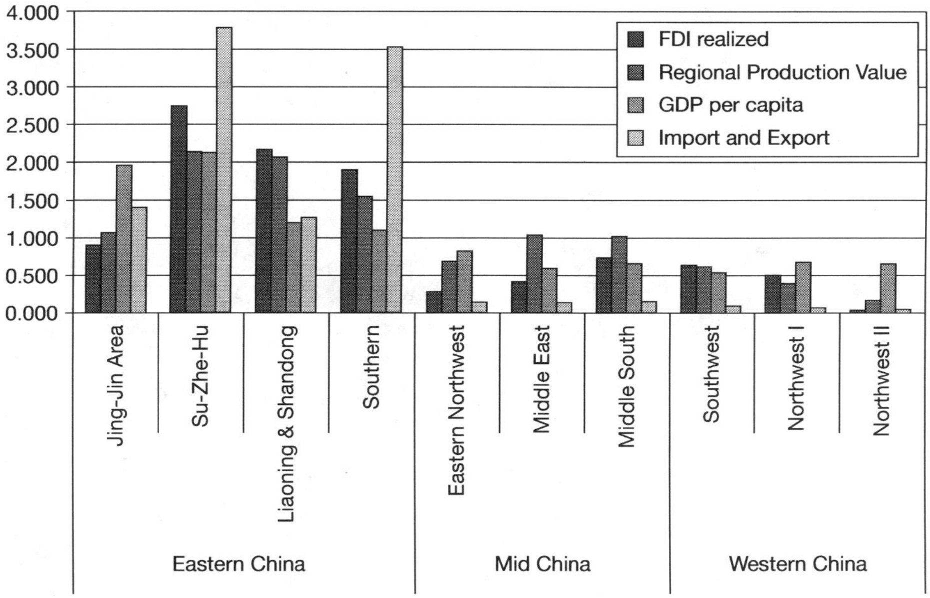

Figure 12.5 Comparison of ten typical regional economies: FDI vs. Impt&Expt volume, compared with Western.

Sources: *China Statistical Yearbook,* 2009, China Statistic Press, 2010.

In order to contrast difference between more economically developed regions (Eastern and some Mid regions) and Western China, total average economic and innovation indicators are used as benchmark or baseline to reveal gaps between regions in China. Figure 12.5 is provided under this framework, with typical input and output measures (in year 2008) on regional economic development. It is obvious that among various indicators, economically opening up FDI and international trade related parameters are the most significant indicators to divide Eastern China into two other regions.

Innovation based comparison over ten typical regions

Degree of innovation performance based dispersion/convergence over the ten sub-regions is further examined with comparison of the Western region, in order to find the important intrinsic effects of innovation capabilities as a whole in certain regions and the nature of economic development.

It should be noted that data are also calculated here as indexed measures, relative to the baseline (level in overall Western China), as shown in Figure 12.6. It can be clearly seen that there are larger differences across regions on innovation output indicators than input indicators between Western and Eastern China. The highest dispersed case appears on patent applications and inventions.

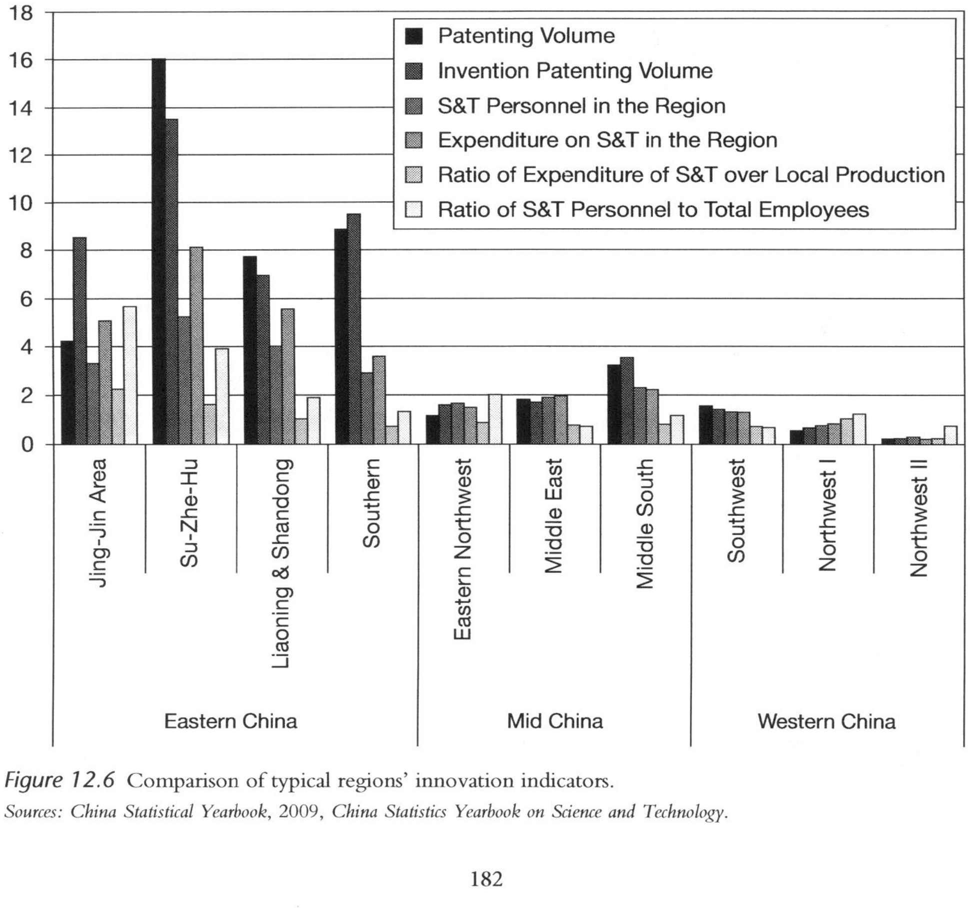

Figure 12.6 Comparison of typical regions' innovation indicators.

Sources: China Statistical Yearbook, 2009, *China Statistics Yearbook on Science and Technology*.

In fact, if only patenting features are concerned, the patterns in different regions in China are very diversified. This patenting based distribution indicates that clusters of innovation output are more likely to be concentrated in typical cities, and although the three geographical regions (Jing-Jin as capital region, Su-Zhe-Hu region, also known as Yangtze River Delta region, and South Sea Costal or Pearl River Delta region) are still the largest clustering areas in patenting, there are other regions in the Northeast, Southwest, and Mid regions in China, where both local and overseas patentees are active, especially local patentees in inner land cities in recent years.

Diversified regional technological innovation capacities and their related economic output

Regional characteristics can be clarified by examining both intra-region and inter-region differences, as shown in Figure 12.7, with contrast across Eastern, Mid, and Western regions in China. These Gini coefficients do not change much between years, as proved by this study over the time period between 2001 and 2008. It is well known that, in general, only policy oriented measures such as expenditure on S&T activities are gradually converging over different regions nationwide; other output measures such as patenting volume and economic output are significantly dispersed over regions. Therefore, in innovation and economic output measures, especially on outward performance, differences and corresponding gaps between typical regions are actually expanding. Regarding input and output measures, output indicators are more diversified than input ones in different regions, which reveals that although policy oriented inputs for innovation in different regions are comparatively steady, or converging, the efficiency of those inputs is significantly different, which in turn provides sound support that innovation capability is rather geographically bounded, not easily transferred or spilled over.

Generally speaking, Western China regions are significantly weak in terms of economic indicators, and this dispersed gap with other regions and within the region is expanding. On

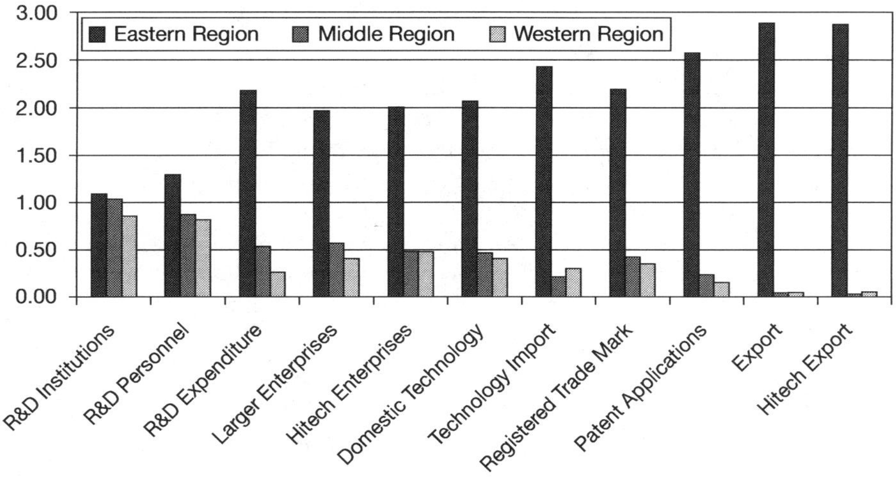

Figure 12.7 Gini Parameters (to indicate dispersion level) on innovation indicators across the three typical regions in China.

Source: the authors' own calculation based on data from *China Statistical Yearbook*, 2006.

the other hand, those economically developed regions are apparently more attractive to economic sources as well as innovation sources in the market place.

Regional innovation clustering in China: university oriented science and technology resource as a potential driving force

Today, universities are increasingly considered as an important resource to support national as well as regional innovation and emerging economic development, by academic researchers, high tech resource based entrepreneurs, and relevant policy makers. The University–Industry–Government (UIG) triplex system or simply University–Industrial consortium keeps attracting attention across developed and developing countries. Key issues in such research and practical policy movement can be technology transfer and technology diffusion between universities and industries, and decisive roles played by universities in university–industry collaborations.

Studies and important findings in empirical as well as in theoretical fields on university–industry collaboration can be found by scholars in various countries such as Japan (Motohashi 2005;[4] Woolgar 2007[5]), UK (D'Este and Patel 2007[6]), Italy (Abramo et al. 2009[7]), and China (Motohashi 2008;[8] Lei et al. 2011[9]), in international literature. Typical studies by Mowery (2001),[10] Lei et al. (2011) and Petruzzelli (2011)[11] attempted to inquire into the patterns and impact of university–industry collaboration upon local economies, based on patent analysis. In particular, Lei et al. (2011) conducted a co-patent research on China's case and found that collaboration between university and industry has become stronger and more intensified in recent years, but other forms of collaborations are weak.

At the same time, there have been important conceptual and theoretical research outputs regarding entrepreneurial universities, especially based on North American and European practices. In recent years, there have been continual efforts from central and regional government in China on the university–industry consortium, together with the development of increasingly larger scale high tech zones all over the country.

Development structures of Chinese universities

According to the statistical yearbook on higher education in China, by 2012 there were 884 publicly owned, formal four-year bachelor degree universities, 1,288 three year bachelor program colleges, 298 privately owned higher educational institutes and 62 branch universities, in total, 2,492 higher education institutions. Especially in the first group of universities, 103 universities (later extended to 113 universities) are selected as member universities in the so-called 211 consortium, and among them 37 universities (later extended to 39 universities) that are further chosen as even more prestigious member universities in the "985" group,[12] representing a group of the best universities in China in terms of advanced scientific research and well developed educational systems (refer to Table 12.2 for those universities in typical regions in China).

Industrial funding for universities' research as important linkage for university–industry consortium

In China, research funds in universities are commonly achieved in a competitive basis from government supported sources (generally basic research as well as applied research oriented) and also from industrial firms, which is more current or future market oriented. The funding from industries can be considered as a clear sign of university–industry collaboration, which is often

Table 12.2 Advanced Chinese universities in typical regions

Typical 10 regional groups	*Universities in 985 group*	*Universities in 211 group*
Jing-Jin regions: Two cities and one province;	**10 (25.6%)**	**31 (27.4%)**
Su-Zhe-Hu region (Yangtze River Delta region) 2 Provinces + 1 city;	7 (17.9%)	21 (18.6%)
Mid Southern regions (or MS region) 4 provinces	6 (15.4%)	14 (12 .4%)
Eastern Huanghai regions (or EH region) 2 provinces;	4 (10.3%)	7 (6.2%)
North West I regions (or NW I region) 3 provinces;	4 (10.3%)	9 (8.0%)
Southern Coastal region (or SC region) 3 provinces;	3 (7.7%)	7 (6.2%)
South Western regions (or SW region) 4 provinces and 1 city;	3 (7.7%)	10 (8.8%)
Northeast regions (or NE region) 2 provinces	2 (5.1%)	7 (6.2%)
Mid Eastern regions (or ME region) 3 provinces	0 (0.0%)	3 (2.7%)
North West region II (or NW II region) 3 provinces.	0 (0.0%)	4 (3.5%)
Total	**39** (100%)	**113** (100%)

Source: wenku.baidu.com.

referred to as the most direct collaboration from existing industries. Table 12.3 provides typical features of industrial funding to Chinese universities in different groups.

Table 12.3 reveals that industrial funding increased faster in recent years. In total, funds from industries increased sharply from 1.8 billion RMB in 2006 to 3.2 billion RMB in 2010, but the percentage share from industry is decreasing. The reason for this is because of the greater increases from other sources, especially from government sources. In terms of the absolute fund volume, "211" university group as well as engineering university group owned the largest funding from industries.

There are other interesting phenomena in research funding for universities, regarding the three modes in different university groups across geographical regions. Typical "211" universities

Table 12.3 Research funds from industries (2006–2010) (0.1 billion RMB)

	2006	*2008*	*2010*	*Average growth (%)*
Total	45.73	65.45	94.03	43.4%
"211" Universities	32.36	46.46	67.93	44.9
Other Universities	13.17	18.66	25.52	39.2
Colleges	0.21	0.33	0.57	64.9
MOE Universities	24.16	34.76	52.19	47.0
Regional Univ.	16.09	22.99	31.27	39.4
Comprehensive Univ.	14.6	21.29	32.17	48.5
Engineering Univ.	24.38	34.37	46.7	38.4

Note: Value of "Total" is a summation of 211 Universities, Other Universities, and Colleges. MOE (Ministry of Education of China) universities are those universities directly under the Ministry of Education, and there are other universities locally owned by regional government. Comprehensive University is the university that covers wider range of scientific and training disciplines, typically on nature sciences and social sciences.

Source: *Statistical Yearbook on Higher Education University S&T*, 2007–2011.

develop larger sized collaborative projects with wider scope of geographical regions, based on their advanced position in academic output and from important government support, especially for universities in Beijing and Shanghai; while regional universities, usually supported by local government, generally focus more on local industries, which can be shown by a higher ratio of industrial funding. And there is another group of universities that develop not only larger government supported projects but also tremendous industrial collaborated projects. Figure 12.8 is provided to indicate such distributions. The chart is produced based on information on 31 provinces and key municipal areas (directly under central government). Up to early 2015, in total there are 2,491 publicly owned higher educational institutions in China,[13] among them there are 1,170 universities offering degree programs. Figure 12.8 shows situations based on 1,074 degree program universities in 2009, among them 710 were publically owned. Three indicators are used in this chart. Ratio to Total (right scale) indicates ranks of those regions where universities received different volumes of research funding from both government and industries; while Ratio to Total Enterprises' Funding (right scale) indicates ranks of industrial funding in relevant regions, which shows the importance of those regions where universities in the region received diversified volumes of industrial funds. The most important one is Funding Ratio from Enterprises (left scale) which indicates the ratio of industrial funding to total funding by universities in the region. Apparently, only limited numbers of universities in a few important regions control larger amounts of research funds from both government and industries, while other universities from most regions use limited research funds primarily from industries. In fact, universities in six provinces and key municipal areas (namely in ranking, Beijing city, Shanghai city, Shandong Prov., Shaanxi Prov., Hubei Prov., Zhejiang Prov.) control 55.4 percent total research funding and 55.2 percent of industrial funding respectively. Other universities in the rest of the regions rely on funds with a comparatively higher ratio from industries.

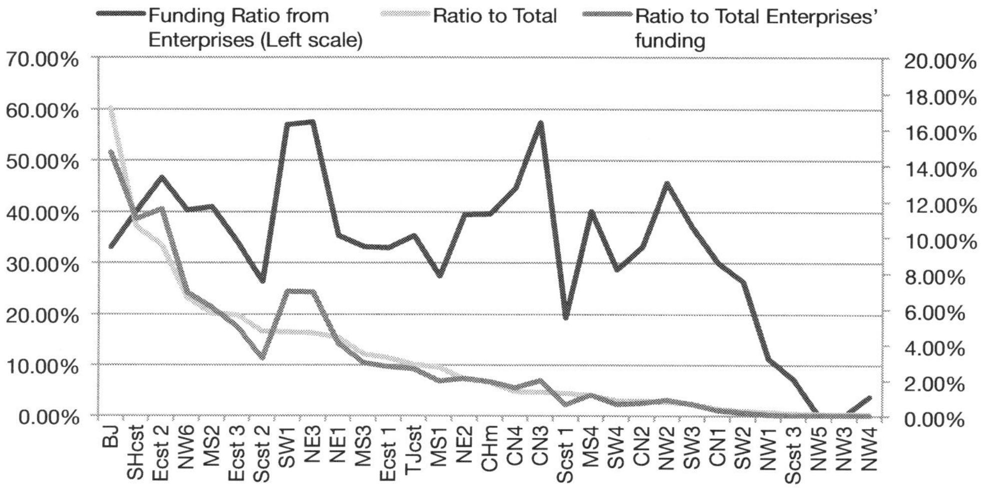

Figure 12.8 Universities' funding from industries in China: contrast among different groups of geographical regions (2006–2009) (ranked by total funding volume received by universities in the region).

Source: based on *China Higher Education Statistical Yearbook*, 2010.

Joint innovation output between university and industries

Joint innovation output, particularly measured by patent licensing or joint patenting, are more important indicators for reflecting universities' collaboration with industries. Based on the authors' research, Figure 12.9 provides a detailed comparison of universities across regions in 55 typical cities in China on both university patenting (in a particular year) and joint patenting with industries. Local production value (used as a basis for regional ranking in this chart) and numbers of local universities are used for reference. This chart is produced based on relative measures, e.g., value in all four indicators are transformed into the percentage of total volume in the relevant indicator.

It is obvious that numbers of universities are rather evenly distributed across these typical regions; however, in terms of patenting volume, especially joint patenting, which is more representative in market oriented collaborations between universities and industries, it is highly diversified and basically dependent upon economic development in the region. On the other hand, there are exceptions in different cities. It can be found that for Beijing, although local universities' funding from industries is less than 40 percent, the volume of funding is big, and especially the joint patenting level with industries is significantly the highest. This can be attributed to the nature of the capital city in more concentrated science and technology resources, and

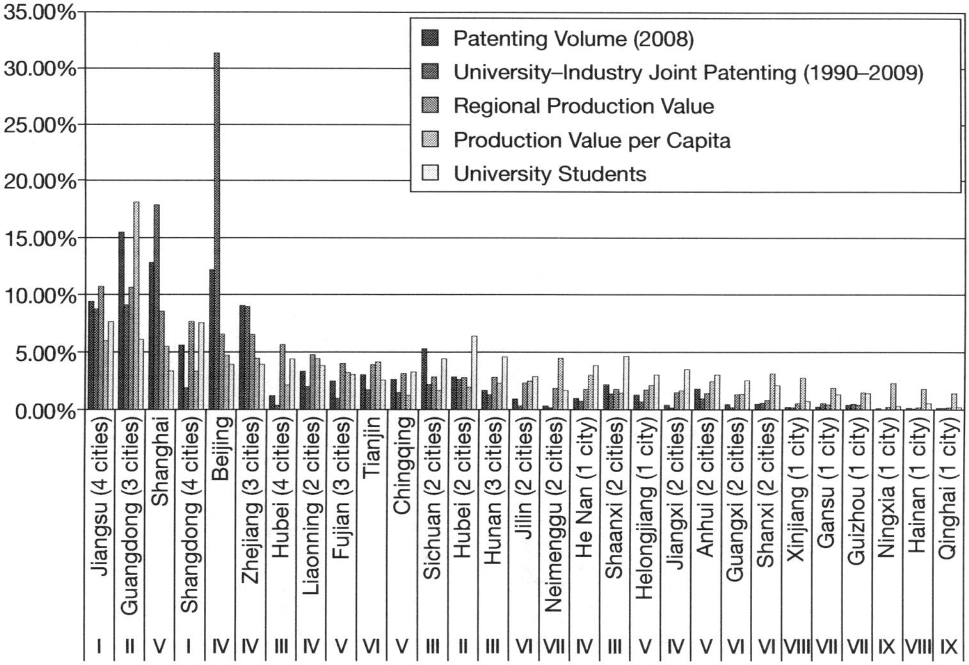

Figure 12.9 Joint patenting by university–industrial collaboration in China, with reference to local production value and distribution of university students in 55 typical cities (% of total).

Note: regions in this chart are ranked by regional production value, and I, II, and so on until IX are used to mark different levels of the regions in terms of university student numbers, with group I the largest number and IX the least number of university students in the region, based on the information of a total 1,394 universities in these 55 cities during 2009.

Source: authors' own data collection and processing, based on data from SIPO website, www.sipo.gov.cn.

also implies that universities with a larger share of national projects (other than funding from industries) are more widely accessible for innovative knowledge diffusion and transferring advanced research to industrial institutions at a greater distance. Universities in Beijing generally collaborate with industrial firms almost all over China, not limited to nearby regions; this is similar in typically big cities with more advanced universities. However, again, such a capable university hub is highly concentrated in limited regions.

Along with rapid growth in university patenting as well as joint patenting with industries, the volume of licensing agreements from universities to industries has also been increasing at a faster pace (refer to Figure 12.10 and 12.11); among them, naturally, engineering universities are major licensors.

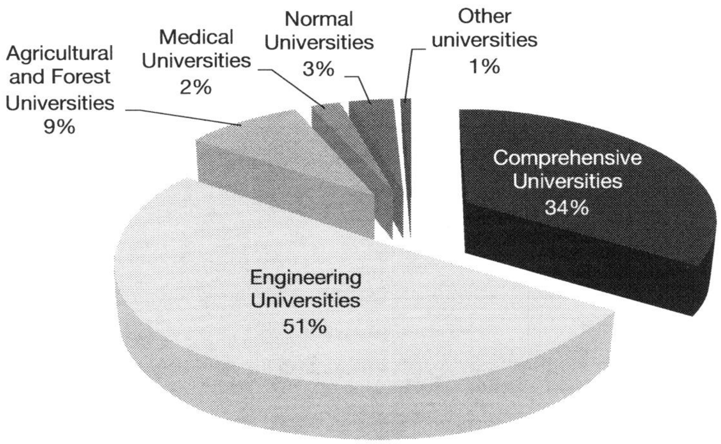

Figure 12.10 University licenses by types of universities.
Source: *China Higher Education Statistical Yearbook*, 2007–2011.

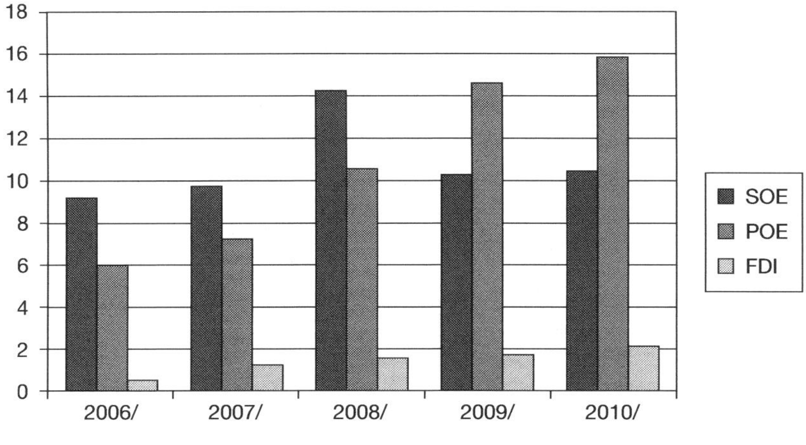

Figure 12.11 Universities' technology transfer by recipients (2006–2010).
Note: SOE: state owned enterprise, POE: private owned enterprise, FDI: foreign direct investment firms.
Source: *China Higher Education Statistical Yearbook*, 2007–2011. Billion RMB.

It is interesting to note that universities' licensing revenue develops faster than licensing project numbers, which implies that value-added effect is increasingly significant. Another interesting feature is that although two major recipient groups share most of the technologies provided by Chinese universities, major recipient groups are privately owned enterprises (POEs) and this group of recipients gradually outperforms state owned enterprises (SOEs) in terms of payment to university licensors in recent years.

The third effective way for universities to operate with industries is to directly run their own companies, usually so called Start Up's on newly developed products or technologies based on universities' own intellectual property resources. In fact, there are in total 85 national science parks in typical cities all over China, where universities play important roles. Again, these university run enterprises are highly concentrated in either company assets or market revenue. For example, among the top 100 university-run high tech companies, the top ten companies own 84 percent of total assets, and among the 100 leading companies backed by universities, total asset share by the top 14 companies is already well above the average (1.60 billion RMB). In terms of revenue, concentration ratio is even more keen; the top ten firms control 94 percent of total revenues among nation-wide university-run enterprises, while revenues by even just the top seven companies are above the average (2.47 billion RMB) in that 100 group.

In summary, Chinese universities are increasingly transferring from more traditional learning and academic institutions to an important position in national as well as regional innovation systems, with unique features in collaborating/participating with industries via joint patenting, commissioned research, and university-run enterprises. In terms of regional innovation performance, besides an advanced university group (e.g., the "211" consortium) as the major driving force in national and regional technology innovation, more local or regional universities have also been playing crucial roles in regional innovation; however, such technology transfer functions may still be unbalanced among different university groups across regions. At the same time, universities' function in industrial innovation can be influential beyond geographical boundaries, especially for those highly advanced university groups.

Conclusion

Based on these three section reports, the following conclusions can be made:

1 Quality of regional economic development, usually reflected from innovation and technology contents in the regional economic movement, is determined jointly by various kinds of driving forces, namely, local and overseas companies for the local market, universities for knowledge creation potentiality, and regional government as well as national government in their innovation policies. This needs to be understood as a strong process of socio-economic development in a rather opening up economic system, with continual influence and interactions from the overseas global knowledge and commodity market.
2 Offshore investment inflows usually overlap with regional economic development if the local market is more promising and local companies are clustering in innovation; thus in developing countries, the technology contents and innovation capacities of those overseas companies are usually highly demanding, if compared with stronger competitive partners from local firms, such as in China's case, where both FDI firms and local companies are transforming into more active technology based collaboration and competition, especially in coastal regions. However, due to the highly diversified nature of Chinese regions in both economic and innovation output, there are also exceptional trends of such a clustering

situation, where local policies and regional universities may also be decisive and active in regional innovation performance.

3 It should be noted that university–industrial collaboration and local regional innovation capacity in China are increasingly strengthened, along with the rapid development of local companies' progress in advanced manufacturing technologies. Therefore, it is strongly suggested from this study that regional diversification in economic and innovation clusters needs to be investigated more dynamically, rather than stably.

Notes

1 de Bresson, C., Sirilli, G., Hu, X. and Luk, F.K., 1994: Structure and location of innovative activities in the Italian economy 1981–1985. *Economic System Research* 6(2), pp. 135–138.
2 Nelson, R.R., Winter, S.G., 1982. *An Evolutionary Theory of Economic Change*. Cambridge, MA: Harvard University Press.
3 Patel, P. and Pavitt, K., 1996: Pattern of technology activity: their measurement and interpretation. In: Stoneman, P. (Ed.): *Handbook of Economics of Innovation and Technological Change*. Blackwell Publisher.
4 Motohashi, K., 2005: University–industry collaborations in Japan: the role of new technology-based firms in transforming the National Innovation System. *Research Policy* 34(5), pp. 583–594.
5 Woolgar, L., 2007: New institutional policies for university–industry links in Japan. *Research Policy* 36(8), pp. 1261–1274.
6 D'Este, P. and Patel, P., 2007: University–industry linkages in the UK: What are the factors underlying the variety of interactions with industry?. *Research Policy* 36(9), pp. 1295–1313.
7 Abramo, G., D'Angelo, C., Di Costa, A. and Solazzi, F.M., 2009: University–industry collaboration in Italy: a bibliometric examination. *Technovation* 29(6–7), pp. 498–507.
8 Motohashi, K., 2008: Assessment of technological capability in science industry linkage in China by patent database. *World Patent Information* 30(3), pp. 225–232.
9 Lei, X., Zhao, Z., Zhang, X., Chen, D., Huang, M. and Zhao, Y., 2011: The inventive activities and collaboration pattern of university–industry–government in China based on patent analysis. *Scientometrics*, 90(1), pp. 231–251.
10 Mowery, D.C., 2001: Patenting and licensing university inventions: lessons from the history of the research corporation. *Industrial and Corporate Change*, June, pp. 317–355.
11 Petruzzelli, A.M., 2011: The impact of technological relatedness, prior ties, and geographical distance on university–industry collaborations: A joint-patent analysis. *Technovation* 31(7), July, pp. 309–319.
12 The 211 scheme, named after 21 (the 21st century) and 1 (100 universities in China), was initiated in 1993 and aimed at well developing advanced universities in the twenty-first century through continual effort by the Chinese government. The "985" scheme was initiated in May 1998 by the Chinese government to well promote internationally advanced universities; first 34 universities were included and later the name list was extended by an additional 5 selected universities, all over China.
13 According to the website of the Ministry of Education of China, www.moe.gov.cn/publicfiles/business/htmlfiles/moe/s8493/201412/181591.html.

13

PUTTING SINGAPORE ON THE GLOBAL INNOVATION MAP

The shifting role of the state in the rapidly changing environment

Lai Si Tsui-Auch, Sherwin Ignatius Chia and Anica Liu

Introduction

Globalization presents both advantages and disadvantages to the role of state in managing a knowledge-based economy through innovation and technological development. Although globalization has allowed collaborations to take place more easily through technological improvements, nations seeking to sustain the growth of their economies have to face intensive competition – both regionally and globally – in terms of the cost of doing business as well as attracting and retaining both foreign investments and talents.

In this chapter, we focus on the role of the developmental state in developing technologies and pursuing innovation in the context of global and regional competition. We choose Singapore as a case for three reasons. First, Singapore is a unique nation in which there are no natural resources and no hinterland to support a domestic market, but yet is located in a thriving Asian region that constitutes a growing market, and attracts and provides both investments and human resources. Next, it is a well-known city-state in its attempt to catch up with high-technology development. Last, it has been an exemplar of the state-led development strategy in directing technological and industrial upgrading for late-industrializing nations in the past four decades. Unlike South Korea which has adopted a 'go big' strategy (by relying on *chaebol* for innovations) and Taiwan which has chosen a 'go small' strategy (by harnessing small and medium-sized enterprises for entrepreneurial undertakings), Singapore has been persistent with its 'go global' strategy, through attracting FDI and importing foreign talents (Wong 2011).

This chapter is aimed to present the trajectory of technological development since the 1970s and to analyse how it has been shaped by the developmental state amid global and regional competition and how it has in turn changed the role of the state. We review and update the state's past success in developing the electronics industry and information technology, its subsequent bet on biotechnology and its most recent new pickings in clean technology. Drawing on the typologies of R&D (Amsden and Tschang 2003), we contend that the evolution from production-related R&D to applied research has generally taken place due to policies of the developmental state and an adaptation of the Triple-Helix nexus (Etzkowitz *et al.* 2000) in a small open economy (Wong 2007). However, the attempted shift from a manufacturing economy to a knowledge-based economy has been fraught with critical challenges.

Based on an analysis of the development of these key industries, we discuss two issues: (1) In what ways has the state enabled or inhibited industrialization and technological development in the context of regional competition for foreign talents and markets? (2) Has there been a retreat of the developmental state amid profound uncertainties in developing science-based industrialization?

The Singapore context

After independence in 1965, the government assumed the role of a developmental state alongside its counterparts in Taiwan, South Korea, Japan and Malaysia (Woo-Cummings 1999). To speed up economic modernization and to deal with unemployment at the time of independence, the state established government-linked corporations (in which the government takes equity) and enticed multinational corporations (MNCs) to invest in the country. As Singapore has a smaller domestic market than Hong Kong and Taiwan and has no hinterland since its separation from the Malayan Federation in 1965, it has attempted to overcome its natural weakness by offering an entry to the Southeast Asian market through creating an international business and language (English) environment, efficient telecommunication and transportation systems, as well as business-friendly government policies.

After two decades of independence, Singapore shifted from being a developing country to joining the league of Asian newly industrialized countries. As a very small country lacking a 'natural' hinterland for cheap labour and land supply, Singapore had fewer alternatives other than shifting from IT/electronics manufacturing towards knowledge-intensive industries since the mid 1980s, being increasingly integrated into the global system of knowledge production and exchange (Phillips and Yeung 2003; Wong 2007; Wong 2011).

However, unlike Japan and South Korea in which the development of knowledge-intensive industries stem from the private sector, Singapore's private sector, which faces financial constraints, has been weak in technological upgrading and knowledge-intensive industries. Unlike the bank-centred financial system of Germany in which firms rely on banks to finance investments (Casper 2000), Singapore's banks have not offered patient finance. Moreover, the country has not established a vibrant venture capital industry. Unlike the US venture capitalists who are willing to accept high technological uncertainty and short- to medium-term financial losses in return for the prospect of very large gains in the future, most of the venture capitalists in Singapore/Asia have been risk-adverse.

Other than the constraints in finance, the development of knowledge-intensive industries has been hampered by a lack of qualified scientists. The government fostered education in engineering, business, finance and banking rather than natural science. Whereas Taiwan has been able to attract its US-educated professionals who have competed in Silicon Valley to return home to set up their own businesses, Singapore has continued to suffer from brain drain, and has few alternatives but to adopt liberal immigration laws to foster the recruitment of foreigners.

Despite the structural constraints, Singapore does have geographical, political and institutional 'advantages' over other countries in undertaking science-based industrialization such as the biomedical industry. Geographically, its unique geographic location (on the sunbelt), which provides Singapore with radiation of 50 per cent more than that in Germany and Japan (the other two major hubs for solar technology located at temperate regions), enhances its opportunity to develop 'clean technology' (Ng 2010).

Politically, given the dominance of a ruling party without credible opposition parties (Worthington 2003; Gourevitch and Shinn 2005) and the absence of protests and non-governmental organizations that lobby against genetic engineering, the Singapore government and research institutes have been largely free from ethical and political debates on biotechnology development.

Institutionally, the state evolved a capability through identifying a nodal agency, the EDB, to spearhead industrial and economic development (Tsui-Auch 2004). Being established as a statutory board in 1968, it has enjoyed a clear political mandate for its mission and has been endowed with the power to coordinate and command other state agencies to accomplish tasks. As a nodal agency with financial and decision-making power, the EDB can offer financial incentives and physical facilities to MNCs and secure their entry into Singapore. It could seek cooperation from the Jurong Town Corporation to establish industrial infrastructures; the Development Bank of Singapore for financing; the state-led National Trades Union Congress to restrain labour unions and the tripartite National Wage Council to regulate wages and to upgrade labour skills (Lim 1987); the Ministry of Education to boost the promotion of science education; the Ministry of Science and Technology to spearhead scientific research; the National Science and Technology Board and its successor, the Agency for Science, Technology and Research (A*STAR), to manage research across universities and public research institutes and steer research towards 'world class' standards. Internationally competitive compensation packages have been offered to lure star scientists to Singapore.

Singapore's path to participation in the innovative world

Joining the electronics/IT industrial development race

The electronics segment, which has remained one of the main pillars of economic growth, began in the late 1960s, whereas the IT segment started in the 1980s. FDI in the electronics segment contributed greatly to the economic growth in Singapore especially during the initial years. The initially functional role of IT in the civil service has led to the important economic role of IT as a service provider. It has also led to the service sector playing an increasingly important role in Singapore's economy. Overall, state intervention has generally been successful in these two industries.

Electronics segment

The electronics segment has a backwards linear trajectory of R&D based on Amsden and Tschang's (2003) categorization of R&D, starting with advanced development and moving towards applied research. Its development can be divided into three main periods so far.

1960s to 1979: from survival to growth

Given Singapore's situation, a focus on labour-intensive manufacturing was the most attractive option to reduce unemployment and increase economic growth in the early 1960s (Lim and Pang 1981). The EDB's heavy promotion of Singapore as a low cost manufacturing base (Chan 2002), coupled with generous tax incentives (Lim 1987), attracted substantial investments from large foreign MNCs (Lim and Pang 1981). Over time, the state pushed for more diversification, by pursuing the manufacturing of consumer and industrial electronics. By the mid 1970s, component manufacturing and consumer electronics manufacturing were the two largest subdivisions (Lim and Pang 1981). A recession struck in the mid 1970s and employers were forced by the state to retrench foreign labour (Lim 1987). This increased labour costs and labour shortage made Singapore less attractive for labour-intensive manufacturing (Lim 1987; Chalmers 1991; Chua 2012). Subsequently, it triggered a shift from a development paradigm anchoring on lower value-added production by cheap labour to one emphasizing techno-industrial innovation by academic labour force. Thus in 1979, the state advocated skills upgrading and created incentives to attract investments towards higher value-added and skill-intensive production such as integrated circuits designs and wafer fabrication (Lim 1987; Chalmers 1991). The JTC announced the building of a new science park to encourage more R&D between academia and industry (Phillips and Yeung 2003). The NWC allowed suppressed wages to increase towards market rates (Lim 1987).

1980s to 1989: promotion of R&D

In the 1980s, the state merged and established universities to produce engineering talents. The EDB provided additional incentives for MNCs to use Singapore as their regional headquarters leading to foreign MNCs expansion towards the late 1980s (Chalmers 1991).

Subsidiaries of MNCs in Singapore began to engage in R&D activities, but primarily in advanced and exploratory development such as product design and fabrication (Mathews 1999). Electronic goods manufacturing began to diversify towards computer printed circuit board assemblies and hard disk drive manufacturing (A*STAR 2012a). However, cutting edge R&D activities were still lacking in local firms and subsidiaries of MNCs.

1990 to present: innovation and knowledge-led growth

The EDB re-emphasized its commitment by aiming ‘to develop Singapore into a world-class electronics manufacturing hub with end-to-end R&D capabilities’ (EDB 2011: 1). Several public research institutes engaging in applied research were established in the early 1990s (A*STAR 2012a). However, R&D activities were confined to advanced and exploratory development, with the exception of the storage industry moving towards applied and basic research.

However, the electronics segment was hit badly first by the global health crisis inflicted by SARS in 2003 and then by the recent global economic crisis with a significant drop in output and increase in unemployment rates (Jordan 2009). The NWC announced wage reduction to cope with the SARS outbreak (Lim 2013), and the state introduced several measures to preserve jobs during the recession (Jordan 2009).

IT segment

The IT segment followed the similar R&D trajectory of the electronics segment. However, the state’s intervention through deliberate planning was more obvious in this segment. Its development can be classified into two periods.

1960s to late 1990s: the birth of IT

In the 1960s, IT referred to telephone services, and the telecommunications company was state-owned. However, efforts were made to use IT as one of the key technologies in enabling economic growth by the late 1970s (Chua 2012). When the state’s information and communication technology master plan was launched, research institutes were established in collaboration with foreign MNCs initially to train IT talents but subsequently to engage in applied research. For example, IBM was engaged to assist National University of Singapore to establish the Institute of Systems Science in 1981. The Information Communication Institute of Singapore was established in collaboration with AT&T Bell labs in 1989 (Wong 1992; Wong 1996; A*STAR 2012a).

Late 1990s to present: IT as an economic pillar

This period saw the civil service's reduction of front desk manpower through online platforms and the provision of IT services (i.e. e-business and business productivity consultancy services) as a potential economic growth sector (iDA 2000; Chua 2012). In addition, the late 1990s saw the gradual liberalization of the telecommunications industry with the state-owned telecommunications provider becoming privatized to form SingTel (Chua 2012). Although full liberalization of the telecommunications industry took place in 2000, strict regulations inhibited initial competition growth (Chua 2012). Temasek Holdings's (the largest government-linked holding in Singapore – SingTel's parent company) acquisitions of stakes in telecommunications companies across Asia and Australia generated hostility from host country governments and nationals and, specifically in Thailand, provoked a deep political crisis that subsequently led to Temasek's high financial loss (Lau 2001).

RESULTS

Obviously, in both the electronics and IT segments, the state played a crucial role in attracting R&D investments and developing R&D capabilities (starting with exploratory development) through the control and coordination of various agencies and utilization of the Triple-Helix nexus (Etzkowitz *et al.* 2000).

For a small open economy, the results have been remarkable. The electronics segment contributed almost a third of the manufacturing output in 2011. The IT segment drew revenue of S$70.39 billion in 2010, of which 66 per cent was contributed outside of Singapore (iDA 2011). FDI abroad has also been increasing with manufacturing and info-communications contributing 24 per cent and 5.1 per cent respectively.

In particular, there has been a state-led change towards a modern research and science-based economy employing university trained personnel for higher value added process. Researchers grew almost nine-fold while R&D expenditure rose almost twelve-fold between 1982 and 1992. R&D expenditure in the engineering and technology research areas, which are related to the electronics and IT industry, accounts for 62.8 per cent of total R&D expenditure in 2011 (see Table 13.1). However, the majority of the expenditure was devoted to exploratory development and was mostly contributed by foreign companies.

There are two main challenges facing the electronics and IT industry. The first challenge is to strengthen local firms and public institutions, and grow their R&D capabilities across all categories of R&D. Local firms and public institutions contributed less than a quarter of R&D expenditure in engineering and technology research. The ability to create value and produce global technology leaders through basic and applied research especially among local firms is still in transition. The second challenge is to navigate through political sensitivities while acquiring foreign assets that are strategic to their national economies. This is illustrated in the outward foreign investments by government-linked SingTel and its parent company, Temasek Holdings, which have generated hostility in host economies for their telecommunications investments abroad.

Table 13.1 R&D expenditure in Singapore[a,b]

	1992	*1996*	*2001*	*2006*	*2011*
GDP (Current prices) (S$mil)[c]	84724.7	134207.6	157136.1	231580.6	326832.4
R&D Expenditure indicators					
Current prices (S$mil)	959.54	1792.14	3232.68	5009.70	7448.48
per cent of GDP	1.13	1.34	2.06	2.16	2.28
per cent of GDP by public sector	0.44	0.37	0.39	0.74	0.86
per cent of GDP by private sector	0.68	0.44	0.71	1.42	1.42
per cent of GDP by local firms	N.A.	42.96	42.39	31.85	24.28
per cent of GDP by foreign firms	N.A.	57.04	57.61	68.15	75.72
Breakdown by R&D type					
Basic research (per cent)	N.A.	11.78	15.36	20.63	19.06
Applied research (per cent)	N.A.	39.56	31.34	31.93	32.91
Exploratory research (per cent)	N.A.	48.67	53.50	47.44	48.03

Notes: All sources are taken from the respective year of A*STAR's national survey of R&D in Singapore unless indicated otherwise.
[a]Industry was used instead of research area in 1992 and 1996.
[b]Research area classification was changed in 2006 and Energy was added in 2011.

[c]Sources from World Bank.

Towards a science-based industrialization: participating in the biotech revolution

The developmental state of Singapore surely did not want to miss the 'biotech revolution'. As with its counterparts in South Korea and Taiwan, it has envisioned its economy as a biotech hub, being a gateway into the growing China market. Singapore's biotechnology development, however, has diverged from that for the electronics and IT industry which followed the typical approach of late-industrializing economies that progresses from production and development-type research to product design. To foster biomedical development since the late 1980s, the state has established the whole value chain, embracing not only the 'D' part (exploratory development and advanced development) of the 'R&D' but also the 'R' part, fostering basic research and applied research. Its development can be classified into three periods.

1988 to 1997: a broad-based approach

In this initial period, a broad-based approach towards biomedical development was adopted. Other than high value-added pharmaceuticals and diagnostics, the EDB aimed to foster agricultural and food biotechnology to meet the needs of local small- and medium-sized enterprises in the food sector.

The EDB offered financial incentives to attract MNCs to establish R&D processes in the country, and enticed those that had already established manufacturing facilities in the country to invest in R&D. To aid the commercialization of inventions, it set up a venture capital fund to make direct equity investments in viable biomedical projects both locally and abroad. The JTC developed four science parks to foster exchanges between industry, academia and the government. The NSTB was tasked to oversee public research, and started to fund the establishment of three large research institutes, covering various steps of the value chain of the bio-pharmaceutical industry.

1997 to 2006: refocusing and resource orchestration

The Asian financial crisis of 1997 devastated the property sector and banks in Singapore. The political turmoil in Indonesia rendered Singapore's grand scheme of regional division of labour in manufacturing risky. Expecting the relatively unscathed China to become an industrial and technological powerhouse, the Singapore government felt the urgent need to develop knowledge-based industries to maintain its competitiveness.

In early 1999, the EDB launched an economic blueprint that aims to develop Singapore into a vibrant and robust global hub of knowledge-driven industries. It identified biomedical industry (including pharmaceuticals, medical devices, health care and biotechnology) as one of the four pillars of the economy. The shift from a broad-based approach, which includes agro-biotechnology to an approach that focuses on human health-related life science (particularly on cancer research), represents an attempt to define a niche and to pool resources to yield results in a shorter time span.

A new focus was to nurture domestic start-ups, which deviated from the conventional approach to attract FDI only. The EDB has adopted the resource orchestration approach, designing policies to provide start-ups with seed funding, access to incubation space in a new science park (the Biopolis), technical advice, business consultancy, and networking opportunities.

To support the new focus, the EDB set up an International Advisory Committee that included representatives from MNCs. With respect to the state sector, the A*STAR invested in three new research institutes and merged two existing institutes to build a biomedical science base. Scientists in the existing institutes were strategically directed to strengthen biomedical sciences. The educational institutions from primary schools to universities were mobilized to nurture future technopreneurs and qualified scientists. To build an academic labour force, life science has been incorporated into every subject taught from Primary 1 to pre-university. To entice young students to study biomedical sciences, the government has offered scholarships to recipients studying biochemistry, biophysics and developmental biology.

2007 to present: changing state approach to organize science-based industrialization

Despite the state's highly coordinated efforts for two decades, value-added investment in terms of R&D and value-added gains have been limited. Some industry stakeholders started to complain about the slow pace of commercial growth and questioned whether the investment in biomedical science was worth undertaking, whereas others criticized the state strategy for being too ambitious (Wong 2011). Although the state has attempted to promote 'stars' – star start-ups, star scientists and world class partnerships – to portray success in the biomedical science, the acrimonious dissolution of the A*STAR and Johns Hopkins University partnership in 2006 came as a severe setback to its foreign talent-dependent industrialization strategy.

The state's management of biomedical science development began to change in 2007. The extraordinary technological and market uncertainties have rendered the developmental state's past practices of picking winners impractical. While its financial commitment to nurture biomedical industry has continued to increase, the proportion allocated to biomedical science and disbursement of public funding indicated a change in its management of science and technology development. For example, while S$332 million, i.e. over half of all R&D funds to public research institutes, was allocated to biomedical research in 2005, that for this research stream dropped to S$263 million in 2006, amounting to about 42 per cent of all funds allocated to public research institutes and the proportion has remained as of 2011 (A*STAR 2006, 2007, 2012b). Moreover, instead of centralizing power in the EDB and A*STAR for allocating funds in a coordinated fashion, the government has created new funding streams. This suggests that the sector's technological and market uncertainties have rendered a decentralization of expertise, which has subsequently led a more horizontal distribution of authority in shaping science-based industrialization (Wong 2011).

RESULTS

The state's approach to build up its biomedical science base is consistent with its proven strategy of harnessing Singapore's location advantages in the attraction of MNCs to strengthen its domestic technological capacity and to foster the growth of local supporting industries. MNCs accounted for 79 per cent of the private sector R&D spending, and employed 69 per cent of researchers in the biomedical industry (A*STAR 2012c). So far, nearly all the large pharmaceutical companies have operations in Singapore, including twenty-eight biopharmaceutical plants as of January 2013. However, most companies made investments in manufacturing rather than those in R&D, despite the government's hopes for the opposite. As with the case for electronics manufacturing and IT industry, the entry of MNCs has triggered the growth of SMEs as suppliers of materials and research services for MNCs rather than as innovators in the biomedical industry.

The development of the biomedical industry has enabled the state to diversify its manufacturing base; biomedical output surpassed that of electronics, accounting for 25.5 per cent of last year's manufacturing output (Chia 2013). However, growth in commercial biomedical output has increasingly concentrated in lower value-added manufacturing, contrary to the expectation of the state. Value-added constituted nearly 75 per cent of the value of total biomedical manufacturing output in 1999; its share was, however, only 46 per cent in 2010 (EDB 2012a).

With respect to public research, the public research institutes have shown significant achievements. Scientists have published several papers in prestigious international refereed journals. However, the research institutes have encountered difficulty in attracting and retaining foreign scientists as scientists have to cope with constantly changing missions, goalposts and foci, as well as a lack of transparency in organizational change management (Tsui-Auch 2004). The constant promotion of technopreneurship, rosy job prospects and scholarships might lure Singaporean students to study biomedical science. Yet it remains to be seen whether the pragmatic students can be persuaded to pursue scientific discovery.

Diversifying the science-based industrialization: creating an Asian clean technology hub

Given the tremendous market and technological uncertainties in science-based industrialization, the Singapore government has worked to diversify into technologies other than biotech. Essentially, its 'hub development strategy' applies not only to the biomedical science but also to clean technology. Nowadays an environmentally sustainable economic development and the need for alternative clean and renewable energy have become urgent for nations worldwide as a result of global climate change, urbanization and the depletion of fossil fuels (Jung *et al.* 2000; Kannan *et al.* 2007). In this context, Singapore, a highly urbanized country that lacks natural resources, has identified the clean technology industry as a new strategic economic growth area, with clean energy (such as solar energy and biomass) as an important sector since the mid 2000s

(EDB 2012b). The ultimate aim is to turn Singapore into Asia's carbon hub and global hub where clean energy solutions are developed, tested and imported overseas.

The nation has several advantages to support its clean technology development. First, the nation's industrial infrastructures have provided a firm base for this new industry, including the existing strengths in electronics, precision engineering and chemicals industries for the manufacturing of solar wafers, cells and modules (EDB 2012b). Second, Singapore has the potential to become an Asia-Pacific carbon hub given its strategic connectivity to carbon markets, as the Southeast Asian region is one of the biggest sources of carbon credits after China and India with nearly 29 per cent of the global net carbon release from deforestation as well as the strength in providing financial and legal services (Phat *et al.* 2004; Hextall 2009; Cho 2011). Being embedded in the Asian region, Singapore can take advantage of its strategic location to provide culturally and socially acceptable technologies to its neighbouring countries.

2007 to present: the birth of clean technology industry

Singapore has been promoting clean technology industry from three aspects since 2007: creating an institutional environment, providing financial incentives and supporting higher education institutions. First of all, several agencies have been set up to support the new focus. The Energy Innovation Programme Office (EIPO), which was established in 2007, is a key inter-agency workgroup to implement and coordinate the various research programmes, and to leverage on the strengths of different government agencies for a comprehensive approach to developing clean technology (NRF 2007). In 2007, government's initial funding on the clean technology industry amounted to S$35 million, amounting to 5.5 per cent of the total R&D expenditure, with the blueprints being composed of five key pillars: innovative research and development, developing manpower, grooming Singapore-based enterprises, branding the industry internationally and growing a vibrant industry ecosystem. In 2011, the EIPO announced the allocation of an additional S$195 million to promote R&D in the energy sector in the five-year period to 2015 (EDB 2011). Moreover, in 2009, the Monetary Authority of Singapore issued a circular providing details of the Enhanced Tier Fund Tax Incentive Scheme, which included emission derivatives while previously it was limited to tangible commodities such as oil, metals and agro-commodities (PWC 2009; Sethuraman 2009). In 2012 the JTC established the construction of CleanTech park, which serves the function of fostering a conducive environment for collaboration between industry and academia (JTC 2012). Moreover, the government also supports higher education institutions, including the establishment of research institutes such as the Energy Research Institute and the Solar Energy Research Institute of Singapore.

Currently, researchers across disciplines are targeting different aspects of R&D, from advanced development to applied science and even to pure science. The government actively positions the nation as a 'living laboratory' for companies to test and commercialize innovative energy solutions that are customized for the urban tropics (Goh 2012). By 2015, the clean technology industry is expected to meet the targets of creating S$3.4 billion value-add to the GDP and 18,000 jobs across a broad range within the industry (EDB 2012b).

RESULTS

The outcomes of the development of clean technology are encouraging so far. It has attracted a significant number of foreign and local SMEs and MNCs that are leading companies in various sub-fields in clean technology. Many of them have selected Singapore as the regional headquarters or hub (EDB 2012b). Some leading MNCs have set up collaborative projects with local academic institutes. However, challenges and uncertainties still exist in this new field. For example, Vestas, one of the giants in wind industry, which celebrated in 2008 the opening of an Asian R&D centre in Singapore with a plan to invest up to S$500 million in Singapore to advance research in wind power, closed the centre and laid its employees off in 2012 (Vestas 2008; Dvorak 2012).

A state-led innovation system: achievements and challenges

Notably, the nation has evolved the R&D capability from scratch towards applied research for electronics, IT, clean technology and biomedical industries. The global competitiveness report by the World Economic Forum provided some evidence of this success: Singapore has steadily increased its global competitiveness ranking from fifth in 2008 to second in 2012. The state has also been partially successful in creating an ecosystem of R&D, which is indicated by data presented in Tables 13.1 and 13.2. Total portion of R&D expenditure per GDP has been increasing from 1.13 per cent in 1992 to 2.28 per cent in 2011. While public R&D expenditure increased about twofold from 0.37 per cent in 1996 to 0.86 per cent in 2011, private R&D expenditure increased threefold from 0.44 per cent to 1.42 per cent. However, foreign firms still account for 75.7 per cent of the private R&D expenditure and constituted the majority in all categories of R&D in 2011.

The national innovation system helped to increase the level of skilled expertise for the industries. The triple helix model is also starting to show some success. Public research institutes have been engaging in collaborations with the academy and the industry (A*STAR 2012a). The total researchers, scientists and engineers (RSE) grew from 15,366 in 2001 to 29,482 in 2011 (with Singapore citizens and permanent residents RSE decreasing from 79 per cent in 2001 to 73.6 per cent in 2011). Exploratory R&D, which is the major category of R&D, accounted for over 45 per cent of the total R&D expenditure throughout the last two decades. Total patents awarded increased from twenty in 1992 to 855 in 2011. Sales revenue from commercialized products showed that foreign firms contributed over 75 per cent over the past two decades, whereas the local firms yielded below 25 per cent. Licensing revenue from patents showed that local firms contributed 29.2 per cent in 2006 but this increased to 51.4 per cent in 2011. Although local firms show improvements in terms of licensing revenue, the sales revenue is dominated by foreign firms. This suggests that local firms have difficulties in translating their patents into commercial success.

Table 13.2 R&D output in Singapore

	1992	*1996*	*2001*	*2006*	*2011*
Patents awarded	20	91	461	933	855
Sales revenue from patents(S$mil)	N.A.	88360.66	16638.00	25672.53	13466.72
per cent by local	N.A.	24.96	15.34	21.55	24.58
per cent by foreign	N.A.	75.04	84.66	78.45	75.42
Licensing revenue from patents (S$mil)	N.A.	N.A.	N.A.	137.41	92.78
per cent by local	N.A.	N.A.	N.A.	29.19	51.36
per cent by foreign	N.A.	N.A.	N.A.	70.81	48.64

Note: All sources are taken from the respective year of A*STAR's national survey of R&D in Singapore unless indicated otherwise.

In summary, the technological development in Singapore has gained critical acclaim. The country has established a comparatively strong R&D establishment in fewer than two decades, established collaborations with renowned research institutes and industrial players, recruited prominent scientists from all over the world and built an academic labour force constituted by Chinese, Indians and Malaysians other than the locals. It has also attracted substantial FDI and sustained some local start-ups and large firms (see Table 13.3). The state has no doubt achieved considerable short term success in applied, advanced and particularly in exploratory research. However, its innovation system, for example, in biomedical science, is hampered by constant changes in policy and goalposts, difficulty in attracting and retaining scientists, the dominance of MNCs that focus on manufacturing or downstream R&D and few home grown start-ups. The Singapore government has long realized that it is necessary to develop local firms in the event that 'footloose' (Caves 2007) foreign MNCs relocate their operations. Several local MNCs are created, although most are government-linked. Yet when they expanded beyond Singapore by making overseas acquisitions, they tended to arouse hostility among foreign nationals and governments, particularly for the telecommunications industry. In addition, Singapore companies have yet to be in the fifty most innovative companies as indicated in the report by Fast Company, whereas local firms from China (TenCent in 2012, Huawei in 2011, Alibaba in 2010), Korea (Samsung in 2010 and 2011) and Taiwan (HTC in 2010) have been making headlines as global

Table 13.3 A sample of prominent foreign MNCs and local companies in Singapore across the selected industries

	Electronics	*IT*	*Biomedical*	*Clean Technology*
Foreign	*Semicon* Globalfoundries UMC Micron Infineon Mediatek Components 3M Sony Hitachi Chemical HP Dell Showa Denko Western Digital Seagate *Systems* Foxconn Philips	IBM HP Tata Consultancy Services	Abbott GSK Lonza Merck Sharp & Dohme Novartis Pfizer Sanofi-Aventis Amgen MedtronicEdwards Life Sciences Siemens Medical Instruments Wyeth-Ayerst Applied Biosystems Genetech Lonza Biologics Schering-Plough Becton Dickinson	Renewable Energy Corporation Soitec Trina Solar Black & Veatch Nestle Oil
Local Enterprises and *Startups*	Creative Technologies Singapore Technologies Engineering Venture	*Muvee* Singtel	*AWAK* MerLion Pharmaceuticals Lynk Biotechnologies S* Bio Singapore Biotech	*Alphafuels* Hyflux

Note: Local startups are in italics.

Sources: EDB factsheets, company websites and media reports.

innovation leaders. This is surprising because in the innovation and sophistication sub index of the global competitiveness report, Singapore has been maintaining its ranking while China's, Korea's and Taiwan's rankings have been declining. This could suggest other factors that might have inhibited Singapore from producing innovative companies in technology.

We argue that a strong, activist state with a centralized approach to managing technological and economic development can be a double-edged sword, enabling the prompt development of the manufacturing economy up to the 1980s, but inhibiting science-based industrialization, local innovations and overseas expansion of its own government-linked corporations in the recent decades.

The shifting role of the state in a rapidly changing environment

While a top-down, centralized approach of state management of technological and industrial development has fostered prompt decision making, it has rendered bureaucratic action insensitive to the changing environment. Essentially, the state has locked into its past success with developing foreign-capital dependent, labour-intensive industries. Lock-in can be advantageous when the environment remains more or less the same. However, it can have negative consequences in case of radical changes in the environment.

The 'lock-in' has prompted the bureaucrats to maintain a low-risk investment strategy that defeats its claim to nurture local start-ups. Driven by risk avoidance, the EDB and its other agencies adopted some strategies that are unfavourable to nurturing a science-based industrialization. First, unlike its Korean and Taiwanese counterparts which were tasked to develop local capacity, the EDB favoured foreign companies over local start-ups. Hence, most domestic companies tend to tie up with MNCs and lose their small firm dynamic. Second, it favoured government-linked spin-offs over privately funded start-ups, reflecting the mentality to 'make' winners. Next, it tended to fund projects in the lower-risk market segments rather than the higher risk segments. Last, with an imperative to ensure performance and yield quick returns, the government agencies tended to subject research institutes to great pressure to prompt commercialization and imposed constant organizational change as seen in the development of biomedical science. However, science-based industrialization depends more on public science than many other technologies (McMillan *et al.* 2000). Scientists who lose trust in the establishments often seek positions elsewhere. When their exit is not well managed, the reputation of the institutes is often eroded, rendering it difficult for them to recruit scientists in the future.

Notably, the strong state management also inhibits overseas expansion of the government-linked enterprises. Although the government-linked corporations could gain financial and policy support from the state for their overseas expansion, it was hindered by the government-linked label. For instance, SingTel's failure to acquire Cable & Wireless of Hong Kong Telecom was attributed mainly to China's reluctance to allow a Singaporean entity to control its telecommunications assets (see Jayasankaran 2001; Mauzy and Milne 2002), given the ownership and control links between SingTel, the government and the political (Lee) family in Singapore (Yeung 2004). In another case, Temasek Holdings's acquisition of a controlling stake in Thailand's Shin Corp., which was owned by the family of the nation's then Prime Minister Thaksin Shinawatra, triggered a deep political crisis that subsequently led to a military coup in 2006. That Thailand's strategic industry was sold to a company that was wholly owned by a foreign government intensified the opposition. The political consequences that unfolded after the coup resulted in numerous stumbling blocks for Temasek's investments in Thailand. The Shin's share price fell drastically, reportedly leading to paper losses for Temasek of over S$800m as of November 2006 (Arnold 2006). These two incidents show that government-linked corporations were at times impeded by their ownership structure and the relative lack of political experience in operating in foreign countries. The Singapore political culture moulded by the one-party state without credible opposition parties (Worthington 2003; Gourevitch and Shinn 2005) might sustain the political insensitivities that government-linked corporations portray towards political resistance in the host economies.

Given the increasing complexity in regional and global economic competitions in technological and industrial development and increasing nationalism in neighbouring countries, the Singapore state has had to rethink its role in the economy. As stated above, the states of the newly industrialized economies compete to develop themselves into regional hubs or springboards into the Chinese market, and have been willing to invest heavily in this race. Nevertheless, the development of science-based industrialization is very different from that of electronics and the IT industry. For the electronics/IT industry, the development of electronics manufacturing paved the way for that of IT industries, and the market for such products and services were rather certain and quick financial returns can be generated. Both the biomedical industry and the clean technology industry, however, have been fraught with great uncertainties in market, product development and regulatory environments. Moreover, the Singapore government officials have to catch up with new development in academic knowledge in these fields. Together with the factors including weak science tradition and small domestic market, the Singapore state, as with its South Korean and Taiwanese counterpart, has gradually made a 'strategic retreat' of the developmental state (Wong 2011: 13). Whereas it has continued to invest heavily in biomedical industry, it has diversified its bet into new areas such as clean technology and has retreated from picking and creating winners. In addition, it has scaled back its ambition to venture into basic research in a wide range of fields, and has become more realistic in focusing on the niche of cancer research. This refocusing on profitable innovations rather than basic research is also shown in the development of clean technology. By so doing, its approach resembles the niche approach that has been adopted by its Taiwanese counterpart, and continues to deviate from South Korea's long-standing approach to developing a broad base covering both upstream, basic research and downstream, industry focused development. However, whereas the Taiwanese state thrives on its 'go local' strategy, depending on the thriving SMEs to capture the niches, the Singapore state has been facing uphill battles to create local technopreneurship and has continued to depend on inward FDI. Although the Singapore state has been inspired by the Korean *chaebol* and nurtured large domestic business groups such as the government-linked corporations, they tend to engage in commercial expansion rather than technological deepening and have thus been unable to produce global innovative giants.

To support the strategic retreat, the Singapore state has gradually changed its approach to organize and manage technological, industrial and economic development. The technological and market uncertainties of both the biomedical industry and the clean technology industry have rendered a decentralization of expertise that has subsequently led a more horizontal distribution of authority in shaping science-based industrialization (Wong 2011), rather than a singular reliance on the bureaucratic commanding agency of the EDB and its allies (Tsui-Auch 2004). This has brought Singapore to resemble its counterparts, shifting from past practices of top-down command and control towards a decentralized approach to managing science and technology development, and to allowing a diversification of bets into recent new pickings.

Moreover, the state has gradually reduced its ownership of and control over the government-linked corporations. As the government-linked corporations are increasingly commercially driven and involved in overseas acquisitions, the government has gradually reduced its stake in some of them including SingTel. In addition, these corporations have reduced their recruitment of directors of the board and top management personnel from the civil service sector and increased that from the corporate sector (Tsui-Auch and Yoshikawa 2010). In the face of increasing nationalism in neighbouring countries, the Temasek Holdings announced the adoption of a 'three-pronged strategy' to meet the challenges that includes avoiding investment in 'iconic' companies, tying up with local partners and seeking minority stakes (Chua 2007).

Conclusion

In this chapter we have documented the technological and industrial development of Singapore in the past four decades with examples from three key industries – electronics/IT, biomedical and clean technology. We have shed light on the role of the state as a double-edged sword, both enabling and inhibiting such development. We argue that the strong developmental state has been instrumental in successfully establishing an electronic/IT industry for the manufacturing economy but has been facing severe challenges in developing science-based industrialization for the knowledge economy. The state's venture into science-based industrialization has in turn reshaped its role in organizing science and technology as well as the economy. As shown in the analysis, the state has gradually made a strategic retreat in picking winners, changed its approach in organizing science-based industrialization and loosened its control over the government-linked corporations.

References

A*STAR, 2006: *National Survey of R&D in Singapore 2005*. Singapore: Agency for Science, Technology and Research.

A*STAR, 2007: *National Survey of R&D in Singapore 2006*. Singapore: Agency for Science, Technology and Research.

A*STAR, 2012a: *20 Years of Science and Technology in Singapore*. Singapore: Agency for Science Technology and Research.

A*STAR, 2012b: *National survey of R&D in Singapore 2011*. Singapore: Agency for Science, Technology and Research.

A*STAR, 2012c: *National Survey of Research and Development in Singapore 2011*. Singapore: Agency for Science, Technology and Research.

Amsden, A.H. and Tschang, F.T., 2003: A new approach to assessing the technological complexity of different categories of R&D (with examples from Singapore). *Research Policy* 32(4), pp. 553–572.

Arnold, W., 2006: Bangkok insists phone deal broke law. *International Herald Tribune*. New York: The New York Times Company.

Casper, S., 2000: Institutional adaptiveness, technology policy and the diffusion of new business models: the case of German biotechnology. *Organization Studies* 21(5), pp. 887–914.

Caves, R.E., 2007: *Multinational Enterprise and Economic Analysis*. 3rd edn. New York: Cambridge University Press.

Chalmers, I., 1991: International and regional integration: The political economy of the electronics industry in ASEAN. *ASEAN Economic Bulletin* 8(2), pp. 194–209.

Chan, C.B., 2002: *Heart Work*. Singapore: Singapore Economic Development Board.

Chia, Y.M., 2013: Biomed output overtakes electronics. *The Straits Times*. Singapore: Singapore Press Holdings.

Cho, E., 2011: Singapore's prospects as a regional carbon hub. Available online at: http://siew.sg/energy-perspectives/energy-singapore/singapores-prospects-regional-carbon-hub (accessed 28 May 2013).

Chua, J., 2012: The e-transformation journey of Singapore. In: Hanna, N.K. and Knight, P.T. (eds): National Strategies to Harness Information Technology: Seeking transformation in Singapore, Finland, the Philippines, and South Africa. New York: Springer, pp. 41–76.

Chua, M.H., 2007: Temasek's strategy to counter nationalism. *The Straits Times*. Singapore: Singapore Press Holdings, p. 3.

Dvorak, P., 2012: Sad sign of the times: Vestas closing R&D facilities. Available online at: www.windpowerengineering.com/policy/sad-sign-of-the-times-vestas-closing-rd-facilities/(accessed 28 May 2013).

EDB, 2011: *Factsheet: Electronics*. Singapore: Economic Development Board of Singapore.

EDB, 2012a: *Biomedical Sciences: Singapore the biopolis of Asia*. Singapore: Economic Development Board of Singapore.

EDB, 2012b: *Clean Energy: Factsheet 2012*. Singapore: Economic Development Board of Singapore.

Etzkowitz, H., Webster, A., Gebhardt, C. and Terra, B.R.C., 2000: The future of the university and the university of the future: evolution of ivory tower to entrepreneurial paradigm. *Research Policy* 29, pp. 313–330.

Goh, C.K., 2012: Singapore: Asia's clean power growth frontier. Available at www.edb.gov.sg/content/edb/en/resources/downloads/articles/asias-clean-power-growth-frontier.html (accessed 28 May 2013).

Gourevitch, P.A. and Shinn, J., 2005: *Political Power and Corporate Control: The new global politics of corporate governance*. Princeton, NJ: Princeton University Press.

Hextall, B., 2009: China, Singapore may beat Sydney in carbon-hub race. Available online at: www.reuters.com/article/2009/10/28/us-carbon-asia-hub-idUSTRE59R0Z320091028 (accessed 28 May 2013).

iDA, 2000: *Infocomm21 Singapore: Where the digital future is*. Singapore: Infocomm Development Authority of Singapore.

iDA, 2011: *Annual Survey on Infocomm Industry for 2010*. Singapore: Infocomm Development Authority of Singapore.

Jayasankaran, S., 2001: Blueprint for an Asian superbank. *Far Eastern Economic Review*, pp. 48–51.

Jordan, R., 2009: Singapore in its worst recession for years: the effects of the current economic crisis on the city-state's economy. *Journal of Current Southeast Asian Affairs* 28(4), pp. 95–110.

JTC, 2012: Real estate solutions: CleanTech park. Available online at: www.jtc.gov.sg/RealEstate Solutions/CleanTech-Park/Pages/default.aspx (accessed 25 April 2013).

Jung, T.Y., La Rovere, E.L., Gaj, H., Shukla, P.R. and Zhou, D., 2000: Structural changes in developing countries and their implication for energy-related CO2 emissions. *Technological Forecasting and Social Change* 63(2–3), pp. 111–136.

Kannan, R., Leong, K.C., Osman, R. and Ho, H.K., 2007: Life cycle energy, emissions and cost inventory of power generation technologies in Singapore. *Renewable and Sustainable Energy Reviews* 11(4), pp. 702–715.

Lau, D., 2001: SingTel Wins Cable & Wireless Optus Bid. Available online at: www.forbes.com/2001/03/26/0326global.html (accessed 8 April 2013).

Lim, K., 2013: CPF contribution rates to be restored. *The Business Times*. Singapore: Singapore Press Holdings.

Lim, L.Y.C., 1987: Capital, labor and the state in the internationalization of high-tech industry: The case of Singapore. In: Douglass, M. and Friedmann, J. (eds): *Conference on Transnational Capital and Urbanization on the Pacific Rim*. Center for Pacific Rim Studies, University of California, Los Angeles, March 26–27.

Lim, L.Y.C. and Pang, E.F., 1981: Technology choice and employment creation: A case study of three multinational enterprises in Singapore. Multinational Enterprise Program Working Papers. Geneva, Switzerland, International Labour Office.

McMillan, G.S., Narin, F. and Deeds, D.L., 2000: An analysis of the critical role of public science in innovation: the case of biotechnology. *Research Policy* 29(1), pp. 1–8.

Mathews, J.A., 1999: A silicon island of the East: Creating a semiconductor industry in Singapore. *California Management Review* 41(2), pp. 55–78.

Mauzy, D.K. and Milne, R.S., 2002: *Singapore Politics under the People's Action Party*. London: Routledge.

Ng, S.K., 2010: A new solar hub? Singapore ramping up research and manufacturing. *Solar Industry Magazine*, pp. 26–29. Oxford, CT: Zackin Publications.

NRF, 2007: Introduction to the clean energy programme. Available online at: https://rita.nrf.gov.sg/ewi/cepo/default.aspx (accessed 25 April 2013).

Phat, N.K., Knorr, W. and Kim, S., 2004: Appropriate measures for conservation of terrestrial carbon stocks: analysis of trends of forest management in Southeast Asia. *Forest Ecology and Management* 191(1–3), pp. 283–299.

Phillips, S.-A.M. and Yeung, H.W.-c., 2003: A place for R&D? The Singapore Science Park. *Urban Studies* 40(4), pp. 707–732.

PWC, 2009: *Harvest★ Investment Management Industry Updates Issue 3*. Singapore: PriceWaterHouseCoopers.

Sethuraman, D., 2009: Singapore may start carbon trading on new exchange. Available online at: www.bloomberg.com/apps/news?pid=newsarchive&sid=av1AZd7aAfhI (accessed 28 May 2013).

Tsui-Auch, L.S., 2004: Bureaucratic rationality and nodal agency in a developmental state. *International Sociology* 19(4) pp. 451–477.

Tsui-Auch, L.S. and Yoshikawa, T., 2010: Business groups in Singapore. In: Colpan, A.M., Hikino, T. and Lincoln, J.R. (eds): *The Oxford Handbook of Business Groups*. New York: Oxford University Press, pp. 267–293.

Vestas, 2008: Press release from Vestas Wind Systems A/S No. 8/2008. Available online at: www.vestas.com/files//Filer/EN/Press_releases/VWS/2008/081103-PMUK-08.pdf (accessed 28 May 2013).

Wong, J., 2011: *Betting on Biotech: Innovation and the limits of Asia's developmental state*. Ithaca, NY: Cornell University Press.

Wong, P.-K., 1996: Implementing the National Information Infrastructure vision: Singapore's experience and future challenges. *Information Infrastructure and Policy* 5(2), pp. 95–117.

Wong, P.-K., 2007: Knowledge sources of innovation in a small open economy: the case of Singapore. *Scientometrics* 70(2), pp. 223–249.

Wong, S.H., 1992: Exploiting information technology: A case study of Singapore. *World Development* 20(12), pp. 1817–1828.

Woo-Cumings, M., 1999: *The Developmental State*. Ithaca, NY: Cornell University Press.

Worthington, R., 2003: *Governance in Singapore*. New York: RoutledgeCurzon.

Yeung, H.W.-c., 2004: *Chinese Capitalism in a Global Era*. London: Routledge.

PART 4

Policy instruments

How to realize techno-industrial innovation

14

GOVERNMENTAL POLICIES AND TECHNOLOGICAL INNOVATION

Biotechnology and fast breeder reactor technology revisited

Cornelia Fraune

Introduction

Although governmental innovation policies are historically a rather new phenomenon (Mayntz 2001: 13), the crucial role of the government in innovation processes is being discussed more and more within innovation literature. It is argued that governments influence innovation processes proactively and to a great extent (Hilpert 1991a: 4; Mazzucato 2011: 70). This is especially true for the initial phase of innovation processes, since basic research is the most important source of innovation (Rammert 1992: 22), but is also valid for further phases of innovation.

The emphasized role of the government is explained by the uncertainty that is inherent to innovation (Hilpert 1991a; Mazzucato 2011). The main characteristic of innovation is that it has not yet been applied in a certain manner. Thus, as long as no technological breakthrough happens, it is far from clear whether an innovation will be a success or failure. Moreover, even if a technological breakthrough takes place, economic success is not yet assured. Hence, why do governments agree to this uncertainty and commit themselves to innovation processes? Mostly it is argued that governments are motivated by the prospect of economic growth (Mazzucato 2011: 70), but this is only one of many reasons. From a political point of view, the objective of government innovation policies is to provide welfare. From an economic point of view, the competitiveness of the national economy is fostered by innovation policy. In this regard, participation in international economic development is the main objective (Hilpert 1991b: 86).

Astonishingly, the leading role of the government is not necessarily restricted by technological progress but by international economic interdependency. Against the background of a more liberal international framework and increasing transnational operating companies, governments have to be more sensitive in regard to international innovative developments in order to avoid an economic disadvantage (Barben 2007a: 61). But this does not mean that the government does not possess any room for maneuver: "even when deregulation, flexibilization, or privatization were the guiding principles in policies of promoting competitiveness, they could be implemented in different ways, and be complemented by additional principles, such as balancing social and economic disparities" (Barben 2007a: 61). It rather means that international innovative developments require governmental reaction.

It is the aim of this contribution to show that the uncertainty inherent in innovation is not the only reason for the crucial role of the government in innovation processes. This claim implicates that the impact of governmental policies is not reduced to the initiation of innovation processes but is also given in later phases within this process. Furthermore, it will be shown that the impact of the government is not only supporting by nature but can also be detrimental. Governments' interest in innovation is not only diverse but also dynamic.

The diversity and dynamism of governmental interest in innovation will be shown by exploring the development of two different technologies: biotechnology and fast breeder reactor technology. These technologies are quite different by nature and both document different paths of technological as well as innovative development. Therefore, both have caused different challenges for governments. Moreover, each of these innovative developments will be analyzed by a comparison of governmental policies within the United States, Germany, and Japan. Although the initial conditions of these countries differed in regard to both technologies, they became important actors within the international race of innovation and technology. If governmental policies had an impact on technological development in both cases, considerable evidence for the crucial role of the government will be given. This is also true for the diversity and dynamics of governmental interests in innovation processes.

Biotechnology

The investments needed for biotechnological developments are relatively small. Moreover, it has mainly emerged as a business area of small, newly established firms instead of large, established companies, and it is a distributed rather than a centralized technology (Bauer 1995: 9–10). Nevertheless, governments have played a crucial role in implementing new biotechnology[1] since its developmental process was characterized by high uncertainty and required new and innovative structures of production. In contrast to business, governments were willing to take the risk because their interest in innovation is diverse and dynamic. By funding basic research and implementing new entrepreneurial structures they provide the basis for biotech-innovation.

Different political contexts—different political aims

Although the USA was and still is the most successful nation regarding biotechnology, the government was rather late in coming to it (Sharp 1987: 282). In fact, the German government was the first that supported biotechnology (Barben 2007b: 121). By 1966, the OECD report "Government and Technical Innovation" had already been published, which recommended biotechnology as an important technology for future economic development (Giesecke 2000: 206).[2] Against the background of saturated indigenous markets and growing international competition from industrialized as well as newly industrialized countries, the German government followed this recommendation and launched its first program in 1968 (Giesecke 2001: 167). But the most important key actors for implementing innovation—industry and scientists—were rather skeptical about new biotechnology. Both industry and science not only had a strong tradition but were also very successful in fermenting technology and enzymology.

Regarding science, the skepticism was reinforced by the institutional structure of the university. New biotechnology requires interdisciplinary cooperation which was inhibited by the division of research along disciplinary boundaries within faculties (BMBF 2008: 15). Furthermore, DECHEMA, an industry association for chemical engineering, had a great influence on the public program since it advised the government regarding biotechnology. As a result, the public development programs were focused rather on traditional than on innovative biotechnological development (Adelbergera 2000: 107–108; Giesecke 2001: 169).

In contrast to the German or the Japanese government, the US government never implemented a public program targeted on new biotechnology (Collins 2004: 107). But basic research was massively funded by the U.S. National Institutes of Health (NIH) after World War II. The main purpose of this funding was to find new possibilities of treatment for curing diseases (Kaiser 2008: 209). Applicability of basic research was not particularly a condition for funding (Giesecke 2000: 214; Barben 2007b: 113) and therefore provided a basis for both modern products and innovative industries. On the basis of this publicly funded basic research, Stanley Cohen and Herbert Boyer developed recombinant DNA technology in 1973 which is described as the starting point of biotechnology industry (Müller 2001: 2; Lange 2006: 194). By hindsight, basic research funding of the NIH is seen as one of the major reasons for the competitive advantage of the United States in biotechnology (Lange 2006: 195).

International competition as driving force for innovation policy

The success of new biotechnology as innovation was finally implemented by gaining political relevance. Within the United States, the profitability of new biotechnology came to the fore. Since the late 1970s, a great number of small biotechnology companies, so called New Biotechnology Firms (NBF), were established (Acharya 1999: 32–33). Those NBFs were proven to be highly profitable, especially by the stock market launch of one of the first NBFs, Genentech, in 1980 when the value of the shares increased persistently (BMBF 2008: 10). Against the background of these developments, new biotechnology gained political relevance internationally. At the beginning of the 1980s, Japan and Western Europe recognized that they had significantly lagged behind the US in the development and commercialization of biotechnology and launched different governmental development programs (Sharp 1987: 283; Collins 2004: 132).

The Japanese government especially made great efforts to catch up with the US.

> Through link-ups between Japanese and American companies, particularly with some of the larger NBFs; through a substantial programme of training doctoral and post-doctoral students abroad, particularly in the U.S.; and through a deliberate programme by government to raise the awareness of Japanese industry to developments and to involve them in promoting a Japanese presence in the industry.
>
> *(Sharp 1987: 286)*

It was precisely these Japanese efforts that brought the US government to the scene concerning biotechnology since it feared losing the technological progress race and thus international competitiveness (Leff 1983: A-8; U.S. Congress 1984: 7; Bartholomew 1997: 256; Collins 2004: 126; Kaiser 2008: 212).

The US government reacted to this challenge by implementing new regulations. Although these regulations were not explicitly targeted at biotechnology they were aimed at complementing the strong U.S.-research and strong U.S.-government programs. On the one hand, technology transfer was strengthened;[3] on the other hand, genomes science was supported in order to accelerate scientific progress and to secure commercialization in biotechnology (Loeppky 2005: 282). Furthermore, by means of the Small Business Innovation Research program launched in 1982 the venture capital market was legitimized (Giesecke 2001: 180; Kaiser 2008: 210–211). Finally, the government supported biotechnology indirectly by establishing new entrepreneurial structures and by funding basic sciences. These supporting measures were crucial to consolidate both its innovative capacity and commercialization and to strengthen the position of the national biotech-industry within international competition.

One size does not fit all

In a nutshell, the importance of biotechnology as innovation became implemented at the beginning of the 1980s when a great number of governments committed themselves to supporting the development of biotechnology. At that time, it became obvious that biotechnology was an important policy field within international competition. But it also became clear that governmental commitment as such is a necessary but not a sufficient condition for developing innovation. Its commitment has to be focused on the creation of something new and not on the support or advancement of existing structures or knowledge. It has to be accepted by governments that uncertainty is inherent to innovation. This is shown by both the German and the Japanese programs. The German one was not crowned with success until the government abandoned traditional paths of biotechnology support and oriented its policies on the determinants of the success of new biotechnology within the U.S. (Adelbergera 2000: 110; Giesecke 2001: 186–188; Casper 2009: 382–282; Motohashi 2012: 223). In the Japanese case, the problem was a structural one. Different ministries got involved and each one launched its own program. In consequence, public funding was inconsistent. Furthermore, these programs mainly aimed to get knowledge and were focused on the production of me-too products. Institutional prerequisites enabling cutting-edge research were not created. The Japanese research system emphasized applied science more than basic research and strict regulation inhibited cooperation between universities and industry (Müller and Fujiwara 2002: 702). In consequence, this strategy of biotechnological progress was not sustainable and thus ended by the middle of the 1980s: "The inability to mount a genome project worthy of the country's size and scientific status became a source of embarrassment, which prompted a rethinking of the government's entire approach to biotechnology" (Collins 2004: 137).

Biotechnology nationally restarted

Against the background of the continuing economic success of US NBFs, both the German and Japanese governments tried again to establish a biotechnology economy within their nations. In 1981, the German biotechnology policy changed as a consequence of the "Hoechst shock," in order to support basic research and to strengthen science–industry cooperation gene centers were funded (Giesecke 2001: 174). In the 1990s the government decided to become the most competitive nation within biotechnology in Europe (Adelbergera 2000: 110). In consequence, public funding was increased through new policy initiatives. The "BioRegio" competition demonstrated the success of the former gene centers which were the main beneficiaries. But BioRegio also constituted the basis for both regional concentration and situations of regional cooperation between research, industry, capital, and government even in those regions that were not funded (Giesecke 2001: 183–185; Barben 2007c: 76).

Although they were not related to each other, the second initiative was complementary to the BioRegio program since it was focused on the knowledge and technology transfer between research institutes and industry. On the one hand, a program was implemented that encouraged scientists to patent their findings. In contrast to the US, property rights of scientific findings and patent law restrained such activities. On the other hand, the set-up of service centers for knowledge and technology transfer at universities were financially supported (Giesecke 2001: 186). The third initiative aimed at encouraging a venture capital market in Germany. Government-owned banks were established in order to provide capital for NBFs. They became equity providers under the condition that private venture capital was also engaged. Since they assumed the risk of undertaking, it became much easier for newly established firms to find a private equity provider. This program was complemented by the implementation of "New Market" (Adelbergera 2000: 112–113; Giesecke 2001: 187–188). In contrast to the first governmental initiative these programs were successful because they were tailor-made for new biotechnology instead of for the interests of the traditional chemical industry.

In 1997, the Japanese government mentioned biotechnology as one of the key sectors for economic development under the Action Plan for Economic and Structural Reform. Now, structural restraints were abolished. Funding programs of different ministries were coordinated through "basic guideline for the creation of a biotechnology industry," with a special emphasis put on extending basic research (Müller and Fujiwara 2002: 701). Furthermore, the commercialization of scientific findings by intellectual property regulations was encouraged (Casper 2009: 382) and access to capital by creating a venture capital market was facilitated (Caspar 2009: 383; Motohashi 2012: 223). Of course it took a certain amount of time until the establishment of appropriate structures at the different levels (university, technology transfer, and capital market) were completed and became effective. The USA is still the leading nation in biotechnology. But in both countries, Germany (among other EU member states) and Japan, the biotechnology sector increased and both became competitors within the international innovation race (Lynskey 2006; Zika et al. 2007; OECD 2011).

Determinants of the technology in question in different contexts

In a nutshell, government policies founded the basis for progress within biotechnology in all three countries. In the United States, the government involvement was not targeted directly at biotechnology but its initiatives paved and shaped the way for biotechnological innovation. It was even the indefiniteness of the governmental programs that enabled the emergence of new biotechnology since innovations are marked by novelty in different dimensions (production process, economic structures, products, etc.). By funding basic research and creating the regulatory framework for both university–industry cooperation as well as the venture capital market, the government initiated the innovation process. Other actors did not enter the process until innovation was substantiated.

The rise of international competition implemented the innovative nature of biotechnology. Due to its success, US biotechnology provided a model and was the main incentive for the German and Japanese governments to redirect or to launch their own programs. This aimed to overcome a situation in both countries in which both science and industry were not interested in new biotechnology until its innovative and commercial potential was shown by US NBFs. But at that point in time both countries were lacking the necessary structures to compete with the USA. Due to different national contexts the programs for establishing a biotechnology industry were quite different.

The development of new biotechnology shows that the government played a crucial role in each of the three countries but also that the national contexts and challenges differed completely. Without the commitment of the government new biotechnology would not have emerged in one of the countries, at least to its actual extent. The incentive for government support differed not only in dependence on the national situation but also on international development. Within the USA the initial incentive for supporting basic science was curing diseases. When the commercial potential of biotechnology became obvious and other governments discovered biotechnology as a growth sector, the US government strengthened its commitment. US biotechnology provided a model but the German and the Japanese governments both had to implement new structures of public funding, in science as well as in business instead of just initiating basic research and supporting emergent economic structures. They had to enforce these reforms not only against traditional routines but also against corporate actors that recognized the innovative capacity of biotechnology rather late.

Fast breeder reactor development

In contrast to biotechnology, it is of course a truism that the government was the most important driving force for the development of civilian nuclear energy since different properties inherent in the technology in question restrained industrial commitment: its military origins, its high-risk potential, its technological complexity, and its high capital intensity (Joppke 1992: 257). From a technical point of view, it is still not clear if the fast breeder reactor technology completely failed or if much more research and time is necessary to make it work (Hippel 2010: 12). But the developmental path of the fast breeder reactor exemplifies that governmental interest in technological innovation is multidimensional and can vary over time, even more or less independently from technological progress.

After World War II, fast breeder reactor technology was perceived as an innovative technology because two developments occurred more or less at the same time. On the one side, there existed the assumption about an imminent world energy problem. The limited supply of conventional energy resources such as oil and gas was recognized. Furthermore, access to these resources was not equally distributed so that different kinds of international dependencies evolved (Nemzek et al. 1974; Kaiser 1978; Suzuki and Suzuki 1986). On the other side, scientists thought about the possibility of using nuclear fission to generate electricity and thus to produce power by research and development independently of fossil resources (Cochran et al. 2010: 89). The main problem of using nuclear fission as an energy source was seen in the scarcity of fissile material. Alternative nuclear reactors were only fueled with U-235 which was able to fissile with slow neutrons. But U-235 made up only 0.7 per cent of natural uranium. Since 99.3 per cent of natural uranium consisted mainly of U-238, its usage was proposed to increase the raw material resources. But U-238 is only fissionable with fast neutrons, and although the reactor configuration that permitted this kind of fission seemed possible it still had to be developed. It was also recognized that this kind of reactor would be able to produce more fissile material than it would consume since U-238 would be converted into plutonium-239. Since plutonium-239 is fissionable it can replace U-235 after reprocessing as fuel in nuclear reactors (Schulte 1977; Cochran et al. 2010: 89).

Governments hoped for fossil resource independent, uranium-efficient energy production from fast breeder reactors in order to consolidate or achieve national energy autonomy. That is the reason why the Japanese government was one of the first to make a strong commitment to the fast breeder reactor technology in the 1950s. Japan had only limited indigenous energy resources at its disposal. Consequently, it was highly dependent on foreign sources and was not able to exert influence on a reliable energy supply to a sufficient extent. The fast breeder reactor technology appeared to allow self-reliance on nuclear power and thus promised to become a "semi-domestic energy source" (Suzuki and Suzuki 1986: 25; Lidskya and Miller 2002: 127). Therefore, the fast breeder reactor program became the central element of the governmental nuclear program. As a result, the public R&D funds for nuclear reactor technology were mainly allocated to fast breeder reactor technology (Suzuki and Suzuki 1986: 26–27; Suzuki 2010: 54). In contrast to Japan, the question about energy autonomy was not recognized by either the US government or the German one as an urgent political problem.[4] Furthermore, an immediate or foreseeable impact of the fast breeder reactor was lacking. These were the main reasons why both the US and the German government did not pay great attention to this technology although both funded the basic research and scientists and the nuclear industry were rather enthusiastic about it[5] (Kitschelt 1986: 78).

Beyond national energy autonomy, the governments of the United States, Germany, France, and the United Kingdom especially were also interested in the fast breeder reactor technology for export. Within the 1960s it was still not possible to predict technological progress reliably. It seemed possible to develop a commercial fast breeder reactor within the next decade. Since there existed a huge international demand for this innovative, science-based technology for energy production, being the first nation to offer a commercial fast breeder reactor would have yielded national economic growth and enhanced international competitiveness (Keck 1980: 280).

The first phase of fast breeder reactor technology development for civilian purposes of energy production can be narrowed down from the middle of the 1940s to the beginning of the 1970s. From a technological point of view, this phase was characterized by a high degree of uncertainty since its developmental path was still experimental. From an economic point of view, both the huge amount of capital to be invested as well as the uncertain prospects of success and profit impeded business commitment. From a political point of view, the promise of a fossil resource independent, science-based mode of energy production implicated increasing energy autonomy. On the one hand, governments appraised the fast breeder reactor as a device for dealing with the supposed conventional fossil energy resource scarcity as well as with the nuclear one. On the other hand, they appreciated it as an instrument for achieving international independency; even governments that had relatively large conventional and/or nuclear fossil energy resources available were interested in this technology. Due to the huge international demand on commercial reactors, a kind of design and development race between highly developed countries existed. These wanted to push their national economic growth and to strengthen their international competitiveness. Thus, the effects the fast breeder reactor technology would have brought about concerned vital governmental interests.

In consequence, governments all over the world fostered technological development by national programs, almost independent from technological progress. Because of politically highly relevant promises technological innovation was pushed by governments all over the world although their individual interests may have been different.

Changing situations—changing political priorities

The rise and failure of fast breeder reactor technology took place within a rather short period of time. At the beginning of the 1970s, the question of energy supply independence became politically urgent in the oil-dependent countries. The importance of nuclear power as a source of energy grew significantly. First of all, the US government increased its commitment to fast breeder reactor technology in 1971 due to the fact that more oil was imported than exported (Kitschelt 1986: 71). In the aftermath of the first worldwide oil crisis in 1973/74, this development occurred all over the world since fast breeder reactor technology was seen as the key to deal with energy scarcity (Kaiser 1978: 86). Strikingly, the "rise of the fast breeder reactor technology" took place at a time when its technological progress was delayed significantly all over the world. It became apparent that the realization of the theoretically developed fast breeder reactor technology was even more difficult than imagined (Nemzek et al. 1974; Marth and Koehler 1998).

Nevertheless, this second phase of fast breeder reactor development is characterized as the "rise of fast breeder reactor technology" because governmental commitment was intensified all over the world. At the beginning of the 1970s fast breeder reactor technology was no longer just a scientific experiment that promised future societal benefits but a technological innovation that realized technological opportunity[6] for solving a present problem (Kitschelt 1986: 87). Moreover, alternative solutions to the worldwide problem of energy scarcity did not exist or had not been perceived. In consequence, the governments aimed at accelerating technological progress by increasing their programs.

Paradoxically, the rise of fast breeder reactor technology induced its failure as innovative technology. Just as it was being implemented as innovative technology, its decline was caused by political decisions. Due to its international implementation as an innovative technology to meet national problems of independent and reliable energy supply, the concern about nuclear weapons proliferation came to the fore again: "While for most countries, fast breeders and reprocessing were now necessities of rational energy policy, to others they appeared to be a direct path to nuclear hell" (Kaiser 1978: 86). The government of the USA especially feared to lose its control of nuclear weapons proliferation implemented by the Treaty on the Non-Proliferation of Nuclear Weapons. As a result, the decline of fast breeder reactor technology was introduced by the US government from the middle of the 1970s.

In 1977, the US government abandoned its fast breeder reactor technology program. Against the background of international dispute about proliferation and growing public resistance against nuclear power,[7] a group of experts was asked to review the entire question of basic nuclear options. As one result, the so-called Ford-Mitre Study rejected the assumption of scarcity of uranium supply, concluding that the uranium supply would not draw to an end within the next thirty years (Kaiser 1978: 94–95). Against the background of this result the argument of the scarcity of uranium supply was paid off by the question about its access. Since the USA have a large proportion of the world's uranium share at their disposal, the question about access was not that important for them (Kaiser 1978: 95).

International interdependency

Although the situation of energy supply in regard to uranium as well as in regard to conventional energy resources was different in many other nations, the decision of the US government to abandon their fast breeder reactor technology program made an international impact. Facing growing domestic opposition, foreign governments were put under pressure by the decision of "the biggest oil consumer in an increasingly petroleum-scarce world" to review their own nuclear policy (Kaiser 1978: 94–95). But the discussion was still dominated by technological uncertainty. On the one hand, significant technological progress had not yet been reached. In consequence, other nuclear energy technologies such as the Light Water Reactor were more efficient in regard to energy supply as well as cost effectiveness. On the other hand, scientists were still convinced of future benefits. Moreover, several countries had already invested large sums in the development of fast breeder reactor programs (Kaiser 1978: 96).

But significant technological progress did not appear. Furthermore, several nuclear incidents stirred up political and public resistance, especially the Chernobyl accident. Finally, the fast breeder reactor technology lost its priority in many countries and became insignificant as innovative technology for solving the problem of an independent and reliable energy supply. Nevertheless, in Germany, as in other countries, a kind of political reinsurance was maintained due to prevailing technological uncertainty (Marth and Kohler 1998: 606). Moreover, fast breeder reactor technology is still discussed internationally as one possible option for nuclear waste disposal—the focus is now on burning plutonium instead of breeding. But this debate is also still accompanied by political concerns about proliferation as well as technological uncertainty (Cochran et al. 2010). Thus, the history of the development of fast breeder reactor technology shows that government policies have a great impact on technological development. Fast breeder reactor technology development was enabled by governments as long as they perceived this technology as an instrument to serve their own vital interests and to deal with societal challenges; while conversely, they withdrew public funding when they no longer expected that their interests would be served or when the interests opposed to fast breeder reactor technology became more relevant.

Technological innovation as object of political decision making

Originally, fast breeder reactor technology was developed for military purposes within the United States in World War II. The extension of this technology to civilian purposes—energy production—was fostered by scientists who gained some public funding from the US government. Due to the capital-intensive investments needed for its development, fast breeder reactor technology was never pursued by business actors alone. Thus, political commitment was needed in order to implement the fast breeder reactor as innovative technology. Overall, fast breeder reactor technology promised to be a fossil-resource independent, science-based mode of energy production at a time when the scarcity of fossil resources was supposed to be an urgent problem. Consequently, an international tendency to national nuclear programs emerged.

Significantly, not only the national programs but also the individual national interests differ. The Japanese government was mainly focused on the possibility of decreasing international dependency on foreign fossil resources and increasing the means to a reliable energy supply. Thus, the Japanese government was mainly interested in the application of the fast breeder reactor. With the exception of the first oil crisis, this does not apply to either the US or the German government. For them, this technology was more important as an instrument to get economic and technological advantages in international competition. But in all three cases, vital governmental interests are at stake. Thus, governments push technological innovation by public funding. Strikingly, this governmental support is carried out relatively independently from actual technological progress.

By contrast, governmental support is revoked if governmental interests lose their priority. The United States abandoned their fast breeder reactor program because their concern regarding proliferation became more relevant than technological supremacy in international competition.[8] Due to the abandoning of fast breeder reactor technology by the United States the German interest also decreased since the most important competitor had opted out. Moreover, increasing public protests challenged its legitimacy. Finally, the development of the fast breeder reactor was not triggered by technological invention but by government policies. It had been and still is at the mercy of governmental support. Thus, as long as from a technological point of view "the breeder reactor dream is not dead but . . . has receded far into the future" (Hippel 2010:

12), a recovery of the fast breeder reactor induced by governmental decision seems to be conceivable.[9]

Conclusion

The case studies on biotechnology and fast breeder reactor development both confirm the crucial role of government policies within innovation processes. Its policies pave and shape the way for innovation, especially in those cases where science and business are not enabled or motivated to initiate innovation processes due to the uncertainty inherent in innovation (Mazzucato 2011: 65). It is even a characteristic of innovation that "it breaks away from old routines or standards rather than perfecting existing ones" (Mintzberg 1983: 210). But both case studies have also shown that government policies are indeed a necessary but not a sufficient condition for innovation.

Innovation is a bottom-up rather than a top-down process. Techno-scientific progress cannot be induced top-down by government but evolves from bottom-up initiatives (Hilpert 1991b: 98). But government policies enable innovation by implementing or reinforcing institutions necessary for these bottom-up initiatives. Structural conditions given in each country differ. In some they might be beneficial for innovation, in others not. The government is the only actor that is qualified to create these conditions. Furthermore, governmental policies are relatively independent from actual technological progress. If a government favors a certain innovation because its promises are highly relevant for political interests then it pushes the technology in question more or less disregarding the hitherto existing development. Thus, government policies might be costly and inefficient. Of course, this kind of government support depends on the relevance of actual political interests and alternative technologies available to meet these interests and thus might change due to context dependent developments.

Furthermore, an international interdependency of innovation exists. The main reason for this interdependency is of course international competition. Governments are interested in the participation of their economy in new or emerging markets in order to accelerate economic growth. In this regard, they fear competitive disadvantages if they have lagged behind. Thus, governments observe each other and compare themselves. If and to what extent government policies converge depends on the similarity of actual national interests. This is not only true for successful innovations but also for failures. The decision of a government to abandon the support for a certain technology can also trigger a domino effect. Beyond economic concerns these considerations are also true for welfare.

This diversity of interests as well as their dynamism promotes the crucial role of the government within innovation processes. In contrast to science and business the commitment of the government is not limited to one purpose. Science is not prepared to induce innovation processes since cutting-edge research continuously requires new structures in order to generate new knowledge. In order to satisfy this demand, budgetary resources are required that science is not able to generate from own resources (Gläser and Lange 2007). Industry on the other hand would be in a position for inducing innovative processes. But such budgets will be provided in expectation of attractive profits. Otherwise the characteristic of a capital-investment—to create added value—will not be fulfilled. Regarding both technologies, biotechnology and fast breeder reactor, industry did not provide starting capital because it was rather uncertain whether economically exploitable results would be created.

Finally, the crucial role of the government in innovation processes is not reduced to agreeing "Knightian uncertainty" (Mazzucato 2011: 70) in innovation processes but to pave and shape the way for innovation in dependence on its diverse and dynamic interests. Thus, the government influences innovation not only defensively but also proactively (Mazzucato 2011: 70); but the variety of measures a government can take in order to exert this influence has not been systematically analyzed yet. For a better understanding of new technologies and processes of innovation, the contribution of governments through enabling policies has to be identified. Furthermore, particular attention has to be paid to the interplay between government, science, and the reference industry.

Notes

1 New biotechnology has to be differentiated from "modern" biotechnology that refers to the discovery and application of micro-organisms and their application in fermentation processes (Barben 2007b: 64–66).

2 In 1971, the interest of the Japanese government was aroused by the Council for Science and Technology which identified biotechnology as an important research area. But policy initiatives did not occur until the 1980s (Yuan and Dibner 1990: 19).

3 In this regard, three legislative initiatives are important: the Bayh–Dole Act (1980), the Stevenson–Wydler Technology Innovation Act (1980) and Federal Technology Transfer Act (1986) (Bozeman 2000: 634; Loeppky 2005: 268, 276). The Bayh–Dole Act permits universities and small businesses to patent inventions resulting from R&D funded by the federal government. The Stevenson–Wydler Technology Innovation Act regulates the granting of title to inventions made by federal laboratories and private research institutes collaboratively. The Federal Technology Transfer Act enables national laboratories to conclude cooperative R&D agreements and licensing agreements (Bozeman 2000: 634; Mowery and Sampat 2004: 237).

4 This might be surprising since the USA was the first nation that developed the fast breeder reactor. Clementine, the world's first fast-neutron reactor, went critical in 1946. In 1953, the EBR-I reactor was the first reactor that produced more plutonium than it consumed uranium (Cochran et al. 2010: 89–92).

5 Due to the proliferation threat, the government of the United States supported the innovative fast breeder reactor technology only to a limited degree and was rather preoccupied with the control of international development (Kaiser 1978: 84). It (as well as the French government) got room for maneuver concerning their own supply of weapons-grade plutonium since they "already controlled other technologies that supplied plutonium in sufficient quantities for their military program" (Kitschelt 1986: 79).

6 This description follows Walker's definition of innovation: "the creation and realization of technological opportunity" (Walker 2000: 833).

7 The rapid growth of nuclear power programs as a result of the first oil crisis caused growing public resistance against nuclear power (Kitschelt 1986: 87).

8 Of course, technological progress was delayed, but this was already the case during the first oil crisis when the US increased their program.

9 In the aftermath of the Fukushima accident in 2011, the Japanese energy policy was also critically reviewed against the background of international developments such as the renewable energy policy in the USA and the EU (Shadrina 2012: 77).

References

Acharya, R., 1999: *The Emergence and Growth of Biotechnology: Experiences in industrialised and developing countries.* Cheltenham: Edward Elgar.

Adelbergera, K.E., 2000: Semi sovereign leadership? The state's role in German biotechnology and venture capital growth. *German Politics* 9(1), pp. 103–122.

Barben, D., 2007a: Changing regimes of science and politics: comparative and transnational perspectives for a world in transition. *Science and Public Policy*, 34(1), pp. 55–69.

Barben, D., 2007b: *Politische Ökonomie der Biotechnologie. Innovation und gesellschaftlicher Wandel im internationalen Vergleich.* Frankfurt: Campus.

Barben, D., 2007c: Innovationsregime der Biotechnologie im internationalen Vergleich Herausforderungen und Probleme verwertungsorientierter Strategien. In: Feuerstein, G. (Ed.): *Strategien biotechnischer Innovation. Analysen, Konzepte und empirische Befunde*. Hamburg: Hamburg University Press, pp. 67–89.
Bartholomew, S., 1997: National systems of biotechnology innovation: complex interdependence in the global system. *Journal of International Business Studies* 28(2), pp. 241–266.
Bauer, M., 1995: *Resistance to New Technology: Nuclear power, information technology and biotechnology*. Cambridge: Cambridge University Press.
Bozeman, B., 2000: Technology transfer and public policy: a review of research and theory. *Research Policy* 29 (2000), pp. 627–655.
Bundesministerium für Bildung und Forschung (BMBF) (Ed.), 2008: *Wege in die Biotechnologie. 25 Jahre Nachwuchsförderung*. Berlin: Bundesministerium für Bildung und Forschung.
Casper, S., 2009: Institutional frameworks and public policy towards biotechnology: Can Asia learn from Europe? *Asian business & management* 8(4), pp. 363–394.
Cochran, T.B., Feiveson, H.A. and Hippel, F. von, 2010: Fast reactor development in the United States. In: Cochran, T.B., Feiveson, H.A., Patterson, W., Pshakin, G., Ramana M.V., Schneider, M., Suzuki, T. and Hippel, F. von (Eds.): *Fast Breeder Reactor Programs: History and status. A research report of the International Panel on Fissile Materials*, pp. 89–111. Available online at: http://fissilematerials.org/library/rr08.pdf (accessed 29 May 2015).
Collins, S.W., 2004: *The Race to Commercialize Biotechnology. Molecules, markets and the state in the United States and Japan*. Abingdon: Routledge-Curzon.
Giesecke, S., 2000: The contrasting role of government in the development of biotechnology industry in the US and Germany. *Research Policy* 29 (2000), pp. 205–223.
Giesecke, S., 2001: Wandel in der deutschen Biotechnologie-Politik: Ist der Staat lernfähig? In: Abele, J., Barkleit, G. and Hänseroth, T. (Eds.): *Innovationskulturen und Fortschrittserwartungen im geteilten Deutschland*. Köln: Böhlau, pp. 165–192.
Gläser, J. and Lange, S., 2007: Wissenschaft. In: Benz, A., Lütz, S., Schimank, U. and Simonis, G. (Eds.): *Handbuch Governance: Theoretische Grundlagen und empirische Anwendungsfelder*. Wiesbaden: VS Verlag, pp. 437–451.
Hilpert, U., 1991a: The state, science and techno-industrial innovation: a new model of state policy and a changing role of the state. In: Hilpert, U. (Ed.): *State Policies and Techno-Industrial Innovation*. London: Routledge, pp. 3–40.
Hilpert, U., 1991b: Economic adjustment by techno-industrial innovation and the role of the state: solar technology and biotechnology in France and West Germany. In: Hilpert, U. (Ed.): *State Policies and Techno-Industrial Innovation*. London: Routledge, pp. 85–108.
Hippel, F. von, 2010: Overview: the rise and fall of plutonium breeder reactors. In: Cochran, T.B., Feiveson, H.A., Patterson, W., Pshakin, G., Ramana, M.V., Schneider, M., Suzuki, T. and Hippel, F. von (Eds.): *Fast Breeder Reactor Programs: History and status. A research report of the International Panel on Fissile Materials*, pp. 1–15. Available online at: http://fissilematerials.org/library/rr08.pdf (accessed 29 May 2015).
Joppke, C., 1992: Models of statehood in the German nuclear energy debate. *Comparative Political Studies* 25(2), pp. 251–280.
Kaiser, K., 1978: The great nuclear debate: German-American disagreements. *Foreign Policy* 30, pp. 83–110.
Kaiser, R., 2008: *Innovationspolitik. Staatliche Steuerungskapazitäten beim Aufbau wissensbasierter Industrien im internationalen Vergleich*. Baden-Baden: Nomos.
Keck, O., 1980: The West German fast breeder programme. A case study in governmental decision making. *Energy Policy* 8(4), pp. 277–292.
Kitschelt, H., 1986: Four theories of public policy making and fast breeder reactor development. *International Organization* 40(1), pp. 65–104.
Lange, K., 2006: Deutsche Biotech-Unternehmen und ihre Innovationsfähigkeit im internationalen Vergleich: eine institutionentheoretische Analyse. Proefschrift ter verkrijging van het doctoraat in de Bedrijfskunde aan de Rijksuniversiteit Groningen. Available online at: www.rug.nl/research/portal/publications/deutsche-biotechunternehmen-und-ihre-innovationsfahigkeit-im-internationalen-vergleich%28c1e9ba3e-3f41-4453-9549-a431151ddc4f%29.html (accessed 29 May 2015).
Leff, D. (Ed.), 1983: *Biobusiness World Data Base*. Draft Report by a U.S. government Interagency Working Group on Competitive and Transfer Aspects of Biotechnology. Amsterdam: Elsevier.
Lidskya, L.M. and Miller, M.M., 2002: Nuclear power and energy security: a revised strategy for Japan. *Science and Global Security* 10(2), pp. 127–150.

Loeppky, R., 2005: History, technology, and the capitalist state: the comparative economy of biotechnology and genomics. *Review of International Political Economy*, 12(2), pp. 264–286.

Lynskey, M.J., 2006: Transformative technology and institutional transformation: coevolution of biotechnology venture firms and the institutional framework in Japan. *Research Policy* 35(9), pp. 1389–1422.

Marth, W. and Koehler, M., 1998: The German fast breeder program (a historical overview). *Energy* 23(7/8), pp. 593–608.

Mayntz, R., 2001: Triebkräfte der Technikentwicklung und die Rolle des Staates. In: Gerd Simonis, G., Martinsen, R. and Saretzki, T. (Eds.): *Politik und Technik: Analysen zum Verhältnis von technologischem, politischem und staatlichem Wandel am Anfang des 21. Jahrhunderts. Politische Vierteljahresschrift Sonderheft* 31, Wiesbaden: Westdeutscher, pp. 3–18.

Mazzucato, M., 2011: *The Entrepreneurial State*. London: Demos.

Mintzberg, H., 1983: *Structure in Five: Designing effective organizations*. Englewood Cliffs, NJ: Prentice-Hall.

Motohashi, K., 2012: A comparative analysis of biotechnology startups between Japan and the US. *Social Science Japan Journal* 15(2), pp. 219–237.

Mowery, D.C. and Sampat, B.N., 2004: The Bayh-Dole Act of 1980 and university–industry technology transfer: a model for other OECD governments? In: Link, A.N. and Scherer, F.M. (Eds.): *Essays in Honor of Edwin Mansfield. The Economics of R&D, Innovation, and Technological Change*. New York: Springer. pp. 233–245.

Müller, C., 2001: *The Biotechnology Industry in Germany and Japan*. Arbeitspapier Nr. 11, Oktober 2001. Available online at: http://doku.b.tu-harburg.de/volltexte/2006/152/(accessed 29 May 2015).

Müller, C. and Fujiwara, T., 2002: The commercialization of biotechnology in Japan. *Drug Discovery Today* 7(13), pp. 699–704.

Nemzek, T., Squire, A., Iacobellis, S., Wolfe, B., Landis, J. and Taylor, J., 1974: The US fast breeder reactor development programme. In: IAEA Bulletin 164: pp. 37–43. Available online at: www.iaea.org/sites/default/files/publications/magazines/bulletin/bull16-4/16405393743.pdf (accessed 29 May 2015).

Organization for Economic Cooperation and Development (OECD), 2011: Key Biotechnology Indicators. Paris: OECD. Available online at: www.oecd.org/science/innovationinsciencetechnologyandindustry/49303992.pdf (accessed 29 May 2015).

Rammert, W., 1992: Wer oder was steuert den technischen Fortschritt? Technischer Wandel zwischen Steuerung und Evolution. *Soziale Welt* 43(1), pp. 7–25.

Schulte, K., 1977: Zur Geschichte des Brüters. *Physik unserer Zeit* 8(4), pp. 97–101.

Shadrina, E., 2012: Fukushima fallout: gauging the change in Japanese nuclear energy policy. *International Journal Disaster Risk Science* 3(2), pp. 69–83.

Sharp, M., 1987: National policies towards biotechnology. *Technovation* 5(4), pp. 281–304.

Suzuki, T., 2010: Japan's plutonium breeder reactor and its fuel cycle. In: Cochran, T.B., Feiveson, H.A., Patterson, W., Pshakin, G., Ramana, M.V., Schneider, M., Suzuki, T. and Hippel, F. von (Eds.): *Fast Breeder Reactor Programs: History and status. A research report of the International Panel on Fissile Materials*, pp. 53–60. Available online at: http://fissilematerials.org/library/rr08.pdf (accessed 29 May 2015).

Suzuki, T. and Suzuki, A., 1986: Japan's nuclear energy policy. *Science and Public Policy* 13(1), pp. 25–32.

U.S. Congress, 1984: *Commercial Biotechnology: An international analysis*. Washington, D.C.: U.S. Congress, Office of Technology Assessment, OTA-BA-218, January.

Walker, W., 2000: Entrapment in large technology systems: institutional commitment and power relations. *Research Policy* 29(7–8), pp. 833–846.

Yuan, R.T. and Dibner, M.D., 1990: *Japanese Biotechnology: A comprehensive study of government policy, R&D and industry*. New York: Stockton Press.

Zika, E., Paptryfon, I., Wolf, O., Gomes-Barbero, M., Stein, A.J. and Bock A.-K., 2007: *Consequences, Opportunities and Challenges of Modern Biotechnology for Europe*. JRC Reference Reports EUR 22728 EN. Luxembourg: European Commission.

15

KOREAN GOVERNMENT AND SCIENCE AND TECHNOLOGY DEVELOPMENT

Sunyang Chung

Introduction

Korea has evolved from being a very poor country into a developed country. The GDP per capita of Korea increased from 80 US$ in 1962 to 20,591$ in 2011. There has been no other such remarkable story in the world. What are the reasons for this phenomenon? There are two important reasons for Korea's success: technological innovations and the active role of the government. These two factors are interrelated and the Korean government has supported very actively the generation, improvement and utilization of technological innovations.

The Korean government has implemented a series of good S&T policies, increased R&D investment on a large scale and made great efforts to nurture and produce well qualified scientists and engineers. Based on their technological capabilities, Korean companies have introduced good products and services to international markets.

There are many unique characteristics in the Korean approach to technological innovations. For example, the role of government has been essential in the technological development of Korea. The Korean government has increased its R&D investment and induced private companies to increase their R&D investment. It has established public research institutes according to major S&T areas in order to develop relevant technologies effectively. The government has also made a great effort in activating the collaboration among industrial companies, public research institutes, and universities, as a result of which Korean industrial companies have increased their technological capabilities. This chapter will discuss this Korea-specific approach to technological innovations.

Literature review on technology and politics from Korean perspectives

At the beginning of Korean industrialization, especially in the 1970s and 1980s, there were several studies on the role of technological innovations in the economic development of developing countries such as Korea (Clark 1985; Westphal et al. 1985; Dahlman et al. 1987; Amsden 1989; OECD 1992). For example, Clark (1985) emphasized the role of government in increasing investment in technological innovation and establishing S&T infrastructure. In those years, the concept of *"appropriate technology"* was on the rise. Many experts argued that imported technologies should fit well with the degree of economic development and the level of adopting capabilities of developing countries.

In line with the concept of appropriate technology, experts emphasized that developing countries should accumulate indigenous technological capabilities in order to digest and utilize imported technologies from advanced countries. Here the role of government is essential in securing and motivating industrial companies, public research institutes, and universities to learn advanced technologies and accumulate technological capabilities. In this regard, Bell (1984) stressed that technological innovations could be attained by purposeful investment of scarce resources of developing countries. In this sense, developing countries should mobilize their R&D resources very actively and utilize them as efficiently as possible. He also argued that governmental intervention was very effective to the economic development of developing countries, but it was not systematic due to the lack of experiences of those countries. In addition, OECD (1992) also stressed that not so many discussions were conducted on the role of technological innovations in the development of developing countries, even though there were many studies on developing countries.

Around the end of the 1980s, a system approach to S&T policy was raised, especially after analyzing the Japanese success in the 1970s and 1980s. Freeman (1987) argued that the Japanese success at that time resulted from a close cooperation among government, academia, public research sector, and industry. He named the cooperation model as a *national innovation system*. It implies that Japan was successful in formulating and implementing a national innovation system that led to economic success. Under the concept of a national innovation system, Lundvall and his colleagues carried out a series of theoretical studies on national innovation systems, especially focusing on interactive learning and institutional change (Lundvall 1992). Nelson (1993) carried out wide-spread international comparisons between different national innovation systems.

There were also several studies on the Korean national innovation system. Analyzing the Korean national innovation system, Kim (1993) emphasized that Korea was moving into the phase of creative innovation and should get into the phase of innovation. Chung and Lay (1997) emphasized that S&T policies should be based on country-specific frame conditions, especially national innovation systems, and compared the influences of the country-specific frame conditions on S&T policies between Korea and Germany.

In the 1990s, many scholars started to investigate regional innovation systems (Chung 1996, 1999; Cooke et al. 1997; Braczyk et al. 1998). This reflects well the increasing importance of regions in S&T, business, and economic activities. The regional innovation system will also be a good policy concept to generate, implement, and appropriate efficient sectoral innovation systems in regions, because regions develop different economic sectors due to their economic conditions (Chung 2002). Therefore, many regional governments in the world have tried to formulate their own regional innovation systems in terms of various policy instruments. This concept has also been studied by scholars in economic geography (Storper 1995; Koschatzky 2002).

In Korea, there have been several important studies on regional innovation (Chung 1999, 2002; Lee and Chung 2000). In particular, Chung (2002) analyzed Korean regional innovation systems and concluded that the Korean national innovation systems were relatively weak, as there were only three advanced regional innovation systems, six fast developing regional innovation systems and seven less developed regional innovation systems. He emphasized that Korean regional innovation systems should be refined and further developed based on active support by the central government, active interactive learning between innovation actors, and also close cooperation between the central and regional governments.

In those days, the discussion on S&T policy was moving to *sustainable development*. Grey (1989) argues that technological innovations have *paradoxical effects*: they produce not only positive effects such as economic development but also negative effects such as environmental problems. He emphasizes that only technological innovations can solve the paradoxical effects. Freeman (1992) also emphasizes the harmony among economic, technological, and environmental changes and calls the discipline for this purpose the *economy of hope*. Chung (1998) adopts the concept of sustainability to national innovation system and emphasizes that government should strive to formulate and implement a *sustainable national innovation system* in order to attain sustainable development effectively. Weber and Hemmelskamp (2005) also emphasize that governments should make an effort to implement environmental innovation systems.

Role of Korean governments in S&T development

Technology policy is a result of the role of government in S&T areas. However, it does not fully reflect the relationship between technology and politics. There will be several important actors in this relationship such as the central government, regional government, political parties, and other interest groups. From the perspectives of Korea, the central government has been playing a crucial role in S&T areas, while the Korean general assembly has played only a meager role. Therefore, in order to analyze the relationship between technology and politics in Korea, the role of the central government should be analyzed. The Korean government has not only set the goals of its S&T policies but has also implemented a series of national R&D programs. We will analyze how much and what kinds of role the Korean government has played in the development of the Korean national innovation system.

Korean economy in general

Korea has developed remarkably since the beginning of its economic development. Many of the champion products in international markets, e.g. CDMA, semiconductors, automobiles, and steel, are made in Korea. Success has been based on technological capabilities, which have been actively supported by the central government. Korea has been accumulating its strong technological capabilities since the end of the 1960s and especially in the 1980s and thereinafter. Such technological capabilities have been transformed into new products and services that are competent in international markets.

Table 15.1 shows the major indicators of the Korean economy for the five decades since its industrialization. First, Korea's population increased significantly from 25.01 million people in 1960 to 48.58 million people in 2010. This indicates about a twofold increase over five decades. However, we can observe that the rate of increase has decreased dramatically since the beginning of the 1990s. Nowadays, Korea is worrying about the low birth rate.

Second, GDP has increased dramatically from 2 billion US$ in 1960 to 1,014 billion US$ in 2010. This indicates 507 times increase of total GDP over five decades. The growth rate of GDP has always been surprising in Korea's history of industrialization. The year 1960 showed only 2.2 percent of annual growth rate of GDP. However, the 1970s, 1980s and 1990s always showed two-digit growth rates. However, the GDP growth rates diminished in the 1990s, especially since the economic crisis of the late 1990s. The year 2000 showed only 8.5 percent growth rate and the year 2010 6.2 percent. As a result of rapid economic development, the Korean GDP per capita has also increased dramatically. The GDP per capita increased from 80 US$ in 1960 through 11,134 US$ in 2000 to 20,759 US$ in 2010. This is a 259.5 times increase of GDP per capita between 1960 and 2010.

Table 15.1 Major economic indicators in Korea

	1960	*1970*	*1980*	*1990*	*2000*	*2010*
Population (1000)	25,012	32,241	38,124	42,869	45,985	48,580
GDP (US$, billion)	2	8	62	253	512	1,014
Growth rate of GDP (percent)	2.2	17.2	21.8	20.6	8.5	6.2
GDP per capita (US$)	80	248	1,632	5,900	11,134	20,759
Trade balance (US$, million)	-65	-597	-4,384	-2,004	11,787	41,172
Exports (US$, million)	32	660	17,214	63,124	172,268	466,384
Imports (US$, million)	97	1,256	21,598	65,127	160,481	425,212

Source: National Statistical Office (Each Year).

Third, Korea had suffered from trade deficits till the beginning of the 1990s, because it had needed lots of resources for its industrialization and imported them from foreign countries. Since the Korean economy switched into high-tech oriented structures in the 1990s, however, Korea has shown a positive trade balance. The year 2000 shows 11,787 million US$ of trade balance and the year 2010 41,172 million US$. This confirms the competitiveness of the Korean economy in international markets.

One of the crucial factors for the Korean success is the effective involvement of the Korean government. The Korean government has formulated an effective legal framework for technological innovations and the economic activities of Korean innovation actors and implemented relevant policy programs for promoting innovation and economic activities. The Korean government has been an essential component of the Korean national innovation system. Therefore, in this chapter, we will examine the role of the Korean government in the development of the Korean national innovation system.

Role of the government

As a centralized country, the Korean government has increased its efforts to enhance technological capabilities. Several methods might be adopted to classify and describe the historical role of the central government in the area of science and technology. It could be described in terms of changes in the administration of a central government or in terms of decades. According to our studies, there has been a tendency for changing policy directions in many countries with the change in decades (Bruder and Dose 1986; Chung and Lay 1997).

There have been some studies and reports on the historical development of Korean innovation policies, e.g. MOST (1990), OECD (1996), and Chung and Lay (1997). They discuss the role of government in Korea's accumulating technological capabilities in terms of decades. Table 15.2 shows the role played by the Korean government in science, technology, and innovation in terms of decades. This indicates that the Korean government has been actively involved in developing S&T and innovation.

In the 1960s: beginning of building S&T infrastructure

It was not until the beginning of the 1960s that the governmental efforts for the promotion of S&T and innovation were initiated in line with the First Five Year Plan for Economic Development, which was introduced in 1962. Since then, the Korean government has intervened very strongly in the areas of S&T and innovation. The government has applied a strong

Table 15.2 Role of Korean government in national innovation system

Periods	*Major S&T policies in Korea*
1960s	Beginning of scientific education Beginning of S&T infrastructure construction (e.g. KIST, MOST)
1970s	Establishment of government-sponsored research institutes Technical, scientific, and further education (e.g. KAIS) Establishment of Daedock Science Park Beginning of industrial R&D
1980s	Promotion of key technologies through National R&D Program Establishment of KAIST by merger between KIST and KAIS Activation of industrial R&D Mass production of high-qualified R&D personnel Expansion of S&T-related ministries
1990s	Expansion of R&D investment and increase the need to coordinate S&T policies among ministries Promotion of academic R&D potentials, for example by introducing ERC program Introduction of regional innovation policies Introduction of Research Council system for government-sponsored research institutes (GRIs)
2000s	Enactment of Basic Law of Science and Technology Expansion of regional innovation strategies Adoption of Deputy Prime Minister of Science and Technology and establishment of Science & Technology Innovation Office (STIO) Brain Korea 21 and NURI programs Establishment of Ministry of Education, Science and Technology(MEST) by merger of MOST and Ministry of Education (MOE) Promotion of low-carbon and green growth Nurturing R&D Special Zones and International Science Business Belt Strengthening National S&T Commission (NSTC) for better Coordination Establishment of Institute of Basic Science (IBS) for basic sciences
2013–Present	Establishing the Ministry of S&T, ICT, and Future Planning (MISIP) for Creative Economy

Source: Revised and improved from Chung, S. (2003), "Innovation in Korea" in: Shavina, L.V. (Ed.), *The International Handbook on Innovation*. Oxford: Pergamon, p.893.

technology-push approach in the construction and improvement of the national innovation system. Korean economic policies in the 1960s were characterized by an import substitution and export orientation. At this time, automobile production (1960), shipbuilding (1967), mechanical engineering (1967), and electronics industry (1967) were the central concern of governmental promotion (Byun 1989; Song 1990).

In order to realize this economic policy effectively, an institutional framework in the area of science and technology began to be established. In 1967, the Korea Institute of Science and Technology (KIST) was founded as the first *government-sponsored research institute* (GRI); it carried out comprehensive R&D activities, especially in the technology areas mentioned above. In order to provide the base of S&T and innovation activities, the Korean government enacted the Law for Science and Technology Promotion in 1967 as the first S&T law in Korea. In 1968, the Ministry of Science and Technology (MOST) was established for the first time in developing countries, whose task was formulating and implementing S&T policies.

At the same time Korean universities attempted to produce as many engineers as possible, because there was a great shortage of qualified engineers, who were indispensable for the development of the Korean economy. Korea concentrated on the digestion and imitation of imported technologies from advanced countries. There were no concrete S&T policy measures and programs in the Korean system. Most technological needs were covered by KIST, which was the only public research institute in Korea.

In the 1970s: establishment of government-sponsored research institutes

In the 1970s the Korean government placed the main emphasis of its industrial policy on the establishment and expansion of heavy, chemical, and export-oriented industries (Byun 1989; Song 1990). These industries were technology-oriented and needed a certain level of domestic technological capabilities.

With a view to meeting the needs of these industries, the Korean government founded several corresponding GRIs according to the KIST model, e.g. Korea Institute of Machinery and Materials (KIMM), Korea Research Institute of Chemical Technology (KRICT), and Electronics and Telecommunication Research Institute (ETRI). These GRIs were the grounding stones of the Korean national innovation system. During this period, the major emphasis of the S&T and innovation policy shifted from the simple imitation of imported technologies to their complex adoption and the domestic development of simple, less complex technologies. Creative imitation started in this period (Kim 1997).

In this period, Korea lacked well-qualified manpower to support the development of heavy and chemical industries. Therefore, the Korean government established the Korea Advanced Institute of Science (KAIS) in 1971, which was the predecessor of the Korea Advanced Institute of Science and Technology (KAIST). The establishment of KAIS stimulated the competition with Korean major universities in nurturing and producing researchers and engineers. Since then, Korean universities including KAIST have trained and supplied a sufficient number of good scientists and engineers in the Korean national innovation system. As the Korean economy has expanded very rapidly, there has been no serious brain drain in Korea.

In 1973 the Korean government initiated and implemented a very ambitious plan to establish the Daedock Science Park which is about 150 km south of Seoul. This was the first innovation cluster in Korea and many of the GRIs and KAIS mentioned above would be expected to move into this science park. Some private research institutes would also be expected to be established in this innovation cluster. The Korean government hoped this park would become a growth engine for the national economy by generating technological and innovation synergies between GRIs and private institutes. However, because of the two oil crises, in the middle of the 1970s and the beginning of the 1980s, it was not until the middle of the 1980s that the establishment of the Daedock Science Park was activated.

Around the end of the 1970s, some big Korean industrial enterprises, especially those in the industries mentioned above, for example Samsung and LG, began to carry out their own R&D activities. Those industrial companies recognized the importance of technological innovations in securing and enhancing their competitive advantages in international markets.

In the 1980s: enhancement of industrial R&D capabilities

The 1980s were characterized by a very strong increase of industrial R&D activities within the Korean national innovation system. Using several policy instruments, the Korean government motivated industrial enterprises to establish their own R&D institutes, so that the number of private research institutes rose dramatically from 53 in 1981 to 966 institutes in 1990 (KITA, each year). In line with this strong increase of industrial R&D capabilities, the government tried to shift the Korean industrial structure away from traditional sectors towards high technology areas.

In 1982 the MOST initiated the first big project in the areas of S&T and innovation, National R&D Program based on the Law for Promoting Technological Development. This program aimed at developing not only high technologies but also big technologies (MOST 1987). In this program the industrial key technologies that industrial companies could not deal with alone were developed through joint projects, especially between industrial companies and government-sponsored research institutes. As a result of strong R&D efforts in the public and private sectors in this period, Korea was able to attain a certain level of innovation capabilities to compete with advanced countries in some advanced technology areas such as semiconductors (STEPI 1991).

Since the end of the 1980s, several ministries, particularly the Ministry of Commerce, Industry and Energy (MOCIE) became concerned with science, technology, and innovation. In 1987, this ministry initiated the Program for Developing Industrial Base Technologies based on the Law for Industrial Development. Following the MOCIE, other ministries started to initiate their own programs to activate technological innovations in their areas of jurisdiction. It made a great contribution to enhancing technological capabilities in many industrial sectors. However, the problem of duplication of R&D resources had begun in this period, as these ministries competed very strongly with each other to collect more R&D resources.

In the 1990s: activation of academic research

Despite the greatly increased importance of industry, the Korean government intervened in the 1990s more actively than before in the areas of S&T and innovation. Based on some successes in the last decade, the Korean government recognized the importance of technological innovations in economic development. The government tried to step up national R&D expenditures, with the result that in 1991 the share of national R&D expenditures in GDP exceeded 2 percent for the first time in Korea's history (MOST, each year).

Based on the strong increase in industrial R&D capabilities, in the 1990s industrial companies took over major areas of R&D activities that were previously performed by GRIs. Criticism of the role of public research institutes rose in this period and there were frequent reorganizations, mergers, and disorganizations of Korean public research institutes (Chung et al. 2001; Song et al. 2001; Chung 2002; Yu et al. 2002). Therefore, in March 1999, the Korean government introduced a new public research system, the Research Council system, by benchmarking Germany's *Gesellschaft* system, to secure the autonomy of GRIs and avoid the direct influences from the government on them by establishing an umbrella organization between the government and GRIs.

In this period, the Korean government very strongly promoted R&D and innovation capabilities of Korean universities, which had been the weakest point of the Korean national innovation system until this period (Chung 1996; OECD 1996; Chung and Lay 1997). In order to strengthen academic R&D capabilities, the government initiated the excellent research center (ERC) program for the most advanced research centers in universities in 1990. This program consists of Science Research Centers (SRCs) in the area of basic science and Engineering Research Centers (ERCs) in the area of engineering and applied research. When a center in a university is accepted as an excellent research center, it can be supported by a very large amount of money for ten years. As there was a hierarchy in the level of research capabilities in Korean universities, a few of the best universities, especially in Seoul, dominated the excellent research centers. Therefore, the Korean government initiated the Regional Research Center (RRC) Program in 1995 in order to strengthen the R&D and innovation capabilities in universities in other regions. As of 2001 there are 25 SRCs, 34 ERCs, and 45 RRCs (MOST 2001). These centers have played an important role in enhancing R&D capabilities of Korean universities.

In the middle of the 1990s, the Korean government started to initiate regional innovation policies. Korea had developed in the middle of the capital city, Seoul, and its outskirts; the development of politics, economy, society, and culture was centered in these areas, so that the regional level of industry, science, and technology was still very low. The central government was always a dominant player in S&T and innovation policy and there had been no regional S&T policy in Korea. Even in 1999, the R&D budget of total regional governments represented only 6.8 percent of the national S&T budget (MOST 1999). Korean research organizations were located in and around Seoul and in Daedeock Science Park. Therefore the Korean government initiated the Master Plan for Promoting Regional Science and Technology in 1999 and motivated regional governments to implement their own S&T policies, increase their R&D investment, and establish an organization for promoting technological innovations in their regional administrations (MOST 1999). In this period, six Technoparks were established in Korean regions, which were expected to become innovation clusters for Korean regions. At the same time regional governments also started to recognize the importance of S&T for the economic development of their regions, especially since the inauguration of the Local Government System in March 1995. As of 2000, eight among 16 regional governments established an independent organization for promoting technological and innovation capabilities in their regional administrations (MOST 1999 Chung 2002).

In the 2000s: further strengthening of the national innovation system

Turning to the twenty-first century, Korea initiated a very ambitious plan to enhance technological and innovation capabilities more systematically. The Korean government enacted a comprehensive law, the Basic Law of Science and Technology in January 2001, which aimed at more systematic promotion of science and technology. This law prescribed to formulate the Basic Plan of Science and Technology every five years by comprising detailed S&T plans of all S&T-related ministries (MOST 2001). The first *Basic Plan of Science and Technology* was formulated in December 2001. It had a comprehensive goal and implementation strategies for enhancing technological capabilities for the next five years, e.g., from 2002 to 2006. Korea selected six technology areas, i.e., information technologies (IT), biotechnologies (BT), nanotechnologies (NT), space technologies (ST), environmental technologies (ET), and cultural technologies (CT), which would be essential to the knowledge-based twenty-first century.

As technological innovations were promoted by many ministries and lots of budget was invested in S&T and innovation, it was necessary to coordinate S&T policies among major S&T-related ministries. Therefore, the National Science and Technology Commission (NSTC), which was a presidential commission, was established in 1999 to better coordinate S&T and innovation policies among ministries. As the chairman of this new commission was the President of Korea, a much better coordination was anticipated.

With regard to the general S&T policy goals, future-oriented goals, e.g., enhancing quality of life in terms of science, technology, and innovation, were seriously pursued for the first time in the Korean S&T and innovation policy. That implies that the Korean government fully recognized the importance of science, technology, and innovation in the development of the Korean economy and society.

In December 2004, Korea undertook a big experiment by adopting a new S&T administration structure. The Minister of Science and Technology was promoted to Deputy Prime Minister in order to effectively coordinate S&T policies among diverse S&T-related ministries. For this purpose, the Science & Technology Innovation Office (STIO), whose mission is S&T policy coordination among ministries, was established under the Deputy Minister of Science and Technology (MOST).

At the beginning of the 2000s, the Ministry of Education and Human Resources Development (MOE and HRD) initiated two important programs for strengthening the R&D and innovation potential of Korean universities. The first was the Brain Korea (BK) 21 program. It started in 1999 in order to upgrade the research infrastructure and graduate-level training of Korean universities. This program was evaluated as very successful in strengthening the R&D potential of Korean universities (MOE and HRD 2005). Therefore, the second phase of the Brain Korea (BK) 21 Program started for a period of seven years between 2005 and 2012 in order to raise Korean graduate schools to a global level. As the BK 21 program was concentrated on universities in Seoul and its outskirts, the Korean government initiated the New University for Regional Development Innovation (NURI) program in 2004 in order to support regional universities (MOE and HRD 2005).

In 2008, the Korean government established the Ministry of Education, Science and Technology (MEST) by merger of MOST and the Ministry of Education (MOE). It tried to generate synergy effects by integrating R&D and HRD promotion policies. The Korean government strengthened the function of the NSTC in order to coordinate S&T policies more effectively by making NSTC a standing commission and giving it the right to distribute R&D resources. In order to strengthen the Korean academic R&D capabilities, the government introduced the World Class University (WCU) program, in which world-class scientists and engineers could be invited to Korean research-intensive universities.

In addition, the Korean government recognized the importance of sustainable development in national and social development in Korea and initiated the Five Year Masterplan for Green Growth for 2009 and 2013 in 2009, which was foccused on low-carbon and green growth development. In order to support the governmental policy for green growth, the Korean government enacted the Basic Law for Low-Carbon and Green Growth in January 2010. The Master plan had a vision of being rated seventh greenest country by 2020 and fifth by 2050 (Presidential Committee on Green Growth 2009).

As for regional innovation policy, the Korean government implemented lots of institutional and policy programs in the 2000s. First of all, the Korean government put the contents on regional innovation strategies in the Basic Law of Science and Technology. It prescribed that the central government should formulate and implement a Master Plan for Promoting Regional Science and Technology every five years and establish the Committeee for Regional S&T Promotion NSTC to evaluate and coordinate regional innovation policies and programs. Based on the law and master plans lots of policy programs for regional S&T and innovation have been introduced. For example, the Korean government authorized the Daedock Science Park as a R&D Special Zone in 2005, which was called Innopolise, based on the Special Law for Nurturing R&D Special Zone of Daedock and Others. Special incentives, for example tax exemption, simplification of start-up process, and so on, were given to the R&D Special Zone in order to activate start-ups and technology commercializations. In 2011, in addition to the Daedock Innopolis, two additional R&D Special Zones were authorized: Gwangju Innopolis and Daegu Innopolis.

Based on the competent national innovation system, Korean industrial companies, especially big enterprises, have introduced very competent products in international markets. Some big companies could lead the markets in diverse industries, for example semiconductor (Samsung Semiconductor, SK Hynix), electronics (Samsung Electronics, LG Electronics), shipbuilding (Daewoo Shipbuilding and Marin Engineering, Samsung Heavy Industries, Hyundai Heavy Industries), petrochemical (SK Innovation, Samsung Petrochemical, LG Chem, GS-Caltex), automobile (Hyundai Motor, Kia Motors, Ssangyong Motor), steel making (POSCO, Hyundai steel), and so on. These big enterprises have accumulated their technological capabilities by operating their own research institutes and increasing their R&D investment to a large scale.

In the 2010s: transforming into the creative national innovation system

Around the end of the 2000s, Korea recognized the importance of basic science and research in the development of the Korean economy and society. In those days, several studies emphasizes that Korean national innovation should move from an imitation-oriented system to an innovation-oriented system. In order to compete with advanced countries, Korea had to implement the creative national innovation system. The Korean government recognized the importance of basic research and science for this purpose and established the Institute of Basic Science (IBS) for promoting basic science and research, which were the weakest points of the Korean national innovation system. The Korean government expects that IBS could develop and accumulate as high a level of basic research capabilities as those of the *Max Planck Society* in Germany.

In February 2013, the new governmental administration came into office and announced that the Korean economy should be a creative economy. For this purpose, the Korean government established a big ministry, the Ministry of S&T, ICT, and Future Planning (MSIP), which would be in charge of preparing for the creative economy. The functions for promoting S&T, innovation, information and communication technologies, and future planning, as well as those of the the NSTC moved to this ministry.

In addition, most Korean GRIs should be under the jurisdiction of this ministry and are expected to play a crucial role in attaining a creative economy. Some big enterprises have been conducting global R&D and innovation activities. For example, Samsung established a research complex in Silicon Valley in order to recruit world-best innovative talent and to carry out its R&D and innovation activities, especially on S/W and design, more effectively.

Increase in R&D resources

The role of the government in S&T policies can also be described in terms of R&D investment of the government. Science and technology are public goods, and as a result, the government tends to invest lot of resources in them. This is particularly true when a national economy is in the phase of underdevelopment; in this case the government should lead a national innovation system by increasing its R&D investment. Of course, the governmental R&D investment is based on the legal framework and national R&D programs.

Table 15.3 indicates the national R&D investment of Korea since the beginning of Korean industrialization. The national R&D investment increased from 4 million US$ in 1963 to 37.9 billion US$ in 2010. This is a remarkable increase, representing about a 9,484 times increase in about 50 years. Therefore, the share of national R&D investment in GDP increased from 0.25 percent in 1963 to 3.74 percent in 2010. As a result, Korea is now one of the most R&D-intensive countries in the world. At the beginning of the development of the Korean national innovation system, the government played a leading role in R&D investment. Up to the beginning of the 1980s, the Korean government invested much more money in R&D activities than the private sector. For example, in 1980, 64 percent of the national R&D investment in Korea was financed by the government. This indicates that the Korean government has played a crucial role in the development of the Korean national innovation system and the accumulation of technological capabilities in Korea.

However the private sector has increased its R&D investment on a large scale, especially since the middle of the 1980s, and in 1990 about 81 percent of the national R&D investment was made by the private sector. However, the Korean government increased its R&D investment more aggressively since the beginning of the 1990s and the governmental share in the national R&D investment is 28 percent in 2010. This confirms that the Korean government has played an essential role in the recent development of the national innovation system. In order to implement a creative national innovation system, the Korean government should more actively engage in implementing a national innovation system.

The total amount of governmental R&D investment increased from 9.7 million US$ in 1970 to 13.7 billion US$ in 2010. The share of the governmental R&D investment in GDP increased 0.35 percent in 1970 to 1.17 percent in 2010. It is noteworthy that the Korean government has increased its R&D investment very significantly since 1990. Based on the successful economic growth, the government was able to effectively increase its R&D investment. This confirms that the government has played an essential role in the development of the Korean national innovation system. The new governmental administration, which started in February 2013, has emphasized a creative economy, and the promotion of basic sciences and research will be a very important national agenda. Therefore, it seems that the Korean government will play a more significant role in national innovation systems and its R&D investment will be increasing on a larger scale.

Since 1980, the Korean private sector has also increased its R&D investment dramatically and much stronger than the Korean government. The role of the private sector has become more important in the national innovation system than the Korean government. In particular, there has been a tendency for a concentration of R&D investment in big enterprises: The portion of top ten enterprises in total industrial R&D investment was 34.8 percent in 2000 and 31.2 percent in 2010 (MOST, each year).

The volume of R&D manpower increased dramatically from 3,072 persons in 1963 to 500,124 persons in 2010. This represents an increase of about 163 times. It deserves to be mentioned that Korea has almost doubled it every ten years since 1990 after it attained a high level of

Table 15.3 Increase in R&D resources in Korea

	1963	*1970*	*1980*	*1990*	*2000*	*2010*
GERD	4	33	428	4,676	13,849	37,935
(Share of GDP)	(0.25)	(0.38)	(0.77)	(1.87)	(2.39)	(3.74)
Government: Private	97:3	71:29	64:36	19:81	25:75	28:72
Governmental R&D investment	n.a.	9.7	183.7	921.3	4,197.4	13,701.4
(Share of GDP)	n.a.	(0.35)	(0.47)	(0.48)	(0.70)	(1.17)
Number of R&D personnel	3,072	12,922	30,473	125,525	237,232	500,124

Note: Units: million US$, percent, persons.

Source: MOST (Each Year), Report on the Survey of Research and Development in Science and Technology, Seoul.

economic development. This indicates that Korea's success has resulted from the active accumulation of technological capabilities.

Conclusions

Korea's development has been based on its technological capabilities. In this chapter, we investigated how Korea has accumulated its technological capabilities since the beginning of its industrialization. The Korean government has played a crucial role in the development of the national innovation system and national economy as a whole. We can identify several characteristics of the Korean government's involvement in technological innovations as follows.

First, the Korean government has implemented a systematic approach to promote technological innovations. It has enacted relevant laws, initiated a series of national R&D programs, and increased its R&D investment in order to effectively promote S&T development and innovations in Korea. In this sense, the concept of a national innovation system is well applied for Korea, as it has adopted a systemic approach to S&T and innovation.

Second, the Korean government has enlarged its S&T policy contents continuously. At the beginning of Korea's industrialization, i.e., in the 1960s and 1970s, the Korean S&T policy focused on establishing S&T infrastructure, especially the government-sponsored research institutes (GRIs). In the 1980s, the Korean government actively initiated a series of policies for strengthening R&D and innovation capabilities of industrial companies. In the 1990s, Korean academic R&D capabilities were strengthened by the Korean government. The Korean government implemented active regional innovation policies in the 2000s. Since the end of the 2000s, the Korean government has focused on promoting green growth very actively.

Third, the Korean public research institutes, which are called GRIs, have played a pivotal role in the development of the Korean national innovation system and the national economy as a whole. The history of the Korean national innovation system started from establishing the first GRI, the Korea Institute of Science and Technology in 1967. The major technological successes, for example CDMA, nuclear energy, and so on, originated from those GRIs. In this sense, public research institutes have been good S&T policy instruments for the Korean government. It confirms the arguments of Mazzoleni and Nelson (2007), which emphasize the role of public research institutes in economic catch-up.

Fourth, Korea has made a great effort to learn from the successful national innovation systems of advanced countries, e.g., the USA, Japan, and Germany, and finally it can have a relatively competent national innovation system. There have been a series of systematic researches on advanced national innovation systems, which were supported by the government, and many successful policy contents were benchmarked and creatively implemented in the Korean S&T policies. In particular, Korea has actively benchmarked German S&T policies and systems, for example the S&T governance system, innovation policies for SMEs, public research system and so on. However, considering the hectic competition between countries to attain and implement the best national innovation system in the world, Korea should continue to learn from other advanced national innovation systems.

However, it is necessary for the Korean government to make a more careful involvement in S&T development. For example, it should have a more systematic and sustainable coordination system of S&T policies, as almost every ministry has been involved in S&T development. The government should implement more efficient S&T policies for Korean SMEs, as their technological and innovation capabilities are still low even though there have been diverse policy measures for Korean SMEs. In addition, the Korean government should strengthen international S&T cooperation, especially with developing countries.

As a whole, Korea is a very innovative and dynamic country. Based on the active and successful involvement of the government, it has established and implemented a relatively competent and dynamic national innovation system in a very short period. Korea has invested a lot of resources in order to enhance the efficiency of its national innovation system and increase the innovation capabilities of major innovation actors. The national innovation system as a whole and its major actors are very innovative and produce a lot of innovative results, products, and so on. We can ascribe the dynamic development of the Korean economy in this globalized economy to the efficient national innovation system. Basically we can identify some cultural factors for the success of Korea. From historical perspectives, Korean people have been very eager to educate their children and Korean society has been appreciating science and knowledge. Korea's success could be repeated by developing countries too. However, they must appreciate the importance of S&T and innovation beforehand in their economic and social development.

References

Amsden, A.H., 1989: *Asia's Next Giant: South Korea and late industrialization.* New York and Oxford: Oxford University Press.

Bell, R.M.N., 1984: "Learning" and the accumulation of industrial technological capacity in developing countries. In: Fransman, M. and King, K. (Eds.): *Technological Capacity in the Third World.* London: Macmillan, pp. 187–209.

Braczyk, H.J., Cooke, P. and Heidenreich, M. (Eds.), 1998: *Regional Innovation Systems.* London: UCL Press.

Bruder, W. and Dose, N., 1986: Forschungs- und Technologiepolitik in der Bundesrepublik Deutschland. In: Bruder, W. (Ed.): *Forschungs- und Technologiepolitik in der Bundesrepublik Deutschland.* Opladen: Westdeutscher Verlag.

Byun, H.Y., 1989: Industry. In: Byun, H.Y. (Ed.): *The Korean Economy.* Seoul: Yoopoong Publishing Co., pp. 263–290.

Chung, S., 1996: Technologiepolitik für neue Produktionstechnologien in Korea und Deutschland. Heidelberg: Physica-Verlag.

Chung, S., 1998: Towards a "sustainable" national system of innovations: theory and Korean perspectives. In: Lefebvre, L.A., Mason, R.M. and Khalil, T. (Eds.): *Management of Technology, Sustainable Development and Eco-Efficiency.* Amsterdam–New York: Elsevier, pp. 321–330.

Chung, S., 1999: *How to Formulate Regional Innovation Systems in Korea.* Seoul (Korean): Science and Technology Policy Institute (STEPI).

Chung, S., 2002: Building a national innovation system through regional innovation systems. *Technovation* 22(8), pp. 485–491.

Chung, S., 2003: New Management System of Korean Public Research Institutes. Paper presented at the Portland International Conference on Management of Engineering & Technology (PICMET 03), July 20–24.

Chung, S. and Lay, G., 1997: Technology policy between "diversity" and "one best practice": a comparison of Korean and German promotion schemes for new production technologies. *Technovation* 17, pp. 675–693.

Clark, N., 1985: *The Political Economy of Science and Technology.* Oxford: Basil Blackwell.

Cooke, P., Uranga, M.G. and Etxebarria, G., 1997: Regional innovation systems: institutional and organisational dimensions. Research Policy 26(4–5), pp. 475–491.

Dahlman, C.J., Ross-Larson, B. and Westphal, L.E., 1987: Managing technological development: lessons from the newly industrializing countries. *World Development* 15(6), pp. 759–775.

Freeman, C., 1987: *Technology Policy and Economic Performance: Lessons from Japan.* London and New York: Pinter Publishers.

Freeman, C., 1992: *The Economics of Hope: Essays on technical change, economic growth, and the environment.* London and New York: Pinter Publishers.

Grey, P.E., 1989: The paradox of technological development. In: Ausubel, J.H. and Sladovich, H. (Eds.): *Technology and Environment.* Washington, DC: National Academy Press, pp. 192–204.

Kim, L., 1993: National system of industrial innovation: dynamics of capability building in Korea. In: Nelson, R.R. (Ed.): *National Innovations System: A comparative analysis*. New York: Oxford University Press, pp. 357–383.

Kim, L., 1997: Imitation to Innovation: The dynamics of Korea's technological learning. Boston, MA: Harvard Business School Press.

Korea Industrial Technology Association (KITA) (Each Year), Annual Report on Industrial Technologies. Seoul (Korean).

Koschatzky, K., 2002: Regionsorientierte Innovationspolitik und Innovationsoriente Regionalpolitik: Zwei Wege in die gleiche Richtung? Seminarberichte: Beiträge zum Sommerseminar vom 24. bis 25. September 2001 in Bremen, Gesellschaft für Regionalforschung, Heidelberg, pp. 7–30.

Lee, J. and Chung, S., 2000: *How to Cooperate in Regional Innovation Policies between the Central and Regional Governments*. Seoul (Korean): Science and Technology Policy Institute (STEPI).

Lundvall, B.-A. (Ed.), 1992: *National Systems of Innovation: Towards a theory of innovation and interactive learning*. London: Pinter Publishers.

Mazzoleni, R. and Nelson, R.R., 2007: Public research institutions and economic catch-up. *Research Policy* 36, pp. 1512–528.

Ministry of Education and Human Resources development (MOE and HRD), 2005: A Plan for the Second Stage Brain Korea (BK) 21 Program, Seoul (Korean).

Ministry of Science and Technology (MOST), (Each Year), Annual Report of Regional Science and Technology. Seoul: MOST (Korean).

Ministry of Science and Technology (MOST), (Each Year), Report on the Survey of Research and Development in Science and Technology. Seoul: MOST (Korean).

Ministry of Science and Technology (MOST), 1987: Five Years Report of the "National R&D Program," Seoul: MOST.

Ministry of Science and Technology (MOST), 1990: Introduction to Science and Technology. Republic of Korea. Seoul: MOST.

Ministry of Science and Technology (MOST), 1999, Report on the Survey of Research and Development in Science and Technology. Seoul: MOST (Korean).

Ministry of Science and Technology (MOST), 2001, Science and Technology Annual, Seoul: MOST (Korean).

National Statistical Office (Each Year), Major Statistics of Korean Economy. Seoul.

Nelson, R.R. (Ed.), 1993: *National Innovation Systems: A comparative analysis*, New York and Oxford: Oxford University Press.

OECD, 1992: *Technology and Economy: The key relationship*. Paris: OECD.

OECD, 1996: *Reviews of National Science and Technology Policy: Republic of Korea*: Paris: OECD.

Presidential Committee on Green Growth, 2009: The Five Year Master Plan for Green Growth, July, Seoul.

Science and Technology Policy Institute (STEPI), 1991: Evaluation of National R&D Program (1982–1989), Seoul: STEPI.

Song, B., 1990: *The Rise of the Korean Economy*. Hong Kong: Oxford University Press.

Song, H., Cho, M., Kim, H. and Kim. K., 2001: A Study on Operation Status and Improvement of Government-sponsored Research Institutes. Seoul: Office for Government Policy Coordination (OPC).

Storper, M., 1995: Regional technology coalitions: an essential dimension of national technology policy. *Research Policy* 24, pp. 895–911.

Weber, M. and Hemmelskamp, J. (Eds.), 2005: *Towards Environmental Innovation Systems*. Heidelberg: Springer.

Westphal, L.E., Kim, L. and Dahlman, C.J., 1985: Reflections on the Republic of Korea's acquisition of technological capability. In: Rosenberg, N. and Frischtak, C. (Eds.): *International Technology Transfer: Concepts, measures, and comparisons*. New York: Praeger Publishers.

Yu, S., Son, T. and Lee, J., 2002: New Management Model for Research Councils and Government-sponsored Research Institutes, KRCFST/KRCIFT/KRCPST, Seoul.

16

TWENTY-FIRST CENTURY UNIVERSITIES AS DRIVERS FOR INNOVATION

The dimensions of learning, research, and collaboration

Paul M.A. Baker, Shiri M. Breznitz, Art Seavey and Keith R. Bujak

Nodes of innovation in a global economy

Universities have historically been seen as bastions of stability and anchors of traditions (DeMillo 2011). In the twenty-first century, universities are increasingly expanding their traditional roles of teaching and research to include technology transfer, economic initiatives, and workforce development, partially in response to technological and global economic factors. They have become drivers of innovation both physically, in their immediate locales, as well as virtually, in terms of dissemination of knowledge. In many places, the university's strengths of teaching and pure research represent untapped opportunities to collaborate with other actors across institutional boundaries, leveraging sector strengths (Cross 2013). Public perception of what the university of the twenty-first century can do has not always kept up with these changes, and is a potential barrier to industry–university partnerships (Baker et al. 2012). The influence of universities beyond their immediate physical environs is not a new idea in the geographic literature (e.g., Audretsch et al. 2005; Mueller 2006), but is magnified by the adoption of information and communications technologies (ICT), as noted by Castells (2010). Consequently, this influence is shifting beyond the impact of knowledge creation to actual changes in the manner in which higher education is produced, practiced, and disseminated (Baker et al. 2012).

This paper explores several crosscutting themes: First, universities are exceptionally well suited to satisfy the needs of new markets for knowledge competencies. This includes the granting of degrees as well as preparing learners with a mix of competences that meet the needs of individuals and the workforces required by innovative industries. Second, universities must expand their reach, via virtualization of audience; that is, through digital technologies, they must increase adoption of virtual teaching and research approaches. In addition, development of university courses can contribute to the dissemination of both knowledge and competencies. This can yield an enhanced supply of university trained individuals locally as well as in under-served areas and around the globe. And finally, the role of the university as nexus of social networks, one of the "value-added" characteristics of engagement in university life.

Twenty-first century universities

Universities are complex communities; transmission of knowledge is merely one of their many roles. The integration of research into curriculum, collaboration across systems, and cultivation of relationships with non-traditional educational partners, and cross-disciplinary initiatives, are all critical components of university functioning.

Institutions of higher education interact with a wide array of actors: faculty, researchers, governments and industry, NGOs and foundations. Innovation in education and research have been driven by advances in ICT which augments the type of interactions possible between teacher and student, between student and content, between researchers collocated or distant, as well as between university researchers and industry. Accessible online education and training offers possibilities for learning to those who are not able to take advantage of traditional in-person education. Of further impact is the potential for increased workforce development and maintenance of professional skills. Although university activities are occasionally dismissed as "just education," many of these technologies and practices have application beyond the classroom, for workforce and employment training, as well as enhancing team and collaborative activities.

Institutional innovation and change

Universities expend significant resources on keeping pace with, and meeting the needs of an ever-changing world. But considering the rapidly changing economic landscape that challenges the skill-base of workers and professionals today, these institutions must change quickly—anticipating the needs of the populations they serve. Underutilized infrastructure could be reprogrammed for community uses, for instance to house project or entrepreneurial incubators, or even surplused. There will most likely be efforts to focus on and refine the notion of a "geographic" or physical campus. Online activities such as educational activities or collaborative research not only enable access to the best teachers and most robust material but also facilitate the formation of peer-to-peer communities of learning, virtual collaborative teams, and new forms of investigational endeavors.

For instance, open (free or low cost) online learning represents an alternative to traditional face-to-face learning experiences, and has generated a push back from traditional instructional faculties. In places that lack sufficient specialized educational options they represent a very real, and viable, route to economic and industry growth. While many of these online options are still predominantly in English, local institutions of higher education could provide translations in forums and localized learning communities; a low cost expansion of educational opportunities. Local universities could develop customized learning and training opportunities to increase the competitiveness of a workforce that otherwise might not have the opportunity to improve their skills.

Key issues facing policy makers include issues of socio-economic status (Morgan and Carey 2009; Chesters and Watson 2013; Leach 2013), which has long been a barrier to higher education. What accommodations might be made for those without the necessary technology? Cross-cultural collaborations are becoming easier and more common, but how will various parties interact, given language barriers? Finally, those with disabilities and functional limitations can potentially benefit from the proliferation of educational technologies, but how do we design learning environments to support access for all learners?

Markets for knowledge competencies

Virtually all online education material is in a digital format, generating streams of data that can be used to provide instructor feedback, identify difficult concepts, as well as improving learning outcomes. As software based digital instruction becomes more sophisticated, it is critical to remember that the availability of content is necessary, but not sufficient, to learning. Consumption of content does not automatically equal learning. Conversely, this affords universities the opportunity to develop and facilitate online learning experiences, particularly at fundamental or basic levels, freeing faculty to focus on more advanced or nuanced in-person experiences. The learning communities forming around these educational experiences can occur both virtually or physically with respectively different advantages, and disadvantages.

We propose a conceptual framework consisting of several components, including the learner/student, learning approaches and evaluative analytics, learning technology and knowledge networks that contribute to the development innovation in higher education. Internationally, there is not a consensus on the definitions of "twenty-first century skills," despite being mentioned in regulations and guidelines with frequency (Ananiadou and Claro 2009). One model identifies three dimensions of skills as critical: cognitive (problem-solving and critical thinking), interpersonal (collaboration with peers, situated problems), and intrapersonal (e.g., self-discipline, adaptability) (Koenig 2011). So while technologies of content delivery and connectivity have advanced dramatically, one of the key characteristics of universities is the capacity to help develop these critical thinking and collaborative social skills. A globally competitive workforce demands more than just academic knowledge in a field, but also a mastery of the current technology used. This is another of the opportunities that the twenty-first century university can provide: freeing the delivery of educational, learning, and training experiences from the potentially geographically limited context of the institution.

Employers are beginning to look to work experience as much as academic success (Hodges 2011) as an indicator of work readiness. Surveys of employers suggest a perception that higher education is failing in teaching transferable skills to new graduates—and that they need additional on-the-job training before they can be relied on to contribute meaningfully to the workplace (Hodges 2011). While ICTs facilitate learning of content, universities still maintain an advantage in being able to instil community based soft and social skills such as teamwork and collaborative problem solving. While critical thinking and problem solving are not new skills, as they have been necessary components of human progress throughout history (Rotherham and Willingham 2010), they are considered to be even more critical as twenty-first century skills.

Increasingly, degrees are seen not as endpoints but rather *starting points* for lifelong learning. New technologies in the workplace demand new skills to use the technology and to be able to adapt to new work practices afforded by these technologies. These changes require workers to have a constantly refreshed set of skills. There are cases where an individual course—or even a series of workshops—may satisfy this need. The traditional four-year undergraduate degree, while still meaningful, leaves room for innovation in higher education content and practice. But this is a doubled-edged sword, as employers face an expanded set of credentials and certifications, and employees struggle with demonstrating the knowledge and skills they possess.

New pathways have been proposed that recognize competency as recognized by certificates and credentials, as well as via the traditional degree. Participation in a non-traditional (online) learning experience offers the opportunity to acquire basic knowledge. But as pathways open up this kind of process could lead to a traditional degree for some people and something completely different for others. Drawing on Clayton M. Christensen's concept of a product or service that is "good enough,"—not necessarily ideal, but sufficient to meet the needs of the user: adaptive learning that occurs just as it is needed rather than in a pre-packaged "degree" might serve larger social objectives of an appropriate prepared and competitive workforce.

The ability to aggregate, manipulate, and analyze large data streams, quantified and captured by learning platforms, is an enabling factor behind the development of learning analytics (Ferguson 2012). Software based learning analytics allows direct assessment and evaluation of the efficacy of various different kinds of learning approaches and content delivery. Learning analytics can potentially quantify factors leading to unsuccessful collegiate careers, enabling institutions to better understand why students drop out, and universities are closing the feedback loop by using the results of data analytics to help students change behaviors and habits (Johnson 2013).

Learning analytics are useful for generating insights on actual learning and for prediction of future behavior, but they can also be transformative, driving change of instruction, assessment, and administration (Siemens and Long 2011). The insights generated by learning analytics could potentially streamline the transition from community college to a four-year institution by identifying important skill sets necessary for a successful transition. Further, learning analytics are tools that could help instructors more quickly and accurately assess the range of student knowledge (Strader and Thille 2012), more readily linking teaching approaches to outcomes. Analytics can bring actionable feedback to students, instructors, instructional designers, and learning scientists, creating communities of learning (Strader and Thille 2012). A robust strategy of online collaborative activities could expand the portfolio of university IT departments in a facilitative function helping to manage higher education data analytics, especially if they engage other, non-traditional, research functions, and more broadly, external industry and interested parties.

Competencies, assessment, and documentation

Although accreditation models have focused to some degree on student learning outcomes, competency-based assessment focuses solely on the direct assessment of student knowledge. Motivated students could teach themselves, crafting unique bodies of knowledge, using aggregation of instructional material they find on the Internet or through other sources. Currently there are efforts to move in this direction, but they are primarily associated with courses in the more traditional sense. Several (US) state legislatures have proposed legislation to allow for assessment-for-credit options for basic education requirements, and currently there are regulations in place, federally for application for recognition from the Department of Education for self-paced, online, competency-based degree programs (DOE 2013).

The efficacy of many of the alternative approaches hangs on the development of valid and reliable assessments. Partnerships such as those between online education providers such as Coursera and accrediting bodies such as American Council on Education (ACE), designed to experiment with alternative learning certifications, have increased the urgency for developing assessments that measure what students know and can do, and are fundamental to competency-based programs. Developing high quality assessments is much harder to do than many realize. One concern is that institutions run the risk of granting degrees for test taking skills rather than for the skills and mastery of knowledge the tests are intended to measure. While there are some ideas that might help ensure test quality, such as massive test banks for online courses, the use of portfolio-based assessments for some fields, and peer evaluation of work, there is much work to be done in this area.

The decision on how and where to learn shifts a greater responsibility to the student who must decide on the venue of learning, as well as on the best channel or provider of learning. Globalization also opens up markets for learning and education, so that more convenient, timely or matched opportunities become possible in a wider range of locations and contexts. Well-informed choices require objective, accurate data to make decisions on optimal paths to learning. A variety of external agents currently evaluate, assess, and categorize the various opportunities. There exist, however, significant differences in perceptions among academics, business leaders, and policy leaders about how this should work—a condition that complicates innovation. While there is agreement on the *importance* of accountability, they disagree how best to achieve these objectives (Bogue and Hall 2012).

An increasingly common viewpoint, as expressed, for instance, in the New America Foundation's *Cracking the Credit Hour* holds that traditional accreditation is not well equipped to address the ever-evolving nature of higher education (Laitinen 2012). This raises the question of how the traditional accreditation model might be re-envisioned to be more responsive. While some accrediting bodies *are* taking strides toward updating their standards, such as the Western Association of Schools and Colleges (WASC) (US),[1] other groups are taking more innovative approaches that range from lawmakers pushing for the accreditation of individual courses to educational technology developers supporting portable badges, or e-portfolios, that recognize and document specific accomplishments (Chatham-Carpenter 2010; Cheng and Chau 2013).

The interplay between place and virtuality

One of the most intriguing uses of information and communication technologies is the way in which they enable new communities and networks of interaction (Baker and Ward 2002). Collaborations, partnerships, and classrooms all involve forms of group interactions that are in essence, communities. Online and digital interactions are additional overlays of communications that run as counterparts to traditional face-to-face communities and partnerships, and allow engagement with collaborators that may or may not be physically located. So research activities and developmental partnerships that might be otherwise hindered by the divide between universities and surrounding industry and employers can be enhanced by a strategy of enabling virtual trans-disciplinary and inter-institutional communities.

The impact of virtual communities is especially evident in learning and education settings, but also illuminating in terms of less specialized collaborative processes (Liu 2007). Further, it appears that other factors, such as the implementation approach, impact the efficacy of online education. A meta-analysis of the literature (Means et al. 2013) found that, on average, students in online learning conditions performed modestly better than those receiving face-to-face instruction. It was interesting to note that the advantage over face-to-face classes was significant in those studies contrasting blended learning with traditional face-to-face instruction but not in those studies contrasting purely online with face-to-face conditions.

Insights gained from the ways in which communities of learning organize and operate can inform other kinds of collaborative community activities. This suggests the advantage of the two different approaches—online education as a potential expansion of the mission and outreach of the university to underserved populations, and the value that the university provides in terms of in-person, proximate learning communities, serving as a repository of knowledge for local industry.

The emergence of cheaper alternatives to traditional residential university education noted by Hanna (1998) has only grown more evident by the emergence of alternatives such as less expensive, non residential access-oriented community colleges, proprietary for-profits, and both online venues offered by physical institutions and those that are purely online. New educational and learning opportunities, particularly ones such as MOOCs that are free or very low cost have great appeal. "Free," ironically may also have associated costs as noted in a recent essay "Information wants to be free, but the world isn't ready" (Sirius 2013).

A variety of business models are beginning to arise to deal with the issue of sustainability and affordability. For instance, one proposed system would be one of delayed payment—students only begin to pay off their tuition costs after they are making a certain level of income. This is not a new idea; there are examples of this extant in the United States, such as receiving medical education in exchange for military service, or providing medical services in remote or underserved areas. Online education offers this as an avenue (Moore 2005). Innovations such as the open courseware movement have the potential to dramatically increase student access to university resources, but are limited by society's view of the purpose of teaching and education (Rhoads et al. 2013).

Universities, *continuous* education, and workforce innovation

Workforce development has historically been associated with industrial change, iteratively as both a driver and consequence of industry innovation. It is in this regard that a concerted effort could be made to reach across institutional boundaries to allow coalitions of universities as well as other actors to develop collaboratively based synergies centered on the role of new applications of knowledge (Eyster et al. 2013). These collaborations also offer enhanced opportunity for social knowledge distribution via virtual learning communities, as well as facilitating the integration of regional proximate, and online virtual communities. Workforce development can be defined as the delivery of an educational experience, such as professional education, that leads to graduates capable of commanding higher value in the labor marketplace. Conventional wisdom suggests that traditional faculty, representing a key constituency of the university, have not seen the development of work specific skills as a central mission. Demand for "real-world, applied skills" has been viewed as a threat to the construct of the traditional university.

Employers use degrees as a low-cost sorting mechanism in an increasingly crowded and complex global marketplace, underscoring inherent workplace value in the specific knowledge, skills, abilities, and dispositions gained through the process of higher education. The wage gap itself between a university graduate and a worker with only a high school diploma has increased over the same time period from 40 percent in 1980, to 74 percent in 2010, with the expectation that by 2025 this gap will further widen to 96 percent (Carnevale 2011). Employment data from the United States consistently shows college graduates unemployment rates at less than half that of their high-school diploma only peers (BLS 2013). This gap suggests that there is an unfilled opportunity in terms of workforce development, that is, the provision of training and educational experiences delivered in virtual, or blended virtual and in-person contexts.

This increasingly workforce, skill-focused orientation of universities, especially in the United States, is in part because of increased degree attainment internationally. OECD member countries from 1997 through 2012 have increased tertiary education attainment from 18 percent to 28 percent (OECD 2012). In other words, globally competitive pressures from the success of universities in workforce development, accelerated through globalization of labor, intensifies demand for workforce development.

Students and parents increasingly see the university in this workforce development role, perhaps in an effort to justify the time and monetary investment in higher education. A 2010 Gallup and Lumina Foundation for Education poll reports that 69 percent of adults "strongly agree/agree" with the statement "Having a college degree is essential for getting a good job in this country." On a more granular level, 86 percent of respondents list "to earn more money" or "to get a good job" as "the main reason why students get education beyond high school" (English 2011). Given global trends, this further supports the argument that institutions of higher education need to expand knowledge translations to individuals and regions that could economically benefit from expanded avenues to learning and skill development, in addition to tailoring learning options to the needs of different constituencies.

The formation of Western Governor's University (WGU) in the United States in 1997 and its recent evolution, is an example of the reconceptualization of higher education organization and function. WGU, based on an online, competency based approach, provides select workforce-oriented degrees under a model that is learner-paced, rather than a pace set by administrators and faculty. The model values prior learning (competency) to determine starting points in knowledge acquisition, and disaggregates the role of faculty into teams of instructional designers, mentors, and assessors. WGU, although designated as a university, does not perform traditional research and has limited fields and degree offerings. Despite this limitation, the institution is formally supported by nineteen state governors, with 38,000 students currently enrolled (WGU 2013).

WGU, and other such programs (e.g., Southern New Hampshire University, and Wisconsin's and Florida's adult degree completion programs) align with professional literature from organizations promoting "completion" primarily for purposes of workforce development, with equity often as an underlying ultimate motivation. These sources include: the Lumina Foundation for Education, the Bill & Melinda Gates Foundation, Complete College America, the Council on Adult and Experiential Learning, and the National Governor's Association, among others. The changing role of a university could be one where emphasis is placed on the following functions: assessor and certifier of knowledge, rather than creator and transmitter; facilitator of individualized learning and a pace of progression largely determined by the student; and, improvement in affordability and workforce relevancy of programs.

The confluence of advances in ICT and educational delivery platforms are not just bystanders in the changing workforce development role, but enablers as well. WGU, for example, is entirely online, regionally agnostic, and logistically possible because of advances in ICT. It represents a step on the path toward a larger movement typically referred to as competency-based or, outcomes-based education. Competency-based approaches to education have the potential for assuring the quality and extent of learning, shortening the time to degree/certificate completion, developing stackable credentials that ease student transitions between school and work, and reducing the overall cost of education for both career–technical and degree programs (Bergeron 2013).

Universities face a combination of challenges and opportunities: demand for more targeted skill sets from employers, students, and politicians; an ICT ecosystem that enables fulfillment of these demands; a policy and regulatory landscape growing more amendable to new approaches; and, growing competitive pressures from non-traditional entities. Discussions of the role of the university and workforce development seem to have relied on an overly simplified assumption that workforce development always equates to specific training and anything of utilitarian value in the job marketplace does not belong in the university. Despite other potential benefits to students and faculty, the employment of new models of learning, including competency-based education, even when not strongly aligned with workforce needs, may therefore be met with skepticism and suspicion.

Employer surveys signal increasing demand for skills that help produce "innovation in the workplace" and acknowledgment that roles today are more complex (Humphreys and Carnevale 2013); the rapid pace of economic change and unpredictability of needs calls for graduates that are adept at learning quickly and adaptable to new situations (DOL-BLS in Humphreys and Carnevale 2013); finally, employers also acknowledge the value of a balance of broad knowledge with specific skills (Humphreys and Carnevale 2013).

While specific skill based job training might provide short term benefits, it is unclear whether the individual and the public are better off with an education system that practices this separation and locks a subset of the population into a specific track. An alternative approach to workforce development focuses on continuous lifelong learning opportunities, as well as opportunities that can enhance and increase the competitiveness of regional economies and workforces.

Steps such as the Degree Qualifications Profile[2] in the US, and the Tuning Process[3] in Europe hint at ways to provide for a more connected student experience at different levels of higher education. The predominately post-baccalaureate user base of online educational learning could be viewed as a signal for unmet demand for lifelong learning opportunities. For the university of the twenty-first century hoping to remain relevant, a set of promising strategies emerges: a reinforcement of general education; embracing of the idea of continuous, lifelong learning, development of pathway partnerships to specific training institutions or employer developed certificates; disaggregation of roles allowing focus on learning and research; and adoption of tools for assessment and communication of valued skills and knowledge.

University innovation and community economic impact

In addition to the historic, inward facing role of student education, universities also operate with an outward facing role as drivers of innovation both physically, in their immediate locales as well as in terms of dissemination of knowledge. The historic university strengths of teaching and conduct of research, especially in some European countries, are reliant on state funding rather than on university–industry collaborations (Muscio et al. 2013), represent relatively untapped opportunities to collaborate with other actors across institutional boundaries. This is not a novel idea—universities have long existed as venues in which original ideas are developed, philosophical and ethical issues are debated, and creativity is rewarded (Breznitz and Feldman 2012).

A key avenue for the diffusion of innovation lies in the commercialization process. Universities' engagement in commercialization of research began in the nineteenth century, following the two world wars (Breznitz and Ram 2013). Universities' contribution to society during the wars had significant local economic impact. In particular, products and services were a result of university knowledge spillovers (Goldstein and Renault 2004; Lawton Smith and Bagchi-Sen 2011). Many believe that the economic impact of universities has a deeper root in the institutions' mission statements and the way they perceive themselves as part of their region (Feldman and Breznitz 2009; Franzoni and Lissoni 2009; Breznitz 2011) originally in a geographic, but increasingly, in a virtual sense as well.

As noted above, universities contribute to their region through the education and job training of students, as well as in training and professional development efforts. Building a strong workforce is an immense contribution by universities to society and local economic growth. In remote areas, where universities may be the only option for job training and retraining, this makes their contribution indispensable. However, training a qualified labor force is typically an expensive endeavor; it requires increasingly greater investment. As a rule no individual company can support such an investment, and therefore individual companies are not likely to make such an investment, especially if the output benefits other corporations (Kenney 1986). This condition helps support the rationale for university–industry partnerships, cross-industry partnership, and public–private partnerships, in addition to the traditional public sector, or NGO based efforts.

Modern industrial economic growth requires a highly trained workforce, something universities were in a position to provide (Scott 1977). The main source of university funding for applied research and the training of students has historically been governmental funding (Muscio et al. 2013). However, this reliance on public funding created a pressure on universities to make a return to society. As part of "paying back the community," universities make contributions through teaching, research and development (R&D), collaborations, and technology transfer to industry (Minshall et al. 2007).

Research universities can become engines of local economic growth, through innovative efforts toward higher education, as well as professional development and on-going fine-tuning of existing worker skills, in addition to the more traditional deployment and commercialization of their research output. The outcome of these efforts can be seen in an analysis of universities' ability to commercialize technology, a specific endpoint of the collaborative partnership between universities and industry. However, studies on universities' commercialization practices and output indicate that technology commercialization is not performed equally at all universities nor is it equally rewarding everywhere (Feldman and Desrochers 2003; Lawton Smith and Bagchi-Sen 2011).

Many university faculty believe that they should conduct research for the sake of research, and as such they shun commercialization, and focus on skill development and technical training, while others embrace the commercialization opportunity and the ability to collaborate with industry. Some universities are more geared toward research and others toward commercialization (Lawton Smith and Bagchi-Sen 2011; Breznitz and Ram 2013). It is important to note that society's expectations from universities are double edged: that universities will work on the most "disruptive" research and come out with the most revolutionary inventions, but at the same time they are expected to make direct economic contribution. These demands maybe found to be too much for universities to handle (Breznitz and Feldman 2012). It is the universities that successfully adapt to these changes that stand to survive as successful universities of the twenty-first century.

A major part of universities' involvement in innovation is through its relationships with industry. By viewing these relationships in the context of national and regional innovation systems and the triple-helix theories, the environment in which universities operate and the relationship between firms and institutions emerge as important factors in influencing their ability to innovate and bring products to market (Nelson 1993; Etzkowitz 1995). Many academics, government officials, and industry representatives believe that universities should be involved with industry, and that there should be a relevant flow of information and knowledge from universities to industry (Schimank 1988; Jaffe et al. 1993; Saxenian 1994).

University science parks, in which the university is placed in a physical location suited to collaborative activities, are another method of collaboration with regional impact. In many cases universities provide land or funding for the construction of this kind of facility where companies and universities have a direct and simple way to collaborate. University incubators, on the other hand, are spaces within or in close proximity to universities in which university related spinouts are host. The fact that the move from a university laboratory to become a commercial firm, located in close proximity to a university provides stability and options for university–industry collaborations and in many cases is the basis for a firm's success (Massey et al. 1992; Rothaermel and Thursby 2005).

University–industry collaborations take many forms, including ones that emphasize human capital. Companies recruit university students (through internships and co-op programs, for instance), and graduates of universities. By placing their graduates in companies, universities build social networks that allow for future hires and possible funding through research projects and licensing. In turn, industry needs access to universities to acquire the best research, as well as employees who are knowledgeable in new technologies (Feldman 1999). It is only recently that universities have begun to build on the tremendous unrealized value of these networks—a resource that could have tremendous development potential. Further, universities license their technology to firms, and spin out firms based on universities' research, and universities and industry collaborate on joint research projects. In some cases, universities have a particular project funded by a corporation and managed by academics at a university laboratory; in others, companies such Hitachi at the University of Cambridge, UK have established their own laboratories within a university department. In cases where these joint research projects result in a commercial invention, the university intellectual property (IP) policy will determine whether companies may have first right on inventions and a pipeline agreement (Hatakenaka 2002).

Partnerships, universities, and change

New partnerships and collaborations across systems, the cultivation of relationships with industry and non-traditional educational partners, and cross-disciplinary initiatives are critical to the sustainability of these new innovation based approaches to university functioning. The practicality of these collaborative efforts diverge globally due to a variety of cultural, social, and economic reasons, not all due to reluctance on the part of universities. A recent survey in Mexico, for instance, suggested that key reasons for lack of industry–university partnerships include lack of awareness of programs and opportunities, problems with matching students to opportunities and "lack of interest on the part of businesses" (University World News 2013).

We can expect that going forward, successful universities will be those that implement a diversified portfolio of functions and objectivities. Most fundamentally, it is a willingness to recognize and meet the changing needs and characteristics of learners in a globally connected context. This can be accomplished by awareness of the new markets and options for learners both inside and outside of the university, as well as by taking advantage of new forms of technology driven assessment and instructional approaches. A second key is to embrace the idea that learning needs to be lifelong and continuous. Skills and knowledge rapidly decay at the rates of global change; universities are well poised to take the lead in developing the idea of lifelong learning and the need to retune and retrain the workforce. Underscoring all this is the role of the university in developing knowledge, deploying applied approaches to the knowledge and as a node of innovation; critical to community and regional economic impact. Active outreach to industry will also serve both sectors well.

In consideration of the above, a variety of policy related questions are fertile ground for researchers working on the boundaries of politics, innovation, and economic development, given unpredictable levels of state (i.e., public sector) support, and the consequential appeal of alternative private–public and industry funding. What potential impact will these factors have on the independence of universities? What ICT based tools and practices will facilitate virtual research and development collaborations? What are the policy impacts of the changing higher education sector, not only on universities, but more broadly on industry innovation and workforce development? How much of the variation seen in the higher educational systems is a function of size and geography of the nations they are embedded in, and what does this say for innovative practices? How will the changing approaches to learning and the dissemination of knowledge impact developing countries, both positively and negatively?

Changes in technology, an emerging view of the university as providing lifelong, continuous learning, as well as professional development, and the opportunities offered by competing channels for information flow have converged to challenge the roles and function of the traditional university. In order to survive in this competitive global marketplace, traditional institutions of higher education must proactively explore innovative and effective approaches not just to facilitate learning, but to be seen as a node for collaborative innovation and regional diffusion of knowledge. Conversely, the historic ambivalence of industry and government sectors to network with universities can result in missed opportunities to draw on the pure and applied research expertise of university researchers, and thus potentially be a barrier to enterprise innovation.

Notes

1 See, for instance a series of papers commissioned on the redesign of accreditation, www.wascsenior.org/redesign/conceptpapers.

2 http://degreeprofile.org/.

3 www.unideusto.org/tuningeu/.

References

Ananiadou, K. and Claro, M., 2009: 21st Century Skills and Competences for New Millennium Learners in OECD Countries. OECD Education Working Papers, No. 41, OECD Publishing. Available online at: http://dx.doi.org/10.1787/218525261154 (accessed June 11, 2013).

Audretsch, D., Lehmann, E. and Warning, S., 2005: University spillovers and new firm location. *Research Policy* 34(7), pp. 1113–1122.

Baker, P.M.A. and Ward, A.C., 2002: Bridging temporal and spatial "gaps": the role of information and communication technologies in defining communities. *Information Communication and Society* 5(2), pp. 207–224.

Baker, P.M.A., Bujak, K.R. and DeMillo, R., 2012: The evolving university: disruptive change and institutional innovation. *Procedia Computer Science* 14, pp. 330–335.

Bergeron, D., 2013: Applying for Title IV Eligibility for Direct Assessment (Competency-Based) Programs. United States Department of Education, Dear Colleague Letter GEN-13-10. March 19. Available online at: http://ifap.ed.gov/dpcletters/GEN1310.html (accessed June 11, 2013).

BLS, 2013: Economic News Release: Table 4-a Employment status of the civilian population 25 years and over by educational attainment. United States Bureau of Labor Statistics. Available online at: www.bls.gov/news.release/empsit.t04.htm (accessed June 11, 2013).

Bogue, G. and Hall, K., 2012: Business, political & academic perspectives on higher education accountability policy. *College and University* 87(3), pp. 14–23.

Breznitz, S.M., 2011: Improving or impairing? Following technology transfer changes at the University of Cambridge. *Regional Studies* 45, pp. 463–478.

Breznitz, S.M. and Feldman, M.P., 2012: The engaged university. *Journal Of Technology Transfer* 37, pp. 139–157.

Breznitz, S.M. and Ram, N., 2013: Enhancing economic growth? University technology commercialization. In: Audretsch, D.B. and Walshok, M.L. (Eds.): *Creating Competitiveness*. Northampton, MA: Edward Elgar.

Carnevale, T., 2011: The Undereducated American. Georgetown Public Policy Institute Center on Education & the Workforce. Available online at: www9.georgetown.edu/grad/gppi/hpi/cew/pdfs/undereducatedamerican.pdf (accessed June 26, 2011).

Castells, M., 2010: *The Information Age: Economy, society and culture,* Volume 1: *The Rise of the Network Society*. 2nd ed. Oxford: Wiley Blackwell.

Chatham-Carpenter, A., 2010: Avoiding the pitfalls: current practices and recommendations for ePortfolios in higher education. *Journal of Educational Technology Systems* 38(4), pp. 437–456.

Cheng, G. and Chau, J., 2013: Exploring the relationship between students' self-regulated learning ability and their ePortfolio achievement. *Internet & Higher Education* 17, pp. 9–15.

Chesters, J. and Watson, L., 2013: Understanding the persistence of inequality in higher education: evidence from Australia. *Journal of Education Policy* 28(2), pp. 198–215.

Cross, S., 2013: A leadership model for the research university. In: *Proceedings of the 3rd International Conference on Leadership, Technology and Innovation Management*, pp. xix–xxvii. Istanbul, Turkey.

DeMillo, R., 2011: *Abelard to Apple: The Fate of American Colleges and Universities*. Cambridge, MA: MIT Press.

Department of Education (DOE), 2013: DCL ID: GEN-13–10 Applying for Title IV eligibility for direct assessment (competency-based) programs, March 19, 2013. Washington DC: United States Department of Education.

English, C., 2011: "Most Americans See College as Essential to Getting a Good Job." Gallup with the Lumina Foundation. Available online at: www.gallup.com/poll/149045/americans-college-essential-getting-good-job.aspx (accessed June 11, 2013).

Etzkowitz, H., 1995: The Triple Helix—university–industry–government relations: a laboratory for knowledge based economic development. *EASST Review* 14, pp. 9–14.

Eyster, L., Anderson, T. and Durham, C., 2013: Innovations and future directions for workforce development in the post-recession era. Urban Institute working paper no. 7, Washington D.C.: the Urban Institute. Available online at: www.urban.org/publications/412884.html (accessed June 11, 2013).

Feldman, M.P., 1999: *The New Economics of Innovation, Spillovers and Agglomeration: A review of empirical studies*. London: Routledge.

Feldman, M.P. and Breznitz, S.M., 2009: The American experience in university technology transfer. In: Mckelvey, M. and Holmén, M. (Eds.): *European Universities Learning to Compete: From social institutions to knowledge business*. Cheltenham: Edward Elgar, pp. 161–186.

Feldman, M.P. and Desrochers, P., 2003: Research universities and local economic development: lessons from the history of Johns Hopkins University. *Industry and Innovation* 10, pp. 5–24.

Ferguson, R., 2012: Learning analytics: drivers, developments and challenges. *International Journal of Technology Enhanced Learning* 4(5/6), 304–317.

Franzoni, C. and Lissoni, F., 2009: Academic entrepreneurs: critical issues and lessons for Europe. In: Varga, A. (Ed.): *Universities, Knowledge Transfer and Regional Development: Geography, entrepreneurship and policy*. Cheltenham: Edward Elgar Publishing, pp. 163–190.

Goldstein, H.A. and Renault, C.S., 2004: Contributions of universities to regional economic development: a quasi-experimental approach. *Regional Studies* 38, pp. 733–746.

Hanna, D.E., 1998: Higher education in an era of digital competition: emerging organizational models. *Journal of Asynchronous Learning Networks* 2(1), 66–95.

Hatakenaka, S., 2002: Flux and flexibility: A comparative institutional analysis of evolving university–industry relationships in MIT, Cambridge and Tokyo. Ph.D. Dissertation, Massachusetts Institute of Technology Sloan School of Management.

Hodges, D., 2011: The assessment of student learning in cooperative and work integrated learning education. In Coll, R.K. and Zegwaard, K.E. (Eds.): *International Handbook for Cooperative and Work-Integrated Education: International perspectives of theory, research and practice*. 2nd ed. Lowell, MA: World Association for Cooperative Education, pp. 53–62.

Humphreys, D. and Carnevale, A., 2013: The Economic Value of Liberal Education. Association of American Colleges & Universities. 2013 edition. Available online at: www.aacu.org/leap/presidentstrust/documents/EconomicCaseUpdated2013.ppt (accessed June 11, 2013).

Jaffe, A.B., Trajtenberg, M. and Henderson, R., 1993: Geographic localization of knowledge spillovers as evidenced by patent citations. *The Quarterly Journal of Economics* 108, pp. 577–598.

Johnson, J.A., 2013: *Ethics of Data Mining and Predictive Analytics in Higher Education* (SSRN Scholarly Paper No. ID 2156058). Rochester, NY: Social Science Research Network. Available online at: http://papers.ssrn.com/abstract=2156058 (accessed June 2013).

Kenney, M., 1986: *Biotechnology: The university–industrial complex*. New Haven, CT: Yale University Press.

Koenig J.A., 2011: *Assessing 21st Century Skills: Summary of a workshop*. Washington, DC: The National Academies Press.

Laitinen, A., 2012: *Cracking the credit hour*. Washington, DC: New America Foundation. Available online at: http://newamerica.net/publications/policy/cracking_the_credit_hour (accessed June 11, 2013).

Lawton Smith, H. and Bagchi-Sen, S., 2012: The Research University, entrepreneurship and regional development: research propositions and current evidence. *Entrepreneurship and Regional Development* 24, pp. 383–404.

Leach, L., 2013: Participation and equity in higher education: are we going back to the future? *Oxford Review of Education* 39(2), pp. 267–286.

Liu, X., Magjuka, R., Bonk, C. and Lee, S., 2007: Does sense of community matter? An examination of participants' perceptions on building learning communities in online courses. *The Quarterly Review of Distance Education* 8(1), 9–24.

Massey, D., Quintas, P. and Wield, D., 1992: *High-Tech Fantasies: Science parks in society, science and space*. London: Routledge.

Means, B., Toyama, Y., Murphy, R.F. and Baki, M., 2013: The effectiveness of online and blended learning: a meta-analysis of the empirical literature. *Teachers College Record* 115(3), pp. 1–47.

Moore, B., 2005: Web-based education in the human services: models, methods, and best practices. *Journal of Technology in Human Services* 23(1), 2.

Morgan, T. and Carey, S., 2009: From open content to open course models: increasing access and enabling global participation in higher education. *The International Review of Research in Open and Distance Learning* 10(5). Available online at: www.irrodl.org/index.php/irrodl/article/view/632 (accessed June 11, 2013).

Mueller, P., 2006: Exploring the knowledge filter: how entrepreneurship and university–industry relationships drive economic growth. *Research Policy* 35(10), pp. 1499–1508.

Muscio, A., Quaglione, D. and Vallanti, G., 2013: Does government funding complement or substitute private research funding to universities? *Research Policy* 42(1), pp. 63–75.

Nelson, R.R., 1993: *National Innovation Systems: A comparative analysis*. New York: Oxford University Press.

OECD, 2012: Education at a Glance. Available online at: www.uis.unesco.org/Education/Documents/oecd-eag-2012-en.pdf (accessed June 11, 2013).

Rhoads, R.A., Berdan J. and Toven-Lindsey, B., 2013: The open courseware movement in higher education: unmasking power and raising questions about the movement's democratic potential. *Educational Theory* 63(1), pp. 87–109.

Rothaermel, F.T. and Thursby, M., 2005: University–incubator firm knowledge flows: assessing their impact on incubator firm performance. *Research Policy* 34, pp. 305–320.

Rotherham, A.J. and Willingham, D., 2010: 21st century skills: the challenges ahead. *Educational Leadership* 67(1), 16–21.

Saxenian, A., 1994: *Regional Advantage: Culture and competition in Silicon Valley and Route 128*. Cambridge, MA: Harvard University Press.

Schimank, U., 1988: The contribution of university research to the technological innovation of the German economy: societal auto-dynamic and political guidance. *Research Policy* 17, pp. 329–340.

Scott, P., 1977: *What Future for Higher Education*. London: Fabian Tracts.

Siemens, G. and Long, P., 2011: Penetrating the fog: analytics in learning and education. *EDUCAUSE Review* 46(5), pp. 30–32.

Sirius, R., 2013: Information wants to be free, but the world isn't ready. *The Verge*. Available online at: www.theverge.com/2013/1/23/3899518/information-wants-to-be-free-world-world-isnt-ready (accessed January 23, 2013).

Strader, R. and Thille, C., 2012: The open learning initiative: enacting instruction online. In: Oblinger, D.G. (Ed.): *Game Changers: Education and information technologies*. Washington, DC: EDUCAUSE, pp. 201–213.

University World News, 2013: Missed opportunities for university–business partnerships. Available online at: www.universityworldnews.com/article.php?story=20130110110144741 (accessed May 27, 2013).

WGU, 2013: The WGU Story. Western Governor's University. Available online at: www.wgu.edu/about_WGU/WGU_story (accessed June 11, 2013).

17

REGIONAL INNOVATION POLICY AND PUBLIC–PRIVATE PARTNERSHIPS

Iryna Kristensen,[1] *Ronald W. McQuaid and Walter Scherrer*

Introduction

For innovation policies to become effective, smoothly functioning interfaces between innovation agents, assembling resources from diverse sectors of the economy, and sound strategy development and policy implementation are all required. Connecting independent innovation agents is a core feature of several theories of innovation, for example: systemic approaches to innovation (Freeman 1988; Lundvall 1992; Nelson 1993; Cooke 2002; Asheim et al. 2011); the triple-helix approach (Etzkowitz and Leydesdorff 1997); the learning region approach (Florida 1995, 2002; Morgan 1997), and the smart specialization approach (Foray et al. 2009). Further, innovation is usually characterized by increasing returns to knowledge implementation and diffusion, which typically takes on both public and private goods attributes. Forming partnerships for innovation and balancing public and private interests can play a significant part in combining innovation-relevant resources such as technical expertise, production capacities, regulatory power, user requirements, and finance which are spread out among multiple agents. An instrument for connecting agents in innovation policy is public–private partnerships (PPP), which are—loosely defined—a cooperative institutional arrangement between public and private sector agents (Hodge and Greve 2007).

PPPs have been used by government in the field of innovation policy for a variety of purposes from providing the organizational frame for 'producing' innovations: developing a new product, a new process, a new form of economic organization etc. and bringing it to the market. However, as discussed below, there are variations in PPPs along divergent institutional, political, historical, and cultural settings as well as along differing strategic objects of the PPPs. The rest of the chapter presents an overview of PPPs, before considering PPPs specifically in relation to innovation policy and then concluding.

PPP: a general overview of the concept

Definitions and types of PPP

History provides many examples of public and private sector cooperation that may even date back to the biblical era.[2] Despite the extensive literature that has developed since the second half of the 1990s (e.g. Montanheiro et al. 1995; Osborne 2000; Rosenau 2000; Akintoye et al. 2003; Grimsey and Lewis 2005), a universally accepted definition of public–private partnership does not yet exist[3] as the term covers a variety of conceptually distinct forms of relationship. The OECD defines a PPP largely in terms of a contractual relationship as:

> an agreement between the government and one or more private partners (which may include the operators and the financers) according to which the private partners deliver the service in such a manner that the service delivery objectives of the government are aligned with the profit objectives of the private partners and where the effectiveness of the alignment depends on a sufficient transfer of risk to the private partners.
>
> *(OECD 2008: 17)*

In a broader sense PPPs cover all kinds of arrangements that work within the framework of cooperation and involvement of partners in order to map out a strategy and a framework for accomplishing a common goal defined by public and private agents (Kolzow 1994; Grimsey and Lewis 2004: 6). Therefore the concept of PPP—on which this paper is based—also includes joint organizations of public and private partners.

Innovation policy relies on the assumption that stakeholders cooperate to fortify regional or national competitiveness and places a strong emphasis on 'bargained cooperation' and 'political exchange' (Marshall 1996; Fogelberg and Thorpenberg 2012). However, private participation is often opposed by governments' fear of losing regulatory control, which results in 'multiple grammars' to the meaning of PPP across countries (Linder 1999). For instance in Victoria, Australia, PPPs are argued to have nothing to do with privatization, while in the market-liberal political environment in the UK the Treasury sometimes speaks of PPPs as directly equivalent to privatization (Hodge and Greve 2007). In Sweden's corporatist organization of society the term 'partnership' is sometimes deliberately avoided and the more moderate connotation of 'association' or 'cooperation' is preferred, motivated by the fact that the term partnership is imported from the EU. At the same time, however, public–private partnerships are considered 'merely a new formulation of a longer tradition and working mode of the Swedish welfare model' where the responsibility for economic development is usually shared between public and private sectors (Fogelberg and Thorpenberg 2012: 348).[4]

According to their organizational structure, PPPs can be categorized into two types: contractual and organizational PPP. In a '*contractual*' PPP a partnership is solely based on contractual links between public and private agents and is regulated by administrative contract(s). Contractual PPPs were significantly used first in Anglo-Saxon countries. Britain's Public Finance Initiative (PFI) projects have been prototypical in which the state claimed to retain control over the activity through complex contracts while operational tasks have been delegated to the private sector. Such PFI projects were frequently used for providing infrastructure in a rather broad sense including transport, waste water disposal, schools, hospitals, and jails. In innovation policy contractual PPPs have been used particularly for the provision and/or operation of infrastructures and services that are important for the general business environment, and thus also for innovation. This is confirmed by the survey of Swedish municipalities' innovation policy (see below). An '*organizational*' PPP is manifested in the establishment of an entity jointly owned by the public and private parties and is regulated by the shareholder agreements. This type of PPPs is characterized by a potentially more direct government influence in the PPP and is used in regional innovation policies especially for the establishment and operation of enabling organizations that provide common ground between the public, private, and third sectors to promote economic and social development policies. Our empirical results for Swedish municipalities' innovation policies support this assumption. Beyond these more supply-side-focused tasks, both contractual and organizational PPPs can also focus on stimulating demand in order to promote regional innovation activity. Hence PPPs are seen as one of a number of options to assist national and regional innovation in different circumstances.

The economic rationale for and major lines of critique of PPPs

PPPs comprise a broad range of institutional arrangements that emphasize different general characteristics or mechanisms and reflect a variety of economic, social, and political reasons and motives for their growth (McQuaid and Scherrer 2010). We distinguish three groups of explanations based on: first, micro-economic arguments concerning the efficiency and effectiveness of public spending; second, budget or macro-economic factors focusing on the availability of public resources; and third, arguments concerning the coordination of public and private agents.

Microeconomic motivations postulate that PPPs make it possible—as the UK Treasury (2000) formulates—to tap into the disciplines, incentives, skills, and expertise that private sector firms have developed in the course of their normal everyday business, while releasing the full potential of the people, knowledge, and assets in the public sector. The private sector involvement should result in greater commercial incentives for delivering efficient and effective services, a greater focus on customer requirements, and innovative approaches to providing services or infrastructure. Government retains the basic responsibility and democratic accountability for deciding and defining objectives, delivery standards required, and safeguarding wider public interests (McQuaid and Scherrer 2010: 29). Thus PPP fits well into the 'enabling view' of government, and microeconomic drivers of PPPs have been an instrument for spreading New Public Management concepts in the public sector (McQuaid 2010).

However, the long-term character of PPPs and complex financial structures, entailing risk- and cost-sharing among the partners, results in high transaction costs that may exceed the potential advantages compared to other forms of public service delivery. Transaction costs are largely fixed cost and raise the efficient minimum size of a PPP, thus giving rise to organizational economies of scale (e.g. the organization having breadth and depth of experience) or economies of scale related to the physical project (e.g. it may be technically more efficient to construct and/or maintain a series of buildings rather than doing one), or to economies of scope (as a PPP may involve a range of activities including, for instance, construction and operation). The occurrence of economies of scale and/or scope may lead to governments favoring larger firms that have acquired specialized PPP-specific knowledge whereas learning effects will mostly occur in large government units due to repeated implementation of PPPs. This results in asymmetries in information about and experience with PPPs between the public partners (particularly if small authorities are involved) and the private sector (particularly if large experienced private firms are involved) that can be exploited by the private partners. The complexity of projects over their life cycles may also lead to poor protection for public interests (Da Cruz and Marques 2012). Establishing dedicated PPP units in government (OECD 2010b) and the standardization of PPP contracts (van den Hurk and Verhoest 2012) can help alleviate these problems.

Risk sharing between the public and the private sectors is a fundamental micro-economic constituent of PPPs. Compared to other ventures an extra element of risk—technical risk—appears in projects that either develop or are based on or implement a new technology. Therefore the private sector's desire to share risks with (public) partners is particularly strong when projects that involve new technologies are concerned. If such projects are considered politically or economically 'important' governments have an incentive to save them from failing; huge infrastructures (e.g. infrastructures in the fields of energy, transport or communication technologies) and networking organizations (e.g. cluster organizations) are potential candidates. Therefore, in technologically risky PPPs (but also in other PPPs) the taxpayer tends to be the ultimate risk-taker. From a technology perspective it is important to note that long-term contracts restrict changes in the future because an organization is tied into a specific type of technology thus reducing flexibility and making the introduction of newer technologies in the future depend on costly re-negotiations (McQuaid and Scherrer 2010: 32).

Major *macroeconomic explanations* of the use of PPP are its attractiveness for government because it is a way of off balance sheet funding that does not appear as capital expenditure in the year in which it occurs, but rather as a series of smaller annual 'revenue' expenditures over the project's life. This is particularly attractive in times when new technologies emerge and demand for related infrastructure raises investment requirement of the public sector. Official public debt can be kept low which might improve the government's standing in the international financial markets and will facilitate meeting formal fiscal requirements such as the deficit and debt limits of the European Monetary Union rules on Member States.[5] Further, the overall tax burden could be reduced in the medium term if PPP turns out to be a more cost-effective mode of providing public services compared to traditional public procurement. Finally, deregulation and economic structural change has made previously sheltered sectors—which usually undergo major technological innovations through this phase—attractive for PPPs (McQuaid and Scherrer 2010: 30). Anglo-Saxon countries (e.g. United Kingdom, Australia, New Zealand) have long-time experience with PPPs because they privatized and liberalized utilities sectors relatively early and used PPP as an instrument of infrastructure delivery, which contrasts with other countries that mainstreamed PPPs later and in divergent ways.

Empirical evidence on whether PPPs alleviate public finances is mixed.[6] Efficiency gains of PPPs from non-finance-related activities would at least have to compensate for the cost disadvantage that PPP-financing has compared to traditional government finance (e.g. the interest to be paid usually is higher for private than for public debtors) in order to break even with other forms of providing public infrastructure. Further, off-budget financing gives way to a kind of 'fiscal illusion' as the financial burden related to PPPs does not show immediately in public budgets but is indiscernibly dispersed over a long period into the future (McQuaid and Scherrer 2010).

A third explanation of the wide use of PPP emphasizes their *coordination function* between public and private agents and is particularly relevant for regional innovation policies. PPPs act as vehicles to promote a policy that is mostly based on a more bottom-up orientated approach, taking into account the different interests of the parties involved in innovation. The coordination function explanation of PPP distinguishes itself from pure microeconomic theorizing as it reflects 'a willingness to share some forms of public authority with citizens and communities' (Considine 2005: 90). In innovation-related PPPs, the public partners' benefits are derived primarily through the improvement of innovative capacity for regional competitiveness and growth and exploitation of skills and knowledge of the private partners. On the side of the private stakeholders, apart from risk- and cost-sharing advantages in developing new technologies, products, and services, commercial profits are gained by the utilization of new market opportunities and the expansion of the regional market.

The alignment of interests between partners reflects also the *political nature of PPP formation* as different interests are involved. The alignment of interests ought to be achieved by creating and fostering partnerships and networks, involving public and private agents in goal and strategy definition, project development and selection, and project or policy implementation. This means more than merely restructuring and economizing the contracting relations between government and private suppliers but aims at establishing and fostering regional networks, forming social capital, and facilitating cross-sectoral local and regional governance. European Union policies that seek to establish such public–private networks at the local, national and European Union levels to promote their goals particularly in the areas of regional innovation policy and research and development are a good example of fostering this type of PPP.

Yet, despite the widespread use of PPPs, there is still much debate on their connotation and applicability in different contexts. In Anglo-Saxon market-oriented societies, for instance, PPP is usually commenced through competitive selection of private stakeholders and is characterized 'by very detailed contracts and . . . monitoring institutions' founded with the purpose to 'supervise' this cooperation; whereas continental forms are more flexible and often initiated by the government who acts as regulator and provider of legislation, at the same time enabling private participation in joint execution of operational functions (Beliczay and Pál 2006). The decline of corporatist governance alters the relationship between various organizations and public authorities making them 'less formal' and more competitive 'for attention from politicians' (Hodge and Greve 2007: 446). If there is a matching interest between public and private entities then PPP reflects that match.[7] Private sector lobbying becomes more important in influencing the political decision-making process; what projects eventually materialize is a highly political issue. 'In some cases governments will not choose the most able firms that would have been selected through the market process but will select those actors that are most influential in lobbying' (Hospers et al. 2008: 443).

PPP in innovation policy

Types of PPP in innovation policy

PPPs are widespread in the field of research and development policy (which may differ from innovation policy) where the cooperation between public and private sectors has a long history (see e.g. Stiglitz and Wallstein 1999; Hagedoorn et al. 2000). PPPs are also a key ingredient of (regional) innovation policy: technology-based economic development policies have traditionally been implemented in the United States as PPP (Briem and Singh 2016), regional innovation systems 'should be based on PPP' (Landabaso et al. 1999), and there exist 'cases of regions' where 'close public–private partnership and policy networking operate' (Cooke 2004: 512). PPPs are 'an essential instrument for fostering innovation in OECD countries' (OECD 2004), they are relevant at both the national and regional levels, and 'have become increasingly popular in R&D and innovation' (OECD 2010a: 104). Surprisingly, in the register of a recent *Handbook of Research on Innovation and Clusters* (Karlsson 2008), the only entry for 'Public–Private Partnership' refers to the role of PPP in place marketing. Surprisingly, too, PPP was considered an 'emerging instrument' in regional innovation policy recently, arguing that technology centers have been created that do not focus exclusively on new technology development but also on 'exploitation in the business sector, emphasizing the co-creation of new knowledge between public and private actors' (OECD 2011: 94). This section sets out some conceptual issues concerning PPPs and how these relate to our empirical results in the Swedish survey.

In order to achieve a general overview of the use of PPPs in innovation policy at the regional level within a whole nation, all 290 Swedish municipalities were surveyed. Sweden is characterized by a long history of corporatist governance and innovation policy, by a high degree of autonomy of players in the innovation system, by considerable regional diversity in terms of innovation activity, and by a favorable overall innovation performance in international comparison (EU 2012a). This suggests that a broad variety of PPP uses for innovation policy purposes exist in Sweden and therefore this country provides a good example for such an investigation. In total, 63 municipalities or 21.7 per cent responded, 21 (one third) municipalities reporting to have no PPPs in innovation policy. The remaining 42 municipalities reported 68 cases of public–private cooperation of which 50 cases meet the requirements of our understanding of PPP.

PPPs are used for a variety of purposes in the field of innovation policy. First, PPP is a mode of *fostering the generation and exploitation of innovation activities* by providing the organizational frame for 'producing' innovations: developing a new product, a new process, a new form of economic organization etc. and bringing it to the market. Research partnerships between private firms and private research institutes on the one hand and the public sector (particularly universities and other public research bodies) on the other hand are—if the venture is not confined to basic research but is market oriented—a good example for a traditional form of an innovation-producing PPP. Like other innovation policy instruments PPPs could reduce variety by selecting specific industries and technologies as targets of direct policy intervention, but establishing cooperation between agents from different sectors induces variety (which is a prerequisite for innovation). Government takes a particularly active role in technology and innovation policy in this context: The economic rationale for PPP here is based on market failure that entails a large gap between private and social returns of R&D. If properly implemented (particularly with regard to risk allocation), government-industry R&D programs could potentially yield enormous benefits (Stiglitz and Wallsten 1999: 70). Of innovation-related PPPs in Swedish municipalities 44 per cent focus on generation and 20 per cent on exploitation of innovation activities; 36 per cent of innovation-related PPPs of Swedish municipalities carry out joint generation/exploitation of innovation.

Generating and exploiting innovation activities might also necessitate the use of different organizational structures of PPP as well as different roles being assigned to the partners involved. Swedish municipalities' PPPs that aim at generating innovation are carried out under both contractual and organizational forms of PPP with a slight difference in responsibility structures. In organizational PPPs tasks assigned to the private sector are widely scattered across a range of categories varying from operative tasks to R&D and commercialization, whereas in contractual PPPs there is a clear-cut line of responsibilities between the partners with the public sector actively engaged in the early stages of cooperation (e.g. creation of conditions for innovation output and R&D) and the private sector assuming the risk for further development of the innovation outcome. Swedish municipalities' PPPs aiming at exploiting innovation, by contrast, seem to require closer ties between partners that go beyond merely contractual relationships (such as joint equity) and that might facilitate the appropriation of economic benefits by the partners involved. Consequently, organizational PPPs are in the vast majority of exploitation cases preferred over contractual ones. They are characterized by joint execution of operational functions (e.g. management, production planning etc.) and testing and networking, occasionally solely assigned to the private sector. PPPs with 'mixed' modes of innovation (i.e. where generation and exploitation of innovation are combined), are predominantly of organizational form, too, where both partners jointly execute operational tasks. In contractual PPPs the research and development task is performed jointly while operational and design tasks are primarily carried out by the private sector.

Second, PPP is used in the field of innovation policy as a *mode of providing innovation-related, mostly physical infrastructure*. This function has a long tradition, particularly in the build-up of infrastructure for the diffusion of key technologies that were the drivers of 'long waves' in economic development (e.g. railway networks, telecommunication; see Scherrer 2016) and that have been accomplished through close cooperation between the public and private sectors. Twenty per cent of innovation-related PPPs of Swedish municipalities focus on providing innovation-related infrastructure; empirical results indicate that structural properties of a PPP usually govern the scope and remit of public–private arrangements in providing and operating innovation-related infrastructure. For example, in organizational PPPs, R&D and project design are primarily carried out by public sector agents whereas the transmission of tacit knowledge by means of joint activities (e.g. workshops) is assigned to the private sector. In contractual PPPs, operational responsibilities are often jointly executed by both sectors; additionally, the private sector is also in charge of designing the infrastructure for the public sector (occasionally building and operating it as well). Cooperative research and marketing of innovation is not a major objective for this form of public–private cooperation.

Finally, PPP is a *mode of policy delivery* in the field of innovation—often with a focus on technology transfer—comprising innovation strategy development, and program and project implementation. Innovation support programs, such as those typical of the European Union that aim at enhancing R&D and regional innovation, are conducive to the establishment of PPPs because they usually require forming networks in which both private and public partners are to be integrated. Therefore, the policy delivery-type of PPPs' primary objectives of innovation advancement and fostering regional competitiveness are best managed in the proximal context of interaction between the public and private agents. Eighty per cent of innovation-related PPPs of Swedish municipalities focus on policy delivery aspects. Strategy development and program delivery that aim at strengthening regional competitiveness and improving innovative capacity are only carried out under organizational PPPs. Operational tasks usually are jointly executed by public and private partners, the responsibilities of the private sector are widely scattered across various functions, indicating that every launch of a new program activity requires specific functions performed by the private partner, for example, R&D, marketing, or commercialization of the innovation outcome. PPPs in innovation project implementation are strongly commercially oriented with research tasks falling mainly under the competence of the public sector partner(s) and commercial application of research results is the private partners' task. The majority of PPPs in project implementation are contractual, which can be explained by their degree of specificity and efficiency. Project implementation requires the achievement of a single, clearly defined goal through execution of inter-reliant activities; therefore, the contractual links between partners enable appropriate resource planning and management control over the entire process of project implementation (Wysocki 2009).

Spatial aspects of innovation and PPP

Spatial aspects of innovation have become major issues in innovation theory, particularly since the discussion on the national innovation systems approach emerged in the 1990s (Hassink and Ibert 2009). This approach claims that national patterns of production specialization are not caused by differences in factor proportions (as standard neoclassical theory would assume) but by differences in the knowledge bases across nations (Lundvall 1998). A major family of approaches emergent from the literature on national innovation systems, which is particularly relevant for the discussion of the role of PPPs as an instrument of innovation policy, has its focus on innovation at the sub-national level. This focus is reflected in approaches of economic geography and regional economics such as 'Industrial Districts,' 'Innovative Milieus,' 'Clusters,' 'Learning Regions,' 'Regional Innovation Systems' (Cooke 2002; Moulaert and Sekia 2003; Rutten and Boekema 2007), and 'Learning in space' (Hassink and Klaerding 2012).

The regional dimension has also become highly relevant in practical innovation policy at all levels of government: at the supra-national level within the EU programs on regional technology plans (RTP), regional innovation strategies (RIS), and regional innovation and technology transfer systems (RITTS), and at the level of national states in programs to support innovation in regions (Dohse 2007). PPPs have emerged as a preferred mode of innovation policy delivery, particularly in research and development policies and in cluster policies (OECD 2011). In addition to supply side measures, which are traditional in innovation policy, PPPs also include demand side policy elements as public procurement exerted by means of PPP can be targeted at stimulating technological innovation in the private sector (Edquist et al. 2000). PPP might serve as a policy vehicle both as contractual and organizational PPP and is likely to stimulate mutual exchange of knowledge between partners.

The use of PPP as an instrument of innovation policy and its concrete designs vary across regions and reflect different regional preferences, different regional structural characteristics, and differences in public entities' ability to incur debt. The major expression of regional preferences with reference to PPPs is that the use of partnerships—particularly those allowing participation in decision making by members of the civil society—is likely to increase the legitimacy of actions (McQuaid 2000). For each service, local and regional governments need to make pragmatic decisions based on their own circumstances within their constitutional boundaries. The principle of local self-government enables local and regional authorities to decide democratically the best means of delivering local public services, including decisions to use companies they own or control and contract based arrangements with private partners. Regional innovation policy in such circumstances means mostly moderating and stimulating processes and brokering ideas to set incentives for cooperation to the most important and competent agents in a region. A more decentralized approach to PPPs is expected to increase its focus and accountability and to involve agencies with a more narrow range of objectives (McQuaid 2000, 2010), to allow more targeted interventions (Silva and Rodriguez 2005), and to increase effectiveness and efficiency; accordingly, growth of PPPs should occur mainly at the local and regional levels (Carroll and Steane 2000). Concerning the importance of regional structural characteristics it was found that Swedish municipalities' PPPs in the field of innovation policy cover a broad spectrum of industries both in manufacturing and services reflecting the respective region's economic structure. Furthermore, smaller public entities such as municipalities might have an incentive to prefer PPPs over traditional public procurement because of limited access to credit and capital markets (McQuaid and Scherrer 2008).

An economic impact on innovation at the regional level arises also from PPPs that are initiated at the supranational level (e.g. the European Union's PPPs for advancing technology in the automotive, manufacturing and construction sectors; EU 2012b) or at the national level but that are implemented at the regional level (e.g. examples quoted in OECD 2011). Regional differences in implementation of central government-initiated innovation-related PPPs may be expected to occur both in centralist and federalist states. The impact of such programs differs across regions depending on a region's structural characteristics. As there emerge regional spillovers from decisions that are made outside of the region the choice of using PPP as a mode of delivery for public services therefore does not only reflect regional preferences.

Finally, PPPs have an impact on regional innovation because of the substantial fixed cost of negotiating contracts. Thus the efficient minimum size of provision is high, too, particularly so if the provision of large infrastructure and/or advanced technology is concerned. The regional economy might be negatively affected as small firms from the region tend to be crowded out by national or international contractors.

PPP—a systemic instrument of regional innovation policy

In an innovation environment that is characterized by a linear view of innovation, PPPs' primary role is to connect agents at similar stages of the innovation process (e.g. several research agents) or to connect agents in neighboring stages of the innovation process (e.g. basic research and applied research, government that is interested in a new technology and private partner(s) who deliver). PPP here is primarily a mode of 'producing' innovation. Further, within a linear model of innovation PPP can have a role in providing innovation related infrastructure, frequently used to foster innovation capacity for regional competitiveness and business growth.

After the rise of systemic approaches in innovation research the scope for PPP in innovation activity has widened. Innovation policy now focuses not only on individual organizations or on the relation between two organizations, but also on the system's level (Smits and Kuhlmann 2004: 11). Thus emphasis shifted from project and individual firm oriented support of innovation towards a more systemic understanding of the innovation process in the expectation that systemic instruments will improve the functioning of the entire (innovation) system (Wieczorek and Hekkert 2012: 74). For a PPP to unfold its systemic potential, proximity of agents is considered important because it is supportive of cooperation between innovation agents, such as universities, research institutions, innovating firms, and the public sector (Simmie 2005). Proximity facilitates the exchange of different forms of knowledge and expertise and the development of productive relationships; it is much more than merely a spatial or territorial concept. Boschma (2005) distinguishes five dimensions of proximity (cognitive, organizational, social, institutional, and geographical) and shows that agents should seek an optimum, rather than a maximum of proximity on each dimension.

Systemic instruments of innovation policy ought to accomplish five functions (Smits and Kuhlmann 2004: 11ff): First, managing interfaces between the agents involved in the innovation process; second, building and organizing (innovation) systems; third, providing a platform for learning and experimenting; fourth, providing an infrastructure for strategic intelligence; and finally, stimulating demand articulation, strategy and vision development. By their very nature alone, PPPs have the potential to fulfill at least two functions of a systemic instrument of innovation policy: the management of interfaces and the building and organizing of innovation systems. PPP is fundamentally about cooperation building among agents involved in the innovation process, and addressing the build-up and strengthening of relationships between the public and private sectors. The other three systemic functions can be addressed by using PPP as a mode of policy delivery, too, particularly those that are concerned with strategy development (PPP can be a mode of policy delivery most of all if a bottom-up approach is applied) and with the stimulation of demand for goods based on specific new technologies.

The survey among Swedish municipalities suggests that PPPs may in fact be considered systemic instruments of regional innovation policy:[8] Only one out of 50 cases of PPP is reported that does not fulfill any systemic function, while the other 49 PPPs perform at least one systemic function. On average a PPP in regional innovation policy fulfills approximately two (out of four) systemic functions, organizational PPPs slightly more than contractual type PPPs (2.29 vs. 1.95). Nearly 90 per cent of PPPs contribute to innovation system building and nearly 60 per cent to managing interfaces; 46 per cent of PPPs aim at developing strategic intelligence, demand articulation, strategy and vision development, and a quarter of all PPPs provide a platform for learning and experimenting. When the total amount of systemic functions performed by all PPPs is considered, approximately 40 per cent are related to innovation system building, 25 per cent to managing interfaces, another 25 per cent to strategic intelligence, demand articulation, strategy and vision development, and less than 10 per cent of systemic functions performed by PPPs are related to providing a platform for learning and development.

PPPs of Swedish municipalities aiming at *generating* innovation on average fulfill 2.45 systemic functions. This is well above the results for PPPs focusing on *exploiting* innovation (where the small number of cases makes the result less meaningful) and those combining generating and exploiting innovation. The different modes and intensities of private participation, as well as different degrees of uncertainty, which are inherent in every innovation process, imply differing properties of PPPs. All PPPs that focus on generation *and* exploitation of innovation fulfill a function in innovation system building reflecting the necessity to harmonize the interests and competencies of the agents who seek long-term economic relations that appear in the process of innovation generation on the one hand and cost advantages through exploitation of regional innovation potential on the other hand.

All forms of PPP in innovation policy concentrate on innovation system building, particularly so in innovation project implementation. PPPs used in *innovation program delivery* on average fulfill 2.53 out of four possible systemic functions which is far more than PPPs in innovation project implementation and, to a lesser extent, in innovation-related infrastructure do. PPPs in innovation programs are preferred when management of independent subsystems and facilitation of bargains between various stakeholders ought to be offered. Most PPPs in *innovation project implementation* are carried out as contract-type PPPs; they are usually commercially oriented with a relatively small number of stakeholders, and therefore only in a minority of cases managing interfaces is a systemic function to be performed within these projects. Platforms for learning and experimenting tend to be mostly created by organizational PPPs in innovation programs and projects.

Conclusions

Despite the increased use of different types of PPP in regional innovation policy, little scholarly attention has been devoted to the systemic characteristics of PPP in the innovation processes. In part this can be attributed to differences in definitions of PPP and the dissimilarity of application in innovation policy across countries and regions, and the balance of micro- and macro-economic and co-ordination motivations underlying them.

The systemic approach to innovation instigates complex interactions between the public and private actors as well as their external environments, thereby gradually advancing partnership schemes. PPPs can meet most requirements of a systemic instrument of innovation policy, and our empirical evidence indicates that nearly all cases of PPP in regional innovation policy involve at least two systemic functions. Organizational PPPs are more likely than contractual PPPs to exert systemic functions, especially managing interfaces and acting as a platform for learning and experimenting. Generators of innovation carry out more systemic functions on average than exploiters or joint generators and exploiters of innovation.

For a better understanding of the role of PPP in regional innovation policy further quantitative and qualitative research is needed. As current empirical research consists nearly exclusively of case studies, more quantitative research (covering more nations and larger samples of PPPs) would improve the generalizability of results. More detailed qualitative information should improve the understanding of internal power dynamics and changing dynamics of PPPs over time. Comparative analyses should identify the impact of macro-institutional influences (e.g. culture, socio-economic model, state structure, political system, macro-economic conditions, administrative history) and the impact of policies, regulation, and supporting institutions that are relevant for establishing PPPs in innovation policy.[9] From a policy perspective, a better understanding of whether PPPs can be realized in specific situations, and whether they can only be applied in certain situations and circumstances, is needed.

Notes

1 Support by the Humer Foundation is gratefully acknowledged.
2 Based on Wettenhall (2003), Hodge and Greve (2007: 545) mention:

> Mathew the private tax collector from the Bible; the private cleaning of public street lamps in 18th-century England; the private railways of the 19th century; or the fact that 82 per cent of the 197 vessels in Sir Francis Drake's fleet, which successfully conquered the Spanish Armada in 1588, were private contractors to the Admiralty

as early forms of cooperative partnerships and examples of innovation in organization structures.
3 For an overview of further definitions see OECD (2008: 15–17).
4 Accordingly, many left-wing municipalities in Sweden report strong involvement of the public sector in innovation-related PPPs going beyond financial aid, including also one or several other functions such as planning design, research, and development, but only rarely the commercialization of innovations, which is given to the private domain. In essence, PPP is then an improved method of service procurement by means of joint efforts between the public and private sectors which is more than just a new form of funding of public services. The role of the private sector is no longer to simply comply with the predefined set of criteria in service delivery but also to share responsibilities and risks in service operations and quality management and sometimes in the development of services.
5 Although this may be influenced by international financial reporting standards; see McQuaid and Scherrer (2010: 30–31).
6 For a survey of evaluations of contract-type PPPs see Hodge and Greve (2007).
7 This might also help explain why ex-post evaluations of PPPs based on information given by stakeholders usually indicate that PPP is superior to other forms of public procurement.
8 In this analysis, only four categories of systemic functions are used instead of five by Smits and Kuhlmann: the functions 'infrastructure provision for strategic intelligence' and 'demand articulation, strategy and vision development' are merged in his paper into one category 'Strategic Intelligence, Demand Articulation, Strategy and Vision Development.' The other functions—managing interfaces, innovation system building, and providing a platform for learning and experimenting—are as in Smits and Kuhlmann (2004).
9 See Verhoest et al. (2013) for PPPs in a non-innovation policy context.

References

Akintoye, A., Beck, M. and Hardcastle, C. (Eds.), 2003: *Public–Private Partnerships: Managing risks and opportunities*. Oxford: Blackwell.

Asheim, B., Coenen, L. and Vang, J., 2007: Face-to face, buzz, and knowledge bases: socio-spatial implications for learning, innovation, and innovation policy. *Environment and Planning C* 25, pp. 655–670.

Asheim, B., Lawton Smith, H. and Oughton, C., 2011: Regional innovation systems: theory, empirics and policy. *Regional Studies* 45(7), pp. 875–891.

Beliczay, E. and Pál, J., 2006: *Public–Private Partnership: Trick or opportunity?* Clean Air Action Group. Budapest, November 2006.

Boschma, R., 2005: Proximity and innovation: a critical assessment. *Regional Studies* 39(1), pp. 61–74.

Briem, C. and Singh, V.P., 2016: The role of universities in the evolution of technology based economic development policies in the United States. In: Hilpert, U. (Ed.): *Routledge Handbook of Politics and Technology*. London: Routledge, pp. 132–45

Carrol, P. and Steane, P., 2000: Public–private partnerships: sectoral perspectives. In: Osborne, S. (Ed.): *Public–Private Partnerships: Theory and practice in international perspective*. London: Routledge, pp. 36–56.
Considine, M., 2005: Partnerships, relationships and networks: understanding local collaboration strategies in different countries. In: OECD (Ed.): *Local Governance and the Drivers of Growth*. Paris: OECD, pp. 89–109.
Cooke, P., 2002: *Knowledge Economies: Clusters, learning and co-operative advantage*. London: Routledge.
Cooke, P., 2004: The role of research in regional innovation systems: new models meeting knowledge economy demands. *International Journal of Technology Management* 28(3/4/5/6), pp. 507–533.
Da Cruz, N.F. and Marques, R.C., 2012: Mixed companies and local governance: no man can serve two masters. *Public Administration* 90(3), pp. 737–758.
Dohse, D., 2007: Cluster-based technology policy: the German experience. *Industry and Innovation* 14: 69–94.
Edquist, C., Hommen, L. and Tsipouri, L. (Eds.), 2000: *Public Technology Procurement and Innovation*. Dordrecht: Kluwer Academic Publishers.
Etzkowitz, H. and Leydesdorff, L. (Eds.), 1997: *Universities in the Global Economy: A triple helix of university–industry–government relations*. London: Cassell Academic.
European Commission, 2012a: *Regional Innovation Scoreboard 2012*. Brussels: Directorate-General for Enterprise and Industry.
European Commission, 2012b: *New Public–Private Partnerships for Research in the Manufacturing, Construction and Automotive Sectors: European PPP research supports economic recovery*. Progress Report, Directorate-General for Research and Innovation, Unit G2 'New Forms of Production'. Luxembourg: Publication Office of the European Union, July.
Florida, R., 1995: Toward the learning region. *Futures* 27(5), pp. 527–536.
Florida, R., 2002: *The Rise of the Creative Class*. New York: Basic Books.
Fogelberg, H. and Thorpenberg, S., 2012: Regional innovation policy and public–private partnership: the case of Triple Helix Arenas in Western Sweden. *Science and Public Policy* 39, pp. 347–356.
Foray, D., David, P.A. and Hall, B., 2009: *Smart Specialization: The concept*. Knowledge Economists Policy Brief no. 9, June.
Freeman, C., 1988: Japan: A new national innovation system? In: Dosi, G., Freeman, C., Nelson, R.R., Silverberg, G. and Soete, L. (Eds.): *Technology and economy theory*. London: Pinter, pp. 330–344.
Grimsey, D. and Lewis, M. (Eds.), 2005: *The Economics of Public Private Partnerships, International Library of Critical Writings in Economics*, Volume 183. Northampton, MA: Edward Elgar.
Hagedoorn, J., Link, A.N. and Vonortas, N., 2000: Research partnerships, *Research Policy* 29, pp. 567–586.
Hassink, R. and Klaerding, C, 2012: The end of the learning region as we knew it: towards learning in space. *Regional Studies* 46(8), pp. 1055–1066.
Hassink, R. and Ibert, O., 2009: Innovationssysteme. Zum Verhältnis von Innovation und Raum in subnationalen Innovationssystemen. In: Blättel-Mink, B. and Ebner, A. (Eds): *Innovationssysteme. Technologie, Institutionen und die Dynamik der Wettbewerbsfähigkeit*. Springer, pp. 159–175.
Hodge, G.A. and Greve, C., 2007: Public–private partnerships: an international performance review. *Public Administration Review* 67(3), pp. 545–558.
Hospers, G.-J., Sautet, F. and Desrochers, P., 2008: Silicon somewhere: is there a need for cluster policy? In: Karlsson, C. (Ed.): *Handbook of Research on Innovation and Clusters*. Cheltenham: Edward Elgar, pp. 430–447.
Karlsson, C. (Ed.), 2008: *Handbook of Research on Innovation and Clusters*. Cheltenham: Edward Elgar.
Kolzow, D.R., 1994: Public/private partnership: the economic development organization of the 90s. *Economic Development Review* 12(1), pp. 4–6.
Landabaso, M., Oughton, C. and Morgan, K., 1999: Learning Regions in Europe: Theory, Policy and Practice through the RIS Experience, 3rd International Conference on Technology and Innovation Policy, Austin, TX.
Linder, S., 1999: Coming to terms with public–private partnership: a grammar of multiple meanings. *American Behavioral Scientist* 43(1), pp. 35–51.
Lundvall, B.-A., 1998: Why study national systems and national styles of innovation? *Technology Analysis and Strategic Management* 10(4), pp. 407–421.
Lundvall, B.-A., 1992: *National Systems of Innovation: Towards a theory of innovation and interactive learning*. London, Pinter.
McQuaid, R.W., 2000: The Theory of Partnerships – Why have Partnerships. In: Osborne (Ed.), *Managing Public–Private Partnerships for Public Services: An international perspective*. London: Routledge pp. 9–35.

McQuaid, R.W., 2010: Theory of organisational partnerships: partnership advantages, disadvantages and success factors. In: Osborne, S.P. (Ed.): *The New Public Governance: Emerging perspectives on the theory and practice of public governance*. London: Routledge, pp. 125–146.

McQuaid, R.W. and Scherrer, W., 2008: Public and private sector partnership in the European Union: experiences in the UK, Germany, and Austria. *uprava* 6(2), pp. 7–34.

McQuaid, R.W. and Scherrer, W., 2010: Changing reasons for public private partnerships. *Public Money and Management* 30(1), pp. 27–39.

Marshall, M., 1996: The changing face of Swedish corporatism: the disintegration of consensus. *Journal of Economic Issues* 30(3), pp. 843–858.

Montanheiro, L., Nunes, R., Owen, G. and Rebelo, E. (Eds.), 1995: *Public and Private Sector Partnerships in the Global Context*. Sheffield: Pavic Publications.

Morgan, K., 1997: The learning region: institutions, innovation and regional renewal. *Regional Studies* 31(5), pp. 491–503.

Moulaert, F. and Sekia, F., 2003: Territorial innovation models: a critical survey. *Regional Studies* 37(3), 289–302.

Nelson, R.R. (Ed.), 1993: *National Innovation Systems: A comparative study*. Oxford: Oxford University Press.

OECD, 2004: Public/Private Partnerships for Innovation, Chapter 3. In: *OECD Science, Technology and Industry Outlook 2004*. Paris: OECD.

OECD, 2008: *Public–Private Partnerships*. Paris: OECD.

OECD, 2010a: *Innovation Strategy*. Paris: OECD.

OECD, 2010b: *Dedicated Public–Private Partnership Units: A survey of institutional and governance structures*. Paris: OECD.

OECD, 2011: *Regions and Innovation Policy*. Paris: OECD.

Osborne, S.P. (Ed.), 2000: *Managing Public–Private Partnerships for Public Services: An international perspective*. London: Routledge.

Rosenau, P.V. (Ed.), 2000: *Public–Private Policy Partnerships*. Cambridge, MA: MIT Press.

Rutten, R. and Boekema, F., 2007: *The Learning Region: Foundations, state of the art, future*. Cheltenham and Northampton, MA: Edward Elgar.

Scherrer, W., 2016: Technology and socio-economic development in the long run: a 'long wave'–perspective. In: Hilpert, U. (Ed.): *Routledge Handbook of Politics and Technology*. London: Routledge, pp. 501–64.

Silva, M.R. and Rodriguez, H., 2005: Public–private partnerships and the promotion of collective entrepreneurship. Paper presented at the 11th International Conference on Public and Private Partnerships: Iasi.

Simmie, J., 2005: Innovation and space: A critical review of the literature. *Regional Studies* 39, pp. 789–804.

Smits, R. and Kuhlmann, S., 2004: The rise of systemic instruments in innovation policy. *International Journal of Foresight and Innovation Policy* 1(1–2), pp. 4–32.

Stiglitz, J.E. and Wallsten, S.J., 1999: Public–private technology partnerships: promises and pitfalls. *American Behavioral Scientist* 43(1): pp. 52–73.

Treasury, 2000: *Public Private Partnerships: The government's approach*. London: GSO.

van den Hurk, M. and Verhoest, K., (2014) The challenge of using standard contracts in public–private partnerships. *Public Management Review* 5(3), 1–22.

Verhoest, K., van den Hurk, M., Carbonara, N., Lember, V., Petersen, O.H. and Scherrer, W., 2013: National context for PPPs—policy, regulation and supporting institutions. COST Action TU1001—2013 Discussion Papers: Part I, Country Profiles: pp. xii–xxv.

Wettenhall, R., 2003: The rhetoric and reality of public–private partnerships. *Public Organization Review: A Global Journal* 3, pp. 77–107.

Wieczorek, A.J. and Hekkert, M.P., 2012: Systemic instruments for systemic innovation problems: a framework for policy makers and innovation scholars. *Science and Public Policy* 39(1), pp. 74–87.

Wysocki, R.K., 2009: *Effective Project Management: Traditional, agile, extreme*. Indianapolis, IN: Wiley Publishing.

18

ECOSYSTEMS OF OPEN INNOVATION

Their applicability to the growth and the development of economies within small countries and regions

Bill O'Gorman and Willie Donnelly

Introduction

In essence this chapter addresses what Oughton, Landabaso and Morgan (2002) call the 'regional innovation paradox'. The innovation paradox refers to the concept whereby it is clear that certain regions and small countries need to invest heavily in R&D, innovation and the commercialisation of research if they are to close the income and wealth creation gaps compared to 'wealthier', 'more sustainable' regions and countries; however, these regions and countries do not have the capacity nor capability to effectively manage such investments. This may be due to a lack of experience and/or being at a stage of development whereby neither the region's or small country's enterprise and innovation policies nor infrastructures are conducive to effectively utilise investments geared for R&D, innovation and the commercialisation of research. Specifically, from a regional perspective the innovation paradox often exists as the result of centralised government and policies and/or a country's economy being dominated by an advanced and well performing capital city, large urban area(s), or region(s) that overshadow(s) weaker and underperforming regions (O'Gorman 2005).

Most developing economies transition from a policy of protectionism through to a focus on foreign direct investment (FDI) (O'Gorman and Cooney 2007). Indeed many such developing economies find it difficult to transition beyond the focus on FDI to the detriment of indigenous enterprise and innovation (O'Hearn 1998; O'Sullivan 2000). However, in a globalised economy, where the boundaries between regions and economies are blurring, in order to remain competitive and to sustain their economies regions and small countries need to realise that the capability and capacity to innovate and commercialise research is essential.[1]

National and regional boundaries often generate restrictions to commerce, trade, innovation, technology development and the commercialisation of research. But in the current information age of cloud computing, and the relative ease of brain circulation (physical and electronic) across boundaries how do we define 'region'? What is a region? Is a region an area or territory constrained by geography such as rivers, mountains and seas, or is it merely a mental picture used to classify the real world? Or is a region a 'space' bounded by economics, social constructs and culture?[2] There are many definitions and interpretations of what a 'region' is.[3] For the purposes of this chapter the authors have chosen the Organisation for Economic Co-operation and Development (OECD 2011) concept of region as being based on economic linkages that may not match political borders but can span regional or even national boundaries.

However, the definitions, while once adequate, are now questionable in an era marked by phenomena such as globalization, unbundling of production cycles and processes, open innovation systems, brain circulation, factors triggering and feeding innovation and regional development are increasingly found 'elsewhere' rather than within the internal network of relations that have traditionally been the main focus of regional development (Bellini and Hilpert 2013). Bellini and Hilpert suggest that in order for a region (or small country) to create, maintain, increase or reshape its 'relational assets' such aspirations must be added to a region's (small country's) objectives of their modern regional economic policy. They continue that regional development should be defined in terms of space: *economic space*, *innovation space*, *political space*, and *culture and identity space*.

The focus of this chapter is primarily on *innovation space* and thus the determination of an ecosystem of open innovation for regions and small countries. The main argument throughout this chapter is that, for small countries and regions, it is often more difficult to build the required capacity to innovate. These limited innovation capacities and capabilities have a significant impact on a region's (country's) development and competitiveness with regional performance being hampered as a result. Driven by the increased intensity of international competition in a globalising economy, the shortcomings of traditional regional development models, and the emergence of successful clusters of firms and industries in many regions around the world (Enright 1994), considerable attention is now being paid to the concept of regional innovation systems (RIS) and specifically, as discussed in this chapter, ecosystems of open innovation as a conducive method of building the required capacity and capability to innovate and commercialise research.

It is the contention of the authors of this chapter that developing and implementing an ecosystem of open innovation that is conducive to business growth and regional economic and social development, will assist small countries and regions to overcome the *regional innovation paradox*. However, 'such processes [will] demand highly innovative labour, collaboration and an exchange of ideas and competencies, which refer to a particular region's profile in scientific research and technology and a particular stock of innovative knowledge' (Hilpert 2013: 3). Equally those tasked with the role of enhancing a region's economy and sustainability need to enmesh all relevant stakeholders to embrace and develop an environment whereby the region's boundaries of porous and permeable capacities and capabilities can absorb and disseminate innovative labour, knowledge and technology.

Strong regions contribute to national development. In particular regions that are open and prepared to engage and collaborate with 'outside' leading institutions can attract expertise and specialisms into their respective regions thus enhancing economic development, growth and sustainability for their region and their country. Therefore whereas most previous research and literature pertaining to this subject area has focused on large successful regions, this chapter focuses on how small countries and regions can enhance their competitiveness and sustainability through the development and implementation of an ecosystem of open innovation in their respective domains.

Innovation, policies and the development of small countries and regions

Innovation can be defined in many ways;[4] however, we contend that it is not the innovation itself that is key but rather the process and location of innovation and the commercialisation and internationalisation of research outputs. The locus and catalyst of innovation systems and the commercialisation of research is in fact within the region, as opposed to solely at a national or supranational level. Therefore supranational, national, regional and local innovation policies need to be aligned (Sternberg 2009). In 2011, the OECD stated that policy makers at all levels need to support both innovation and regional development at the same time to ensure that regions can become functional agents of change, keeping pace with global markets and trends.

Doloreux and Parto (2005) posit that much of our understanding of regions as a locus of innovation comes from research into innovation milieu, learning regions, clusters, industrial districts and regional innovation systems. However, such studies are by no means conclusive and are largely based on metropolitan areas or exemplary regions such as Silicon Valley, Emilia-Romagna and Baden-Wurttemberg, to mention but a few (Cooke and Morgan 1998) that are conducive to the development of innovation systems. On the other hand, small countries and/or peripheral regions are considered to be inferior and lack the dynamics, actors and infrastructure to avail of inward investment to create and develop effective regional innovation systems. Such regions (and small countries) consist mainly of traditional industries with low levels of innovation and R&D capacity, are often over-reliant on FDI (where innovation and R&D are jealously guarded by those in the home nation's HQ) and are therefore considered to be less developed in terms of possessing the resources, supports, networks, education infrastructure, or knowledge support systems to develop a cohesive, interactive triple helix of regional (or national) actors to internationalise and commercialise technology and knowledge transfer.[5] Even though these peripheral regions and small countries are operating in open economic systems they are still mostly 'inward looking' and find it difficult to break out of the 'innovation paradox' cycle.

Regional innovation systems that are successful make extensive use of endogenously generated as well as exogenously available knowledge to strengthen their competencies and to remain competitive in a global economic environment (Doloreux and Parto 2005). Whereas, not so long ago, the demarcation between endogenously and exogenously generated influencers on the development of regions and countries was clearly evident, in the current high-tech, information age the endogenous–exogenous boundaries are blurring. This is especially so when one considers the possibility and actuality of R&D, innovation, and new product development commercialisation in multi(national) site locations. The world wide web (www), cloud computing and other technology and communication advances have enabled this multi(national) site feature of product development and commercialisation to become a reality, to the extent that the definition of 'region' becomes even more confusing and complex. Indeed the role of local, regional and national politics and its influence over delineating and implementing innovation policies, taking local, regional and national nuances into consideration, becomes even more questionable. Thus there is the absolute need for the relevant triple helix of stakeholders of peripheral regions and small countries to generate RTD and innovation policies of cooperation and collaboration to create an environment whereby *ecosystems of open innovation* can thrive.

Evolution from innovation milieu to ecosystems of open innovation

The evolution to what we today call ecosystems of open innovation has taken many guises over the last several decades. The first incarnation is what was referred to as *innovation milieu*. This is a concept developed in the late 1980s and early 1990s by a group of economists known as GERMI.[6] The innovation milieu is the socio-economic environment of a region produced by the interactions of firms, institutions and labour. It is the relationships and interactions between these entities that creates the innovative capacity of the *milieu*. However, to date, it is still not clear how an innovation milieu comes into being, whether through luck or historical accident. It is also not clear whether they represent a general model of regional development or a specialised model suited to unique circumstances (Bergman 1991).[7]

Next came the concept of the *industrial district* – a term used to describe a location where workers of heavy industry lived and worked, e.g. Northern England, Northern Italy. It is a geographically localised productive system, based on a strong local division of work between small firms specialising in different aspects of the production and distribution cycle of an industrial sector. However, in more recent times the term was used to imply the ways in which economic specialisation arises through clustering in a particular industry-zoned area/region. But the key aspects to innovation in the district lies with the SMEs themselves and relationships, trust and reciprocity between the SMEs. The concept of *industrial districts* stresses that a region's economic development is dependent on the trust and opportunism between SMEs, the role of culture as a vehicle for change, and the way in which agents (firms) who behave inappropriately are penalised for their actions.[8]

The concept of *local production systems* assumes that for its creation a region (locality or district) already has production factors and resources, technology capability, leading firms, a dynamism of local demand and appropriate institutional actions (and interactions). Leading firms are a critical factor in this concept as it is supposed that these are the catalysts for the development of human capital, the creating and development of the supply infrastructure and the generation of spin-offs. However, it appears that within this concept, it is the leading firms solely that are the drivers of economic growth in isolation from other institutions within the *local system*.[9] On the other hand, in the 1990s, the concept of *new industrial spaces* (also referred to as the theory of *new economic geography*) was based on the social division of labour, the proliferation of small to medium sized industries and the re-agglomeration of production and services industries, in particular high-technology industries that made use of information technology, employed large numbers of highly skilled and educated staff and actively engaged in inter-firm networks. The use of technology by highly skilled and educated staff was core to the development of business and social networks across regional and international boundaries. As a result, in the late 1990s and early 2000s, the movement of people and especially the sharing and use of technology and knowledge across firm, regional and national boundaries became even more prolific leading to globalised industrialisation, innovation and commercialisation of research as we know it today.[10]

Clusters of innovation, *learning regions* and *regional innovation systems* are concepts that are often used interchangeably and confused. Based on Porter's work on *clusters of innovation* in the early 1990s governments in general and organisations such as the OECD and EU in particular have embraced the notion that *clusters of innovation* are key to the economic development of regions. *Clusters of innovation* are geographic concentrations of firms, suppliers, service providers and supporting institutions involved in the same or similar industry sectors (Porter 1998). However, the mere existence of these entities in a single geographic area alone, while supporting a region's economic development, does not guarantee a region's longevity nor its sustainability. Rather, it is *the learning region*, i.e. the interaction between these entities, the formal and informal networking between their employees, and particularly the transfer of technology and knowledge between the entities, and the two-way sharing of knowledge supported by learning and dissemination institutions such as universities and research centres that fuels the economic development and growth of regions. An essential ingredient to this regional development, growth and long term sustainability is finance and the access to finance. Creating the financial infrastructure whereby firms, and supporting institutions have the capacity and capability to gain access to and use necessary venturing capital to generate endogenous innovation is what constitutes a *regional innovation system* (Andersson and Karlsson 2004).[11]

This brings us back to the question of the '*regional innovation paradox*' and how peripheral regions and small countries can innovate and compete successfully in an open globalised economy against *regional innovation systems* such as Silicon Valley, Route 128, Emilia-Romagna and Baden-Wurttemberg, which have the venturing capital, human capital, technology and infrastructures to create an environment to generate endogenous innovation within their regions.

Equally, where a regional innovation system expands its own boundaries through a process of economic integration, globalisation, and attraction and dissemination of innovative labour and technologies, and 'brain exchange' in a sharing, collaborative and complementary process with other regional innovation systems, reinforces its innovation capacity and capability. The process becomes a spiral of ever increasing creation, innovation and commercialisation.

However, as stated earlier, peripheral regions and small countries, because of their governance (which is usually centralised), the small size of their markets, their reliance on FDI and exports, and their lack of access to adequate venture capital, find it difficult to nurture an environment that leads them to being a competitive, effective regional innovation system.

Current research and dialogue about regional innovation systems suggests that, in an environment of international markets and multi-(international)-site production, delivery and innovation systems where knowledge flows freely and boundaries (at firm and regional levels) are blurred, ecosystems of open innovation are the new way forward if regions are to compete successfully and assure their sustainability.

Ecosystems and innovation ecosystems

Preparing the way for ecosystems of open innovation is the concept of 'Islands of Innovation'. Islands of Innovation are regions where the most advanced industries and R&D facilities are located, where there are attractions to maintain and/or draw in scientists and high-skilled and innovative labour, and effective government policies support innovation policies (Hilpert 2003) and where brain exchange and brain circulation exist. However, since the mid 1990s economists, researchers and policy makers have attempted to use the notion of ecosystems to define a new and emerging generation of innovation systems. Many have intimated that any capitalist economy can be viewed as a living ecosystem consisting of competition, specialisation, cooperation, exploitation, learning and growth as being central to economic life. They suggest that the basic mechanisms of economic change are similar to those found in nature with the main difference being speed and that economic development, and the resulting social change, are not shaped by society's genes, rather by the accumulation of technical knowledge.[12]

A key feature of any ecosystem is its ability to adapt to change, be it caused exogenously or endogenously and a variety of distinct species must exist to ensure that at least part of the population can cope with any new environmental change (Peltoniemi and Vuori 2004). The 'variety of distinct species' consists of firms (from a variety of industry sectors and not just a single cluster), consumers, suppliers, R&D centres and supporting economic, cultural, educational and legal institutions. The nutrients required to develop, regulate and balance the equilibrium of innovation ecosystems are: entrepreneurial capacity, business acumen, risk capital, R&D enterprises, technology commercialisation, human capital, physical infrastructure, an industrial base, global linkages, networking opportunities, a culture that fosters innovation and a community mindset, networking, capital, knowledge and technology transfer processes,[13] professional services, support infrastructures, supportive government policies and a balanced quality of life (Jackson 2011; TECNA 2011). Another key aspect to the development and maintenance of innovation ecosystems is the development of trust, cooperation, collaboration and co-evolution of the species and organisms constituting the ecosystem and the management of the complex relationships arising from these interactions.

By the same token there is a need for decentralised decision making and self-organisation within the ecosystem. But, just as in the biological ecosystem, innovation ecosystems are characterised by the large number of interconnected participants who depend on each other for their mutual survival. If the ecosystem is healthy and functioning well individual species (organisations) prosper. On the other hand if the ecosystem is unhealthy this will result in fragmentation, a reduction in interconnectedness, reduced cooperation and increased competition (Iansiti and Levien 2004). However, some innovation ecosystems are often built around one single organisation that is highly connected (Power and Jerjian 2001) and seen to be the engine at the heart of the whole (eco) system (Gossain and Kandiah 1998).

Jackson (2011) suggests that innovation ecosystems comprise two distinct economies (i) the research economy and (ii) the commercial economy (see Figure 18.1). The research economy is driven by fundamental research, whereas the commercial economy is driven by the needs of the marketplace. However, the innovation ecosystem will be thriving and healthy when the resources invested in the research economy (either from private, government or direct business funds) are subsequently replenished by innovation induced profit increases in the commercial economy. Such practices allow for the discovery of innovations to be capitalised upon and commercially introduced to the marketplace.

An essential ingredient to create the 'innovation ecosystem spectrum' is appropriate active government enterprise policy and government infrastructures to support R&D, innovation, commercialisation, internationalisation, the nurturing of innovative labour, and industry. An equally important ingredient for the sustainability of an 'innovation ecosystem spectrum' is to create an environment and culture of 'free movement' of scientific and innovative labour across boundaries. This will be discussed in more detail later in the chapter under the heading *a blueprint for ecosystems of open innovation*.

Whereas it is very important to note that successful, thriving innovation ecosystems are based on decentralised decision making and self-regulation, it is the constantly evolving relationships between a wide range of innovation partners (local, regional, national and international) that affect knowledge creation, the rate of knowledge diffusion, and knowledge transformation into innovation and commercialisation. It is also important to note that it is essential that regional innovation ecosystems must leverage off local, regional, national and international infrastructures to fuel the regional innovation process through the collaboration of multiple partners including research parks, universities, large research-driven firms, start-ups, investors and other professionals (Wolfe 2009).

However, much of what is expressed above is based on highly urbanised metropolitan regions where well established institutional organisations and knowledge-intensive firms known for their creativity, share information and knowledge, resulting in high levels of success and economic prosperity (Doloreux and Dionne 2008). Much of the research on innovation ecosystems, presented to date, does not take into account the unique features of small countries, sub-regions nor peripheral regions. Neither does the research explain how innovation ecosystems might emerge in such locations, which very often lack the basic requirements conducive to the fostering of an innovation culture, what Oughton *et al.* (2002) referred to as the 'regional innovation paradox'. For example, small countries, sub or lagging regions, and peripheral regions often do

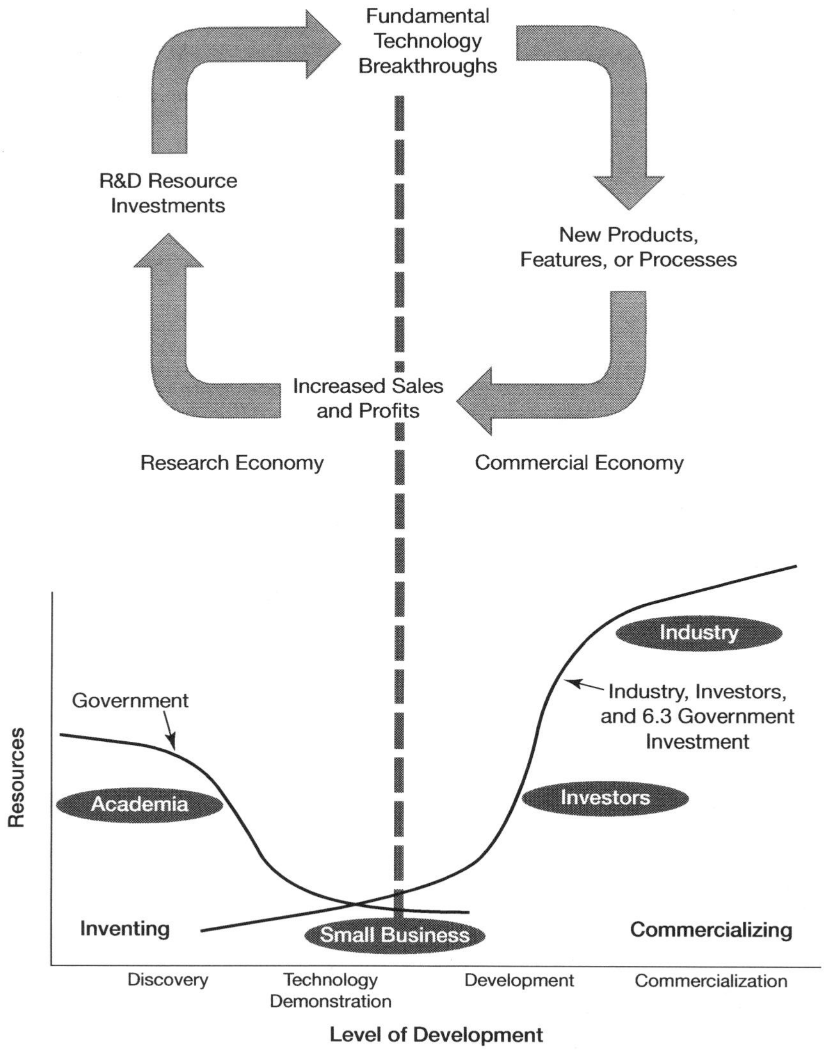

Figure 18.1 Innovation ecosystem spectrum.
Source: Jackson 2011: 8.

not have the dynamics, actors or support organisations conducive to developing an innovation system. Such regions are less developed in terms of innovation, lacking the resources and supports required, for example networks, technology transfer supports, and knowledge support systems. Frequently, such regions lack specialised services and have poor technology transfer links between the public and private sectors. Less developed regions and countries often have a larger portion of SMEs in traditional industries with little R&D and low absorptive capacity, with levels of innovation frequently lower in comparison to urbanised regions (Tödtling and Trippl 2005). Innovation in lagging regions tends to be small scale, incremental and normally takes place through the application of existing knowledge (Asheim and Coenen 2005). Therefore, it can be difficult to attract high-skilled jobs to such regions resulting in reduced productivity

(Doloreux and Dionne 2008), with the possibilities of entrepreneurial growth often limited due to the lack of local competition in product markets, the limited scale and scope of local market opportunities, combined with lengthy distances to larger markets (North and Smallbone 2000).[14] A major challenge therefore for governments of small and/or developing countries and regions is how to increase that country's or region's attractiveness to draw in scientists, innovative labour, technologies and know-how. A key question for such governments is what is the catalyst to start the 'brain circulation' process.

Ecosystems of open innovation – comparing regions and countries

Based on the above analysis we believe the five essential ingredients to develop an ecosystem of open innovation are: *connectedness* between individuals, organisations and support institutions, *infrastructure* provided at a local and regional levels, an *environment* conducive to business, economic and regional development and growth, a *culture* that supports innovation and knowledge exchange, and *governance* that offers the mechanisms for regional economic and social development in a sustained and supported manner. To test this theory we selected sixteen regions/countries selected from the Regional Innovation Scoreboard (RIS 2012) based on their classification as either innovation leaders, innovation followers, moderate innovators or modest innovators. Innovation leaders tend to be located in the most well developed and economically prosperous countries, whereas modest innovators tend to be located in poorer, less developed countries and/or in peripheral regions. Table 18.1 shows the comparison between the sixteen regions/countries based on the five factors we identified as being critical to creating and developing an ecosystem of open innovation.

Connectedness

The presence of a high level of cluster development, where organisations and key stakeholders collaborate and cooperate, share information and have common goals and objectives is essential for a region to remain competitive and be at the forefront of technological change. Regions that have demonstrated the benefits of cluster development include Silicon Valley and Route 128 in the US. Both regions have well established clusters of businesses and key support organisations that work in tandem, aiding regional growth and development in a sustained manner.

The presence of key indigenous industries contributes enormously to a region's growth and development, in-flux of venture capital, attraction of public and private sector investments, attraction of skilled human capital, and the region's governance; for example Apple, Microsoft and HP in Silicon Valley; General Electric in Boston on Route 128; Nokia in Finland; and Bosch, Damlier and SAP in Baden-Wurttemberg.

Infrastructure

The presence of pro-business institutions that actively encourage the set-up and support of new firms is crucial to regional development, especially in regions seeking to transition and develop their innovation capacity. Silicon Valley grew as a direct result of a pro-business environment (Herbig and Golden 1993) that fostered a collective, team-driven approach to doing business. Inter-regional linkages and cooperative employer–employee relationships, supported by consensus in politics and business also facilitated growth and development in Baden-Wurttemberg, Germany (Krauss and Wolf 2002). Additionally, the presence of tertiary education and research organisation is important to a region's development of its innovation capacity and

Table 18.1 Ecosystem of open innovation – five-factor analysis of countries and regions

	Silicon Valley, California	*Route 128 Boston*	*Eastern Region United Kingdom*	*Switzerland*	*Horedstaden Denmark*	*Southern Region Sweden*	*Singapore*	*Norway*	*Israel*	*Baden-Wurttemberg Germany*	*Tampere Finland*	*Sophia Antipolis France*	*Northern Ireland*	*Bucuresti-Ilfor Romania*	*Latvia*	*South East Ireland*
RIS 2012 Classification																
Innovation Leader	X	X	X	X	X	X				X	X					
Innovation Follower							X	X				X				X
Moderate Innovator									X				X	X		
Modest Innovator															X	
CONNECTEDNESS																
High level of cluster development	X	X		X	X	X	X	X	X	X	X		X			
Presence of major indigenous organisation	X	X	X	X	X	X		X		X	X	X		X		
INFRASTRUCTURE																
Presence of pro-business institution	X	X	X		X			X		X	X	X	X			X
Presence of university/higher education institution	X	X	X	X	X	X	X	X	X	X	X	X	X	X	X	X
High level of university/HEI – industry research collaboration	X	X	X	X	X	X	X	X	X	X	X	X				
High level of FDI and technology transfer	X	X	X	X	X	X	X	X	X				X	X		X
ENVIRONMENT																
High level of population with tertiary education	X	X	X	X	X	X		X	X	X	X	X	X			X
High level of R&D expenditure in the public sector as per cent of GDP			X	X	X	X	X	X	X	X	X	X				
High level of R&D expenditure in the private sector as per cent of GDP	X	X	X	X	X	X	X	X	X	X	X					X

INNOVATION CULTURE																
High propensity for supporting innovation	X	X	X	X					X	X						X
High capacity for innovation	X	X		X		X			X	X	X	X				
Regional attractiveness	X	X	X	X		X				X	X					X
Critical mass of industry	X	X	X	X			X			X	X					
High level of SMEs innovating in-house	X	X	X	X	X	X			X	X	X					X
High level of innovative SMEs collaborating with others	X	X		X	X	X		X		X	X					X
GOVERNANCE																
Low level of government regulation	X					X		X		X						
Decentralisation of economic policy making	X	X			X	X		X		X	X					

Source: authors.

capability. Examples include Stanford University near Silicon Valley and Massachusetts Institute of Technology (MIT) near the Route 128 region in Boston. Although it is clear that all regions examined benefited from the presence of a university/HEI, those regions characterised as *innovation leaders* or *followers* reported higher levels of university/HEI – industry research collaboration. Collaborative research relationships between such institutions and the business community is of significant importance to the development of regional innovation systems. A similar argument is presented in terms of FDI and technology transfer. Those same regions (innovation leaders and followers) that benefit from greater levels of research collaboration reported higher levels of FDI and technology transfer.

Environment

Exemplar regions known for their innovation, technology and knowledge transfer tend to report higher levels of their population having tertiary education that are skilled and capable to engage in the workforce (Bramwell *et al.* 2012). Having a well educated and skilled workforce that can develop and disseminate new knowledge is critical to the development of a culture of innovation, conducive to business growth and regional economic and social development. Additionally, the investment in R&D from both the public and private sectors is equally important to ensure regional development and growth. Regions that reported higher levels of R&D expenditure in the public and private sectors (as per cent of GDP) are more likely to be regions and countries characterised as innovation leaders.

Innovation culture and regional attractiveness

In this instance culture refers to an embedded spirit of entrepreneurship and the supports to foster a collaborative approach to the creation and development of innovation processes and systems. Fostering a regional culture of innovation, where knowledge is generated, diffused and exploited will assist business growth and therefore benefit the region's economy (Zhang 2012). This in turn positively impacts the attractiveness of a region and enables synergies to develop with other stakeholders both within and external to the region, thus leading to greater levels of inward, institutional and government investment in the region. Table 18.1 shows that regions and countries classified as innovation leaders, and to a lesser extent innovation followers, report a high propensity for supporting innovation and therefore have a high capacity for innovation.

Studies of regional attractiveness are often based on socio-economic, social life and living standard indices. Good public services, a low crime rate, a clean environment and low levels of unemployment are all contributing factors to a region's attractiveness. Equally, individuals, businesses and investors are often attracted to regions with a strong social and cultural identity. For instance, the sun and sea climate was identified as a significant factor in attracting industry to Silicon Valley and Sophia-Antipolis (Longhi 1999). For example, highly skilled graduates from Taiwan, Japan, Korea and Vietnam located in Silicon Valley in search of better living standards, whereas Boston was noted as offering a pleasant living environment for migrants (Herbig and Golden 1993).

However, regional attractiveness is not all about sunshine and pleasant living environments, it is also about jobs – the availability of good paying, good quality jobs and interesting jobs. The attractiveness of a region is also about its capability to offer innovative labour the opportunity for career, experience and qualification advancement. In a study performed by Bernard, Patockova and Kostelecky (2013) about what motivates Czech researchers and scientists to migrate abroad to innovation regions they found 'professional development and qualifications' to be the most significant and dominant factor (148).

Governance

The quality of regional governance makes a significant difference to the success of regional innovation systems. The primary concern should be to establish the best governance that offers the mechanisms for regional economic and social development in a sustained and supported manner. Government regulations can advance or hinder regional development and growth intentions. Some regions favour a centralised approach (e.g. UK, France, Ireland) viewing regional government as yet another layer of bureaucracy that often results in a slowdown of decision making and policy implementation. Such regions favour an approach that consolidates municipalities and regions to form larger entities in anticipation of benefits of scale. On the other hand, some countries (e.g. Sweden, Denmark, USA) favour a more regional/localised approach to governance.

However, the effects of the style of governance are inconclusive (see Table 18.1). For example, some successful regional innovation systems report low levels of government regulation with a high degree of decentralised economic policy making i.e. Silicon Valley, USA; Southern Sweden; Baden-Württemberg, Germany. Other successful regional innovation systems report the opposite, having a system of high government regulation with a low regional level of economic policy making, i.e. Eastern UK; Switzerland; Singapore.

It must be noted and understood that the role government adopts and the tone, content and implementation of its enterprise, research and innovation policies has a huge impact on economic regional performance and, as a result, the performance on the country's economy. In particular, policy makers need to be aware of the knock-on effect on restrictive policies. To ameliorate the effect of such policies and practices government leaders and policy makers need to become more integrated with industry and in particular international business good practices and processes.

A blueprint for ecosystems of open innovation for small countries and regions

According to Hilpert (2013), Islands of Innovation are centres of competence and locations where knowledge is applied and new knowledge is generated. They are also centres that attract innovation labour. But ecosystems of open innovation need to be more than this, they need to have porous and permeable boundaries that can, at the same time, absorb new knowledge and expertise while equally disseminating knowledge about their own specialisms to international centres of research and trade. No small or developing region or country has the capacity or capability to efficiently develop the five-factors of ecosystems of open innovation outlined above. To be successful these regions and small countries need to rely on international support.

Therefore, in our opinion, for regions and small countries to become ecosystems of open innovation they need to embed themselves in a process of international mobility of innovative labour. There are probably three parallel processes that must be adopted to achieve this, (i) build a wealth of sought after knowledge of regional specialisms and nuances, (ii) increase the attractiveness of the region (or small country) by creating and continuously developing leading edge research centres, improving the quality of tertiary education beyond international standard levels, and providing high-value and interesting jobs, and (iii) entering an arrangement with international partners whereby there is an equitable process of brain exchange.

However, the question is how can a lagging region or small country achieve such specialisms and open innovation systems? Such ecosystems of open innovation take time to develop. Figure 18.2, depicts the upward positive spiral effect of the necessary interaction between government policy and funding, research, industry investment and education needed to develop an ecosystem of open innovation. The dotted boundary suggests the need for porosity and permeability to facilitate the inward and outward flow of innovative staff. This flow of innovative staff consists of (i) brain drain where well educated scientists, researchers, engineers and other professionals leave the region/country. This activity is prevalent in countries and regions of low economic status, lagging regions, peripheral regions and emerging economies; (ii) brain gain where 'outsider' scientists, researchers, engineers and other professionals are attracted into the region/country. For example Singapore has built its economy on a strategy of a combination of foreign direct development (FDI) and attracting foreign talents into the city state;[15] (iii) brain exchange whereby there are collaborative agreements for the mutual exchange of scientists, researchers, engineers and other professionals between the region/country and relevant international partners; and (iv) 'free' brain circulation within, out of, and into the region/country. All of this leads to knowledge spillover, job mobility and wealth creation.

Coupled to this is the need to create a supportive, collaborative balance between the research economy and commercial economy. These are complementary, not mutually exclusive, economies. Finally, immersing the regional/national community into an evolving entrepreneurial culture is essential, particularly policy makers, entrepreneurs, business owners, employers and

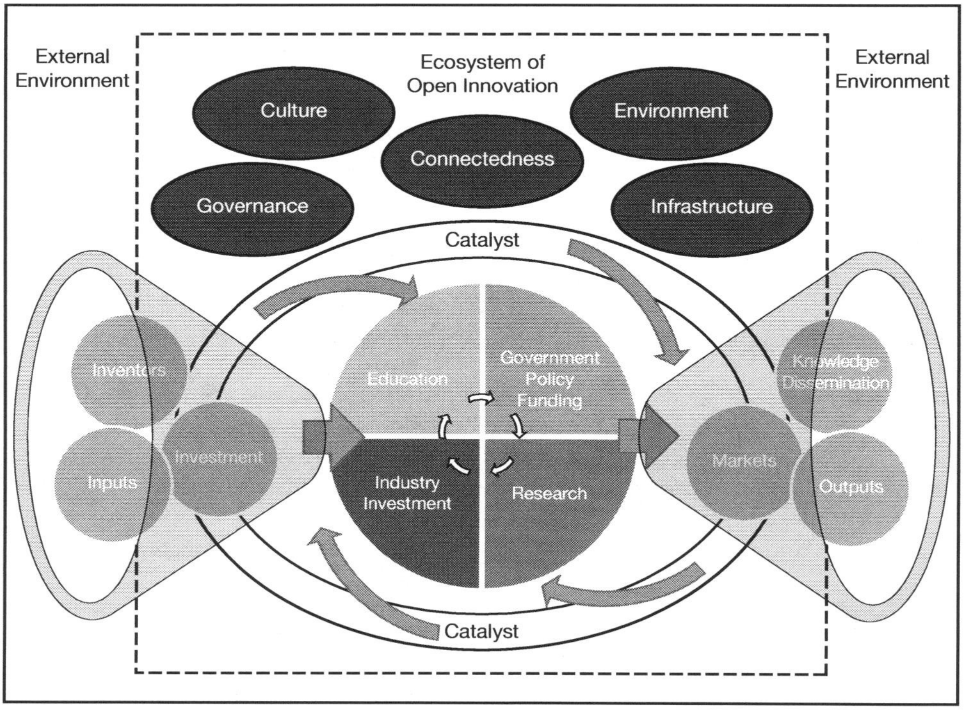

Figure 18.2 Ecosystem of open innovation for small countries and regions.
Source: authors.

citizens have got to embrace the concept of job mobility, brain circulation and labour/skill circulation. Instead of putting barriers in place to hinder mobility and free flow of personnel, stakeholders should encourage it knowing that the circulation of knowledge, skill and labour is what is required to build regional wealth and sustainability – it is the ecosystem of open innovation.

A central entity in making this happen is the *catalyst* (see Figure 18.2) that is needed to create and implement the policies to nurture the environment and provide the nutrients to develop the ecosystem of open innovation. The catalytic agent could be an institution, a group of institutions, an industry, or a group of industries or government. In the opinion of the authors of this chapter, it is best if government are the catalytic agent, but government must create, develop and implement an all inclusive process of engagement of all regional stakeholders, supported by appropriate enterprise, research and innovation policies that encourage growth rather than hindering it.

In summary

Policy makers, policy implementers and academics should expand their horizons beyond the limiting view that the outputs from innovation and regional innovation systems (RIS) are new forms of technology, technology processes, improved manufacturing processes and delivery systems. They should equally explore innovation in low-tech industries, public sector organizations, service industries and the delivery of services to consumers at large. There is also the need to embrace the broader aspects of social innovation (SI) and in particular to use imaginative thinking, creativity and innovation in the reshaping of social interactions.[16]

In order to nurture a sustainable ecosystem of open innovation there is also the need for 'brain circulation' and that, not alone should the consumer/citizen be embraced as a key element of the innovation process, but also that the innovation process must be multidisciplinary, multi-organisational, multi-sectoral, and multi-institutional.[17] However, to realise this potential the region's/small country's institutions need to be adaptable and responsive to international networks of collaboration. Governments (local, regional and national) need to play an important role as a catalyst of different potentials and activities to induce innovation and the development of new technologies and new applications of these technologies.

Notes

1 See Montana *et al.* (2001).

2 For further discussion on the determination of 'region' see for example Maskell (1998); Wolfe and Gertler (1998); Latouche (1998); Cooke and Schienstock (2000); Niosi (2000); Cooke (2001); Simmie (2001); Asheim and Isaksen (2002); Doloreux and Parto (2005a, b); Paasi (2009).

3 A few such examples are: Cooke, Uranga and Etxebarria (1997) classified region as 'a territory less than its sovereign state, possessing distinctive supralocal administrative, cultural, political, or economic power and cohesiveness, differentiating it from its state and other regions'. Johansson (1992, 1998) writes about a region having a high intensity of economic interaction and connectivity of nodes via economic networks and networks of infrastructure. According to Andersson and Karlsson (2004), region is a territory in which the interaction between the actors and the flow of goods and services, create a regional economic system whose borders are determined by the point at which the magnitude of such interactions and flows change from one direction to another.

4 For example some say it is the introduction of new products and services in the market (Bannock 1992), or the implementation of change in practice (Suranyi-Unger 1982), or thinking outside the box through creativity and design (OECD 2011).

5 For further reading on this concept see for example Landabaso and Reid (1999); Cooke, Boekholt and Tödtling (2000); Etzkowitz and Leydesdorff (2000); Isaksen (2001); Doloreux (2003); Asheim and Coenen (2005); Tödtling and Trippl (2005); Doloreux and Dionne (2008).
6 GERMI = Groupement Européen des Milieux Innovateurs.
7 For further reading about the *innovation milieu* see for example Camagni (1995); Maillat (1998); Crevoisier (2001); Moulaert and Sekia (2003); Konstadakopulos (2004).
8 For further reading about *industrial districts* see for example Bagnasco (1977); Becatinni (1981); Kafkalas (1998); Moulaert and Sekia (2003).
9 For further reading about *local production systems* see for example Bouchara (1987); Porter (1998); Courlet (2000); Viesti (2000); Lombardi (2003).
10 For further reading about *new industrial spaces* (and the theory of *new economic geography*) see for example Storper and Scott (1988); Bathelt and Hecht (1990); Krugman (1991); Moulaert and Scott (1997); Kaufman and Karson (2000); Gatefield and Yang (2006).
11 For further reading about *clusters of innovation* see for example Porter (1990, 1998); Enright (1994); Saxenian (1994); Karlsson (2001); Andersson and Karlsson (2004); for *learning regions* see for example Storper (1995); Sternberg (1996, 2009); Morgan (1997); Florida (1995); Cooke (1998); Konstadakopulous (2004); and for *regional innovation systems* see for example Meeus, Oerlemans and van Dijck (1999); Edquist (1997); Ladendijk (1998); Doloreaux and Parto (2005); Doloreux and Dionne (2008).
12 See for example Rothschild (1990); Peltoniemi and Vuori (2004).
13 It is extremely important that these knowledge and technology transfer processes facilitate *all* four of the following scenarios (i) firm – firm, (ii) institution – firm, (iii) firm – institution, and (iv) institution – institution.
14 For further reading about ecosystems see for example Rothschild (1990); Moore (1996, 1998); Gossain and Kandiah (1998); DeLong (2000); North and Smallbone (2000); Power and Jerjian (2001); Mileton-Kelly (2003); Ianisti and Levien (2004); Peltoniemi and Vuori (2004); Asheim and Coenen (2005); Tödtling and Trippl (2005); Doloreux and Dionne (2008); Wolfe (2009); Jackson (2011); Mercan and Goktas (2011); TECNA (2011); Bramwell, Hepburn and Wolfe (2012).
15 See Tsui-Auch *et al.* (2013).
16 O'Gorman, B. and Donnelly, W, 2013, Knowledge-based networks: The jewel on the regional development crown, presentation to the Directing Committee of the Cooperative Action Programme on Local Economic and Employment Development (LEED), Derry-Londonderry.
17 Ibid.

References

Andersson, M. and Karlsson, C., 2004: Regional innovation systems in small and medium-sized regions: a critical review and assessment. In: Johansson, B., Karlsson, C. and Stough, R.R. (eds): *The Emerging Digital Economy: Entrepreneurship, Clusters and Policy*. Springer-Verlag: Berlin.

Asheim, B.T. and Coenen, L., 2005: Knowledge bases and regional innovation systems: comparing Nordic clusters. *Research Policy* 34, pp. 1173–1190.

Bellini, N. and Hilpert, U., 2013: *Europe's Changing Geography*. Routledge: London.

Bergman, E., Maier, G. and Tödtling, F. (eds), 1991: Regions Reconsidered: Economic networks, innovation, and local development in industrialized countries. London: Mansell.

Bernard, J., Patockova, V. and Kostelecky, T., 2013: Islands of innovation in the Czech Republic. In: Hilpert, U. and Lawton-Smith, H. (eds): *Networking Regionalised Innovative Markets*. Routledge, London, pp. 136–59.

Bramwell, A., Hepburn, N. and Wolfe, D.A., 2012: Growing innovation ecosystems: university–industry knowledge transfer and regional economic development in Canada. Knowledge Synthesis Paper on Leveraging Investments. In: HERD, Final Report to the Social Sciences and Humanities Research Council of Canada.

Cooke, P. and Morgan, K., 1998: *The Associative Region*. Oxford: Oxford University Press.

Doloreux, D. and Dionne, S., 2008: Is regional innovation system development possible in peripheral regions? Some evidence from the case of La Pocatiere, Canada. *Entrepreneurship and Regional Development* 20(3), pp. 259–283.

Doloreux, D. and Parto, S., 2005a: Regional innovation systems: current discourse and unresolved issues. *Technology in Society* 27(2), pp. 133–153.
Doloreux, D. and Parto, S., 2005b: *Regional Innovation Systems: A critical review*, Maastricht: INTECH United Nations University, Institute for New Technologies.
Enright, M.J., 1994: Regional clusters and firm strategy. Paper presented at the Prince Bertil Symposium, The Dynamice Firm, Stockholm.
Fujita, M., 2010: The evolution of spatial economics: from Thunen to the New Economic Geography. *The Japanese Economic Review* 61(1), March.
Gossain, S. and Kandiah, G., 1998: Reinventing value: the new business ecosystem. *Strategy & Leadership* 26(5), pp. 28–33.
Herbig, P.A. and Golden, J.E., 1993: The rise of innovation hot spots: Silicon Valley and Route 128. *International Marketing Review* 10(3), p. 35.
Hilpert, U., 2003: Globalisation and selective localisation of industry and innovation: the role of government in regionalising socio-economic development. In: Hilpert, U. (ed.): *Regionalisation of Globalised Innovation: Locations for advanced industrial development and disparities in participation*. London: Routledge, pp. 3–28.
Hilpert, U., 2013: Exchange of knowledge and the building of networks. In: Hilpert, U. and Lawton-Smith, H. (eds.): *Networking Regionalised Innovative Markets*. London: Routledge, pp. 3–32.
Iansiti, M. and Levien, R., 2004: The Keystone Advantage: What the new dynamics of business ecosystems mean for strategy, innovation, and sustainability. Boston, MA: Harvard Business School Press.
Jackson, D., 2011: *What is an Innovation Ecosystem?* Arlington, VA: National Science Foundation. Available online at: www.erc-assoc.org/docs/innovation_ecosystem.pdf.
Krauss, G. and Wolf, G.H., 2002: Technological strengths in mature sectors: an impediment or an asset for regional economic restructuring? The case of multimedia and biotechnology in Baden-Wurttemberg. *Journal of Technology Management* 27(1), pp. 39.
Longhi, C., 1999: Networks, collective learning and technology development in innovative high technology: the case of Sophia-Antipolis. *Regional Studies* 33(4), pp. 333–343.
North, D. and Smallbone, D., 2000: The innovativeness and growth of rural SMEs during the 1990s. *Regional Studies* 34(2), pp. 145–157.
OECD, 2011: *Regions and Innovation Policy*. Brussels: OECD Publishing.
O'Gorman, B., 2005: Developing entrepreneurial regions – towards a model of modernisation and sustainable growth. *Conference Proceedings*, Guangxi University of Technology, China.
O'Gorman, B. and Cooney, T., 2007: An anthology of enterprise policy in Ireland. In: Cooney, T. (ed.): *Special Edition of Irish Journal of Management*. Dublin: Blackhall Publishing.
O'Gorman, B. and Donnelly, W., 2013: Knowledge-based networks: The jewel on the regional development crown. Presentation to the Directing Committee of the Cooperative Action Programme on Local Economic and Employment Development (LEED), Derry-Londonderry.
O'Hearn, D., 1998: *Inside the Celtic Tiger. The Irish Economy and the Asian Model*. London: Pluto Press.
O'Sullivan, M., 2000: The sustainability of industrial development in Ireland. *Regional Studies* 34(3), pp. 277–290.
Oughton, C., Landabaso, M. and Morgan, M., 2002: The regional innovation paradox: innovation policy and industrial policy. *Journal of Technology Transfer* 27(1).
Peltoniemi, M. and Vuori, E., 2004: Business ecosystem as the new approach to complex adaptive business environments. In: *Proceedings of 4th Annual Conference eBRF (eBusiness Research Forum)*, Tampere, pp. 267–281.
Porter, M., 1998: Clusters and the new economies of competition. *Harvard Business Review* 76(6), pp. 77–90.
Power, T. and Jerjian, G., 2001: *Ecosystem: Living the 12 principles of networked business*. London: Pearson Education.
Sternberg, R., 2009: Regional dimensions of entrepreneurship. *Foundations and Trends in Entrepreneurship* 5(4), pp. 211–340.
TECNA (Technology Councils of North America), 2011: Jobs and Innovation Ecosystems – Implementation within TECNA Regions. Available online at: http://ct.typepad.com/files/tecna--jobs-and-innovation-ecosystemss-6–1-2011.pdf (accessed July 2012).
Tödtling, F. and Trippl, M., 2005: One size fits all? Towards a differentiated policy approach with respect to regional innovation systems. *Research Policy* 34, pp. 1203–1219.

Tsui-Auch, L.S., Chai, S.I. and Liu, A., 2013: Putting Singapore on the global innovation map: the shifting role of the state in the rapidly changing environment. In Hilpert, U. (ed.): *Routledge Handbook of Politics and Technology*. Oxford: Routledge. pp. 191–206.

Wolfe, D., 2009: *21st century cities in Canada: The geography of innovation*. Ottawa: Conference Board of Canada.

Zhang, Q., 2012: An evolutionary perspective on knowledge networks of university spin-offs: Literature review and a proposal for the empirical study of Wales. *RENT Proceedings*, Lyon, France.

PART 5

Effects of new technologies

Dynamism and change as outcomes of government policies

19

METROPOLITAN LOCATIONS IN INTERNATIONAL HIGH-TECH NETWORKS

Collaboration and exchange of creative labour as a basis for advanced socio-economic development

Ulrich Hilpert

Introduction

New technology is always based on new ideas, findings, research and development strategies, appropriate skills and availability of the necessary labour, user industries as reference industries to apply such opportunities successfully, and, of course, markets that are ready to absorb such new products. While industrial structures and available markets are fundamental when such technologies are being prepared (to generate their economic potential), academic labour, research structures and the funding of techno-scientific research is both prior and fundamental to economic exploitation. Since new technologies generally provide a wide range of business opportunities and diverse applications, there are plenty of strategies for techno-industrial innovation that policy makers can utilise. No matter what strategy is decided upon finally, because of limited resources (in budgets, personnel and equipment) there is always a problem of there being more new ideas and opportunities than could be realised at a single location. This applies no matter how strong their research base might be – or whether they are engaged in certain areas of research from very early stages. Even nation states may be confronted with limitations that are formed by available personnel and outstanding research locations.

While facing this problem collaboration has become a fundamental element of research, innovation and technology development. This allows a realisation of projects with partners from different countries and locations based on both merging outstanding competences and making use of scientific researchers from different locations (Straubhaar 2000; Avveduto 2001; Criscuolo 2005; Millar and Salt 2008; Breschi and Lissoni 2009). The problem of lacking both geographic proximity and the agglomeration of such personnel and competences can be offset and additional creativity, based on divergent and heterogeneous research strategies or academic traditions, will find its way into such collaborative projects (Audretsch and Stephan 1996; Hilpert and Bastian 2007). Thus, it will further contribute to the quality of research as well as providing new findings and new ideas. This, in the end, is more than just a compensation for deficits in both university personnel trained at the forefront of research or outstanding research facilities; such collaboration provides the basis for further, and constantly increasing, creativity and expanding competences that encourage highly attractive collaborative projects in the future (Hilpert 2012a).

Thus, the development of a new technology becomes a collaborative activity that simultaneously, and perhaps paradoxically, is rather exclusive. Only locations and countries are involved and can contribute that provide attractive research opportunities and where scientific researchers or engineers contribute at a significantly high level to a global body of scientific knowledge (Mahroum 1999; Rolfe 2001; Laudel 2005; Favell *et al.* 2006). Government policies that are focused on the development of a new technology can build a strong, competitive position and provide for a country's participation in a new technology, if such necessary conditions are established at highly regarded locations or regions. Scientific excellence plays an important role, to prepare for such processes of networked technology development and to benefit from the exchange of leading edge scientific knowledge (Williams *et al.* 2004; Mason and Nohara 2008). Centres of excellence emerge as nuclei of future technology development and are fundamental for processes of techno-industrial innovation (Mahroum 1999, 2000a, 2000b; Williams *et al.* 2004).

Such processes and future tendencies can be clearly identified in the case of biotechnology which has become a key technology for future industrial innovation and development. It also indicates how such a technology concentrates at particular locations. It points to the role of government policies for such processes and over several decades. It allows one to identify how countries and locations continue to participate in the sector. The case of biotechnology also provides an understanding of whether new centres of excellence and scientific research emerge by producing new scientific knowledge, and whether such centres are recognised as new partners for collaborative research. Such new locations, and their contribution to networked processes of innovation, knowledge production and technology development, also provide a better understanding of the role of government policies both in those countries that were among the first to innovate and those that joined later as highly regarded contributors to the R&T network.

Government policies and the building of Islands of Innovation: the geographical agglomeration of funding and continuity over time

While research facilities are basic to the realisation of research strategies and the search for new knowledge, new solutions to existing problems or simply different ways to understand and handle situations, it is public funding of scientific and technological research that plays an important role in generating progress and new opportunities when applied to marketable products (Hilpert 1998; Bercovitz and Feldman 2006). Such competences are related to particular places that are indicated by research equipment (e.g. laboratories, buildings) and the presence of researchers and engineers. There they work on such scientific and technological issues and transform their research questions into new findings and better knowledge of theoretical or practical value (Bercovitz and Feldman 2006). Private enterprises, of course, do not engage in such research unless they can reliably predict the development of marketable products (Mazzucatto 2011); whereas it is in the public interest to make available such knowledge because it can provide for advanced socio-economic development and high economic value added (Caragliu and Nijkamp 2012).

Regional and national government policies are oriented towards this aim, while they also have to bear in mind a global race in innovation. Competing enterprises based in other countries will also be interested in such leading edge knowledge for its economic exploitation. Thus, the generation of new knowledge is not just a matter of research and better understanding, it is also a research process that, in particular, can impact directly on competitiveness both in quality and timing. This provides for the particular public attractiveness of new techno-scientific opportunities, because these might be exploited economically. The socio-economic importance of technologically relevant knowledge demands strategies that can engage with the internationally leading edge research. National and regional governments, and also programmes launched by the European Union, clearly aim at strengthening research at the highest international level.

Consequently, competitions for public research funding leads towards those institutes, universities and locations where star scientists and well recognised institutions provide a situation where outstanding findings are to be expected. Such research funding further contributes the strengthening of such techno-scientific competences and provides for the continuation of both these outstanding competences and the international recognition of these places. Clearly, it is the new scientific breakthrough that matters, and the participation of scientific research institutes and universities during early periods of development that put such locations in a particularly strong position. Once such windows of opportunity are opened, and a region or location is prepared to take advantage of newly emerging funding opportunities, an agglomeration of funding will take place (Hilpert 2012a).

The limited number of places, and the absence of additional emerging locations within a short period of time, will channel the funding to such places and allow them to become even more outstanding and to continue their leading position over time. This makes them to appear like Islands of Innovation in particular areas of research and technologies (Hilpert 1992). In the early period of scientific research, when there is an absence of economic exploitation, public funding becomes fundamental for both future techno-scientific progress and the regional concentration and continuity of research competences.

The case of biotechnology clearly indicates such a process in Europe and North America. Government funding of biotechnology programmes in the US and Germany, which cover a period of three decades, indicate such processes. A few places of great competence in various areas of biotechnology attract the major shares of funding. During the period 1976 to 1980 these Islands of Innovation in biotechnology received about three quarters of the federal funds in biotechnology in the US and in Germany (see Table 19.1 and 19.2). Although the funding of the biotechnology programmes in both countries has increased significantly, during the period 1986 to 1991 the share that was concentrated on the Islands of Innovation remained almost unchanged, still accounting for about three quarters of funding provided by the national governments. The dominant position of the Islands of Innovation continues even after a quarter of a century, or when almost three decades of research have passed and when a huge growth of funding has taken place – which of course has opened opportunities for plenty of new initiatives. Even then the share of funding still converges at about two thirds for the Islands of Innovation in the US or in Germany, even though biotechnological knowledge has been disseminated and used far more widely.

Thus, certain locations are not just important for conducting research that is fundamental for new technologies, but furthermore these locations continue to be outstanding and fundamental for the processes of technology development that follow from these early findings. Here, at the Islands of Innovation, most attractive research is concentrated and an outstanding body of knowledge is available because of both the location's own research and that it is based on transfer of knowledge from earlier collaboration with other Islands of Innovation. This makes

Table 19.1 Distribution of biotechnology research funding, USA

Period	*Funding NIH to US Islands of Innovation (million $)*	*Funding NIH to US Islands of Innovation (%)*	*Total NIH funding (million $)*
1976–1980	365.9	75.8	482.8
1986–1991	5,371.9	75.8	7,085.6
2000–2003	41,906.3	64.2	65,252.8
2014	3,923.4	67.0	5,852.4

Note: data for 2014 from a new National Institute of Health (NIH)-dataset, URL: http://report.nih.gov/categorical_spending_project_listing.aspx?FY=2014&ARRA=N&DCat=Biotechnology, last accessed 18 August 2015.

Source: Hilpert (2012b: 42), for last row see note above.

Table 19.2 Distribution of biotechnology research funding, Germany

Period	*Funding to German Islands of Innovation*	*Funding to German Islands of Innovation (%)*	*Total funding*
1976–1980	107,541,184.14 m DM	77,6	138,538,789.82 m DM
1986–1990	309,185,548.67 m DM	73,0	423,490,280.20 m DM
2001–2005	550,784,120.95 m €	68,8	800,003,014.18 m €
2010–2015	100,966,210.00 m €	62,4	161.882.713,00 m €

Note: data for 2010–2015 from a new dataset of the German federal government: Förderkatalog der Bundesregierung, URL: http://foerderportal.bund.de/foekat/jsp/StartAction.do, last accessed 16 July 2015. After 1990 the German government provided particularly strong support to former East Germany to build capable research institutions. Thus, data on West German were used to examine the process.

Source: Hilpert (2012b: 42), for last row see note above.

these locations the home of attractive partners for research that provides for a continuation of their favourable position in global R&T development. It is in these locations that outside enterprises, institutes and individual academic researchers will search for partners when aiming at collaboration.

Within the broad area of research in biotechnology such Islands of Innovation develop divergent patterns of specialisation that are based on new opportunities or on existing competences. These are equipped to provide further contributions to regional or national economic development. Localisation of Islands of Innovation follows from existing expertise in scientific research that has a potential for new technologies; in addition it indicates opportunities for a particular location to contribute to networked technology development as well as adding higher value because of its participation in techno-industrial innovation. Patterns of specialisation become the basis that allows the development of outstanding expertise (Abel and Deitz 2009). The existence and identifiability of these locations with clear R&T strengths both creates and subsequently maintains the necessity of collaboration, and enables the generation of both new knowledge and scientific progress, which consequently reaches out across countries and borders. A system of Islands of Innovation emerges through agglomeration of techno-scientific research and collaboration. Government funding that has permitted such academic research is fundamental to establish such a system that allows for building strong Islands of Innovation and internationally recognised centres of excellence.

Networking Islands of Innovation: a collaborative process of technology development

Once such an agglomeration of funding at places of outstanding techno-scientific expertise is realised, these centres of excellence continue to develop their individual research strategies and, in addition, they search for partners with whom to realise their research projects. Universities and public research institutes play an important role in the generation of new findings and knowledge, as well as providing for the creation of newly founded research based enterprises. Based on academic research in different areas of biotechnology, this provides the basis for a widely recognised body of knowledge concerning strong partners for research at the different Islands of Innovation. Collaboration across different locations, which refer to divergent research traditions, allows for synergy based on different areas of expertise in new products and technologies. Consequently, such collaboration includes regions where there are potential partners who are ready to add leading edge knowledge and research competences. Both the collaboration among partners located at Islands of Innovation, and the collaboration between those located at different Islands of Innovation and sometimes at other places of less intensively concentrated research competence further contribute to both the outstanding position of these centres of excellence and their strength in technology development. Because there are more opportunities for application and synergy of the new knowledge that is produced, and also when knowledge is increasingly spread out through collaboration, this position is continued (Caragliu and Nijkamp 2012).

Thus, the building of Islands of Innovation through government policies comes to be more than just strategies for participation in innovation and attractive socio-economic development; rather they become constitutive to the process of innovation itself. Collaboration among partners from different location permits the development of new technologies both despite and because of which country, region or metropolis they are located in (Bercovitz and Feldman 2006). The exchange of knowledge and competence and, in addition, the generation of new leading edge knowledge and findings will continue and thus provide for continuation of their strong positions in a global race for techno-scientific progress. This, again, contributes to both their outstanding situation and their difference from regions and locations that do not emerge as an Island of Innovation. Clearly, such networks of collaborative research among enterprises refer strongly to existing centres of excellence (see Figure 19.1). Techno-scientific knowledge indicates a strong relationship to the locations previously established through successful agglomeration of research funding and the capability to continue over long periods of time.

Once such a position (in a collaborative process of both the production of a new body of knowledge and the generation of new techno-scientific progress) is established, based on previous government policies, there follows a concentration of economic exploitation (Florida 2002; Berry and Glaeser 2005; Lawton Smith and Waters 2005). Consequently, economic effects follow from patterns of competences and are based on the successful search for partners to pursue collaborative economic strategies. Thus, of course, there is a first preference for places, where such expertise is located. Although the process of techno-scientific research may differ from a technology-based strategy of commercialisation, the generation of a new technology and its presentation in markets can be realised only where there is an outstanding level of competence. This might include additional partners from elsewhere, or with different, complementary competences, but such a search needs to focus predominantly on locations where such competences are agglomerated at a particularly high level of competence. Following earlier processes, and based on the legal situation of those included in these processes, a network emerges that again uses the Islands of Innovation as an important basis for the economic exploitation of new technologies (see Figure 19.2).

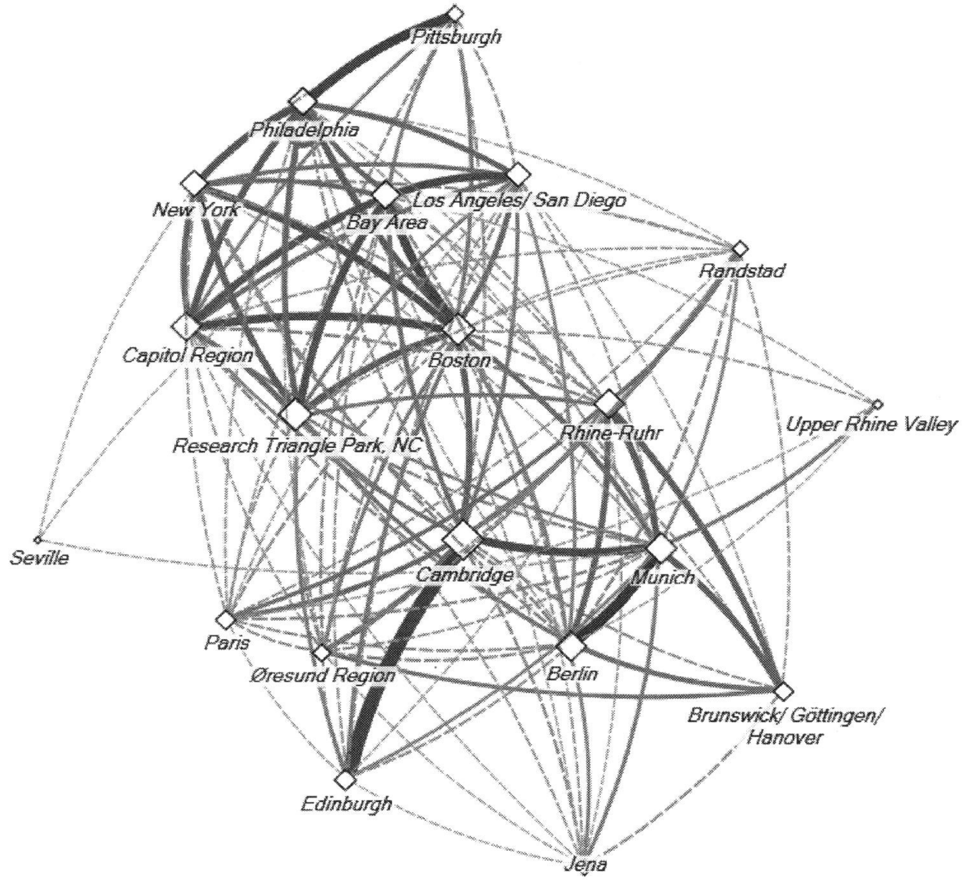

Figure 19.1 Networks of collaboration in research among enterprises (N = approx. 2,800 collaborations).
Note: N=3216, equal to 67.2 per cent of all collaborations in research, N=4786.
Source: Author.

As with techno-scientific research, so economic exploitation is realised as a network that pays little reference to borders, but rather emerges from the individual interests of the partners involved. Although they emerge because of the capability of governments to establish such centres of internationally recognised scientific excellence, of collaborative research and of the search for strong partners, the process of technology development has also emerged as a process that is not addressed to countries or regions. Such national or regional effects thus follow from the building of Islands of Innovation and their international recognition as locations where outstanding competences and economic capability can be found. A national or regional participation in new technologies, such as biotechnologies, is introduced because of the expertise involved in research and development. The body of knowledge established and the competences in research acquired are fundamental to the contributions that are made to the development of leading edge technologies. Once these contributions are made, open markets allow for a joint exploitation of economic opportunities – and further contribute to the attraction of networked innovation.

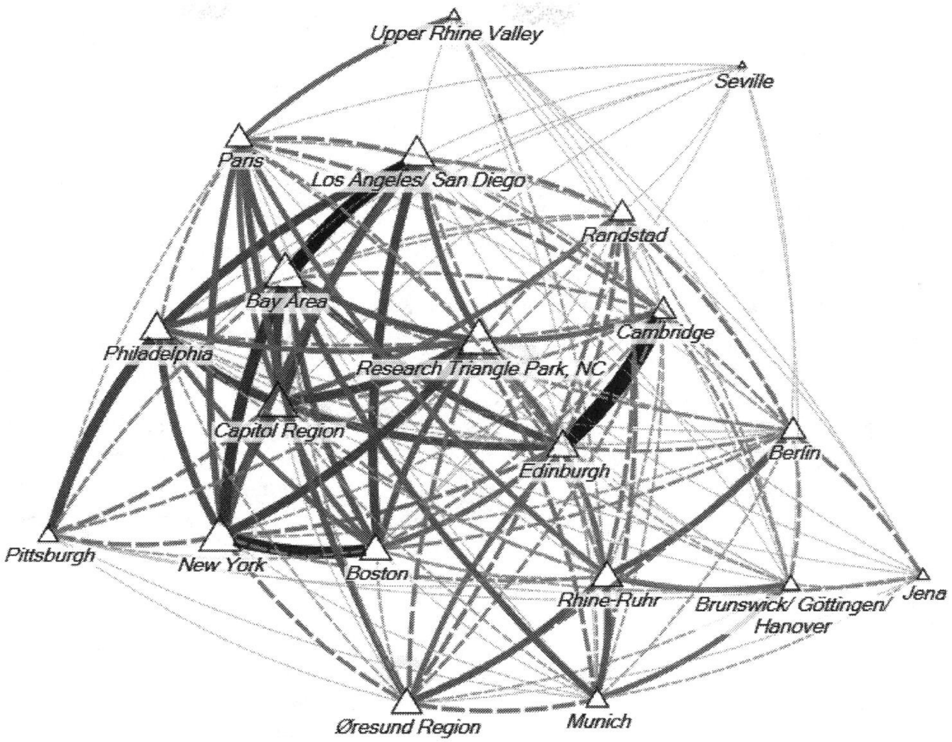

Figure 19.2 Networks of collaboration in economic exploitation among enterprises.
Note: N=1213, equal to 63.5 per cent of all collaborations in economic exploitation, N=1911.
Source: Author.

Cross fertilisation through the mobility of creative human capital: the exchange of innovative labour

The fundamental role of scientific competences, and a rich body of leading edge knowledge for the participation in new technologies such as modern biotechnologies, clearly indicates the importance of continuously producing new research findings and techno-scientific progress, which is able to provide the next steps in innovation. Since governments can provide research funding according to their budgetary capacities, and laboratories might be established, research ideas and strategies need to be created by individual knowledge workers (Avveduto 2001; Lawton Smith and Waters 2005; see also Ackers 2005; Breschi and Lissoni 2009). Traditions in research and particular areas of expertise, as well as patterns of specialization of individual locations or Islands of Innovation, indicate existing variations in both paths of innovative development and contributions to networked processes of technology development (Hilpert 1992). While there are competing interests among individual top scientists, it is recognised that a particular highly recognised academic or star scientist who is an extremely innovative resource at one location, yet may have little to contribute at a different location with different characteristics at this particular point of technology development (Hilpert 2012a).

An existing research environment, a specialisation in a particular area of technology (e.g. in a particular area of biotechnology) and an established industrial structure or situation of newly founded research-based enterprises – which allow for highly individual technological applications – require particular competences, orientations and experiences even from such highly creative personnel. Technology development and innovation relate closely to the opportunities that exist at an Island of Innovation and other locations of innovative potential at a particular point in time. Such a window of opportunity demands an appropriately innovative labour force; and such requirements may change once the existing innovative opportunity has been used and a new technological opportunity has been developed. While a window of opportunity needs particularly creative labour, this labour may not have the same impact anymore at the location once the technology is established (Hilpert 2012a); whereas it might be equipped to make an extraordinarily important contribution in a different situation at a different location (Trippl 2012).

This creates a constantly changing demand for particular competences and creative ideas as the process of innovation and technology development continues. The wide body of knowledge accumulated by an individual researcher makes them a highly valuable contributor to a situation characterised by a new and divergent environment (Hilpert 2012a). Thus, an exchange of labour can be found among locations. Since outstanding competences and particularly interesting bodies of knowledge can be acquired at highly respected locations, outstanding personnel from research institutes and leading technology enterprises in Islands of Innovation are of particular interest for recruiters (Caragliu and Nijkamp 2012). Based on their experience and competence such knowledge workers may provide new and creative impact in different situations (Audretsch and Stephan 1996; Criscuolo 2005; Breschi and Lissoni 2009). Consequently, in biotechnology the exchange of labour through recruitment can be recognised predominantly among Islands of Innovation (see Figure 19.3). In Europe and the US the recruitment of academics in biotechnology at universities and public research institutes hardly changes and indicates that about two thirds are from institutions located at Islands of Innovation. After about a quarter of a century of biotechnology research has passed, and the funding of such research has increased extraordinarily, these locations and their institutions still dominate in academic research, education of next generation of top-researchers, and are outstanding locations to exchange knowledge, to organize research networks and exchange academic labour. This spreads both the availability of scientific findings and the access to techno-scientific progress in biotechnology among these locations.

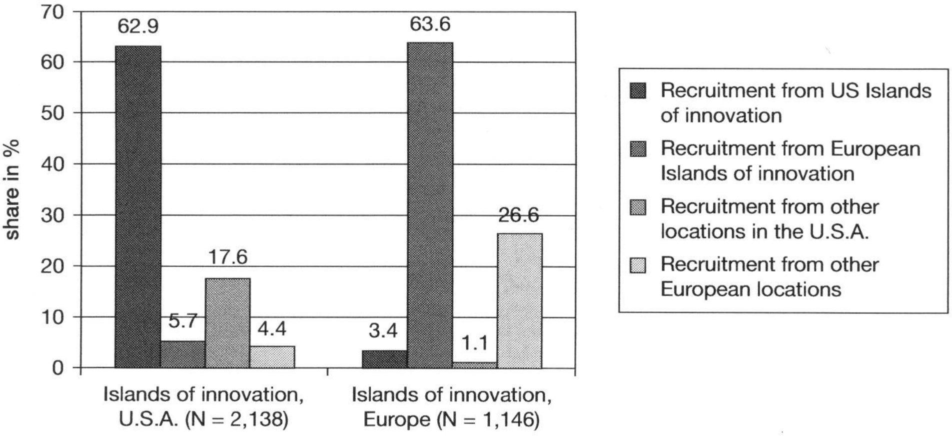

Figure 19.3 Recruitment of academics at Islands of Innovation by type of sending location.
Source: Author.

Funding of biotechnology research in Europe and the US thus was not only important during an early period of research and during the entire lifespan of biotechnology, it also allowed the employment of top researchers who prefer locations that are highly scientifically attractive and foster a vital exchange of expertise and findings, and that are also well placed in global research networks (Mahroum 1999, 2000b; Williams *et al.* 2004; Trippl 2012). In future, based on the highly creative academic personnel, contributions to biotechnology development will be made predominantly from these locations which act as a network of Islands of Innovation (Figure 19.4).

The increasing importance of research-based enterprises, which are founded on the basis of university research or of other publicly funded research institutes, provides a particularly advantageous situation. Outstanding academic research at these locations and their embeddedness in global networks allows for participation in technology development and economic exploitation at the forefront of science-based innovation. A particularly close relationship between leading edge academic research and enterprises, which are drivers of innovation, provides for the basis to continue the dynamic situation of a location characterised by innovative processes of advanced industrial development. In addition, this again helps to continue participation in the process of networked innovation.

A close relationship between academic research, education and economic exploitation, including newly founded enterprises, characterises the situation of innovation in biotechnology.

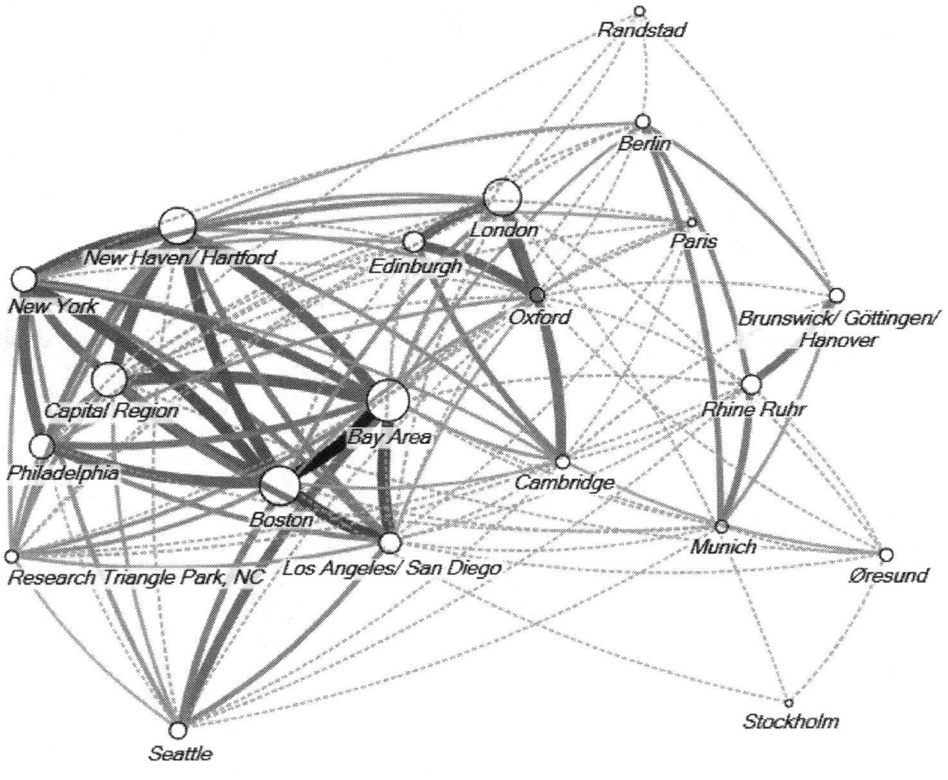

Figure 19.4 Patterns of recruitment among Islands of Innovation.

Note: N=2235, equal to 68.1 per cent of all recruitments, N=3284.

Source: Author.

Once this is achieved, and an Island of Innovation maintains its strong position within the global network, it will both contribute to future technology development and participate in economic exploitation. Particular competences that helped compete successfully for research funds and the attraction of knowledge workers from other Islands of Innovation (Hilpert 2012b; Trippl 2012) are fundamental to a situation where competences constantly modernise and expand in a way that is required to continue to participate in the changing world of biotechnology. The changes are introduced by innovation, and partners, locations and institutions continue to be involved to the extent they can assist in the generation of new knowledge and findings.

New locations of knowledge production in biotechnology: the flexibility of a research-based network

While modern biotechnology was developed in its various areas and opportunities for application predominantly at Islands of Innovation located in the leading Western industrialised countries of Europe and in the US, the situation in academic knowledge production passed through changes. In the early years of the new millennium fewer than 5 per cent of collaborations included partners from outside these countries. Nevertheless, this situation has changed and new countries and locations have emerged. East Asian industrialising countries have paid particular attention to university education and their young scholars were encouraged to spend time in established Western centres of biotechnology research to learn from internationally recognised academics about this important technology. The strong economic development of these countries allowed them to accumulate a sufficient amount of capital and to provide sufficient public budgets that allowed academic researchers who returned to their home countries to carry out research to international standards. Thus they became recognised by the established centres of biotechnology research.

The situation of knowledge production in biotechnology became characterised by contributions from countries and centres of excellence that did not exist before. Since academic research and the production of new knowledge provides the basis for technological competence and future opportunities in participation in technology development and economic exploitation, today, changes in the global structure of academic knowledge production are important indicators regarding future development. Publication of scientific research findings in recognised journals indicate the quality of the research carried out; in addition, co-publication indicates whether the authors are regarded as strong partners. Thus, co-publication also points to their potential to contribute to networked technology development.

While, from the 1970s until the turn of the millennium, research in biotechnology was clearly dominated by a number of Islands of Innovation located in the US and Western Europe, the current situation indicates some significant changes (see Table 19.3). In 2010 North America accounted for 38.1 per cent of the global co-publications (US: 34.3 per cent; Canada: 3.8 per cent) and continued its leading position in biotechnology. In Europe the centres that were already in existence before the political changes on the continent in 1990 still continued their dominant position; these Western European countries (United Kingdom, France, Germany, Italy, The Netherlands, Belgium, Switzerland and the Scandinavian Countries) contribute 31.7 per cent to the total global co-publications; an additional 5.1 per cent are contributed by the other European countries. Including some other Western countries, the global situation, which existed from the beginning, had broadly been maintained. These countries still contribute about three quarters of the total co-publications.

Nevertheless, some significant changes have emerged within just a decade. Countries such as China, South Korea or Taiwan, which were not contributing to a significant extent before,

Table 19.3 Contribution to global co-publication on biotech research in 2010, Top 20 countries

Rank	*Country*	*Total of Inst Share* 43,164.2	*Per cent of total Inst Share* 100.0
1	UNITED STATES	14,824.2	34.3
2	GERMANY	2,852.2	6.6
3	UNITED KINGDOM	2,665.1	6.2
4	JAPAN	2,432.2	5.6
5	CHINA	2,415.0	5.6
6	FRANCE	1,963.2	4.5
7	ITALY	1,666.5	3.9
8	CANADA	1,633.8	3.8
9	SPAIN	1,212.0	2.8
10	NETHERLANDS	1,169.8	2.7
11	AUSTRALIA	1,155.5	2.7
12	KOREA	914.7	2.1
13	SWITZERLAND	650.9	1.5
14	BRAZIL	604.9	1.4
15	SWEDEN	592.9	1.4
16	BELGIUM	513.3	1.2
17	TAIWAN	501.5	1.2
18	INDIA	477.0	1.1
19	DENMARK	385.1	0.9
20	ISRAEL	346.7	0.8
	TOP 20 Countries	38,976.6	90.3

Source: own calculation based on Thomson Reutters Citation Index.

in 2010 account for about a tenth of all co-publications. This strong position is even more significant, because simultaneously the number of publications has increased fundamentally (between 1980 and 2010 the number of co-publications has more than tripled). This clearly indicates the extraordinary efforts made in East Asia and the strong dynamism in academic research that is going on in this region. Clearly, there are new contributors emerging that will both contribute to the global body of knowledge and benefit from technology development based on a global network of research, and the exchange of knowledge and expertise through collaboration.

This globally extended process of knowledge production in biotechnology is still characterised by the established Islands of Innovation which are now complemented by additional locations that are predominantly located in East Asia. The core locations that were identified almost a quarter of a century ago (Hilpert 1992) are still outstanding and contribute almost 30 per cent of all co-publications (see Table 19.4). While the strongest Islands of Innovation in the US and Europe contribute to the global body of co-publications in biotechnology at a similar level to many nation states, they continue to be elements of a global system rather than performing as dominant individual drivers of academic research. Similarly to the early processes of biotechnology oriented research and development, the newly emerging strong contributors in East Asia are characterised by centres of excellence. This enables these countries to perform as both contributors and participators in relation to a growing global body of knowledge in biotechnology.

This situation was formed on the basis of government policies of both countries newly emerging in global biotechnology research, and countries already well established within the

Table 19.4 Contribution to global co-publication on biotech research in 2010, Islands of Innovation

Rank	*Island of Innovation*	*Total of Inst Share*	*Per cent of total Inst Share*
1	Boston	1,299.6	3,0
2	Capitol Region	1,202.9	2.8
3	London	1,131.6	2.6
4	New York City Conurbation	1,130.0	2.6
5	Los Angeles-San Diego	1,084.3	2.5
7	San Francisco Bay Area	836.7	1.9
8	Paris (Ile de France)	769.9	1.8
9	Austin–Dallas–Houston–San Antonio	662.3	1.5
11	Amsterdam/Rotterdam	531.0	1.2
12	Philadelphia	517.9	1.2
16	Chicago–Milwaukee	469.0	1.1
17	Research Triangle Park, NC	462.2	1.1
19	Rhine-Ruhr	377.0	0.9
21	Milan	372.9	0.9
24	Seattle	349.8	0.8
27	Copenhagen/Øresund	323.8	0.8
28	Munich	317.4	0.7
40	New Haven-Hartford	248.1	0.6
46	Karlsruhe/Heidelberg/Stuttgart	229.9	0.5
50	Lyon–Grenoble	202.7	0.5
52	Marseille	191.3	0.4
91	Darmstadt–Frankfurt	103.4	0.2
131	Torino	76.4	0.2
	Islands of Innovation total	12,890.2	29.9

Source: own calculation based on Thomson Reutters Citation Index.

global network and continue to participate in government programmes (in Europe complemented by the programmes of the European Union). Because of newly emerging locations this indicates that there are global changes to be found that take advantage of the existing collaborative networks. As new and recognised contributors they can also participate in the existing collaborative networks of competence. The expansion of the network again is characterised by regional concentration and the building of centres of excellence. Locations such as Seoul in South Korea, Beijing, Hong Kong and Shanghai in China, or Singapore contribute between 1.3 and 0.5 per cent to the global number of co-publications. This indicates the highly dynamic economic processes in East Asia where capital accumulated based on the success of traditional industries in international markets, but today it is heavily re-invested through such government technology programmes. The recognizable contribution of places such as São Paulo and Rio de Janeiro in Brazil (0.6 per cent) indicates that such processes can also be induced elsewhere. Since this is the only example outside East Asia, this indicates that there is an uneven global participation in the changing network, which presently favours East Asia.

Research findings and contributions to a global body of publications in biotechnology are, of course, indicators for new centres of competence and excellence in countries that were not strong in biotechnology before. Nevertheless, this does not yet provide a clear picture of the quality of the work being done and does not clearly indicate the extent of its innovative effects. Still a difference in creativity, innovative impact and leading edge research might be involved. But, what is clearly indicated is that there are new centres and they are related to particular areas of competences and patterns of specialization.

While such new centres emerge, they adapt to the existing networks. Again, as a basis, these innovative metropolises establish a strong research structure that provides for a participation in the network of knowledge production. The strength in research and the concentration of both well recognised research programmes and academics help to make a location well known and enable their inclusion within such networks (see Table 19.5). The share of co-publication with partners based in their own location or region is rather similar to the share of intra-regional collaboration that could be found concerning research and economic exploitation among biotechnology enterprises in Europe and the US. And indeed, these leading, established geographical centres of research are also home to important collaborators for these newly emerging centres. On average about one third of all co-publications refer to a relationship between these newly emerging centres and partners at locations in Europe or in North America.

Although partners from these continents play an important role in these emerging relationships the recognition from partners based at the established Islands of Innovation is much less than that to be found within the well-established collaborative networks. While in the case of collaborations between these new locations and North America at least a majority relates to established Islands of Innovation; it is much less when the relationship with European partners is considered, where only about one third refers to collaborations that include established European Islands of Innovation. These emerging networks might indicate a divergent pattern of network participation. Almost one third of their co-publications together with authors based at these locations are with partners from Asia; again, the concentration is not particularly strong or dominant, while in some cases other locations than the newly emerging Asian centres are the basis for partners in co-publication.

This strong relationship of these newly emerging Asian locations in biotechnology towards partners from locations that are neither from an established European nor an American Island of Innovation, but towards partners that are not based at the newly outstanding Asian biotechnology locations, appears to reflect a particular modification to the previous situation. Here, again, concentration is an important basis for participation in pre-existing networks, but de-concentrated locations play a more important role as home for partners in co-publication. Nevertheless, the concentration of knowledge again provides an advantage and helps to establish a relationship with the leading American and European research fairly rapidly.

Whereas processes of biotechnology driven innovation in Europe and North America indicate tendencies towards continentalisation with about three quarters of all collaborations taking place among partners from the same continent, this is not equally strong with regard to the Asian locations – although it can sometimes be detected. Besides the case of Singapore, researchers from these locations work with Asian partners to an extent that at least equals their numbers of co-publications with Western partners. Although such co-publications indicate a certain national preference with regard to China and Chinese locations, this is neither particularly strong nor to be noticed clearly at other emerging strong locations in Asia. Activities indicate attempts both to participate in existing networks and to contribute to the processes achieved within this global system of collaboration. Thus, these newly emerging locations finally tend to add to and to integrate into established networks while introducing a certain change of network structures.

While such new contributors join these networks there is also a continuing problem of the migration of academic labour and of other knowledge workers towards the Western industrialised countries and the US or the United Kingdom in particular. Star scientists are predominantly to be found at Islands of Innovation and other research intensive locations in the US and Europe (Trippl 2012). In addition, such star scientists, who are regarded as particularly important contributors to science-based innovation, demonstrate a strong tendency to migrate towards

Table 19.5 Participation of new locations in existing networks, 2010

Metropolis	*North America*		*Europe (incl. EU, Switzerland and Norway)*		*Asia*				*Other emerging metropolises in biotech*	
	Total[a]	*Share of IoI*[b]	*Total*[a]	*Share of IoI*[b]	*Total*[a]	*Selected Asian Metropolises*[c]	*Collaboration at the own Metropolis*[d]	*Other Asian Locations*	*Sao Paulo and Rio de Janeiro*[e]	*Collaboration at the own Metropolis*[d]
Singapore	967 (26.2)	671 (69.4)	891 (24.14)	327 (36.7)	1516 (41.04)	1137 (75)	938 (61.87)	379 (25)	7 (2.21)	–
Shanghai	840 (26.32)	476 (56.67)	319 (9.99)	85 (26.65)	1942 (60.84)	1201 (61.84)	749 (38.57)	741 (38.16)	1 (1.1)	–
Seoul	1083 (16.95)	608 (56.14)	470 (7.36)	158 (33.62)	4761 (74.52)	2573 (54.04)	2402 (50.45)	2188 (45.96)	5 (6.67)	–
São Paulo	450 (19.58)	265 (58.89)	424 (18.45)	139 (32.78)	89 (3.87)	(19) (21.35)	–	70 (78.65)	792 (59.33)	709 (53.11)
Rio de Janeiro	205 (19.61)	109 (53.17)	186 (17.8)	67 (36.02)	29 (2.78)	(5) (17.24)	–	24 (82.76)	382 (61.12)	299 (47.84)
Beijing	1267 (25.74)	707 (55.8)	640 (13)	200 (31.25)	2878 (58.46)	1599 (55.56)	1014 (35.23)	1279 (44.44)	6 (4.35)	–
Hongkong-Shenzen	793 (15.94)	419 (52.84)	545 (10.95)	194 (35.6)	3365 (67.64)	2524 (75.01)	1995 (59.29)	841 (24.99)	5 (1.84)	–

Note: per cent values in brackets.

[a] Share of co-publications with partners from North America/Europe/Asia in all co-publications of the location.

[b] Share of co-publications with partners from North American/European Islands of Innovation in all co-pubs with partners from North America/Europe.

[c] Share of co-publications with partners at the here selected Asian metropolises in all co-publications with partners from Asia.

[d] Percentages are related with the share of contributions in co-pubs from the own location with others from Asia/not from USA, European Union or Asia.

[e] Share of co-publications with partners not from North America, Europe or Asia.

Source: own calculation based on Thomson Reutters Citation Index.

such places. India is well known as a major exporter of highly trained academic labour (Khadria 2001). In Silicon Valley there is also a large number of Indian and Chinese entrepreneurs who have founded highly innovative and research-based new enterprises (Saxenian 2002; see also Malecki 1989). Newly emerging locations clearly have to face the challenge that the participation in such networks brings, and that recognition by the existing centres of expertise and by leading Islands of Innovation may create a highly specialised brain drain away from these countries and their innovative locations (Mahroum 1999, 2000b; Williams *et al.* 2004).

Only a few might return to their home countries and locations. Although they may continue relationships with their home countries (Simonen and McCann 2008), they contribute first of all to the strength of the locations where they are located. Thus, the participation by newly emerging Asian research locations may contribute to existing networks, but the situation they face might continue to be different from Western locations for a foreseeable future. New fields of research and strongly growing fields where these new technologies are applied, in general, demonstrate a high demand for such labour (Hilpert 2012a). Thus, newly developed research centres contribute both additional knowledge and partners for collaboration, as well as being additional sources of university trained labour which is frequently attracted to migrate to Islands of Innovation and to provide the additional labour that is required to continue the processes of research and development related with biotechnology.

Conclusions: a globally expanding network provides widening opportunities for participation

Biotechnology is regarded as a key technology for the twenty-first century. It is clearly based on scientific breakthroughs and requires the existence of particular local conditions regarding the demand for academic labour, and networks of collaboration and knowledge exchange. Additional resources at new locations, and the technology's close relationship with economic exploitation, reduce the lead time from research to new products or to new areas of application. The speedy processes of knowledge production incorporate new locations into established networks as soon as these are recognised as centres of both expertise and excellence, which can contribute effectively to ongoing or new research projects. Thus, institutions, enterprises and individual researchers are constantly alert to identifying such potential contributors – at least in certain areas of research. New technologies have often been regarded as a field where leading industrialised countries improve their international competitiveness, whereas newly industrialising countries will have to overcome technological barriers to entry to participate in such socio-economic development.

In the electronics industries, the case of Samsung indicates that new technologies are maturing and a particular country's dominating position need not necessarily continue. It might occur that a newcomer enters the scene and challenges existing providers. Since such development is based on scientific research this also allows participation from locations that supply the context necessary although there may not be a long tradition in leading edge research. Singapore, South Korea or China provide interesting examples of government policies that invested significant funds that were acquired earlier from the manufacture of less advanced products. Government policies were fundamentally important for both the original generation of biotechnology and the creation of Islands of Innovation in leading Western industrialised countries. Today, government policies are important for the participation of some newly emerging industrialised countries. Policies based on the education of academic labour – the introduction of effective systems in education and research – and the building of infrastructures of scientific research, allow for a widening of the established global network of collaborative innovation.

Simultaneously such additional contributors and new locations of research can be successfully developed only in exchange with the already existing Islands of Innovation and the body of knowledge exchanged within the established networks of collaboration. Consequently, among these additional countries and locations no clear tendencies towards continentalisation can be identified. Nevertheless, although there is a strong element of collaboration and complementarity in the competences involved when such networks of innovation emerge and grow, of course, there is also economic competition among the contributors and the locations included within networks. Biotechnology helps one to understand that international division of labour in a new technology is both competitive, based on the excellence of research, and collaborative, based on the exchange of knowledge for the generation of mutual benefits. This allows for a more detailed understanding of both the international division of labour and the opportunities for government policies that help to place a country and its leading research locations within such a global system.

It is, of course, interesting that such positive effects of different policies that contribute to biotechnology-based innovation are to be found in countries that are characterised by open economies and networked technology development. It is this formal and cultural openness that allows collaboration as the fundamental basis for mutual benefits. The free exchange of ideas and the openness to collaboration helps to identify complementary competences that may help to enrich existing research strategies. Such a situation is favourable for both large and small countries, as well as for technologically advanced countries and newly emerging countries, and for new locations of excellence. As Samsung demonstrated, a new economic actor did not ruin the US-American electronics industry – rather it might have contributed to further attempts at innovation. Thus, new biotechnology provides opportunities for a rich variety of government policies in different countries and different situations; but, such economic opportunities for techno-industrial innovation have always followed on from clear and focused government policies.

The process of networked innovation in biotechnology raises a number of new research questions that help one to compare and understand both the processes and its effects better and to learn about the specifics of individual technologies, as well as more general tendencies. Obviously, industrial profiles and patterns of specialization in academic and applied research are important to enable participation in such processes that are based almost immediately on scientific progress. There is still an open question, however, about how fundamentally new such a technology needs to be to permit the growth of new locations and countries as contributors to its networks. By contrast, one could easily imagine that a new technology based on a close relationship with existing research and industry structures may vary from the biotechnology example. This would help to provide a better understanding of the needs for variations in government policies.

In addition, there is the question of time frames which needs to be investigated more thoroughly. While an early participation in both the forefront of research and in new technologies undoubtedly provides an advantage, there could emerge a situation where more countries have strong academic and applied research capabilities, so that such advantages do not last as long as indicated in biotechnology. This will have an important impact on the return on investment that was required from a new technology by public and private investors.

Nevertheless, both publicly funded academic research in areas of high potential for new technologies, and an effective education system involving as many gifted people as possible, and allowing as many people as possible to make use of their intellectual capabilities, tend to be important in a situation that demands knowledge workers and requires techno-scientific progress. This may have highly divergent impacts on the policies of particular countries and on the politics that are fundamental to foster techno-scientific development. It is, of course, clearly related to the research and knowledge intensity of a new technology and its application. This is an area from where the new technological and economic advances might be made. Thus, technology policies and the generation of new technologies and the academic research they require clearly link to the political interests and orientations of a society. The integration into a networked system and the mutually beneficial situation of participation in innovative products with high value added may generate political effects that are so far unknown and awaiting identification.

References

Abel, J. and Deitz, R.R., 2009: *Do Colleges and Universities Increase Their Region's Human Capital?* New York: Federal Reserve Bank of New York.

Ackers, L., 2005: Promoting scientific mobility and balanced growth in the European research area. *Innovation: The European Journal of Social Science Research* 18(3), pp. 301–317.

Audretsch, D.B. and Stephan, P.E., 1996: Company–scientist locational links: the case of biotechnology. *American Economic Review*, 86(3), pp. 641–652.

Avveduto, S., 2001: International mobility of PhDs. In: OECD (eds): *Innovative People: Mobility of skilled personnel in national innovation systems*. Paris: OECD.

Bercovitz, J. and Feldman, M., 2006: Entrepreneurial universities and technology transfer: a conceptual framework for understanding knowledge-based economic development. *Journal of Technology Transfer* 31, pp. 175–188.

Berry, C. and Glaeser, E., 2005: The divergence of human capital levels across cities. NBER working paper series. National Bureau of Economic Research. Cambridge, MA: Cambridge Press.

Breschi, S. and Lissoni, F., 2009: Mobility of skilled workers and co-invention networks: an anatomy of localized knowledge flows. *Journal of Economic Geography* 9, pp. 439–468.

Caragliu, A. and Nijkamp, P., 2012: From Islands to Hubs of Innovation: connecting innovative regions. In: Hilpert, U. and Lawton Smith, H. (eds): *Networking Regionalised Innovative Labour Markets*. London and New York: Routledge, pp. 119–135.

Criscuolo, P., 2005: On the road again: researcher mobility inside the R&D network. *Research Policy* 35, pp. 1350–1365.

Favell, A., Feldbaaum, M. and Smith, M.P., 2006: Mobility, migration and technology workers: an introduction. *Knowledge Technology and Policy* 29, pp. 3–6.

Florida, R., 2002: The economic geography of talent. *Annals of the Association of American Geographers* 92(4), pp. 743–755.

Hilpert, U., 1992: *Archipelago Europe – Islands of Innovation*, Synthesis Report. Prospective Dossier No. 1: Science, Technology and Social and Economic Cohesion in the Community. Brussels: Commission of the European Communities.

Hilpert, U., 1998: Regieren zwischen Problemnähe und Regierungsrationalität. Die EU-Politik im Geflecht veränderter intergouvernementaler Arbeitsteilung. In: Hilpert, U. and Holtmann, E. (eds): *Regieren und intergouvernementale Beziehungen*. Opladen: Leske und Budrich, pp. 193–214.

Hilpert, U., 2012a: Networking innovative regional labour markets: towards spatial concentration and mutual exchange of competence, knowledge and synergy. In: Hilpert, U. and Lawton Smith, H. (eds): *Networking Regionalised Innovative Labour Markets*. London and New York: Routledge, pp. 3–31.

Hilpert, U., 2012b: Labour for regional innovation: the role of researchers for development and patterns of recruitment. In: Hilpert, U. and Lawton Smith, H. (eds): *Networking Regionalised Innovative Labour Markets*. London and New York: Routledge, pp. 35–57.

Hilpert, U. and Bastian, D., 2007: Innovation und Beschäftigung, Jena: Unpublished research report.

Hilpert, U. and Holtmann, E. (eds), 1998: *Regieren und intergouvernementale Beziehungen*. Opladen: Leske und Budrich.

Hilpert, U. and Lawton Smith, H. (eds), 2012: *Networking Regionalized Innovative Labour Markets*. London and New York: Routledge.

Khadria, B., 2001: Shifting paradigms of globalization: the twenty-first century transition toward generics in skilled migration from India. *International Migration* 39(5), pp. 45–71.

Laudel, G., 2005: Migration currents among the scientific elite. *Minerva* 43, pp. 377–395.

Lawton Smith, H. and Waters, R., 2005: Employment mobility in high-technology agglomerations: the cases of Oxfordshire and Cambridgeshire. *Area* 37(2), pp.189–198.

Mahroum, S., 1999: Global magnets: science and technology disciplines and departments in the United Kingdom. *Minerva* 37, pp. 379–390.

Mahroum, S., 2000a: Scientists and global spaces. *Technology and Society* 22, pp. 513–523.

Mahroum, S., 2000b: Scientific mobility: an agent of scientific expansion and institutional empowerment. *Science Communication* 21, pp. 367–378.

Malecki, E.J., 1989: What about people in high technology? Some research and policy considerations. *Growth and Change* 20(1), pp. 67–78.

Mason, G. and Nohara, H., 2008: What's left of internal labour markets for scientists and engineers? New evidence from the UK and France. Paper prepared for IWPLMS conference at Porto, 8–10 September 2008. Available online at: www.roa.unimaas.nl/workshoplabourmarkets/papers/MASON_nohara.pdf (accessed 21 August 2009).

Mazzucatto, M., 2011: *The Entrepreneurial State*. London: Demos.

Millar, J. and Salt, J., 2008: Portfolios of mobility: the movement of expertise in transnational corporations in two sectors – aerospace and extractive industries. *Global Networks* 8 (1), pp. 25–50.

Rolfe, H., 2001: Qualifications and international mobility: a case study of the European chemicals industry. *National Institute Economic Review* 175, pp. 85–94.

Saxenian, A., 2002: Silicon Valley's new immigrant high-growth entrepreneurs. *Economic Development Quarterly* 16(1), pp. 20–31.

Simonen, J. and McCann, P., 2008a: Firm innovation: the influence of R&D cooperation and the geography of human capital inputs. *Journal of Urban Economics* 64(1), pp. 146–154.

Straubhaar, T., 2000: International mobility of the highly skilled: brain gain, brain drain or brain exchange. HWWA Discussion Paper 88/2000, Hamburg: Hamburg Institute of International Economics.

Trippl, M., 2012: Star scientists, Islands of Innovation and internationally networked labour markets. In: Hilpert, U. and Lawton Smith, H. (eds): *Networking Regionalised Innovative Labour Markets*. London and New York: Routledge, pp. 58–77.

Williams, A.M., Baláz, V. and Wallace, C., 2004: International labour mobility and uneven regional development in Europe: human capital, knowledge and entrepreneurship, *European Urban and Regional Studies* 11(1), pp. 27–46.

20

GOVERNANCE OF BIOFUEL PRODUCTION IN THE UNITED STATES

Sharmistha Bagchi-Sen and Peter Kedron

Introduction

Until now, U.S. ethanol production has remained tied to the location of the industry's primary resource, corn.[1] However, abundant corn is not enough to make a U.S. region an ethanol production center. Industrial scale production was not economically viable until federal and state policies created captive markets that incentivize regional production. Furthermore, the emergence of a unique set of policy conditions conducive to the development of a regional ethanol industry depended on the coming together of technological, operational, and business knowledge of agri-processing corporations and the close connection between farmers, industry, and policy makers. This chapter examines how U.S. policies at both the federal and state level interact to create convergent and divergent forms of regional non-renewable energy production pathways. Using a comparative approach that contrasts how multiple regions respond to federal policies, this chapter contributes toward an understanding of the space–time evolution of policy, technology, and industrial development within the United States.

Regional interest groups shape regional concentrations of ethanol production by aligning local policies with the regulatory and market frameworks created by federal environmental governance structures. That is, regional concentrations of ethanol production depend on the coordinated development of policies executed by different levels of government, with each level addressing different industry needs. Both convergent and divergent patterns of regional policy formation and industrial structure exist. Divergence results from prior variation in the pre-existing structure of related industries, interest group organization, and policies among regions.

This chapter has two goals. First it examines national and regional patterns of ethanol production and innovation. Second, this chapter analyzes regionalization of ethanol development by examining causal mechanisms. Emphasis is placed on convergent and divergent industrial development patterns within the United States' largest ethanol producing region. In the Midwest, a six state region represents 70 percent of all U.S. ethanol production, and 50 percent of all U.S. ethanol facilities (RFA 2013). Analysis of this region and its relationship with differing forms of national environmental governance provides insight into regional patterns of government induced techno-industrial pathways.

To understand why regional variation in industry structure exists and how it relates to the environment, we must understand the evolution of industrial development policies and environmental governance in each state. To do so we must move beyond separate research on economic and environmental impacts and refocus on the development of governance (Bridge 2008; Coenen et al. 2012; Truffer and Coenen 2012; Patchell and Hayter 2013). Such a focus raises three questions that guide this chapter (i) what policies exist, (ii) how do those policies seek to promote ethanol development, and (iii) what does the focus of those policies tell us about how and why the United States' leading ethanol producing region is incorporating environmental concerns into industrial policies?

Characteristics of ethanol production

Biofuels account for 22 percent of U.S. renewable energy consumption and 45 percent of U.S. biomass energy production (USEIA 2013). Corn-based ethanol, produced through the fermentation of starch rich corn kernels, currently accounts for 98 percent of U.S. biofuel production and consumption (USEIA 2013). Blended with conventional forms of energy, ethanol contributes to domestic heating and electricity use. However, ethanol's principle use is as a transportation fuel oxygenate.

In the United States, ethanol production occurs in regional clusters supported by inter-regional innovation systems and promotional government policies organized around existing agricultural interests. A number of particular interest groups constitute the main actors promoting the regional clustering of production. First, industrial farming interests and developers of genetically modified crops generate abundant ethanol feedstocks at reduced cost leading to the concentration of production in corn-rich regions. Second, corn farmers operate cooperatively owned ethanol biorefineries with production capacities under 100 million gallons per year (mgy) as value-added extensions of their agricultural businesses. Third, related industry interests (e.g., grain processing companies, oil refineries) operate multiple biorefineries with production capacities greater than 100mgy as secondary business interests. For both ethanol producer groups, small and large, biorefinery operation permits integration of suppliers and distributors, and internalization of up- and down-stream market risks. Furthermore, such internalization reduces transportation costs associated with moving grain to market. However, internalization through ethanol production is only feasible in the presence of government policies that create and maintain markets. The federal government mandates ethanol production as a means of emissions reduction and industrial development. State policies promote regional production systems to meet such policy-constructed market needs.

The effectiveness of ethanol production as a form of either industrial development or environmental governance remains contested. Low and Isserman (2009) suggest new biorefineries have very different direct and indirect economic impacts that arise with existing regional economic complexity, although research suggests that these impacts may be less than often claimed (Swenson 2006; Swenson and Eathington 2007). Job multiplier estimates for the ethanol industry vary from 3.4 to 50, an indication of the variation among study assumptions and findings (Swenson 2006). Similarly the environmental impacts of industrial scale ethanol production remain unclear. Estimates of the industry's net energy balance and net emissions reduction vary greatly (Hammerschlag 2006; Hill et al. 2006; Koh and Ghazoul 2008; Searchinger et al. 2008). Corn-based ethanol's intensive use of agricultural crops has also increased concern about its impact on food prices and agricultural land use (Cassman and Liska 2007; Thompson 2012).

Development of a new techno-economic paradigm

Networks of firms, institutions, and end users organize the external coordination of production through the use of information and communication technologies (Freeman and Perez 1988; Freeman 1992; Hayter 2008). However, Bridge, Cooke, and Hayter argue that in the future this currently dominant form of industrial production will integrate environmental concerns into industrial networks and renewable energy will be considered in every transaction (Bridge 2002; Hayter and Le Heron 2002; Cooke 2002, 2004; Hayter 2004). Within a "green" techno-economic paradigm competitiveness will depend on the ability to leverage both environmental and industrial change into favorable market conditions. Renewable energy industries face unique investment barriers (e.g., resistant energy interests) that limit the effectiveness of market centered industrial development policies (Esslezbichler 2012; Simmie 2012). Without industry adoption and support the impact of environmental regulation is likewise limited. Effectiveness depends on the convergence of industrial development and environmental policy, and their emergence as a form of combined governance. The process that leads to convergence between industrial and environmental governance giving rise to a new techno-economic paradigm is of interest in understanding the emergence of industrial pathways and regional development (Rodriguez-Pose and Storper 2006; Rafiqui 2009).

The role of federal policy

Federal government policies created a governance framework favoring the development of selected alternative energy industries over others. Responding to lobbying by farmers and agri-processors, government officials built a system of biofuel subsidization alongside existing support for agricultural production. Initial policies focused on market formation insulated ethanol producers from foreign competition, and reduced start-up costs by providing tax credits and subsidized financing. Environmental concerns (e.g., greenhouse gas emissions) expanded government support for alternative energies but initially had limited direct impact on production.

Ethanol production remained at a commercial scale until 2003 when a change in environmental regulation created a captive market for the fuel. Prior to 2003 oil refineries commonly used two alternative fuel oxygenates, ethanol and MTBE, to meet emissions reduction standards put in place for major metropolitan areas in the Clean Air Acts of 1970 and 1990. Reacting to groundwater contamination concerns, the USEPA began a planned phase-out of MTBE in 2000. In 2003, New York and California announced plans to ban MTBE, which ultimately led to twenty-five states banning the chemical's use as a fuel oxygenate (EIA 2003; USEPA 2004, 2012). Ethanol then captured the fuel oxygenate market as the primary oxygenate viable for industrial scale production.

Federal policies shifted to further support ethanol industry development. The Energy Policy Act of 2005 established a national renewable fuel standard (RFS) that mandated production of 7.5bgy of renewable fuel by 2012, a target later expanded to 36bgy by 2022 in the Energy Independence and Security Act of 2007. Alignment of interest group and policy maker interest coalesced into initiatives such as 25×25, a broadly supported (U.S. Congressional Members, farmers, ethanol refiners, university members) agenda calling for 25 percent of the U.S. energy supply to come from renewable sources by 2025 (25×25 2013). Expanded legislative support for production and infrastructure development followed. Until 2012, refineries blending ethanol into fuel received a \$0.45 per gallon tax credit. Small ethanol producers received a \$0.10 per gallon tax credit for operations producing 60mgy or less.

Despite rapid growth, uncertainty about the economic viability and environmental impact of ethanol remained. In response, federal policy shifted focus to improving the economics of ethanol production absent policy support, and its impact on emission levels, food prices, and land use. In particular, policy placed emphasis on cellulosic technologies that produce ethanol using non-food feedstocks and an improved net energy balance. For example, the Food, Conservation, and Energy Act targets ethanol research by making available $300 million for cellulosic ethanol research, and $250 million in loan guarantees for renewable energy investments. Similarly, the Biomass Research and Development Act of 2000 aimed specifically at ethanol research projects by setting aside funding of $200 million per year. Policy changes were similarly incorporated into the RFS. The 2007 Energy Independence and Security Act amended the RFS to include a progressive shift to "advanced biofuels" based primarily on cellulosic production technologies.

There are currently twenty-three federal policies in operation that directly focus on some segment of the ethanol industry value-chain (Table 20.2). Of those policies, eleven are grant and loan programs, and ten are regulations. In the six states making up this chapter's study region there are sixty-two ethanol related policies.

The emergence of regional patterns of U.S. industrial ethanol production

Promotional federal policies align environmental and industrial interests to support the development of ethanol production within existing agriculturally intensive regions. Corn-rich regions capitalize on that policy framework through regional policy initiatives that draw necessary investment and innovation to sites of ethanol production.

Like other resource-based industries, ethanol refineries have agglomerated in regions rich in their primary resource. The largest ethanol producing region in the United States (Iowa, Nebraska, Illinois, Indiana, Minnesota, South Dakota) accounts for 70 percent of national ethanol production (9.9 bgy), 68 percent of national corn production (8.4 billion bushels), and 55 percent ($1.47 billion) of national corn subsidies (USDA 2012; EWG 2013; RFA 2013). In addition, those states received $55.6 billion in corn subsidies from 1995–2012, two-thirds of all national corn subsidies during that time (EWG 2013). Table 20.1 outlines the distribution of ethanol

Table 20.1 Industry characteristics of the largest U.S. ethanol producing states

	*Ethanol production**			*Corn production***		
	Total	*Local*	*Non-Local*	*Acres*	*Bushels*	*Subsidies*
Iowa	3,573 (40)	897 (11)	2,793 (29)	13.7	2,350	$370
Nebraska	1,917 (24)	186 (03)	1,731 (21)	9.6	1,540	$259
Illinois	1,374 (13)	93 (02)	1,281 (11)	12.4	1,950	$298
Indiana	1,038 (13)	0 (00)	1,038 (13)	5.7	840	$149
Minnesota	1,032 (21)	532 (10)	500 (11)	7.7	1,200	$287
South Dakota	1,012 (15)	220 (04)	792 (11)	4.9	650	$265
United States	13,819 (209)			83.9	12,360	$2,700

Source: compiled by authors from EWG (2013); Nebraska Energy Office (2013); RFA (2013); USDA (2012)

* Production in millions of gallons per year with the number of facilities in parentheses
** Corn acreage, bushels, and subsidies in millions

and corn production within these states for the year 2012. Iowa is the largest U.S. producer of ethanol and corn, and receives the greatest amount of corn subsidization from the U.S. government, $370 million in 2012. By comparison, the average ethanol refinery in the state of Minnesota has a production capacity, 56mgy, roughly half that of the average Illinois refinery, 103 mgy.

There are 126 biorefineries operating in these six states (RFA 2013). Industry growth occurred unevenly through time. In 2003 only thirty-three biorefineries operated within the region. Expansion occurred rapidly between 2004 and 2007. By 2007 the number of ethanol refineries operating in the region increased to ninety-four (RFA 2007). The rate of growth slowed as the 2008 financial crisis restricted funding. However, increasing refinery numbers only capture a portion of overall regional growth. Average production capacity at a plant within the region rose from 65mgy in 2003 to 80mgy in 2012. Two factors contributed to that rise. First, early entrants undertook capacity expansion projects to match technological changes within the industry. Second, new ethanol refineries incorporated those advancements into their designs. By 2012 a new biorefinery typically opened with an annual production capacity of 100mgy (RFA 2013).

The financial crisis also impacted the organization of the ethanol industry in the region. Local-ownership as a proportion of total ethanol production declined as related industry interests consolidated their position within the industry. Unable to secure project funding from tightening credit markets and unable to control the prices of their commodity inputs (e.g., corn) or their commodity products (ethanol), biorefineries suspended production or filed for bankruptcy protection. Recognizing an ongoing need for ethanol supplies, agri-processors and oil refiners seized the opportunity to vertically integrate failing biorefineries into their larger operations. Three producers Archer Daniels Midland, POET, and Valero now account for one-third of all U.S. biofuel production (RFA 2013).

Divergent regional policies and industrial patterns

While federal policy encourages ethanol production in the U.S. corn-belt, state policy differentiates production within that region. A divergent industrial pattern emerges as state-to-state policy variation selectively echoes, amplifies, and extends promotional federal policies. Alternative state policy configurations develop as officials and regional interest groups coordinate government action to support the varied interests of related pre-existing industries and emerging ethanol production structures.

Table 20.2 Distribution of state regulations and production of ethanol in the United States

	Tax incentives	*Grants and loans*	*Regulations*	*Total*
Iowa	4	3	5	12
Nebraska	2	1	2	5
Illinois	3	3	10	16
Indiana	2	2	8	12
Minnesota	1	3	6	10
South Dakota	0	2	5	7
Federal	2	11	10	23

Source: compiled by authors from US AFDC (2012); USEIA (2013).

The role of state-level policies

States within the region vary in the number and focus of their existing ethanol industry regulations. Table 20.2 organizes existing ethanol support policies of each state within the region. Each state provides policy support but incentives focus on different avenues. While states continue to provide a range of incentives there appears to be a preference for regulations at this time. Iowa's continued use of tax incentives and loans is notable in this respect, although some of these programs target cellulosic ethanol development specifically. How these policies will extend into the future is unclear. For example, following a long history of support for the ethanol industry, Minnesota is currently reassessing many of its ethanol policies. Table 20.3 provides further detail on selected policies of each state. States share a policy focus on market creation measures, production subsidies, and research credits for cellulosic ethanol development. However, the implementation of these policies varies by state, and this variation produces divergent regional industrial structures.

Production policies

Recognizing the opportunity industrial development of corn-based ethanol provided to the United States' largest corn producing region, state governments enacted supportive policies that matched and at times preceded the intent of federal ethanol governance. Each state in the region mirrored federal market creation efforts with policies designed to facilitate access to ethanol and mandate its use. The most expansive policies amplified the federal government's renewable fuel standard by instituting larger state usage mandates. For example, the Minnesota legislature passed a law mandating that 20 percent of state's transportation fuel use is replaced with ethanol by 2013. Although this target was later amended to 2015, the policy exceeds related federal targets that remain limited by the E10 and E15 blend walls. Selected states match Minnesota's policies. In Iowa the state government has targeted a 25 percent reduction in state gasoline usage by 2020.

To achieve overarching ethanol usage goals, state policy makers instituted regulations facilitating the supply and use of ethanol. In 1997 Minnesota extended emissions reduction mandates within the Clean Air Act to the entire state. The federal legislation targets reduction in only metropolitan areas. Combined with a state-wide ban on MTBE use in 2000, three years before other states banned the chemical, Minnesota created a state-wide market for ethanol. States paired general market creation strategies with incentives that targeted demand through the purchase and use of vehicles capable of operating on higher ethanol mixtures (flexfuel vehicles). For example, Indiana provides direct monthly payments to state agencies based on the number of flexfuel vehicles they operate. Iowa mandates 60 percent of all state-owned vehicles use E85. However, these targets cannot be met without infrastructure alterations. Existing fueling stations cannot dispense higher blend ethanol mixtures through pumps dedicated to lower blend fuels. Recognizing this gap, state governments provide direct loans and tax credits to encourage development and expansion of these distribution facilities. In Iowa, the 2006 Biofuel Infrastructure Program provided grants up to $50,000 for ethanol equipment installation. Similar legislation in Illinois funds the retrofitting of fuel stations to manage the sale of higher ethanol blends.

State policy similarly extended beyond federal policy in direct payments supporting ethanol production. For example, Minnesota, Nebraska, and South Dakota all administered direct payment or tax credit programs to ethanol producers. Minnesota's direct payment program operated from 1987 to 2012, and distributed $350 million to local ethanol refineries. That program paid ethanol producers a $20 per gallon direct payment for each gallon of ethanol produced. Similarly,

Table 20.3 Ethanol policies of selected states

Policy	*Date*	*State*	*Description*
Nebraska Ethanol Board	1971	NE	Institution created to promote, support, and manage development of the Nebraska ethanol industry.
Ethanol Development Fund	1986	MN	Provided direct payments of $0.20 per gallon of ethanol to producers. 2000, closed to new applicants.
Ethanol Production Incentive (South Dakota Statutes § 10–47B)	1989	SD	Provides an incentive of $0.20 per gallon to ethanol producers with a maximum of $1 million per facility.
Ethanol Production Incentive Fund	1990	NE	Incentive program to attract/develop Nebraska ethanol refineries.
Alternative Energy Loan Program (Iowa Code § 476.46)	1996	IA	50 percent funding for ethanol refinery development project cost, up to $1 million.
Office of Renewable Fuels (Iowa Code § 159.A3)	1997	IA	Established Office of Renewable Fuels and Co-Products.
Biofuels Production facilities grants (Illinois Statute § 689/1 to 99)	2003	IL	Funds the construction of production facilities (Min 5mgy) with grants of up to $4 million.
Ethanol Blend Mandate (Minnesota Statute § 239.761)	2003	MN	Mandates all gasoline sold in Minnesota must contain 10 percent ethanol, rising to 20 percent in 2015.
State Agency Petroleum Reduction (Executive Order 04–08, 04–10)	2004	MN	State agencies must achieve a reduction in gasoline use of 25 percent by 2010 and 50 percent by 2015.
Domestic Energy Research Initiative	2005	NE	Funds renewable energy projects within the state of Nebraska.
Iowa Renewable Fuels Standard (Iowa Acts 2006 § 2241)	2006	IA	Establishes an Iowa renewable fuels standard to replace 25 percent of gasoline by 2020.
Biofuels Infrastructure Program (Iowa Code § 15G.202–15G.204)	2006	IA	Provide grants of up to $50,000 to upgrade and install ethanol infrastructure equipment.
Iowa Office of Energy Independence (House File 918)	2007	IA	Established Iowa Office of Energy Independence and appropriated $100 million for ethanol research.
Biofuels Promotion (House Resolution 1010)	2008	SD	Support of the state legislature for the "25×25" initiative.
E85 Retailer Tax Credit (Iowa Code § 422.11O)	2010	IA	Provides a tax credit of $0.20 per gallon to fuel retailers selling E85 ethanol.
Cellulosic Investment Tax Credit (House File 2695)	2010	MN	Tax credits up $250,000 in support of cellulosic ethanol R&D.
Corn-to-Ethanol Research Plant (Illinois Statutes § 520/6.5 to 6.6)	2010	IL	Funds operation of a pilot plant focused on R&D to reduce the costs of ethanol production.

Source: compiled by authors from state legislative databases.

Nebraska's Ethanol Incentive Cash Fund distributed $190 million until its closure in 2012. The goal of both programs was to expand in-state ethanol production after tax credits provided to consumers failed to provide sufficient incentive to increase supply. The direct payments also indirectly addressed entry barriers by raising the operating margins of new producers, which improved their ability to manage market volatility. Loan programs that provided start-up funding of up to $0.5 million in Minnesota and $1 million in Iowa for new refinery projects further bolstered these payments.

Administration of related policy measures varies by state, which produces divergent patterns of industrial ethanol production. States established special agencies to coordinate payment programs, infrastructure expansion, and industry promotion efforts. Agencies such as the Nebraska Ethanol Board, Minnesota Ethanol Commission, and Iowa Office of Renewable Fuels and Co-Products pursue similar mandates to promote and facilitate ethanol industry development in their respective states. However, coordinating agencies pursue alternative pathways to development. For example, the Minnesota ethanol commission pursues what Bevill (2008) calls the "Minnesota Model" of ethanol development. The commission targets program support at small local producers in order to ground ethanol profits within the state and insulates biorefineries from price fluctuations in grain and oil markets and competition from established industry interests. Unlike other states, Minnesota's direct payment program targets funding to locally owned refineries. The ownership disclosure requirement was put in place after Archer Daniels Midland's 2002 purchase of a local refinery that previously received direct payments. Similarly, as early as 1994 the Commission helped administer the state's stock loan program, which sought to facilitate farmer-ownership of cooperative ethanol refineries through the coordination of bank loans. As a result of these policies, half of Minnesota's ethanol production capacity remains locally owned.

In contrast, direct payment programs in other states do not distinguish payment by ownership type. For example, Nebraska provided direct payments to all ethanol producers. Variation relates to the structure of related industry interests during the establishment of the regional ethanol industry. Minnesota instituted policies favoring local-ownership as a reaction to the early concentration of ethanol production in nearby states. Prior to 2000, the majority of ethanol production was concentrated in Iowa, and operated by ADM. ADM used ethanol as a value-added extension to its primary grain business and placed production facilities near its major trans-shipment points throughout the state. The company made direct appeals to the federal government for ethanol industry support.

Research policies

Variation in policy support for ethanol research is also responsible for divergent industrial development patterns. National support for ethanol research focuses primarily on development of cellulosic ethanol technologies. However, uncertainty about cellulosic technologies disconnected federal policy support from corn-rich regions, connecting it instead with centers of biotechnology innovation or alternative feedstock abundance. To counteract this trend, policies of corn-rich states support research focused on development of corn-based cellulosic technologies. This amplifies divergence as states select policies that further the interests of related industries and existing industrial structures.

Iowa has been particularly aggressive in its pursuit of cellulosic ethanol research that amplifies existing industrial trajectories. Through Iowa's Enterprise Zone Program a variety of tax credits, exemptions, and refunds are available for ethanol production projects. As part of the Enterprise Zone Program it is possible to double research tax credits given to ethanol projects. The Iowa

Power Fund appropriated $100 million dollars to be distributed in support of ethanol industry research projects. The fund provided $14 million in research funding for POET's development of a cellulosic ethanol plant in Emmetsburg Iowa. Research policies also target other segments of the value-chain. The state's AFV demonstration grants fund research that aims to improve ethanol use in vehicles. Iowa similarly funds development of cellulosic technologies that can be added to existing production facilities. The Power Fund provided $2 million to an algae-based cellulosic project that captures carbon emissions from corn-based ethanol production, and uses them in algae growth.

In contrast to Iowa, Minnesota's policy makers are beginning to question past government support programs for the ethanol industry. In a 2009 report, the state Office of the Legislative Auditor raised a series of questions about how the state should support the ethanol industry (Christiansen 2009). In particular that report noted subsidization of ethanol production continued even as the industry recorded significant profits. The report also brought into question the environmental impacts of state ethanol production, highlighting the uncertainty surrounding real environmental benefits and the potential for improved results through expansion of cellulosic production. Recent state policy changes are more in line with the report's findings. Minnesota instituted a cellulosic investment tax credit in 2010 (H.F. 2695) that provides up to $250,000 in support of cellulosic ethanol R&D. However, those projects target alternative markets outside the traditional transportation fuels sector. For example one project explores the possibility of using cellulosic technologies to develop the industrial chemical butonal.

Discussion and conclusions

The need for resources ties the ethanol industry to specific locations, but the customization of regional policies to match related industry interests and regional histories geographically differentiates development of industrial scale ethanol production and its environmental impacts. Broadly, the shift in state policies matches the federal reorientation in support for cellulosic ethanol development. However, unlike federal ethanol policies that do not differentiate among industrial feedstocks, regional policies target development of corn-based technologies, or technologies compatible with current forms of ethanol production. Whether differences in federal and regional research policies produce inter-regional divergence or convergence remains unclear. If multiple cellulosic technologies become economically viable, regions may converge in their total ethanol production, albeit along different technological trajectories. Such equalization in regional production would likely shift production toward the U.S. South, where cellulosic feedstocks are abundant and multiple cellulosic research projects are already underway. If one technology emerges or becomes dominant through policy manipulation ethanol production may remain tied to the current production region or shift to another. In either case divergent national patterns would result. Must environmental governance be tied to industrial development policy to produce meaningful environmental, economic, and social impact?

These are industrial development policies that are acting in lieu of environmental governance policies. Policies and governments create environments but firms are principle agents making decisions that structure industries. In such an industry, expanded policy support for the development and transfer of applied research that firms have the capacity to absorb and leverage is likely to produce greater social returns (Rodriguez-Pose 1999; Jensen and Tragardh 2004). Methodologically, this chapter highlights the need for policy analysis to examine the relationship between energy policies and industrial structures. The implementation and impact of energy policies depend on their incorporation into existing industry interests that are themselves varied in both space and time. Methods emphasizing governance and how and why policies favor some interests over others are needed to understand energy–industry relationships as producers incorporate environmental consideration into decision making.

This chapter contributes to theoretical discussions about the role of regional governance on development of innovation and industrial development. The need to consider how multiple scales of governance interrelate to produce both convergent and divergent regional industrial development trajectories is highlighted. In collaboration with regional interest groups policy makers design interventions that capitalize on opportunities created by national policy frameworks. Variation in regional interests (e.g., large/small farmers, agri-processing firms) differentiates those interventions and the coordination of policy mechanisms. Although not examined in this chapter, those interest groups and regional policy makers also work to alter national policies in their favor. A further examination of that dynamic in relation to the development of cellulosic ethanol policies with clear inter-regional competition is one area of possible future research. Avenues for comparative research exist to show how regional pathways have developed in North America, Europe, and Brazil. With globalization, companies are investing in each other's markets and collaborating with unusual partners and new industries (e.g., oil refineries, biotechnology) are entering this market. International comparative work exploring how national and state level policies of different countries interact to structure global ethanol industry development would be of particular interest.

Note

1 In other parts of the world, a variety of feedstocks are used for biofuel production such as sugarcane in Brazil.

Bibliography

25x25 Alliance, 2013: 25x25 Alliance. www.25x25.org (last accessed September 15 2013).

Bevil, K., 2008: Building the Minnesota model. *Ethanol Producer Magazine* April, pp. 114–120.

Bridge, G., 2002: Grounding globalization: the prospects and perils of linking economic processes of globalization to environmental outcomes. *Economic Geography* 78, pp. 361–386.

Bridge, G., 2008: Environmental economic geography: a sympathetic critique. *Geography Compass* 39, pp. 76–81.

Cassman, K. and Liska, A., 2007: Food and fuel for all: realistic or foolish. *Biofuels, Bioproducts, and Biorefining*, pp. 18–23.

Christiansen, R., 2009: Minnesota auditor says shift funding from corn-based to cellulosic ethanol. Available online at: *Ethanol Producer Magazine* www.ethanolproduer.com (last accessed October 1, 2013).

Coenen, L., Benneworth, P. and Truffer B., 2012: The geography of transitions: addressing the hidden dimensions of socio-technical transformations. *Research Policy* 41(6), pp. 955–967.

Cooke, P., 2002: Regional innovation systems: general findings and some evidence from biotechnology clusters. *Journal of Technology Transfer* 27, pp. 133–145.

Cooke, P., 2004: The regional innovation system in Wales. In: Cooke, P., Heidenreich, M. and Braczyk, H.C. (Eds.): *Regional Innovation Systems: The role of governance in a globalized world*, 2nd ed. London: Routledge, pp. 214–233.

Energy Information Agency (EIA), 2003: Status and impact of State MTBE Bans. Available online at: www.eia.gov/oiaf/servicerpt/mtbeban/ (last accessed September 20, 2013).

Environmental Protection Agency (USEPA), 2004: State actions banning MTBE. EPA420-B-04–009.

Environmental Protection Agency (USEPA), 2012: Methyl Tertiary Butyl Ether (MTBE). Available online at: www.epa.gov/mtbe/ (last accessed September 20, 2013).

Environmental Working Group (EWG), 2013: Available online at: www.ewg.org/farmsubsidies (last accessed October 1, 2013).

Esslezbichler, J., 2012: Renewable energy technology and path creation: a multi-scalar approach to energy transition in the UK. *European Planning Studies* 20(5), pp. 791–816.

Freeman, C., 1992: *The Economics of Hope: Essays on technological change, economic growth, and environment*. London: Pinter Publishers.

Freeman, C. and Perez, C., 1988: Structural crises of adjustment, business cycles and investment behaviour. In: Dosi, G., Freeman, C., Nelson, R., Silverberg, G. and Soete, L. (Eds.): *Technical Change and Economic Theory*. London: Pinter, pp. 38–66.

Hammerschlag, R., 2006: Ethanol's energy return on investment: a survey of the literature 1990–present. *Environment, Science, and Technology* 40, pp. 1744–1750.

Hayter, R., 2004: Economic geography as dissenting institutionalism: the embeddedness, evolution, and differentiation of regions. *Geografiska Annaler B* 40, pp. 1–21.

Hayter, R., 2008: Environmental economic geography. *Geography Compass* 2, pp. 831–850.

Hayter, R. and Le Heron, R., 2002: Industrialization, techno-economic paradigms and the environment. In: Hayter, R. and Le Heron, R. (Eds.): *Knowledge, Industry, and the Environment: Institutions and innovation in territorial perspective*, London: Ashgate, pp. 11–30.

Hill, J., Nelson, E., Tilman, D., Polasky, S. and Tiffany, D., 2006: Environmental, economic, and energetic costs and benefits of biodiesel and ethanol biofuels. *Proceedings of the National Academy of Sciences* 103 (30), pp. 1106–1110.

Jensen, C. and Tragardh, B., 2004: Narrating the Triple Helix concept in "weak" regions: lessons from Sweden. *International Journal of Technology Management* 27(5), pp. 513–530.

Koh, L.P. and Ghazoul, J., 2008: Biofuels, biodiversity, and people: understanding the conflicts and finding opportunities. *Biological Conservation* 141, pp. 2450–2460.

Low, S. and Isserman, A., 2009: Ethanol and the local economy: industry trends, location factors, economic impacts, and risks. *Economic Development Quarterly* 23, pp. 71–88.

Nebraska Energy Office, 2013: Ethanol production by state archive. Available online at: www.neo.ne.gov (last accessed October 1, 2013).

Patchell, J. and Hayter, R., 2013: Environmental and evolutionary economic geography: time for EEG^2. *Geografiska Annaler B* 95(2), pp. 111–130.

Rafiqui, P., 2009: Evolving economic landscapes: why new institutional economics matter for economic geography. *Journal of Economic Geography* 9, pp. 329–353.

Renewable Fuels Association (RFA), 2007: *Ethanol Industry Outlook 2007*. Available online at: www.ethanolrfa.org February 2007 (last accessed September 20, 2013).

Renewable Fuels Association (RFA), 2013: *Ethanol Industry Outlook 2013*. Available online at: www.ethanolrfa.org February 2013 (last accessed September 20, 2013).

Rodriguez-Pose, A., 1999: Innovation prone and innovation averse societies: Economic performance in Europe. *Growth and Change* 30(1), pp. 75–105.

Rodriguez-Pose, A. and Storper, M., 2006: Better rules or stronger communities? On the social foundations of institutional change and its economic effects. *Economic Geography* 82, pp. 1–25.

Searchinger, T., Heimlich, R., Houghton, R.A., Dong, F., Elobeid, A., Fabiosa, A., Tokgoz, S., Hayes D. and Yu, T., 2008: Use of US croplands for biofuels increases greenhouse gases through emissions from land-use change. *Science* 319, pp. 1238–1240.

Simmie, J., 2012: Path dependency and new technological path creation in the Danish wind power industry. *European Planning Studies* 20(5), pp. 753–772.

Swenson, D., 2006: *Input-Outrageous: The economic impacts of modern biofuel production*. Ames, IA: Iowa State University.

Swenson, D. and Eathington, L., 2006: *Determining the Regional Economic Values of Ethanol Production in Iowa Considering Different Levels of Local Investments*. Ames, IA: Iowa State University.

Thompson, P., 2012: The agricultural ethics of biofuels: the food vs. fuel debate. *Agriculture* 2, pp. 339–358.

Truffer, B. and Coenen, L., 2012: Environmental innovation and sustainability transitions in regional studies. *Regional Science* 46(2), pp. 1–22.

U.S. Department of Agriculture, 2012: Available online at: www.usda.gov/wps/portal/usda (last accessed October 1, 2013).

U.S. Department of Energy – Alternative Fuels and Advanced Vehicles Data Center, 2012: Available online at: www.afdc.energy.gov/afdc/fuels/index.html (last accessed September 15, 2013).

United States Energy Information Administration, 2013: Available online at: www.eia.doe.gov (last accessed September 20, 2013).

21

COMPETITION IN INTERNATIONAL AUTOMOTIVE AND AEROSPACE TECHNOLOGIES

Desmond Hickie

Introduction

This chapter is a brief review of technology policy in the automotive and aerospace industries, seeking to explain what policies governments use in order to influence technology development, and what impact these policies may have. It analyses the issues around aerospace and automotive industry technology policies in three steps: first, the key features that characterise the automotive and aerospace industries; second, the range of policy instruments governments use in order to foster R&D and technology development in these industries; and third, assessing the impacts of these policies, not only on the development of particular technologies, but more broadly on the structures, competitiveness and geographies of both industries.

The nature of the aerospace and automotive industries

The automotive and aerospace industries are both assembly industries, manufacturing thousands, even millions, of parts and assembling them into technically complex vehicles. As such they have broad structural characteristics, and even participant companies, in common. Each consists of: primary manufacturers (primes) broadly capable of designing, developing and assembling whole vehicles, and integrating the technical systems they embody; a range of specialist suppliers of components; and specialist research and training facilities. The automotive industry is fundamentally a consumer goods industry. By contrast, the aerospace industry is overwhelmingly a producer goods industry, manufacturing vehicles to be used as producer goods by airlines, and a manufacturer of military aircraft for governments.

Both industries are mature with oligopolistic characteristics, having been subject to industrial concentration over recent decades. The primary manufacturers in both sectors are globally recognisable names (e.g. Boeing, Lockheed Martin, EADS in aerospace; Ford, Toyota, Mercedes, Fiat-Chrysler in automotive). In the automotive industry the demands for greater economies of scale in design and manufacturing have driven the process of industrial consolidation since the 1960s. By 2005 it was estimated that a globally competitive automotive manufacturer, producing a full range of vehicles, would need an annual production of 3 million vehicles. However, consolidation has not resolved the industry's persistent problem of low profitability. Its most established markets (in Europe, the US and Japan) are saturated, but high capital intensity dictates high production volumes, despite flagging demand and low returns on capital (Nieuwenhuis *et al.* 2006). In aerospace, consolidation has been driven more strongly by the costs and complexity of R&D, although recent and anticipated cuts in military spending are adding further pressures.

Two key differences in the respective patterns of concentration are ownership and geography. In aerospace, strategic considerations make national ownership and control critical for governments (e.g. in late 2012, merger talks between EADS and BAE Systems appear to have foundered because of governmental concerns about loss of national control). Similarly, the US Government seems reluctant to allow much further concentration of ownership among its primary suppliers (*Financial Times* 2012a). Policy focuses on the retention of national capability. By contrast, in automotive, weak companies such as Chrysler can be passed from one overseas partner to another without a government veto. In the automotive industry production is dispersed. The major automotive manufacturers, while tending to keep core engineering and design functions close to their headquarters, have major production facilities outside their home markets, close to the customer. They also conduct some research and design activities abroad, in markets that have particular customer requirements or technical expertise to draw on. Increasingly, they conduct these activities in both the 'continentalised' European and North American markets, and in emerging markets such as China and Brazil (Sturgeon *et al.* 2008). In aerospace key R&D functions are retained at home, as is commercially and security sensitive assembly work.

Supporting the primes in both sectors are complex networks of subcontractors that are fundamental to their competitiveness. For example, car makers typically only manufacture 25 per cent of the value of the vehicles they build (Maxton and Wormald 2004). Subcontractors provide a vast range of products and services for both industries from the technologically unsophisticated to the highly complex. These suppliers are organised into tiers, with the first tier suppliers often being major, high technology businesses (e.g. Bosch, GKN). As one moves down the supply chain, there are more regionally based and low technology suppliers. Both cars and aircraft have become increasingly dependent upon electronics and computing to run and manage vehicles. This has drawn major specialist suppliers into both sectors, and has made the primes increasingly dependent upon them to provide subsystems critical to product competitiveness.

Both industries present very high barriers to potential new entrants. The dominant firms benefit from formidable economies of scale. As Sperling and Gordon (2009: 213) comment, 'One can't launch a car company from a backyard garage like one can a software or internet company.' Such barriers are arguably more severe in aerospace, because of the high R&D costs associated with the development of a new aircraft, and the long payback period (typically fifteen years) to recover that investment. Overcoming these barriers requires a growing home market, strategic vision, persistence and, usually, extensive government support. Among developing nations, currently these conditions are, arguably, best met in China, which has long-term growth potential and has pursued clear objectives about the particular market segments to be developed and the technologies needed in both sectors (Maxton and Wormald 2004; Cliff *et al.* 2011). India, while having many similar advantages, has pursued a less focused national strategy (e.g. Mani 2010).

For both industries R&D is critical, being the key to product differentiation and so to competitiveness. It is hugely expensive, complex and frequently path-dependent. 'The creation and introduction of a new [automotive] vehicle is a mammoth project, involving very big commitments of time and money – it is quite capable of breaking a company if it goes wrong' (Maxton and Wormald 2004: 141). Similarly Newhouse (1982) referred to the aerospace industry as 'The Sporty Game', because developing a new aircraft involved 'betting the company'. Both sectors share some key research priorities, in particular reducing vehicle weight, increasing fuel economy and reducing the lifetime cost of vehicle ownership (Price Waterhouse Coopers 2012a). These involve, for example, the development of new, lighter, materials, electronic engine management systems, the replacement of hydraulic with electrical controls, and the development of new, non-hydrocarbon-based fuels (Price Waterhouse Coopers 2011). Currently, Boeing and Airbus are both developing new variants of their short-haul jets (the 737 MAX and the A320 NEO) using new more efficient engines, while the automotive industry is developing both electric cars (e.g. the Nissan Leaf) and hybrid fuel cars (e.g. the Chevrolet Volt) (*Economist* 2013).

The aerospace industry has the longest project lead times of any manufacturing industry, typically about ten years (as well as the most complex supply chains) (Price Waterhouse Coopers 2010). Successful aircraft also have exceptionally long product life cycles. The Boeing 747 has been manufactured for forty years. The industry is still riding the 'innovatory wave' generated by the advent of the jet engine, and its associated aerodynamic developments (e.g. swept wings), that entered service in the 1940s. However, the industry has also received major innovatory impetus from the advances in IT and new materials technologies since the 1970s. The effect of high project start-up costs and long payback periods is that aerospace companies are unlikely, even unable, to proceed with major new product developments without public subsidy. Although they have become much more complex, cars remain technologically simpler than aircraft, but are mass produced in volumes unimaginable in aerospace. Greater product simplicity results in: much shorter times to market; shorter product life cycles; a wider range of products in manufacture; and, an industry where production technologies have a greater saliency. R&D activity in automotive has been generally more a single company-based process than in aerospace. This is essentially because production volumes are incomparably greater in relation to R&D costs, and projects are technologically simpler. Given the importance of R&D to both industries, neither is well suited to short-termism in management decision making, which can lead to a neglect of technological innovation (because payback is uncertain and may be years away) and a loss of long-term competitiveness (e.g. Boeing between launches of the 777 and 787).

Policy instruments

The technologies of both industries have been greatly influenced by government policies. However, the policy instruments that governments have used to influence them, and the extent of that influence, have varied. It is not possible to understand the aerospace industry, even civil aerospace, without understanding its symbiotic relationship with government. In the automotive industry government influence has been less than all pervasive. This section will now explore the policy instruments used by governments to influence technological development in both sectors as follows: influence over the ownership and structure; subsidies; government research facilities and universities; aircraft purchasing; and regulation.

Both the automotive and aerospace industries enjoy high levels of political saliency. In countries where they are large, or are a focus for economic development, governments recognise them as having key roles to play in economic policy, industrial policy, technology policy, employment policy and regional policy. As Maxton and Wormald (2004: 95) commented, 'Ownership and control in the automotive sector are very important political, economic and social issues.'

Aerospace enjoys an even greater saliency because of its strategic importance. In addition, its very long time horizons, together with the incremental, path-dependent, nature of much technical improvement, place a high priority on organisational stability, keeping research, design and production teams and facilities together. This necessitates not only a steady stream of work, but also a stable organisational context. These organisational considerations apply in the automotive sector, but the shorter time horizons, greater autonomy of automotive companies, and the lack of a defence imperative, make them less salient for public policy, at least among nations with an established car industry. Few developing economies are likely to have the capability to develop an internationally competitive and substantially autonomous industry in either sector. For developing nations attempting to enter either sector, the ways in which they structure infant aerospace or automotive industries will critically impact upon their capacity to develop or acquire the necessary technologies.

Between 1945 and the 1960s, a 'national champions' policy was common in Western Europe for both sectors. The implication was that the national champion companies would dominate their national markets while attempting to export. However, from the 1960s in automotive, mass production and the internationalisation of markets forced concentration in the industry. At the same time in aerospace, rising costs (especially R&D), and increasing technological complexity, rendered national champions incapable of developing major new aircraft independently. Public ownership was frequently used as a means of protecting national champions that had become uncompetitive (e.g. Rolls Royce), and nationalisation was often justified in terms of protecting national technological competitiveness. Even though European governments have not been able to maintain autonomous aerospace companies, some retain an element of public ownership (e.g. Finmeccanica in Italy). State ownership impacted directly on the governance of Airbus, and later of EADS, reflecting a reluctance by partner governments to cede national control of their aerospace champions. Where governments have not taken ownership in aerospace companies, as in the US, they have still exercised considerable influence over the industry's structure. The US Government has at times encouraged mergers (e.g. Boeing's takeover of McDonnell Douglas) and currently appears to be discouraging them between its major primes (*Financial Times* 2012a).

Because it lacks the defence significance of aerospace, and has been less dependent upon government funding, a more liberal policy regime has generally been applied by governments to ownership and control in automotive. This has not precluded taking automotive companies into full or partial state ownership (e.g. the French Government currently owns 15 per cent of Renault). Nevertheless, in general it has been easier for major automotive companies to merge with and take over foreign competitors (e.g. Land Rover has been owned by BMW, Ford and now Tata). In addition it has been easier to set up not only production plants but also R&D facilities abroad. Both of these strategies have led to an international diffusion and sharing of automotive technologies.

For developing economies attempting to enter either sector, ownership and control are highly significant in enabling them to acquire or develop the necessary technologies. The Chinese Government's Tenth Five Year Plan specifically set out the pathway for automotive industry development to 2006, including: the sectors of the market to be pursued; the role of joint ventures; and, the pace and directions of technology development (Maxton and Wormald 2004). Governments in other developing countries have used similar methods, such as state ownership (e.g. Hindustan Aeronautics), partial state ownership of joint ventures (e.g. Maruti Motors in India, Proton in Malaysia), and restrictions on the foreign ownership of joint ventures (currently 26 per cent in Indian aerospace) (Mani 2010). What appears to distinguish the Chinese approach is the coherence and persistence with which its development strategy in the automotive and aerospace industries has been pursued. For smaller developing economies, attempting to enter these huge, well established industries is, if anything, even more daunting. They need a 'Chinese' consistency of purpose, but also a keen perception of the niche opportunities in which they are likely to be competitive (e.g. maintenance, repair and overhaul for ST Engineering in Singapore).

Both industries receive public subsidies to support their technological development, but to varying extents. The significance of public R&D subsidies in aerospace cannot be overestimated. In military aerospace national governments are the primary customers for their industry's aircraft. In civil aviation project start-up periods are long, R&D costs huge, and payback periods long, hence private capital markets have failed consistently to invest sufficiently in such very long-term and relatively high risk projects, so necessitating public subsidy. The patterns of aerospace subsidy between the US and Europe vary markedly. In Europe, subsidies have tended to be direct financial aid in the form of cheap loans to pay part of aircraft development costs. Given the oligopoly and market dominance of American civil aircraft manufacturers in the 1960s, Airbus could not have achieved a competitive and sustainable market position without it. In addition, the EU subsidises joint pre-competitive research in aerospace, such as the joint EU–aerospace industry Clean Sky Initiative which will be worth 1.6 billion euros across the aerospace supply chain. In the US, financial support for civil aerospace R&D has tended to be more indirect, not least via the funding of military and space R&D. Clearly, knowledge both of design and manufacturing can pass between complementary projects. As the Arnold and Porter Report (1991) commented, there is 'massive, systematic support to the US commercial aircraft industry pursuant to a long-standing US policy of striving to maintain US superiority in all areas of aeronautics technology' (quoted by Lawrence and Thornton 2005: 116). More recently, however, Boeing has additionally become heavily reliant on direct public subsidies to support the 787 project, from the state governments of Kansas and Washington and from the governments of Japan and Italy. This jockeying for market share and technological advancement, using different forms of subsidy, has led to a series of international trade disputes between the US and Europe over the past two decades. Clearly, facing such heavy subsidies paid to the market leaders, new entrants are themselves inevitably heavily dependent upon such subsidies in order to break into the industry. For example, the Indian Government will pay 80 per cent of R&D costs on its defence contracts, plus a tax benefit of 150 per cent of the contractor's internal R&D costs (Confederation of Indian Industry and Price Waterhouse Coopers 2009).

The automotive industry receives significant public subsidies, but there are two key differences to the aerospace sector: first, subsidies are smaller and less all pervasive upon the industry's priorities; and second, their priority is largely towards the support of manufacturing facilities. For about two decades public R&D subsidies to automotive, especially in its three dominant markets, have prioritised new technologies to reduce dependence on petroleum. The motivations for this have been: environmental, economic (to equip domestic manufacturers to compete more effectively with cars that are cheaper to run) and strategic (to reduce dependency on oil imports). These subsidies cover a wide range of measures necessary to introduce the new technologies (e.g. for new manufacturing technologies, for developing less polluting fuels). They are also large (e.g. the US electric car specialist Tesla received a $465 million loan from the Department of Energy, and its Model S is subsidised for consumers by a $7,500 federal tax credit (*Financial Times* 2013a); in Japan, lithium-ion battery manufacturer GS Yuasa has received a loan of $3.5 billion from the Ministry of Economy, Trade and Industry, mainly to support the production of these batteries for hybrid vehicles (*New York Times* 2013)). Following the financial crash of 2008, the widespread use of 'scrappage' schemes (subsidising consumers to buy new vehicles, while trading in older ones for scrap) were often explicitly linked to the replacement of the older vehicle by one that was more fuel efficient, thereby boosting demand for vehicles embodying greener technologies.

Of course, countries in the early stages of developing an internationally competitive automotive industry need a more broadly based strategy to acquire the necessary technologies, as the Japanese industry ministry MITI did in its 1955 five-year plan to develop the automotive industry that included substantial access to cheap capital for new technology development. Currently the Chinese Government is working to make up the shortfall in indigenous automotive R&D; however, the sums being spent are still small (e.g. $100 million on fuel cell, electric car and hybrid vehicle technologies; Sperling and Gordon 2009). Currently their policy focus is primarily on the acquisition of existing technologies via joint ventures.

Apart from research subsidies to companies, governments directly conduct aerospace and automotive research and fund it in universities. Again there is, however, some difference in the scale and intensity of such activities. The military significance of aerospace, and the priority for technological and engineering developments, led governments to create their own industry-based research institutions in the early decades of the last century (e.g. the US Langley Research Center), rather than rely solely on companies and universities. Government research laboratories and testing facilities have been critical to technological advance in aerospace (e.g. the Office National d'Etudes et de Recherches Aerospatiale in France, India's National Aerospace Laboratories at Bangalore). Government laboratories both conduct projects of direct value to particular companies (e.g. the Langley Research Center works very closely with Boeing; Newhouse 2007), and pursue a wide range of more generally useful research projects, from 'blue skies' research to technological developments of relevance to the next generation of products. The automotive industry also frequently benefits from the work of government research laboratories, but such laboratories are more likely to be focused on related scientific disciplines, rather than the specific needs of the automotive sector (e.g. in the US the National Laboratories at Argonne and Oak Ridge, both controlled by the Department of Energy, provide research support for various industries, including automotive, in fields such as future engine technologies and alternative fuels).There are generally fewer, more bespoke, government laboratories specifically serving the automotive industry, such as the China Automotive Technology and Research Center at Tianjin.

Universities have tended to play a subordinate, but still appreciable, role in both aerospace and automotive research, as well as being key sources of highly skilled labour. Their involvement tends to be greatest towards the 'blue skies' end of the research spectrum, where their expertise is greater, and which does not require a large industrial engineering infrastructure. So university links to the industries can be very close and multifaceted (e.g. between the University of Washington and Boeing, between Cranfield University and Jaguar). Such research can be critical in developing leading-edge technologies, such as in Alcoa's collaboration with Stanford University to develop airframe fasteners that function additionally as sensors to reduce the need for manual monitoring of aircraft in service (Price Waterhouse Coopers 2011). Universities also play a key role in supplying highly skilled, technological labour, but again governments have specifically prioritised the supply of skilled labour in aerospace, by creating and funding specialist educational and research institutions (Sup'aero in France, the Beijing University of Aeronautics and Astronautics), as well as supporting engineering education more broadly through their general funding of higher education. A large supply of highly skilled engineering labour is seen as a key area of potential competitive advantage for emerging economies such as India and China. This is particularly significant in aerospace, where the leading manufacturers are suffering skilled labour shortages (Price Waterhouse Coopers 2011).

Governments' role as a purchaser of (mainly military) aircraft, and their ability to persuade airlines and foreign governments to buy particular aircraft, is a critical feature of the aerospace industry that has no parallel in automotive. Military contracts have generally been the lifeblood of the aerospace industry, because airlines have tended to buy aircraft in smaller numbers. Military priorities have greatly affected the development of the industry as a whole. In particular, technologies developed for military purposes have been used on many civil projects (e.g. technology for the B2 Stealth Bomber has been used on the Boeing 787). This position has gradually been changing since the end of the Cold War, both because of reductions in military orders, and because of the rapid growth of air transport. Since the 2008 economic downturn, cuts in military budgets in Europe, and the prospect of severe cuts in the US, have reinforced these trends, so that increasingly, major aircraft manufacturers are coming to depend more on commercial sales (Price Waterhouse Coopers 2012b).

In the past, when many airlines were publicly owned, governments often required them to buy planes made by their domestic aircraft industry. Even now when there are fewer state-owned airlines, governments continue to exercise significant influence on commercial aircraft purchases (e.g. the US Government has been very persuasive in support of Boeing's dominance of Japanese airline fleets). However, this influence is most obviously present in China, where airliner purchases remain an arm of broader public policy. For example, one or more of Chinese state airlines will be obliged to buy the new, Chinese single-aisle COMAC C919 airliner (Cliff *et al.* 2011). Worldwide, now that there are fewer state-owned airlines, and airlines are generally more economically deregulated, government influence over their purchases is less direct, and arguably less significant, but it remains important.

It is also important to recognise that aircraft purchasers can be well placed to use their purchases to foster industrial and technological policy objectives. Purchasers use aircraft purchases to negotiate 'offsets' (where the aircraft manufacturer agrees to set up manufacturing facilities in the purchasing country). Such 'offsets' can form the basis for aerospace clusters. China is perhaps the best example for civil but not military aircraft, because its domestic market is potentially so large. Cliff *et al.* (2011: 42) have commented: 'Certainly, Chinese aviation industry leaders have made no secret of their desire to trade market access for technology, and joint ventures are their vehicle for gaining access to advanced Western technologies.' For example, Airbus has built its first non-European assembly line in Tianjin. Similarly, in India defence contracts specify that 30 per cent of the value of the contract must be spent with Indian companies or joint ventures. In automotive, FDI has often also been a price for market access (e.g. Japanese transplants in the US and Europe; European transplants in China) though here, of course, the government is not itself the key purchaser of vehicles – its citizens are (Sturgeon *et al.* 2008).

Governmental regulation of the aerospace and automotive industries is significant and impacts on technology development in both sectors. It has primarily focused on international trade, on product safety, on environmental pollution, and on the protection of intellectual property. In aerospace, international trade regulations are mostly a civil matter, since military exports are governed by national regulations protecting security interests. Jockeying for market share and technological advancement, using different forms of subsidy, has led to a series of recurring disputes between the US and Europe for over two decades. A bilateral agreement about subsidy levels was reached by the EU and US in 1992, but the US (at Boeing's behest) withdrew its agreement in 2004, leading to parallel claims disputes about Boeing and Airbus subsidies being taken to the WTO. In 2012 the WTO found that both parties were guilty of illegal subsidies ($18 billion to Airbus and $4 billion to Boeing). The dispute appears to have moved on to issues of compliance, but may eventually be settled bilaterally, avoiding mutual trade sanctions (*Financial Times* 2012b).

In the automotive industry governments have regularly protected their manufacturers, but the primary focus in international trade has been on tariff barriers, and sometimes quotas, to cut imports, rather than on subsidies to encourage exports. In Europe the opening up of the single market and the Eurozone were effective in reducing national protectionism. Both the US and the EU held down Japanese imports through 'voluntary' export quotas in the 1980s and 1990s. This was, however, only a temporary protection. The opening of Japanese transplants in Europe and North America, allied to strong consumer demand for Japanese cars, rendered these restrictions superfluous. Tariff barriers on automobiles are difficult under WTO rules, hence China cut its tariffs on new car imports from 80 per cent to 25 per cent and also increased its import quotas after joining the WTO in 2001 (Maxton and Wormald 2004). However, cutting tariffs does not by itself open up automotive markets. The Japanese abandoned import tariffs on cars in 1978, but their market remains notoriously 'the most closed auto market in the world' (Steve Biegum, Ford Vice-President for International Governmental Affairs, *Financial Times* 2013b), significantly due to strict and particular vehicle testing regulations that raise the costs of vehicle imports.

National and international environmental regulation has become increasingly important, and has acted as a major spur to technological innovation in both sectors, designed to improve engine efficiency, reduce vehicle weights with new, lighter materials, and develop new fuels. In both sectors environmental concern has focused very largely on noxious emissions from vehicles (e.g. carbon monoxide, nitrogen oxides). However, in aerospace there has also been concern about noise pollution, especially around airports, dating back to the 1960s. Because air travel is largely international, the International Civil Aviation Organization has played a key role in developing the regulatory framework, but so have national governments (in particular the US) and increasingly the EU (e.g. the inclusion of aviation in the EU Emissions Trading Scheme in 2012). In automotive the key sources of environmental regulation have been national, or sometimes local, governments (e.g. California, Shanghai), although in Europe the EU has also been a significant player (e.g. setting carbon dioxide reduction targets). California passed the first laws controlling vehicle emissions in 1959, and the California Air Resources Board has played a continuing innovatory role in regulating traffic pollution (e.g. the Zero Emission Mandate re the availability for sale of electric and hybrid cars). In the developing world, governments have begun to regulate pollution, but standards tend to be lower, because local manufacturers often cannot meet more challenging standards, existing vehicle owners object, and the necessary infrastructures are unavailable (e.g. a ready supply of unleaded petrol; Sperling and Gordon 2010).

In practice automotive manufacturers have often been more reluctant to introduce greener technologies than their aerospace counterparts. They have argued in the past that such innovations would not work (e.g. catalytic converters, electric cars) and that consumers would not pay for them. Their attitude is understandable in that they have huge investments and sunk costs in existing powertrain technologies that would be rendered obsolete by a technology that replaced the internal combustion engine (Zapata and Nieuwenhuis 2010). However, over time they have developed and successfully introduced quite radical technologies (e.g. replacing carburettors and distributors with fuel injection and electronic engine management systems; Maxton and Wormald 2004), not least under pressure from regulators and consumers. The industry has also radically transformed its production technologies (from mass production, to lean production, to build-to-order production). Nevertheless, the volume of auto manufacturers' vehicles still use steel-based structures and internal combustion engines. Rising oil prices have helped encourage manufacturers by increasing demand for smaller cars. However, regulation has also had unintended consequences. For example the CAFE (corporate average fuel economy) standards introduced in the 1970s to reduce the size of US automobiles were effective in reducing the size of cars, but also drove up demand for SUVs which were not governed by the same regulations. In aerospace it may be argued that cleaner technologies were easier to accept, because lighter aircraft with more efficient engines were clearly a source of competitive advantage when selling to airlines seeking to cut costs. Arguably, airlines were more price sensitive to aircraft running costs than car owners were to automobile running costs. Hence environmental regulation can be seen to be a major driver of technological change in both sectors, but as especially significant in automotive where government R&D subsidies and purchases lack the impact they have in aerospace.

Both industries have been subject to safety regulation for many years, much applying to vehicle users rather than manufacturers (e.g. drivers' and pilot's licences). In various other ways, safety regulation in both sectors mirrors environmental regulation. For example, in aerospace ICAO plays a leading role in setting safety standards and reviewing their implementation, while the EU in Europe (through the European Safety Agency) and national governments (e.g. the Federal Aviation Administration in the US) also regulate key areas of the industries' activities. Critically, safety regulation involves giving type approval to aircraft and cars, and to their components, and without it planes, cars and components cannot go into service. Obtaining type approval makes meeting the requirements of regulators an essential objective for engineers when designing vehicles. However, cars remain much less safe in use than aeroplanes. As with environmental regulation, the automotive industry was not necessarily enthusiastic about safety improvements (e.g. independent crash tests). However, pressure from governments, consumers, insurers and consumer champions (notably Ralph Nader) drove both increased regulation and technological improvement.

The regulation of intellectual property arises in two respects, one affects both sectors, and the other only aerospace. The first, affecting both, is the protection of intellectual property rights (IPRs) (e.g. in an overseas joint venture). This is critical, so that products are not cloned or pirated. The most obvious recent cases in this respect have been in automotive in China, where both GM and Volkswagen have found even whole vehicles have been cloned. The best regulatory protection is likely to be that of the technology importing country, and China has strengthened its IPR laws since joining the WTO. Nevertheless they are widely recognised as weak (Sperling and Gordon 2009), which impacts on their capacity to acquire new technologies (e.g. China attracts markedly fewer foreign aerospace investments for R&D than for manufacturing; Price Waterhouse Coopers 2010). The second aspect of IPR regulation, significant in aerospace, is the refusal of domestic governments to allow their aerospace industries to export products that may lead to the leakage of technology to unfriendly states. This problem is most acute in the US, where government regulations can, for example, restrict sales of civil aircraft that contain a single component designated as restricted under the US International Traffic in Arms regulations. Compliance becomes even more complicated when companies have to meet both US and European technology export regulations. In practice this has led to some SMEs avoiding the more restrictive US regulations by not seeking contracts that involve compliance with them.

Policy impacts: technologies, competitiveness, structure and geography

Technological competitiveness is only one consideration for technology policy makers concerned with the aerospace and automotive industries. These are key industries, both in industrialised and developing societies. Automotive is the largest manufacturing industry, while aerospace is critical for national defence and can drive a range of other technologies. Technology policy here critically affects the achievement of a much wider range of policy objectives, such as exports, employment, environmental protection, defence, citizens' safety and national prestige. Hence, governments adopt a wide range of policy instruments that impact upon the technological development of these industries. In aerospace, Price Waterhouse Coopers (2011: 9) conclude 'We see the government as playing a key role in driving research priorities in the aerospace sector . . . – both through regulation . . . and through joint efforts to promote environmentally-friendly R&D'. Governments do not generally exercise the same degree of control over technology development where automotive manufacturers are well established, as the industry can afford its own R&D, and government is not a key customer. Nevertheless, via regulation governments drive an environmentally friendly agenda. In countries with developing automotive industries, the position is closer to that in aerospace. If they are to overcome high technological and financial barriers to entry, they need consistent government support.

Clearly such policies can directly impact on R&D activities in general as well as individual projects. In aerospace, governments can profoundly influence the direction and pace of technological advance. In military aerospace, government both decides what projects will be pursued as end user, and pays directly for R&D. In civil aerospace, the government is no longer usually the customer, but the character of the industry's technologies affords it opportunities directly to influence what projects will be pursued and using what policy instruments. Furthermore, regulatory activities set the industry a whole range of R&D priorities (e.g. emissions). In addition military R&D can provide direct spin-offs to aid civil aerospace, though the current decline in US and European military expenditures may reduce its capacity to do so. In the automotive industry, the role of government is less all-embracing, in particular where companies are already established competitors in world markets. But, government regulatory concerns, accompanied by substantial subsidies, are driving longer-term R&D priorities (e.g. lean burn engines). In addition, the official sanctioning, and implementation of non-tariff barriers (e.g. in Korea and Japan) encourages R&D in general, by enabling manufacturers to amortise its costs over longer production runs for domestic markets.

In developing economies, both sectors usually need government support to acquire new technologies. Apart from subsidies, this can be done by restricting imports (as far as the WTO's credulity will allow), and offering market access in return for access to the necessary technologies. This is most likely to happen for production technologies (as foreign investors are less likely to set up R&D facilities overseas – except to meet particular local market requirements). Nevertheless, much can be learned even on this basis. However, such learning requires government to create the necessary infrastructure of universities, and research laboratories that will provide the highly skilled labour, research facilities, etc. to understand and use the technologies being made available. A developing country's ability to acquire and use knowledge and skills from overseas, especially if it is unable or unwilling to protect intellectual property, should make potential foreign investors very cautious in deciding how much of their critical IPRs they are willing to transfer, regardless of promises of market access (Price Waterhouse Coopers 2011). In more advanced economies, universities and government research laboratories play a somewhat different role in R&D, focusing more on 'blue skies' and 'leading edge' research, where they have greater expertise, and where firms are less immediately interested, because paybacks are less clear. Government technology policies play a key role though, both because they fund academic research, and because they fund collaborative, public–private projects designed: to focus academic researchers on projects with potential economic value; to shape public–private interactions; and to facilitate the transfer of research findings into industry.

The aerospace and automotive markets are ones where technological advance is key to product differentiation and hence to competitiveness. Thus, technology policy has a key role to play in influencing the size and shape of the industry. The extent of this influence is somewhat less in automotive, not least because it is a consumer industry where other factors (e.g. branding) affect competitiveness. In aerospace, government R&D funding is the 'ticket price' for competitiveness. Firms cannot afford to pay for enough R&D on their own. In periods of contraction and consolidation (as at present in US and European military aerospace) government policy is critical in determining not only what technologies will be pursued, but which companies will be allowed to pursue them, and what will be the resulting structure of the industry. Clearly, this involves broader considerations than technology policy, but decisions about industrial policy, employment policy and regional policy have to be taken in a technology policy context.

In the automotive industry the role of technology is more contingent, both on the strength and competitiveness of the industry, and the broader context of public policies. Where firms are internationally competitive and profitable, they can in principle pay for the technology necessary to design and manufacture their next generation of vehicles. However, in market conditions of over supply and falling profit margins, this is likely to apply to fewer manufacturers. It is unlikely to apply to new entrants to the industry in developing economies. Perhaps the most interesting contra-indication to this is the Indian Tata Group that has both developed the Nano car for the domestic market and gained access to advanced technologies by buying Jaguar and Land Rover from Ford. For developing economies, possessing a competitive, indigenous aerospace or automotive industry can play an important role in national economic development and industrialisation. But the experience of the Malaysian automobile industry illustrates the challenges of trying to enter such industries as a primary manufacturer. Ultimately, few nations are likely to have the domestic markets, or technological and industrial capabilities necessary. China may well achieve autonomy in both industries. India, through Tata, may do so in automotive, but seems less likely to do so in aerospace. Russia has a major aerospace sector, but whether it can become a global player in aerospace or automotive markets is unclear. Perhaps the most interesting developments in either sector are the current Brazilian, Chinese, Russian, Japanese and Canadian attempts to enter the single-aisle airliner market to compete with the A320 and Boeing 737. Were one (or more) of these to prove internationally successful, it would represent, inter alia, a remarkable achievement of technology policy.

Looking at technology policy beyond the strict confines of the automotive and aerospace industries, the trajectories of technological development in both offer the prospect of spin-off technological and economic benefits into adjacent sectors. Aerospace, in particular, has generated a wide range of technological advances that benefit other sectors (e.g. wind turbines). If anything, the trend of technological developments in both sectors, which has seen Tier 1 and 2 suppliers adopting more salient roles, enhances the opportunities for inter-sectoral spin-offs, because these suppliers may already be serving other sectors.

Finally, it is important to recognise that technology policy impacts upon the geography of the aerospace and automotive industries in two distinct ways. First, the security implications of aerospace are such that its R&D has a distinctly national or continental focus. In practice, the commercial aircraft industry is dominated by two essentially continental industries in Europe and the US. In military aviation Governments wish to retain their own R&D capabilities at home, within their borders and being conducted by indigenous companies but, as EADS illustrates, very few states have this capability. In automotive, the lack of security considerations has allowed a somewhat more international approach in R&D. International mergers and acquisitions permit R&D to be conducted in one location but to be freely disseminated internationally within the company. Equally, companies that set up major manufacturing facilities abroad can readily set up R&D facilities there, even if only to serve a particular, local market. Nevertheless, there is strong evidence of continentalisation in automotive (e.g. European manufacturers moving production to the EU periphery; US manufacturers moving production to Mexico). Assembly transplants (e.g. German and Japanese assembly plants in the US) are built to serve continental markets, while core design and engineering functions are retained in the company's 'home' market (Sturgeon *et al.* 2008). Second, both industries demonstrate the importance of clustering. Such clusterings can involve leading manufacturers, their suppliers, and supporting R&D facilities (company, university and government run). The development of such clusters is likely to be, at least in large part, a function of public policy. The best single example is probably Toulouse, which became France's hub for civil aerospace as a result of a deliberate act of public policy (Hickie 2006).

What this brief review of the automotive and aerospace industries illustrates is the range of policy instruments governments can use to influence, and even drive, technology development in both sectors. Furthermore it demonstrates how a judiciously focused technology policy, determinedly pursued over time, can impact upon: the direction, focus and pace of technology development; the international competitiveness and structure of both sectors; and the capacity of governments to retain or develop internationally successful manufacturers in either sector.

References

Cliff, R., Ohlandt, C. and Yang, D., 2011: *Ready for Takeoff: China's advancing aerospace industry*. Washington DC: Rand Corporation.

Confederation of Indian Industry and Price Waterhouse Coopers, 2009: *Changing Dynamics: India's aerospace industry*. New Delhi: Price Waterhouse Coopers.

Economist, 2013: Difference Engine: Tailpipe Truths. 20 April.

Financial Times, 2012a: Gelles, D. and Crooks, E., UD Defence Groups Reassess Strategy, 19 September, p. 12.

Financial Times (electronic edition), 2012b: Politi, J. and Chaffin, J., WTO Affirms Ruling on Illegal Boeing Subsidies, 12 March.

Financial Times, 2013a: Foy, H. and Waters, R., Electric Shock, 5 September, p. 9.

Financial Times, 2013b: Steve Biegum, Vice-President for International Governmental Affairs, quoted in Politi, J. and Stanley, A., Ford Aims Trade Talks Barb at Japan, 17 July, p. 6.

Hickie, D., 2006: Knowledge and competitiveness in the aerospace industry: the cases of Toulouse, Seattle and North-west England. *European Planning Studies* 14(5), pp. 697–716.

Lawrence, P. and Thornton, D., 2005: *Deep Stall: The turbulent story of Boeing commercial airplanes*. Aldershot: Ashgate.

Mani, S., 2010: The Flight from Defence to Civilian Space: Evolution of the Sectoral System of Innovation of India's Aerospace Industry. Working Paper 428, available online at: www.cds.edu (accessed 20 May 2013).

Maxton, G. and Wormald, J., 2004: *Time for a Model Change: Re-engineering the global automotive industry*. Cambridge: Cambridge University Press.

Newhouse, J., 1982: *The Sporty Game*. New York: Alfred Knopf.

Newhouse, J., 2007: *Boeing versus Airbus*. New York: Alfred Knopf.

New York Times, 2013: Stewart, J., Japan's Role in Making Batteries for Boeing, 25 January. Available online at: www.nytimes.com/2013/10/26-/business (accessed 21 June 2013).

Nieuwenhuis, P., Wells, P. and Vergragt, P., 2004: Technological change and regulation in the car industry. *Greener Management International* 47, pp. 5–11.

Price Waterhouse Coopers, 2010: *A & D Insights: Accelerating global growth*. London: Price Waterhouse Coopers.

Price Waterhouse Coopers, 2011: *A & D Insights: Gaining technological advantage*. London: Price Waterhouse Coopers.

Price Waterhouse Coopers, 2012a: *Aerospace and Defence: 2011 year in review and 2012 forecast*. London: Price Waterhouse Coopers.

Price Waterhouse Coopers, 2012b: *A & D Insights: A new intensity. Programmes under pressure*. London: Price Waterhouse Coopers.

Sperling, D. and Gordon, D., 2009: *Two Billion Cars: Driving toward sustainability*. New York: Oxford University Press.

Sturgeon, T., van Biesebroeck, J. and Gereffi, G., 2008: Value chains, networks and clusters: reframing the global automotive industry. *Journal of Economic Geography* 8, pp. 297–321.
Zapata, C. and Nieuwenhuis, P., 2010: Exploring innovation in the automotive industry: new technologies for cleaner cars. *Journal of Cleaner Production* 18, pp. 14–20.

22

NANOTECHNOLOGY FOR GREEN AND SUSTAINABLE GROWTH

A recent example on the co-evolutionary development of a technology

Oliver Pfirrmann, Stephan Heinrich and Eva Schindler

Introduction

Nanotechnology has been regarded as a key technology for radical innovations leading to economic growth and employment since the 1990s. Up to the present time, large technological advances have been made. Many countries are trying to participate in the worldwide race for this interdisciplinary and knowledge-based technology in order to benefit from its potentials. Such countries launch, for instance, public programs to generate new products and production processes based on nanotechnology. Furthermore, they fund firms to generate cross-border networks in nanotechnology and support universities to establish new study courses in relevant disciplines such as physics and chemistry.

However, a deeper look at the issues that are linked closely to the analyses and predictions focusing on nanotechnology exhibits the following:

- Many analyses rely on differing or in some cases unspecific definitions of nanotechnology. It is an acknowledged fact that nanotechnology is a general purpose technology (Youtie et al. 2008) that has an inherent potential for technical improvements in a number of industrial sectors. Different definitions, however, often lead to incomparable results and sometimes to an overestimation of the economic potentials of nanotechnology.[1]
- From a technological point of view nanotechnology is not completely new. It considers technological developments on a nano-scale, which have been, for instance, fundamental to the development of chemical products for decades. The application of nano-scale developments for established products such as tyres, cosmetics or sports equipment, the scaling-up in production and the marketing of these innovative solutions are what can be called new nanotechnology developments.

In the past few years, nanotechnology developments have been predicted to have large impacts.[2] Among these, the use of nanotechnology for green and sustainable growth is a new area of application. It is assumed that with nanotechnology-based developments, solutions for green and sustainable growth will become available. These solutions aim at the reduction of climate change impacts.[3]

From an economic point of view, nanotechnology is still emerging. However, as outlined, many industrialized as well as developing countries have launched initiatives and support programs to capture the economic potentials of nanotechnology. The combination of nanotechnology with green and sustainable growth may be regarded as a recent variation of existing public initiatives. As Aghion et al. (2009: 1) have pointed out, established and often inefficient technologies are not an adequate answer to reduce the costs of climate change. They call for "radical new emissions-free 'backstop technologies' to strengthen the 'green innovation machine'" and, in this context, nanotechnology is seen as one great promise to green and sustainable growth (see also Shapira and Youtie 2012).

Given the assumption that the degree of availability of nanotechnology for all countries affects the influence of green growth, this leads to the central questions of our investigation:

- Does technology develop easily under specific conditions, e.g., science and industry structures, mechanisms for technology transfer, or a national framework for innovation funding, to name a few?
- Can we assume an interaction between these drivers of nanotechnology development and is there evidence for a prominent role of government policy for nanotechnology?

However, before we go further into details we have to outline some preliminaries of our analysis. The first one is concerned with the countries of investigation. From a global perspective nanotechnology cannot be regarded as homogenous. While in industrialized countries nanotechnology is mainly discussed as a stimulus for growth, less developed countries often fear they are missing participation in the global "nano-race." There is an ongoing debate of the so-called nano-divide. This debate reflects the fear that the introduction of a new technology such as nanotechnology may cause substantial inequalities between "nano haves" and "nano have nots."[4] For this paper we have chosen three countries for a deeper investigation on the relationship between nanotechnology and green growth. The three countries are Germany, the US, and South Korea. All countries have a significant potential for nanotechnology products and, from the perspective of industrialization, they can be regarded as more or less similar. They also have appropriate industry sectors for the application of nanotechnology, e.g. chemical industry, energy industry, and electronic industry. Nevertheless, they differ with regard to the relevance of these industry sectors. For the first two, we could build on a recent publication that intended to demonstrate the relevance of nanotechnology for industrial growth in Germany.[5] Thus detailed material was available. In the case of South Korea we have based our work on a study for the OECD. However, the present contribution does not present "old wine in new bottles" but has carried out new research, based on the collection of existing information.

A second preliminary concerns our understanding of technological development. With regard to the relationship between technology and society, two polar explanations of technical development are often discussed: on the one hand, technological determinism argues that technology determines society. It is the notion of a social potency of the underlying technology. Accordingly, technical development proceeds as an intrinsically dynamic program—regardless of sociocultural influences. The social constructivist approach assumes, on the other hand, that society (and also policy) determines technology (Bijker et al. 1987; Bijker and Law 1992). Social constructivism treats technology as a product of social processes of negotiation and neglects determining effects of the specific technology. Largely ignored by radical social constructivism is that new technology always arises from old.

Today, the two radical positions are in retreat against intermediate models. Social constructionists include technology as a determinant among other factors in their models, and treat it as a necessary but not sufficient condition of sociocultural development. One speaks, for example, of a "co-evolution" of technology and society (Rip and Kemp 1998; Mayntz 2009). Technology is changing over time, it varies from place to place, and it is subject to many influencing factors that are related in various ways of interacting with each other. Each influences the other: technology certainly has an impact on society and society on technology. The analysis presented here follows these considerations. In this context light is shed specifically on the role of policy for the diffusion of nanotechnology. As we will see, in the new application area for nanotechnology, policy makers fulfill certain tasks to overcome diffusion barriers. Thus, the social dimension of technology construction is subject to a specific "policy" extension.

The last preliminary concerns the level of investigation in nanotechnology. As mentioned above, we regard the state of diffusion of nanotechnology as too early for a detailed empirical analysis. In addition, reliable data on nanotechnology for green and sustainable growth does not exist (Prognos 2012). Thus we have instead chosen a more qualitative way of investigation for measuring contributions of nanotechnology to growth. In the present analysis, we have selected two specific examples for our country case studies that seem most suitable for analyzing the relationship between nanotechnologies on the one hand and green and sustainable growth on the other. These examples are:

- organic photovoltaics (OPV) and
- lithium-ion (Li-ion) batteries.

We are aware of the fact that these examples do not represent a complete analysis of nanotechnology applications for green and sustainable growth. However, they demonstrate recent and important technological developments such as organic photovoltaics for energy supply and Li-ion batteries for electro-mobility. The example of OPV shows a low cost source for sustainable energy in which nanotechnology is relevant for cells and production. Nowadays there are small and mobile devices available. In a long term perspective it could contribute to a net-independent energy supply. The example of Li-ion batteries shows that batteries are only one small component in car or transport systems. But there is a systemic importance to storage technologies: they are a precondition for electro-mobility and, more generally spoken, for an energy mix (renewable energies, e.g., wind or solar) and therefore hold important impulses for green and sustainable growth.

Based on these preliminaries we aim to investigate the development process of nano-technology applications for green growth in selected countries. Our preferred perspectives are specific conditions for this development that lie outside nano-laboratories, the role of actors in science and industry, their structures of operation, mechanisms for technology transfer, national innovation strategies, and specifically frameworks for innovation funding.

Country studies

Nanotechnology as a part of the national innovation and competitiveness strategy: the example of Germany

The actors in science, industry, and policy

In the scientific field, Germany has a very diverse and broad regional infrastructure. In the field of Li-ion batteries, there are no fewer than six academic centers. They offer expertise in electrochemical materials, long lasting experience in the development of material and battery manufacturing and optimization of materials for batteries and supercapacitors as well as battery management and packaging and system integration; in some cases in close cooperation with large energy companies.[6] In OPV numerous universities and other research institutions from different disciplines are working in Germany. Among the important R&D players are, for example, Fraunhofer Institutes[7] as well as a leading research institute in the field of basic and applied research on organic semiconductors at the Technical University Dresden. In this framework set by universities and research institutions, small and medium enterprises (SMEs) fulfill an important role in the development of OPV. On the one hand, they act as a supplier of small quantities of nanomaterials necessary for development. On the other hand these firms often have special knowledge that is important for further development steps. Many spin-offs maintain long-term cooperation agreements with large companies. Research and development in nanotechnology takes place in various research institutions, without a clear application focus. This is also due to the fact that (non-nanotechnology) products are already on the market, and their development and optimization is strongly influenced by the issue of competition between firms and their R&D strategies. The disciplinary origin of the research institutions cooperating with those companies is manifold. Especially in the field of OPV, strong thematic links to other disciplines such as electric engineering or chemistry and industrial sectors can be found.

Due to its long tradition in industry, especially in the chemical and manufacturing industry, Germany is one of the world's major players in nanotechnology development. However, with regard to the different examples of nanotechnology application in products, which this paper is focused on, the industry landscape tends to correspond with the maturity of the application. We also note country specific notions. The corporate landscape in the field of Li-ion batteries corresponds with the relatively late start of this technology in Germany, compared to countries such as Japan or South Korea. Joint ventures of original equipment manufacturers (OEMs) in the automobile industry are the main actors operating in the field of Lithium-ion batteries. They either serve niche markets, or enter the production phase jointly with a major partner. This is due to the high development and investment costs of the construction. Beyond the automobile industry the growing renewable energy sector is engaged in storage, i.e., battery technologies (Bundesministerium für Bildung und Forschung und Bundesministerium für 2008b). Unlike in many other areas of nanotechnology-based products, the importance of SMEs is hence more likely to be low. As mentioned above, OPV is still in the development phase. Germany is an attractive location both for production as well as R&D, due to its long tradition in photovoltaics. Both research and development activities as well as the start-up and spin-off landscape are very dynamic. Moreover, the global players in the chemical industry and engineering, such as BASF and Bosch are major actors in the production.

The German government is the largest national funder of nanotechnology in Europe. The main activity of the federal government moved from basic research funding in the 1990s to a more application based funding as well as the organization of network activities. An important role has been assigned to the Innovation Alliance Carbon Nanotubes whose objective is to develop Germany as a globally leading market and technology hub. The same objectives are being followed by the Innovation Alliance Organic light-emitting diodes (OLED) and OPV, and the Innovation Alliance for Li-ion batteries. Nevertheless a certain amount of project oriented funding continues. The central instrument for green and sustainable growth and nanotechnology is the so-called High Technology Strategy (HTS) as strategic framework of the federal government. Within the HTS, nanotechnology is addressed as one of seven key technologies. As in other countries, the strategy focuses on different goals. The support and funding it offers is thematically oriented. The mission-oriented funding is based on issues with a high priority in the areas of climate, energy, health and food, mobility, safety and security, and ICT. There is also a "Masterplan Green Technologies," to foster the development of Green Tech. This masterplan acts as a framework for other funding and support activities. Currently it is undergoing an evaluation that is crucial to further development. Also there is a Nanotechnology Action Plan 2015, a national strategy within the HTS, that focuses strongly on an intensive integration of science and economy. It particularly addresses topics such as climate and energy, health and nutrition, mobility, as well as security and communication. Its objectives lie in effective technology transfer and the commercialization of nanotechnology.

Networks and jointly arranged strategies

In Germany, due to the so-called "Energiewende," i.e., the phase-out of nuclear power, the stationary sector, especially for storing electricity from renewable sources, has become an equally important field of application, besides energy for e-mobility. Thus, for industrialized countries such as Germany the relevance of stationary storage capacity for electricity is an important goal of the national energy policy. One example is the objective of the German government to raise the share of renewable energy to 50 per cent of the entire German energy mix by 2050. Due to the enormous potential and the key role high-performance Li-ion batteries can play for environmental and resource-saving mobility and energy concepts, a number of funding opportunities exist on the federal, state, and EU level. Major political players are the Federal Ministries for Education and Research as well as for Economics and Technology. They both offer various support programs for Research and Development (R&D) and innovation and try to capture so-called cluster activities between science and industry partners in strategic partnerships.[8] In addition, a large technology support push was initiated by the Federal Government when it announced the provision of a package of EUR 500 million as an economic stimulus for the electric mobility program in 2009. Of these funds, the German Ministry for Education and Research (BMBF) provides EUR 60 million for the development of production technology for Li-ion batteries. Another technology example is the German strategic research agenda for the years 2014–2017 for OPV. This agenda aims at the integration of organic solar cells into building surfaces. Currently, several examples for the installment of solar sails on rear walls of public buildings exist. It is further planned to integrate solar cells into glass areas such as large windows. In the long-term perspective for the year 2020, OPV could be established in so-called energy farms and therefore contribute to an energy supply independent of the grid (Geelhaar 2009: 23).

For the technologies of Li-ion batteries and OPV we see a tight interaction between policy, industry, and science. Especially the latter two operate in networks and clusters, mainly initiated and supported by public funding based on various support instruments. There is no doubt that these joint activities between academia and industry are dedicated to green growth in the context of important social objectives. Nevertheless, it is also clear that without policy objectives towards society and an adequate public funding, the commitment of industry and science would not reach the same level. Nanotechnology in Germany has a strong base in the chemical industry. The application areas described above are mainly business areas of other industry sectors along the value chain (automotive, energy, electrical engineering, medical technology). In order to support these downstream industries, public policy emphasizes the role of nanotechnology. While public support for green and sustainable growth in Germany is a most welcome effect, the central focus by the use of nanotechnology is to strengthen the competitive ability of these export-intensive industries. Thus governmental support for nanotechnology in Germany is not only a device to open up the innovative potentials, but also a vehicle to strengthen competitiveness of export-intensive industry sectors.

Nanotechnology as a means to continue a path towards world class products: the case of South Korea

The actors from science, industry, and policy

South Korea has set itself the political goal to become one of the worldwide leading countries in the development of nanotechnology (MoSt 2011: 8f). The support of existing scientific and economic actors and structures represents the starting point in achieving this goal. It is not the establishment of entirely new industries and technology fields that lies in focus, but rather the transfer of expanded or new technologies into established industries. In this regard, a path of industrial development and technology advancement is continued. Thus, the strategy supports existing strengths and transfers them into other industries. The main actors of this strategy are governmental ones that address actors in science and industries.

The key enabling ministries, the Ministry of Education, Science and Technology and the Ministry of Knowledge Economy have widely supported the development of R&D infrastructure, research, and development as well as industry efforts for early commercialization. Without their continuous impulses on science and industry to enhance technology transfer, R&D capacities at universities and outside universities such as R&D labs in Seoul and outside (e.g. Daegu, Dankook, Pohang) would not have the relevance that they have today (Ministry of Education, Science and Technology Korea (n.d.): 13f). Within this context, it is interesting, that South Korea is going to copy R&D structures from abroad such as the Institute of Basic Science in Daejon, which in its development and structure is oriented towards the German Max Planck Institutes.

However, Korean research and development activities are also very much internationally aligned. In 2010, Dankook University signed a cooperation agreement with the University of Michigan (UM) in order to work on efficiency and cost reduction for OPV cells (OSA DIRECT 2010). The University of Konkuk built a joint testing laboratory for OPV and DSSC cells in cooperation with the German Fraunhofer Institute for Solar Research (Das 2011).

On the industry side, a range of companies can be identified, most of which reflect the focus of Korean research centers on materials development. Companies in Korea are predominately among the World leaders in displays, followed by photovoltaics, organic TFTs, and equipment. A wide range of materials are being explored (Ibid.). Advanced Nano Products Co. develops nano materials for OPV, ELPANI & Co. Ltd. produces conducting metallic polymers (Ibid.). Sunic System, a leading Korean producer of vacuum deposition equipment for OLED, established a cooperation in OLED and OPV research with the German Fraunhofer Institute for Photonic Microsystems in Dresden in 2008 (Bundesministerium für Bildung und Forschung

2008a). Chemical company Dongjin has set up a pilot plant for the production of DSSC cells that has been operative since 2011 (Das 2011).

Although the initial work regarding the development of nanotechnology was done in Europe and the United States, Asian countries have been successful in acquiring technology since the 1980s, when they started the process of technology acquisition in the field of consumer electronics, e.g., for batteries. Manufacturing competence and capacities were also built up all over Asia, mainly driven by the support of governments and the protection of local markets. Another important factor in these developments are vertically integrated companies in consumer electronics such as Samsung or LG Chem in Korea, which today are the biggest battery producers (Kassatly 2010: 54ff; Steinbusch 2012). Both aspects are supported by evolving science, which leads to a high share of patents related to Li-ion batteries held by companies in Korea (Millard et al. 2012: 15). This way, governmental actions as well as a high demand by the established consumer electronics industry, secured the market share on Li-ion batteries-related nanotechnology for Korean actors in nanotechnology (Kassatly 2010: 54ff; Millard et al. 2012: 10ff; Steinbusch 2012). Their domination of Li-ion battery industries for consumer electronics regarding the key indicators of market share and know-how, as well as science with strong industry links, is a big advantage for Asian companies. In Korea, it was the starting point to launch electric vehicle industries. Additionally, strategic alliances with automotive producers in Asia, USA, and Europe were used to spur development (Kassatly 2010: 63). The example of Korea shows how public funding and support measures are used to transfer new and improved technologies to new fields of application in established industries and related R&D. This results in a publicly funded research system with strong links to existing industries. Overall, it is the systematic use of a techno-industrial innovation complex driven by policy.

Compared with Germany both research/science and industry in Korea have a strong focus on rapid recovery and production while German actors are more focused on research on complex systems. This is illustrated by the example of the joint venture between Samsung and Bosch that existed between 2008 and 2012. The joint venture was terminated due to different views on the business strategy, the cell production remained at Samsung, and Bosch continues to focus on battery systems and their development (Herz and Mayer-Kuckuk 2008; Quodt 2008; HB 2012).

In general today there are overcapacities in battery production in Asia, so new companies and industries outside Asia are hardly ever founded or built up. Some scholars are of the opinion that overcapacities will lead to "price wars" and only large and established players will be able to invest enough in future R&D.[9] On the other hand, there is also the opinion that comprehensive public support programs for battery production and necessary research and development are set up in Korea (Millard et al. 2012: 13ff).

The development of OPV is usually part of research on printed electronics, an established topic in R&D connected to existing industries with many applications in production and consumer products. R&D activities reflect the yet rather early stage of the technology, as a major focus is on materials research. As part of the Nanotechnology Initiative, the Korea Advanced Nano Fab Center (KANC) and Korea Printed Electronics Center were set-up. They are major government supported research and development facilities that are researching inter alia printed electronics, thin film electronics development etc. (MoSt 2011). Much of the research is still focused on basic research concerning materials. The CHO Research Group (Polymer Surface and Organic Electronics Lab 2013) at POSTECH—Pohang University of Science and Technology in Pohang—develops OPV cells, e.g., High Performance Organic Photovoltaics via Interface Engineering or High Performance Organic Photovoltaics via Morphology Control

(Polymer Surface and Organic Electronics Lab 2013). Other important actors in materials research are located at Seoul National University (Seoul National University 2013) as well as the Nano Practical Application Center in Daegu, which develops organic electronics for a variety of applications (Nano Practical Application Center 2013). The Korea Photonics Technology Institute develops, inter alia, dye-sensitized solar cells (KOPTI 2012).

Networks and commonly arranged strategies

As outlined before, nanotechnology development in South Korea is strongly driven by political forces and includes a relatively strong regulation of important actors in science and industry. A good testimonial is the Korea National Nanotechnology (NT) Initiative that started in December 2000. The NT was implemented by the National Science and Technology Council (NSTC) that is mainly driven by actors from the Ministry of Education, Science and Technology and the Ministry of Knowledge Economy as well as some scientists. The "NT Development Plan" with two five to ten years plans was approved by the NSTC in 2001. It was a ten-year plan for the development of nanotechnology as a next-generation technology. The support focused on selected areas, related to the most commercial potential, such as nanoelectronics and nanomaterials (Lee 2002). However, it was not until 2009, when the National Strategy for Green Growth was launched, that nanotechnology was adopted as a vehicle for green and sustainable growth. The National Strategy has a mid- to long-term (2009–2050) national agenda that is to be implemented through the collaborative efforts between various governmental organizations, industries, and civil society.[10] It is structured into several Five-Year Plans and its first phase runs from 2009 to 2013 and includes the support and enforcement of several new technologies, among them nanotechnology as well as communications technology and biotechnology.

The National Strategy for Green Growth envisages three main objectives. The first objective is to effectively deal with climate change and attain energy independence. It calls for actions such as setting mid- to long-term mitigation goals, increasing the use of new and renewable energy sources, as well as efficient management of demand for energy. The second objective is to create new engines of growth on multiple fronts. This includes the development of green technology, greening of industries, transition to a more advanced industrial structure, and laying the groundwork for a green economy. Emphasis will be placed for example on increasing strategic investments in the R&D of the green sector, development of green small and medium enterprises, a cutting-edge convergence industry, and a high value-added service industry as well as laying the structure for green finance and tax incentives for eco-friendly activities. The third objective is to raise the overall quality of life for the people and to enhance the contributions to the international community through strong advocacy for green growth. Efforts will be directed towards greening the land and water and building a green transportation infrastructure (e.g. green vehicles, more bicycles as main means of city transportation). Campaigns will be conducted to promote public awareness and acceptance of green lifestyles. Furthermore, Korea will strive towards building its national image as a role-model for green growth by redoubling its efforts for mitigating climate change and assisting developing countries to effectively deal with the adverse impacts of climate change.

In Korean policy, nanotechnology is regarded as a promising force for the "greening" of existing industries and promotion of green industries. Nanotechnology should act as the key base technology for highly efficient solar cells, fuel cells, rechargeable batteries for electric cars, LED lights and light ultra-high strength materials for fuel efficient automobiles. Nanotechnology is also regarded as a vehicle for new developments in medical technology (nanorobots for the immune system). Strategically, large as well as small firms (start-ups) should play a major role in implementing this strategy. With regard to the industrial structure in Korea with its dominating form of business conglomerates – the so called "*chaebols*" – the main activities in implementing nanotechnology for green growth are being carried out by large companies. However, priority setting often happens on the national level, because of missing "long term planning and foresight" activities in these large companies. The management of nanotechnological innovation and its implementation in products and processes is nevertheless performed by industry (Park and Son 2006: 12).

Mission oriented policies as a key factor to spread new technologies and enabling further applications: the example of nanotechnology in the US

The actors from science, industry, and policy

Nanotechnology support in the US is highly prioritized by political initiatives. The central instrument is the National Nanotechnology Initiative (NNI). It was initiated by the US government in 2001. As a framework or "umbrella" institution the NNI brings together different initiatives on nanotechnology and tries to concentrate on defined issues. These issues cover topics such as Environmental Protection, Sustainable Energy (Clean Energy), and Manufacturing as well as Healthcare. Within NNI, risk and security research as well as the new focus on health (e.g., medical engineering, "Personalised Medicine") are increasingly important (Shapira and Wang 2008; Sargent 2011). With reference to the case studies the following remarks focus on OPV and Li-ion battery activities.

The major scientific players in the field of Li-ion batteries are Argonne National Laboratories, National Renewable Energy Laboratory, and Sandian National Laboratories (Kassatly 2010: 104). International cooperation agreements are held with many laboratories and universities all over the world, e.g., with Chinese and Korean ones (Sheng et al. 2013; SZ 2013).

In the last decade, the United States have established comprehensive public support for battery production (Millard et al. 2012: 13ff). Nowadays, the battery industry is clearly dominated by cooperation or joint ventures with Asia-based firms and focuses on battery pack assembly. Asian companies built up production plants in the USA mainly with the strategic target of cooperation with the automotive industry (Kassatly 2010: 61f; Millard et al. 2012: 13; Schulte 2012). Until 2012 there was one important firm for Lithium-ion batteries in the USA, a spin-off from the Massachusetts Institute of Technology (MIT) (Kassatly 2010: 68). The company filed for bankruptcy in 2012, but had previously been declared to be one of the world's top five Lithium-ion battery companies (Schulte 2012). Besides this firm, a lot of small companies and start-ups have begun innovative research and development since the late 1990s. Most were supported by DARPA (Defense Advanced Research Projects Agency) and federal programs. They aim mainly at niche markets such as military or medical applications. In most cases technology transfer is supported by cooperation with Asian companies. Now, however, companies with a history in lead battery development and production are also moving towards lithium-ion based batteries (Kassatly 2010: 61ff).

Research on the development of OPV in the USA is concentrated on a limited number of high profile institutes. A working group at Stanford School of Engineering was one of the pioneers in OPV R&D. Similarly, Harvard University, the University of Chicago as well as UCLA are important actors and are mostly working closely with venture and start-up companies developing OPV. A working group at the University of Chicago, for example, cooperates with the new US firm Solarmer on the development of OPV (Science Watch 2011).

US companies have been among the first to commercialize organic photovoltaics and have thus been recognized as market leaders for the past ten years. However, the still early stage of development of the technology has proven to cause difficulties. Konarka Technologies, founded in 2001, was the first company to market a number of products such as a bag with an integrated OPV-cell to charge mobile phones "on the go." It was also planning to develop the area of building integrated organic photovoltaics, an area that a number of companies see as having future market potential. In 2012, Konarka was forced to file for bankruptcy because it failed to successfully commercialize the technology on a large scale (Ibid.). Three companies remain the key players in OPV development in the US: Plextronics, Solarmer, and Polyera. While the first two are university spin-offs from Carnegie Mellon University and UCLA respectively, Polyera is an electronics supplier. Plextronics and Solarmer work mainly on improving the cell efficiency, Polyera's main focus is the flexible use of OPV for building integration. One of the areas of OPV application is seen in the provision of electricity in less populated regions (Polyera Corporation 2012).

Nanotechnology policies in the US have moved through several stages (ObservatoryNano 2010, 2012). Furthermore, the main actors changed slowly with the different stages. A difference can be detected, i.e., between federal and state or regional actors. While federal actors mainly focus on R&D and development of infrastructure, state and regionally based actors concentrate on commercialization activities for nanotechnology (Shapira and Wang 2008: 4).

The before mentioned role of the NNI as an "umbrella" institution for bringing together different actors is not limited to actors from science and industry but also includes initiatives on nanotechnology policy and institutions from public policy. In addition to the NNI, the Department of Energy (DOE) is currently of central importance among policy actors on the federal level. The DOE directs and coordinates R&D activities for conventional and renewable energy. In addition, it has a leading role in the development of a national energy strategy (Rave et al. 2013). DOE covers energy issues as well as core programs and initiatives for vehicles technologies such as the Electrical Drive Vehicle Battery and Component Manufacturing Initiative or the Batteries for Advanced Transportation Technologies Program. Important US companies in the battery business have been supported by these programs (Kassatly 2010: 68, 102ff). Other important participants in nanotechnology policies are, e.g., National Science Foundation, National Aeronautics and Space Administration, Department of Commerce, National Institute of Standards and Technology, as well as the Environmental Protection Agency (Shapira and Wang 2008: 17f; Sargent 2011: 5).

While DOE activities concentrate on the use of nanotechnology in energy aspects such as storage and batteries and photovoltaic, the NNI Strategic Plan dated from 2011 has a wider focus. Support for R&D in basic research is accompanied by application-driven research, which is of growing importance. Furthermore, topics such as solar energy and photovoltaic emerging as significant breakthroughs are expected in these areas.[11]

Networks and commonly arranged strategies

It becomes obvious that these technologies and their release into the market are a focus of the parent nanotechnology strategies. In addition, there are other strategies and network approaches that are used to support or address the purpose of photovoltaic and battery development. They are mainly concentrated in or around the automotive industry. Notably, the US Advanced Battery Consortium is connected to the US Council for Automotive Research. It is a collaboration to develop electrochemical energy storage technologies in long term R&D. It is anticipated that these technologies will support commercialization of fuel cell, hybrid, and electric vehicles

(Kassatly 2010: 66f, 100f). In 2008 the National Alliance for Advanced Transportation Battery Cell Manufacture was formed by fourteen battery related companies and the Argonne National Laboratory. The aim was to strengthen and improve competitiveness and expedite battery development (Kassatly 2010: 71). For many companies, R&D activities and collaborations, the Electrochemical Energy Storage Technical Team Technology Development Roadmap, published by the FreedomCAR Initiative in 2006, has played an important role.

In summary it can be stated that nanotechnology activities regarding energy in the US are connected to automotive and in particular to battery topics. In general, photovoltaic development is also being addressed as a key issue by important actors. While basic research is an ongoing high priority, application-driven research and market aspects have become increasingly important in the last five years.

Overall, nanotechnology support in the US as in South Korea is prioritized and pushed by political initiatives and governmental programs. The difference between the two countries' policies lies in the formulation of strategies and policies. With the NNI as a central instrument, defined issues or missions are addressed. Partly the missions fit in energy issues, such as environmental protection or sustainable energy, but other topics such as manufacturing of nanotechnologies, healthcare or security research, are also addressed (Shapira and Wang 2008; Sargent 2011). The mission-orientation of NNI favors the diffusion of nanotechnology in established industries and R&D structures, but also opens up the space for radical innovations and building up new industries. Many different actors of R&D and industries are brought together and supported by partial but additional strategies.

This results in government policies providing mainly for the modernization of existing structures and the use of nanotechnologies in a variety of application areas (National Economic Council 2011; National Science and Technology Council Committee on Technology 2011). By doing so, a multitude of application and research findings is generated. This knowledge is accumulated via the instrument of national and international networks in a limited number of selected places, institutes, and industries of the US. The US position is based on government policies regarding nanotechnology, which helps to continue the country's leading position in technology—based on policies that can be addressed towards existing reference industries and centers of scientific excellence.

Divergent paths of policies to execute their fundamental role in techno-industrial innovation

In conclusion, several key findings can be drawn from our analysis. In all country studies a number of activities on nanotechnology were carried out by actors in science, industry, and policy. Concerning the first research question of our analysis we can reject the assumption that technology develops easily under specific conditions regardless of the wider framework. This is not a question of the perspective, represented by our analysis. The development and diffusion of nanotechnology cannot be understood without taking into account industry, market, and policy conditions. The energy example with its traditional focus on large technical systems (Mayntz 2009) shows that without public activities towards green growth, nanotechnology for renewable energies would not be as important as it is today.

While the role of public policy is therefore important for the development of this relatively new general purpose technology, different policy strategies on nanotechnology in the countries of observation prevail. In South Korea a National Strategy for Green Growth took up nanotechnology issues and thus enhanced the scientific importance of it. In contrast, Germany shows a variety of support activities that involve nanotechnology; however, not as a strategic topic towards green and sustainable growth, but rather as an industry stimulus. The key difference in between the two countries as well as with regard to the US, is that in Germany no national nanotechnology initiative exists beyond the nanotechnology action plan within the strategic research agenda, the HighTech-Strategy. South Korea and the US both have a national concept of nanotechnology building on a national nanotechnology initiative (NT and NNI). In these initiatives, actors from science and industry work together on different value chains in order to develop nanotechnology solutions in areas such as photovoltaic or battery technology for industry applications. Especially in South Korea, a regulated technology approach dominates, similar to the build-up of the national economy in the 1960s and 1970s on national development plans.

The central focus in the use of nanotechnology in Germany is to strengthen the competitive ability of export-intensive industries such as automotive, energy, electrical engineering. This approach is similar to other technology developments in the past years and can be called diffusion-oriented, taking into account those industries and application areas that are important for the German economy.[12] From an instrumental perspective new measures are applied, i.e., the merging of science and industry in large alliances or regional clusters. This is relevant in South Korea, too, but more a result of the industry structure, reflected by large industrial combines (*chaebols*). In the US, an umbrella institution such as the NNI provides an inclusion of relevant actors from science and industry. Here, research has demonstrated a mix of basic research and applied research as well as industry competition issues. However, more central to the development of nanotechnology as well as other technologies, is the mission-oriented approach in the United States, building on specific topics such as new energy sources or storage capacities for batteries and the complete value chain from research to industrial application (Ibid.).

We have shown that the development of nanotechnology in all three countries takes into account an industry perspective. A major difference can be traced back to the relevant market size. Especially in the automotive and energy industry, export is a precondition of success for South Korea and Germany due to the relatively small size of their home markets. The US home market is large enough to absorb new technological developments that might be more expensive (and therefore not competitive) than existing ones.

Summarizing these results, the influence of policy for nanotechnology development cannot be regarded as isolated. It is influenced by the type of market economy with regard to the state of regulation, framework conditions such as national market size and innovation policy approaches (diffusion-oriented vs. mission-oriented). Looked at in more detail, these differences become smaller, however, because of the inclusion of all the main steps of the specific value chain.

Concerning our second research question, we found some evidence for an interaction between market, industry, and policy factors. However, we are not able to derive causal relationships between these factors. What can be stated thus far is that, especially in South Korea and the US, government policies initiated innovative activities in nanotechnology to support green and sustainable growth. In Germany this is at least the case for related activities. What can be mentioned is the example of education for basic knowledge in chemistry for batteries that have been neglected by universities and would not have been started without public support.

Clearly another deficit of this paper is that, with regard to the relatively early state of the development of nanotechnology, it was not possible to precisely assess the importance for green and sustainable growth. Many applications are either produced as small charges or as technical demonstrators that are not ready for industrial applications. Many of them require further R&D in a number of aspects. Nevertheless, the analyzed activities towards nanotechnology in all cases had linkages to green growth. What seems surprising at the end of our analysis is the fact that the complete life cycle was not considered for any single product. The recycling of nanotechnology is usually not mentioned when new products are developed. However, its contributions not only to green but also to sustainable growth as outlined before seem an important and contemporary question for policy makers all over the world.

Notes

1 This paper is based upon the following definition of nanotechnology: nanotechnology includes all procedures and processes that deal with the production, investigation and use of structures and materials in an order of magnitude between 1 and 100 nanometers. In this size range partially drastic characteristic changes from materials and components can occur and nanotechnology here is used for a optimization of technological components; see for this definition Grimm et al. (2011: 15); BMBF (2009: 4).

2 See Hullmann (2006) for an overview on different market studies.

3 In the following the OECD definition for Green Growth is used:

> Green growth is about fostering economic growth and development while ensuring that the natural assets continue to provide the resources and environmental services on which our well-being relies. To do this it must catalyze investment and innovation which will underpin sustained growth and give rise to new economic opportunities.

See for this definition OECD (2011: 9).

4 See for this debate for instance: Invernizzi and Foladori (2000); Miozzo et al. (2003); Maclurcan (2005).

5 The examples are taken from our book Grimm, Heinrich, Malanowski, Pfirrmann, Schindler, Stahl-Rolf and Zweck (2011): Nanotechnologie: Innovationsmotor für den Standort Deutschland, Baden-Baden and with regard to the issues of the study and recent technological developments revised and actualized.

6 For example, at RWTH Aachen University the stationary energy storage has a strong academic home, not least because of the commitment of the energy supplier E.ON, Institute for Energy Research.

7 See for detailed information: www.fraunhofer.de/en/institutes-research-establishments/groups-alliances/nanotechnology.html (accessed July 22, 2013).

8 Both Ministries offered nearly Euro 80 Mio. for specific programs. However all amounts for this application in Germany are not easy to assess due to other various programs funding technology in an indirect manner and programs on the federal state level. This holds true for the other areas of nanotechnology application.

9 See Schulte (2012); Roland Berger Strategy Consultants (2012); first effect can be seen in the bankruptcy of A123Systems, a US-based battery producer. This firm was mentioned as one of the five world key-players (see Kleese 2012; Trechow 2013).

10 Detailed figures on public nanotechnology expenditures were not available, but official statistics claim that funding of nanotechnology is the second biggest asset after funding of information technology (see MoSt 2011).

11 See Nanoscale Science, Engineering and Technology Subcommittee; Committee on Technology, National Science and Technology Council (2011).

12 See for the contribution of "mission-oriented vs. diffusion-oriented policy" to the innovation policy debate: Chiang (1991).

References

Aghion, P., Hemous, P. and Veugelers, R., 2009: No green growth without innovation. *Breugel Policy Brief* 2009/7, p. 1–8.

Bijker, W.E. and Law, J. (Eds.), 1992: *Shaping Technology/ Building Societies: Studies in sociotechnical change.* Cambridge, MA: MIT Press.

Bijker, W.E., Hughes, T.P. and Pinch, T.J. (Eds.), 1987: *The Social Construction of Technologcial Systems: New directions on the sociology and history of technology.* Cambridge, MA: MIT Press.

Bundesministerium für Bildung und Forschung, 2008a: Sunic System gibt strategische Kooperation hinsichtlich OLED Beleichtungs- und Solarzellen-Fertigungsanlage mit dem Fraunhofer IPMS bekannt. Suwon, Korea. Pressemitteilung am 24. Juni 2008.

Bundesministerium für Bildung und Forschung und Bundesministerium für Umwelt, Naturschutz und Reaktorsicherheit (Ed.), 2008b: Masterplan, Green Tech, Berlin.
Bundesministerium für Bildung und Forschung, 2009: nano.D-Report 2009, Berlin.
Bundesministerium für Bildung und Forschung (Ed.), 2011: Action Plan Nanotechnology 2015, Berlin.
Chiang, J.T., 1991: From "mission-oriented" to "diffusion-oriented" paradigm: the new trend of U.S. industrial technology policy. *Technovation* 11(6), pp. 339–356.
Das, R., 2011: Printed Electronics in Korea. Available online at: www.idtechex.com/contact/team/raghu_das.asp (accessed April 22, 2014).
Geelhaar, T., 2009: *Strategische Forschungsagenda für Organische und Grossflächige Elektronik. Für Grüne Elektronik aus Deutschland.* VDI-TZ (Ed.), Düsseldorf.
Grimm, E., Heinrich, S., Malanowski, N., Pfirrmann, O., Stahl-Rolf, S. and Zweck, A., 2011: *Nanotechnologie: Innovationsmotor für den Standort Deutschland.* Nomos: Baden-Baden.
HB, 2012: Batteriegeschäft: Bosch und Samsung begraben Gemeinschaftsprojekt. Frankfurt. Handelsblatt.com, September 5.
Herz, C. and Mayer-Kuckuk, F., 2008: Gemeinschaftsunternehmen: Bosch-Chef schmiedet Batterie-Pakt, Frankfurt. Handelsblatt.com, June 16.
Hullmann, A., 2006: *The economic development of nanotechnology: an indicator based analysis* (DG Research eds.). Brussels.
Invernizzi, N. and Foladori, G., 2000: Nanotechnology & the Developing World: Will Nanotechnology Overcome Poverty or Widen Disparities?, *NANOTECH. Law & Business* 2(3), pp. 101–110.
Kassatly, S., 2010: The lithium-ion battery industry for electric vehicles. Master Thesis, Massachusetts Institute of Technology.
Klesse, H., 2012: US-Batteriehersteller: Ist die Pleite von A123 Systems der Anfang vom Ende der E-Mobilität? *Wirtschaftswoche Online* (accessed October 18, 2012).
KOPTI, 2012: Optical Applications, Seoul. Available online at: http://eng.kopti.re.kr/index.sko?menuCd=AC01001001000 (accessed June 3, 2015).
Lee, Jo-Won, 2002: Overview of nanotechnology in Korea—10 years blueprint. *Journal of Nanoparticle Research* 4, pp. 473–476.
Maclurcan, D.C., 2005: Nanotechnology and Developing Countries Part 2: What Realities? *AZoNano—Online Journal of Nanotechnology*. Available online at: www.azonano.com/Details.asp?ArticleID=1429 (accessed August 14, 2012).
Mayntz, R., 2009: The changing governance of large technical infrastructure systems. In: Mayntz, R. (Ed.): *Über Governance. Institutionen und Prozesse politischer Regelung.* Frankfurt a.M.: Campus, pp. 121–150.
Millard, J., Larsen, P., Pedersen, K., Kidmose, B., Rytz, J., Vet, M., Vodovar, M., Wymenga, P., Hay, G. and Stenning, J., 2012: Study on internationalisation and fragmentation of value chains and security of supply. European Commission: DG Enterprise and Industry.
Ministry of Education, Science and Technology (Korea), 2011: Road to Our Future: Green Growth National Strategy and the Five-Year Plan (2009~2013).
Miozzo, M., Dewick, P. and Green, K., 2003: Globalisation and the environment: the long-term effects of technology on the international division of labour and energy demand. In: ASEAT. Manchester. eScholarID:2b567.
Nano Practical Application Center, 2013: Development of Nano Component and Device Technology.
Nanoscale Science, Engineering and Technology Subcommittee; Committee on Technology, National Science and Technology Council, 2011: National Nanotechnology Initiative Strategic Plan.
National Economic Council, Council of Economic Advisers, and Office of Science and Technology Policy, 2011: A STRATEGY FOR AMERICAN INNOVATION: Securing Our Economic Growth and Prosperity.
National Science and Technology Council Committee on Technology, Subcommittee on Nanoscale Science, Engineering, and Technology, 2011: National Nanotechnology Initiative – Strategic Plan.
ObservatoryNano, 2010: Economic Report: Public Funding of Nanotechnology.
ObservatoryNano, 2012: Public Funding of Nanotechnology, March 2012.
OECD (Ed.), 2011: Towards Green Growth: Monitoring Progress.
OSA DIRECT, 2010: University of Michigan, GPEC and South Korean organisations partner to develop organic photovoltaic devices.
Paris President's Council of Advisors on Science & Technology 2011: Report to the President on ensuring American Leadership in Advanced Manufacturing.

Park, Byeongwon and Son, Seok-ho, 2006: Korean Technology Foresight for Science and Technology Policy Making. Second International Seville Seminar on Future-Oriented Technology Analysis: Impact of FTA Approaches on Policy and Decision-Making – Seville, September 28–29, 2006.

Polyera Corporation, 2012: Polyera Achieves 5.2 per cent All-Polymer Organic Solar Cells. *Pressemitteilung*, September 5, 2012.

Polymer Surface and Organic Electronics Lab, 2013: Overview Organic Photovoltaics, Pohang.

Prognos, 2012: Nanotechnology for Green growth. An analytical paper on the potential contribution of nanotechnology to sustainable growth (prepared for the OECD), Berlin.

Quodt, J., 2008: Automobilindustrie: Bosch und Samsung gründen Joint Venture. *Merger & Acquisitions Review* 8–9, p. 432.

Rave, T., Triebswetter, U. and Wackenbauer, J., 2013: Koordination von Innovations-, Energie- und Umweltpolitik. *Studien zum deutschen Innovationssystem* 10. Available online at: www.e-fi.de/fileadmin/Innovationsstudien_2013/StuDIS_10_2013_ifo.pdf (accessed June 3, 2015).

Rip, A. and Kemp, R., 1998: Technological change. In: Rayner, S. and Malone, E.L. (Eds.): *Human Choice and Climate Change. Two: Resources and technology*. Columbus, OH: Batelle Press, pp. 327–399.

Roland Berger Strategy Consultants, 2012: Lithium-ion batteries: the bubble bursts. Stuttgart.

Sargent, J., 2011: Nanotechnology: A Policy Primer, CRS Report for the Congress RL34511.

Schulte, A., 2012: Wettkampf um den besten Akku – Viele Kooperationen zur Entwicklung von Batterien für Elektroautos kämpfen mit Schwierigkeiten, Frankfurt. Handelsblatt.com, September 18, p. 49.

Science Watch, 2011: Luping Yu discusses Organic Photovoltaic Research.

Seoul National University, 2013: Website Department of Materials Science and Engineering.

Shapira, P. and Wang, J., 2008: *The Policy Mix Project: Case study nanotechnology in the USA*. European Commission: DG Research.

Shapira, P. and Youtie, J., 2012: The Economic Contributions of Nanotechnology to Green and Sustainable Growth. OECD/NNI International Symposium on Assessing the Economic Impact of Nanotechnology Background Paper 3, March 27–28, 2012, Washington DC.

Sheng, X. et al., 2013: Stretchable batteries with self-similar serpentine interconnects and integrated wireless recharging systems. *Nature Communications*, February 26. Available online at: www.nature.com/ncomms/archive/subject/npg_subject_25/2013/02/index.html (accessed June 3, 2015).

Steinbusch, A., 2012: Elektromobilität: Boom der Batteriefabriken. *Wirtschaftswoche Online*. Available online at: www.wiwo.de/technologie/auto/autoderzukunft/elektromobilitaet-der-boom-der-batteriefabriken/6722518.html (accessed 20 June 2012).

SZ, 2013: Biegsame Batterie: Energiespeicher lässt sich ohne Schaden dehnen und falten, München. *Süddeutsche Zeitung*, March 4, p. 16.

Trechow, P., 2013: Batterieproduktion für Elektromobile sucht Abnehmer, Düsseldorf. *VDI-Nachrichten*, February 15, p. 9.

Youtie, J., Iacopetta, M. and Graham, S., 2008: Assessing the nature of nanotechnology: can we uncover an emerging general purpose technology? *The Journal of Technology Transfer* 33(3), pp. 315–329.

PART 6

Important players and driving forces for science and innovative development

Stability and change

23

THE POLITICS OF TECHNOLOGICAL INNOVATION

The case of U.S. solar industry

Joseph S. Szyliowicz and James M. Ohi

Introduction

Global economic and per capita income growth will lead to increasing world energy needs and emissions of greenhouse gases that, in turn, will accelerate and intensify the consequences of climate change. Research and development of renewable energy technologies are a matter of global concern and interest because deployment of these technologies can ameliorate or break the link between economic development and local, regional, and global environmental damage. Furthermore, renewable energy sources can provide the quantity, form, and quality of energy needed to meet demands for economic growth and can be sustainable if they are based on forms of solar energy that are replenished on a timescale on the order of a human lifespan. If so done, there will be minimal net increase in greenhouse gas emissions and further disruption of the radiative energy balance of the earth's atmosphere. The use of renewable energy will allow economic development and mitigation of climate change to proceed in synergy rather than in opposition.

Any state seeking to meet the twin challenges posed by economic development and climate change must decide how to guide and support the innovation process involving renewable energy technologies. The content of such decisions is shaped by two primary factors, the nature of the technologies themselves that define possibilities and options and the political decision making system that includes institutional structures, the values of decision makers, and the power of various organized groups. Thus a study of how the U.S. has attempted to promote solar technologies provides a useful case that permits us to analyze the relationship between technological innovation and the ways in which a government functions influences this process.

The nature of solar energy technologies

Renewable energy can be defined in the broadest sense as any form of primary energy that is derived directly or indirectly from the sun. In this sense, renewable energy sources such as biomass, hydropower, and wind are different forms of solar energy. The most familiar forms of energy used around the globe, such as wood, oil, gas, and coal are embodied forms of solar energy that have been gathered, transformed, and stored by natural processes. Emissions of greenhouse gases from converting and using energy resources become a global concern when the rates of conversion of stored solar energy to more usable forms (heat, electricity, fuels, and chemicals) far exceed those of formation.[1]

The surface of the earth receives about 1kW/m^2 of solar energy at peak intensity, and there is no constraint of resource availability; in one hour, the earth receives more energy from the sun than the total annual global consumption of energy.[2] Solar panels and other collection devices are used to capture the incoming solar energy and convert this energy into useable electricity. Electricity from solar energy can also be used to produce hydrogen, which can be used as a fuel (in place of gasoline) in zero-emission fuel cell engines or to store the electricity and help overcome the intermittency of solar energy. Electricity and hydrogen are particularly valuable energy carriers because they are interchangeable.[3]

Electricity from renewable resources can be generated by large facilities such as wind farms and concentrating solar energy plants. Photovoltaic (PV) technologies offer a direct path to renewable and sustainable electricity generation. Among solar energy technologies, PV systems possess typical characteristics, such as zero emissions and modularity, but also those that are unique, such as no moving parts, fluids, or gases; high power-to-weight ratio; and instantaneous output.[4] Solar panels are modular and can generate electricity for an individual building, for a village, or for larger communities. Hence, policies that lead the development and widespread use of this technology will have very beneficial effects on the environment and on climate change.

Small solar systems can be located to take advantage of locally available solar energy resources and adjusted to best fit the local environmental and energy situation. A distributed energy system of interconnected groups of solar panels, for example, results in a much more robust power generation system that is less vulnerable to disruptions whether they are due to natural or man-made disasters.[5] Such decentralization clearly offers significant technological advantages, especially if coordinated on a national level but doing so requires careful coordination between local political entities and a central authority, a condition that may often be difficult to meet, especially when the former enjoys a high degree of autonomy as is the case in the U.S. as well as in other states with federal systems.

Although the widespread deployment of solar technologies will have multiple and synergistic economic, societal, political, and environmental benefits, nations whether industrialized or developing will not be able to realize such benefits unless they act individually and collectively to address a host of policy issues, including those that directly or indirectly affect technological innovation. Photovoltaic technologies also present a number of policy issues involving technology R&D and innovation.

Hence, in this chapter we analyze the choices that governments, primarily the U.S., have made in seeking to promote the development and diffusion of this specific subset of solar energy technology. We do so in order to answer such questions as 1) what policies did the U.S. adopt and how effective were they? 2) why did the U.S. adopt such policies? And, 3) what lessons emerge on how governments seeking to promote technological innovation should proceed? In order to do so we shall consider in detail the specific ways in which U.S. policy has evolved and the factors that have shaped its evolution. However, to understand the policy issues, it is necessary to consider the ways in which technological innovation occurs and the role of national policies therein.

The nature of technological innovation and national policies

If the dream of solar energy is to be realized, technological innovations are required, but doing so successfully is no easy matter. Though governments everywhere seek to develop policies to promote technological innovation, examples of policy failures can easily be found throughout the globe. The problem is that innovation is a complex activity that involves a high degree of uncertainty.

In addition to the political issues that complicate the difficulties of devising and implementing effective policies in any technological sector, conceptual issues further complicate this task. This complexity is reflected in the fact that scholars disagree even on the meaning of terms as well as on the conceptualization of the process. Though there is general agreement that it involves a number of stages, no consensus exists on the number of stages or on the nature and extent of the feedback loops that are involved. The simplest categorization posits a linear model with three stages—Research and Development, Commercialization, and Diffusion. These stages are also known as R&D, Market Formation, and Diffusion. A slightly more elaborate model identifies four stages—Research, Development, Demonstration, and Commercialization.

In Auerswald and Branscomb (2003), a more sophisticated model identifies a five stage process with various feedback loops. Whatever the conceptualization, each stage requires various inputs, and, hopefully, yields an output that, at the end of the process, has led to a commercially viable product.[6] Scholars also agree that a simple linear process does not capture the complexities of the innovation process for it is necessary to incorporate feedback loops and interactions among the stages. A sophisticated version of this type is developed by Gallagher et al. (2012: 140) for the energy sector.

Not only is there agreement that the process does not flow smoothly but many scholars have labeled the stage that lies between a successful output from basic research and its successful commercialization as the "valley of death." As the name vividly implies, this is the final resting place for many innovations. Though effective government policies can help to overcome this formidable barrier, whether and how a government should be involved is often a very controversial ideological issue whose outcome will determine to a significant degree whether such policies will be adopted. Conceptual problems compound this difficulty for it is not at all clear how the process of technological innovation can best be operationalized. Beard et al. (2009), for example, seeking to analyze the "valley of death" phenomenon, found it necessary to limit the innovation process to three stages—basic research, "the valley of death," and diffusion.

It is, however, also possible to conceptualize this complex overall process with its stages and feedback loops through two simple analytical models. The first, a "discovery push" model, stresses the importance of research and development activities that are focused to a greater or lesser degree on specific technologies, some of which may be pursued by scientists with no clear market in mind yet often turn out, as in the case of the laser, to have profound impacts on national and international economies and societies. Such research is often conducted in university laboratories. Governments, however, also frequently play an important role in this model, sponsoring research and development activities that are focused on a specific perceived need, even creating R&D organizations for this purpose (Szyliowicz 1981). The establishment of the National Renewable Energy Laboratory by the U.S. government is a prime example. The second is the "demand-pull" model, most often characteristic of industrial research and development activities where a company's sales force has identified a potentially profitable gap that remains to be filled and its research and development section set to work to develop a suitable product or process. Recently, however, the demand side has received increased attention as experts have identified various obstacles at the last stage(s) of the innovation process that prevent the wide diffusion of technologies that have escaped the "valley of death." Accordingly various policies designed to eliminate or minimize the impact of the barriers that limit market introduction and diffusion and to increase the demand for a new product have been proposed (OECD 2011).

Choosing and implementing an appropriate set of policies is clearly a complex issue though it is important to recognize that scholars have established certain important points. First, as noted above, it is essential to recognize that linkages are critical and that success is more likely when government, industry, and academia interact cooperatively. Second, is the importance of recognizing that it is necessary to take a holistic perspective and recognize that even policies in another area can have positive or negative impacts. Thus any government seeking to influence the technological process in a specific sector must pay attention to at least two sets of policies. The first, difficult enough, involves selecting and developing the most appropriate policies to impact the innovation process of a particular technology. The innovation process, however, is also influenced by a range of indirect impacts resulting from policies that have been adopted in other sectors such as, for example, import regulations.

This point is underscored by a recent study performed by two Federal Reserve Bank associates that sought to measure the impact of technology policies on aggregate output over time. They found that government policies designed to support research and development activities by firms were effective only if the tax and regulatory environments were also supportive. Thus, since policies sometimes came into conflict, it is critical to examine both direct and indirect policies to ensure that they are mutually reinforcing rather than negating each other.

Such complexity does not negate the need for such policies as evidenced by the results of a recent study of the sources of innovation in the U.S. It found that large corporations are no longer the major contributors. From 1971 to 2006, the number of awards for innovation won by the 500 largest US firms fell from about 40 to four. And, the proportion of U.S. corporate patents by such traditional technologically innovating firms such as G.E., Kodak, AT&T, DuPont, G.M., Dow Chemical, 3M, United Technologies, and Ford fell from 10 percent to 4.5 percent during the same period. Furthermore, technological innovations are increasingly federally funded and the result of cooperative interactions made possible by linkages between the private sector, federal laboratories, and academic researchers (Block and Keller 2008). The evidence that public policy has a powerful impact on technological innovation has also been demonstrated by a sophisticated cross national analysis of several OECD countries over a five year period, using patent data, though it found that the impact varies depending upon the policy and the type of technology involved. Specifically, the authors state:

> Our empirical results indicate that public policy has had a very significant influence on the development of new technologies in the area of renewable energy. Using the composite policy variable, statistical significance at the 1 percent level is found for all renewable energy sources, except biomass (where it is significant at the 5 percent level). However, the results suggest that instrument choice also matters. With respect to patent activity in renewable energy overall, taxes, obligations and tradable certificates are the only statistically significant policy instruments.
>
> *(Johnstone et al. 2008; also see Gallagher et al. 2012: 149ff).*

The politics of science and technology policy in the U.S.

The U.S. has for decades adopted various policies to promote technological innovation. In this sector and others, U.S. policies have fluctuated over time but they can essentially be assigned to three major categories. The first, Direct Government Funding of R&D, includes R&D

contracts with private firms, contracts and grants with universities, Intramural R&D conducted in government laboratories, R&D contracts with industry-led consortia or collaborations among two or more of the actors above. The second, Direct or Indirect Support for Commercialization and Production and Indirect Support for Development includes patent protection, R&D tax credits, tax credits or production subsidies for firms bringing new technologies to market, tax credits or rebates for purchasers of new technologies, government procurement, and demonstration projects. The third category involves Support of Learning and Diffusion of Knowledge and Technology. This includes education and training, codification and diffusion of technical knowledge, technical standard setting, industrial or technology extension services, publicity, persuasion, and consumer information (Alic 2002). Which of these tools should be used and to what degree is a question that has always been answered by the nature and functioning of the political system. And, since there is often little agreement beyond the view that governments should create an environment that facilitates technological innovation, the specific policies that have been adopted have always been a function of the nature of the dominant ideology and the distribution of political power at any given time.

Most of the literature dealing with technological innovation, however, is not the work of political scientists so that political considerations are seldom discussed in a way that adequately considers the policy and decision process. The authors of an important detailed study on the Energy Technology Innovation (ETIS), for example, discuss the political dimension as follows:

> Actors and institutions strongly affect the ETIS. The roles and importance of different actors and institutions vary among innovation systems, and also change over the lifecycle of an innovation . . .. Typically, for example, as innovation systems increase in maturity, the importance of private actors increases . . .. New energy technologies often face resistance from actors with vested interests in incumbent systems. To build up innovation systems, actors, particularly from non-governmental organizations (NGOs) and industry, can counteract this inertia though political lobbying and advocacy coalitions. Public institutions may also contribute, as in the case of planning agencies advising regional or national governments to develop supporting policies for emerging technologies.
>
> *(Gallagher et al. 2012: 143)*

Although this discussion identifies some of the key actors, it merely hints at the political nature of the process or the ways in which the structure and functioning of the relevant organizations and the worldviews of their elites shape outcomes. The nature of power relations determines policy choices but those relations are the result of a potent mixture of specific ideas, interests, personalities, and institutional structures. It is therefore necessary to discuss the nature of the U.S. political system because, like any such system, it possesses distinct features and characteristics.

One of these involves an important characteristic of any political system—how power is distributed vertically. Essentially there are two basic patterns. In some the central government monopolizes power, in others, power devolves to regions or states, as is the case in Germany and the U.S. where the individual states have significant latitude in making policy decisions in many areas including energy. California, for example, a leader in environmental protection has often led the way in establishing new environmental standards. It has now committed itself to "reducing of statewide greenhouse gasses (GHG) emissions to 1990 levels by 2020 and to 20 percent of 1990 levels by 2025 and providing 33 percent of our electricity demand in 2020 from renewable resources."[7] Policy making at this level, however, is similar to that at the center, with a variety of actors possessing different ideologies and resources seeking to determine outcomes. This is certainly commonplace in the American system—the case of ethanol in Iowa, discussed in Chapter 20, provides a vivid illustration of this phenomenon.

These forces also operate at the national level of any state. In the U.S., the government's power is divided among three branches—the judiciary, the executive, and the legislative with its two bodies, the Senate and the House of Representatives. Legislation has to be approved by both bodies and signed by the President. As head of the executive branch, he is the most powerful person in the state but that power is circumscribed not only structurally (for example, he possesses a veto power but it can be over-ridden by a two-thirds vote in the Senate) but also by many political forces.

Herein lies the answers to how and why the "valley of death" discussed above is such a major feature of technological innovation in the U.S., why so many potentially important technologies that have emerged from an earlier stage apparently do not receive adequate funding and thus never make a successful entry into the marketplace. Beard's research led him to conclude that: "the Valley of Death is a phenomenon that may be a consequence of the US Government focusing its R&D investment activities upon early stage, basic research, with less attention paid to intermediate-stage projects" (Beard et al. 2009: 355). But why is this the case? The answer lies in the nature of the horizontal governance structures that characterize the U.S. political system. A recent study found that the separation of powers prevents the essential coordination required if innovations are to successfully navigate the "valley of death." As the authors noted, "Today, many of the specifics of energy research, development, and demonstration (RD&D) programs are decided by the Department of Energy (DOE) headquarters[8] while many of the most important deployment incentives are decided in Congress or by federal and state standard-setting agencies" (Anadón et al. 2010: 1). In short, despite its important role in developing and administering energy policies, the DOE may perhaps be considered as "primus inter pares."

This division of power, where many layers and actors influence technological policy making, clearly complicates any effort to create and implement a strategy that is based on a rational, integrated long term approach. Moreover, the President has the power to shape energy policy and to influence the DOE's activities, sometimes with unfortunate consequences, as was vividly illustrated by the widely publicized Solyndra affair which also reveals the difficulties that confront the Obama administration (indeed any government) seeking to promote technological innovation.[9]

The nature of the political parties adds additional powerful actors since they are themselves internally divided into various factions over which there is little hierarchical control. Thus, though the policy process is driven by the ideas, aims, and orientation of the government in power, with the President as the key policy maker, the degree to which he is able to actually shape policy is a function of his ability to gain the support of other powerful actors including economic and political interests (Congress and even elements within the bureaucracy) and ultimately the public. Thus the American political system is characterized by frequent conflict as personalities, ideologies, and organizations clash. Under these conditions it is not surprising that business and other interests that naturally seek to influence the policy process are often able to do so very effectively both at the state and the federal level.

One scholar has attempted to bring analytical order to this complexity by building on the concept of "issue networks" and has identified eight "arenas" or groups of primary actors – "legislative," "executive," "regulatory," "academic-professional," "corporate-managerial," "judicial," "labor," and "public mobilization." Each has its own power structure, perspectives, interests, and possesses different power and access to the decision making process. The basic technology strategy that leads to a focus on particular kinds of technologies as well as the technology policies designed to promote the development of a specific area is produced by the interaction of these groups whose perspectives and positions change according to the technology involved (Hamlett 1992). In reality, the process is even more complicated, for these "arenas" contain sub sets of actors who often disagree, as evidenced by the Solyndra case discussed below. And, to understand the role of Congress, it is not only essential to understand such factors as its committee system and their jurisdictions, the role of the filibuster in the Senate, the power of private sector lobbyists and of public interest groups, but the ways in which Senate and House members frame the issue as well.

The area of science and technology clearly reflects this general pattern. It is characterized by sharp ideological divisions, between and to some degree within the political parties, and attempts by powerful business groups and non-governmental organizations to influence policy. Of particular concern is a key issue—should the U.S. government play an active role at this stage of the innovation process or should it permit only market forces to operate. The outcome of such a debate has important implications because each ideological position contains very different perspectives, each of which inexorably leads to particular policies that will profoundly affect the character of future technological development.

A large majority of the Republican Party's Congressional delegation and its supporters argue that national government action should be limited, that it should act only to the extent that its policies facilitate the work of the private sector since that is where most innovations originate. Its 2012 platform articulated this perspective in no uncertain terms:[10]

> We look to government—local, State, and federal—for the things government must do, but we believe those duties can be carried out more efficiently and at less cost. For all other activities, we look to the private sector; for the American people's resourcefulness, productivity, innovation, fiscal responsibility, and citizen-leadership have always been the true foundation of our national greatness. For much of the last century, an opposing view has dominated public policy where we have witnessed the expansion, centralization, and bureaucracy in an entitlement society. Government has lumbered on, stifling innovation, with no incentive for fundamental change.

If such an ideology prevails, then the basis is laid for the emergence of a wider range of technologies than would otherwise be the case. In other words, action by the national government should be limited, it should act only to the extent that its policies facilitate the work of the private sector since that is where most innovations originate. It should, at most, promote basic research and help ensure that an adequate supply of trained scientists and technologists is available but it should exercise great care to adopt only policies that do not hinder the private sector's innate ability to innovate; it should not interfere in any way in the operation of free markets since by doing so, it will hinder the creation and diffusion of new technologies by erecting barriers and distorting the efficient allocation of resources (Block and Keller 2008: 1–2).

Proponents of an active policy argue that markets do not always work efficiently and point to the important contributions that government policies have historically made to the emergence of technological innovations in defense and other sectors. Accordingly, they argue:[11]

> If networks involving government research and development (R&D) programs and scientific and technical experts have been at the heart of the innovation economy, then policies that limit or even roll back government involvement in innovation are counterproductive. Instead, effective technology policies would require active

> government support of targeted R&D programs and collaborative mechanisms that support innovation.

The key, in their view is to create an environment that links universities, the private sector, and the government into a dynamic and mutually reinforcing relationship.

This ideological perspective is shared by many in the Democratic Party, which is committed to the view that the government must play an active role in promoting technological innovation. Its 2008 platform, for example, stated that it would "fast-track investment of billions of dollars over the next ten years to establish a green energy sector that will create up to five million jobs," and said the party was "committed to getting at least 25 percent of our electricity from renewable sources by 2025" (Malakov and Sachdev 2012). Such a commitment highlights the relationship between particular ideologies and the nature and scope of technological development.

Upon coming to power, President Obama attempted to develop and implement such a policy because of the state of the economy and his recognition that new technologies lead to economic growth. His policy has also been motivated by the growing awareness of the threat posed by climate change though many powerful actors continue to argue that human activity is not responsible for the changes that are evidently taking place. Such arguments are widely held by many Republicans and continually advanced by well financed groups who advance such arguments through all possible channels including the distribution of such free books (including a DVD) as *The Mad, Mad, Mad World of Climatism: Mankind and climate change mania*. It argues that "contrary to what our newspapers, our professors, or *our political leader* [my emphasis] tells us, global warming is natural and cars are innocent." Indeed President Obama is explicitly listed, along with Angela Merkel and David Cameron as being one of the "World Leaders Captured by Climatism" (Goreham 2013: 10–11).

President Obama has clearly earned such a designation, and has often stressed the need to promote the development of renewable energy. Soon after coming to power, his administration published a formal policy statement on this topic (2009) and, in February 2011 issued an update. Entitled "A Strategy for American Innovation: Driving Towards Sustainable Growth and Quality Jobs," it emphasized the potential of solar energy and reflects an awareness of the need for an active government role, albeit one that promotes and does not hinder the effective operation of the market. It stated:

> A modern, practical approach recognizes both the need for fundamental support and the hazards of overzealous government intervention. The government should make sure individuals and businesses have the tools and support to take risks and innovate, but should not dictate what risks they take.

It focused on three policy areas: 1) enhancing investments in fundamental research (with 3 percent of GDP as the goal), education, and infrastructure in science and technology, 2) increasing market based innovation by creating an entrepreneurial environment in both the private and public sector, supported by exports and capital markers, and 3) promoting national priorities in such areas as clean energy through government action when market failures occur.[12]

Although the President has outlined a specific strategy that fits clearly into the three major categories discussed above that have traditionally guided U.S. technology policy—Direct Government Funding of R&D, Direct or Indirect Support for Commercialization and Production and Indirect Support for Development and Support of Learning and Diffusion of Knowledge and Technology, its successful implementation requires the participation of many actors, notably Congress which wields considerable power in establishing technological and other policies through its ability to create new programs, exercise legislative oversight, and provide funding. Thus, the President can present a budget that incorporates increases for energy R&D but it is Congress that will determine how much will actually be allocated and under what conditions. Similarly, the President can propose new standards and regulations but these may require Congressional assent.

Under these circumstances, two points deserve to be emphasized, one theoretical, the other practical. First, the process of technological innovation cannot be separated from its political context because the technology that emerges in the market place is one that has found enough political support to help it overcome particular barriers in the innovation process. Second, it is by no means clear that Obama's innovation strategy will be implemented as he has outlined, given the nature of the American political system. An important variable that mitigates against success is the fact that the Republican Party controls the House of Representatives and an overwhelming majority of its members believe (despite the evidence to the contrary) that an active government policy is inherently counterproductive as it creates barriers to innovation and to the operation of the market that, left alone, is the most efficient producer of successful innovations.

Even so, the President has, because of his administrative responsibilities, a wide set of tools that essentially give him the power to create and enforce what amount to new laws. These include issuing Executive Orders, Presidential Proclamations, Signing Statements, and Regulatory Reviews. Thus, though a partisan deadlock between Democrats and Republicans may aggravate the structural separation of powers and create legislative paralysis that prevents the passage of new legislation, the President can still wield great influence over the ways in which technology policy is implemented (Flanagan 2011).

In terms of energy generally and solar energy specifically, such Presidential actions will be targeted largely at The Department of Energy (DOE). It is the major bureaucratic actor in the energy sector and is responsible for a large number of initiatives designed to improve the environment. It is therefore, involved in technology R&D and innovation for photovoltaics.

U.S. policy towards solar energy: meeting the foreign challenge

Any consideration of the role of solar energy in the U.S. in coming decades must take into account the activities of international competitors. At this stage, due to limited and inconsistent solar policies, the deployment of solar energy in the U.S. during the past decade has lagged behind that in European and Asian countries, which have instituted stronger policies to promote solar energy and thus pose a continuing challenge to the American effort. The two major players are China and Germany.

Germany's renewable energy policies were first crafted in the early 1970s. The German strategy has been to promote the development of marketable products, thus creating a new market, domestically and internationally. It has, therefore, sought to foster the deployment of renewable energy (RE) sources, with the Feed-in-Tariff (FiT) being the central approach. Reinforcing the FiT has been an array of additional policies to increase public support for R&D of PV technologies, as well as measures to spur investments by manufacturing plants. Initiated in 2000, the Renewable Energy Sources Act (EEG) applies to electricity generated from RE sources, and established FiT levels for each specific RE source with the FiT levels for PV being the highest. The PV tariffs are paid for a 20-year period, with levels determined based on the type of installation (ground or roof-top) and the kW threshold capacity of the system (30 kW, 100kW, and 1000 kW). The tariffs are to decrease at a scheduled rate during the specified time period, to account for decreasing costs associated with increased technological innovation. The German government decided to cut the tariff three times during 2010, instead of the scheduled reduction of roughly 9 percent, as system prices were falling much faster in 2009 than originally expected; the total reduction from the 2009 level was approximately 23 percent by the end of 2010. The years 2011 and 2012 also saw stronger decreases, at 24 percent and 15 percent, respectively (Avril et al. 2012: 249–250). The government subsidized this tariff at an average annual cost of €4,270 million from 2003–2009. The EEG was amended in 2004 and 2009 to adapt to changing technologies and market circumstances, in order to ensure the more efficient deployment of RE sources. The 2004 amendment saw an increase in the PV FiT, and the 2009 amendment adjusted the schedule due to the drastic fall in system prices. PV installations increased greatly following both of these changes (Grau et al. 2009: 26–28; Laird and Stefes 2009: 2622–2624). Moreover, one cannot ignore various additional market stimulation measures and investment support policies nor the role of the EU. Despite these efforts, there is a fear in Germany that the FiT and its resulting large PV deployment is creating high costs for German electricity consumers, while also benefiting Chinese manufacturers instead of the development of German industry (Grau et al. 2009: 21).

China's first major PV policies date back only to 2009 and 2010 when the central government established the Golden Sun Program and some large-scale FiT programs. These were market policies designed to operationalize the medium- and long-term strategy initiated by the National Development and Reform Commission in 2007. The goals of these PV policies are the national deployment of 5 GW of PV electricity installed by 2015, and 20 GW by 2020. While there have also been some PV manufacturing investment incentives and market policies established by city and regional governments, R&D continues to have the smallest budgets at both national and regional levels (Grau et al. 2009: 30–35). However, the amount of government funding for R&D has been expanding for state owned enterprises (SOEs) (Anadón 2012: 3). Accordingly, though China has been able to produce and export large amounts of inexpensive solar panels, there is the concern that a strong domestic innovation capacity is being neglected as many technologies and much manufacturing equipment is being imported from Germany (Grau et al. 2009: 21).

Regardless of the Chinese and German concerns, their policies have had a profound impact on the U.S. whose market share of PV module supply has declined significantly during the past decade, falling from 30 percent of global shipments in 2000 to 6 percent (about 1000 MW) in 2010, a decade in which global shipments grew at a compound annual rate of 53 percent and reached 17 GW in 2010. In 2010, solar energy provided less than 0.1 percent of the electricity demand in the U.S., which is comparable to that provided by nuclear energy in 1960.

In an attempt to develop a long-term, multi-mission national program that will enable the U.S. to regain the technological lead in solar energy, the DOE is implementing the SunShot Initiative.[13] Incorporating both the "discovery push" and "demand pull" approaches to technology innovation, it purposely invokes President Kennedy's "moon shot," a policy objective that has become emblematic of a concerted—and successful—effort to achieve a challenge worthy of a great nation. Announced by Secretary of Energy Steven Chu in February 2011, this initiative explicitly recognizes that "America is in a world race to produce cost-effective, quality photovoltaics" and seeks "significant improvements in solar cell efficiency, reliability, and cost [and] to move novel PV devices and systems to pilot production as well as advance market-ready technologies into mass production." The SunShot initiative will enable the U.S. to achieve these goals by:

> spurring American innovations to reduce the costs of solar energy and re-establish U.S. global leadership in this growing industry. . . . It will boost our economic competitiveness, rebuild our manufacturing industry and help reach the President's goal of doubling our clean energy in the next 25 years.

If the cost targets are reached, it is estimated that solar energy has the potential to meet roughly 14 percent of electricity demand by 2030 and 27 percent by 2050 in the contiguous U.S. (excluding Alaska and Hawaii).[14]

Both evolutionary and revolutionary technologies changes will be required to achieve the cost and deployment targets of the initiative. Of the steps in the innovation process, the key findings of the Vision Study focus more on market formation and diffusion than on R&D and demonstration, on an attempt to successfully cross the valley of death. It seeks to do so by attempting to achieve efficiency improvements, material substitutions, and expanded material supplies through "technological advances," but this advancement may be more difficult than anticipated. The technological pathways to revolutionary improvements in PV technologies are not known today and will require more R&D with a sustained focus on meeting the cost target (Vision Study 2012: xxviii). Acquiring the resources for such activities will, as always, become a political matter whose outcome will be determined by a struggle between various more or less powerful actors.

Sensitivity analyses conducted by the Vision Study reveal the major weakness of this and other initiatives devoted to a particular technology or set of technologies (Vision Study 2012: xxii). The level of solar energy deployment for electricity generation envisioned by the SunShot Initiative is contingent on how aggressively cost reductions for other renewable electricity generation technologies, especially wind, and conventional technologies are pursued and achieved by actors and institutions in both the public and private sectors. At certain price thresholds, which differ among renewable energy technologies, deployment increases non-linearly with cost reductions, particularly for wind.[15]

Conclusion

This analysis of the difficulties confronting the U.S., as well as its achievements, as it strives to promote the commercialization of solar energy, permits us to derive some important generalizations about the role of public policy in technological innovation. These can be divided into the two major dimensions identified above—the nature of the technology and the structure and functioning of the political system that shapes the policies that are adopted.

It is clear that different technologies pose different challenges along the innovation chain because of their different risk profiles, thus creating difficult challenges concerning the type and level of government support that is most effective. Any effort by the government to promote the innovation process must be based on a coherent long term strategy. To be successful, such a strategy must be based on economic rationality and consider the risk-bearing tendencies of private sector actors as well as the positive externalities that are involved with innovation activity. Moreover, given the nature of the innovation process and its various stages, different specific policy prescriptions are likely to be required for each stage and, probably, for different industrial sectors as well.

The ability to develop and implement long term, rational policies, however, is obviously not a universal attribute. Policies are the output of a political system. Developing and implementing such a technology policy approach requires a particular kind of decision making process if it is not to be frustrated by the political and ideological orientations of political parties and decision makers as well as those of various private actors.

An important variable in this regard is the issue of the structural distribution of power, whether the state is "federalist" or "centralist." Superficially it can be argued that the latter type is more likely to develop a more effective science and technology policy but this is not necessarily the case for there are many examples of such states, e.g., France, that are generally considered as lagging in this area. As to the former, states in the U.S. have considerable power and can be valuable crucibles of innovation though political considerations at this level can also lead to distorted policies.

Thus, the power of the vested interests within a political system and their ability to shape policy to further their own ends emerges as a critical variable. If they do not share a commitment to long term scientific and technological innovation or if they are so ideologically divided in a manner that prevents compromise, then that state is unlikely to prosper in today's international environment where heated competition not only in solar energy but in so many other technological sectors is the norm.

Notes

1 Detailed discussions of the technological issues presented in this paper are to be found in the Home Page, posted on the website. The specific items are listed there as #1, #2, etc. For a technical discussion of solar energy, see #1.
2 This has important implications for the developing world. See Home Page, #2.
3 For more information on energy carriers, see Home Page #3.
4 On the PV effect see #4.
5 David Sanborn Scott has coined the term, "hydricity," for the "twin energy currencies, hydrogen and electricity, ultimately manufactured from sustainable, non-carbon energy sources" (www.whec2012.com/wp-content/uploads/2012/06/SCOTT-WHEC-V.2.pdf). See Home Page, #4 for more information and discussion on solar energy and photovoltaic technology and the role of the Department of Energy therein.
6 For a discussion and diagram of this process see "The Nature and Importance of Innovation" pp. 6–7, http://press.princeton.edu/chapters/s9221.pdf.
7 California's Clean Energy Future, CEC-100-2010-002; www.cacleanenergyfuture.org/documents/CACleanEnergyFutureOverview.pdf.
8 On the history and achievements of the DOE see the Home Page #5.
9 The details of the Solyndra affair are to be found in the Home Page, #6.
10 www.gop.com/2012-republican-platform_reforming/.
11 www.gop.com/2012-republican-platform_reforming/.
12 www.whitehouse.gov/administration/eop/nec/StrategyforAmericanInnovation.
13 For a detailed discussion of this project, see Home Page #7.
14 These estimates are to be found on p. xx of the SunShot Vision Study (2012), a detailed analysis of the issues and problems that have to be dealt with to attain the Vision's goals. See Home Page, #8.
15 See Home Page #9 for a discussion of their significance.

References

Alic, J.A., 2002: Policies for innovation: learning from the past. In: Norberg-Bohm, V. (Ed.): *The Role of Government in Technology Innovation: Insights for government policy in the energy sector.* Belfer Center for Science and International Affairs, Harvard University, Table 2, pp. 25–26.

Anadón, L., 2012: Missions-oriented RD&D institutions in energy between 2000 and 2010: a comparative analysis of China, the United Kingdom, and the United States. *Research Policy* 41(10), pp. 1742–1756.

Anadón, L., Bunn, M., Jones, C. and Narayanamurti, V., 2010: *U.S. Public Energy Innovation Institutions and Mechanisms: Status & Deficiencies.* Belfer Center for Science and International Affairs, Harvard University.

Auerswald, P.E. and Branscomb, L.M., 2003: Valleys of death and Darwinian seas: financing the invention to innovation transition in the United States. *Journal of Technology Transfer* 28(3–4), pp. 227–239.

Avril, S., Mansilla, C., Busson, M. and Lemaire, T., 2012: Photovoltaic energy policy: Financial estimation and performance comparison of the public support in five representative countries. *Energy Policy* 51, pp. 244–258.

Beard, T.R., Ford, G.S., Koutsky, T.M. and Spiwak, L.J., 2009: A Valley of Death in the innovation sequence: an economic investigation. *Research Evaluation* 18(5), pp. 343–356.

Block, F. and Keller, M.R., 2008: Where do innovations come from? Transformations in the U.S. national innovation system, 1970–2006. The Information Technology & Innovation Foundation, July 2008. Available online at: www.itif.org/files/Where_do_innovations_come_from.pdf (accessed February 4, 2012).

Flanagan, S., 2011: The administrative power of the President: environmental policy from Clinton to Obama. Available online at: www.thepresidency.org/storage/Fellows2011/Flanagan_Final_Paper.pdf (accessed February 8, 2012).

Gallagher, K.S., Grübler, A., Kühl, L., Nemet, G. and Wilson, C., 2012: The energy technology innovation system. *Annual Review of Environment and Resources* 37(1), pp. 137–162.

Goreham, S., 2013: *The Mad, Mad, Mad World of Climatism: Mankind and climate change mania*, Special Edition. Lenox, NY: Ne Lenox Books.

Grau, T., Huo, M. and Neuhoff, K., 2009: Survey of photovoltaic industry and policy in Germany and China. *Energy Policy* 51, pp. 20–37.

Hamlett, P.W., 1992: *Understanding Technological Politics: A decision-making approach*. New York: Prentice Hall.

Johnstone, N., Hascic, I. and Popp, D., 2008: Renewable Energy Policies and Technological Innovation: Evidence Based on Patent Counts. Working Paper No. 13760, National Bureau of Economic Research. Available online at: www.nber.org/papers/w13760 (accessed February 8, 2012).

Laird, F. and Stefes, C., 2009: The diverging paths of German and United States policies for renewable energy: sources of difference. *Energy Policy* 37(7), pp. 2619–2629.

Malakoff, D. and Sachdev, M., 2012: Democratic Party platform mostly looks back on science. *Science Insider* 4. Available online at: http://news.sciencemag.org/scienceinsider/2012/09/democratic-party-platform-mostly.html (accessed February 9, 2012).

OECD, 2011: Demand Side Innovation Policies. Available online at: www.oecd.org/sti/demand-sideinnovationpolicies.htm (accessed February 12, 2012).

Szyliowicz, J.S., 1981: Technology and the nation state. In: Szyliowicz, J.S. (Ed.): *Technology and International Affairs*. New York: Praeger.

Vision Study, 2012: SunShot Vision Study. U.S. Department of Energy, DOE/GO-102012–3037, February 2012.

24

CLUSTERS, UNLIKE DIAMONDS, ARE NOT FOREVER

The European way to global competition

Alberto Bramanti[1]

Introduction

The 'European way to global competition' appears to be narrow and burdensome. Manufacturing of the labour intensive variety, no matter the tax subsidies, will never return to EU-15, while 'talent' and creative skills are what matters most.

It is precisely the role played by innovative workers that changes the economy of cities and regions and enables them to attract further skilled workers, until territories leap into the knowledge-based world and become 'winners'.

While Europe is still discussing how to repay those huge budget deficits that are the legacy of the 2008 financial crisis, it is quite clear that many existing EU clusters of SMEs will either need restructuring in depth, or will fade away. One major problem is that there is limited room for dramatic changes in production costs: microeconomic efficiency is largely under control. Differently, major problems are hidden in the *total factor productivity* (TFP) issue (see § 1) and the perception that millions of work places are at risk – under the pressure of low cost products from extra-EU countries – is basically right (Farshchi *et al.* 2009; Dettori *et al.* 2013). The European dilemma cannot be, therefore, 'austerity' versus 'no austerity'. It is rather about Europe phasing in a long-term plan that balances its need to protect the most vulnerable in this generation, while funding most opportunities for the next generation, and still creating growth.

And to do so Europe has to change its policy, and to go quickly and fast towards a new season of *place-based policies* (PBPs), within a shared frame of simplified taxes, simplified regulations and more accountable government (Barca 2009). It is typically a multilevel governance policy problem, with a strong role for regions as main actors in the process, as they are the subject best positioned to manage such new policies: large enough to matter and small enough to care.

The 'European way to global competition' needs to better exploit the existing specific assets Europe is endowed with: the presence of *Islands of Innovation* (IoI) (Hilpert 1991; Caragliu and Nijkamp 2012) strongly intertwined with SMEs (also) operating in low-medium and medium-tech (LMT) industries (Cappellin and Wink 2009; Robertson *et al.* 2009).

The present chapter is structured into six sections. The first section offers a view on the major problem of TFP which plunges its roots well before the recent global downturn and sees Europe (on average) striving with America. The second section looks at the R&D and patent issue in a quite critical way, showing that R&D is not the only (nor the most fruitful) means to innovate, and these considerations open the way to discuss two features characterising the European landscape (the third section): soft innovation and LMT sectors.

The next section is dedicated to the territorial dimension of innovation systems and the emergence of 'IoI'. While strong reinforcing mechanisms are surely at work within those 'Islands', the section raises doubts about the trigger elements that can allow an accumulation process to start when a territory is positioned well below a minimum threshold. An implication of these difficulties is that Europe should balance an 'endogenous innovation pattern in scientific network' with the 'creative application pattern' (see the previous section) in order to fully exploit its manufacturing competences.

The fifth section throws light on the need for a new PBP, discussing its economic rationale and the need for a European governance of the process, while the final section shortly resumes the main conclusions of the chapter.

Scanty productivity and the role of technological innovation

The recent global downturn has definitely brought into the light major problems in European competitiveness and, particularly, a scanty trend in productivity that dates back at least twenty years.

During the decade 1995–2005, ICT investments contributed twice as much to aggregate labour productivity growth in the USA as in Europe: earlier adoption of ICTs in the USA, largely related to a more intensive use of high-skilled labour, contribute to a gap in labour productivity between the EU market economy and the USA of 37 per cent (Timmer *et al.* 2010).

A large part of the enduring gap is explained by the differences in the efficiency with which labour and capital are used, as measured by TFP, and within this aggregate measure, it has clearly emerged that business services account for a significant part of the difference, so that we can surely conclude that future growth in Europe will crucially depend on the path taken by market services. Also within Europe we have to record important national differences. Estimated TFP levels point out a concentration of high values around Switzerland, the Netherlands, Western Germany and Norway, while Mediterranean countries are falling short.

While the declining European employment trend was reversed in the first half of the 1990s – due to a widespread deregulation process of labour markets – a malicious trade-off between jobs and productivity has rapidly grown: it is frequently argued that the price paid for the European 'employment miracle' was a drop in labour productivity growth.

Different experts have also insisted on institutional characteristics of educational and innovation systems in Europe (Niosi 2010), arguing that European slowdown is mainly related to difficulties in switching from growth based on 'imitation' to growth based on 'innovation', but this idea is largely controversial, particularly if we assume a narrow view of innovation, mainly considered as a barely technological problem.

The convergence between human capital and technological innovation leads to the idea of 'IoI' (Hilpert 1991, 2003) and the role of territories in shaping firms' competitiveness.

Specifically, a distinctive advantage of winning territories is their ability to produce, attract and retain those workers who provide the ideas, know-how, creativity and imagination crucial to economic success.

There is a large debate on the role of high-tech – jobs, firms, sectors – on regional performance and this debate is particularly vivid in the US. Enrico Moretti (2012) explores the 'brains hubs' phenomenon, offering an answer to the old but still intriguing question: *why are some places more prosperous than others?* That can be doubled with: *why does American urban renaissance look more effective (and conducive to growth) than the still lagging Europe response?*

The shareable starting point of the analysis is that the future and the destiny of urban areas will depend heavily on the degree of education of their citizens, and the difference among even similar urban areas has increased more rapidly over the last decades.

The powerfulness of American high-tech markets – hauled by state-of-the-art technologies and the research and patents system staying behind – is concentrated in no more than two dozen communities of innovators. A handful of cities (see Table 24.1) with the 'right' industries and a solid base of human capital, keep attracting good employers and offer them high wages: all of them share high-skilled professionals, innovative firms and a thick professional labour market.

European clusters actually result in fast innovation-takers and slow innovation-makers and, in addition, we have to remark that *clusters are not forever*, as they can no longer compete by squeezing productive costs while they rather need to strongly innovate.

As directly experienced in the last downturn, European regions with the 'wrong industries' and a limited human capital base have been struck with dead-end jobs and low average wages. Moreover, a great divergence in education levels – as witnessed by the most recent OECD study (2013) – is causing an equally large divergence in labour productivity (and therefore in salaries). Obviously, these territories evidence some worrisome lock-in, and it is by no means easy to plan a new development for them.

The bright side of the moon: R&D and patents

R&D, notwithstanding its important role as a determinant of innovation, accounts for barely a quarter of the total expenses aimed at obtaining product innovation (Kleinknecht and Mohen 2002) and the choice of other innovation activities, beyond formal R&D effort, is all the more important for the innovation process of a large number of industries.

Anyway, when we concentrate on R&D activity as an input of the innovation process – and on patents as the main output deriving from R&D – there are many unavoidable points to be mentioned, and because discussion on these themes without hard evidence will inevitably be constrained to simple speculation, let the numbers tell us a story.

The PatVal EU survey[2] delivers different enlightening interesting information, to some extent 'contra intuitive' for non experts in the field. We would like to simply summarise three main points (Gambardella 2009).

1. 30 per cent of the overall European innovations are not the result of specific R&D projects and, within this group, 8 per cent of the patents are the outcome of *pure creativity* without any investment; 70 per cent are the expected results of R&D projects but, again, a good half of this 70 per cent represents a by-product of the principal investigation line. Ultimately, half of the research effort comes up from unexpected innovation: *pure serendipity!* That's to say only one third of the innovations comes out exactly where scientists, researchers and technicians are searching, and – even more important – where investors are putting their money, while at least two thirds of the innovations are less formal and unstructured, and they also count for a large share within structured R&D projects.
2. Large firms (more than 250 employees) hold more than two thirds (70.2 per cent) of all registered patents – while universities as well as individual inventors play a very marginal

role, with a share of 3.3 per cent and 3.1 per cent, respectively – and they use only a short half of their patents portfolio.[3] So, once again, we have many more 'ideas' (patented innovations) than the number of applications actually delivered to the markets. If we could only find out good market applications for at least one fourth of the already patented innovations we would be able to increase the productivity of the whole R&D system dramatically.

3 A final point is related to the value of patents.[4] There exists a very small number of great value innovations and a huge number of low value innovations: the greatest number of patents share a value around 6,000 euros (*mode*), while 380,000 euros is the *median* on the distribution. High value innovations more frequently belong to large firms because they systematically invest in research activities, and we know from the literature (Gambardella *et al.* 2008) that the value of patents primarily depends on R&D expenditures.

To cut a very long story short, most large firms and research institutions have drawers full of unexploited patents, and the value of used patent is, on average, quite small. R&D, therefore, it appears is not the only way to be innovative (nor necessarily the most fruitful). This is to underline that R&D is far from being an 'efficient process'; it is rather characterised by a very high component of 'serendipity' and randomness: a too exclusive attention on R&D is not that interesting for knowledge exploitation, and patents are only a starting point towards a successful market adoption.

At the European level, the simple comparison of the geographical concentration (at Nuts 2 level) of R&D expenditures on GDP (a standard input indicator of the innovative effort) and the spatial dispersion of the share of firms introducing product and/or process innovation (a standard measure of innovative outcome) is quite enlightening. A largely expected result is that the geography of knowledge and the geography of innovation do not necessarily overlap in space (Caragliu and Lenzi 2013).

It is a further evidence that a dramatic increase in the generation of ideas has not been matched with a corresponding increase in the exploitation of such ideas (Gambardella 2009). What we need exactly is not a simple increment of R&D investments but an increase in the productivity of research activities, as it is typically a field in which the simplistic judgement 'the more the better' is not true.

The Norway case is quite enlightening (Bhidé 2008). Its national innovation system does not perform particularly well on a benchmark basis. R&D intensity is relatively low, the number of patents is modest, the share of scientific publications has been decreasing since the mid 1990s, and the scientific productivity is evidently not outstanding. Nevertheless, Norwegian productivity per hour worked is among the highest in the world. Norway has been able to fully integrate ICTs in its economy, dramatically increasing the service sector contribution to total factor productivity: a promising case of being outstanding users of innovative technologies while being late comers as producers of them.

A generalisation of the Norway experience can be condensed into a simple statement: in order to grow, European countries should better increase the TFP rather than further enhance the frontier of already advanced sectors. And in Europe, to address backwardness (especially in the services sector) may be a very fruitful way to close the still persisting productivity gap with other non-EU competitors, especially advanced ones (USA, Canada, Japan, Israel, etc.).

European assets: LMT industries and soft innovation

Two major issues clearly emerge at this stage. *First*, the high-tech debate has fallen short in interpreting what is going on in many advanced, well developed, industrial economic systems, where technology and innovation are playing a major role in rejuvenating mature regions and mature sectors. *Second*, there is a type of innovation, labelled 'soft innovation', primarily concerned with change in products of an aesthetic or intellectual nature. This soft innovation – for which R&D is not a good indicator at all – has emerged to play a major role in the innovation map of a large number of developed countries (NESTA 2009; Stoneman 2010).

Following Capello and Lenzi (2013) we can distinguish three conceptual archetypes of territorial patterns of innovation: i) an *endogenous innovation pattern in a scientific network* that frequently takes the form of 'IoI'; ii) a *creative application pattern* in which innovation performances consist of the skillfulness to exploit knowledge spillovers in a creative way, by recombining, integrating and enriching the local knowledge base with new knowledge coming from outside. It is precisely this creative application pattern that quite often generates 'soft innovation'; and iii) an *imitative innovation patter* that mainly consists in adopting and imitating different innovations developed elsewhere. This last one is a kind of innovative profile strongly present in the most proactive firms in LMT industries.[5]

Starting from the last territorial pattern of innovation (iii), it is worthwhile stressing the role of LMT sectors that are an overwhelming presence in the European manufacturing scenario. Not only are they the dominant sectors for European exports into the global markets, but they are still the fastest growing sectors in international trade (Cappellin and Wink 2009). In different cases these LMT industries are characterized as 'mature' regions that experience industrial restructuring and transformation and are populated by SMEs.

At the same time, LMT sectors are far from being internally homogeneous. We can find a number of well performing firms, focusing on an expansion of knowledge that goes beyond maintaining the absorptive capacity that LMT firms need for successful adoption of innovations developed elsewhere. Innovation has in fact evolved from context-free linearity to embedded complexity, and effective innovation within LMT firms is often rooted in the exploitation of their problem solving capabilities, deriving from a long history of learning-by-doing processes. European LMT firms have largely contributed to the competitive race with 'integrative technologies' that are the bridge to applying general insights of high-tech to concrete and very specific engineering problem solutions (Robertson *et al.* 2009).

Innovation is therefore an expression of capabilities gained with interactions with other actors, through the processing of experience and tacit knowledge. It is not easy to put together forms and materials, and the way to do so – the only way to do it – is to build objects, to be a 'maker' and this is undoubtedly a very strong asset of European firms and clusters.

One of the main challenges for the future therefore regards innovative products, highly customised, manufactured on very small lots, supplied by a new generation of firms in between high-tech enterprises and craftsmen (Micelli 2011). So, products are no more sold as simple objects: they are stories, technologies, culture and even art; they are the true expression of a territory.

In a recent study on EU regional innovation patterns (Caragliu and Lenzi 2013), it emerges that regional structural elements matter more than sector-specific characteristics in shaping a region's innovation pattern. The implication is the emerging need for a place-based approach to innovation and industrial policies rather than supporting their non-neutrality.

We have previously referred to a *creative application pattern* in which talented, smart and creative entrepreneurs are able to identify new needs and unmet demands, and it is precisely here that 'soft innovation' may be an appropriate answer.

Two main implications derive from this innovative behaviour. First, soft-innovation is frequently interlinked with more consolidated technological innovation, in the sense that the first derives from the second and that, for any new true technical innovation, we can discover a whole family of descending soft-innovations.

Second, we need a new metrics to measure the dimension and the impact of soft innovation on the productive system and on society. Due to a very high intra-sectoral heterogeneity, we need to conduct firm level analysis rather than sectoral level analysis (Bramanti 2015).

So, if we think that soft innovation may also produce good performances[6] for firms, and enhance good jobs for society, we have an answer reversing the standard technological approach towards a new inclusive one: in order to prosper, European clusters should exploit talent and creativity to make wonderful new objects that meet new needs and the unknown wishes of affluent consumers, so that they 'will buy like crazy when they see them'.

The emergence of 'IoI': agglomeration and networking

To some extent, 'hard science' and 'soft innovation' should and could proceed hand in hand, that's to say that an *endogenous innovation pattern in a scientific network* and a *creative application pattern* may walk side by side, towards a converging territorial perspective and this seems to be a particularly promising path for European competitiveness future.

The traditional top-down, linear innovation model has come to an end. It was a perspective in which knowledge supply played the major role without a real function for demand articulation.

Differently, more cyclical and open innovation models look at the triangular structure incorporated in the Triple Helix model (Etzkowitz 2008) in which knowledge sector, industry (the productive platform) and government are linked together.

When adding the *spatial dimension* to innovation systems we are stressing economies of scope, tacit knowledge, communities of practice and thick labour markets. We can recognise the existence of a 'local buzz', that is a knowledge and communication ecology created by face-to-face contacts and the co-presence and co-location of a variety of stakeholders in the local milieu, which cannot be easily reproduced at any location.

All these ingredients, interacting together, shape what have been called 'IoI', where local networks and open access to modern technology give rise to a local cooperative learning process. Here emerges a reinforcing co-existence of scientific and industrial expertise (Caragliu and Nijkamp 2012).

It is quite easy to understand that – in order to preserve their dynamic control of evolving technologies and knowledge accumulation – such IoI have to bridge, to strengthen horizontal linkages, to network together at least at a continental scale.

Peter Nijkamp (*et al.* 2011) suggests calling these networks among nodal areas 'creative hotspots', where creativeness is a cognitive ability that may lead to new ways of thinking and acting, while connectivity among clusters of innovation plays a central role in implementing a regional innovation policy. A creative hotspot derives its innovation and growth potential from three major sources: i) *economies of density* in a given 'IoI' or metropolitan knowledge region; ii) *economies of synergy* as a result of complementarities among different areas; iii) *economies of linkages* in satellite locations through specialised supply of, or demand for customised goods, not available in the core agglomerations themselves.

A fundamental implication of this joint presence of leading research institutions, and competitive firms able to fully exploit the available innovation potential, is that such 'IoI' – or creative hotspots – are able to educate, attract and retain not only a 'creative class' but also 'star scientists' (Zucker and Darby 2006; Trippl 2012, 2013). It is important to highlight that scientific elite is highly mobile and tends to concentrate geographically in only a few places worldwide; a handful of major urban areas in both the US and Europe are connected by such unique conditions and – even more important – they seem to be rather stable over time (Hilpert 2009).

Table 24.1 Number of star scientists employed in US and European 'IoI'

Top Islands (USA and Europe)	*Total*	*Natural Sciences*	*Medical and Health Sciences*	*Engineering and Technology*	*Social Sciences*	*Agricultural Sciences*
New York, NY	35	14	10	4	6	0
Los Angeles/San Diego, CA	32	13	8	7	2	1
San Francisco Bay Area, CA	29	17	4	6	1	1
Washington, DC/ Baltimore, MD	29	13	13	2	1	0
Boston, MA	21	10	4	1	5	0
Dallas/Houston/San Antonio, TX	19	10	4	2	3	0
Chicago, IL/ Milwaukee, WI	14	7	3	2	2	0
Raleigh-Durham, NC	12	7	2	2	1	0
Total for top US Islands	*191*	*91*	*48*	*26*	*21*	*2*
Total for the United States	**390**	**197**	**94**	**44**	**45**	**5**
London, UK	26	13	9	1	1	2
East Anglia, UK	12	9	2	0	0	1
Munich, D	8	5	3	0	0	0
Copenhagen, DK	7	3	1	2	1	0
Glasgow/Edinburgh, UK	7	3	3	0	0	1
Paris/Île-de-France, F	6	4	0	1	0	0
Amsterdam/ Rotterdam, NL	5	3	2	0	0	0
Milan/Turin, IT	4	2	2	0	0	0
Total for top European Islands	*75*	*42*	*22*	*4*	*2*	*4*
Total for Europe	**197**	**113**	**51**	**17**	**5**	**9**

Source: our elaboration on Trippl (2012).

It is instructive to compare US and Europe 'IoI' as top researchers have surely a strong potential to be key drivers of science-based innovation. Following a recent empirical study (Trippl 2012), the US and Europe together account for 85 per cent of all star scientists included in the sample[7] and the large majority is densely concentrated in the top 8 + 8 creative hotspots (see Table 24.1). Top Islands are major locations of star scientists with a concentration that is higher in the US than in Europe (also for the persistent differences among twenty-seven national innovation systems).

One further point is that an important number of European star scientists have been working in US Islands for a while (on average six years) and finally they have chosen to relocate back home. In doing so, they reinforce networking relations between transcontinental Islands, while linkages between European Islands are almost negligible.

In addition, within 'IoI' multinational firms in recent years have started offshoring R&D activities. This new behaviour – jointly with 'super stars' mobility – has allowed some form of reverse technology transfer. A recent study on 262 EU regions (Castellani and Pieri 2013) has shown to what extent productivity growth is related to the creation of R&D labs abroad. The main result is that there is a positive correlation and European regions are still in the phase of increasing returns of the process.

From a policy perspective, European 'IoI' – which already act as gateways and hubs towards external research excellence – should play a role as facilitators of the participation of EU firms to global R&D projects.

In order to reach the planned objective, policies should go beyond past experience, not entirely satisfying. Over recent years innovation policy has frequently become an 'umbrella policy' where functional dimensions and traditional policy areas have become mixed in a disappointing mess. Scholars and practitioners have repeatedly observed major shortcomings of the past experience of regional innovation policies in Europe (Bellini and Landabaso 2005):

- too narrow in scope and small in resources, with the interesting exception of the French experience of the *pôles d'innovation*;
- too ambitious, too unrealistic, and too uncertain in their results. Ultimately, they have seemed too vague and with an over emphasising of best practices syndrome;
- too difficult to manage, even for the significant presence of financial and legal constraints.

When we widen the horizon of our observations beyond such well performing 'IoI', a further critical question will arise. We can help a cluster fairly well with 'after care' policies – once it is already established – but we will have a hard time in the start-up and upgrading phases, till the cluster reaches its critical mass. In addition, and equally worrisome, clusters, unlike diamonds, are not forever! The current winners can be losers unless they manage to adapt, perpetually: they too are subject to Schumpeterian 'creative destruction' and to the competitive pressure arising from a rapid diffusion of technological standardisation and a growing quality in follower regional competitors.

So, the main challenging questions for policy makers are related to the possibility of nurturing a creative hotspot. It is the theory of 'big push' and we have to recognise that, in recent years, a large number of cities and regions have tried in their personal way to reach a critical mass in whatever sector or cluster is representing at least a potential winner. In doing so in the past few decades, the world has been mantled with 'draft copies' of Silicon Valley, none of which has been shown to work properly: there are always some missed ingredients or linkages. In the end serendipity, luck and the good fortune to have a successful, innovative, platform company located in your region, is what creates a 'brain-hub'.

Towards a new PBP[8]

Global competition delivers the same challenges to America and Europe, and a number of converging trends are framing the developing paths of both the Atlantic shores: i) the clear spatial clustering of innovative ventures with an increasing density of the agglomeration process; ii) the role played by top research universities in producing, attracting and retaining star scientists; iii) the relative stability over time of top 'IoI', both American and European ones; iv) the overwhelming difficulties met in replacing manufacturing sectors that have eroded their competitive advantages in relation to the new global 'division of labour' (with some difference between the US and Europe).

Beyond these shared features, deep differences also appear (Hilpert 2009). The shift from America to Europe plunges the analyst in a world populated by so many SMEs, frequently operating in LMT sectors, with a remarkable presence in the light industries (clothing, furniture, household appliances, rubber and plastic products, etc.), many of which are bravely facing global competition, but restlessly asking for new injections of creativity and novelty.

Moreover, Europe is the sum of twenty-seven different national innovation systems and markets that are still marked by significant differences in terms of purchasing power, tastes and preferences, consumers' habits, communication strategies as well as advertising sensibilities (Niosi 2010).

The American system has been always connoted by a high flexibility in capital and labour markets – the 'hire and fire' feature that makes creative knowledge workers more footloose – and the result is the possibility of experiencing new combinations of factors but, at the same time, also quick competence destruction. As a consequence, the American system is much more prone to radical innovation and new sectors, where firms need to be able to change strategies at short notice.

When the pace of technical changes is so accelerated, a standard consequence is the rising of increasing diversities. A large number of regions seem to be in a difficult position towards evolution, and will probably be swept away by the rising concentration of valuable immaterial assets in a small number of 'state-of-the-art' places (Moretti 2012).

To remain prosperous, a society needs to keep climbing the innovation ladder, but not all cities (or regions) have been able to attract some innovative workers (or firms) to begin the process of growth. In addition, focusing on R&D investment, or on human capital, is not per se a solution for European clusters competing in light industries and with small firms.

Europe mostly needs 'embedded policies' since institutional and technological regimes are deeply interrelated, where institutions may be differently designed, according to the respective nation's framework.

Within such a scenario, a good policy, enhancing productivity and fostering competitiveness, cannot be based on the simple idea of softening traditional factor costs, labour and capital. European firms have already at their disposal the best machinery in the world (mostly produced in Germany, Switzerland and Italy), the availability of excellent designers and a very high skilled workforce.

In old Europe, clusters of SMEs in LMT sectors would be better supported by public–private partnerships and by intermediate bodies representing the beneficiaries and being the subjects responsible for the implementation of a true *cluster strategic programme*[9] (Florio and Ozzimo 2006).

The contemporary approach to PBP stresses: additionality; inclusiveness (strategy designed and delivered by a partnership between regional and local players); projects and solutions (bottom-up orientation with local actors proposing and accepting risk); and first rate quality.

This attention to enhancing competitiveness of clusters (also) in LMT sectors – and strongly connecting them with 'IoI' (the frontier of innovation research and patenting activity) – seems to be the only feasible goal in order to improve connectivity so that positive effects from such integration enhance the innovative potential of local economies. Such PBPs, without any deterministic view on the path that a single place should choose, have to recognise the values of a place's own history, idiosyncrasies, endowments and capabilities.

An increased attention to 'IoI' – jointly with clusters of SMEs in LMT sectors – represents a sound declaration of what has been called a PBP: a programme to foster successful networks, or clusters of business, at the regional level. PBPs target the prosperity, equity, sustainability and liveability of places, how well or how poorly they function as places and how they change over time. They should promote the supply of integrated goods and services, tailored to contexts, as this triggers institutional changes; and leverage investments in targeted places, drawing on the compounding effect of cooperative arrangements.

If European territories need this new course of PBPs, within a multilevel governance approach, Europe represents the most appropriate layer for designing and monitoring them: why? Because: i) it is better able to take account of over-the-border interdependencies; ii) it can manage the need for rapidly produced techno-scientific progress intensifying the search for partners and trans-regional collaboration and allowing trans-Islands (of Innovation) collaboration to emerge; and finally iii) it can counterbalance the pressure of local interest groups that may distort or obstruct the development path pursued (Barca 2009).

Any experience of economic growth finds its enabling conditions in a rich set of complementary institutions, shared behavioural norms and public policies. Competitiveness oriented policies are not an exception; they offer their maximum contribution when technological progress is matched with innovation and changes in organisational models and institutions. The spring of productivity is almost always linked to complementary innovations in other technologies and in organisational routines (Dettori *et al.* 2013).

Concluding remarks

The chapter has developed an analysis of European disappointing productivity jointly with the role of innovation, broadly considered, as an answer to the challenges of global competition, passing through a discussion of some specific assets that Europe is endowed with – soft innovation and the making capability of clusters in LMT industries. Their future should be linked with the presence of 'IoI' which play a major role as hubs in the international networks of star scientists and science-based research.

To properly innovate Europe needs talented workers, endowed with high-skilled competences, a lively curiosity and imagination, and strong problem solving capabilities. European 'IoI' seem to be well positioned to contribute to both the creation and attraction of 'smart human capital' and to enable it to produce 'smart new products', provided they strengthen their networking with the largest number of SME clusters.

But theory is much further ahead than practice. While scholars and practitioners know many things about the innovation process, on the intertwined relations between 'talents' and technological advances, on the emergence of 'IoI', on the needs expressed by territorial SME clusters, they barely know how to design, implement and manage a supportive and competitiveness-oriented policy.

That's why European PBPs are strongly needed, even when this looks like a trial-and-error approach, when they try to experiment and to open new ways of facing global competition.

Within this frame the chapter has introduced the idea of a 'cluster strategic programme', discussing the conditions for maximising its *ex-ante* success possibilities. As specific innovation sectors, jobs, occupations and firms will come and go, live and die; there are no specific clusters that may be expected to prosper endlessly: a 'Great Divergence' is clearly in front of us.

A major consequence is a corresponding geographic rising inequality between the brilliant interaction of college educated, talented, innovative, highly skilled, highly waged, longest living, healthiest individuals, who gravitate to innovative brain hub metropolitan areas, and the other side of the moon: people living outside the brain hubs and characterised by mediocrity, lower wages, sickness and decline.

The 'European way to global competition' is still hindered by three main courses:

- the rapid transformation from manufacturing platform towards a service economy (with the derived problems of diminishing productivity) and a further shift towards the small dimension of enterprises (as the big ones are closing and delocalising);
- the dramatic rise of territorial differences (in opportunities, good jobs, and GDP per capita) with a small number of new winners and a large and widespread mass of losers (in terms of firms, cities and regions). Here the greatest divergences are all concentrated on the job market, showing unbelievable and unbearable, higher than ever youth unemployment rate;
- the emergence and consolidation of 'Islands of Innovation' (within an everlasting dialectic between agglomeration effects and networking) and their limited positive spillover effects towards surrounding territories.

This increased attention to 'IoI' – jointly with clusters of SMEs in LMT sectors – represents a sound declination of what has been called a PBP. It is a programme to foster successful networks, or clusters of business, at the regional level. European PBPs target the prosperity, equity, sustainability and liveability of places, how well or how poorly they function as places and how they change over time. They should promote the supply of integrated goods and services, tailored to contexts, which triggers institutional changes. They leverage investments in targeted places drawing on the compounding effect of cooperative arrangements.

We know that technological progress can contribute to meaningful changes in productivity if it is matched with innovation and changes in organisational models and institutions. The spring of productivity is almost always linked to complementary innovations in other technologies and in organisational routines. Many times positive productivity outcomes derive not only from technological upgrades but more deeply from new conditions to enable interactions and exchange of information within the work force.

The maximum degree of productivity change derives from the complementarities among three different kinds of investments: computer, high-skilled labour and organisational decentralisation. Overall productivity rises – both at the micro level of the firm and at the macro level of the productive system – when these three investments are soundly balanced, and this is the task and the challenge for the European Commission – to implement such a new PBP.

Notes

1 I'm deeply indebted to Nicola Bellini and Ulrich Hilpert for having discussed with me the advances of the chapter at different stages. The first idea has already been presented at a Workshop in Pittsburgh (June 25–26, 2009): many thanks to all the participants for their valuable comments and suggestions. I'm grateful to CERTeT, at Bocconi University which has supported my research programme during the last two years. The usual disclaimer applies.

2 The PatVal EU survey represents one of the more exhaustive and inclusive field analyses on patents in Europe. It was developed in 2003 focusing on European patents with priority years 1993–1997 (in order to allow the right delay for the exploitation of the patent). The final sample includes 9,550 patents gathered with a stratified sampling design that allows inference on the whole population (Giuri 2007; Gambardella *et al.* 2008).

3 When the main source of inspiration is innovators' clients, the share of used patents rises up to 61 per cent. That is to say: if innovation is a clear answer to a specific problem (raised by potential clients) the likelihood of an effective exploitation is higher.

4 It is not easy to appreciate patents' value, but there are two main ways to approximate it. The *first* is to ask the inventor what is the price at which he/she would sell the patent to his/her competitor (and we know that we normally gather overestimate values). The *second* is to look at the other side of the market, asking the buyer to express his/her willingness-to-pay or, better, collecting data on the prices registered in the patents' auctions when they occur.

5 As a matter of fact, we should not fall into the trap of equating low-tech industries with low-tech firms. High, medium and low-tech firms are widely spread across high, medium and low-tech sectors.

6 Despite the little evidence on the commercial impact of soft innovation, there are important clues that soft innovations can generate significant returns.

> This positive payoff from soft innovation casts doubt on the validity on analysis that concentrates on traditional business innovation alone. By excluding or ignoring soft innovation, they incorrectly attribute any benefits of soft innovation to changes in technological products and processes.
>
> (Nesta 2009: 6)

7 Star scientists are identified by the number of citations in ISI journals (1981–2002). A worldwide survey accounts for some 720 top researchers, and among them the US hosts no fewer than 57 per cent, while the EU accounts for 28 per cent. As a matter of fact the US offers more favourable institutional conditions for attracting and retaining star scientists and it critically depends on the provision of excellent employment opportunities for outstanding researchers.

8 'A place-based policy is a long-term strategy aimed at tackling persistent underutilization of potential and reducing persistent social exclusion in specific places through external interventions and multilevel governance.' (Barca 2009: vii).

9 A cluster strategic programme is characterised by some distinctive features aiming at: i) addressing the firms' cluster and not the individual SME (also establishing a monitoring mechanism of its performance); ii) identifying a managing body in charge of the implementation of the strategy; iii) guaranteeing the presence of one (or more) financial investors ready to co-finance the project against a share in its future revenues; iv) allowing a cluster to experience a strong degree of freedom in selecting the specific interventions best suited to achieve its competitiveness targets.

References

Barca, F., 2009: An Agenda for a Reformed Cohesion Policy. Independent report prepared for Danuta Hübner, Commissioner for Regional Policy, Brussells.

Bellini, N. and Landabaso, M., 2005: Learning about innovation in Europe's Regional Policy. *In-SAT Working Paper N. 3*, Scuola Superiore S. Anna, Pisa.

Bhidè, A., 2008: *The Ventursome Economy: How innovation sustains prosperity in a more connected world*. Princeton, NJ: Princeton University Press.

Bramanti, A., 2015: Innovation policies deserve a sound monitoring system: an agenda for policy makers. In: Hilpert, U. (ed.): *Routledge Handbook of Politics and Technology*. London: Routledge (forthcoming).

Cappellin, R. and Wink, R., 2009: *International Knowledge and Innovation Network*. Cheltenham: Edward Elgar.

Capello, R. and Lenzi, C., 2013: Territorial patterns of innovation: a taxonomy of innovative regions in Europe. *Papers in Regional Science* 51(1), pp. 119–154.

Caragliu, A. and Lenzi, C., 2013: Structural elements and dynamics in territorial patterns of innovation: a perspective through European case studies. *Regional Science Policy & Practice* 5(4), pp. 1–15.

Caragliu, A. and Nijkamp, P., 2012: From islands to hubs of innovation: connecting innovative regions. In: Hilpert, U. and Lawton Smith, H. (eds): *Networking Regionalised Innovative Labour Markets*. London and New York: Routledge, pp. 119–135.

Castellani, D. and Pieri, F., 2013: R&D offshoring and the productivity growth of European regions. *Research Policy* 42, pp. 1581–1594.

Dettori, B., Marrocu, E. and Paci, R., 2013: Total factor productivity, intangible assets and spatial dependence in the European regions. *Regional Studies* 46(10), pp. 1401–1416.

Etzkowitz, H., 2008: *The Triple Helix: University–industry–government innovation in action*. London: Routledge.

Farshchi, M.A., Janne, O.E.M. and McCann, P. (eds), 2009: *Technological Change and Mature Industrial Regions*. Cheltenham: Edward Elgar.

Florio, M. and Ozzimo, E., 2006: Innovation Strategies for SMEs and Clusters: The Challenge of a Globalised Europe. *Working Paper, N. 16*. Milan: Università degli Studi di Milano.

Gambardella, A., 2009: *Innovazione e sviluppo. Miti da sfatare. Realtà da costruire*. Milano: Egea Editore.

Gambardella, A., Harhoff, D. and Verspagen, B., 2008: The value of European patents. *European Management Review* 5(2), pp. 69–84.

Giuri, P., 2007: Inventor and invention processes in Europe: results from the PatVal-EU survey. *Research Policy* 36(8), pp. 1163–1183.

Hilpert, U., 1991: *Archipelago Europe: Islands of Innovation*. Brussels: EU, Fast Report.

Hilpert, U. (ed.), 2003: *Regionalisation of Globalised Innovation*. London and New York: Routledge.

Hilpert, U., 2009: A Differentiation of Regionalised Processes on Innovation in Europe and the US. Paper presented at the 4th Workshop of the Research Network on Transatlantic Comparison of Continental Innovation Models. 13–14 November, Oxford.

Hilpert, U. and Lawton Smith, H. (eds), 2012: *Networking Regionalised Innovative Labour Markets*. London and New York: Routledge.

Kleinknecht, A. and Mohnen, P. (eds), 2002: *Innovation and Firm Performance. Econometric explorations of survey data*. London: Palgrave.

Micelli, S., 2011: *Futuro artigiano. L'innovazione nelle mani degli italiani*. Venice: Marsilio Editori.

Moretti, E., 2012: *The New Geography of Jobs*. Boston, MA: Houghton Mifflin Harcourt.

NESTA, 2009: *Soft Innovation: Towards a more complete picture of innovative change*. Research Report, July, London.

Nijkamp, P., Kourtit, K., Lowik, S., van Vught, F. and Vulto, P., 2011: *From Islands of Innovation to Creative Hotspots*. Research Memorandum, N. 41. Amsterdam: Vrije Universiteit.

Niosi, J., 2010: *Building National and Regional Innovation Systems*. Cheltenham: Edward Elgar.

OECD, 2013: OECD Skills Outlook 2013. *First Results from the Survey of Adult Skills*. Paris: OECD.

Robertson, P., Smith, K. and von Tunzelmann, N., 2009: Introduction: Innovation in low- and medium-technology industries. *Research Policy* 38, pp. 441–446.

Stoneman, P., 2010: *Soft Innovation: Economics, product aesthetics, and the creative industries*. Oxford: Oxford University Press.

Timmer, M.P., Inklaar, R., O'Mahony, M. and van Ark, B., 2010: *Economic Growth in Europe*. Cambridge: Cambridge University Press.

Trippl, M., 2012: Star scientists, islands of innovation and internationally networked labour markets. In: Hilpert, U. and Lawton Smith, H. (eds.): *Networking Regionalised Innovative Labour Markets*. London and New York: Routledge, pp. 58–77.

Trippl, M., 2013: Islands of innovation as magnetic centres of star scientists? Empirical evidence on spatial concentration and mobility patterns. *Regional Studies* 47(2), 229–244.

Zucker, L.G. and Darby, M.R., 2006: Movement of Star Scientists and Engineers and High-Tech Firm Entry. *NBER Working Paper Series*, Cambridge, MA.

25

INSTITUTIONAL TRANSFORMATIONS OF TECHNOLOGY POLICY IN EAST ASIA

The rise of the entrepreneurial state

Alexander Ebner

Introduction

Japan and the East Asian 'dragon economies' Korea, Taiwan and Singapore have been subject to a historically unique process of catching up with the Western economies. The institutional foundations of this process involve technology policies exercised by developmental states with a focus on the assimilation of new technologies. The rationale of this policy approach has been shifting recently as the capability for generating technological innovations becomes essential for sustaining economic growth, based on science-based technologies such as biotechnology. Accordingly, the East Asian developmental states are transformed into new types of entrepreneurial states. In discussing these issues, the chapter proceeds as follows. The first section addresses the East Asian developmental states and related technology policies. The second section takes on the institutional transformations of these policies. The following two sections address country examples: Japan as well as Korea, Taiwan and Singapore. The final section interprets these observations in terms of the Schumpeterian concept of the entrepreneurial state.

Technology policies and developmental states in East Asia

Following the decades of high performance growth from the 1970s to the 1990s, the high-performing East Asian economies witnessed the Asian financial crisis in 1997. Yet Korea, Taiwan and Singapore have regained their growth performance while Japan still serves as the regional centre of high-value added manufacturing and service operations – with China's development providing both stimuli and challenges. This 'East Asian Renaissance' holds even in the aftermath of the global financial crisis of the late 2000s (Gill and Kharas 2007: 12–16; Asian Development Bank 2013: 3–5). Nonetheless, challenges in the domain of technology are eminent. Do institutional settings that have been effective during catch-up growth match the tasks of technological leadership in the context of new technologies, such as biotechnology, which are science-based and require distinct entrepreneurial efforts? Indeed, technological leadership is exercised by countries that fit the requirements of a dominant techno-economic paradigm, that is, a hegemonic mode of organising production and innovation most effectively (Freeman 2002: 193f). The responsiveness of technology policy to the productive needs of the private sector stands out in this regard, especially concerning the provision of R&D and a supportive institutional framework (Nelson 2004: 370f). Yet the East Asian economies differ beyond common patterns of export-orientation and strategic policy coordination. Japan's systemic approach to technology policy combined industrial structures dominated by large enterprises, *keiretsu*, with cooperative relations between government and business (Freeman 1987). Korea's industrial structures have been dominated by large enterprise conglomerates, *chaebol*, subject to intense government interventions. Taiwan's local enterprise networks have met comparatively lower degrees of government intervention. Singapore has been dominated by large foreign enterprises and local government-linked companies, combining government intervention with international openness (Hobday 1995: 196f).

This diversity has formed the basis for coping with the specificity of technological change in catch-up growth as East Asian firms have entered the international product life cycle in the phase of standardisation, reversing its sequence until they exhibit developed productive capabilities, including R&D (Hobday 1995: 40f; Kim 1999: 112–5). Diverse modes of technological learning prevail as the Gerschenkronian latecomer advantage allows for skipping the original costs of innovation (Hobday 2003: 297–300; Hobday *et al.* 2004: 1454f; Mathews 2006: 313f). In this context, the East Asian innovation systems have come to share the following characteristics: an expanding education system with an emphasis on tertiary education and engineering; the rapid growth of business in-house R&D; a share of industrial R&D above 50 per cent of gross expenditures on R&D; the basic development of science and technology infrastructures; strong influences of Japanese models of organisation; high levels of domestic investment with high shares of Japanese foreign direct investment; major investment in advanced telecommunications; growth of export-oriented electronic industries; increasing participation in international technology networks (Freeman 1996: 178). These commonalities include a high degree of government involvement in the economy with a focus on the strategic upgrading of technologies (Reslinger 2012: 387–389). The World Bank's report 'East Asian Miracle' has provided influential arguments on these issues. It states that technological change benefitted from policies that would highlight cost–benefit considerations and performance criteria, thus moderating the distorting effects of policy interventions (World Bank 1993: 5–8).

The concept of the developmental state reflects these issues, originally applied to the case of Japan. It maintains that states in late industrialising economies could promote goal-oriented strategies for administratively guiding industries and markets. The quality of these policies draws on the coherence of the economic bureaucracy and communication with the private sector (Johnson 1982: 19–21, 312f). A further interpretation of these mechanisms is provided by the notion of 'embedded autonomy', which addresses the policy pattern of a Weberian type of bureaucracy that is embedded in social relationships with the private sector (Evans 1995: 12, 146–9). This functional imperative also characterises late industrialisation in Korea and Taiwan with its efforts at assimilating technologies already in use abroad (Amsden 1989: 3f). Exemplified by Korea, an interventionist developmental state implements performance standards on private sector firms that receive subsidies in a reciprocal relationship (Amsden 1989: 8, 13f). The notion of 'governed markets' addresses a corresponding location of innovative initiatives with government, stimulating the private sector under its leadership. Associated strategies technological foresight involve the study of technology development in leading as well as competing countries

– with Japan as role model for Korea and Taiwan (Wade 1990: 28f, 334f). Thus, developmental states exercise a transformative capacity to coordinate economic development in accordance with the shifting conditions of international competition. The corresponding mode of governance involves a catalytic mechanism of public–private cooperation (Weiss 1998: 7f, 67; Chang 1999: 186f). A major component in these governance structures are intermediary institutions for private sector coordination, as pioneered in Japan and adapted all across East Asia. These deliberation councils highlight knowledge on coordination failures in the assessment of technological opportunities, among others by the establishment of technological standards (Aoki *et al.* 1997: 8f, 22f). Yet the inherent technological and institutional dynamics of catch-up growth feed back on the developmental state, thus heralding its institutional transformation.

Technological change and the transformation of the East Asian development model

Technology policy in catch-up growth becomes ever more complex as technology gaps are reduced. It needs to change emphasis towards the generation of new technologies, which requires a different policy framework (Freeman 2002: 208f). Thus, across East Asia, policies have shifted from resource mobilisation in support of industrialisation to the building of science and technology infrastructures, accompanied by the deregulation and internationalisation of industries and markets (Amsden and Hikino 1993: 259; Amsden 1995: 27f; Hobday 1995: 200f; Weiss 2000: 22). This is accompanied by a less hierarchical governance approach in technology policy involving an extended participation of both local and foreign enterprises, as government and private sector identify promising technological trends and learning externalities (Weiss 1998: 64f; Chang 2001: 73–5). Therefore, the state may persistently stimulate the upgrading of technological capabilities, moulded by legal and fiscal affairs, among others (Lall 2000: 14; Wade 2005: 110f; Thurborn and Weiss 2006; Beeson 2009: 38). In particular, the support of technological innovation requires a combination of public–private interactions, local coherence and international connectedness, while major policy challenges relate to the cultivation of entrepreneurship (Yusuf and Evenett 2002: 181f; Yusuf *et al.* 2003: 29). As government support of R&D in latecomer economies is biased towards applied research and product development, the expansion of basic research is eminent (Dodgson 2000: 402f; Amsden and Chu 2003: 162f). Also, the availability of venture capital in the funding of new technologies becomes a requirement (Beeson 2004: 35f).

All of this proceeds in a technological context that is marked by the emergence of a new techno-economic paradigm based on information and communication technologies as well as science-based technologies such as biotechnology (Perez 2003: 8–10). Their network patterns of organisation do not fit hierarchical patterns of resource mobilisation that matched resource-intensive industries of the past (Coriat *et al.* 2003: 231f; Carlsson 2012: 9f). These tendencies also matter for the spatial dimension of technology policy. The promotion of linkages between universities and industries focuses on knowledge-intensive agglomerations of innovative activities (Masuyama and Vandenbrink 2001: 40f; Hu and Mathews 2005: 1346f; Vang 2006: 16f). This cluster-oriented policy approach resembles a pattern of state-led networking in combining physical, knowledge and social capital (Yusuf *et al.* 2003: 249–254; Ebner 2013: 1f). At the same time, East Asian production networks take part in multi-layered 'global networks of networks' with clusters serving as network hubs (Ernst and Kim 2002). In effect, a 'modular economy' emerges that combines diverse regional, national and transnational models of economic organisation (Ganne and Lecler 2009: 22; Kuchiki and Tsuji 2011: 2–4).

In facing these challenges, efforts in the upgrading of knowledge and innovation infrastructures have been enormous. Adding to the effects of export-orientation and transnational economic integration, this expansion of the knowledge base contributes to competitive performance most sustainably (Brahmbhatt and Hu 2010: 178f). The GDP ratio of gross expenditures on R&D was increasing above OECD average all across East Asia during the 2000s. Japan's GDP share of Gross Domestic Expenditures on R&D rose slightly from 3 per cent in 2000 to 3.39 per cent in 2011. Korea's share even rose from 2.3 per cent in 2000 to 4.03 per cent in 2011. Taiwan's increased from 1.94 per cent to 3.02 per cent, Singapore's from 1.85 per cent to 2.23 per cent (OECD 2013: Table 2). All these economies have exhibited a high share of the private sector way above OECD average, settled between 60 and 75 per cent of R&D expenditures (Gil and Kharas 2007: 146–152; Roy *et al.* 2012: 105). Also, entrepreneurial conditions have improved. For instance, costs of business start-up have further decreased from already low levels (Asian Development Bank 2013: 314–315); in effect, in addition to Japan, Korea and Taiwan having already emerged as innovating economies in fields such as semiconductor industries since the 1990s (Mathews 2006: 328f). By 2004, Korea and Taiwan were the fourth and fifth biggest recipients of patents granted in the United States, predominantly in electrical and electronics technologies as well as in computers and communications, ranking only behind the United States, Japan and Germany (Gill and Kharas 2007: 154–160). Still, the question is whether a common East Asian system of innovation emerges. Korea and Taiwan decreased reliance on Japanese technology during the 1990s, adding local technology content as well as foreign direct investment from the United States (Mahmood and Singh 2003: 1031f). Also during the 2000s, the United States remained the largest source of patent citations with a share of 60 per cent, followed by Japan's share of 20 per cent. However, citations among the East Asian economies increased to a share above 5 per cent, focusing on electronics as well as information and communication technology (Gill and Kharas 2007: 163–7; Brahmbhatt and Hu 2010: 184). The institutional dimension of these tendencies points to transformations of technology policy in Japan as well as Korea, Taiwan and Singapore.

Institutional transformations of technology policy in Japan

Japan has served as a role model for systemic approaches to technology policy. The concept of the developmental state has addressed Japanese policies for industrial and technological change, highlighting administrative guidance by the Ministry of International Trade and Industry (MITI) (Johnson 1982: 315–9). In this vein, the Japanese development state is viewed as an epitome of 'governed interdependence' between the state and the private sector in an institutionalised mode of cooperation on technological upgrading (Weiss 1998: 38f). These aspects have also informed the systems of innovation perspective and its pioneering research on Japanese technology policy that discussed the interdependence between the policies of MITI, the organisation of company R&D, national education and training schemes, and the evolution of industrial structures (Freeman 1987: 4). Nonetheless, the Japanese innovation system has been persistently confronted with deficits in basic research and its commercial application. Already since the 1980s, the lack of cooperation between universities and industries has been singled out as an area of policy reform (Okimoto 1989: 67; Fransman and Tanaka 1995: 13f). Indeed, Japanese technology policy has been under pressure as Japan's internationally competitive and technologically advanced firms have outgrown the institutional conditions of the developmental state (Callon 1995: 147f; Aoki 2002: 2).

Flexibilisation, decentralisation and the competitive reorientation of governance structures have become prominent since the 1990s, also driven by a restructuring of the political–

administrative system (Whittaker 2003: 80f). MITI was actually refurbished as Ministry of Economy, Trade and Industry, METI; a measure that could be interpreted as a branching out of its policies (Elder 2000: 5f). These efforts have been paralleled by an opening of competitive structures, resulting from deregulation, privatisation and a renewed concern with competition policy. The internationalisation of Japanese R&D adds to this openness (Odagiri and Goto 1996: 268f; Porter and Sakakibara 2004: 35–36; Vogel 2006: 217–218). The corresponding transformation of Japanese technology policy reflects a shift from applied research under MITI's guidance towards a new approach that strengthens the local knowledge base in science-based industries by means of the cooperation between universities, industries and government. In governing these affairs, METI's competences in industrial policy, energy and nuclear power are met by the new Ministry of Education, Science and Technology that administers university policy, basic research, and the general support of science and technology. In promoting the new approach, Science and Technology Basic Plans have been implemented since 1996. The lack of high-quality research infrastructures is singled out as a key problem in promising fields such as life sciences, materials, information and communication as well as environment (Okimura 2005).

The regional differentiation of technology policy proceeds with an emphasis on internationally interlinked knowledge agglomerations, exemplified local centers such as Tsukuba Science City and transnational efforts such as the East Asia Science and Innovation Area Initiative. A related strategic thrust points at small business innovation and venture capital in regional innovation networks (Council for Science and Technology Policy 2010; Tung 2013: 62f). All of this should further the generation of new knowledge through university–industry links and its diffusion through entrepreneurial start-ups beyond the operations of established large firms. Competitive funding of research centers and administrative autonomy for selected universities add to this scheme (Elder 2000: 18–21; Odagiri 2006: 213–221; Holroyd and Coates 2007: 35–37). The support of local innovation capabilities knowledge agglomerations builds on preceding projects such as the Technopolis Plan. However, METI's Industry Cluster Plan, which has been running since the early 2000s, actually differs from earlier efforts. It allows for a regional decentralisation of governance and interactions, framed by transnational linkages with clusters in Asia, Europe and the United States (Kitagawa 2007; Fujita and Hill 2012: 29–39). Corresponding bottom-up initiatives in science-based clusters are predominantly driven by entrepreneurial start-ups, quite in line with METI's entrepreneurship and innovation strategies (Ibata-Arens 2004: 4f, 2005: 92–94; Holroyd and Coates 2007: 46–48, 129–131). In effect, the technology policy of the developmental state is transformed into a new model of governance. The cases of Korea, Taiwan and Singapore point in a similar direction.

Institutional transformations of technology policy in Korea, Taiwan and Singapore

Both the Korean and Taiwanese developmental states have operated in authoritarian terms well until the early 1990s, thus differing from Japan with its democratic political system. Also, both in Korea and Taiwan, the completion of catch-up growth has made the private sector less dependent on government, thus allowing for a reconfiguration of government–business relations beyond the confines of the developmental state. In this vein, Korea and Taiwan have been going through country-specific changes in reorganising the steering capacity of government and administration (Amsden 1989: 80f; Evans 1995: 230f). Korean economic policies have been subject to market-oriented reforms, also stimulated by the Asian Financial Crisis since the late 1990s. Financial instruments of technological upgrading such as preferential credit have become largely ineffective. This has been framed by a reform of corporate governance, aiming at the *chaebol*, as well as by a further opening of the Korean economy for international trade and investment. Still, national development remains a most relevant policy goal (Lee and Han 2006: 322–323; Seliger 2013: 116–123). In this context, Korean technology policy has been shifting from an 'industrial learning paradigm' to a 'technology creation paradigm' in the drive for a knowledge-based economy (Wong 2004: 491f; Wong *et al.* 2004: 46). Since its inception in the 1970s, Korean technology policy has focused on applied research and technology transfer. The bulk of R&D expenditures has been carried by the private sector, that is, primarily by the *chaebol* with Samsung alone accounting for a quarter of private R&D expenditures. Since the 1990s, R&D operations have become less concentrated due to the entry of new entrepreneurial ventures undertaking R&D operations (Johann 2012: 54–57). Scientific research infrastructures have emerged as prominent policy features of university–industry–government interactions in local knowledge agglomerations. Corresponding efforts are differentiated with regard to firms, industries and markets, thus reflecting the diversity of the *chaebol*. Entrepreneurial ventures in science-based industries, embedded in regional networks, add to this profile (Hobday *et al.* 2004: 1455–1456; Lee 2011: 31–35; Nahm 2011: 160f). Crucially, Highly Advanced National Projects promote large-scale support of high-technology products in areas such as electronics consumer durables, including HDTV. Biotechnology, environment and materials are part of this strategic thrust, which has been institutionalized in the shape of the Korean National Science and Technology Council and its strategic plans since the early 2000s. Two new executive organs, the Ministry of the Knowledge Economy and the Ministry of Education, Science and Technology, have operated with the same orientation since 2008 (Hemmert 2007; Lee and Yoo 2007; Johann 2012: 179f).

Korean concerns with biotechnology and other science-based industries are shared by Taiwan's technology policy. It highlights similar goals, although the Taiwanese industrial structure is more network-oriented and involves more foreign firms. Yet the segmentation of the value chain of the bio-pharmaceutical industry has provided both economies with opportunities for attracting high-value added operations. In this regard, Taiwan's technology policy stands out in combining the support of technological learning with a state-guided internationalisation of industrial structures (Wade 2000: 12; Tung 2013: 70f). Paralleling Japanese and Korean policy strategies, Taiwan has also been nurturing high-tech industries yet with a more pronounced emphasis on building international linkages for local knowledge agglomerations. Thus, Taiwan persistently utilises knowledge flows of global production and innovation networks that are set to stimulate entrepreneurial capabilities (Amsden and Chu 2003: 1f; Hu and Mathews 2005: 1347; Wang and Ma 2011: 286f). However, Taiwan's promotion of the bio-pharmaceutical industry has exhibited an incremental character in line with the prevailing small and medium-sized enterprise networks – and quite different from the Korean policy approach that retreated from the concerted focus on *chaebols* only recently in favour of promoting new science-based ventures and their networks (Wang *et al.* 2009). Nonetheless, biotechnology firms in both Taiwan and Korea are still in an early stage of industry evolution, which means that they have not yet generated sustainable income and employment effects. Still, these firms are part of a new innovation regime that redefines the relationship between local and global economic affairs across East Asia (Wong *et al.* 2004: 46; Wong, J. 2011: 166–168).

The logic of combining local and global resources in the strategic outreach of technology policy is most prominently represented by Singapore's city-state economy. The Singaporean development model highlights the vision of a local knowledge agglomeration in a globalised knowledge-based economy. Singapore actually belonged to the pioneers in attracting foreign direct investment as a strategy for technological upgrading. Multinational enterprises serve as driving forces of economic development, paralleled by local operations of government-linked companies in a market-friendly setting. In line with the institutional patterns of the developmental state, the Singaporean Economic Development Board, EDB, has been guiding policy efforts in industrial restructuring and technological upgrading (Ebner 2004: 56–9). Singapore thus combines governmental steering capacity with the competitive logic of markets, while leveraging on foreign direct investment as a means of technological upgrading (Wong 2001: 564). Current tendencies in the transformation of this developmental model also pinpoint the emergence of a knowledge-based economy. This includes extended interactions between universities, research institutes and local as well as foreign enterprises. The nurturing of technology-intensive start-ups contributes to the new sets of policy goals that emphasise issues of entrepreneurship and creativity in the formation of Singapore as a globally interlinked knowledge agglomeration (Low 2004: 166f; Yeung 2006: 284f). Singapore's efforts at promoting a local science base for biotechnology, among others, represent this recombination of public knowledge infrastructures and private innovation strategies quite well, for university–industry linkages become a key strategic variable in a perspective of technology policy that is set to nurture entrepreneurial ventures (Koh and Wong 2004: 275–280; Wong, P.K. 2011: 256f).

The rise of entrepreneurial states in East Asia

Various concepts have been proposed in addressing the institutional transformation of developmental states and technology policies in East Asia. For instance, it is argued that a new type of 'transitional developmental state' balances state autonomy and private sector dynamism in a shift from interventionism to liberalisation – which may even strengthen state capacity in the enforcement of the market order (Wong and Ng 2001: 43–47). Also, exemplified by Taiwan, the formation of a revamped developmental state with post-industrial, innovation-driven and democratic credentials is proposed. It utilises governance mechanisms of competition and decentralisation in order to further its steering capacity in a rapidly changing technological environment (Wong 2005: 170–173). In associated terms, a 'neo-developmental state' is said to operate in high-tech industries, promoting economies of scale, industrial R&D and skilled employment. It is complemented by a liberal type of 'regulatory state' that regulates liberalised services, competition and international openness (Amsden and Chu 2003: 167–172). Also, a complete transition of the developmental state towards a market-oriented type of regulatory state has been projected (Jayasuriya 2005). In summary, East Asian developmental states are going through country-specific transformation processes, rooted in the dynamics of catch-up growth, that recombine their institutional components in line with prevailing economic, social and political constellations (Green 2007: 35–36). A further specification may require the exploration of strategies, capabilities and financial patterns of innovative enterprises as well as a reconsideration of the regulatory and developmental roles of states across the OECD (Lazonick 2008: 27f). Indeed, according to Chalmers Johnson's concept of the developmental state, the state functions of the latter cover only a fraction of government activities. Beyond the dichotomy of the developmental state with its industrial guidance and the regulatory state with its market regulation, diverse combinations of policy actors, goals and instruments are possible (Johnson 1982: 305). The transformation of policy approaches and governance patterns thus resembles a recombination of co-evolving institutional components in the formation of state functions (Ebner 2008: 301f).

This perspective points to the Schumpeterian notion of the entrepreneurial state, which addresses historically specific state functions in the creation of technological innovations. According to Schumpeter, the entrepreneurial state carries out entrepreneurial functions by promoting the introduction of technological innovations in an established economic setting (Ebner

2006: 510f). In the East Asian context, the emergence of entrepreneurial states and the related transformation of technology policies reflect a shift from catch-up growth to technological leadership. Also, it is set in the context of a new techno-economic paradigm of information and communication technologies and science-based industries such as biotechnology with distinct institutional implications (Ebner 2007: 103f). In reconsidering relevant state functions in support of technological change, then, regulatory, developmental and entrepreneurial states may be distinguished. They may be simultaneously present, yet they will be subject to constellations of hegemony and institutional tension. With regard to the matter of technology policy, these types of states may be approached from different angles, including the state as a normative order as well as a set of organisations and rules that influence technological change by regulatory, fiscal and other institutional means (Hart 2002: 181f). This typology of state functions in technology policy is depicted in Table 25.1.

The developmental state, which has been prevalent during East Asian catch-up growth, exhibits a normative orientation towards developmentalism, an ideology that perceives industrial development as a goal of nation-building. Its policy rationale highlights the mobilisation of the factors of production, labour and capital, in furthering an extensive type of economic growth. Fiscal instruments include taxation and subsidies as well as the channelling of credit and interest. Governance modes exhibit a hierarchical relationship between an interventionist state and the private sector. Technological dynamics reflect the assimilation of new technologies. In contrast to this, the regulatory state regulates the market system, as exercised in industrialised Western economies. Recently, it has also gained in relevance across East Asia. Its normative orientation leans towards market liberalism while the policy rationale focuses on resource coordination through the enforcement of market competition. Fiscal instruments focus on taxation and subsidies. Governance modes put the hierarchy of state and private sector in a rule-based framework. In this manner, technology dynamics reflect market competition.

With regard to East Asian technology policies, however, a specific set of state functions has become hegemonic, namely the entrepreneurial state and its concern with the generation of technological innovations. Being relevant all across the industrialised and emerging economies, it is most prominent in post-developmental East Asia with its shift from the assimilation of technological innovations to their entrepreneurial creation. The normative orientation of the

Table 25.1 A typology of state functions in technology policy

	Type of State		
Characteristics	*Regulatory*	*Developmental*	*Entrepreneurial*
Normative Orientation	Market Liberalism	Developmentalism	Entrepreneurialism
Policy Rationale	Resource Coordination	Factor Mobilisation	Innovation
Fiscal Instruments	Taxation, Subsidies	Taxation, Subsidies, Credit, Interest	Taxation, Subsidies, Venture Capital
Governance Mode	Rule-Based Hierarchical	Interventionist Hierarchical	Communicative Networked
Policy Scale	National	National	Multi-Scalar
Technological Dynamics	Competition	Assimilation	Creation

Source: author.

entrepreneurial state addresses an ideology of entrepreneurialism that promotes creativity and novelty. Its policy rationale underlines technological innovation in an intensive type of economic growth. Fiscal instruments utilise taxation and subsidies as well as public venture capital. A hierarchical governance mode is combined with communicative networking. This goes together with a multi-scalar policy scale that strengthens local and regional as well as transnational interactions and thus differs from the national focus of both the developmental and regulatory states. Technological dynamics highlight the creation of new knowledge and its productive application in the generation of technological innovations. Technology policy then promotes innovations by strategic interventions as well as by providing institutional and physical infrastructures. However, innovation is a social process. Thus, democratisation and participatory structures gain in relevance as means for mobilising decentralised knowledge and innovation capabilities (Ebner 2007: 118–120, 2009: 382f).

Conclusion

As outlined above, current transformations of technology policy in East Asia may be approached in terms of the emergence of an entrepreneurial state. This notion entails the following propositions:

- The concern with technological leadership becomes a crucial feature of technological policy, which involves market interventions as well as the provision of institutional and physical infrastructures for innovation.
- Governance structures evoke a network pattern in the relations between government, business and civil society, based on knowledge flows that support policy learning.
- Technology policies of entrepreneurial states reflect the logic of globalisation in addressing the innovation capabilities of both local and foreign firms, universities and research institutes in knowledge-based agglomerations.

Entrepreneurial states in East Asia demonstrate diverse national varieties that range from Japan as pioneering late industrialiser via Korea and Taiwan as second generation tiers of catch-up growth to Singapore's high-performing city-state economy. All these entrepreneurial states exhibit country-specific combinations of governance modes that combine hierarchies, markets, networks and associations, among others, and thus add to the diversity among and within the evolving entrepreneurial states (Walter and Zhang 2012: 16–19). In this regard, technology policies in East Asia will be persistently challenged by the co-evolution of technological and institutional change in an economic setting that is subject to both regionalisation and globalisation.

References

Amsden, A., 1989: *Asia's Next Giant: South Korea and late industrialization*. New York: Oxford University Press.

Amsden, A., 1995: 'Post-Industrial' Policy in East Asia, Council on Foreign Relations Asia Project Working Paper. New York: Council on Foreign Relations.

Amsden, A. and Chu, W., 2003: *Beyond Late Development: Taiwan's upgrading policies*. Cambridge, MA: MIT Press.

Amsden, A. and Hikino, T., 1993: Borrowing technology or innovating: an exploration of the two paths to industrial development. In: Thomson, R. (ed.): *Learning and Technological Change*. New York: St Martin's Press, pp. 243–266.

Aoki, M., 2002: Japan in the Process of Institutional Change, *Miyakodayori* 31, 25 January 2002, Tokyo: Research Institute for Economy, Trade, and Industry. Available online at: www.rieti.go.jp/en/miyakodayori/031.html (accessed: April 14, 2014).

Aoki, M., Murdock, K. and Okuno-Fujiwara, M., 1997: Beyond the Asian Miracle: introducing the market-enhancing view. In: Aoki, M., Kim, H.-K. and Okuno-Fujiwara, M. (eds): *The Role of Government in East Asian Economic Development*. Oxford: Clarendon Press, pp. 1–37.

Asian Development Bank, 2013: *Key Indicators for Asia and the Pacific 2013*. Manila: ADB.

Beeson, M., 2004: The rise and fall of the developmental state: the vicissitudes and implications of East Asian interventionism. In: Low, L. (ed.): *Developmental States: Relevancy, redundancy or reconfiguration?* New York: Nova Science, pp. 29–40.

Beeson, M., 2009: Developmental states in East Asia: a comparison of the Japanese and Chinese experiences. *Asian Perspectives* 33(2), pp. 5–39.

Brahmbhatt, M. and Hu, A., 2010: Ideas and innovation in East Asia. *The World Bank Research Observer* 25(2), pp. 177–207.

Callon, S., 1995: *Divided Sun: MITI and the breakdown of Japanese high-tech industrial policy, 1975–1993*. Stanford, CA: Stanford University Press.

Carlsson, B., 2012: A systems framework for the study of economic and social dynamics of biotechnology. In: De la Mothe, J. and Niosi, J. (eds): *The Economic and Social Dynamics of Biotechnology*. New York: Springer, pp. 9–27.

Chang, H.-J., 1999: The economic theory of the developmental state. In: Woo-Cumings, M. (ed.): *The Developmental State*. Ithaca, NY and London: Cornell University Press, pp. 182–199.

Chang, H.-J., 2001: Rethinking East Asian industrial policy: past records and future prospects. In: Wong, P.-K. and Ng, C.-N. (eds): *Industrial Policy, Innovation and Economic Growth: The experience of Japan and the Asian NIEs*. Singapore: Singapore University Press, pp. 55–84.

Coriat, B., Orsi, F. and Weinstein, O., 2003: Does biotech reflect a new science-based innovation regime? *Industry and Innovation* 10(3), pp. 231–253.

Council for Science and Technology Policy, 2010: *Japan's Science and Technology Basic Policy Report*. Tokyo: Council for Science and Technology Policy.

Dodgson, M., 2000: Innovation policies in East Asia. In: Conceição, P. *et al.* (eds): *Science, Technology, and Innovation Policy: Opportunities and challenges for the knowledge economy*. Westport, CT and London: Quorum, pp. 399–413.

Ebner, A., 2004: Development strategies and innovation policies in globalisation: the case of Singapore. In: Mani, S. and Romijn, H. (eds): *Innovation, Learning and Technological Dynamism of Developing Countries*. Tokyo: United Nations University Press, pp. 48–76.

Ebner, A., 2006: Institutions, entrepreneurship and the rationale of government: an outline of the Schumpeterian theory of the state. *Journal of Economic Behavior and Organization* 59(4), pp. 497–515.

Ebner, A., 2007: Public policy, governance, and innovation: entrepreneurial states in East Asian economic development. *International Journal of Technology and Globalisation* 3(1), pp. 103–124.

Ebner, A., 2008: Institutional evolution and the political economy of governance. In: Ebner, A. and Beck, N. (eds): *The Institutions of the Market: Organisations, Social Systems, and Governance*. Oxford and New York: Oxford University Press, pp. 287–308.

Ebner, A., 2009: Entrepreneurial state: the Schumpeterian theory of industrial policy and the East Asian 'miracle'. In: Cantner, U., Gaffard, J.-L. and Nesta, L. (eds): *Schumpeterian Perspectives on Innovation, Competition, and Growth*. Berlin: Springer, pp. 367–388.

Ebner, A., 2013: Cluster policies and entrepreneurial states in East Asia. In: Eriksson, S. (ed.): *Innovation, Clusters and Economic Growth in Asia*. Aldershot: Elgar, pp. 1–20.

Elder, M., 2000: METI and industrial policy in Japan: change and continuity. *The Japanese Economy* 28(6), pp. 3–34.

Ernst, D. and Kim, L., 2002: Global production networks, knowledge diffusion and local capability formation. *Research Policy* 31(3), pp. 1417–1429.

Evans, P., 1995: *Embedded Autonomy: States and industrial transformation*. Princeton, NJ: Princeton University Press.

Fransman, M. and Tanaka, S., 1995: Government, globalisation and universities in Japanese biotechnology. *Research Policy* 24(1), pp. 13–49.

Freeman, C., 1987: *Technology and Economic Performance: Lessons from Japan*. London: Pinter.

Freeman, C., 1996: Catching-up and falling-behind: the case of Asia and Latin America. In: de la Mothe, J. and Paquet, G. (eds): *Evolutionary Economics and the New International Political Economy*. London: Pinter, pp. 160–179.

Freeman, C., 2002: Continental, national and sub-national innovation systems: complementarity and economic growth. *Research Policy* 31, pp. 191–211.

Fujita, K. and Hill, R.C., 2012: Industry clusters and transnational networks: Japan's new directions in regional policy. In: Park, B.-G., Hill, R.C. and Saito, A. (eds): *Locating Neoliberalism in East Asia: Neoliberalizing spaces in developmental states*. Oxford: Wiley, pp. 26–58.

Ganne, B. and Lecler, Y., 2009: From industrial districts to poles of competitiveness. In: Ganne, B. and Lecler, Y. (eds): *Asian Industrial Clusters, Global Competitiveness and New Policy Initiatives*. Singapore: World Scientific, pp. 3–24.

Gill, I. and Kharas, H., 2007: *An East Asian Renaissance: Ideas for economic growth*. Washington DC: World Bank.

Green, A., 2007: Globalisation and the changing nature of the state in East Asia. *Globalisation, Societies and Education* 5(1), pp. 23–38.

Hart, D.M., 2002: Private technological capabilities as product of national innovation systems: four ways of looking at the state. *Science and Public Policy* 29(1), pp. 181–188.

Hemmert, M., 2007: The Korean innovation system: from industrial catch-up to technology leadership? In: Mahlich, J. and Pascha, W. (eds): *Innovation and Technology in Korea*. Heidelberg: Physica, pp. 11–32.

Hobday, M., 1995: *Innovation in East Asia: The challenge to Japan*. Aldershot: Elgar.

Hobday, M., 2003: Innovation in Asian industrialization: a Gerschenkronian perspective. *Oxford Development Studies* 31(3), pp. 293–314.

Hobday, M., Rush, H. and Bessant, J., 2004: Approaching the innovation frontier in Korea: the transition phase to leadership. *Research Policy* 33(4), pp. 1433–1457.

Holroyd, K. and Coates, K., 2007: *Innovation Nation: Science and technology in 21st century Japan*. Basingstoke: Palgrave Macmillan.

Hu, M.-C. and Mathews, J.A., 2005: National innovative capacity in East Asia. *Research Policy* 34(3), pp. 1322–1349.

Ibata-Arens, K., 2004: *Japan's Quest for Entrepreneurialism: The Cluster Plan, JPRI*. Working Paper No. 102. Encinitas, CA: Japan Policy Research Institute.

Ibata-Arens, K., 2005: *Innovation and Entrepreneurship in Japan: Politics, organizations, and high-technology firms*. Cambridge: Cambridge University Press.

Jayasuriya, K., 2005: Beyond institutional fetishism: from the developmental to the regulatory state. *New Political Economy* 10(3), pp. 381–387.

Johann, D., 2012: *The Reconfiguration of a Latecomer Innovation System: Governing pharmaceutical biotechnology innovation in South Korea*. Frankfurt am Main: Lang.

Johnson, C., 1982: *MITI and the Japanese Miracle: The growth of industrial policy, 1925–1975*. Stanford, CA: Stanford University Press.

Kim, L., 1999: Building technological capability for industrialization: analytical frameworks and Korea's experience. *Industrial and Corporate Change* 8(1), pp. 111–136.

Kitagawa, F., 2007: The regionalization of science and innovation governance in Japan? *Regional Studies* 41(8), pp. 1099–1114.

Koh, W.T.H. and Wong, P.K., 2004: Competing at the frontier: the changing role of technology policy in Singapore's economic strategy. *Technological Forecasting and Social Change* 72(2), pp. 255–285.

Kuchiki, A. and Tsuji, M., 2011: Introduction. In: Kuchiki, A. and Tsuji, M. (eds): *Industrial Clusters, Upgrading and Innovation in East Asia*. Cheltenham: Elgar, pp. 1–12.

Lall, S., 2000: Technological change and industrialization in the Asian newly industrializing economies: achievements and challenges. In: Kim, L. and Nelson, R. (eds): *Technology, Learning, and Innovation: Experiences of newly industrializing economies*. Cambridge: Cambridge University Press, pp. 13–68.

Lazonick, W., 2008: Entrepreneurial Ventures and the Developmental State: Lessons from the Advanced Economies, United Nations University World Institute for Development Economics, Research Discussion Paper 2008/01.

Lee, J.-H., 2011: Issues and policies in the STI leadership phase. *STI Policy Review* 2(4), pp. 29–38.

Lee, S.-K. and Han, T., 2006: The demise of 'Korea, Inc.': paradigm shift in Korea's developmental state. *Journal of Contemporary Asia* 36(3), pp. 305–324.

Lee, S.H. and Yoo, T., 2007: Government policy and trajectories of radical innovation in dirigiste states: a comparative analysis of national innovation systems in France and Korea. *Technology Analysis and Strategic Management* 19(4), pp. 451–470.

Low, L., 2004: Singapore's developmental state between a rock and a hard place. In: Low, L. (ed.): *Developmental States: Relevancy, redundancy or reconfiguration?* New York: Nova Science, pp. 161–177.

Mahmood, I.P. and Singh, J., 2003: Technological dynamism in Asia, *Research Policy* 32(4), pp. 1031–1054.

Masuyama, S. and Vandenbrink, D., 2001: Industrial restructuring for East Asian economies in the twenty-first century. In: Masuyama, S., Vandenbrink, D. and Yue, C.S. (eds.): *Industrial Restructuring in East Asia: Towards the 21st century*. Singapore: ISEAS, pp. 3–54.

Mathews, J.A., 2006: Catch-up strategies and the latecomer effect in industrial development. *New Political Economy* 11(3), pp. 313–335.

Nahm, K.-B., 2011: Regional innovation policy in South Korea: building science and technology based entrepreneurial development capabilities. In: Mian, S.A. (ed.): *Science and Technology Based Regional Entrepreneurship: Global experience in policy and program development*. Aldershot: Elgar, pp. 160–186.

Nelson, R.R., 2004: The challenge of building an effective innovation system for catch-up. *Oxford Development Studies* 32(3), pp. 365–374.

Odagiri, H., 2006: Advance of science-based industries and the changing innovation system of Japan. In: Lundvall, B.-Å., Intarakumnerd, P. and Vang, J. (eds): *Asia's Innovation Systems in Transition*. Cheltenham: Elgar, pp. 200–226.

Odagiri, H. and Goto, A., 1996: *Technology and Industrial Development in Japan: Building capabilities by learning, innovation, and public policy*. Oxford: Clarendon.

OECD, 2013: *Main Science and Technology Indicators*. Paris: OECD.

Okimoto, D.I., 1989: *Between MITI and the Market: Japanese industrial policy for high technology*. Stanford, CA: Stanford University Press.

Okimura, K., 2005: Japan's science and technology policy. *Japan Economic Currents* November/December (5), pp. 1–4.

Perez, C., 2003: *Technological Revolutions and Financial Capital: The dynamics of bubbles and golden ages*. Cheltenham: Elgar.

Porter, M.E. and Sakakibara, M., 2004: Competition in Japan. *Journal of Economic Perspectives* 18(1), pp. 27–50.

Reslinger, C., 2012: Is there an Asian model of technological emergence? *Socio-Economic Review* 11(1), pp. 371–408.

Roy, K., Blomqvist, H. and Clark, C., 2012: *Economic Development in China, India and East Asia: Managing change in the twenty-first century*. Aldershot: Elgar.

Seliger, B., 2013: *The Shrimp that Became a Tiger: Transformation theory and Korea's rise after the Asian crisis*. Frankfurt am Main: Lang.

Thurbon, E. and Weiss, L., 2006: Investing in openness: the evolution of FDI strategy in South Korea and Taiwan. *New Political Economy* 11(1), pp. 1–22.

Tung, C.-M., 2013: The national innovation system and policy implications for entrepreneurship in Taiwan and Japan. *STI Policy Review* 4(1), pp. 54–73.

Vang, J., 2006: Asia's systems of innovation in transition: an introduction. In: Lundvall, B.-Å., Intarakumnerd, P. and Vang, J. (eds): *Asia's Innovation Systems in Transition*. Cheltenham: Elgar, pp. 1–20.

Vogel, S.K., 2006: *Japan Remodeled: How government and industry are reforming Japanese capitalism*. Ithaca, NY: Cornell University Press.

Wade, R., 1990: *Governing the Market: Economic theory and the role of government in East Asian industrialization*. Princeton, NJ: Princeton University Press.

Wade, R., 2000: Governing the Market: A Decade Later, London School of Economics and Political Sciences Development Studies Institute. LSE-DESTIN Working Paper No. 00–03. London: LSE.

Wade, R., 2005: Bringing the state back in: lessons from East Asia's development experience. *Internationale Politik und Gesellschaft* 8(2), pp. 98–115.

Walter, A. and Zhang, X., 2012: East Asian capitalism: issues and themes. In: Walter, A. und Zhang, X. (eds): *East Asian Capitalism: Diversity, continuity and change*. Oxford: Oxford University Press, pp. 3–25.

Wang, J., Chen, T.-Y. and Tsai, C.-J., 2009: In search of an innovative state: the development of the biopharmaceutical industry in Taiwan, South Korea and China. *Development and Change* 43(2), pp. 481–503.

Wang, J.-C. and Ma, D., 2011: Taiwan's industrial innovation policy and programs to support research and technology based entrepreneurship. In: Mian, S.A. (ed.): *Science and Technology Based Regional Entrepreneurship: Global experience in policy and program development*. Aldershot: Elgar, pp. 286–305.

Weiss, L., 1998: The Myth of the Powerless State: Governing the economy in a global era. Cambridge: Polity Press.

Weiss, L., 2000: Developmental states in transition: adapting, dismantling, innovating, not 'normalizing'. *The Pacific Review* 13(1), pp. 21–55.

Whittaker, D.H., 2003: Crisis and innovation in Japan: A new future through technoentrepreneurship? In: Keller, W.W. and Samuels, R.J. (eds): *Crisis and Innovation in Asian Technology*. Cambridge: Cambridge University Press, pp. 57–85.

Wong, J., 2004: From learning to creating: biotechnology and the postindustrial developmental state in Korea. *Journal of East Asian Studies* 4(4), pp. 491–517.

Wong, J., 2005: Re-making the developmental state in Taiwan: the challenges of biotechnology. *International Political Science Review* 26(2), pp. 169–191.

Wong, J., 2011: *Betting on Biotech: Innovation and the limits of Asia's developmental state*. Ithaca, NY: Cornell University Press.

Wong, J., Quach, U., Thorsteinsdóttir, H., Singer, P.A. and Daar, A.S., 2004: South Korean biotechnology: a rising industrial and scientific powerhouse. *Nature Biotechnology* 22, Supplement, pp. 42–47.

Wong, P.-K., 2001: The role of the state in Singapore's industrial development. In: Wong, P.-K. and Ng, C.-N. (eds.): *Industrial Policy, Innovation and Economic Growth: The experience of Japan and the Asian NIEs*. Singapore: Singapore University Press, pp. 503–569.

Wong, P.-K., 2011: The dynamism of Singapore's science and technology policy and its quest for technopreneurship. In: Mian, S.A. (ed.): *Science and Technology Based Regional Entrepreneurship: Global experience in policy and program development*. Aldershot: Elgar, pp. 256–285.

Wong, P.-K. and Ng, C.-N., 2001: Rethinking the development paradigm: lessons from Japan and the four Asian NIEs. In: Wong, P.-K. and Ng, C.-N. (eds): *Industrial Policy, Innovation and Economic Growth: The experience of Japan and the Asian NIEs*. Singapore: Singapore University Press, pp. 1–54.

World Bank, 1993: *The East Asian Miracle: Economic growth and public policy*. Oxford: Oxford University Press.

Yeung, H.-W., 2006: Innovating for global competition: Singapore's pathway to high-tech development. In: Lundvall, B.-Å., Intarakumnerd, P. and Vang, J. (eds): *Asia's Innovation Systems in Transition*. Cheltenham: Elgar, pp. 257–292.

Yusuf, S. and Evenett, S.-J., 2002: *Can East Asia Compete? Innovation for global markets*. New York: Oxford University Press.

Yusuf, S. *et al.*, 2003: *Innovative East Asia: The future of growth*. New York: Oxford University Press.

26

CHINA'S PATH TOWARDS BECOMING A MAJOR WORLD PLAYER IN SCIENCE AND TECHNOLOGY

Xiaming Liu

Introduction

Since the adoption of economic reforms and opening to the outside world, China has experienced rapid economic growth. In recent years, China has especially focused on increasing its R&D efforts. For instance, China's spending on research and development (R&D) reached 1.02 trillion yuan (US$162.24 billion) in 2012 (*AsianScientist* 2013), representing 2 per cent of the country's GDP. In addition, China has the second largest number of researchers after the United States (OECD 2008).

China is already a major science and technology (S&T) player in terms of input to innovation, but its output is below levels in OECD countries that have similar levels of R&D (OECD 2008). Compared to the US government, which believes that the market drives innovation, the Chinese government feels that it is public policy that plays a critical role in fostering indigenous innovation, and it is important for the government to define strategic objectives and key parameters for S&T activities (Ernst 2011). The Chinese government has not only encouraged innovation, but also tried to use public policy to address low efficiency and other problems associated with R&D activities in China. Sections 1 and 2 of this chapter discuss the evolution of China's innovation policy and innovation system, and section 3 analyzes China's path towards becoming a major world player in S&T.

China's innovation policy

Definition of innovation policy

There is no consensus on how to define either innovation policy or industrial policy, where the latter is closely related to the former. One official definition is that innovation policy is:

> a set of policy actions, measures, and tools intended to raise the quantity and efficiency of innovative activities and enhance innovative capability, whereby "innovative

> activities" refer to the creation, adaptation and adoption of new or improved products, processes, or services.
>
> (*European Commission 2000: 9*)

These measures not only include traditional support of R&D and provision of intellectual property rights, but actually also include any policy action that would in the end have an effect on innovation (ibid: 4).

Industrial policy can be understood as a set of "government measures aimed at improving the competitiveness and capabilities of domestic firms and promoting structural transformation" (UNCTAD and UNIDO 2011: 34). By this definition, many industrial policies may overlap with innovation policies, as all industrial policy measures aiming to improve the competitiveness and capabilities of domestic firms via the promotion of R&D and innovation can be regarded as innovation policy measures. Of course, industrial policy measures also include those that are not directly related to innovation but to structural transformation.

China's definition of innovation policy is very broad, and is consistent with that of the European Commission (2000). China's Medium- and Long-Term Plan for Development of Science and Technology (2006–2020) (MLP) devotes Part Eight to Major Policies and Measures, and requires that:

> all policies and measures shall be made as such that they are conducive to enhancing indigenous innovation capability, spurring the enthusiasm and creativity of science and technology (S&T) personnel, making full use of S&T resources both at home and abroad, and supporting economic and social development through S&T.

As a result, the discussion of China's innovation policy in this chapter is based on this broad definition.

Evolution of China's innovation policy

Given the broad definition of innovation policy, and very sophisticated bureaucratic system for policy formulation and implementation in China (Lieberthal and Oksenberg 1988; Liu et al. 2011), it is not surprising that there is no consensus on how this policy is governed and has evolved.

Since the founding of the People's Republic of China, the Chinese authorities have held several S&T conferences, issued a number of S&T plans (*guihua*) and specific programs (*jihua*), and made several S&T "decisions" at the national level. These plans were designed for the short, medium or long term, such that several of them could coexist in a particular time period. They could either overlap or complement each other. Special programs have been launched on an irregular basis. All this makes it difficult to clearly trace the evolution of China's innovation policy over time. Table 26.1 lists some of the most important S&T plans, programs and decisions since the 1950s.

The Organisation for Economic Co-operation and Development (OECD 2008: 381–382) divides China's post-1978 era into four periods: 1975–1978; 1979–1994; 1995–2005; 2006–2020, as the S&T conference was held in 1978, 1995, 1999, and 2006, and as the four S&T decisions issued following the 1985, 1995, 1999, and 2006 S&T conferences were the milestones in China's S&T policy. Specifically, 1975–1978 was a "rectification" period during which Deng Xiaoping aimed to rectify the economic, S&T, and education systems damaged by the Cultural Revolution. 1979–94 was a "reform" period for the economic, S&T, and education systems.

Table 26.1 China's major S&T policies since 1956

Year	*Name*	*Key Features*
1956	1956–1967 Science and Technology Development Prospective Plan	Focused on "making scientific advances" (*xiang kexue jinjun*), specifying 57 major tasks and laying the foundations for new S&T sectors, including atomic energy, electronics, semiconductors, automation, computing technology, aviation and rocket technology.
1963	1963–1972 Science and Technology Development Plan	The principle of "self-reliance and working hard to catch up" was set up (*zili gengsheng, yingtou ganshang*) for the development of science and technology, and a view was established that the modernization of science and technology would be the key to achieving modernization in agriculture, industry, national defense, and science and technology. The Plan specified 374 key research projects, 3205 central issues and 15,000 research topics.
1978	1978–1985 National Science and Technology Development Plan	Deng Xiaoping proposed that S&T would be the leading productive force, intellectuals were part of the working class, and S&T would be the key to the "Four Modernizations" drive. The plan specified eight priority areas for development and 108 key research projects.
1985	Decision on the Reform of the Science and Technology System	Focused on developing the market for technology; commercializing technology; and encouraging the linkage between scientific research institutions and enterprises.
1986	1986–2000 Science and Technology Development Plan	Focused on implementing the basic principle that "science and technology must be oriented to economic development and economic development must rely on science and technology," developing a science and technology system with Chinese characteristics. The plan included the 1986–2000 National Science and Technology Development Plan Outline, the 1986–1990 National Science and Technology Development Program Outline, and technology policies in the 12 areas (in 1988, two more areas were added). During this period, the Chinese government approved the establishment of 53 national high-tech industrial development zones. It also formulated the "Spark Program," "863 Program," "Torch Program," "Climbing Program," and established the China Natural Science Funds.
1995	Decision on Accelerating the Progress of Science and Technology	Put forward the strategy of "revitalizing the nation through science, technology and education" (*kejiao xingguo*). In 1996, the "Technology Innovation Project" was established to enhance the technological innovation capability of enterprises.
1999	Decision on Strengthening Technological Innovation, Developing High Technology and Realizing Industrialization	Called for the construction of a national innovation system and the speeding-up of industrialization of S&T achievements.
2006	2006: Medium- and Long-Term Plan for the Development of Science and Technology (2006–2020) (MLP); Decision on Implementing the MLP and Improving Indigenous Innovation Capability	Set up the guidelines of "indigenous innovation, leap-frogging in priority fields, enabling development, and leading the future," aiming to turn China into an "innovation-oriented country" by 2020.

Sources: Li (2006); Li and Li (2008); Liu et al. (2011).

In comparison, 1995–2005 was a "deepening reform" period during which the progress of S&T accelerated: science and education, technical innovation, and high-technology industrialization were strengthened for sustainable development. Finally, 2006–2020 is regarded as an "innovation-driven" period during which the concepts of scientific development and the harmonious society have been proposed, and a strategy for revitalizing the nation by talent has been formulated.

Liu et al. (2011) were interested in the evolution of China's specific innovation policy categories and issuing agencies. For this purpose, they divided the post-reform period into four periods instead: (1) the 1980–1984 period during which there were only 17 innovation policies (six S&T, four industrial, four financial and three tax policies), and there was no formal fiscal policy; (2) the 1985–1994 period during which 76 innovation policies were issued, focusing on S&T and industrial policies; (3) the 1995–2005 period during which the concept of "innovation" was introduced, and a large number of S&T policies were issued together with some industrial, financial, tax, and fiscal policies; (4) since 2006, various central governmental agencies collaborated to produce 79 implementation policies for the MLP among which the majority were S&T policies, followed by industrial policies whose main aims included building up indigenous innovation capabilities, as well as formulating tax, financial and finally fiscal policies. From their analysis of the issues of 366 policies during 1980 and 2008, Liu et al. conclude that China has shifted its S&T and industrial policy-centered innovation strategy towards a series of better coordinated, innovation-oriented economic and technology initiatives. This is partly because China gradually shifted its focus from the initiation of new S&T programs to innovation capacity building and the creation of an innovation friendly environment. The other shift was from dependence on a single policy framework (to support the implementation of specific S&T programs) to the formation of a rich portfolio of diverse policies where financial, tax, and fiscal policies carried the same strategic importance as traditional S&T and industrial policies in the innovation promotion framework.

Adopting the broad definition of innovation policy in China, Peng et al. (2008) selected 423 policies deemed to be closely related to technical innovation from as many as 12,403 policies issued by the central government and its agencies (excluding provincial level regulations and policies) between 1978 and 2006. They aim to provide the trajectory of the evolution of technical innovation policies by classifying these policies using information on the timing of a policy, nature of the issuing organization, legal background and property, guiding ideology, core concept, and measures. They also find that innovation policies from different central government agencies tend to be better coordinated when China attaches increasing importance to innovation.

If we look at Table 26.1, we can find that since the foundation of the People's Republic in 1949, China has seriously attempted to develop its S&T with the aim of realizing the four modernizations. While there is no consensus on how to divide the past 63 years or so into different stages of its innovation policy, the general trend is that China's S&T strategy moved gradually from "closed innovation" to indigenous capability enhancement oriented "collaborative innovation."

China's innovation system

Definition of national innovation system (NIS)

When explaining the rise of Japan as an economic superpower, Freeman (1987, 1995) defines an NIS as the network of institutions in the public and private sectors whose activities and interactions initiate, import, modify, and diffuse new technologies. Since then, a number of different definitions have been proposed, including Lundvall (1992), Nelson (1993), Patel and Pavitt (1994) and Metcalfe (1995). After reviewing these definitions, OECD (1997) suggests that, although there is no single accepted definition, all the widely used definitions emphasize the importance of the web of interaction. The key actors in the web are private enterprises, universities, and public research institutes and the people within them, and "the innovative performance of a country depends to a large extent on how these actors relate to each other as elements of a collective system of knowledge creation and use as well as the technologies they use" (OECD 1997: 9). Given the fact that a large number of multinational enterprises are operating in China, the interaction of these firms with local Chinese firms also needs to be assessed when examining China's NIS.

OECD (2008: 45) suggests that the Chinese innovation system originated in the mid 1980s when China's broader agenda of economic reforms included the reform of the science and technology (S&T) system. However, closely related to the evolution of innovation policy, the origin of China's innovation system could be traced back further. For instance, Zhang and He (1999) and Chen (2002) divide the evolution of China's innovation system into four phases. (1) Formation Phase (1949–1977); (2) Development Phase (1978–1995); (3) National Technical Innovation System Phase (1995–1998); and (4) National Innovation System Phase (1998–).

Their reasoning for these four phases is as follows. The Formation Phase (1949–1977) is characterized by the establishment of various public research institutes and the formulation of S&T development plans. The NIS was gradually formed. In this phase, the mode of innovation was "government-led." Innovations were motivated, planned, financed, and directly controlled by the government based on its understanding of social development and national defense needs. The Development Phase (1978–1995) is featured by the exploration of the NIS development mode and innovation policies. This was a "plan-led" period during which national S&T development plans were formulated and the competition mechanism was introduced into the plans. The fiscal appropriation system was reformed and the market for S&T was nurtured and developed. The focus of the National Technical Innovation System Phase (1995–1998) was the technological innovation capability of enterprises. In this period, the industrialization of S&T achievements was emphasized. The National Innovation System Phase (1998) emphasized knowledge innovation. In this period, China believed that the NIS should include a knowledge innovation system, technological innovation system, and knowledge diffusion and application system.

By definition, the basic feature of an NIS is the formation of a network of actors that can act with each other. It is difficult to judge when such a network emerged in China, and "the reform of China's NIS is far from completed" (Sigurdson 2004: 345). Therefore it is not surprising that there is no consensus on the stages of evolution of China's NIS. Nevertheless, China has been determined to establish and gradually improve its NIS over time. This section briefly assesses the development of China's innovation system, focusing on the evolution of the main aims and actors within this system.

Evolution of China's innovation system

Foundation laying (1949–1955)

When the People's Republic was established in 1949, there were only 30+ specialized research institutions with fewer than 50,000 scientists and technicians (People's Web 2009). At that time, China was "poor and blank." As Mao (1956) explains, being poor meant that China did not have much industry, and its agriculture was not developed. Being blank implied that China was like a blank sheet of paper with low levels of science and technology. A 100 per cent home-made bicycle was hailed as a big technical achievement for 1950 (People's Web 2009). In late 1949, the Chinese Academy of Sciences (CAS) was established. This was the highest scientific authority in China. The Academy then reintegrated all research institutions, reallocated S&T specialists, and reunited the national science community, quickly setting up the first batch of research institutions with CAS being the centre (Li and Li 2008). These institutions were the main actors in China's innovation system. During the early 1950s, the Soviet Union helped China to construct 156 projects, involving the energy, metallurgy, chemical, machinery, military, and light industries. As summarized by Zhang (2009), these projects enabled the transfer of technologies that China urgently needed, and promoted the formation of a relatively complete technical and industrial system. By so doing, the foundation for China's NIS was laid.

Government-led innovation system (1956–1977)

In 1956, China called for "making scientific advances" and formulated its "1956–1967 Science and Technology Development Prospective Plan." For the purpose of national security, China's S&T development in this period favoured military aspects, and specified 57 major tasks, laying foundations for new S&T sectors, including atomic energy, electronics, semi-conductors, automation, computing technology, aviation, and rocket technology. As discussed in Zhang and Li (1999) and Chen (2002), China's S&T development in this stage was "government-led." Specifically, the government directly controlled the division of labor in line with the functions and administrative affiliation of its organizational system. Innovations were motivated by what the government believed were important for national economic and social development and national security. The government was the main source of input in innovations, and resources were allocated strictly according to the plan. The performers as well as organizers innovated in order to fulfill government tasks. Their rewards were not directly dependent on their S&T results, and they did not bear any responsibility for risk or failure of innovations.

The significant milestones of innovation output during this period were the so-called "two bombs (atomic and hydrogen) and one satellite." However, the anti-rightist movement in 1957, the "Great Leap Forward" in 1958, the withdrawal of Soviet experts before 1959, and the 1960–1962 natural disaster badly hurt new China's S&T development. Without Soviet assistance and without contact with western countries, China could do nothing but formulate the principle of "self-reliance" in its "1963–1972 Science and Technology Development Plan." The 1966–1976 "Cultural Revolution" led to the destruction of science and technology and purged intellectuals, severely interfering with and disrupting China's scientific and technological undertakings (Li and Li 2008).

1978–1995: plan-led innovation system

The year of 1978 was hailed as the start of the "spring of science," when Deng Xiaoping proposed that S&T was the leading productive force, intellectuals were part of the working class, and S&T was the key to the "Four Modernizations" drive. Since then, numerous policy measures have been issued with different focuses on different aspects of S&T development. The "1978–1985 National Science and Technology Development Plan" further emphasized the importance of S&T in the Four Modernizations drive. The "1985 Decision on the Reform of the Science and Technology System" aimed to introduce market mechanisms into the state-plan-dominated innovation system. The "1986–2000 Science and Technology Development Plan" called for the orientation of S&T towards economic development and the development of a science and technology system with Chinese characteristics. In these 15 years, several major S&T programs were launched, including the "Spark Program," "863 Program," "Torch Program," "Climbing Program," and the establishment of the China Natural Science Funds. The "1995 Decision on Accelerating the Progress of Science and Technology" emphasized the importance of not only S&T but also education in the revitalization of the nation.

As discussed in Chen (2002) and Zhang and He (1999), the focus of this stage of NIS development was to explore the model of development and related innovation policies, and introduce reform measures. During this period, the innovation mode was "plan-led," namely a competition mechanism was introduced into national S&T plans. Through reforming the funding system, and nurturing and developing the technology market, research institutions vitalized their serving of the economic construction. All this promoted the commercialization of research results, and speeded up the industrialization process, accelerating the development of China's national innovation system. During this period, the main actors seemed to be research institutions.

For any open economy, the NIS is more or less linked with the international S&T community. In the 1950s, China relied very much on technology from the Soviet Union and Eastern European economies, and followed the Soviet Union's model to develop its economy and innovation capabilities. However, having depended solely on the Soviet Union, China was isolated by the Western world and lost the possibility to directly purchase materials, machinery, equipment, and technology from these developed countries. After the relationship with the Soviet Union deteriorated, China had to follow the "self-reliance" ideology for its development (Zhang 2009). After the late 1960s, Western Europe and Japan were the main sources of Chinese technology imports (Andreosso-O'Callaghan 1999).

One important purpose of China's decision to open to the outside world in 1978 was to obtain advanced technologies. Between 1979 and 1981, China initiated the so-called "exchange of market access for technology" (exchange) policy. In 1984, the State Council formally confirmed the strategic importance of this policy: "To exchange partial market access for foreign advanced technologies is a major policy for accelerating our country's technological progress" (Law Institute 1986: 490). This policy allowed a foreign invested firm to sell part of its product on the Chinese market if its technology was regarded as being advanced. China hoped that such market access concession would enable foreign invested firms to transfer their advanced technologies so that China's technological progress could be enhanced (Xia and Zhao 2012).

China also participated in various international S&T networks. For instance, as noted in Blau (2013), the EU and China have closely collaborated in S&T since July 11, 1980 when the European Space Agency and China's National Commission for Science and Technology signed an agreement on the exchange of scientific data. China has actively participated in the EU's Framework Programs since the 1990s.

1996–1999: enterprise-focused innovation system

In 1996, the "Technology Innovation Project" was launched to enhance the technological innovation capability of enterprises. The "1999 Decision on Strengthening Technological Innovation, Developing High Technology and Realizing Industrialization" called for the construction of a national innovation system and the acceleration of the commercialization of S&T achievements.

As noted in Chen (2002) and Zhang and He (1999), the significant characteristic of this stage was to establish the goal of a market economy, starting from enterprise reform, to enterprise system and property rights system reforms, strengthening the innovative features of enterprises.

The S&T management system also underwent a major change: government plans were gradually developed jointly by the departments in charge of S&T and economic development.

1998–2005: knowledge economy-focused innovation system

This period slightly overlapped with the enterprise-focused innovation system period. As reported in Chen (2002) and Zhang and He (1999), in December 1997, the Chinese Academy of Sciences submitted a report that proposed an NIS for the knowledge economy era, including the establishment of a knowledge innovation system, technological innovation system, knowledge dissemination system and knowledge application system. The report was approved by the State Council in 1998, and the CAS was chosen to initiate the knowledge innovation project as the pilot of the NIS.

Indigenous capability-focused innovation system

Most recently, the "2006 MLP" set up the guidelines of "indigenous innovation, leap-frogging in priority fields, enabling development, and leading the future," aiming to turn China into an "innovation-oriented" country by 2020. This latest innovation strategy was further confirmed in Hu Jingtao's speech at the 18th National Congress of the Communist Party of China (Hu 2012). He called for the implementation of the "innovation-driven development strategy," following a path of making innovation with Chinese characteristics and taking steps to promote innovation to catch up with global advances. He also called for a strengthening of China's ability to conduct original innovation, integrated innovation, and re-innovation based on assimilation and absorption of imported technology, as well as more focus on collaborative innovation. In addition, he argued that the reform of the science and technology system needed to be deepened, the construction of a national innovation system accelerated, and an enterprise-dominated, market-oriented, and industry–education–research linked technology innovation system established. Specifically, Hu (2012) argued that, in this system, "enterprises play the leading role, the market points the way, and enterprises, universities and research institutes work together."

Consistent with Hu's speech, the MLP asked universities to act not only as an important base for nurturing high caliber innovative talent, but also as a principal player in basic research and original technological innovation activity and as a commendable force in addressing major S&T issues in the national economy, materializing technology transfer, and effecting technology spin-off and commercialization. The Plan called for support and encouragement for university-based original innovation in basic research, frontier technology development, and public goods research. Universities were also required to fully collaborate with enterprises and research institutes so that they could provide better and more extensive services to economic development at the national, regional, and sectoral levels.

As analyzed in Meng (2011), as part of China's innovation drive, the Chinese government has been fostering S&T research activities in universities, and the innovation policy for the higher education sector experienced three logically related stages of development. The first stage was passive involvement (1996–2001) in line with China's enterprise-centered innovation strategy. In this stage, public research institutions and universities were linked by the government with 1000 enterprises for S&T cooperation for practical use. The second stage was emphasis of roles of prestigious universities (2002–2005) according to China's national innovation strategy. In this stage, the priority was to develop prestigious universities by the reorganization of key national laboratories and the establishment of innovative bases and national large-scale scientific equipment centers in selected universities. The third stage (2006–) was to promote the development of local universities and colleges following China's regional innovation strategy. In this stage, the performance of local universities in S&T innovation was promoted.

In addition to university education and research, the 2006 MPL called for improvement of the scientific and cultural literacy of the entire nation with a view to advancing people's overall development. It emphasized innovation-oriented education, raising teenagers' innovation awareness and capabilities, and providing science and technology related training for the public, including farmers.

Debate about indigenous innovation drive

There has been international debate about China's indigenous innovation drive. As described in McGregor (2010), since the MLP called for enhancing original innovation through co-innovation and re-innovation based on the assimilation of imported technologies, and since the MLP states that the importation of technologies without emphasizing assimilation, absorption, and re-innovation would weaken the nation's indigenous research and development capacity, "the plan is considered by many international technology companies as a blueprint for technology theft on a scale the world has never seen before" (4).

Although there are problems with intellectual property protection in China, the technology theft assertion may be a bit naïve. The gradual phasing-in of the strategy of indigenous capability enhancement oriented collaborative innovation was closely related to the gradual phasing-out of the so-called "exchange of market access for technology" (exchange) policy as discussed earlier. Xia and Zhao (2012) recall that the exchange idea was initiated during the early stage of economic reform and opening to the outside world (1979 and 1981) when China urgently needed advanced technologies from abroad for large scale economic development while its foreign exchange reserves were very limited.

The original purpose of this policy was to promote China's own ability of self reliance by introducing advanced foreign technologies (Economic Group of Research Unit 1985: 200). The designed mechanism was "introduction—digestion—absorption—innovation." However, as Peng et al. (2008) explain, given the agency problem, managers of state owned enterprises (SOEs) as the main receivers of foreign direct investment did not have incentives to digest and absorb foreign technologies. They were interested in maximizing short-run profits while in office. When introducing FDI, they fulfilled their political tasks. The institutional arrangements in China were in favor of SOEs, but not private enterprises. The latter had no chance to introduce foreign technologies, let alone digest and absorb them. The ignorance of digestion and absorption was the main reason for the failure of the exchange policy.

On the other hand, Xia and Zhao (2012) argue that, via the technology introduction–digestion–absorption–innovation mechanism, the exchange policy did bring some benefits to China. For instance, from 1980 to 1984, China caught up with the world's advanced levels in the Chinese language laser typesetting system, colour TVs, NC phones, and containers. However, whether a foreign investment project was technology advanced was determined by individual local governments in much of the post-1978 era, and the amount of FDI attracted was an indicator of local government performance, so that local governments raced for inward FDI projects without considering whether they were just repeats from other provinces, and no attention was made to their digestion and absorption. So long as such projects could quickly bring in profits, speeding up GDP growth, local governments would launch them. As a result, in the 1980s there were repeat introductions of colour TV production lines, wind energy equipment, automobiles, and general equipment manufacturing facilities in different regions.

Zeng and Li (2000) also highlight several problems with the implementation of the exchange policy: (1) a small number of MNEs with advanced technologies strictly control their core technologies; (2) some Chinese firms are not only unable to introduce advanced technology, but suffer from the technological lock-in effect, relying on MNEs' production technologies; (3) foreign invested firms established in China before the 1990s were mainly labor-intensive processing enterprises without advanced technologies; (4) there was no significant improvement of international competitiveness of Chinese products; (5) MNEs had already shifted their strategy from product and then capital introduction to brand introduction.

As noted in Xia and Zhao (2012), the exchange policy gradually lost its support by the end of the twentieth century. The feasibility and effectiveness of this policy were questioned and challenged. It was argued that the Chinese market reality following the implementation of the policy was the monopolistic position of big MNEs and local Chinese firms were crowded out. As of 1998, Motorola, Ericsson, NEC accounted for 90 per cent of the Chinese mobile phone and pager market, and foreign firms had a 60 per cent share of the tire market, and similar shares of the drink, washing, cosmetics, and machinery markets (Huang 2008). After 20 years of opening to the outside world, Chinese industries still relied very much on foreign technologies. This dependence was manifested not only by local Chinese firms' imports of a large amount of key technology and equipment, but also by foreign firms' heavy reliance on their home countries' R&D resources. Xia and Zhao (2012) argue that, while the former phenomenon demonstrated very limited technology spillover effects from FDI, the latter implied strict control of the transfer of foreign advanced technologies. The exchange policy failed to achieve its main purpose. Of course, there are studies showing that inward FDI has produced positive productivity spillovers (e.g. Wei and Liu 2006).

On October 31, 2000 China revised its laws and regulations on inward FDI in accordance with WTO rules and WTO accession commitments so that local-content and export requirements for foreign firms were removed. Thus, the exchange policy no longer had its legal foundations.

Under the above background, the Chinese government gradually shifted its strategy towards indigenous capability enhancement oriented innovation. As indicated in the MLP, China "called for placing the strengthening of indigenous innovation capability at the core of S&T undertakings."

> Facts have proven that, in areas critical to the national economy and security, core technologies cannot be purchased. If our country wants to take the initiative in fierce international competition, it has to enhance its indigenous innovation capability, master core technologies in some critical areas, own proprietary intellectual property rights, and build a number of internationally competitive enterprises.

Current issues with China's NIS

As mentioned in the introduction, China's research output is low relative to its input compared to OECD countries. This is believed to be due to deficiencies in China's NIS as China is still in its transition from a planned economy to a market-oriented system (OECD 2008). Some of the identified problems with the NIS are as follows:

1 Enterprises have weak indigenous innovation capabilities and hence are not yet key players in technological innovation (MLP). This is consistent with the observation of Sigurdson (2004) that most patent applications in China have been filed by foreign rather than local

Chinese companies and the US patent data base indicates that applications originated from China received a very minimal level of approval. Chang and Shih (2004) indicate that the key innovation players in China were traditionally public research institutes and Chinese enterprises invested more in importing technology than developing their own R&D capabilities.

2 S&T forces are self-contained and separated, resulting in duplication of efforts and low overall performance (MLP). OECD (2008) suggested that China's NIS seemed like an "archipelago," as many linkages between actors and sub-systems (e.g. regional versus national) were weak. Kuo (2001) identified three types of obstacles that restricted the effect of R&D collaboration in China: sectionalism led to most organizations focusing exclusively on the function and mission assigned by the central government; lack of integrated management systems and a healthy legislation environment; lack of suitable communication channels and intermediaries.

3 S&T management at the macro level is uncoordinated, with an S&T resource allocation pattern and evaluation system falling short of accommodating the needs for the new S&T development and government mandate shift (MLP). This led to a situation where research institutes and universities did not understand the technical needs of industry, while industry was not aware of what research institutes and universities could offer it (Kuo 2001).

4 Mechanisms for rewarding outstanding personnel and encouraging innovation and pioneering activities are not yet consummate (MLP). Chang and Shih (2004) argue that China's S&T policies are centrally developed. As a result, performers of S&T activities are not fully responsible for their failure, nor do they fully benefit from their success.

5 Change in motivation of foreign investment in R&D (OECD 2008). China is a major host of FDI, and following the strategy of "exchange of market access for technology," FDI with advanced technology was strongly encouraged. This not only directly brought in technologies, but also helped local firms to improve their capabilities via knowledge spillovers (Wei and Liu 2006). However, the motivation of foreign investment in R&D has gradually shifted from market access, adaptation of products for the Chinese market, or support of export-oriented manufacturing operations to human resource seeking (OECD 2008). This change in motivation of foreign investment in R&D may result in reduced knowledge spillovers.

6 Insufficient framework conditions for innovation (OECD 2008). Some framework conditions (such as corporate governance, R&D funding, technology-based entrepreneurship, and enforcement of intellectual property rights) for innovation are not very conducive to market-led innovation (OECD 2008). Take the enforcement of intellectual property rights (IPRs) as an example. As discussed in Huang et al. (2004), since the adoption of economic reforms and opening to the outside world, China has formulated a number of laws to protect IPRs, including the US–China Agreement on Intellectual Property Protection (1979), Trademark Law (1982, revised in 1993), Patent Law (1984, revised in 1992), Copyright Law (1990) and Regulation on Computer Software Protection (1991). China joined the World Intellectual Property Organization (WIPO) in 1980, the Paris Convention for the Protection of Industrial Property in 1984, the Washington Treaty on Intellectual Property in Respect of Integrated Circuits in 1989, the Madrid Agreement Concerning the International Registration of Marks in 1989, the Berne Convention for the Protection of Literary and Artistic Works in 1992, the Convention for the Protection of Producers of Phonograms Against Unauthorized Duplication of Their Phonograms in 1993, and the Patent Cooperation Treaty in 1993. China also set up special intellectual property courts in many big cities. This legal regime for IPR protection is relatively comprehensive.

7 However, McGregor (2010) indicates that China's active police or administrative enforcement of IP protection "all too often appears to be deliberately weak" (24) in order to help its indigenous innovation drive. Like the ongoing debate in the economics literature on whether tighter IPR protection will separate developing countries from advanced technologies invented by developed countries (e.g. Helpman 1993), within China there are very different opinions, and one view is that IPR is a concept invented by developed countries to block the transfer of advanced technologies and exploit developing countries (Huang et al. 2004). Some scholars argue for loose IRP to promote Chinese indigenous innovation and catch up as in the case of Japan and South Korea before the 1990s (Sun and Peng 2010). Nevertheless, China's academic, governmental, and industrial sectors are aware that weak IRP could also destroy local Chinese firms' incentives for indigenous innovation. As argued by Chen (Chen, H. 2006), the lack of intellectual property protection, combined with piracy and shoddy counterfeits made it difficult to benefit from any successful technological innovation and significantly dampened an enterprise's enthusiasm for innovation. As emphasized by the Chinese government in its MLP, "protecting intellectual property rights and safeguarding the interests of IPR owners is not only necessary for perfecting the nation's market economy system and promoting indigenous innovation, but also important for establishing the nation's credibility and image in international cooperation." The Chinese government wants to increase public awareness of the importance of IPR, uplifting the nation's IPR management.

Various policy solutions have been proposed to deal with the above problems. The Chinese government has formulated nine specific policy measures in its MLP (1) to implement favourable financial and taxation policies to encourage technological innovation at the firm level; (2) to strengthen assimilation and absorption of imported technologies and re-innovation; (3) to implement government procurement favoring indigenous innovation; (4) to protest intellectual property rights and develop national technology standards; (5) to provide financial support for innovation and pioneering; (6) to accelerate the industrialization of high technologies and the diffusion of advanced appropriate technologies; (7) to perfect the mechanism for combining defense and civilian sectors, and make defense part of the civilian sector; (8) to expand international and regional S&T cooperation and exchange; (9) to improve scientific and cultural literacy of the entire nation and build a social environment conducive to S&T innovation.

However, like the policy of "strengthening assimilation and absorption of imported technologies and re-innovation" being sometimes interpreted as a blueprint for technology theft, policy measure (3) in the above paragraph is criticized by multinational companies as protectionism (McGregor 2010: 20). Following identifying issues and problems with China's S&T drive, OECD (2008) has made a number of specific recommendations for improving framework conditions for innovation; and adjusting, differentiating, and enhancing dedicated policies to promote science, technology, and innovation activities. Given that this OECD review was requested by the Chinese authorities, and carried out as a joint project between the OECD and the Ministry of Science and Technology of China, these recommendations will be taken seriously by the Chinese authorities.

China's path towards becoming a major world player in science and technology

When reviewing its S&T efforts over the past 50 years, the Chinese government listed the following as its major achievements: nuclear weaponry and satellite technology, manned space flights, hybrid rice, theory of oil formation from continental moist depression and associated application, and high performance computers (2006 MLP). When celebrating the 60th birthday of the People's Republic in 2009, the Chinese government summarized its S&T achievements in the following four areas: aerospace (such as space flights and satellite technology), biotechnology (such as synthetic bovine insulin being synthesized for the first time, and hybrid rice), geographic expedition (such as Antarctic expeditions) and resource physics (such as nuclear weaponry, the discovery of anti-Sigma negative hyperons, the electron-positron collider, and thermonuclear reactor—China's artificial sun; http://society.people.com.cn/GB/8217/151316/).

However, the Chinese government clearly realizes that China's overall S&T level still lags significantly behind that of developed nations. The gap includes a low rate of self-sufficiency in key technology supply, a limited number of invention patents, the relatively low quality of scientific research, a shortage of top S&T talents, insufficient investments in S&T and various flaws in the existing S&T system (2006 MLP). China's weak innovative capacity has been caused by various factors, but Chen (Chen, Q. 2006) emphasizes the following: some Chinese large state-owned enterprises lack market incentives for independent innovation due to government protection and the technology gap with foreign enterprises being so large that domestic enterprises belittle themselves, over-rely on technology adoption, and then gradually lose R&D capabilities. Other scholars feel that China's intellectual property protection system is not conducive to business innovation concern (e.g. Kang and Zhang 2009). Comparing internationally, Ernst (2011) suggests that China is still far behind the United States as well as the European Union and Japan in terms of R&D as a percentage of GDP, the number of scientists and engineers/million people and ownership of the worldwide stock of intellectual property.

China aims to address these gaps in order to become a major world player in S&T. As mentioned in MLP, by 2020, China needs to noticeably enhance indigenous innovation capability and S&T levels; noticeably improve comprehensive strength in basic research and frontier technology development; and attain a series of high world impact S&T achievements and join the ranks of innovative countries, thus paving the way to becoming a world S&T power by the mid twenty-first century.

Specifically, China would like to realize the following objectives in some major scientific and technological areas by 2020: 1) mastering core technologies in equipment manufacturing and information industry; 2) making the nation a world leader in overall agricultural S&T capability; 3) achieving technological breakthroughs in energy development, energy conservation, and clean energy, as well as advocating optimized energy structures; 4) establishing technological development models featured with cyclic economy in major sectors and municipalities, and providing S&T support for building a resource saving and environment friendly society; 5) noticeably enhancing the level of major disease prevention and control, curbing the spread of major diseases, striving for breakthroughs in new drugs and key medical equipment; 6) in defense science and technology, meeting the needs in developing modern arms and associated information technology; 7) establishing a world-caliber contingent of scientists and research teams, attaining high-impact innovative achievements in the mainstream of science development, achieving world advanced technological levels in frontier areas such as information, biology, materials, and space; and 8) establishing a number of world-class research institutes and universities, and world-competitive industrial R&D centers.

Based on the MLP, China's total R&D expenditure is expected to rise to 2.5 per cent or above of its GDP with the rate of S&T contribution to the economy reaching 60 per cent or above, and dependence on imported technology reduced to 30 per cent or below by 2020. Furthermore, the annual invention patents granted to Chinese nationals and international citations of scientific papers are expected to be ranked among the top five countries globally by 2020.

China's objectives sound ambitious, but are sometimes criticized. McGregor (2010) regards the MLP as "a rambling plan of breathless ambition," as it "weaves back and forth in a dizzying fashion that packages programs and goals in multiple ways in various sections." For instance, the MLP identifies 11 priority areas (energy, water and mineral resources, the environment, agriculture, manufacturing industry, transport sector, information industry and modern service industry, population and health, urbanization and city development, public security, and national defense) for economic and social development, from which 68 priority topics of clearly defined missions and possible technical breakthrough in the near term have been selected. The Plan then outlines a total of 16 special major projects. It also selects 27 frontiers in eight technological fields (biotechnology, information technology, advanced materials technology, advanced manufacturing technology, advanced energy technology, marine technology, lasers technology, aerospace technology), and 18 basic scientific issues as priorities. To achieve the above objectives, China is determined to deepen S&T system reform by improving relevant policies and measures, increasing S&T investment, strengthening the build-up of S&T talent, and promoting the creation of a truly national innovation system. However, as criticized by McGregor (2010), there is still a lack of clarity in how to implement the plan.

Furthermore, although the MLP projects China to be a world S&T power by the mid twenty-first century, there is no further description of this objective, and the above policy measures seem to be designed specifically for mid-term objectives. The MLP is actually an MP.

The key strategy defined by the Chinese government for China's path towards becoming a major world S&T player is indigenous innovation. Stevenson-Yang and DeWoskin (2005: 10) are very critical of this strategy:

> In its efforts to create "Chinese IP," the government actually obstructs the path to market inventions that are blooming in laboratories and start-up companies all over the country. That's because these conflict with the commercial interests of politically supported state companies that innovate far less than private, entrepreneurial ones.

However, the Battelle Memorial Institute (2009) is very positive about China's innovation policy: "From an R&D standpoint, it's very difficult to find fault or weaknesses in any of the policies China is pursuing." In its latest global R&D funding forecast, the Battlelle Memorial Institute (2012) suggests that "China established a consistent pattern of double-digit R&D funding increases in the 1990s and over the past 20 years has risen from R&D obscurity to challenging the U.S. (and likely succeeding) for global R&D leadership."

Nevertheless, R&D input is just one important factor for success. Another important factor is efficient management of R&D resources (Sigurdson 2004). As identified above, there are management problems within China's innovation system. Therefore, China's path towards becoming a major world S&T player is not easy, although its government is determined to move along this path.

References

Andreosso-O'Callaghan, B., 1999: Technology transfer: a mode of collaboration between the European Union and China. *Europe–Asia Studies*, 51(1), pp. 123–142.

AsianScientist, 2013: Available online at: www.asianscientist.com/2013/02/topnews/chinese-scientific-expenditure-1-trillion-2012/ (accessed September 23, 2013).

Battelle, 2009: 2010 Global R&D funding forecast. *R&D Magazine*, December 2009. Available online at: http://news.thomasnet.com/imt/2009/03/31/global-research-and-development-outlook-forecast-2009-investment-spending-trends (accessed September 10, 2013).

Battelle, 2012: 2013 Global R&D funding forecast. *R&D Magazine*, December 2012. Available online at: http://battelle.org/docs/default-document-library/2012_global_forecast.pdf (accessed September 10, 2013).

Blau, J., 2013: Close—but challenging—Sino-European research collaboration. *Research Technology Management*, January–February, pp. 4–6.

Chang, P. and Shih, H., 2004: The innovation systems of Taiwan and China: a comparative analysis. *Technovation* 24, pp. 529–539.

Chen, H., 2006: Exploring the path for enhancing indigenous innovation capability. *Economics Dynamics* 7, pp. 45–47.

Chen, L. (Ed.), 2002: *Report on China's National Strategy Issues*. China's Social Sciences Publisher.

Chen, Q., 2006: Policy considerations for promoting indigenous innovations of enterprises. *Management World* 7, pp. 1–3 and 52.

Economic Group of Research Unit, Secretariat of the CPC Central Committee, 1985: Collection of open-door policy literature, July 1979 to April 1985. Central Party School Press.

Ernst, D., 2011: China's innovation policy is a wake-up call for America. *AsiaPacific Issues* 100, East–West Center, Hawai'i, pp. 1–12. Available online at: www.eastwestcenter.org/publications/chinas-innovation-policy-wake-call-america (accessed August 20, 2013).

European Commission, 2000: Innovation Policy in a Knowledge-Based Economy, Luxembourg. Available online at: http://ftp.cordis.lu/pub/innovationpolicy/studies/studies knowledge based economy.pdf (accessed April 10, 2009).

Freeman, C., 1987: *Technology and Economic Performance: Lessons from Japan*. London: Pinter.

Freeman, C., 1995: The national system of innovation in historical perspective. *Cambridge Journal of Economics* 19, pp. 5–24.

Helpman, E., 1993: Innovation, imitation, and intellectual property rights. *Econometrica* 61(6), pp. 1247–1280.

Hu, J., 2012: Firmly march on the path of socialism with Chinese characteristics and strive to complete the building of a moderately prosperous society in all respects. Keynote Speech at the 18th National Congress of the Communist Party of China, Beijing, November 2012.

Huang, C., Amorim, C., Spinoglio, M., Gouveia, B. and Medina, A., 2004: Organization, programme and structure: an analysis of the Chinese innovation policy framework. *R&D Management* 34(4), pp. 367–387.

Huang, Y., 2008: Technological advances under open conditions – from technology adoption to indigenous innovation. *World Economy Research* 6, pp. 14–18.

Kang, Z.Y. and Zhang, J., 2009: Institutional deficit, behaviour twist and the lack of independent innovation motivation. *Modern Economic Research* 3, pp. 78–82.

Kuo, X., 2001: *Collaboration for Technology Innovation: A theoretical and empirical analysis of collaboration between universities and enterprises* (in Chinese). Beijing: Economic Management Publishers.

Law Institute, Chinese Academy of Social Sciences, 1986: *Selected Economic Laws of the People's Republic of China in 1984*, Volume 1. Beijing: China Financial and Economic Publishing House.

Li, H.P., 2006: Review of the Republic's Seven Science and Technology Plans, *Chuangxin Keji (Innovation Science and Technology)* 3, pp. 20–21.

Li, L.Y. and Li, Y., 2008: Evolution of state science and technology system and its management. *Chinese Science and Technology Forum* 8, pp. 6–11.

Lieberthal, K. and Oksenberg, M., 1988: *Policy Making in China: Leaders, structures and processes*. Princeton, NJ: Princeton University Press.

Liu, F.C., Simon, D.F., Sun, Y.T. and Cao, C., 2011: China's innovation policies: evolution, institutional structure, and trajectory. *Research Policy* 40(7), pp. 917–932.

Lundvall, B-Å. (Ed.), 1992: *National Innovation Systems: Towards a theory of innovation and interactive learning*. London: Pinter.

McGregor, J., 2010: *China's Drive for "Indigenous Innovation": A Web of Industrial Policies*. Report Commissioned by US Chamber of Commerce 2010, 4. Available online at: www.uschamber.com/sites/default/files/reports/100728chinareport_0.pdf (accessed August 5, 20113).

Mao, Z.D., 1956: On Ten Major Relations, formally published in: *People's Daily*, December 26, 1976.

Meng, H., 2011: Effects of indigenous innovation policy on the S&T outputs in China: evidence from the higher education system. *Technology and Investment* 2, pp. 163–170.

Metcalfe, S., 1995: The economic foundations of technology policy: equilibrium and evolutionary perspectives. In: Stoneman, P. (Ed.): *Handbook of the Economics of Innovation and Technological Change*. Oxford (UK) and Cambridge (US): Blackwell Publishers, pp. 409–512.

Nelson, R. (Ed.), 1993: *National Innovation Systems: A comparative analysis*. Oxford: Oxford University Press.

OECD, 1997: *National Innovation Systems*. Paris: OECD.

OECD, 2008: *OECD Reviews of Innovation Policy: China*. Paris: OECD.

Patel, P. and Pavitt, K., 1994: The nature and economic importance of national innovation systems, *STI Review*, No. 14. Paris: OECD, pp. 1–22.

Peng, J., Sun, W. and Zhong, W., 2008: The evolution of China's technical innovation policy and empirical study of its performance (1978–2006), *Keyan Guanli Zazhi (Scientific Management Journal)* 29(4), pp. 134–150.

People's Web, 2009: New China's Science and Technology Achievements. Available online at: http://scitech.people.com.cn/GB/25509/56813/167036/index.html (accessed January 14, 2013).

Sigurdson, J., 2004: Technological superpower China?, *R&D Management* 34, pp. 345–347.

Stevenson-Yang, A. and DeWoskin, K., 2005: China Destroys the IP Paradigm. *Far East Economic Review*, March, pp. 9–18.

Sun, B. and Peng, J., 2010: Research on the co-evolution of China's intellectual property right protection and innovation policies. *Management World* 1, pp. 33–35.

UNCTAD and UNIDO, 2011: Economic Development in Africa Report 2011: Fostering Industrial Development in Africa in the New Global Environment. United Nations. Available online at: http://unctad.org/en/docs/aldcafrica2011_en.pdf (accessed August 27, 2012).

Wei, Y. and Liu, X., 2006: Productivity spillovers from R&D, exports and FDI in China's manufacturing sector. *Journal of International Business Studies* 37(4), pp. 544–557.

Xia, L. and Zhao, L., 2012: Historical evolution of the "Exchange of market access for technology" policy. *Dangdan Zhongguoshi Yanjiu (Contemporary Chinese History Research)* 2, pp. 27–36.

Zhang, J., 2009: A study of the 156 projects of the modern industrial construction in 1950s. *Journal Of Engineering Studies* 1(3), pp. 213–222.

Zhang, F. and He, C., 1999: *National Innovation System: The engine of second modernization*. Beijing: Higher Education Publisher.

Zeng, F. and Li, J., 2000: Research on the institutional arrangement for "Exchange of market access for technology." *Guanli Shijie (Management World)* 5, pp. 191–203.

27

SCIENTISTS' MOTIVATION TO INNOVATE, CATCH UP AND COLLABORATE

A trans-disciplinary perspective

Saradindu Bhaduri[1]

Introduction

Science, technology and innovation have come to occupy the centre-stage of debates on economic policy making in a major way. The last few decades have observed many drastic policy changes, both by national governments and at the international level, to promote scientific research and technology development. The implementation of trade related intellectual property rights (TRIPS), providing the ambit of patent to public funded university research, and promoting scientific collaboration between countries beyond Europe and North American countries are a few of them. Among the countries in the global South, India has declared the decade 2010–20 as the 'decade of innovation'. It has raised its gross expenditure on research and development, in absolute terms, fourfold to around 8698 million euros in the last ten years, and has become a partner in EU's FP7 programme on scientific collaboration (Krishna 2013). The Department of Science and Technology, the apex decision-making body in science and technology in India has signed agreements for scientific collaborations with 40 countries in the last few years (Bhattacharya 2014). These policies have also presented complex and nuanced questions for development scholars and policy makers for the future of public funded research, technological catch-up and learning.

Despite this policy enthusiasm, we have not seen much in the form of policy research to understand what motivates individual scientists in their pursuits of scientific research and technology development. One may note that studies on motivation of scientists are not only inadequate in number; there is also a lack of coherence among them. The indicators of motivation these studies use are often devoid of much theoretical underpinning. At times, these indicators are meaningful only within the boundaries of a specific discipline. In doing so, these studies do not connect themselves well with the theoretical research on motivation. A systematic research on motivation behind technology development and innovation is important for policy making in this arena. Such a task is, however, not easy given the complexity involved with the nature of technology development and innovation, and the diverse organisational structures that harbour it. State policies, social and organisational norms have all come to influence the work of scientists. In so far as individual scientists work within diverse organisational frameworks, and policy mandates, an analysis of individual motivation would have to be discussed within the broad contours of these mandates, and the constraints and opportunities they provide to individuals.

This chapter intends to provide a trans-disciplinary perspective on individual motivation for new scientific findings and new technologies. For this, one needs to reconcile the various strands of studies on motivation of scientists and technologists with the theoretical formulations of the motivation theories. The second section presents an overview of the effectance motivation theories that enable us to identify the key indicators of motivations. These indicators are then used to analyse individual motivations to carry out basic scientific research and technological innovations in developed industrialised countries (third section), learning and technological catch-up in a developing country context (fourth section), and the motivation of individual scientists for international collaborations and science and technology (fifth section). Bringing these three types of scientific pursuits gives us the scope to assimilate the broadest possible range of factors associated with individual motivations to conduct scientific research that can aid future research and policy discussions. The sixth section rounds up the discussion.

Motivation: a theoretical perspective and national operational indicators

An overview of (effectance) motivation theories

Motivation is 'the psychological process' that causes the arousal, direction and persistence of behavior by stimulating and inhibiting the desire to engage with the behavior. A major branch of motivation research, the effectance motivation theories, revolves around identifying *intrinsic* and *extrinsic* motivating factors for individuals.

The Cognitive Evaluation Theory (CET) argues that the root of intrinsic motivation lies in the satisfaction of the basic psychological feeling of competence (Deci and Ryan 1985). CET further specifies that the feeling of *competence* will not enhance intrinsic motivation unless they are accompanied by a sense of *autonomy*. In particular, appeal for novelty, challenge, or aesthetic value are some of the person-specific criteria, considered crucial for intrinsic motivation to function in the presence of a favourable environment. The refinement to this theoretical framework came in the form of Self Determination Theory (SDT) (Ryan and Deci 2000). Within SDT one is concerned about the goals of the behavior and what energizes this behavior. The SDT has three fundamental assumptions. First, human beings have the tendency to integrate the aspects of their own psyche with other individuals and groups in their social world. Second, social-contextual (which is dynamic in nature) factors may facilitate and enable the integration tendency, or they may undermine this fundamental process of human nature. Third, human beings have three basic psychological needs, the need for *competence*, *autonomy* and *relatedness*. SDT also explains two separate loci of causality – internal and external. In case of 'internal locus of causality', people perceive themselves as the origin of the behaviour they demonstrate. On the other hand, the locus of control is external if people engage in behaviour to achieve rewards or because of external constraints, making the behaviour extrinsically motivated (Gagne and Deci 2005). In other words, whenever behaviour is undertaken to achieve a separable outcome it is assumed to be extrinsically motivated behaviour.[2] While, social/environmental pressures would bind the majority of extrinsically motivated behavior, some can be autonomous (to the environment) or self-determined.

The Organismic Integration Theory (OIT) (Ryan and Deci 2000) presents the various forms of motivation in a continuum, ranging from the least autonomous kind of extrinsic motivation to intrinsic motivation. For the least autonomous extrinsic motivation, namely, 'external regulation', individual behaviour is completely externally regulated and the locus of control is externally guided either by an external demand or externally imposed reward. A more autonomous type of extrinsic motivation is called 'introjected regulation'. Although more autonomous than the previous type, introjected regulation portrays the presence of outside *pressure*. The third type of extrinsic motivation, even more autonomous or self-determined, is 'regulation through identification'. Here a behaviour is undertaken after understanding/accepting the worth of the behaviour completely.

The most autonomous form of extrinsic motivation is 'integrated regulation'. Integration occurs when identified regulations have been fully assimilated to the self. This occurs through the evaluation of a regulation and bringing it in congruence with one's values and needs. Integrated regulation and intrinsic motivation, both being autonomous and non-conflicting, may appear to be identical at times. However, the former is still extrinsic because a behaviour motivated by integrated regulation is done for its presumed instrumental value (Ryan and Deci 2000). Both these motivations often draw a parallel to the concept of duty. Although Deci and Ryan (2004) treat fulfilment of obligation or duty as an externally motivated act (38), Bhaduri and Kumar (2011) cite political economic thoughts in the Indian philosophical tradition that argue that certain kinds of duty towards one's self and society are universally obligatory (integrity, trust, non-neglect of duty etc.). Such duties fulfil the innate psychological needs of a person to forge a relationship with the society (Tagore 1996). In so far as 'relatedness' is a key component of intrinsic motivation, a desire to fulfil these duties may promote one's intrinsic motivation. As opposed to these duties, there are obligations specific to particular conditions of life (e.g. slavery, caste-ism) that reflect the imposition of norms either by some powerful social groups or the state. Performance of duties under these norms would be considered extrinsically motivated acts, even though internalised by oneself. Finally, the intrinsic motivation is the archetype of self-determined activity, and placed in another extreme of the continuum.

It is perhaps in order now to give a brief overview of studies that have attempted to analyse the implications of external environmental interventions on intrinsic motivations of individuals. This discussion is important for two reasons. First it helps us visualise a policy space conducive for intrinsic motivations, and second, it leads us to identify a set of measurable indicators of intrinsic motivations.

One can argue that intrinsic motivations revolve around four key parameters, namely, 'joy of work', 'autonomy', 'duty/relatedness' and 'competence'. Using these parameters, the empirical research in psychology and education has highlighted that extrinsic rewards could undermine intrinsic motivation (Deci 1971; Deci and Cascio 1972).[3] Choice and the opportunity for self-direction, on the other hand, appear to enhance intrinsic motivation by inducing a sense of autonomy (Zuckerman *et al.* 1978).[4] In management studies, Herzberg (1966) argues that the task-environment that promotes *responsibility, challenge, achievement (in the sense of fulfilment), variety and advancement opportunity* may also strengthen intrinsic motivations (Dietz and Bozeman 2005; Lee *et al.* 2010; Gemme and Gingras 2011). Hackman and Oldham (1976) identify parameters that augment intrinsic motivation such as variety, identity, significance, autonomy, and feedback related to tasks. If effectance motivation is not satisfied, one is urged to gain new competencies (Morgan *et al.* 1993).

Similar studies on creativity and innovations are largely conceptual in nature. Kreps (1997) accepts that innovative activities (tasks), which external regulations can guide only in an imperfect manner, are inherently uncertain leaving much to intrinsic motivation. Similarly,

Osterloh and Frey (2000) suggest that *enjoyment* based intrinsic motivation is vital for facilitating creative behaviour such as knowledge generation and sharing, especially when such knowledge is not codified or explicit. 'Trust', 'enjoyment' and 'identification' with an employer's strategic goals, and 'fulfilment of norms for their own sake' here reduce the problems of free riding, and, thereby, the costs of transactions within an organisation.[5] Here, an extrinsically motivated person tends to produce, mainly, stereotyped repetition of a performance (Amabile 1996, 1998; Schwartz 1990). Jong (2006) discusses the role of intrinsic motivation in 'decision to innovate', and argues that 'the more an idea is accompanied by a task and/or outcome that an individual finds intrinsically motivating; the more he or she is likely to decide to implement the idea.'

Bhaduri and Kumar (2011) took the discussion one step forward by constructing a set of measurable indicators for the four key components of intrinsic motivations for creativity and innovative behaviour. The following table (Table 27.1) summarises these indicators. We use these indicators for our discussions in this chapter.

Table 27.1 Measurable indicators of intrinsic motivations for creativity and innovative behaviour

Component of intrinsic motivation	*Measurable indicators*
Joy of work	Research idea driven by 'curiosity'. Engages in open discussion with others without fearing leakage of knowledge. Free and open dissemination of technological output.
Autonomy	Self generated research idea/proposal. Less reliance on outside, time-bound, funding for research.
Duty/Relatedness	Intention to solve a problem faced by community/society without any considerations of private gains. Undertaking open discussion with others without fearing leakage of knowledge. Voluntary disclosure of outcome of research.
Competence/Confidence	Engages in open discussion with others without fearing leakage of knowledge. Willing to absorb uncertainty of R&D, for instance, by investing own funds in research. Willingness to offer solutions to problems faced by society/community without any identifiable private gains.

Source: compiled from Bhaduri and Kumar (2011).

Motivation for scientific research and frontier innovation

This section examines individual motivation to inventive activities in diverse organisational set ups. The literature we use mostly belongs to scientific and technological activities in an industrialised country context where much of the frontier research is undertaken. David Noble (1976) observed that the process of industrialisation in the United States of America was accompanied by a process of corporatisation of innovative activities, where individual scientists compromised their autonomy to the business interests of firms. Thus, the initial entry of scientists to research driven firms did not appear to have promoted intrinsic motivations. These scientists, however, were not averse to reaping the private benefits of their research through patents and commercial application of their research outputs. In fact, the desire for commercial application of every research is what, for Alexis de Tocqueville, separated the scientists of the USA from their European counterparts even during the early years of America's history (Tocqueville 2003). For Tocqueville the reasons lay in the absence of aristocracy in funding scientific research in the US, which necessitated successful commercial application of one's research for sustained efforts towards innovation.[6]

The other, perhaps more dominant, key motivation for scientists in academic institutions has been the sense of autonomy and freedom of work. Ben-David (1971) argues how the quest for freedom and autonomy led to some major transformations in the institutional structures of academic institutions in countries such as England, France and Germany during the last two centuries. Even recent research shows that freedom of work makes people interested in taking up academic jobs with poorer pay (Roach and Sauermann 2010; Gemme and Gingras 2011). Interestingly, even in corporate jobs, often there exists a trade-off between the wages of scientists and their autonomy; wages were lower in cases where the scientists were allowed to publish their work (Stern 1999). It is often suggested about corporate scientists that these individuals (mostly fresh PhDs) often did not fit easily into teaching positions, were averse to taking risks of entrepreneurship, but, at the same time, had a strong inventive potential (Wise 1980), the curiosity to work 'elsewhere' and do the 'real work' (Hakala 2009).

This aspect of doing the 'real work', 'elsewhere' deserves some attention. Science during its early days quite often received credibility and recognition from its application potentials, which kept scientists motivated to do applied research. With the emergence of organised science in university systems in Germany, there emerged a separation between basic research and applied technological research where university scientists chose to remain occupied with abstract theoretical research and corporations gradually emerged to drive the frontiers of applied research. To some extent, a rise in public funding for basic research, post-World War II, may have encouraged such separation, earning universities the title of 'ivory tower', which was believed to provide basic research background to development of technologies in public funded research laboratories or in industrial units. In such a (linear) framework, theoretical research in universities was argued to be guided by the so called Mertonian norms, while private appropriation of intellectual property became the norm for applied research, especially in corporations.[7]

This separation, however, became untenable with the emergence of disciplines such as bacteriology and engineering, where the clear distinction between 'science' and 'technology' became difficult. This *tension* only became acute with the emergence of modern biotechnology, information technology and their growing popularity in biomedical research. Towards the latter half of the twentieth century, private funding of research also became quite common in the universities of the USA and some European countries. This presented before the scientists a dilemma between the norms of open science in universities and the norms of private appropriation preferred by corporations. Gradually, taking patents for research done at the university departments, especially in biomedical research and research funded by corporations, started becoming the vogue of the day (Govind 2006; Bhaduri 2008). Finally, a policy change in the United States in the form of the Bayh Dole Act began a new era in motivation for research in academics. This law formally allowed university scientists to take patents for their inventions.

How do these changes spell for individual motivations of freedom of work and relatedness discussed above? Academic literature is divided on the implications of the Bayh Dole Act such as policies giving patent protection to university research. While many claim that this act facilitated technology transfer from academia to industry some researchers point out that individual scientists have become more secretive about their research and they seem to disclose less in informal discussions as well as in formal conferences (Bhaduri 2008; Ray and Saha 2011). If relatedness and duty to society are identified as intrinsic motivations then these eventualities do point towards a movement away from it. Lam in this context makes an interesting argument: for him, the Mertonian norms should be ideally seen as extrinsic motivation, albeit of the more autonomous type, which in a sense compelled scientists to abide by it (Lam 2011). In such a scenario, scientists who decided to deviate from this norm (to take up, say, entrepreneurship) were, arguably, guided by intrinsic motivations (e.g. autonomy).

The implementation of the Bayh Dole Act legitimised the entrepreneurial aspirations of scientists. Motivation theories predict that an intrinsically motivated person might leave an organisation if he/she finds its rules restricting his/her motivation. Accordingly, one would have expected a huge 'out migration' of professors and scientists to entrepreneurial firms, if the locus of the Mertonian norms were indeed external. Although some indications of such movements exist, post Bayh Dole, they are far from being the dominant trend.[8] In fact, studies acknowledge that for a researcher to take up an entrepreneurial role or even participate in collaboration activities requires the individual to modify their role identity[9] and such modification alters the set of activities that normally constitute a scientist's workload. One can then argue with some conviction that the norms of disinterested peer evaluation were far from being extrinsic. Ideally, more research should be undertaken to study these deeper aspects of scientists' motivation.[10]

Finally, there is not much work on how a patent helps individual scientists/innovators maintain their autonomy in this era of large corporates. Bessen and Meurer (2008) find that small firms and individual innovators realise substantially less value out of patents, compared to big firms, and rely on other means to appropriate innovations. Our 'quasi-random' observation of India's grassroots innovators reveals that people tend to shift their focus away from 'further innovations' to 'commercialisation of existing innovations' after receiving patents or awards. Note that Noble (1976) insisted that individual scientists often had to forgo their (patent) rights to the financial might of corporations. Thus, the role of patents in augmenting the autonomy of individual innovators needs to be scrutinised further before celebrating policies such as the Bayh Dole Act as a hall mark to promote innovative activities by scientists in academics.

Some seem to prefer academics because of its associated job security (Roach and Sauermann 2010); while security in jobs (as opposed to 'hire and fire') can motivate one to undertake fundamental research whose outcomes are uncertain, denoting intrinsic motivation, it is also subjected to adverse selection where incompetent people scrape through the academic selection processes, and indulge in non-performance. This issue, therefore, requires further research to clearly understand the implications of job security for scientific research.

Motivation to (technological) catch-up

The achievement of self-reliance is a major policy motivation for technological catch-up activities in many countries. How these policies, however, relate to the motivations of individual scientists in these situations has been inadequately researched. Here, one may use the motivation theories to understand some of the nuances of individual motivations in this context, largely based on prior research on Indian industries and public sector research institutes.[11]

One major policy attempt in this direction was patent policies. Immediately after independence, the Indian parliament began to discuss the suitability of the Indian Patent Act 1911 for India's industrialisation process. Along with the protection of 'public interest', the protection of national interest also featured intensely in the debate surrounding patent policies of that time (NWGOPL 1988). At least two committees successively expressed concerns over dominance of 'foreign capital' that patent policies ensured. These committees also observed that patent policies in the industrialised countries always served their national interest, which independent India was not able to exploit because of its colonial past. Eventually, India amended its patent policies in the year 1970 for a select group of industries, including drugs and pharmaceuticals, which allowed only process patents. It is well documented that this policy gave a boost to India's generic drug industry. However, one significant outcome of this policy, which unfortunately has not been studied extensively, is the growth of private sector enterprises in the pharmaceutical industry. The majority of these entrepreneurs were spin-offs of two large public sector enterprises, Hindustan Antibiotic Limited and Indian Drugs and Pharmaceutical Limited. These chemists had the confidence in their research capability, found opportunity in the new environment and, presumably, decided to establish their own firms in want of more autonomy. Our personal conversations with many of these entrepreneurs/scientists reveal that identification with the macro policy proposal for 'technological self-reliance' shaped their activities in a major way.

The motivational implications of learning and self-reliance can be better understood if one takes into account the social and technological context of a developing country. In the context of India, this can be understood by looking at the options Indian entrepreneurs have exercised at various points in time. In the pre-independent era, the majority of entrepreneurs relied on imported foreign capital over uncertain activities of indigenous technology generation through learning. Those who opted for the latter path, may, therefore, be argued to have had intrinsic motivations. Some recent evidence has emerged to show that in the province of Bengal,[12] entrepreneurs had filed around 900 patents in areas of Paper, Iron Foundries, Electrical Equipment during the last two decades of the colonial rule (Bhattacharyya 2007), bearing testimony to active participation in the process of technological self-reliance by a sizeable portion of this class. Patents here, in our view, reflect the desire to take 'control' of the surrounding environment, where the foreign capital aided process of industrialisation was the dominant feature, more than seeking private gains. This debate continued in the post-independent era (McCrory 1956; Berna 1960; Gorter 1996). Scholars argue that the majority continued to be driven by 'quick profit opportunity', and 'personalized liquidity preference', presumably demonstrating a lack of 'confidence' in their innovative abilities and absence of the desire for 'autonomy'. A government of India funded research report (Ray 2003) found scientists in public sector institutions in India alleging that private Indian firms do not purchase technologies from them because of the former's preference for 'ready-made' technologies from abroad.

Unfortunately, such reluctance to undertake risky behaviour continues in the era of liberalisation as well. Although glimpses of technological innovations in the Indian corporate sector are available, the dominant behaviour seems to continue to be of a 'rent seeking' nature. Patra (2013) compares the mode of foreign direct investment (FDI) in the information and technology sector in India and China. While in China most of the FDI entered through 'joint venture', in India, it took the form of 'buying out' of domestic firms (Sreedhar *et al.* 2011). According to industry experts, the key reasons for such 'buying outs' are the risk averse attitude of domestic entrepreneurs when it comes to 'heavy investments in brand building', and exploring distant and 'unknown markets'.[13] Since entrepreneurial visions importantly shape the overall policy environment of firms (Witt 2000), primary data based study may be undertaken to analyse how differences in entrepreneurial visions shape intrinsic motivations of scientists within the firms.

Recently, there have been attempts to bring the innovative activities outside the formal sector to academic and policy discussions (Sheikh 2014). Given that around 80 per cent of India's workforce is from the informal sector, it is indeed a welcome step. These studies (Bhaduri and Kumar 2011; Kumar 2012; Kumar and Bhaduri 2014) argue that the key motivations behind India's grassroot innovations are non-extrinsic. Even at the stage of implementation of innovation, when intrinsic motivation seems to be lowest, quite a substantial number of innovators put their innovations in 'the commons', or distribute the innovative outputs without concerns for private gains. Based on these findings, scholars have cautioned against over enthusiasm of policy makers to incentivise large-scale commercialisation or encourage private appropriations of these innovations. They suspect that such incentives, in line with the predictions of motivation theorists, may reduce intrinsic motivations behind such activities, eventually drying up such innovations. In so far as these innovations often respond to the gaps created by existing markets of technology, drying up of such innovations may not spell well for the livelihood of the rural and semi urban communities in India.

Policy makers and activists of grassroot innovations in India are trying to link these innovations with public sector research laboratories to help overcome technical shortcomings of these innovations. Ironically, not many of these collaborations have borne fruit, partly because of the failure of the scientists of these institutes to appreciate the relevance of 'crude' technical specifications of these innovations. As a result, many grassroot innovators find themselves compromising their 'autonomy' and 'freedom to work' in order to sustain these collaborations, forcing them to move apart. Sometimes, however, scientists in these institutes have undertaken research efforts to solve local level problems on their own.

Government policies have also been detrimental to such activities in the public research laboratories. In the last couple of decades, a cut in public funding has forced public sector research institutes to collaborate, rather, with industrial units (often the bigger ones), both domestic and international. Scientists who take advantage of this new environment to engage with the industry in projects determined by the industry, are, arguably, driven by extrinsic motivations. Particularly so, when cost competitiveness (on the part of the funders) guides such forms of collaboration. During our visits to some of these public sector research institutes, many scientists expressed their annoyance with the policy environment, on the grounds of reduced autonomy to choose research area and topics. Especially, in pharmaceuticals it has often meant a shift of focus from the diseases of the poor (e.g. malaria, tuberculosis) to the diseases whose demand for treatment is often confined to the rich (Upadhyaya *et al.* 2002; Ray 2003). Scientists who are reluctant to make this shift, perhaps, feel obligated to the social commons, which may construe intrinsic motivation.

The mobility of students and scientists has gone up tremendously in recent decades. Increased mobility of scientists and research students has posed a new challenge to the process of technological catch-up of many developing countries. Thorn *et al.* (2008) argue that countries at the 'innovation stage' of economic development commit significant resources to graduate education and compete intensely to attract top scientists and researchers.[14] Further, mobility among researchers and scientists is motivated mainly by the content of their work, concrete conditions under which they conduct their research, and institutions that have a reputation for being cutting-edge (Waters and Lawton-Smith 2012). This reinforces the importance of factors such as 'joy of work', and 'autonomy' in influencing the motivation of scientists.

The 2012 report on international migration by the OECD highlights that many Asian countries have put in place specific policies to attract skilled workers back from overseas. However, these policies often focus almost exclusively on extrinsic motivations such as income benefits, while factors such as ensuring autonomy, and 'joy of work' remain neglected. In India, the current policy framework in higher education curtails autonomy of young academicians by obstructing their career progression. Here, many opportunities to 'control one's environment' are linked to one's academic posts where professors and associate professors are preferred over assistant professors for memberships in important policy making bodies. In so far as these opportunities reflect sociopolitical networks, which can influence research priorities and funding, a lack of career progression opportunities for younger scientists can have a negative impact on their confidence, autonomy and the scope for deriving 'joy' from their work. This might curtail the process of reverse migration, and continue to hinder the process of catching up and the acquisitions of technological capabilities.

Motivation for scientific collaboration

Collaborations in the field of science and technology are on the rise, often taking the forms of 'invisible colleges' and 'open system of learning' (Wagner 2008). One observes a policy enthusiasm, both at national as well as at the international level, to promote scientific collaborations. At the national level, such collaborations are fostered by the growing belief that innovations are engines of growth and innovative activities require 'systemic' efforts, often involving industry and academia (Radas 2005; Fraunhofer 2009). Partly, an environment of 'fiscal prudence' is also gearing academia to collaborate with industry in order to self-sustain their research (Upadhyaya *et al.* 2002). Increasingly, research is also becoming multidisciplinary, requiring collaborations. Thus, a brief overview of existing studies on international collaboration is necessary to delineate the motivational factors behind these endeavours.

The Fraunhofer ISI Report (2009) indicates that the motive to expand one's professional network is the most crucial reason for collaboration. These collaborations are guided by familiarity with people or the field of study. The desire to collaborate with 'star researchers' for better visibility is also an important factor for facilitating collaboration. Developing knowledge and expertise in new and emerging areas often, through accessing new equipment of research and by tackling a bigger problem, also motivates collaboration (Beaver 2001). Paradoxically, raising research quality occupies only the third position. Rarely, collaborations are also mandated by the organisational diktats, and policy agenda. Social context seems to be the least important factor. It is, however, not independent of scientists' networks, both formal and informal (Hwang 2008). Outputs from these collaborations can vary; ranging from informal exchanges of ideas and knowledge to codified output in the form of co-patents or co-publications (Glänzel and Schubert 2004; Radas 2005). A recently concluded study on Indo-French scientific collaboration revealed that 333 projects have produced 143 processes, 22 products, 24 patents filed, 27 designs, and 5 per cent of India's top 1 per cent cited papers (Bhattacharya 2014). Collaborations can, therefore, contribute to the emergence of new research locations.

A mix of extrinsic and intrinsic motivations can be identified here. For instance, collaboration to raise quality of scientific inquiry and augment learning can be regarded as intrinsic motivations. On the other hand, the (sole) motivation to work with star researchers may not be 'intrinsic' as one may have to compromise with autonomy and control over the research design and the area of research for sustained collaboration. If, however, the desire is to augment learning, the underlying motivation can be more autonomous, with better integration with the locus of control, which may still lie outside the individual.

However, secondary data often do not adequately reveal the motivational dynamics of individual scientists involved with such collaborations. In other words, to what extent do these research collaborations fulfil the need for autonomy or the need of 'relatedness'? Retaining autonomy would mean having a say in the research idea, design and its implementation. Casual observations suggest that often such collaborations between a developed-country scientist and a developing-country scientist become hierarchical. In such projects, the developing country scientists often end up performing the role of 'data generator/collector' of research designed by scientists in developed countries.

Although as a result of these collaborations, developing country scientists get access to resources, equipment and publications, one can hardly argue that they can retain autonomy of research under these circumstances. Moreover, the experiences of some of the Indian public sector R&D laboratories, where collaborations prompted them to shift focus away from relevant social diseases, mentioned in the last section, does not seem to suggest that collaborations can necessarily foster 'relatedness' or duty. Further research is needed to ascertain these conjectures.

Concluding remarks

This chapter intended to consolidate the direction of research on motivation of scientists and technologists by analysing the research on motivation across disciplines through the lenses of effectance motivation theories. For this analysis, three categories of scientific research were identified, namely, frontier research done in industrialised countries, catch-up and learning activities undertaken in less developed countries, and scientific collaboration, involving developed and developing countries.

The paper tried to categorise intrinsic and extrinsic motivations of individual scientists in all these forms of research undertakings by a set of predetermined parameters. One sees a tendency in the policy environment to promote extrinsic forms of motivation in the form of emphasising private (intellectual) property and commercialisation without clearly understanding their implications for intrinsic motivations such as joy of work or autonomy. This is important, given the theoretical predictions, and some empirical evidence, of trade-off relationships between these two forms of motivation. The impacts of this trade-off on the nature of technological activities and the productivity of scientific research are important areas of future research.

In the context of developing countries with limited technological capability, one may argue that self-reliance driven research would augment learning, autonomy and, therefore, construe intrinsic motivations. One major bottleneck in this regard is lack of risk taking capacity among entrepreneurs of developing countries. In so far as this risk aversion reflects lack of confidence, behavioural patterns associated with such apathy to risk cannot be called intrinsically motivated. However, more research should be carried out to understand the motivational implications of low risk taking attitudes of developing country entrepreneurs on innovative environments within the organisations.

Here also the emergence of a policy environment may be observed that discourages such activities in favour of researches aiming, solely or predominantly, at commercial benefits, private gains or cost competitiveness. This can crowd out efforts towards acquisition of technological capabilities. For informal sector innovations, such policies may further reduce the technological options available to people living in rural and semi urban places by shifting the motivations behind such technological efforts from 'duty to social commons', 'joy of solving problems' to private gains from large scale commercialisation of innovations, which are fraught with numerous challenges.

Recent policies promote international scientific collaborations, often between developed and developing countries. While there exists some evidence that such collaborations help form new centres of research in developing countries, from the secondary data it is not clear whether developing country scientists have to compromise with their autonomy of research topics and designs to avail the opportunities of such collaborations. Further research is needed to investigate the rather provocative claim of Amulya Reddy, a successful scientist, science administrator and a crusader of India's appropriate technology movement, that 'hierarchical modes of functioning almost always vitiate international, particularly, North–South collaborations' (Rajan 2009). Finally, the discussions in the chapter also reveal that further research is needed to understand the various shades of motivations beyond the pure extrinsic and the pure intrinsic ones.

Notes

1 A research grant from Ulrich Hilpert helped immensely to organise the draft during extreme time constraint.
2 By separable we mean outcomes other than the three basic psychological needs.
3 Unexpected reward, however, may have a positive impact on creativity (Cameron and Pierce 1994).
4 Urdan (2003) argues that the evidence of negative effects of extrinsic rewards on intrinsic motivation were artefacts of 'poor operationalization' of the reward as reinforcer, a focus on short term effects without consideration of overall reinforcement history, and neglect for the enormous amount of research showing that reinforcement makes behavior more, not less likely to occur.
5 They, however, state clearly that not all forms of intrinsic motivations would be advantageous in such situations.
6 Quite along the same line, Abraham Lincoln hailed the patent law for 'adding fuel to the fire of (individual) genius'.
7 Machlup, in fact, was dissatisfied with this arrangement where technologists can privately appropriate the outcome of their research while basic research scientists, on whose work these technologies are often based, can't (1958). However, technological implication of science was a key reason for wide institutionalisation of science in many societies, where scientists were honoured for their contribution to technological progress (Ben-David 1971). Therefore, besides public funding, institutionalisation of science may also have motivated the scientists to embrace open dissemination of scientific knowledge rather than secrecy and private appropriation.
8 Saha and Ray (2014) in a study of Indian scientists in public funded universities and research institutes find peer recognition and dissemination of knowledge to be the dominant motivation for publication; 60 per cent of the scientists they surveyed do not undertake consultancies, and 90 per cent do not have any clear preference for private funding of research.
9 Often defined as a self-view or a meaning attributed to oneself in relation to a specific role.
10 See Erdos and Varga (2013) for an interesting exposition of motivational factors in academics. However, in our view, the paper is an empirical exercise, and offers very limited connection with the theories of motivations.
11 This includes field observations of the author not reported formally anywhere so far.
12 Bengal was the first province to be brought under British rule in the year 1757. It hosted the Capital of colonial India (Calcutta, renamed as Kolkata) for about 170 years. Calcutta was the most happening city of nineteenth- and early twentieth-century India until it lost its industrial and political supremacy to Bombay (Mumbai) and New Delhi, respectively.
13 'The great Indian homegrown brand sale' in www.thehindubusinessline.com (accessed on 3 February, 2014).
14 In the US, between 1993 and 2003 this number rose over 70 per cent, the majority of which were in the hard sciences.

Bibliography

Amabile, T.M., 1996: *Creativity in Context*. New York: Westview Press, pp. 1154–1155.

Amabile, T.M., 1998: How to kill creativity. *Harvard Business Review* (September/October), pp. 77–87.

Anderson, M.S., 2011: International research collaborations: anticipating challenges instead of being surprised. Available online at: www.educationarena.com/pdf/sample/sample-essay-anderson.pdf (accessed 3 June, 2015).

Beaver, D.D., 2001: Reflections on scientific collaboration, (and its study): past, present, and future. *Scientometrics* 52(3), pp. 365–377.

Ben-David, J., 1971: *The Scientist's Role in Society*. Englewood Cliffs, NJ: Prentice-Hall.

Berna, J.J., 1960: *Industrial Entrepreneurship in Madras State*. Bombay: Asia Publishing House.

Bessen, J. and Meurer, M.J., 2008: *Patent Failure: How judges, bureaucrats, and lawyers put innovators at risk*. Princeton, NJ: Princeton University Press.

Bhaduri, S., 2008: Patenting biotechnology. In: Patzelt, H. and Brenner, T. (eds): *Handbook of Bioentrepreneurship*. Heidelberg: Springer, pp. 211–248.

Bhaduri, S. and Kumar, H., 2011: Extrinsic and intrinsic motivation tracing the motivation of 'grassroot' innovators in India. *Mind and Society* 10, pp. 27–55.

Bhattacharyya, A., 2007: *Swadeshi Enterprise in Bengal 1921–1947*. Kolkata: Setu Prakashani.

Bhattacharya, S., 2014: *CEFIPRA – Strengthening Bilateral Collaboration and Cooperation in Science, Technology and Innovation between India and France*. New Delhi: NISTADS.

Cameron, J. and Pierce, W.D., 1994: Reinforcement, reward, and intrinsic motivation: a meta analysis. *Review of Educational Research* 64, pp. 363–423.

Deci, E.L., 1971: Effects of externally mediated rewards on intrinsic motivation. *Journal of Personality and Social Psychology* 18, pp. 105–115.

Deci, E.L. and Cascio, W., 1972: Changes in intrinsic motivation as a function of negative feedback and threats. Paper presented at the meeting of Eastern Psychological Association, Boston, MA, 19 April.

Deci, E.L. and Ryan, R., 1985: *Intrinsic Motivation and Self Determination in Human Behavior*. New York: Plenum Press.

Deci, E.L. and Ryan, R., 2004: *Handbook of Self Deterministic Research*. New York: The University of Rochester Press.

Dietz, J.S. and Bozeman, B., 2005: Academic careers, patents, and productivity: industry experience as scientific and technical human capital. *Research Policy* 34(3), pp. 349–368.

Erdos, K. and Varga, A., 2013: The role of academic spin-off's founders' motivation in the Hungarian biotechnology sector. In: Ferrieira, J.M., Rapaso, M., Rutten, R. and Varga, A. (eds): *Cooperation, Clusters and Knowledge Transfers*. Berlin: Springer, pp. 207–224.

Fraunhofer Report, 2009: *The Impact of Collaboration on Europe's Scientific and Technological Performance*. Fraunhofer ISI.

Gagne, M. and Deci, E.L., 2005: Self-determination theory and work motivation. *Journal of Organizational Behavior* 26, pp. 331–362.

Gemme, B. and Gingras, Y., 2011: Academic careers for graduate students: a strong attractor in a changed environment. *High Education* 63, pp. 667–683.

Glänzel, W. and Schubert, A., 2004: Analyzing scientific networks through co-authorship. In: Moed, H.F., Glänzel, W. and Schmoch, U. (eds): *Handbook of Quantitative Science and Technology Research*. Dordrecht: Kluwer Academic Publishing, pp. 257–276.

Gorter, P., 1996: *The Rise of a New Class of Industrialists: Economic and political networks on an industrial estate in West India*. Delhi: OUP.

Govind, M., 2006: *Sociology of Science*. New Delhi: Anmol Publications.

Hackman, J.R. and Oldham, G.R., 1976: Motivation through the design of work: test of a theory. *Organisational Behavior and Human Performance* 16, pp. 250–279.

Hakala, J., 2009: The future of the academic calling? Junior researchers in the entrepreneurial university. *High Education* 57, pp. 173–190.

Herzberg, F.I., 1966: *Work and the Nature of Man*. Oxford: World.

Hwang, K., 2008: International collaboration in multilayered center-periphery in the globalization of science and technology. *Science, Technology, & Human Values* 33, pp. 101–133.

Jong de Jerroen, P.J., 2006: The decision to innovate: literature and propositions, Zoetermeer. *SCALES*, pp. 1–37.

Kreps, D.M., 1997: Intrinsic motivation and extrinsic incentives. *American Economic Review* 87(2), pp. 359–364.

Krishna, V.V., 2013: ERAWATCH Country Report 2012: India, ERAWATCH Network.

Kumar, H., 2012: Exploring motivation, collaboration and linkages for grassroot innovation systems in India, PhD Thesis. New Delhi: Jawaharlal Nehru University.

Kumar, H. and Bhaduri, S., 2014 : Jugaad to grassroot innovations: understanding the landscape of the informal sector innovations in India. *African Journal of Science, Technology, Innovation and Development* 6(1), 13–23.

Lam, A., 2011: What motivates academic scientists to engage in research commercialization: 'gold', 'ribbon' or 'puzzle'? *Research Policy* 40(10): pp. 1354–1368.

Lee, H., Miozzoa, M. and Laredo, P., 2010: Career patterns and competences of PhDs in science and engineering in the knowledge economy: the case of graduates from a UK research-based university. *Research Policy* 39, pp. 869–881.

Machlup, F., 1958: *An Economic Review of the Patent System: A study of the subcommittee of patents, trademarks and copyrights*. Washington DC: US Senate.

McCrory, J.T., 1956: *Small Industry in a North Indian Town: Case studies in latent industrial potential, ministry of commerce and industry*. New Delhi: Government of India.

Morgan, C.T., King, R.A., Weisz, J.R. and Schopler, J., 1993: *Introduction to Psychology*. New York: Tata McGraw-Hill.

Noble, D., 1976: *America by Design: Science, technology and the rise of corporate capitalism*. New York: Galaxy Books.
NWGOPL, 1988: *Conquest by Patent: On patent law and policy*. New Delhi: National Working Group on Patent Laws India.
Osterloh, M. and Frey, B., 2000: Motivation, knowledge transfer and organizational forms. *Organisational Science* 11, pp. 538–550.
Patra, S.K., 2013: Innovation network in IT Sector: a study of collaboration patterns among selected foreign IT firms in India and China. In: Chakraborty, S. and Das, A. (eds): *Collaboration in International and Comparative Librarianship*. Canada: ALIS, pp. 148–170.
Radas, S., 2005: Collaboration between Industry and Science: Motivation Factors, Collaboration Intensity and Collaboration Outcome. This paper was originally published in *Privredna kretanja i eknomska politika* (Economic Trends and Economic Policy) 102, pp. 60–80.
Rajan, R. (ed.), 2009: *Amulya Reddy: Citizen scientist*. Hyderabad: Orient Blackswan.
Ray, A.S., 2003: A Study of R&D Incentives in India: Structural Changes and Impact. Project Report submitted to the Department of Science & Technology, Government of India.
Ray, A.S. and Saha, S., 2011: Patenting public-funded research for technology transfer: a conceptual–empirical synthesis of US evidence and lessons for India. *Journal of World Intellectual Property* 4(1), pp. 75–101.
Roach, M. and Sauermann, H., 2010: A taste for science? PhD scientists' academic orientation and self-selection into research careers in industry. *Research Policy* 39, pp. 422–434.
Ryan, R.M. and Deci, E.L., 2000: Self-determination theory and the facilitation of intrinsic motivation, social development, and well-being. *American Psychologist* 55, pp. 68–78.
Saha, S. and Ray, A.S., 2014: Science Research and Knowledge Creation in Indian Universities: Theoretical perspectives and econometric evidence. CDS Working Paper.
Schwartz, B., 1990: The creation and destruction of value. *American Psychologist* 45, pp. 7–15.
Sheikh, F.A., 2014: Science, technology and innovation policy 2013 of India and informal sector innovations. *Current Science* 106(1), pp. 21–23.
Sreedhar, D., Janodia, M.D. and Ligade, V.S., 2011: Buyouts of Indian pharmaceutical companies by multinational pharmaceutical companies: an issue of concern. *Journal of Young Pharmacists* 3(4), pp. 343–344.
Stern, S., 1999: Do Scientists Pay to Be Scientists? NBER Working Paper No. 7410, October 1999, National Bureau of Economic Research, 1050 Massachusetts Avenue Cambridge.
Tagore, R.N., 1996: The religion of man. In: Das, S.K. (ed.): *The English Writings of Rabindra Nath Tagore* (vol. 3). New Delhi: Sahitya Akademi.
Thorn, K. and Holm-Nielsen, L.B., 2008: International mobility of researchers and scientists: policy options for turning a drain into a gain. In: Solimano, A. (ed.): *The International Mobility of Talent: Types, causes, and development impact*. New York: Oxford University Press, pp. 145–167.
Tocqueville, A. de, 2003: *Democracy in America*, translated by Gerald E Bevan. London: Penguin Group.
Upadhyaya, V., Basu, P., Ray, A.S., Bhadui, S. and Iyer, P., 2002: A Socio Economic Investigation of In-house R&D in Indian Industry: A case study of pharmaceutical sector. A report Submitted to Govt. of India.
Urdan, T., 2003: Intrinsic motivation, extrinsic reward, and divergent reviews of reality. Book review of *Extrinsic and Intrinsic Motivation: The search for optimal motivation and performance*, eds Carol Sansons and Judith Harackiewicz, Academic press, San Diego, CA, 2000, 489 pp, *Educational Psychological Academic Review* 15(3), pp. 311–325.
Wagner, C., 2008: *The New Invisible College: Science for Development*. Washington DC: Brookings Institute.
Waters, R. and Lawton Smith, H., 2012: High-technology local economies: geographical mobility of the highly skilled. In: Hilpert, U. and Lawton Smith, H. (eds): *Networking Regionalized Innovative Labour Markets*. London: Routledge, pp. 96–116.
Wise, G., 1980: A new role for professional scientists in industry: industrial research at General Electric, 1900–1916. *Technology and Culture* 21(3), pp. 408–429.
Witt, U., 2000: Changing cognitive frames–changing organizational forms: an entrepreneurial theory of organizational development. *Industrial and Corporate Change* 9(4), pp. 733–755.
Zuckerman, M., Porac, J., Lathin, D., Smith, R. and Deci, E., 1978: On the importance of self-determination for intrinsically-motivated behavior. *Personality and Social Psychology Bulletin* 4, pp. 443–446.

PART 7

Methods: How to analyse the role of the state and enabling policies

Comparative research and interdisciplinary design

28

INNOVATION POLICIES DESERVE A SOUND MONITORING SYSTEM

An agenda for policy makers

Alberto Bramanti[1]

Introduction

Innovation is surely a matter of 'life and death' in the capitalism of the twenty-first century as it is at the origin of the growing divergence between successful and lagging regions in the EU. There is evidence (Crescenzi and Rodríguez-Pose 2009) that this divergence reflects the differences between innovation-prone regions – where there is a strong policy support for innovative firms and innovation infrastructures – and innovation-averse regions where relevant policy support is much less developed and backward (Rodríguez-Pose 1999).

In addition, in the Europe 2020 Agenda, it is absolutely clear that innovation can help to win the economic challenge to generate more products and firms (not simply to restore growth and jobs lost during the recent recession). Regions, however, need to identify their own 'smart specialization', that is to say to identify niche development strategies allowing regions to satisfy local needs and to meet global high-quality demand, in order to grow, rather than fall behind (Petrella 2000; European Commission 2007).

'Good policies' make the difference and policy makers should be able to select goals, to measure the innovative outcomes, as well as to communicate final results (LC and Ederer 2006; Manning 2009). But to do their job best, policy makers have the necessity of monitoring the innovation process and this implies an appropriate information system (OECD 2009) as well as suitable composite indicators (Bramanti and Tarantola 2012).

The present chapter addresses this necessity developing the following three core issues: innovation policies and the use of a sound monitoring system (first section); the relationship between indicators and policy models (second section); good (composite) indicators as a support in policy design (third section). With 'good indicators' I simply mean indicators: i) enabling the system to be monitored; ii) signalling the targets to be reached; and iii) evaluating the acquired results. A large part of the data needed originate from innovation surveys, and a major task for the near future is exactly the construction of datasets rooted in regional microdata and, possibly, longitudinal (panel) data (fourth section).

Obviously, we can't measure an ill-defined concept and therefore we still need to define the innovation phenomenon better and select an appropriate metrics; we know perfectly well that this is not first and foremost a 'technical problem' but is mainly a shift from expert-dominated to more open, deliberative, shared and involving methods of defining the goals, the objects, and the targets to be evaluated (Henry and Mark 2003; Stiglitz *et al.* 2008).

Innovation policies need sound monitoring systems

Innovation is not a totally independent and market driven process. Due to externalities, spillovers, appropriability regimes, public procurements and public funding of R&D activities (Malerba and Brusoni 2007; Boschma and Martin 2010), innovation policy matters at all the different scales at which competition takes place. Europe – not by chance – has stressed its innovation-driven policies in any strategic plan for competitiveness. But Europe has largely failed to translate world-class science and technology into growth and jobs and the lesson, hardly learned, helped in shifting governments' attention towards a more 'open model' of innovation (Chesbrough *et al.* 2006), a model that is strongly linked to thick networks and strong absorptive capacities (Zahra and George 2002).

The current Europe 2020 Agenda[2] strongly recognizes that innovation is still to be considered the only economic vehicle that can convey the desired expansion in output, incomes and jobs over the next decade. In this way the EU reassesses its commitment to the goal of a dynamic, sustainable, knowledge-based ('smarter') economy (Hofheinz 2009; LC *et al.* 2011).

Almost all countries within the OECD group have adopted in the last decade some version of the 'knowledge economy' pushing down on the accelerator pedal of knowledge creation (DTI 2004), and giving rise to many questions on how to get the maximum return from the money spent.[3] While in the past the term 'knowledge based-economy' prioritized the instrumental use of scientific knowledge for competitive economic advantage, at the present time the very big question among practitioners and policy makers has rapidly changed from the old one – 'how can I foster innovation?' – towards the new one – 'how can I get value from knowledge?' – which is a much more complex and wider task indeed, involving the understanding and organization of the innovation process (invention isn't enough) (DTI 2004; Bessant and Venables 2008). We deal with the ways to obtain an economic return from scientific and technological research and, indeed, economic and social factors are necessary conditions (even if not sufficient) to explain the capitalization of knowledge (Crescenti and Rodríguez-Pose 2009).

The American lesson is still to be metabolized. In the three-year period 2000–2003, real GDP per hour worked grew in the US by 2.6 per cent. Seven sectors (out of fifty-nine) accounted for 85 per cent of the whole growth and, quite surprisingly, among the top performers just one (computer and electronic products) can be considered conventionally R&D intensive. All the other six are 'traditional sectors' – retailing, finance and insurance, wholesaling, administrative and support services, real estate, and professional and scientific services – but have successfully adopted ICT and other organizational innovations within their 'non-innovating' firms.

In addition, we have to recognize that the difference in the productivity growth in the US and Europe, in the past decade, should be mostly attributed to the divergence in services productivity (Bryson and Daniels 2007), not certainly in high-tech sectors (Hughes 2008).

In order to better understand how to get value from knowledge creation, policy makers have become (more) aware of the need of a monitoring and evaluation system (Mettler 2009; Giovannini 2011).

Monitoring is an ongoing process of collecting and assessing qualitative and quantitative information on the inputs, processes and outputs of programmes and policies, and the outcomes they aim to address. This is exactly what the OECD calls 'indicator systems':

> Indicator systems offer regional policy stakeholders a tool for meeting two important challenges, both related to information. The first challenge has a strong vertical dimension. It involves reducing or eliminating information gap between actors at different levels of government in order to achieve specific policy programme objectives. Indicator systems contribute to meeting this challenge by complementing the contractual arrangements between levels of government. The second challenge has a more horizontal dimension. It involves capturing, creating and distributing information throughout a network of actors to improve the formulation of objectives and enhance the effectiveness of the strategies employed. Here indicator systems can bring together and distribute otherwise disparate information and create a common frame of reference for dialogue about regional policy.
>
> *(OECD 2009: 11).*

And we can now finally ask: 'what exactly are indicators?' As shown in Figure 28.1 they are variables representing properties of defined objects that we use to associate a value, so that we can utilize them to judge and assess those objects on the basis of the significance of the observed indicator value (Gudmundsson 2009). According to this definition, indicators differ from both data or statistics (which are to some extent inputs of the process), on the one hand, and information or knowledge (which are interpretable as outputs), on the other hand.

Reliable and functioning indicator systems may contribute to improving the capacity to develop coordination and strategic planning, and enhance the possibility of implementing and fulfilling competitiveness (Manning 2009).

Indicator systems, in fact, may promote learning, where the feed-back process results in being a major help in reaching effectiveness in the management of policies. From this point of view it is much more interesting to use indicators – even if we are conscious of the many faults they closely highlight – than to do without, only relying on humour, moods and contingencies.

Sound policy making, including the setting of targets, requires that the state of innovation will be adequately measured. In this way, feed-back should be used to improve both the policy and the indicator systems themselves. Even if indicators suffer evident shortcomings, they remain

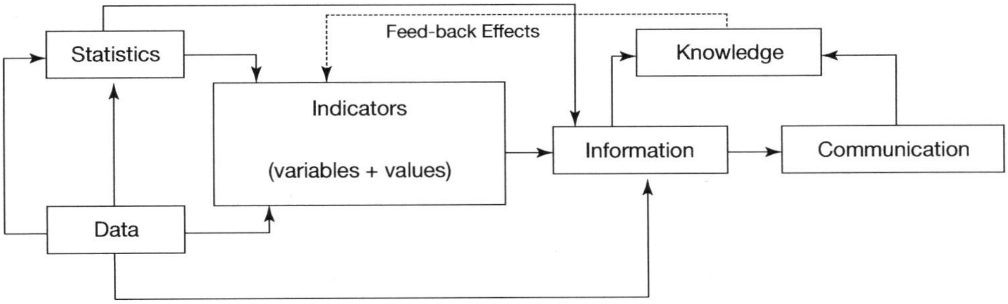

Figure 28.1 The relationships of indicators with other 'knowledge concepts'.
Source: adapted from Gudmundsson (2009).

Table 28.1 Uses of innovation indicators

Uses and their declinations	
1 Theoretical	**3 Ideological/Symbolic**
Understanding and learning about science and technology	Displaying performance
Comparing countries (benchmarking)	Objectifying decisions
Forecasting	Justifying choices
2 Practical (controlling)	**4 Political**
Managing (planning and allocating resources, assessing priorities)	Awakening and alerting
Orienting research	Mobilizing people
Monitoring	Lobbying for funds
Evaluating (accountability)	Persuading politicians

Source: adapted from Godin (2002).

a precious tool for assessing progress and performance. Policy should not be based on hearsay or ideology, but rather rest on some more rooted evidence, calling for measurements and comparisons (Lehtonen 2010).

In Table 28.1 – following Godin (2002) – I present the four different possible uses of indicators when applied to an innovation issue and, specifically, to its quantitative analysis. These uses are: i) theoretical; ii) practical; iii) ideologycal/symbolic and iv) political.

The theoretical one is devoted to the understanding of the phenomenon – we can read behind R&D expenditures statistics, for example, the commitment and de-commitment of public and private sectors; moreover, looking at time series (if available) we can extrapolate future trends. But it is mostly for practical use that data on innovation process and outputs are gathered. The declination of this goal is presented in the second block of Table 28.1, and it is important to remember that a control goal is frequently jointly present, specifically on the total amount of R&D and on the allocation of the public component.

For the private sector the monitoring and evaluating perspective is all the more relevant, as entrepreneurs have to decide where to invest, and to detect and stop unsuccessful works as promptly as possible. The symbolic and potential uses belong to what has been called the 'discoursive–interpretative' policy model and it is the object of the next section.

Within this frame composite indicators represent a step further on this line. They should not claim to have exhausted knowledge and monitoring requirements from policy makers and stakeholders, but they could contribute in speaking 'clearly and aloud' and stressing a more rigorous policy design.

Generally speaking, composite indicators (innovation scoreboards as well as many others built starting from the first decade of the new millennium) may play three different roles in policy (Arundel and Hollanders 2008):

- they can act as an 'early warning' to forerun potential problems;
- they can record changes in strengths and weaknesses (allowing a diachronic analysis of repeated measures); and
- they can spotlight specific questions, attracting the attention of media and policy makers.[4]

Relations between information systems and alternative policy models

So, the nexus between information systems, and specifically composite indicators, and policy goals is very important to this point. In the current debate, the use of information systems and composite indicators in framing policies is habitually called 'evidence based policy'. But this debate is frequently 'ill fated' by a monolithic view of policy making as rational, instrumental, linear and very mechanical problem–solving (Saltelli and Pereira 2011).

According to Boulanger (2007), we can distinguish at least three different models for the use of statistics (and indicators) in policy: i) a rational–positivist; ii) a discoursive–interpretative; and iii) a strategic model.

The first one adheres to a simplified vision of a linear and mechanical way where decision process proceeds from measurement to indicators, and from indicators to decision. In short, policy making as rational problem solving makes use of statistical indicators for the following three complementary goals: i) quantifying objectives; ii) assessing alternative means to reach them (*ex ante*); iii) evaluating effects and impacts (*ex post*).

To some extent we can say that it is a 'policy without politics' model. Even if the rational approach seems to be very promising, we should remember that, up to now, there is no one set of indicators being, at the same time, universally accepted, rooted in a compelling theory, backed in rigorous data collection and analysis, and politically influential.

The third model represents, to some extent, a non-normative conception of politics as a pure competition. In the words of Boulanger (2007: 20) 'there is little room for objective common knowledge and thus for reliable indicators within this model'. The second one – the discoursive–interpretative model – seems to be the more interesting and surely complementary to the first one. Where the rational model looks at technical problem solving, the discoursive–interpretative model:[5] 'sees it as a struggle over the definition, explanation and interpretation of public problems. The core concepts in interpretative policy analysis are the concepts of frame, discourse, narrative, meaning, story, etc.' (Boulanger 2007: 18).

In this frame, indicators and monitoring devices may be, and indeed are, conditioned by social, historical, economic and local factors that intervene at every level of their production (Lehtonen 2010). So, to the discoursive–interpretative model we devote deeper attention.

The new centrality of the 'discoursive–interpretative' policy model

The use of indicators cannot be purely mechanical. On the contrary, they require a massive application of judgement, vastly improving the role of discernment in decision making. If the discursive–interpretative model reads policy making as a struggle over the definition, explanation and interpretation of public problems, then the role of statistics and indicators within this model is a conceptual or 'enlightenment' role, where knowledge provides the information base for decisions, offers conceptual frameworks and fosters different types of learning in the spirit of Habermas' 'communicative rationality' (1984).

In rational policymaking the setting of indicators comes on stage when objectives have already been defined. Differently, in the discoursive–interpretative model, greater emphasis is attached to the way goals are defined, and indicators play a major role in the goal-setting phase of the process.

The subjective word of values, ideas, beliefs, matters and politics has to play its role. Within this approach indicators become important components of policy discourses; they are vehicles of social learning in framing issues, developing new concepts and enhancing legitimacy in the wider political debate (Gudmundsson 2009).

We also have to recognize that while for the researchers technical problems are of the greatest relevance (i.e. the scientific quality of knowledge and, therefore, the accuracy and reliability of data is all that matters), for policy makers, contextual features are of the greatest importance, e.g. communicability, dramatization and resonance of indicators (Henry and Mark 2003).

A first general conclusion is therefore quite obvious: there is no one best composite indicator, partly depending on the goals, partly on the data, and partly on the methodological choices that will be implemented (Bramanti and Tarantola 2012), even if this last one (technical procedures), frankly, is the most workable of the three.

What is much more disputable are the goals that are under the direct responsibility of policy makers. In some cases, when the object of analysis and policy is charged with strong normative assumptions, we meet higher difficulties in the selection of the goals and of the basic indicators. Where the interpretative conceptual models are countless, we have no guidelines for the selection of the relevant information and therefore the offer of a 'unique number' is perceived as highly inappropriate.

The fact that the best composite doesn't exist, can't imply, anyway, that it is useless to construct and to use them in order to learn the proper use of information, choices regarding incentives, and the establishing of clear objectives for the policies. Moreover, statistics and indicators may exert a great influence on policy making (Henry and Mark 2003), the real source of this influence being the dialogical and argumentative processes taking place in the various 'discoursive spheres' in which indicators are produced and used.

Within the policy model we can therefore distinguish six different policy stages ordered from the emergence of the problem to the answering of that problem and the evaluation of the goodness of the solution implemented. Indicators exert different roles depending on the stage of evolution at which they are applied.

Table 28.2 reports this correspondence, recognizing that the three policy models just discussed are more effective at different policy stages. The discoursive–interpretative model, for instance, is more useful in interpreting the legitimization and mobilization phases, while the fourth and fifth stages (formation and implementation on an action plan) may be managed, alternatively, or with a rational–positivistic approach – when there is a large consensus among the different stakeholders – or with a political–strategic model – where the issue is still controversial or when the legitimate interests of powerful stakeholders are at stake. In these cases there is room for opportunistic behaviours (bargaining, strategic-games, log-rolling, etc.).

Table 28.2 Relationships between the stage of policy process, issue characteristics and role of indicators

Policy stages		*Indicators' role*
1 The emergence of the problem	→	Discursive and rationale – enlightenment
2 Legitimisation	→	Conceptual role Discursive-interpretative
3 Mobilisation of the public for action		
4 Formation of an official plan of action	→ Consensus	Instrumental Rational-positivist
5 Implementation of the plan	→ Controversy	Strategic-political
6 Monitoring, evaluation, assessment, appraisal		

Source: adapted from Lehtonen (2010).

Differences between 'use' and 'influence' of indicators

The first model (the rational–positivist one) when referring to the use of indicators in policy explicitly calls for the concept of 'utilization' of indicators. It is an instrumental approach where indicators provide information.[6] But looking at indicators in the light of policy making process it falls short of giving adequate attention to the intrapersonal, interpersonal and societal change processes (Henry and Mark 2003) through which the 'measurement' activity may translate into steps towards regional competitiveness improvement.

Kirkhart (2000) argues that the concept of use is too much result oriented. Despite the relevant efforts made to enlarge its meaning, different unsatisfactory aspects are still present. Instead of continuing to rework the concept of use, she suggests a change in focus from 'use' to 'influence'. Saying it differently, it seems more fruitful to think of the role of indicators in terms of the 'influence' they can exert on policy makers:

> Indicators may not be explicitly 'used' by any stakeholders and yet they can exert powerful influence on policy, for instance through the impacts on frameworks of thought during the indicator design process or the dialogue and argumentation following the release of indicators.
>
> *(Lehtonen 2010: 3)*

The concept of 'influence'[7] (instead of 'use') allows the field of analysis to be broadened to also include the potential negative effects of indicator systems. The issue of performance evaluation, for example, seems to be among the most sensitive, and a number of shortcomings have been highlighted by practitioners (Lehtonen 2010). The message to be learned is that we must stop the finger pointing, as local Governments cannot accept being 'named and shamed' and, as a consequence, Member States frequently do not allow the publication of data considered even potentially controversial or embarrassing.

Differently, the discoursive–interpretative perspective – which better matches with the idea of indicators 'influence' – emphasizes the role of indicators as vehicles of social learning, as a tool designed to open up perspectives and illuminate an issue from a variety of views, as opposed to a closing perspective of achieving convergence around a strictly shared definition of the problem (Stirling 2008).

Good indicators as precious support in policy design and implementation

The focus on innovation calls for proper policies, policies that should have a privileged attention to human capital and entrepreneurship. To give strength to this innovative process we also need good indicators to monitor strategies, but these indicators call for a serious (and wider with respect to the past) engagement of stakeholders. Enrico Giovannini, the past–present President of the Italian National Institute of Statistics (ISTAT) – and Ministry of Labour in the Italian Government of past Prime Minister Letta – has suggested that:

> Statistical indicators chosen through the involvement of stakeholders and shared by all components of the society can play a crucial role in improving policy making and increasing accountability, especially when they deal with the final outcomes that matter to people. . . . Indicators that do not relate to people's lives are seen as irrelevant or, even worse, unfaithful descriptions of what is happening.
>
> *(Giovannini 2011: 10)*

Information systems and indicators have a natural field of application related to benchmarking and its interesting implications. From a methodological point of view it may be very instructive for regional Government to construct and to interpret a composite index on innovation. In fact, there are a number of methodological questions that draw the attention of policy makers towards having a vision on innovation, a clear idea on the undergoing process, and a sound knowledge of the regional innovation system.

In addition, looking at the strengths and weaknesses of the region, help in selecting goals, in identifying the right structure of incentives, in order to have a strategic programming orientation capable of also looking at the medium-long term, not just at the short term political cycle. Regional innovation policy produces outcomes that materialize over an extended period of time (OECD 2009). Obviously in this case data collection may be costly and challenging and we are still searching for the best compromise.

While national statistics still play a role as contextual indicators – and they may be very useful in painting a picture on the international context – the very challenge for the future would be played at the regional level. Here a major shortcoming is always represented by available information. But even to clash with the lack of data (reliable, up-to-date, sound regional data) may create an impulse in the need for a systematic and rigorous statistical effort if we want to take informed decisions.

A guideline for sound indicators

In the light of the previous arguments, the urgency to identify sound indicators is largely understandable: i) indicators that can help in measuring the state of innovative process and its progress both in time and with respect to benchmark territories; and ii) indicators considering targets in relative rather than in absolute terms. It is fundamental to bear in mind that we can't choose the same standards of success for all regions; the 'one-size-fits-all' indicator probably (and hopefully) doesn't exist.

Many innovation measures have been proposed in the literature but we can't choose 'the best'. We can just stress three guiding principles that are worthwhile recalling because they can help in the selection process of the simple indicators.

First of all I'm interested in the regional dimension (NUTS2) of innovation phenomenon. To limit to the country level is not detailed enough for policy purposes, also due to the fact that the overall innovative performance of most countries is determined not by the performance of their leading regions, but by the size of their 'tail' of poor performers.[8]

Second, I have in mind an eclectic and evolutive innovation model (Malerba and Brusoni 2007; Bramanti and Fratesi 2009; Boschma and Martin 2010) where 'hard inputs' (R&D expenditures) are only a part of the story – not necessarily the most meaningful – and 'hard outputs' (patents) are not the ultimate demonstration of innovation success and in any case are very sector/technology specific. The emphasis on increasing R&D spending may not be the most effective way to improve European productivity, and the search for the 'optimal amount' (3 per cent of GDP?) allocated to R&D activities is more an art than a science.

> Are we ultimately using the right indicators to measure a desired policy outcome, or are we only taking into account what can be easily measured, such as R&D spending, and using it as a simplistic proxy for assessing a complex policy phenomenon, like innovation.
>
> *(Mettler 2011: 4)*

A major consequence of this idea of innovation is that more soft factors may be equal (and even more) interesting and, specifically, i) entrepreneurship (as the capacity to bear risks) and ii) high-skilled people (as the human capital asset on which firms may trust) are key assets for regional competitiveness.

Third, the targeting of any measurement exercise would be policy oriented: I'm interested in indicator systems that may have influence on the policy making effort. Policy processes need tangible goalposts so that the progress evaluation can be done on comparable analysis instead of subjective, vague evaluations.

In order to fit these goals we need one (composite) or a small number of simple, easy-to-read, communicative indicators. To increase citizens' awareness, to make performance more transparent, to enlarge the number of stakeholders involved in the process – all these are fundamental ingredients to meeting successful innovation process, or better, to gain the maximum from policies devoted to foster innovation process.

From a policy implications point of view if we look at the data we see that many times the most striking improvements could be obtained by raising the poorest indicators (which frequently have space for manoeuvre) instead of increasing the already best performing assets, which are frequently closer to the 'carrying capacity' of the system. A sound policy implication, in the field of human capital, should be, for instance, the attention given to targeted policies in support of groups that are marginalized in the labour market (i.e. integration of immigrants and minorities), as well as fragile components regarding gender and/or age.

Back to the future: re-starting from the data

Innovative paths differ even among R&D intensive regions as do the final results. Regions' performances, in terms of innovation outcomes, are strongly determined by three main factors:

- the accessibility of knowledge, which is the privileged field of all input indicators (R&D expenditures, but also 'gateway institutions' – such as universities and research centres – and networks, the capacity to attract external assets and innovative firms, etc.);
- the absorptive capacity (Cohen and Levinthal 1990; Zahra and George 2002) (mainly captured by intra-muros research and endowment of high-skilled workers); and
- the capacity to diffuse knowledge and technology (which we are used to measuring with patents, regulatory regimes, clusters and networks of firms, well functioning specialized labour markets).

All the best performing regions share the capacity of mastering these three factors and, specifically, exhibit: i) a high level of skills and effectively functioning professional networks; ii) the presence of knowledge spillovers from nearly technological opportunities; and iii) a strong interdependence among competitors.

'How can we measure all this?' In principle, a small number of indicators – we can roughly guess that ten should be enough – can give a reasonably clear picture of what is going on in this field. In practice, the severe lack of data forces the researcher to use sometimes very disappointing proxies. Instead of gathering a so huge number of poor proxies it would be definitively better to collect new micro data.

The quest for rich and well designed innovation surveys

Innovation surveys (Mairesse and Mohnen 2010) are the only source of this kind of information. They are almost always very useful, providing qualitative and quantitative data on innovation activities. Anyway, there is a heavy job to be done in order to improve these surveys, particularly when we are interested in the regional level (NUTS2) of the analysis.

Apart from the essential requests for more rigorous homogeneity among different territories in running an innovation survey, the most challenging questions surely include: i) merging the innovation survey with firm-based data on economic performance and human capital management; and ii) creating longitudinal datasets.

This last suggestion is the most important, not only because checking our own progress in time is fundamental for policy making, but also because the attention devoted to the issue of the 'persistence of innovation' (Peters 2006; Raymond *et al.* 2006) is dramatically rising. This is another key question in the 'state-of-the-art' innovation research: 'do firms tend to innovate conditionally on past innovation?'. The dynamics of the innovation path is certainly a very challenging problem in the agenda of researchers and we need longitudinal surveys on microeconomic data (firm based) in order to grasp the real outcomes in terms of profitability and competitiveness of innovation efforts (Lööf and Heshmati 2002; Percival and Cozzarin 2010).

In addition, there is also a further 'technical' element in favour of longitudinal datasets: from a statistical point of view it is very difficult to infer strong conclusions regarding causality using only cross-sectional data. Accounting for individual heterogeneity may in fact reverse the conclusions of some analysis. A proper analysis of causality with innovation survey data would require structural modelling in a dynamic setting, which needs the availability of a panel data (Peters 2006). But standard innovation surveys come in waves of cross-sectional data where the same firms are seldom surveyed wave after wave and therefore, panel data should be duly planned and performed in order to fulfil longitudinal surveys.

Closing the Chapter I feel compelled to recommend improving the CIS survey that is now carried out at two-year intervals. CIS 2008 still represents the most recent available version but Eurostat has not yet released the NUTS 2 data. I should remark that the accessibility and timeliness of the data has to be substantially improved. The urgent need for good and easily accessible indicators has never been so necessary as today.

The persistent very large intra-countries variance – particularly on the innovation issue – discourages limiting comparative studies only at the national level, as it is meaningless for policy purposes. As one of the most important goals of indicator systems is to produce information elements that may improve decision making, enhance resources allocation, and increase accountability, we need the CIS survey to carefully stratify its sample in order to guarantee an adequate and uniform coverage of NUTS2 regions.

As also suggested by practitioners (Mairesse and Mohnen 2010), innovation surveys may have a first shared part that is strictly equivalent in all European Countries – which should probably be run yearly – and a second part that goes in depth into the comprehension of innovation processes and results, which should be run at the regional level, maybe on a voluntary basis, at least every two years. I appreciate particularly non-compulsory exercises because they may have a stronger effect in raising awareness of the importance of monitoring and evaluation; and on this field the political and technical challenges to implement a regional indicator system on innovation surely enhance the regional competences in terms of designing systems, selecting indicators, achieving targets, and using explicit financial incentives.

While we know that innovation policy is increasingly designed and implemented at the regional level, the availability of regional data is still discouragingly low. Waiting for a 'new age' of sound, up-to-date, micro-founded regional data, we can work in two complementary directions: i) the first one is a deeper, qualitative scrutiny in 'peer grouping' innovation performance; each region knows which group of regions she belongs to, and can therefore benchmark her direct competitors; ii) the second direction to take advantage of the rather scanty existing data is to raise and improve the most depressed components of the overall innovative performance; any region knows her weaknesses and she can gain time improving these backward aspects. This strategy seems to be a winning one as marginal returns are always greater when starting from low levels, and synergy effects may become widespread when shortening the gap among the different 'ingredients' of the innovative process.

The road ahead

At the very end of this chapter I recall the two main points that have emerged. The question on 'how can we measure innovation results?' is strictly intertwined with the second one 'how can these measures help the design and implementation of policies?'.

While answering these questions seems a technical problem they both imply a policy making problem (Hofheinz 2009; Mettler 2009; LC *et al.* 2011). Different efforts have been devoted to the construction of a composite indicator on innovation activity, and the result may be robust enough, provided the construction process has respected all the methodological requirements of a consolidated technique (OECD–JRC 2008; Bramanti and Tarantola 2012).

But it is still true that any indicator, by definition, can't be better than the data that it relies on, and this uncontestable consideration is open to the point of the availability of good, reliable, timely regional data. These data, to be frank, are not still available at NUTS2 level for all the twenty-seven Member States. Moreover, due to the vision we have embraced on innovation, the date can't be exclusively 'hard data': we need to collect 'microdata', directly gathered at the firm's level, through sound innovation surveys.

The European response to this need has been the CIS survey, certainly a good starting point on which we have to work hard in at least three directions. The first is the necessity of a territorial stratification of the sample in order to cover NUTS2 European regions; the second is to shorten the time lag[9] for the availability of the data; the third direction of improvement is a longitudinal dimension of the analysis, in order to provide panel data.

A final remark addresses directly the policy dimensions. Choosing the 'wrong' indicators means wasting valuable political (as well as financial) capital, but once the 'right' indicators have been chosen, the selection of targets is still to be done and may also be dangerous: the 'one-size-fits-all' approach is totally inappropriate within a European scenario characterized by strong inter- and intra-countries differences. One major point regarding the identification of targets: after an endless debate on the 3 per cent ratio (R&D/GDP), it seems much more feasible to select relative targets (for instance, in terms of rates of growth) instead of absolute ones.

This last point regards the process to be adopted in selecting and implementing the targets. We need to establish dialogic, highly inclusive, strongly participative relationships with all the different stakeholders, and we need to correctly communicate both the process and the final goals, involving local Governments, and reach citizens.

Policy makers know perfectly that regional innovation policy can only be improved by continuously fostering the interface between regional and sectoral innovation systems (i.e. improving the linkages between local and global actors); it is therefore interesting – for the different policy maker levels – to jointly work within a 'dynamic division of labour' where European and National levels deal mainly with 'producing knowledge' and fostering global networks, while regional and local levels focus especially on 'exploiting knowledge' and strengthening internal–external connections.

The new global scenario asks for better informed policy makers (at all levels) but at the regional one we need the full availability of new data (on the innovation phenomenon), thus allowing a contextualized interpretation of the process and avoiding the oversimplification operated by the media and the likely political appropriation of an imprudent and self-assured use of scoreboards and composite indicators.

Notes

1 I'm deeply indebted to Stefano Tarantola from DG Joint Research Centre for having discussed with me the 'composite indicators' issue when I was on sabbatical leave at JRC-IPSC (2010). I'm grateful to CERTeT, at Bocconi University, which has supported my research programme during the last two years. The usual disclaimer applies.

2 'What is needed is a strategy to turn EU into a smart, sustainable and inclusive economy delivering high levels of employment, productivity and social cohesion. This is the Europe 2020 strategy' (Com 2010, 2020 final).

3 The very question, not yet answered in a convincing way, is that related to R&D: 'does the R&D goose really lay golden eggs?'.

4 One important achievement of the Lisbon Strategy – largely portrayed as a policy failure – has been the shift – in policy makers and citizens attention – from the issue of unemployment towards the concept of employment: easier to measure and better reflecting the health and dynamism of the labour market.

5 Following Schön and Rein's (1994) arguments, people facing social problems are engaged in an activity of 'naming and framing'.

> Policy frames are structures of beliefs, perceptions and appreciations that underlie policy positions. Because real situations are complex, indeterminate and ambiguous, people select certain features and relations they consider the most relevant characteristics of the situation and create with them 'stories' that describe and explain the situation.
>
> (Boulanger 2007: 18)

6 During the last twenty years a large debate developed, broadening the concept of 'use' towards a more sophisticated and multi-dimensional construct (Henry and Mark 2003). It is now widely accepted to consider at least four different meanings on the term 'use' (Cummings 2002): i) instrumental (a direct action occurred as a result of the use of indicators); ii) conceptual (something newly learned about the policy); iii) strategic (the justification of a pre-existing position); and iv) process (a direct action occurred, or something newly learned, as a result of participation in the construction of the indicator).

7 The term influence (the capacity or power of persons or things to produce effects on others by intangible or indirect means) is broader than 'use', creating a framework with which to examine effects that are multidirectional, incremental, unintentional, and instrumental.

(Kirkhart 2000: 7)

8 An important consequence, in term of policies, is that by developing attention to the followers as to the leaders, government can drive the innovativeness of their entire economy.

9 In June 2013 the CIS 2008 regional data are the last available data! This delay is quite embarrassing: delivering a black and white 'historical photo' instead of a fresh, up-to-date picture, ends up being useless for policy making.

References

Arundel, A. and Hollanders, H., 2008: Innovation scoreboards: indicators and policy use. In: Nauwelaers, C. and Wintjes, R. (Eds.), *Innovation Policy in Europe: Measurement and strategy*. Cheltenham: Edward Elgar, pp. 29–52.

Bessant, J. and Venables, T., 2008: *Creating Wealth from Knowledge: Meeting the innovation challenge*. Cheltenham: Edward Elgar.

Boschma, R.A. and Martin, R., 2010: *The Handbook of Evolutionary Economic Geography*. Cheltenham: Edward Elgar.

Boulanger, P-M., 2007: Political uses of social indicators: overview and application to sustainable development indicators. *International Journal of Sustainable Development* 12(1/2), pp. 14–32.

Bramanti, A. and Fratesi, U., 2009: The dynamics of an 'innovation driven' territorial system. In: Fratesi, U. and Senn, L. (Eds), *Growth and Innovation of Competitive Regions: The Role of Internal and External Connection*. Verlag Berlin Heidelberg: Springer pp. 59–91.

Bramanti, A. and Tarantola, S., 2012: Regional Innovation Index. Regional Champions within National Innovation Systems, JRC Scientific and Policy Reports, JRC-IPSC, Luxembourg: Publications Office of the European Union.

Bryson, J.R. and Daniels, P.W., 2007: *The Handbook of Service Industries*. Cheltenham: Edward Elgar.

Chesbrough, H., Vanhaverbeke, W. and West, J., 2006: *Open Innovation: Researching a new paradigm*. Oxford: Oxford University Press.

Cohen, W.M. and Levinthal, D.A., 1990: Absorptive capacity: a new perspective on learning and innovation. *Administrative Science Quarterly* 35(1), pp. 128–152.

Com, 2010: 546 final, Communication from the Commission to the European Parliament, the Council, the European Economic and Social Committee and the Committee of the Regions. Brussels: Europe 2020 Flagship Initiative Innovation Union.

Crescenzi, R. and Rodríguez-Pose, A., 2009: Systems of innovation and regional growth in the EU: endogenous vs. external innovative activities and socio-economic conditions. In: Fratesi, U. and Senn, L. (Eds), pp. 167–191.

Cummings, R., 2002: Rethinking Evaluation Use. Paper presented at Australian Evaluation Society International Conference, October–November, Wollongong.

DTI, 2004: *Five Year Programme: Creating wealth from knowledge*. London: Department of Trade and Industry.

European Commission, 2007: *Taking European Knowledge Society Seriously*. Report for DG Research, Brussels.

Giovannini, E., 2011: Turning indicators into action: getting it right this time. In: Mettler, A. (Ed.): *The Lisbon Council (LC), An Action Plan for Europe 2020. Strategic advice for the post-crisis world*. E-brief No. 2. Brussels: The Lisbon Council, p. 10.

Godin, B., 2002: *Are Statistics Really Useful? Myth and politics of science and technology indicators*. WP No. 20, Montreal, Quebec.

Gudmundsson, H., 2009: The Use and Influence of Indicators. A conceptual framework for research. Paper presented at the Ninth Nordic Environment Social Science Conference, 10–12 June, London.

Habermas, J., 1984: *The Theory of Communicative Action*. Boston, MA: Beacon Press.

Henry, G.T. and Mark, M.M., 2003: Beyond use: understanding evaluation's influence on attitude and actions. *American Journal of Evaluation* 24(3), pp. 293–314.

Hofheinz, P., 2009: *The Lisbon Council (LC), EU 2020: Why skills are key for Europe's future*. Brussels: The Lisbon Council.

Hughes, A., 2008: Innovation policy as cargo cult: myth and reality in knowledge-led productivity growth. In: Bessant, J. and Venables, T. (Eds.): *Creating Wealth from Knowledge: Meeting the innovation challenge*. Cheltenham: Edward Elgar, pp. 80–104.

Kirkhart, K.E., 2000: Reconceptualizing evaluation use: an integrated theory of influence. *New Direction for Evaluation* 88, pp. 5–23.

LC, Ederer, P., 2006: *The Lisbon Council (LC), Innovation at Work: The European Human Capital Index*. E-brief No. 2, Brussels: The Lisbon Council.

LC, Ederer, P., Schuller, P. and Willms, S., 2011: *The Lisbon Council (LC), Human Capital Leading Indicators: How Europe's regions and cities can drive growth and foster social inclusion*. Brussels: The Lisbon Council.

Lehtonen, M., 2010: Indicators as an Appraisal Technology: Framework for Analysing the Policy Influence of the UK Energy Sector Indicators. SPRU – Science and Technology Policy Research. Brighton: mimeo.

Lööf, H. and Heshmati, A., 2002: On the relationship between innovation and performance: a sensitivity analysis. *Economics of Innovation and New Technology* 15(4–5), pp. 317–344.

Mairesse, J. and Mohnen, P., 2010: Using Innovation Surveys for Econometric Analysis, WP, 23/2010, UNU-Merit, Maastricht.

Malerba, F. and Brusoni, S., 2007: *Perspectives on Innovation*. Cambridge: Cambridge University Press.

Manning, R., 2009: *Using Indicators to Encourage Development: Lessons from the paradigm of the millennium development goals*. WP DIIS, Copenhagen: Danish Institute for International Studies.

Mettler, A., 2009: *The Lisbon Council (LC), Innovating Indicators: Choosing the right targets for EU 2020*. E-brief No. 4. Brussels: The Lisbon Council.

Mettler, A., 2011: *The Lisbon Council (LC), An Action Plan for Europe 2020. Strategic advice for the post-crisis world*. E-brief No. 2. Brussels: The Lisbon Council.

OECD–JRC, 2008: *Handbook on Constructing Composite Indicators: Methodology and user guide*. Paris: OECD Publishing.
OECD, 2009: *Governing Regional Development Policy: The use of performance indicators*. Paris: OECD Publishing.
Percival, J. and Corazzin, B., 2010: *The Longitudinal Return on Investment on Training to Support Innovation in the Workplace*. Canada: Canadian Council on Learning.
Peters, B., 2006: *Persistence of Innovation: Stylised facts and panel data evidence*, WP No. 6. Aalborg: Danish Research Unit for Industrial Dynamics (DRUID).
Petrella, R., 2000: The future of regions: why the competitiveness imperative should not prevail over solidarity, sustainability and democracy. *Geografiska Annaler*, Series B 82(2), pp. 62–72.
Raymond, W., Mohnen, P., Palm, F. and van der Loeff, S., 2006: *Persistence of Innovation in Dutch Manufacturing: Is it Spurious?* CESifo WP No. 1681, Munich.
Rodgríguez-Pose, A., 1999: Innovation prone and innovation averse societies: economic performance in Europe. *Growth and Change* 30, pp. 75–105.
Saltelli, A. and Pereira, Â., 2011: GDP and Beyond, Seminar on 'Evidence and Decision Making', JRC, Institute for the Protection and Security of the Citizen. Ispra, mimeo.
Schön, D. and Rein, M., 1994: *Frame Reflection*. New York: Basic Book.
Stiglitz, J.E., Sen, A. and Fitoussi, J-P., 2008: *Report by the Commission on the Measurement of Economic Performance and Social Progress*. Paris.
Stirling, A., 2008: 'Opening up' and 'closing down'. Power, participation, and pluralism in the social appraisal of technology. *Science Technology and Human Values* 33(2), pp. 262–294.
Zahra, S.A. and George, G., 2002: Absorptive capacity: a review, reconceptualization, and extension. *Academy of Management Review* 27(2), pp. 185–203.

29

OUTCOMES-ORIENTED INNOVATION POLICY DESIGN

An analytic-diagnostic framework

Sami Mahroum

Introduction: the need for multi-level innovation policy

Over the last two decades, the world has witnessed a proliferation of innovation strategies. Innovation policy has emerged as a distinct area offering a portfolio of instruments to achieve socio-economic goals ranging from raising productivity, to rejuvenating economic regions, through to advancements in environmental, defence and health-related fields. The rise of innovation policy as a distinct policy domain has been the direct result of the popularisation of the concept of a 'knowledge based economy', wherein economies derive competitive advantage through their generation and exploitation of innovations. As a consequence, governments around the world have drafted ambitious plans to spur innovation in their respective economies, pursuing distinct objectives in information and communications technology (ICT), education, infrastructure, finance, and other areas that enable innovation to occur. The ultimate aim of innovation policy is to foster innovation by removing the obstacles that could otherwise hinder its ability to flourish. Innovation policies are, therefore, instruments of government intervention that effectively solve two 'problems'. First, broad socio-economic challenges such as economic growth, and second, barriers and constraints to achieving specific socio-economic goals. For example, an innovation policy instrument that targets the lack of venture capital by making funds available for potential innovators, aims to remove a barrier, which in this case is the lack of funds as well as spurring innovation. This instrument is thus based on an assumption that there is a link between the provision of funds and innovation activity, whereby the lack of the former results in a dearth of the latter.

But all too often such theoretical links are not founded in evidence and innovation policy gets carried away with a focus on what I will call here the 'intermediate problem'. For example, while funding is required for almost any economic activity, funding constraints may improve the quality of policy ideas by driving up competition for limited funds. Furthermore, the shortage of well developed business plans is sometimes a bigger problem than the shortage of funding, where the former drives the latter. In this case, it may be more effective to develop programmes for enhancing skills in preparing business plans.

Thus, such constraints represent 'intermediate problems' that prevent the achievement of socio-economic goals, such as economic growth. Once such intermediate problems have been identified, standard economic analysis is often deployed to design instruments of intervention, such as subsidies, tax breaks or direct funding. In this respect, innovation policy makers have a plethora of funding tools ranging from the mandatory (i.e. stick) to the inducers (i.e. carrots). Some of these instruments are designed to target the supply-side of innovation activity, such as skills, funding and infrastructure, and others target the demand-side such as subsidies, regulations and public procurement.

But if there is a need for innovation why do we need government intervention?

All innovation policies have as their *raison d'être* a problem that may be solved through innovation. The rationale for any government intervention is based on the premises that a 'problem' first exists; which second, 'innovation' may solve, and thirdly that the private sector isn't able to solve the problem on its own. If these three conditions are not present, policy intervention is unwarranted in principal (Edquist 2009). In practice, however, innovation is often held to be a 'public good' where the government is called upon to make a corresponding intervention (Balalaeva 2012).

Yet more often than not, things go wrong where a problem, or its underlying premise, is not well framed, and government intervention cannot be well targeted to make the difference that it intends. For example, it is often incorrectly assumed that economic growth in advanced economies is more of an innovation problem than an efficiency problem (Abramovitz 1956; Solow 1957). However, unlike developing economies, advanced ones have high existing levels of resource mobilisation and utilisation so that they cannot easily achieve greater economic growth by the further mobilisation of resources alone (for a discussion see Fagerberg *et al.* 2010). To improve economic growth it is assumed that these countries need to innovate in order to extract more value from their resources, i.e. their labour, capital or land. This assumption is however only partially true. While internal innovation in this way may achieve marginal gains in productivity, mature economies may achieve higher growth by acquiring and implementing innovations developed beyond their borders (Mahroum *et al.* 2008; Bhidé 2009). The premise that a country needs to innovate in order to grow does not represent an accurate framing of the real problem, which is the need to improve efficiency and productivity. These in fact can be achieved through a variety of means of which innovation is only one. Another such example of a problematic premise that often follows on from the first premise is that insufficient venture capital is a major obstacle to innovation. The prescribed solution is invariably to have more venture capital overlooking an old chicken and egg problem of whether venture capital follows innovation or innovation follows venture capital?

In fact, the experience of many economies, at both national and sub-national, regional, city and state levels, show that higher levels of education sometimes accelerate certain social problems such as 'brain drain' as graduates seek to maximise the benefits of their talent (Molho 1986; Mixon and Hsing 1994; Caponi 2006 using data from Mexico). Graduates in smaller cities flock to larger ones, graduates from poorer states go to richer states, and graduates from poorer countries emigrate to richer economies. In other cases, graduates simply go unemployed or under-employed as a 2013 report by the UK Office of National Statistics shows (ONS 2013). The experiences of internal brain drain in England, Italy, Spain and Portugal attest to this phenomenon (Marinelli 2013), as does the migratory brain drain from Greece, Ireland or Mexico to Australia, Canada, Germany and the US (Caponi 2006).

The misplaced or inflated premises that characterise some innovation policies are too many to enlist here, but we will give one more example. Lack of sufficient research and development (R&D) activity is often seen as a major barrier to technological innovation by most governments around the world. Because R&D is costly, many assume that the marketplace has failed to provide adequate capital, and that governments must directly or indirectly intervene to fund R&D. The premise being that R&D will lead to innovations that in turn translate into new or better goods and services that boost economic growth. The sobering reality is however that R&D does not typically result in such innovations and when it does, most innovations do not culminate in new products and services and the few that do, do not survive on the shelves for more than a year (Cooper 2000). Very little in the way of cost–benefit analysis is usually undertaken to justify government interventions in this domain, when in fact such expenditure is especially vulnerable to free-riders and exploitation and appropriation of return by economic agents external to the home economy (i.e. other regions or countries). A policy to increase the number of graduates, R&D activity or venture funding in one place may in fact result in more value being created elsewhere, sometimes where the ultimate outcome is that a poorer economy subsidises a much richer one.

Too much focus on rationale for intervention and less on causality of factors

Existing studies in designing innovation policy have often been drawn from a single theoretical perspective, such as neoclassical economics (Lipsey and Carlaw 1998; Metcalfe and Georghiou 1998; Hauknes and Nordgren 1999), or systems of innovation (Etzkowitz and Leydesdorff 2000; Lundvall *et al.* 2002; Edquist 2005; Lundvall 2010) to justify government intervention. Some researchers have attempted to integrate these two different theoretical perspectives (e.g. Salmenkaita and Salo 2002; Chaminade and Edquist 2006; Laranja *et al.* 2008; Flanagan *et al.* 2011). These attempts however do not put socio-economic outcomes at the core of the analysis, but instead on the rationale for government intervention. It is like saying that once a problem has been identified as a problem of the market or *systemic failure* (as some would prefer to call it), then the rest of the policy design process becomes straightforward. However, regardless of the conceptual framework underpinning the policy, there remains a design problem wherein innovation per se is often held to be the ultimate desired outcome rather than its tangible benefit to society as a whole and the economy. In this regard, Etzioni (1985) suggests that a multi-variable incorporation should happen at the practical level of policy development and not at the theoretical–disciplinary level (Etzioni 1985: 388).

The following questions become essential for the design of innovation policy:

1 What is the ultimate desired outcome?
2 What are the constraints/barriers/problems preventing us from achieving that outcome?
3 Why does a solution for these problems require a government intervention?
4 What kind of intervention instruments may solve the problem?
5 What objectives should the intervention instruments have?
6 Does reaching the objectives get us closer to achieving the desired outcome?

These six questions represent key essential components of innovation policy design – Outcomes, Constraints, Rationale, Instruments, and Objectives – that link different theoretical underpinnings in innovation policy at a practical level.

The process of innovation policy design begins with identifying the desired outcome before identifying the problem. Problem framing should emerge in the context of appreciating the desired outcome and not in a vacuum as a standalone exercise. For example, a country with a high proportion of STEM graduates may not define this as a problem, whereas in the policy context of lowering youth unemployment, an over-supply of graduates given the particular labour force needs of a country may be defined as a problem. Deciding on whether there is a justification for government intervention should come third and in light of the desired outcome and the nature of the problem. First, policy makers need to establish what their desired outcome is – e.g. cleaner air – and whether the solution resides with a specific innovation – e.g. cleaner engines. Then, it needs to establish what the roots of the problem are, which for example, could be manifold: too many motorists with dirty engines, alternative cleaner engines do not exist or are expensive, cleaner means of transport are not available, and/or too many people living and working in a location. When this is established, an innovative solution can be sought in the form of a cleaner engine, alternative transport, a new economic strategy to reduce population concentration etcetera. Depending on the solution chosen, it can then be decided whether there is a role for government. For example, if the most feasible solution is to adopt cleaner engines, the government may have little leverage if the country does not already have an industrial legacy and infrastructure in mechanical engineering. But a government can help to promote the adoption of alternative lower-tech means of clean transport, including collective transport and bicycles.

The instrument of government intervention is too often determined by what is familiar, with policy makers adopting ineffective instruments because these were the only ones that the government believed it was capable of delivering. In practice, the market failure is matched with a government failure, when in fact no action would have been better than poorly conceived action. This is an important consideration in policy design as it ties the choice of and setting of objectives for policy instruments to what should be achieved in order to reach an ultimate desired outcome.

Designing the policy design

Despite the existence of various frameworks for conducting policy analysis, very few have made their way into innovation policy. While a detailed review of the various available public policy analysis tools lies beyond the scope of this chapter, it is useful to provide a quick overview of some broad categories. First, there are process-based models that attempt to analyse policies as a series of steps (e.g. Bardach 2000). These models have been criticized for being overly linear and simplistic (Graham 1993) and most tend to take a problem as their starting point. Second, there are policy analysis tools designed specifically to determine what is needed to achieve specific targets (i.e. service or function oriented policies), such as minimising ecological impact or reducing traffic fatalities (Simon and Barnard 1976). These are often based on rationalistic (micro-economic) models that define problems as types of market or government failure and then link the problems to sets of possible solutions (e.g. Weimer and Vinning 1999). The problem with the latter is that they become very instrument-target oriented and less comprehensive. As such, instruments may be designed to achieve a target effectively and efficiently, but the choice of target may be wrong. Likewise, a shortfall in achieving the desired outcomes often occurs due to implementation problems that are usually unaccounted for in such analyses.

In many of these analyses, it is also not clear how policy outcomes will be achieved; and explicit consideration of the outcomes is often relegated to the final evaluation stage of the process (Earl *et al.* 2001). While evaluation is important for determining whether or not policies have been successful, they are sometimes not feasible to perform in a robust manner due to the practical problem of monitoring complex causal chains, but more commonly because of implementation problems (McLaughlin 1987). The result is that many policy analyses end up having little if any impact on future policy prescriptions (Salmenkaita and Salo 2002).

Where innovation policy research has been particularly lacking is in the development of analytic frameworks devoted to socio-economic outcomes. This is despite the efforts made by some innovation economists (such as David and Foray 2009) to demonstrate the link between innovation and economic growth, with the latter being defined as a socio-economic problem. Defence, environment, health, security and other varied societal concerns also constitute important objectives in innovation policy. In fact, most government supported mission-orientated innovation programmes fall into one of these categories, albeit with much of the focus of debate around the link between innovation and economic growth being centred on R&D and technology (Ulku 2004). Yet a growing body of research is pointing to economic growth resulting from learning and the exploitation of learning, rather than from original innovations (Lundvall 2007; NESTA 2007; Bhidé 2009). The next section will introduce the theory and literature behind the OCRIO framework to illustrate its applicability to practitioners.

The OCRIO analytic diagnostic framework

As discussed earlier, governments around the world are increasingly adopting broad policies that foster innovation and enhance its economic impact. For example, the EU's Lisbon Agenda, established in 2000, and the 'Innovate America' strategy in the United States of America (USA) in 2005, are initiatives grounded in the rationale that innovation activities contribute positively to socio-economic goals at the macro level (OECD 2007, 2010). As mentioned earlier in the chapter, this widely held belief has meant that innovation policy makers have not felt much need to examine the veracity of the actual linkages between various innovation policy instruments and actual socio-economic goals, especially at the meso-level, i.e. between high level policy making and delivery/implementation agencies.

In the remainder of this chapter, we will describe how the OCRIO structured framework can be used by meso-level policy makers to navigate the multi-layered nature of problem formulation and policy development. The acronym OCRIO stands for the following sequence of steps in an analytic diagnostic framework: **O**utcome, **C**onstraint, ***R***ationale, ***I***ntervention and **O**bjective (OCRIO):

Outcomes refer to the desired ultimate outcome of a policy.

Constraints refer to obstacles and barriers that may prevent or hinder achievement of a desired outcome.

Rationales refer to the justification for governmental intervention, as opposed to other players in an innovation system.

Interventions refer to the type and nature of the policy intervention, e.g. regulatory, financial, etc.

Objectives refer to the change needed to make progress towards the desired ultimate outcome.

The framework takes 'outcomes' as its starting point, rather than 'problems'. This is because the desired outcomes tend to be easier to identify and agree on than problems. Also problems may be hidden, whereas desired outcomes are a matter of subjective expression, collective consensus, or established by vote. More important perhaps, orienting policy development towards outcomes rather than problems leads to different types of policies with different results. The

OCRIO framework is an attempt to constructively sway (innovation) policy discussions away from an orientation towards the intermediate problem (constraints) towards one that is aimed at the ultimate outcome. While at the level of policy instrument (the micro-level) a problem orientation might be a needed exercise that helps design effective policy instruments, at the policy level a greater orientation towards economic and social value creation is needed.

Outcomes

There are numerous examples where the disjoint between innovation policy and socio-economic goals has had a negative impact on actual policy outcomes. For instance, an innovation policy intervention might be successful in removing specific barriers (e.g. high market price) to the adoption of a desired solution (e.g. fuel cell vehicles), but the solution itself does not achieve the ultimate desired outcome (e.g. urban pollution). A more obvious example perhaps is the widespread rise of technology incubators to foster regional economic development. Here the desired ultimate policy outcome is regional economic development, which may be measured by a range of indicators including rapid economic growth, higher employment, increased productivity and improved living standards. While many of these incubators are held up as successful endeavours, only a few can claim to have been successful in delivering a desired level of sustainable economic development (European Communities 2007).

Outcomes can be determined in a number of different ways. Depending on the political system, policy outcomes can be determined democratically, 'technocratically', or by some other consensus. Where outcomes are determined in a democratic system, policy makers are interested in re-election, which influences the choices that they make in the policy process (Burstein 1991). In technocratic political systems, socio-economic goals are determined on the basis of their technical merit in the eyes of expert bureaucrats and others (Forester 1993). Lastly, some socio-economic outcomes are determined in conjunction with high-level committees or planning commissions that engage with the electorate and governments to find consensus about the direction of outcomes.

However, given the plethora of policy analysis approaches available to policy makers, understanding why governments adopt a specific method is still somewhat an enigma. In order to cope with complex problems, policy makers often choose policy instruments that have shown promise in other countries (Walker 1969). Hence, due to the difficulty of rationalising some decisions, policies are sometimes adopted without a clear rationale (Lindblom 1965). Ideology instead plays an important role in determining the kinds of instruments that policy makers adopt. However, aside from replicating policies, policy makers also select policies based on their previous experience. Lastly, ideology also plays a role in influencing policy choices. Governments often seek policies that closely match the preferences of the state. This ideological compatibility is important because it helps governments predict how the electorate will respond to new policies and subsequently helps politicians assess their chances of re-election (Grossback *et al.* 2004). All these factors influence the policy process, starting from policy selection and through to evaluation. Hence there is a pressing need for an innovation policy tool that compels policy makers to link innovation policies, socio-economic outcomes and to justify their policy rationales.

Constraints

Once outcomes have been determined, policy makers can move on to identifying any foreseeable constraints to their achievement. Understanding the constraints for achieving desired outcomes is a crucial aspect of the solution finding process. Identifying the constraints implies understanding the restrictions that may prevent a solution from working as planned. Since ultimate outcomes can be broad and involve many actors, institutions and policy sub-sectors, the nature of constraints will vary in accordance with the perspectives of the various stakeholders (Yanow 2000). What is a problem for some is not necessarily a problem for others. The nature of what constitutes a problem thus becomes more fluid. Policy makers may make use of various evidence-based techniques to support their understanding of the relevant constraints and to try to ensure that their policy is grounded in evidence.

However, there are two key challenges that policy makers face when breaking down complex problems. First, agreeing on the nature of the 'problem'. That is, the way in which a potential barrier to the proposed solution is initially described is critical because it shapes later efforts in the policy action process. Policy makers often have to decide on a variety of issues within a short space of time. They often lack the time and resources to thoroughly investigate the apparent barriers at hand. Furthermore, given that the nature of the 'problem' is defined differently by different groups (Yanow 2000), data collection may be biased by these perceptions and therefore does not ensure that good decisions are made (AbouZahr *et al.* 2007). 'Problems' are often framed in the media, lobby groups, various political forces, or on the basis of an immediate crisis (Dovers 1995; Young and Mendizabal 2009). Problems vary not only in definition, then, but also in perceived seriousness and tractability (McLaughlin 1987). Not all problems merit government attention and nor can all problems be solved by government.

Many innovation initiatives fail because they are either not linked to the broader socio-economic outcomes that they were meant to help to achieve or because they were not linked to any outcome per se. For example, a government may seek to build infrastructure, invest in education and reduce bureaucracy among other outcomes. While each of these outcomes can function as independent goals, policy makers sometimes lack the resources to develop a coherent portfolio that addresses these outcomes in a linked way to maximise the economic contributions. The OCRIO framework is an attempt to help policy makers forge these linkages and frame policy constraints to maximise economic impact, as opposed to value or efficiency based problem framing. By linking desired outcomes to discussions of the nature of constraints, the OCRIO framework emphasises the link between socio-economic goals and the subsequent interrelated decisions that need to be taken (Quinn 1980).

Rationale

In addition to problems with linking innovation policies and socio-outcomes, policy makers also need to switch between different rationales in order to achieve different outcomes. While there is consensus that progress in science and technology is essential for innovation and productivity growth in both the public and private sectors (OECD 2007), there is considerable debate about the role of government in ensuring scientific and technological innovation. Moreover, frameworks for analysis of innovation policy in the academic literature distinguish between two rationales for government intervention: systemic or market failure. However, neither place adequate attention on broader socio-economic goals in the justification for intervention.

According to mainstream neoclassical economics, a government should only intervene in the economy when markets are not efficient, with the underlying assumption that the intervention will improve the efficiency of that national economy. For example, firms won't invest in R&D unless they believe they can recuperate costs and achieve economic gains through the sale of new products or cost savings due to improved production processes.

On the other hand, analyses of systemic failures are better at capturing problems associated with the collective underpinnings of innovation (Edquist 1997; Lundvall *et al.* 2002). According to this systems view, innovation occurs through the interactions among a set of institutions that influences the innovative performance of individual actors (Nelson 1993). These actors include universities, research institutions and corporate research centres as well as firms. A systemic failure is said to occur when the practices, incentives and priorities of these various organisations are incompatible, resulting in a lack of interaction and coordinated activity (Carlsson and Jacobsson 1997; Edquist 1997; Woolthuis *et al.* 2005). The OECD (1997) was among the first to popularise the idea that a *systems of innovation framework* could provide a new rationale for government intervention. Here, governments intervene in order to facilitate knowledge transfer between organisations in the different phases of the innovation process to help prevent systemic failures arising from the lack of interaction and coordination among institutions.

Many innovation scholars consider the theory of market failure inadequate for the purpose of designing government interventions, as it tends to ignore the economic structure or institutional frameworks in which innovation policy arises (Edquist 2005; Woolthuis *et al.* 2005; Lundvall 2010). For example, an innovative solution can be hindered by a clash of cultures between academic institutions and commercial firms. This can happen in the clear presence of a market opportunity.

Neither the framework for analysing market failure nor systems of innovation are used to justify government intervention in innovation from the perspective of the ultimate desired outcome. They are both often used to justify (or object to) government intervention in innovation activities per se. For both frameworks to be useful analytic tools, they need to be applied to a broader context of policy analysis – one that takes into account that innovation itself is an intermediate tool to achieving ultimate desired outcomes. In this regard, the systems of innovation framework can be useful used as a mapping and scanning tool to identify the wider environment in which a barrier and a potential solution exist; whereas the market failure framework helps to identify whether the nature of the barrier requires government intervention, a private solution, or a combination of both.

Intervention instruments

Different policy instruments entail different assumptions about policy problems and their solutions. McDonnell and Elmore (1987) identify four such types of instruments. First, there are instruments based on mandates in which rules are designed to create uniformity and where the policy contains the necessary information for compliance. Here, achievement of the policy objectives can be measured in terms of the degree of compliance. For example, a government may legislate health and safety regulations for the production or consumption of a product that dictates how responsible actors are expected to behave. Such instruments can also be effective in mobilising resources to support policy objectives, such as attracting R&D investment to achieve a particular environmental standard. Second, there are inducements that encourage individuals and agencies to produce innovations when capacity exists but additional resources are needed to mobilise them. In this case, success in achieving objectives can be measured according to the innovation outcomes generated by a specific policy inducement. Third, there are capacity intervention instruments that are designed to build capacity, where knowledge, skills and competence are required to produce value in the future that would not otherwise exist. And finally, there are system changing instruments that are utilised to create new incentives that existing institutions cannot produce.

However, the successful delivery of a solution does not necessarily mean that the solution was the right policy intervention for the economy concerned, nor does success in solving a socio-economic problem necessarily reflect the successful choice of an intervention instrument. Moreover, it is not uncommon for policy intervention instruments to end up acquiring a *raison d'être* of their own, and to continue to exist in isolation of the original outcomes they were meant to help achieve. A successful policy outcome might arrive off the back of an unsustainable policy instrument. For example, tasking universities with supporting innovation activity in the wider economy could help businesses become more innovative, but subject universities to extra costs with little economic return (Abrams *et al.* 2009). Thus, what is needed is a comprehensive approach that links outcomes to constraints, to rationales and to instruments of intervention to ensure that these are interrelated aspects of one analysis rather than separate activities undertaken by different departments and at different points of time.

Objectives

Setting objectives is, fundamentally speaking, a process of identifying targets that when achieved in concert, deliver a desired outcome. Objectives can be linked both to the elimination of constraints and to the direct delivery of outcomes. If capacity is a constraint, then improving capacity by a given factor will arguably address and remove the corresponding constraint. An objective can also be linked directly to an outcome, e.g. reducing CO_2 emissions by a certain factor delivers the ultimate outcome of helping to mitigate climate change. Things become more complicated when objectives are not clearly linked to outcomes, even when constraints are removed due to wrong diagnosis of the problem or the restriction at hand, or when other implementation barriers come into play. In the next few paragraphs, I shed light on some of these implementation barriers.

While it lies outside the scope of this chapter, an OCRIO analytic framework necessitates thinking about the pitfalls of implementation that may derail the best objective-setting mechanisms and result in objectives superseding actual outcomes. In a paper reflecting on the US experience in the 1960s in implementing various social programmes under the Great Society Initiative of the Johnson Administration, McLaughlin (1987) concludes that 'The consequences of even the best planned, best supported, and most promising policy initiatives depend finally on what happens as individuals throughout the policy system interpret and act on them' (172). Policies adopted according to seemingly rational decision making processes can still be circumvented by the actors and conditions that govern their implementation. These include conditions that frame the institutional setting of the implementing system such as environmental stability, competing centres of authority, contending priorities or pressures and other aspects of the social–political milieu that can profoundly influence willingness to implement (Yin 1981). McLaughlin (1987) notes that 'Policy at best can enable outcomes, but in the final analysis it cannot mandate what matters' (188). A lack of buy-in from both policy implementers and the policy target community will inevitably derail implementation objectives and hence stakeholders need to be made aware of the link between objectives and outcomes, particularly the ultimate outcome that a policy intervention is seeking to achieve through its prescribed objectives. It is therefore essential that the macro-level of policy design and development be linked to the micro-level of policy implementation.

Misalignment between a new set of objectives and existing ones or with the objectives of other government agencies can also derail or compromise the implementation of a policy as originally intended. Misalignment can arise from changing political and economic circumstances that give rise to new policy goals that make the original ones seem less relevant or important.

Such a change in circumstances can place pressure on policy makers to serve a new purpose (Beland 2007). The latter phenomenon is often referred to as policy 'drifting' (Hacker 2002). Mahroum *et al.* (2011) expand on the notion of drifting as a form of misalignment, pointing out two common situations, namely 'tactical drifting' and 'strayed drifting', where this occurs. The former takes place when governments are hesitant to undergo widespread policy reform and hence retrofit current policies to reactively meet demands of a new sociopolitical context. The latter occurs when structural or political issues, such as lobbying by a powerful interest group, causes policies to drift unintentionally.

The implementation of innovation policies thus takes place within a wider government apparatus where innovation per se is only a means towards the ultimate goal, which is socio-economic in nature. An innovation policy development process that does not take into consideration the wider institutional setting in which it exists, will likely face implementation problems that, at best, drift the nature of the policy and, at worst, render it irrelevant.

Summary

Innovation policy design should have 'outcomes' at its core and as its focus, rather than using the innovation process itself as a framework to tailor innovation policy around. Accordingly, we have proposed a framework for innovation policy design, geared explicitly around reaching desired outcomes. An innovation policy that is solution-orientated takes as its starting point the desired outcome, and from this creates a roadmap for achieving that outcome in the most efficient way possible.

In this chapter, we have argued that innovation policy is only relevant once (i) the desired outcome is agreed on, (ii) the problem requires an innovation, and (iii) a case for government intervention has been made. Accordingly, innovation policy design should be guided, developed and evaluated on the basis of the ultimate desired policy outcomes, be they in domains of defence, environment, economic development, health or security. The foundation for the case for or against government intervention has to first satisfy the question of whether intervention is actually justified; and second, to determine whether government has the means to intervene, and lastly to ascertain whether or not the options for intervention are likely to be effective in the particular context.

These three layers of analysis collectively form a broader policy development agenda, but they do not necessarily have to follow the same line of theoretical reasoning. Nor do they necessarily have to be conducted within the same departments or ministries in a government. As such it is understandable that these three layers do not typically feature in the policy analysis or rationale that precedes most government intervention in innovation policy, which often tends to skip one or more levels. For example, a case for government intervention in innovation activities might be made in isolation from the first layer of analysis, overlooking the question of whether such intervention is merited or justified. This disjuncture in conceptualisation is often a cause for contention between public policy analysts and scholars in innovation systems.

Furthermore, there is a need for innovation policy to be better linked with the wider policy implementation system and to encompass the range of activities that may play a part in solving the policy problem at hand. Linking innovation policy making to outcomes helps policy makers to identify the specific stakeholders and capacities that matter the most for the successful implementation of a policy intervention. This is important as many policy makers are under pressure to prioritise their efforts in the face of multiple priorities and scarce resources.

The OCRIO framework introduced in this chapter provides a sound structure for linking policy interventions to outcomes and various solution-generating mechanisms. Structuring the design of innovation policy interventions around outcomes makes it easier to capture the relationship between investment in innovation policy instruments and their success in meeting policy objectives. Ultimately, through the OCRIO framework presented in this chapter, it is hoped that governments will be better equipped to ensure that policies not only engender innovation, but better succeed in contributing positively to the broader society and economy.

References

AbouZahr, C., Adjei, S. and Kanchanachitra, C., 2007: From data to policy: good practices and cautionary tales. *The Lancet* 369(9566), 1039–1046.

Abramovitz, M., 1956: Resource and output trends in the United States since 1870. *American Economic Review* 46(2), pp. 5–23.

Abrams, I., Leung, G. and Stevens, A.G., 2009: What drives technology transfer – is it all about the money? *Research Management Review* 17(1), pp. 1–34.

Balalaeva, D., 2012: Innovations as Public Goods Provision with Negative Externalities: Role of Parliamentarism. Higher School of Economics Research Paper No. WP BRP 6.

Bardach, E., 2000: *A Practical Guide for Policy Analysis: The eightfold path to more effective problem solving.* New York: Chatham House Publications.

Beland, D., 2007: Ideas and institutional change in social security: re-purposing, layering, and policy drift. *Social Science Quarterly* 88(1), pp. 20–38.

Bhidé, A., 2009: The venturesome economy: how innovation sustains prosperity in a more connected world. *Journal of Applied Corporate Finance* 21(1), pp. 8–23.

Burstein, P., 1991: Policy domains: organization, culture, and policy outcomes. *Annual Review of Sociology* 17, pp. 327–350.

Caponi, V., 2006: *Heterogeneous Human Capital and Migration: Who migrates from Mexico to the US?* IZA Discussion Paper no. 2446, November 2006.

Carlsson, B. and Jacobsson, S., 1997: In search of useful public policies: key lessons and issues for policy makers. In: Carlsson, B., (ed.): *Technological Systems and Industrial Dynamics.* Dordrecht: Kluwer Academic Publishers, pp. 299–316.

Chaminade, C. and Edquist, C., 2006: Rationales for public policy intervention from a systems of innovation approach: the case of VINNOVA. CIRCLE, Lund University (Paper no. 2006/04).

Cooper, R.G., 2000: Doing it right. *Ivey Business Journal* 64(6), pp. 54–60.

David, P.A. and Foray, D., 2009: Science, technology and innovation for economic growth: linking policy research and practice in STIG Systems. *Research Policy* 38(4), pp. 681–693.

Dovers, S., 1995: A framework for scaling and framing policy problems in sustainability. *Ecological Economics* 12(2), pp. 93–106.

Earl, S., Carden, F., Patton, M.Q. and Smutylo, T., 2001: Outcome mapping: building learning and reflection into development programs. Ottawa: International Development Research Centre.

Edquist, C., 2005: Systems of innovation: perspectives and challenges. In: Fagerberg, J., Mowery, D.C. and Nelson, R.R. (eds): *The Oxford Handbook of Innovation.* Oxford: Oxford University Press, pp. 181–208.

Edquist, C. (ed.), 1997: *Systems of Innovation, Technologies, Institutions and Organisations.* London: Pinter.

Etzioni, A., 1985: Making policy for complex systems: a medical model for economics. *Journal of Policy Analysis and Management* 4(3), pp. 383–395.

Etzkowitz, H. and Leydesdorff, L., 2000: The dynamics of innovation: from national systems and 'mode 2' to a Triple Helix of university–industry–government relations. *Research Policy* 29(2), pp. 109–123.

European Communities, 2007: *Innovation Clusters in Europe: A statistical analysis and overview of current policy support.* Luxembourg: European Communities.

Fagerberg, J., Srholec, M. and Verspagen, B., 2010: Innovation and economic development. In: *Handbook of the Economics of Innovation* 2. Oxford: North-Holland, pp. 833–872.

Flanagan, K., Uyarra, E. and Laranja, M., 2011: Reconceptualising the 'policy mix' for innovation. *Research Policy* 40(5), pp. 702–713.

Forester, J., 1993: *The Argumentative Turn in Policy Analysis and Planning.* Duke University Press Books.

Graham, H.D., 1993: The stunted career of policy history: a critique and an agenda. *The Public Historian* 15(2), pp. 15–37.

Grossback, L.J., Nicholson-Crotty, S. and Peterson, D.A.M., 2004: Ideology and learning in policy diffusion. *American Politics Research* 32(5), pp. 521–545.
Hacker, J.S., 2002: *The Divided Welfare State: The battle over public and private social benefits in the United States*. Cambridge: Cambridge University Press.
Hauknes. J. and Nordgren, L., 1999: Economic rationales of government involvement in innovation and the supply of innovation-related services (STEP Report series No. 199908). Available online at: http://ideas.repec.org/p/stp/stepre/1999r08.html (accessed 2 June 2015).
Laranja, M., Uyarra, E. and Flanagan, K., 2008: Policies for science, technology and innovation: translating rationales into regional policies in a multi-level setting. *Research Policy* 37(5), pp. 823–835.
Lindblom, C.E., 1965: *The Intelligence of Democracy: Decision making through mutual adjustment*. New York: The Free Press.
Lipsey, R. and Carlaw, K., 1998: Technology policies in neo-classical and structuralist-evolutionary models. *OECD STI Review 22*, pp. 31–73.
Lundvall, B-A., 2007: National innovation systems—analytical concept and development tool. *Industry and Innovation* 14(1), pp. 95–119.
Lundvall, B-A., 2010: *National Systems of Innovation: Towards a theory of innovation and interactive learning*. London and New York: Anthem Press.
Lundvall, B-A., Johnson, B., Andersen, E.S. and Dalum, B., 2002: National systems of production, innovation and competence building. *Research policy* 31(2), pp. 213–231.
McDonnell, L.M. and Elmore, R.F., 1987: Getting the job done: alternative policy instruments. *Educational Evaluation and Policy Analysis* 9(2), pp. 133–152.
McLaughlin, M.W., 1987: Learning from experience: lessons from policy implementation. *Educational evaluation and policy analysis* 9(2), pp. 171–178.
Mahroum, S., Huggins, R., Clayton, N., Pain, K. and Taylor, P., 2008: *Innovation by Adoption: Measuring and mapping absorptive capacity in UK nations and regions*. London: NESTA.
Mahroum, S., Goutam, P., Gomes, A. and Doz, Y., 2011: Policy governance in an era of transition: strategies for managing the pitfalls of policy change. INSEAD's Innovation and Policy Initiative. Available online at: www.insead.edu/facultyresearch/centres-/innovation_policy_initiative/events/documents/policy_governance_n_an_era_transition.pdf (accessed 2 June 2015).
Marinelli, E., 2013: Sub-national graduate mobility and knowledge flows: an exploratory analysis of onward- and return-migrants in Italy. *Regional Studies* 47(10), pp. 1618–1633.
Metcalfe, S. and Georghiou, L., 1998: Equilibrium and evolutionary foundations of technology policy. *OECD STI Review 22*, 100.
Mixon, F.G. and Hsing, Y.S., 1994: College student migration and human capital theory: a research note. *Education Economics* 2(1), pp. 65–73.
Molho, I., 1986: Theories of migration: a review. *Scottish Journal of Political Economy* 33(4), pp. 396–419.
Nelson, R.R., 1993: *National Innovation Systems: A comparative analysis*. New York and London: Oxford University Press.
NESTA, 2007: *Hidden Innovation: How innovation happens in six 'low innovation' sectors*. NESTA Research Report.
OECD, 2007: *Innovation and Growth: Rationale for an innovation strategy*. OECD. Available online at: www.oecd.org/dataoecd/2/31/39374789.pdf (accessed 3 March 2015).
OECD, 2010: *The OECD Innovation Strategy: Getting a head start on tomorrow*. Paris: OECD.
Office of National Statistics, 2013: Graduates in the Labour Market.
Quinn, J.B., 1980: *Strategies for Change: Logical incrementalism*. Homewood, IL: R.D. Irwin.
Salmenkaita, J.P. and Salo, A., 2002: Rationales for government intervention in the commercialization of new technologies. *Technology Analysis & Strategic Management* 14(2), pp. 183–200.
Simon, H.A. and Barnard, C.I., 1976: *Administrative Behavior*. Cambridge: Cambridge University Press.
Solow, R.M., 1957: Technical change and the aggregate production function. *Review of Economics and Statistics* 39, pp. 312–320.
Ulku, H., 2004: *R&D, Innovation, and Economic Growth: An empirical analysis*. IMF Working Papers (WP/04/185).
Walker, J.L., 1969: The diffusion of innovations among the American states. *The American Political Science Review* 63(3), pp. 880–899.
Weimer, D. and Vining, A., 1999: *Policy Analysis: Concepts and practice*, 3rd edn. Englewood Cliffs, NJ: Prentice-Hall.

Woolthuis, R.K., Lankhuizen, M. and Gilsing, V., 2005: A system failure framework for innovation policy design. *Technovation* 25 (2005), pp. 609–619.
Yanow, D., 2000: *Conducting Interpretive Policy Analysis*. Thousand Oaks, CA: Sage Publications.
Yin, R.K., 1981: Life histories of innovations: how new practices become routinized. *Public Administration Review* 41(1), pp. 21–28.
Young, J. and Mendizabal, E., 2009: Helping researchers become policy entrepreneurs. ODI Briefing Papers 53, September 2009, Overseas Development Institute. Available online at: www.odi.org.uk/resources/docs/1730.pdf (accessed 2 June 2015).

30

ASSESSING THE IMPACT OF KNOWLEDGE TRANSFER POLICIES

An international comparison of models and indicators of universities' knowledge transfer performance

Ainurul Rosli and Federica Rossi

Introduction

At least since the 1980s, a consensus has emerged among economists and policy makers on the central role of knowledge production and accumulation as a key stimulus to economic growth (Romer 1990). In the new knowledge based economy, intangible investment in the production of knowledge – through the funding of R&D and human capital formation – plays a crucial economic role in order to increase the economy's productive resources, just as physical capital did in the old industrial economy.

Public intervention is often required to ensure that a sufficient amount of knowledge is produced and transferred.[1] For example, governments often fund research carried out in universities and in public research organizations, support firms' investment in innovation and research, promote various kinds of dissemination and knowledge transfer activities in order to ensure that new scientific discoveries are diffused and implemented. Assessing the extent to which government interventions in support of processes of knowledge production and transfer are successful is therefore a very important issue in the knowledge based economy. It is not coincidental that a lot of debates are taking place internationally concerning how to set up appropriate systems to monitor the extent to which the beneficiaries of public funds are able to produce and transfer knowledge successfully and to assess the impact of their activities.

This is, however, a complex task. Not only is knowledge intangible and inherently difficult to measure, but different views and theories about 'what is' knowledge and how best it should be produced and transferred coexist, each of which would suggest different approaches to measuring success in knowledge production and transfer. Choosing the 'right' metrics for performance measurement is particularly crucial because indicators are recognized as playing a performative role (Davis *et al.* 2010; Merry 2011): they signal which behaviours are considered important by policy makers, and which ones may be associated with implicit rewards, such as better reputation and prestige. As such, they can potentially influence the behaviour of the organizations that are monitored.

This chapter discusses how to appropriately measure the effectiveness of public interventions in support of knowledge production and transfer, by focusing on how to monitor and assess the performance of universities in knowledge transfer. This analysis allows us to derive some specific implications for the measurement of universities' performance as well as some more general implications for the assessment of policies in support of knowledge production and transfer.

Models of knowledge transfer and their implications for the choice of performance indicators

The increasing importance and visibility of universities' knowledge transfer activities

As universities are among the most important producers of new knowledge, their contribution to processes of economic growth and development in the knowledge based economy has become more prominent and more debated. Universities are no longer seen as 'ivory towers' where knowledge production is sought purely as an intellectual endeavour detached from practical and commercial applications, but as active agents of economic development (Etzkowitz and Leydesdorff 2000): for most universities, knowledge transfer has become a 'third mission' that complements the traditional research and teaching activities and has gained increasing prominence.

Consequently, ensuring the efficient transfer of academic knowledge to the economic system – so that it can be productively incorporated into the knowledge bases of firms and other organizations and used to generate further innovations, driving productivity increases and opening up new markets – has become an important policy objective. For example, in the United Kingdom, the government has launched a stream of funding (the Higher Education Innovation Fund, or HEIF, appropriately referred to as 'third stream' funding) in order to promote knowledge transfer from universities (Molas Gallart and Castro-Martinez 2007; Kitagawa and Lightowler 2012). In other countries, support for knowledge transfer activities takes place through national project-based funding (for example in Spain; Molas Gallart and Castro-Martinez 2007) and support for the development of a knowledge transfer infrastructure, whether at national level (as in Sweden; Sellenthin 2006), at regional level (as in Germany; Sellenthin 2006) or at State level (as in the US; PACEC 2010).

In order to evaluate the impact of public programmes and to identify whether further interventions are required, policy makers in many countries have launched monitoring and assessment initiatives that often consist of systematic data collection exercises requiring universities to provide quantitative information about their engagement in several activities. In the US and Canada, the Association of University Technology Managers (AUTM) runs a yearly survey of the technology transfer offices of about 200 research universities, mainly focused on technology commercialization activities. In Europe, several associations of technology transfer professionals such as the European Knowledge Transfer Association (ProTon) and the Association of European Science and Technology Transfer Professionals (ASTP) organize their own surveys, usually addressed to the associations' members. Individual countries in Europe organize data collection exercises too. For example, in Spain the Conference of University Rectors distributes an annual survey to the technology transfer offices of universities and public research organizations (Molas Gallart and Castro-Martinez 2007). In the UK a comprehensive survey (Higher Education Business and Community Interaction survey, henceforth HE-BCI) currently managed by the Higher Education Statistics Agency is distributed yearly to all universities in the country; the results of this survey are used to allocate third stream funds to universities. The Australian government runs a biannual survey of universities and public research institutes, and it is currently debating the implementation of indicators similar to those used in the UK (Jensen *et al.* 2009).[2]

Despite the importance of this issue, the choice of appropriate indicators is largely shaped by practical and empirical considerations. In this section, we propose a theoretical discussion both of the different views of knowledge that often implicitly drive the choice of current indicators, as well as of what are the desirable features of indicators. In the following section, we then examine the indicators currently used by several data collection exercises implemented internationally in light of this theoretical analysis.

Different knowledge transfer models

Universities transfer knowledge to external stakeholders in many ways. Even in abstract terms, several possible models of knowledge production and transfer have been identified, according to the nature and properties of knowledge considered (Wang and Peng 2009).

When knowledge is perfectly codified (that is, it has the nature of 'information'), and therefore easily transferrable from one person to another, it shares some features with public goods: differently from tangible goods, it is non rival, because its use on the part of one person does not prevent another person from using it at the same time; and it can be difficult to prevent anyone, including those who have not paid for it, from using it, since it can be transferred rapidly and its marginal cost of reproduction is almost zero (Arrow 1962). This generates a market failure: as knowledge generates positive externalities in the economy, competitive markets do not create sufficient incentives for private agents to produce the amount of knowledge that would be optimal for society.

The market failure in knowledge production can be overcome through government intervention: the government provides public funding for research (by funding universities and public research institutes), and demands that the outputs that result from it are openly disseminated, in the form of publications, reports, books, blueprints, manuals, computer codes, presentations and so on (Dasgupta and David 1994; Antonelli 2008). This model – which we can call the *public knowledge* model – is consistent with the objective to maximize knowledge externalities, and with the assumption that no support mechanisms are needed in order to incentivize knowledge transfer: as knowledge is considered akin to perfectly codified information, economic agents are assumed to be perfectly able to understand it and implement it once it is placed in the public domain.

Another approach to overcoming the market failure in knowledge production is the set up of a system of intellectual property rights. The intellectual property rights system generates at least two types of incentives (Mazzoleni and Nelson 1998; Andersen 2004): the incentive to invest resources in knowledge production (by allowing those who produce knowledge to obtain an adequate economic reward for their efforts) and the incentive to transfer knowledge from one agent to another (by allowing knowledge to be commercialized, for example in the form of patents, copyright, trademarks, design rights that can be sold or licensed). The second incentive is the most relevant in the case of university-generated knowledge (Mowery and Sampat 2005; Schacht 2005). Once intellectual property rights are applied, knowledge is transformed into a quasi-private good for which markets arise spontaneously (Dasgupta and David 1994)[3] – we can call this the ***proprietary knowledge*** model of knowledge transfer.

The view of knowledge as information conceptualizes knowledge transfer as a uni-directional and linear process where the knowledge creator (the university) provides certain 'output' to another party. Therefore, measuring knowledge transfer performance involves quantifying that output – how much output is transferred, to how many users, what is its value. Since this approach presumes that information does not change in the course of the transfer process, the amount of information that is made available and the number of users who have accessed it are considered good measures of the amount of information that is actually received: this suggests that appropriate metrics for universities' intensity and impact of knowledge transfer would be, for example, the number of publications made, accessed and cited, the number of patents and other IPR filed, sold and licensed. It also presumes that the price at which knowledge is sold (or, in case of publicly funded knowledge, the price that the government pays in order to fund it) clearly reflects its value to the user, hence the income that universities derive from knowledge transfer is considered a good measure of its value to society.

Knowledge, however, is not always codified and transmissible like pure information: often, the transmission of knowledge requires practice, active participation and complementary knowledge on the part of the person who is supposed to receive it. In this case, knowledge transfer unfolds over a longer time and usually involves direct interactions between the knowledge holder and the knowledge receiver, in which knowledge is actively constructed rather than simply transmitted – a model of knowledge transfer that we can call *interactive*.

When knowledge transfer requires direct interactions, it can be difficult for free riders to acquire it, even in the absence of intellectual property rights, and this weakens the 'market failure' rationale for public funding: the more knowledge is excludable, the greater are the incentives for its co-production on the part of private firms, as shown by much empirical evidence (Mansfield 1986; Levin *et al.* 1987; Cohen *et al.* 2000).

However, even when markets create sufficient incentives to invest in knowledge production, the economic system may fail to provide sufficient opportunities or resources for agents to interact with other agents (that is, there is a 'system failure'; Klein Woolthuis *et al.* 2005). Appropriate interventions to support interactions may be needed to ensure that knowledge is diffused sufficiently in the economy; since those interactions in turn promote the recombination of existing knowledge, they are potentially able to stimulate the further production of new knowledge.

When knowledge is characterized by tacitness (Ryle 1949; Polanyi 1966), specialization (Cowan and Van der Paal 2000; Cowan *et al.* 2000; Dosi *et al.* 2006), cumulativeness,[4] universities need to directly interact with external stakeholders in order to transfer knowledge effectively. Therefore, the measurement of knowledge transfer performance should not simply focus on the amount and value of outputs that are transferred, but also on the *interaction processes* themselves: that is, the frequency, characteristics and quality of the interactions and the (short and long term) learning processes that all participants in the interactions experience.

Table 30.1 summarizes the main characteristics of the different views of knowledge and their implications for knowledge transfer.

Implications: choosing indicators for different knowledge transfer activities

Some knowledge transfer activities fall quite neatly within one of the models identified in the previous section. It has been acknowledged that the view of knowledge as information is particularly appropriate to describe basic research, which is far from any potential implementation.

Table 30.1 Different views of knowledge and their implication for knowledge transfer

View of knowledge	*Knowledge as information*	*Knowledge as an interactive process*
View of process of knowledge production and transfer	Linear process	Complex, systemic process involving interactions between different knowledge holders
Appropriate way to support knowledge production on the part of universities	Public funding due to market failure in funding of knowledge production	Public or private funding, or a combination thereof
Appropriate way to transfer knowledge on the part of universities	Open dissemination of knowledge outputs *or* assignment of intellectual property rights and trade in IPR markets	Implementation of mechanisms to foster interactions between universities and external agents ('system failure')
Appropriate indicators of knowledge transfer performance	Output-oriented indicators: amount, diffusion and value of outputs transferred	Process-oriented indicators: Number, duration, intensity, characteristics and quality of interactions; learning on the part of all sides of the interaction; involvement of additional beneficiaries; development of further interactions
Theoretical references	Economics of information Linear model of innovation New institutional economics	Economics of knowledge Resource theory of the firm and other heterodox approaches to firm theory Non-linear models of innovation National systems of innovation
Reference period	Since 1950	Since 1990

Source: Authors' own elaboration.

In this case, the market failure in knowledge production is particularly serious (Nelson 1959) and in fact basic research is mostly publicly funded (Haskel and Wallis 2013) and its outcomes are disseminated openly through books, publications, presentations, talks, performances etc., in line with the *public knowledge* model of knowledge production and transfer (for example, much research produced in the humanities may fall within this description). Instead, forms of knowledge that are very tacit and specific to particular users generate very few externalities (Holi *et al.* 2008). Here we find that private organizations are willing to pay universities for contract research, consultancies, the provision of certification and testing services, the provision of training and continuing professional development courses (CPDs), and similar, as in the *interactive knowledge* model described earlier. In other cases, the transfer of knowledge from university to industry occurs simply via the sale of a patent or the licensing of a piece of software or other technology, as in the *proprietary knowledge* model.

But many knowledge transfer activities involve a combination of these approaches. Publicly funded projects such as regeneration programmes and community and cultural events can give rise both to openly disseminated outputs and to interactions with the local communities. Sometimes the effective transfer of knowledge that is codified into a book, or even a patent, requires direct interactions with the researchers who produced it (Cohen *et al.* 2002); hence

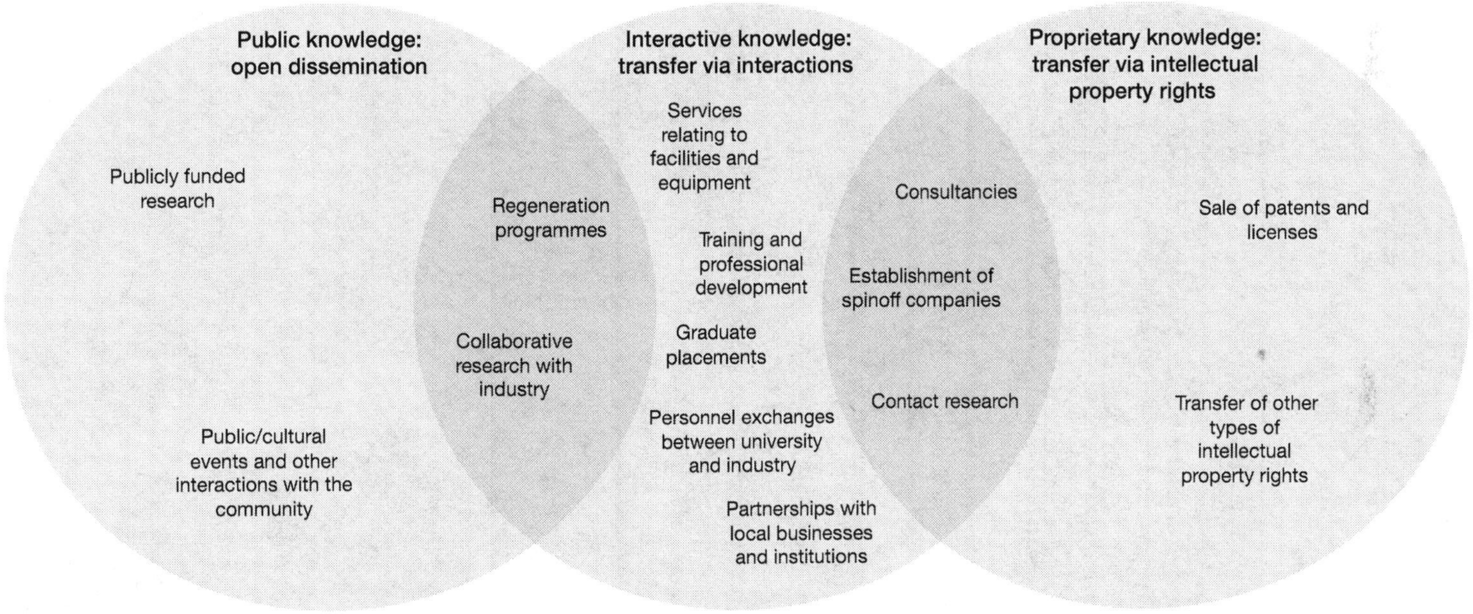

Figure 30.1 Models of knowledge transfer and types of knowledge transfer activities.

Source: authors' own elaboration.

very often informal or even formal interactions develop around the use of published results or around the implementation of a patent licensed from the university.[5] The creation of spin-off companies to exploit the IPR created by universities is another example of a situation where knowledge that is codified into a patent requires the setup of a system of stable interactions to implement it and commercialize it. In the opposite case, the interactions developed around contract research and consultancy may give rise to patents that can be traded and licensed. It is also possible that some interactions between universities and businesses are very standardized and do not involve the production or transfer of new knowledge (for example the rental of rooms and equipment).

Figure 30.1 illustrates how different types of knowledge transfer activities relate to the three models of knowledge transfer identified in the previous section. Because there is no one-to-one correspondence between knowledge transfer activities and theoretical models (and corresponding indicators) of knowledge transfer, the appropriate indicators for each activity must be considered carefully, based on an in-depth understanding of its nature and the channels through which it generates impact.

Implications: choosing indicators for different types of knowledge transfer profiles

The arguments presented suggest that not all knowledge transfer activities can be appropriately measured with the same indicators. For example, the more such activities involve the transmission of tacit knowledge through interactions, the more the characteristics of such interactions matter for the ability of the knowledge transfer process to generate impacts. The more knowledge transfer generates large externalities, the more difficult it is to quantify its impact, and the less likely are private organizations to pay for it: hence, income is less likely to be a good proxy for the value of the knowledge transferred.

The choice of indicators may have important consequences for universities, since the use of a narrow range of indicators may advantage certain types of institutions (those that focus on the activities that are best measured by the chosen indicators) and disadvantage others, according to their knowledge transfer profiles.

A fair and accurate system of assessment of universities' knowledge transfer performance should allow the transfer of different forms of knowledge to be represented and assessed comprehensively (Rossi and Rosli, 2014). First, the range of knowledge transfer activities considered must be broad enough to reflect the variety of activities undertaken by universities: if the choice of activities to be measured is not comprehensive enough, the results may misrepresent the performance of universities that engage in activities that are not measured. Second, for many activities, both output-oriented and process-oriented indicators should be included: the focus on output-oriented indicators may penalize universities that transfer knowledge whose social and economic impact is not accurately reflected by the measurable outputs it generates.[6] Third, the system should be structured in such a way as to avoid the creation of perverse behavioural incentives. If the chosen indicators specifically measure only some knowledge transfer activities and not others, this creates implicit incentives for universities to engage only in the activities that are measured, but these activities may not necessarily be the most effective ways to transfer knowledge for all universities.

These problems are particularly relevant in highly differentiated university systems. Different types of universities, in fact, tend to engage in different types of knowledge transfer activities, for example according to their research orientation (basic vs applied), their research intensity (research-intensive or teaching-intensive; Wright *et al.* 2008), their disciplinary focus (science, technology or the arts and humanities), their geographic localization (urban or peripheral) and their knowledge transfer policies (Di Gregorio and Shane 2003).

In the next section, we show that the systems implemented in several countries (UK, US, Canada, Australia and Europe) in order to assess universities' knowledge transfer performance, generally adopt rather narrow views of what constitute relevant knowledge transfer activities and their impacts. This leads to the selection of indicators that might not allow all institutions to accurately represent their knowledge transfer performance, and in turn it may incentivize universities to focus on the types of knowledge transfer activities whose impacts are measured more accurately.

Case studies: indicators of universities' knowledge transfer performance used in the UK, US and Canada, Australia and Europe

Models of knowledge transfer and choice of indicators in international surveys

In order to showcase the relationship between theoretical knowledge transfer models and the choice of indicators to assess universities' knowledge transfer performance, we consider several surveys implemented in the United Kingdom, the US and Canada, Australia and Europe.

United Kingdom. In the late 1990s, England's main funding agency (the Higher Education Funding Council for England, HEFCE) introduced a systematic UK-wide survey aimed at capturing the exchange of knowledge between higher education institutions, the business community and society at large (the Higher Education-Business and Community Interaction Survey, HE-BCI). Since its existence, the historical HE-BCI data has been used for reference towards grants allocations supporting knowledge exchange. The survey consists of two parts: Part A for strategic and infrastructural data and Part B for financial numeric data, concerning a specific year. The survey has evolved over time, since its inception in 1999. We focus on the indicators contained in the 2010/11 edition of the survey.

United States and Canada. Since the early 1990s, The US based Association of University Technology Managers (AUTM), a non-profit organization, has surveyed North American universities, hospitals and research institutes on their formal knowledge transfer activities. The survey (called AUTM Annual Licensing Activity Survey) focuses on technology transfer activities in the US and Canada, and captures the activities that offices engage in rather than the impact or results of licenses (AUTM 2011). The survey consists of 19 sub-headings and covers six core measures of knowledge transfer activities. We analyse the structure of the survey implemented in the 2011 fiscal year.

Australia. Since 2002, the Australian Government, through the Department of Industry, Innovation, Climate Change, Science, Research and Tertiary Education has conducted a biennial survey (National Survey of Research Commercialisation, NSRC) of 70 Australian publicly funded research organizations (PFROs: universities, publicly funded research agencies and a range of medical research institutes) concerning research commercialization inputs, activity and outputs (NSRC 2012). It consists of two parts: Part 1, which covers the preliminaries of the surveyed institution, and Part 2 for financial and numeric data, concerning a specific year. We focus on the indicators contained in the 2010/2011 edition of the survey.

Europe. Created in 2003 by the European Commission, ProTon Europe, a European Knowledge Transfer Association, coordinates an annual survey of its members across multiple European countries (managed through collaboration with national networks). The survey has evolved over time. Since 2005, it has focused on the performance of technology transfer offices. The survey consists of two parts: Part 1 for core and mandatory questions with three subsections, and Part 2 for optional questions that focus on profiling knowledge transfer activities. We consider the survey implemented in the 2011 fiscal year.

Table 30.2 summarizes the general areas of knowledge transfer engagement included in each of these four surveys. The HE-BCI survey is the most comprehensive in terms of areas considered, although not all of them are investigated with a similar level of detail, as will be clear from our subsequent analysis. The AUTM and NSRC surveys focus very strongly on spin-offs and intellectual property (and to some extent research collaborations, contracts and consultancies) and neglect most of the other areas (the AUTM includes a question on clinical trial services that we consider part of 'facilities and equipment related services' activity; it is however very marginal in this survey). The ProTon survey also focuses mainly on spin-offs, intellectual property, research collaborations, contracts and consultancies, and includes some background information about institutional strategies and infrastructures.

Figure 30.2 shows the shares of questions concerning each area of knowledge transfer activity included in each survey. Questions related to intellectual property (and to a lesser extent, spin-off companies) are prevalent in both the AUTM and NSRC surveys, while the HE-BCI and ProTon survey present a more balanced focus on the different areas, with the HE-BCI being more comprehensive in terms of coverage. Even in the HE-BCI and ProTon surveys, however, intellectual property and spin-offs are relatively more intensely investigated than the other activities.

Table 30.3 compares the four surveys in terms of the models of knowledge transfer represented, and of the types of indicators used. We do not consider questions relating to the institutions' strategies and their infrastructures for knowledge transfer, since these do not relate to specific activities but rather provide the general context in which these activities are performed.

Instead, we focus on the questions concerning the specific knowledge transfer activities that universities perform. In Table 30.3, we have mapped each activity included in the surveys onto the three possible models of knowledge transfer, described in the second section: the *public* model, where knowledge is transferred via open dissemination, the *proprietary* model where knowledge is transferred via trade of intellectual property rights and the *interactive* model, where knowledge is transferred via direct interactions. As illustrated in Figure 30.1, intellectual property-related activities reflect the proprietary model; social, community and cultural engagement activities

Table 30.2 General areas of knowledge transfer activity investigated in the four surveys

Areas of knowledge transfer activity	*HE-BCI (UK)*	*AUTM (US/Canada)*	*NSRC (Australia)*	*ProTon (Europe)*
Strategy	x			x
Infrastructure	x	x	x	x
Intellectual property	x	x	x	x
Spin-offs	x	x	x	x
Collaborations: collaborative research, regeneration programmes, contract research, consultancy	x	x	x	x
Education	x			
Facilities and equipment related services	x	x		
Social, community and cultural engagement	x			

Source: Authors' own elaboration.

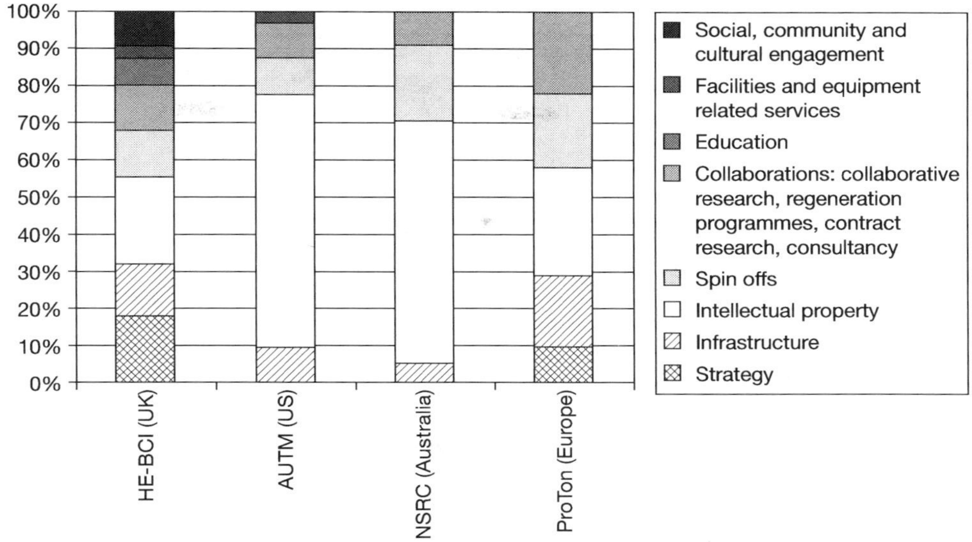

Figure 30.2 Shares of questions relating to each knowledge transfer area.
Source: authors' own elaboration.

and regeneration programmes mainly follow the public model (public financing with open dissemination); the transfer of knowledge via education channels (mostly student placements and CPD), and the provision of facilities and equipment-related services follow the interactive model. The other activities combine different models, for example spin-offs combine the exploitation of intellectual property with the setup of stable interactions around its commercialization; collaborations involve the setup of qualified interactions, but sometimes also open dissemination combined with public funding (in the case of collaborative research) or the creation and transfer of intellectual property (contract research, consultancies).

All four surveys focus on the knowledge-transfer activities that follow the proprietary model. The activities that mainly reflect the interactive model, whether on its own (education-related activities, facilities and equipment-related services) or in combination with the public knowledge model (regeneration programmes, social, community and cultural engagement) are present only in one survey. Collaborations with external stakeholders are present in all four surveys, but if we break them into specific types (collaborative research, regeneration programmes, and contract research and consultancy) we find that only one survey, the HE-BCI, includes all three; the ProTon has some questions on contract research and consultancy while the other two only ask for some general information about research expenditure.

Since most activities combine elements of two or more knowledge transfer models, and most of them are at least partly inspired by the interactive view of knowledge, we would expect the surveys to include a mixture of output-oriented and process-oriented indicators, in order to capture both the outputs transferred as well as the characteristics of the interactions through which the transfer took place. Instead, as shown in Figures 30.3 and 30.4, the majority of indicators capture only the outputs of the knowledge transfer process, whether in the form of knowledge produced (number of disclosures, patents applied and granted, events organized), of income received from the exchange of knowledge, or of impact made upon the business environment (number of licenses executed, number of technologies commercialized, number of companies

Table 30.3 Knowledge transfer activities included in the four surveys, by model of knowledge transfer

Knowledge transfer activities	*Number of surveys that measure the activity*	*Model of knowledge transfer*		
		Public knowledge	*Proprietary knowledge*	*Interactive knowledge*
Intellectual property	4		x	
Spin-offs	4		x	x
Collaborations: collaborative research, regeneration programmes, contract research, consultancy	4	x	x	x
Education	1			x
Facilities and equipment related services	1			x
Social, community and cultural engagement	1	x		x

Source: Authors' own elaboration.

created, employment in companies, etc.). Some indicators capture the cost of the knowledge transfer activity to the university (patent fees, academic staff days invested, etc.) or the inputs in the knowledge transfer process (research personnel, research expenditure). Very few indicators aim to capture some features of the process of knowledge transfer itself; the only information in this sense concerns the number of interactions (in very general terms: number of contracts activated, number of training days delivered) and the identity (SMEs versus other commercial and non commercial organizations, for example) and location (regional versus non-regional) of some of the knowledge transfer partners, as well as some more specific information about the features of the activity performed.

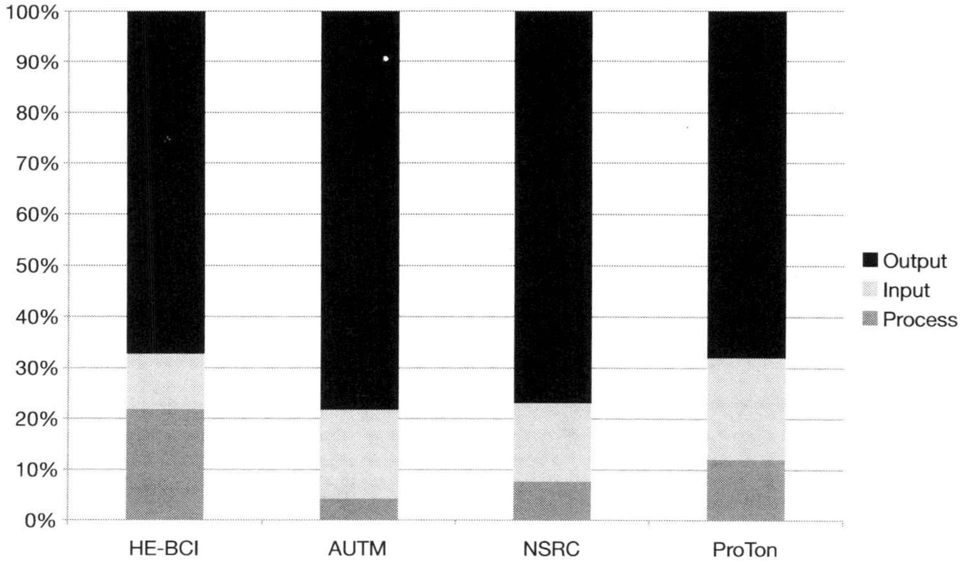

Figure 30.3 Shares of indicators of different types.
Source: authors' own elaboration.

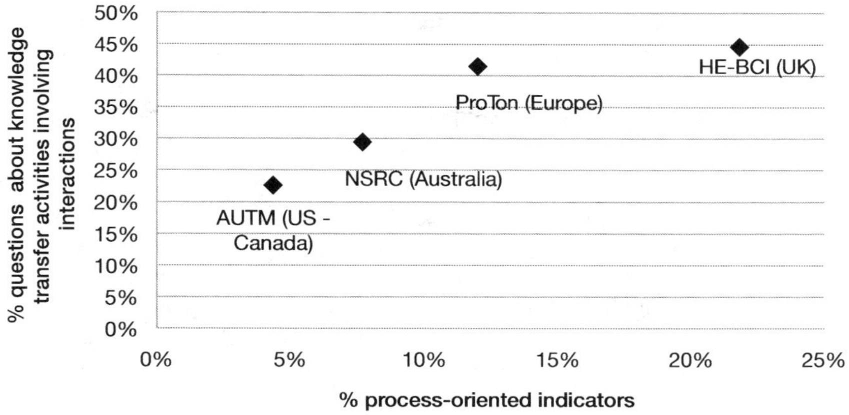

Figure 30.4 Shares of process-oriented indicators vs shares of questions about knowledge transfer activities involving interactions.
Source: authors' own elaboration.

General patterns

Several patterns emerge from our mapping of the knowledge transfer activities and the indicators considered in each survey. No survey is fully comprehensive in terms of the activities considered. The measurement of knowledge transfer via intellectual property rights is attributed high importance in all surveys, as clearly shown in Figure 30.2, particularly in the AUTM and NSRC surveys. This is despite evidence that shows that only a few universities use this model with appreciable intensity and success (Litan *et al.* 2008), as it is suitable to a limited number of scientific fields (Harabi 1995; Brouwer and Kleinknecht 1999). Moreover, the indicators are strongly biased towards patents and software licenses, further skewing the outcomes in favour of a few fields that produce patentable outputs, or software. Little attention is paid to other types of intellectual property rights (design rights, trademarks), to intellectual assets protected by open source or creative common licenses (such as open source software, blogs, wikis, open source film, open source media, open source pharmaceuticals, etc.) and to inventions (for example materials and artefacts) not protected by intellectual property rights (Baghurst and Pollard 2009; Andersen *et al.* 2012). Hence, institutions that are relatively more focused on disciplines, such as the arts and humanities, that are unlikely to generate patents but may generate other forms of intellectual assets, may be unable to correctly represent the amount of intellectual property they produce and transfer.

The public knowledge model is mostly overlooked, especially in the AUTM, NSRC and ProTon surveys, where the only examples of activities that fall within this model are publicly funded collaborative research projects (usually grouped with other types of research activities under the heading 'research expenditure'). In the HE-BCI survey, a few more activities are considered: regeneration programmes as well as knowledge-dissemination activities in the humanities and social sciences. However, these activities represent, together, only around 20 per cent of the overall questions and their impact is mostly measured on the basis of the funding they attract, neglecting other potential outputs.[7] This approach may reflect a concern with keeping a clear distinction between outputs that result from research activities (such as publications) and outputs from knowledge transfer activities, where in practice such distinction is not so easy to make (for example, collaborative and contract research activities and regeneration programmes often have both research and knowledge transfer components). Finding ways to measure the universities' engagement in the open dissemination of scientific outputs resulting from publicly funded research, and to identify their impact more accurately, would be important in order to more precisely assess the outcomes of universities' knowledge transfer engagement. Indeed, empirical evidence shows that 'open science' channels are firms' preferred way to access academic knowledge (Arundel and Geuna 2004; Mowery and Sampat 2005; D'Este and Patel 2007; Abreu *et al.* 2008; Bruneel *et al.* 2009).

In most surveys, very little attention is paid to interactions with different types of external partners (businesses, private non commercial organizations, public organizations, specific communities and even individuals). In the AUTM, NSRC and ProTon surveys, the only interactions considered involve university spin-offs and start-ups and different types of research contracts; in most cases the indicators only quantify the number of companies established and the number of agreements and contracts signed. The HE-BCI is the only survey that attempts to measure numerous types of interactions. Nonetheless, several important direct interactions between university and industry personnel are not included, such as recruitment of university staff members to industry positions, academics' participation in industry conferences and workshops, placements of entrepreneurs and industry personnel in universities, visiting scholarships, and more. Company surveys have shown that firms consider these interactions as important channels in order to benefit from academic knowledge (Bekkers and Bodas Freitas 2008; Boardman and Ponomariov 2009; Jensen *et al.* 2010; Hughes *et al.* 2011), particularly for applied disciplines such as architecture, design, engineering, and medicine. Furthermore, interactions around production and service activities, such as prototyping, clinical trials, testing and design services, would fall within the very generic area of 'Facilities and equipment related services' where they would be grouped with standardized, non-knowledge producing services such as room and equipment rental activities. The minor importance attributed to these activities (if they are considered at all) suggests that the view of knowledge as codified information, easily transferred through economic transactions, is still prevalent, leading policy makers to overlook many activities where the transfer of knowledge occurs in the context of complex, often long term interactions that may not even involve a monetary exchange.

Similarly, the view of knowledge as information shapes the choice of indicators, since all surveys are strongly biased towards output-oriented measures. Knowledge transfer is seen as a linear transmission of information from the university to its external partners, rather than an interactive process that can generate short and long term benefits for both parties and whose outcomes depend on the quality of the interactions themselves. The characteristics and quality of the interactions through which knowledge transfer takes place are not considered. Moreover, the indicators in place only represent uni-directional knowledge transfer from the universities, and no attempts are made to explore the (often non-monetary) benefits that universities derive from these activities.

Conclusions

Performance measurement exercises adopt a narrow view of what constitutes knowledge transfer, and consequently focus on a limited range of activities and impacts. We have illustrated this with reference to four surveys implemented in different international contexts (the UK, the US and Canada, Australia and Europe). In all these surveys, the choice of areas of knowledge transfer to be measured: (i) is strongly inspired by the proprietary model of knowledge transfer based on intellectual property rights, in particular emphasizing patents and software licenses; (ii) only marginally includes activities based on the public model of knowledge transfer (only in relation to the funding attracted to the university and not to the knowledge outputs generated and openly disseminated); (iii) is partly inspired by the interactive model but not inclusive of all possible interactions. Even in the most comprehensive survey (the UK's HE-BCI) not all possible types of knowledge transfer activity are included, and not all types of activities are considered with a similar level of detail.

This rather narrow focus implies that some universities may be at an advantage and others at a disadvantage in representing their knowledge transfer activities, depending on their knowledge transfer strategies. Moreover, universities may be incentivized to focus more on the activities that are measured more accurately, even if this may not be particularly effective for some institutions. Performance measurement exercises should recognize that universities are different, and possibly use different sets of indicators for different groups of institutions, rather than apply the same model of knowledge transfer indifferently to all of them. An alternative approach could be to develop a very broad range of indicators taking into account all possible activities, and let universities themselves choose the profile of knowledge transfer engagement that suits them best (adopting a flexible approach to measurement as suggested, in the more general case of innovation policy indicators, by Rafols *et al.* 2012).

The chapter has also argued that output oriented indicators alone are inadequate to capture the impact of universities' knowledge transfer activities. In particular, the impact of knowledge transfer is not fully captured through monetary measures. Further research should strive to identify indicators that are better able to capture procedural aspects of knowledge transfer rather than just narrowly defined outputs, and that better reflect the multi-directional nature of 'knowledge exchange' processes involving multiple stakeholders rather than unidirectional transfer of knowledge from university to industry.[8] A range of outcome indicators capturing a variety of bidirectional impacts are already deployed in practice, for example by universities attempting to measure their economic and social impacts; these could provide a basis to develop indicators to be adopted more systematically.

We can also derive some implications for the more general issue of identifying appropriate indicators in order to evaluate the impact and success of policies in support of knowledge production and transfer activities. First, different theories of what is knowledge, how it is produced and how it is transferred carry different implications in terms of what indicators should be used to measure relative success. Hence, the choice of indicators needs to be in harmony with the nature of the knowledge whose production and transfer is being monitored. When a wide range of knowledge production and transfer activities are considered, the range of indicators should be broad enough to accurately capture performance in the production and transfer of different types of knowledge. Second, not only indicators should be sufficiently comprehensive, but care should be taken in order to avoid problems of lack of comparability across organizations and of creation of perverse behavioural incentives. Third, countries considering the implementation of performance measurement systems need to be cautious when emulating existing data collection exercises. As this chapter has shown, current exercises suffer from numerous limitations in the scope and types of indicators used. Moreover, each national system is characterized by specific sociocultural arrangements, organizational structures, funding structures, relationships between universities and industry that should be taken into account when designing appropriate systems of performance measurement and assessment.

Notes

1 'Knowledge transfer is about transferring good ideas, research results and skills between universities, other research organisations, business and the wider community to enable innovative new products and services to be developed' (Department for Trade and Industry, UK 2006).

2 See European Commission (2009) for a comprehensive international list of current university knowledge transfer data collections.

3 Whether these markets are efficient and work well, however, is a debated issue: evidence suggests that markets for intellectual property rights suffer from numerous inefficiencies (Andersen and Rossi 2012; Andersen *et al.* 2012).

4 Since the search for new solutions is strongly driven by the knowledge that individuals and organizations already possess, the existing knowledge base is both a driver and a constraint to the development of new knowledge; Nelson and Winter, 1982; Lundvall, 1988).

5 Thursby *et al.* (2001), in a survey of 62 US universities, found that 71 per cent of the inventions licensed from the university to firms required interactions with the inventor in order to be subsequently commercialized.

6 In particular, the assumption that the value of knowledge to those that receive it can be accurately captured by the income that the university accrues from it is debatable: more prestigious institutions may be able to charge more for their services because of reputation, and not because the value of the knowledge is greater; certain forms of knowledge may be transferred for free or at a very low price with the objective to achieve greater diffusion or because they are aimed at people who cannot pay for them, but their value can be high from a social viewpoint; some forms of knowledge may not attract a lot of funding because of their high uncertainty and potential large externalities (Nelson 1959), but they may turn out to have important impacts in the long run.

7 For example, collaborative research can produce joint university–industry publications, support joint workshops and other openly disseminated outputs, and regeneration programmes can have many valuable impacts on the community.

8 For example, some questions could focus on the interactions' duration, the number of partner organizations and people involved, their satisfaction with the interactions, their perception of what they learned from the interactions and the short and long term benefits they received, the long term effects in terms of further interactions generated and of involvement of additional beneficiaries.

References

Abreu, M., Grinevich, V., Hughes, A., Kitson, M. and Ternouth, P., 2008: Universities, Business and Knowledge Exchange. Council for Industry and Higher Education and Centre for Business Research, London and Cambridge.

Andersen, B., 2004: If 'intellectual property rights' is the answer, what is the question? Revisiting the patent controversies. *Economics of Innovation and New Technology* 13(5), pp. 417–442.

Andersen, B. and Rossi, F., 2012: Inefficiencies in markets for intellectual property rights: experiences of academic and public research institutions. *Prometheus* 30(1), pp. 5–27.

Andersen, B., Rosli, A., Rossi, F. and Yangsap, W., 2012: Intellectual property (IP) governance in ICT firms: strategic value seeking through proprietary and non-proprietary IP transactions. *International Journal of Intellectual Property Management* 5(1), pp. 19–38.

Antonelli, C., 2008: The new economics of the university: a knowledge governance approach. *Journal of Technology Transfer* 33(1), pp. 1–22.

Arrow, K., 1962: Economic welfare and the allocation of resources for invention. In: Nelson, R. (ed.): *The Rate and Direction of Inventive Activity*. Princeton, NJ: Princeton University Press, pp. 609–25.

Arundel, A. and Geuna, A., 2004: Proximity and the use of public science by innovative European firms. *Economics of Innovation and New Technology* 13(6), pp. 559–580.

AUTM, 2011: AUTM US Licensing Activity Survey Highlights. Available online at: www.autm.net/AM-/Template.cfm?Section=FY_2011_Licensing_Activity_SurveyandTemplate=/CM/ContentDisplay.cfmandContentID=8731 (accessed 13 June 2013).

Baghurst, D. and Pollard, T., 2009: A Literature Review on the Efficiency and Effectiveness of University Intellectual Property (IP) Models for the Generation, Identification and Exploitation of 'Soft' (Non-Patent and Non-Trademark) IP. SABIP Report.

Bekkers, R. and Bodas Freitas, I., 2008: Analysing preferences for knowledge transfer channels between universities and industry: to what degree do sectors also matter? *Research Policy* 37, pp. 1837–1853.

Boardman, P.G. and Ponomariov, B.L., 2009: University researchers working with private companies. *Technovation* 29, pp. 142–153.

Brouwer, E. and Kleinknecht, A., 1999: Innovative output, and a firm's propensity to patent: an exploration of CIS micro data. *Research Policy* 28, pp. 615–24.

Bruneel, J., D'Este, P., Neely, A. and Salter, A., 2009: The Search for Talent and Technology. AIM research paper (Imperial College London).

Cohen, W., Nelson, R.R. and Walsh, J., 2000: *Protecting Their Intellectual Assets: Appropriability conditions and why U.S. manufacturing firms patent (or not)*. NBER Working Paper No. 7552. Available online at: www.nber.org/papers/w7552 (accessed 4 June 2015).

Cohen, W.M., Nelson, R.R. and Walsh, J.P., 2002: Links and impacts: the influence of public research on industrial R&D. *Management Science* 48(1), pp. 1–23.

Cowan, R. and Van der Paal, G., 2000: Innovation Policy in a Knowledge-based Economy, Publication EUR 17023 of the Commission of the European Communities. Luxembourg.

Cowan, R., David, P.A. and Foray, D., 2000: The explicit economics of knowledge codification and tacitness. *Industrial and Corporate Change* 9(2), pp. 211–253.

Dasgupta, P. and David, P.A., 1994: Toward a new economics of science. *Research Policy* 23(5), pp. 487–521.

Davis, K.E., Kingsbury, B. and Merry, S.E., 2010: *Indicators as a Technology of Global Governance*. Available online from SSRN at: http://ssrn.com/paper=1583431 (accessed 4 June 2015).

Department for Trade and Industry, 2006: *Knowledge Transfer from the Research Base*. London: DTI.

D'Este, P. and Patel, P., 2007: University–industry linkages in the UK: what are the factors underlying the variety of interactions with industry? *Research Policy* 36(9), pp. 1295–1313.

Di Gregorio, D. and Shane, S., 2003: Why do some universities generate more start-ups than others? *Research Policy* 32(2), pp. 209–227.

Dosi, G., Llerena, P. and Labini, M., 2006: The relationships between science, technologies and their industrial exploitation: an illustration through the myths and realities of the so-called 'European Paradox'. *Research Policy* 35(10), pp. 1450–1464.

Dutrénit, G., De Fuentes, C. and Torres, A., 2010: Channels of interaction between public research organisations and industry and their benefits: evidence from Mexico. *Science and Public Policy* 37(7), pp. 513–526.

Etzkowitz, H. and Leydesdorff, L., 2000: The dynamics of innovation: from national systems and 'mode 2' to a triple helix of university–industry–government relations. *Research Policy* 29, pp. 1098–123.

European Commission-DG Research, 2009: *Metrics for Knowledge Transfer from Public Research Organisations in Europe*. Brussels: DG Research.

Harabi, N., 1995: Appropriability of technical innovations: an empirical analysis. *Research Policy* 24, pp. 981–992.

Haskel, J. and Wallis, G., 2013: Public Support for innovation, intangible investment and productivity growth in the UK market sector. *Economics Letters* 19(2), pp. 195–198.

Holi, M.T., Wickramasinghe, R. and Leeuwen, M. van, 2008: *Metrics for the Evaluation of Knowledge Transfer Activities at Universities*. Cambridge: Library House.

Hughes, T., Bence, D., Grisoni, L., O'Regan, N. and Wornham, D., 2011: Scholarship that matters: academic/practitioner engagement in business and management. *Management Learning* 10(1), pp. 40–57.

Jensen, P.H., Palangkaraya, A. and Webster, E., 2009: A Guide to Metrics on Knowledge Transfer from Universities to Businesses and Industry in Australia. Intellectual Property Research Institute of Australia Occasional Paper No. 03/09. Available online at: www.ipria.org/publications/occasional-papers/03-09-Jensen-Palangkaraya-Webster.pdf (accessed 4 June 2015).

Jensen, R., Thursby, J. and Thursby, M.C., 2010: *University–Industry Spillovers, Government Funding, and Industrial Consulting*. NBER Working Papers 15732, Cambridge. MA: National Bureau of Economic Research Inc.

Kitagawa, F. and Lightowler, C., 2012: Knowledge exchange: a comparison of policies, strategies, and funding incentives in English and Scottish Higher Education. *Research Evaluation* 22(1), pp. 1–14.

Klein Woolthuis, R., Lankhuizen, M. and Gilsing, V., 2005: A system failure framework for innovation policy design. *Technovation* 25(6), pp. 609–619.

Levin, R.C., Klevorick, A.K., Nelson, R.R. and Winter, S.G., 1987: Appropriating the returns from industrial research and development. *Brookings Papers on Economic Activity* 1987(3), pp. 783–831.

Litan, R., Mitchell, L. and Reedy, E.J., 2008: Commercializing university inventions: alternative approaches. In: Jaffe, A., Lerner, J. and Stern, S. (eds): *Innovation Policy and the Economy*. Chicago, IL: University of Chicago Press, pp. 31–57.
Lundvall, B.-Å., 1988: Innovation as an interactive process: from user-producer interaction to the national system of innovation. In: Dosi, G. *et al.* (eds). *Technical change and economic theory*. London: Pinter Publishers, pp. 349–369.
Mansfield, E., 1986: Patents and innovation: an empirical study. *Management Science* 32, pp. 173–181.
Mazzoleni, R. and Nelson, R.R., 1998: The benefits and costs of strong patent protection: a contribution to the current debate. *Research Policy* 27(3), pp. 273–284.
Merry, S.E., 2011: Measuring the world: indicators, human rights, and global governance: with CA comment by John M. Conley. *Current Anthropology* 52(3), pp. 83–95.
Molas Gallart, J. and Castro-Martinez, E., 2007: Ambiguity and conflict in the development of 'Third Mission' indicators. *Research Evaluation* 16(4), pp. 321–330.
Mowery, D. and Sampat, B., 2005: The Bayh-Dole Act of 1980 and university–industry technology transfer: a model for other OECD governments? *The Journal of Technology Transfer* 30, pp. 115–127.
Nelson, R.R., 1959: The simple economics of basic scientific research. *Journal of Political Economy* 67(3), pp. 297–306.
Nelson, R.R. and Winter, S.G., 1982: An evolutionary theory of economic change. *Economic Journal* 93(371), p. 437.
NSRC, 2012: The National Survey of Research Commercialisation 2010–2011. Available online at: www.innovation.gov.au/Innovation/ReportsandStudies-/Documents/2010–11NSRCReport.pdf (accessed 13 June 2013).
PACEC, 2010: *Synergies and Trade-offs between Research, Teaching and Knowledge Exchange*. A Report to HEFCE by PACEC and the Centre for Business Research, University of Cambridge.
Polanyi, M., 1966: *The Tacit Dimension*. New York: Doubleday.
Rafols, I., Ciarli, T., van Zwanenberg, P. and Stirling, A., 2012: *Towards Indicators for 'Opening up' Science and Technology Policy*. In: É. Archambault, Y. Gingras and V. Larivière (eds): *Proceedings of 17th International Conference on Science and Technology Indicators (Science-Metrix and OST)*, pp. 675–682. Available online at: http://sticonference.org/Proceedings/vol2/Rafols_Towards_675.pdf (accessed 4 June 2015).
Romer, P., 1990: Human capital and growth: theory and evidence. *Carnegie-Rochester Conference Series on Public Policy* 32(1), pp. 251–286.
Rossi, F. and A. Rosli (2014) Indicators of university-industry knowledge transfer performance and their implications for universities: evidence from the United Kingdom, Studies in Higher Education, DOI: 10.1080/03075079.2014.914914.
Ryle, G., 1949: *The Concept of Mind*. London: Hutchinson.
Schacht, W.H., 2005: The Bayh-Dole Act: Selected Issues in Patent Policy and the Commercialization of Technology. Congressional Research Service Report for US Congress.
Sellenthin, M.O., 2006: Beyond the ivory tower: do patent rights regimes impact on patenting behaviour in Sweden and Germany. *VEST Journal of Science and Technology Studies* 19(3–4), pp. 27–58.
Thursby, J., Jensen, R. and Thursby, M., 2001: Objectives, characteristics and outcomes of university licensing: a survey of major US universities. *Journal of Technology Transfer* 26, pp. 59–72.
Wang, C.F. and Peng, Z., 2009: An empirical study on the relationship between properties of knowledge, network topology and corporation innovation performance. *Management Science and Engineering*. ICMSE 2009. International Conference on Vol. 2, pp. 1230–1237.
Wright, M., Clarysse, B., Lockett, A. and Knockaert, M., 2008: Mid-range universities' linkages with industry: knowledge types and the role of intermediaries. *Research Policy* 37(8), pp. 1205–1223.

31

SIMULATIONS IN POLITICS AND TECHNOLOGY

Innovation policies in the field of photovoltaic cells

Simon Hegelich

Simulations in social science

The aim of this chapter is to highlight the potential of simulations in social science by using the method of simulations on the case study of the market for photovoltaic cells (PV). The simulations used are kept on a very basic level. This means, the analysis presented here is not a "best-practice example." Instead of giving answers to defined research questions the chapter rather tries to use simulations to find interesting questions. Therefore, the reader will not learn a lot about what is going on in the political argument of China and Germany about PV. The main argument is that simulations rely on a different way of thinking about research and the aim of the chapter is to introduce this perspective. To provide some additional hints going beyond the case study, two symbols are used:

Common mistakes in simulation designs and the thinking about simulations are marked with a trap.

Useful hints to apply a simulation approach in another context are marked with a trail.

The core idea of simulations is to create a "virtual world" that is somehow an analogy to the "real world." In analyzing the virtual world of the simulation, it is hoped to find out something relevant for the real world. There are two common misunderstandings in social science of this practice:

- Some critiques argue simulations would take the virtual world for real and therefore reduce the real world complexity in an illegitimate way.
- Others state simulations would only be capable of reproducing their own inputs (data and rules) and therefore were no appropriate tool to produce new insights.

Both critiques are somehow wrong but they do touch relevant aspects of simulation. Axelrod has described simulation as a "third way of doing science" beyond deduction and induction:[1]

> Simulation is a third way of doing science. Like deduction, it starts with a set of explicit assumptions. But unlike deduction, it does not prove theorems. Instead, a simulation generates data that can be analyzed inductively. Unlike typical induction, however, the simulated data comes from a rigorously specified set of rules rather than direct measurement of the real world. While induction can be used to find patterns in data, and deduction can be used to find consequences of assumptions, simulation modeling can be used as an aid to intuition.
>
> *(Axelrod 2003: 5)*

Simulation cannot be a reproduction of the real world. Rules may be deducted from real world experiences, data in the simulation might be taken directly from the real world, but the combination of rules and data is "design" in its fundamental meaning (Simon 2008). Outputs of simulations are not effects of real world causalities but only of the rules of simulation. But nevertheless, these outputs are part of the real world on their own, namely as artificial constructs:

- You can analyze data from simulations and might find interesting interactions that you would not have expected.
- You can formulate expectations about other systems—including real world systems—on the basis of *ceteris paribus* assumptions: To the extent the same rules apply to the simulation and to the compared system, both systems should behave similarly.

Coming back to the notional critiques, it has to be admitted that it is impossible to verify conclusions concerning the real world derived from the virtual world, because the *ceteris paribus* assumption could only be overcome in a one-to-one reproduction of the real world which would be an experiment but not a simulation (Behnke 2009: 175). Therefore, there is always a problem with simulations when it comes to causalities. However—as will be seen—this problem is far from unique to the simulation approach.

Sometimes, scientists using a simulation approach are so convinced of their model that they forget the difference between virtual and real world. They might claim that their simulation has "proved" some real world effect. But because of ceteris paribus the connection to the real world is always questionable. Overestimating the relevance of one's own simulation will make you "easy prey" for any critiques.

In the following sections, I will demonstrate the potential and the weaknesses of simulation approaches in the field of politics and technology. After presenting an example for the validity problem in statistical methods, the paper presents three different simulations highlighting different aspects of politics and solar power. All simulations refer to OECD-data. The first simulation reconstructs the number of patents in the field of photovoltaic from the national R&D-budget on energy. The second simulation reverses this approach and tries to reconstruct the Chinese R&D-budget out of the number of patents. The third simulation uses the approach of agent based modeling to analyze possible effects of different market strategies.

Politics and technology, statistical methods and simulation

When analyzing politics and technology, researchers often have to face the situation that relevant data are not available or that available data do not meet the high standards of comparative approaches, especially concerning the validity of data. Simulations can be used to construct basic models based on fragmented data that help us to identify interesting cases and to pre-test hypotheses. Simulations therefore can be a useful tool to guide the researcher.

I will highlight the difficulties of validity and demonstrate how the weakness of simulations in regard to causality-assumptions can turn out to be a strength as a first example.

The OECD-database (http://stats.oecd.org/) contains information on the R&D-budgets on energy and on the annual number of patents in the field of photovoltaic cells (PV). The assumption is that R&D-spending has a positive effect on patents. Figure 31.1 shows the data.

A regression analysis shows an estimated coefficient of 0.41 (significant at the 1 per cent level) and that nearly 70 per cent of the change in patents can be "explained" by this influence of the budget. Empirical analysis therefore seems to provide a strong argument in this case. So why use simulations?

But there is a problem. The example is only based on data from 2000 till 2009. If all available data are analyzed, the picture is quite different (see Figure 31.2). The R&D-budget on energy had its peak in the early 1980s and has been declining since. But patents on photovoltaic cells started to develop in the 1990s. Of course the estimated coefficient is now negative and our data gives no hint of a positive effect of budget on patents.

Obviously, a serious problem with the validity of data occurs here: The budget-data contains all R&D-spending in the field of energy and PV is only one subtopic with changing relative importance. Without further information—which is not available—inductive methods of data analysis quickly reach their limits.[2]

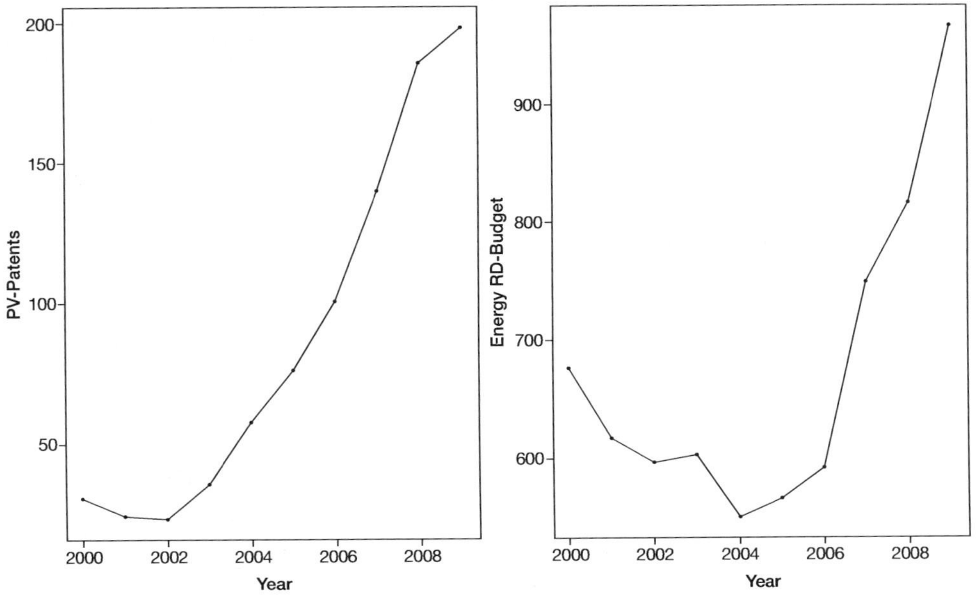

Figure 31.1 German PV-patents and energy R&D-budget.
Source: OECD (http://stats.oecd.org/), own presentation.

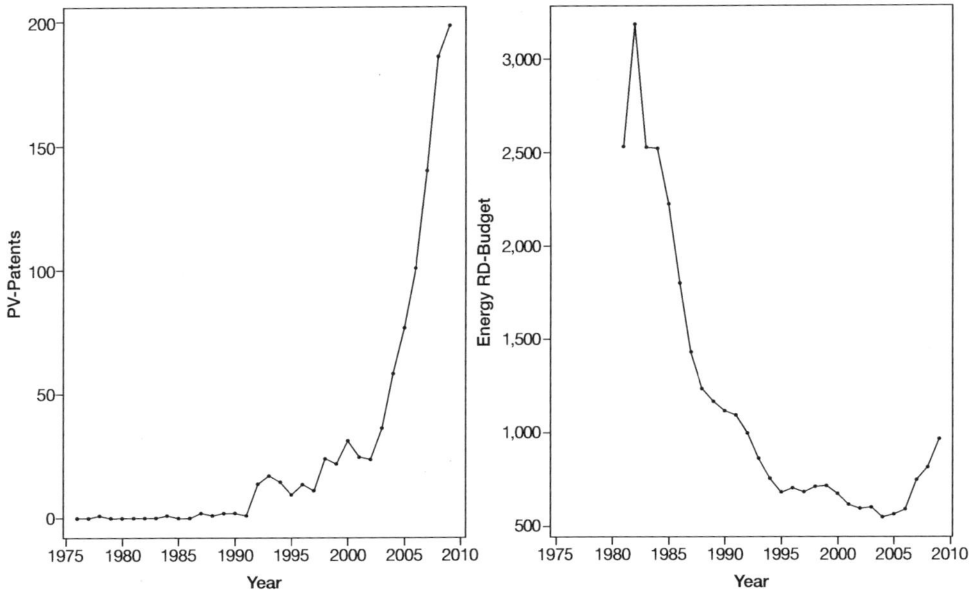

Figure 31.2 German patents and budget from 1975.
Source: OECD (http://stats.oecd.org/), own presentation.

Simulation, however, with its loose connection of virtual and real world may simply take the data "as if" it was presenting the R&D-budget on PV. I will demonstrate the capacities and limits of a simulation approach taking the case of photovoltaic cells and the available OECD data.

Validity asks if a concept corresponds accurately to the real world. Available data often do not represent exactly the part of the real world we would like to measure. In qualitative analysis this has to lead to serious doubts in the quality of the concept applied. Simulations do not claim to deal with the real world in an accurate way and therefore might be a sound way to deal with those problems. But of course you have to keep in mind that for such models the claimed analogy to the real world is very weak.

Simulating innovation policies in the field of photovoltaic cells

The production of photovoltaic cells (PV) is an interesting case of the multiple connections between politics and technology. First, energy is said to be *the* growth market of the future and all industrialized states try to stack a claim for their companies. Second, in many political calculations solar power is a key factor of the energy mix of the future: It is "green energy," it is available when consumption is highest (during the day) and, due to the geographical position of emerging economies such as Brazil, India, China, and South Africa, solar energy has one of the highest growth potentials of all energy sources actually available. Third, PV is a field that has been an object of political interventions for years. Research in this field was initiated by national R&D-budgets. Later, states such as Germany, the USA, and Japan spent huge amounts in subsidies on national markets for PV; the US and German PV-firms, especially, are suffering the effects of Chinese competition and their governments are organizing political support for their national industries.

OECD-data on politics and photovoltaic cells

To analyze the effects of political action and inter-action in the field of PV would be very interesting. But—as in many cases—the available data is not sufficient for empirical comparative analysis. The OECD provides data on the export and import of "photosensitive semiconductor devices, incl. photovoltaic cells whether/not assembled in modules/made up into panels; light emitting diodes," from 1995 onward. This data gives an idea of the activities of national industries in the field of PV, but it is not possible to distinguish between PV-cells and modules as products for the end-consumer. Therefore, the imports to one country might be part of an international production chain and may lead to additional exports. In addition, technical differentiations, e.g. between mono-crystalline and poly-crystalline or film PV-cells might be important. The OECD has data on international patents in the field of PV as well. Again, this data is very interesting but it might be insufficient because it does not reflect different national cultures in dealing with international patents and it does not represent important production steps such as silicon-manufacturing. Finally, the OECD provides data on the states' R&D-budgets in the field of "energy." Here, it is clear that R&D-initiatives for PV will be included, but the relationship between the promotion of solar and other energy sources is not clear. In addition, data on China is missing completely. Figure 31.3 shows these OECD-data budgets for Germany and the United States and on patents (including China).

In simulations, causalities are not inductively derived from data but a deducted causality is used to create data (which might be compared to the "real world" afterwards). The aim is to test whether it is possible to create a model based on simple assumptions that somehow fits the observed reality. In the case of PV, such a model does not need to be very accurate (in the

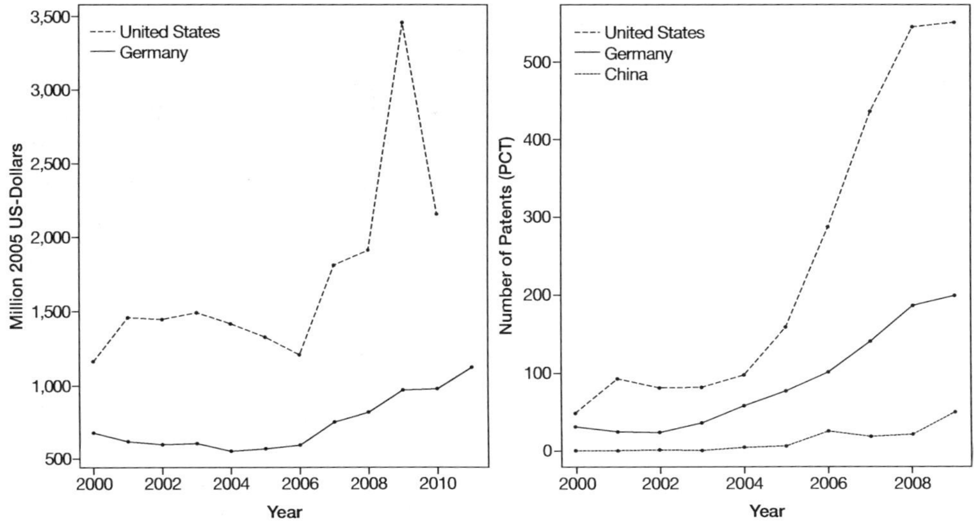

Figure 31.3 R&D energy budgets and PV patents.
Source: OECD (http://stats.oecd.org/), own presentation.

sense of fitting perfectly to the OECD-data), especially because there are serious doubts about the accuracy of the "real world"-data. So, instead of developing more advanced models that fit better to the OECD-data, I will look for breaking-points of the simple models to identify interesting research questions. Thus, the models can help to structure the research process and might even function as a tool to formulate new hypotheses.

Once you have a dataset to work on and a model that is capable of describing the general trend in the data it is always possible to improve the model so that it fits better with the data. But how good is a model that fits perfectly with a dataset that is not perfect at all? The quality of the simulation may decline with its accuracy.

Simulating budget effects on patents

To begin the simulation I assume a simple causality: R&D-budget fosters patents. Second, the necessary variables of the model have to be defined: X is the R&D-budget, Y is the simulated number of patents, a is a country-specific factor, telling us how much is spent on "R&D energy" without an effect on patents, and b is another country-specific factor, telling us how strong the effect of R&D-spending on patents is.

In our Model, Y is a linear transformation of X with country-specific factors a and b.

$$Y_i = a_c + b_c X_i$$

This equation is the standard way to notate a linear transformation (Gelman and Hill 2007: 37–39). a is the intercept. Mathematically it describes the point where the function cuts the Y-axis. In the patent simulation, this means that a budget of zero would result in a patents. b is the coefficient, telling how strongly the budget affects the number of patents. A coefficient of 1 would mean in the simulation that every million US-dollars would result in one additional patent.

The mean and standard deviation are the main indicators for characterizing functions.[3] If X is transformed in a way that the new function has the same mean and standard deviation as the "real world" patent-function, then the virtual and the real world patent function have the same main characteristics. To find out the country specifics a and b I have to use in my model, I therefore transfer X in such a way that the standard deviation and the mean equal the standard deviation and the mean of the patent data of the country. The German R&D-budget has a mean of 736 and a standard deviation of 192. German patent data has a mean of 87 and a standard deviation of 66. For the transformation, I use the following equations:[4]

$$\bar{Y} = a + b\bar{X}$$

$$S_Y = bS_X$$

The value of b can be found by dividing the patent's standard deviation by the budget's standard deviation:

$$b = \frac{66}{192} \cong 0.34$$

Now the first equation can be solved:

$$a = \overline{Y} - b\overline{X}$$
$$\rightarrow a = 87 - 0.34 * 736 \cong -163.24$$

Now the formula can be used (e.g. in Excel) to calculate the simulated values for the German patents:

$$Y_i = -163.24 + 0.34 * X_i$$

This procedure can be used to make scales comparable. However there is an underlying assumption that can cause a lot of problems: The mean and the standard deviation are adequate to describe data that is normally distributed. If the data follows a different distribution other parameters might be more relevant.

The same method is used to simulate the US patents. The results are shown in Figure 31.4.

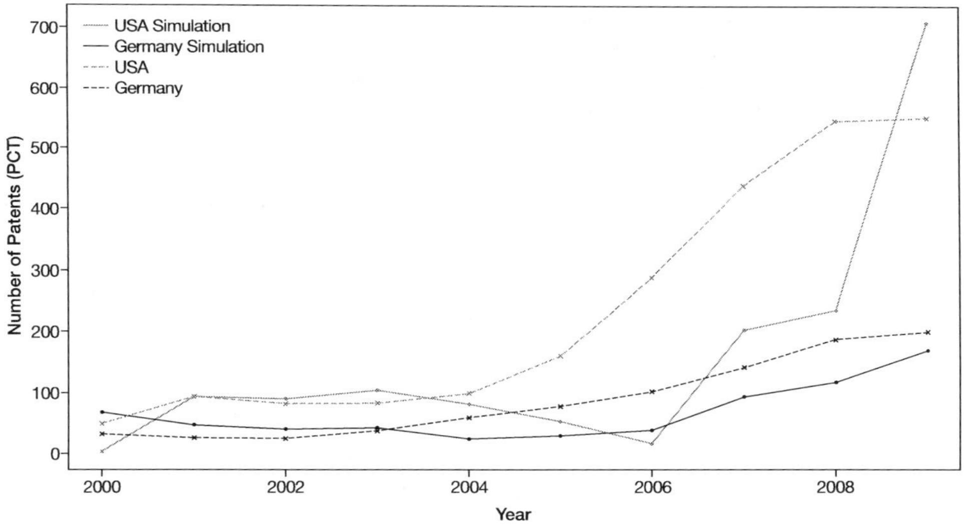

Figure 31.4 Simulation 1.
Source: Own calculation.

Step by step checklist for basic simulations:

- *Rules: Which effect do you want to simulate? What is the underlying causality of the model?*
- *Variables: What variables do you need? How do they correspond to the real world? How can the variables be represented in a formal model?*
- *Scaling: If the variables differ a lot, it is often necessary to make their scale comparable. There are different methods from statistics that can be applied for this step.*

Unsurprisingly, the number of simulated patents is more or less in line with the real development (see Figure 31.5). Instead of arguing that the simulation is a plausible analogy of "what really happens," I will now focus on the most ostensible aberration of the virtual and real world.

From 2005 to 2008 the real number of US-patents is much higher than the simulated number, while in 2009 the simulation exceeds the real data. This means, the United States had been more effective in this period than we would have expected from the experience of the whole decade. So the question arises, what has happened during this time?

There are answers to this question that could be integrated into the simulation. For example, one might argue that there is a time lag that has to be taken into account. But the main point here is that the simulation can be used to identify an interesting case for research. It would be interesting to find out what really happened. Perhaps the relative share of R&D-budgets on PV had increased within the overall energy budget. For example, the Energy Policy Act 2005, the most important US-law on energy policy in the last decades, includes an own chapter on renewable energies.

If a simulation does NOT fit with the real world phenomenon, this might be more interesting than a very smooth model. In the logic of the simulation the points where simulation and real world differ reveal an effect that has not been integrated in the model. Instead of building an artificial effect that leads to a better fit, the first thing to do is always to think about what really happened in the real world and ask whether this effect is systematic (which means it could be integrated in the simulation), erratic (then it should not be part of a general model), or systematically random (it could be integrated as a random variable, but this will lead to a highly complex model and may require methods such as Monte-Carlo simulations that are not covered in this chapter).

This example demonstrated how simulations can be used as a guide for research questions. But the potential of even simple simulations goes far beyond this first demonstration.

Simulating budget from patents

As seen in Figure 31.5, OECD does not provide data on the Chinese R&D-budget. In a second simulation, I will now try to construct these missing data. Therefore, the patent simulation is run in reverse. To work with the model, it is necessary to understand what the variables stand for and how they interact. Let's take a closer look at the country specific factors a and b that were used in the first simulation:

The coefficients for Germany and the United States are 0.31 and 0.35. An additional spending of *ca.* 3 million US-dollars will increase (in the simulation) the number of patents by one. Interestingly, the coefficients do not differ dramatically, so we could suppose that different institutional settings affect the number of patents much less than the total amount of spending.

The country specific a is –168 for Germany and –356 for the USA but these negative values are not very helpful because it does not make any sense to assume a negative number of patents in case of no R&D-spending.

But it would be very useful to know where the function cuts the X-axis: Because this point would tell how high the budget had to be to get zero patents, or in other words, how much of the energy budget has no effect on PV-patents.

$$0 = a_c + b_c X_i$$

$$\leftrightarrow X_i = -\frac{a_c}{b_c}$$

Simulation models that can be represented as linear functions are continuous models. For every X-value, there is exactly one Y-value and normal algebra can be used to identify the values for the points that are of interest.

For Germany, this *X*-value is 484 and for the United States it is 1156. For the simulation I therefore assume that these are the values of the R&D-energy-budgets that are not dedicated to PV-development. Of course, this assumption should not be confused with an assumption on causalities in the real world.[5] But these values can be used to simulate two possible Chinese R&D-budgets now:

As coefficient *b* I take 0.33 or one third, a value that is close to the observed values for the USA and Germany. Because I do not know whether the Chinese budget is more comparable to the German or to the US, I will take both intercepts to define a possible corridor in the following equation which is the basic equation of the linear transformation solved to *X*:

$$X_i = \frac{Y_i - a_c}{b_c}$$

The result can be seen in Figure 31.5.

Of course, there is a great difference between the China 1 budget simulation with the German value as intercept and the China 2 simulation with the US-value. But what is astonishing here is that the simulated budget for China is nearly static in comparison with the US and German budget. This seems to be very unlikely. It is well known that China has increased its R&D-budget in the field of energy enormously. So, it seems to be impossible to deduce the Chinese budget out of the number of patents.[6] Hence, in the German and US case this deduction works. So, again, the simulation leads us to an interesting research question: Why is China different?

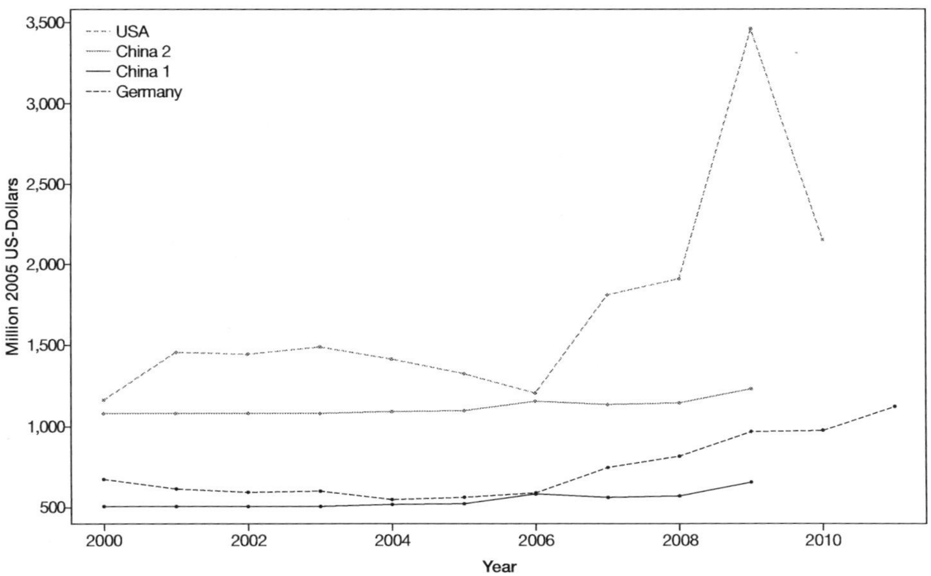

Figure 31.5 Simulation 2.

Source: Own calculation.

One possible answer would be that China uses money in a different way. Here, the accusation that China would not respect foreign intellectual property and instead of inventing new technology foster its low-price economy with state subsidies comes to mind. Obviously, to look simply on budgets is not enough to explain the effect of politics on technological innovation:

> the state when dealing with techno-industrial innovation is completely different from that which designs Keynesian programmes in economic and labour policy. Here it is not the size of the programmes that is important, and whether interest groups are involved in industrial, employment or ecological issues: simply because they do not exist forecasting of the consequences of techno-industrial innovation is highly difficult and uncertain. The policies that this state designs when fostering techno-industrial innovation are concerned with potential markets, capable national industrial structures, innovative academic research and the problem of realizing technology transfer between science and industry. Here the state does not react to strong social interests or to an economic crisis: the state is active, it takes a leading role.
>
> *(Hilpert 1991a: 4)*

A third simulation, using a totally different approach shall demonstrate how simulations could be used to test this and similar assumptions.

ABM of market strategies

In the preceding simulations mathematical equations were used as rules of the model. Those simulations can be described as continuous: For every value of *X*, there is exactly one *Y* and—as demonstrated in the lines of the figures—this is also true for all rational numbers of *X* (e.g. $\frac{5}{8}$). These continuous models are derived from a top-down view of the whole data. Agent based modeling (ABM) is a way to construct bottom-up simulations. ABM does not take datasets as a starting point but focuses on the single agents.

> By definition, ABM looks at a system not at the aggregate level but at the level of its constituent units. Although the aggregate level could perhaps be described with just a few equations of motion, the lower-level description involves describing the individual behavior of potentially many constituent units.
>
> *(Bonabeau 2002: 7287)*

The systemic interaction of the simulation is then derived from the assumptions on the agents and their interaction. In other words: ABM defines the agents of a system and *how* they interact. Then—in general—these agents are set in a timeframe of *discrete* rounds and in every round they deal with the results of their previous action. The virtual world of the simulation therefore constructs data of another "as if"-kind than the previous demonstration. The assumption is: If agents in the real world are guided in their actions by the same rules as in the simulation, the result of their interaction in virtual and real world will—*ceteris paribus*—be similar.

So ABM is a great tool to show that complex results on the macro level might arise from simple heuristics on the micro level:[7]

> At the simplest level, an agent-based model consists of a system of agents and the relationships between them. Even a simple agent-based model can exhibit complex

> behavior patterns . . . and provide valuable information about the dynamics of the real-world system that it emulates.
>
> *(Bonabeau 2002: 7280)*

ABM-basics:

- *Who are the agents? What are the properties of agents?*
- *What is the relationship between them? How does one agent effect the properties of another?*
- *How can this relationship be presented in data?*

I created a simple ABM for the case of the PV market.[8] The idea is to show how different strategies of the states may influence market performance.

As agents, I take Germany, the United States and China. Each state has two basic properties: A value for the import and one for the export of PV devices. Agents do not worry much about the *absolute* values of these properties but they try to maximize their *relative* import and export values. Therefore, agents' properties are interlinked. Figure 31.6 shows the OECD-data on the exports and imports of PV-devices. It can be seen that the United States have lost their leading role and Germany is the biggest importer of PV-devices while China has become the export champion.

The relative value of exports and imports can be understood as the share each state has on the sum of all three import and export values (Figure 31.7). This presentation demonstrates the rise of China and the fall of the US even more clearly.

A third figure is of interest: Assuming the real goal of states is their competiveness in the important strategic field of solar energy, the increase of imports might be seen negatively. On the one hand, it stands for an increasing use of solar power and—as discussed above—might even be a part of a production chain on world market level. On the other hand, the increase

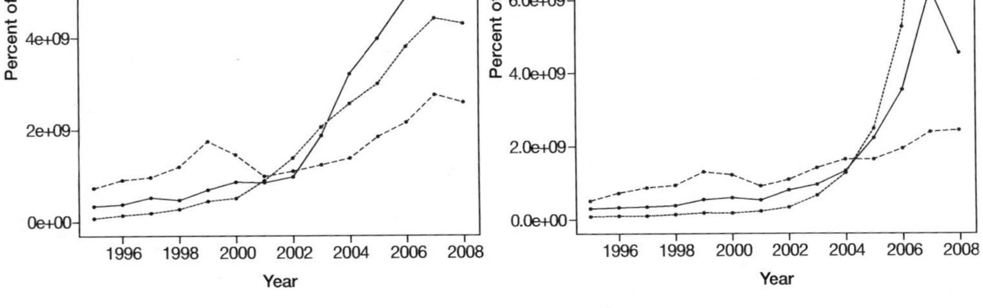

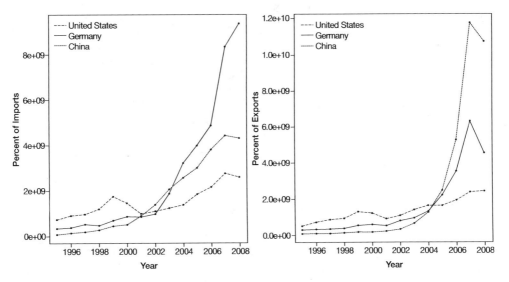

Figure 31.6 Imports and exports of PV-devices.
Source: OECD (http://stats.oecd.org/), own presentation.

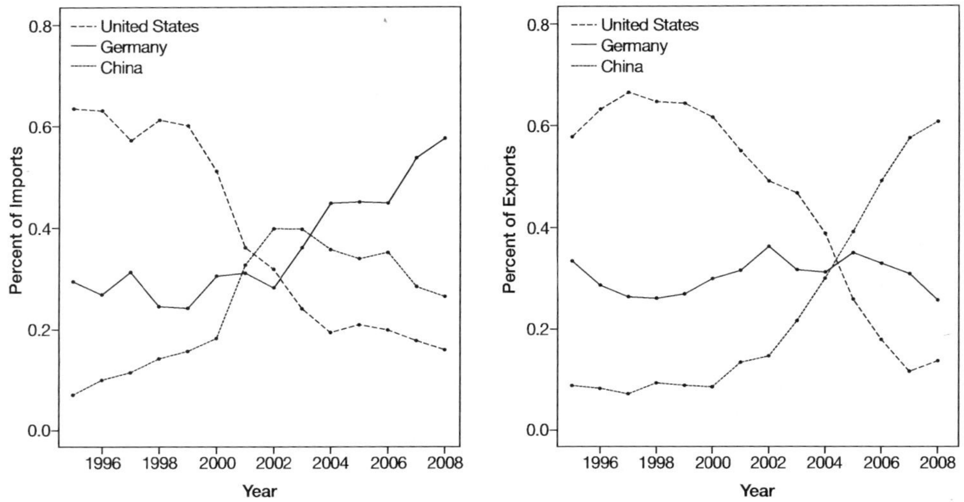

Figure 31.7 Shares of imports and exports.
Source: OECD (http://stats.oecd.org/), own calculation.

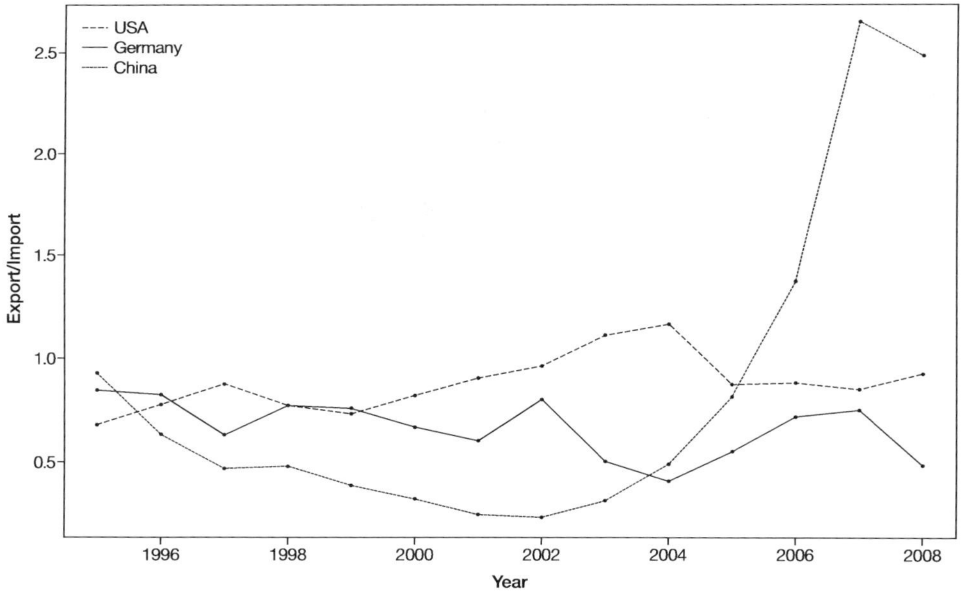

Figure 31.8 Export/import relation.
Source: OECD (http://stats.oecd.org/), own calculation.

of imports could also mean that foreign companies board the domestic market. Therefore, it is interesting to look at the relation of exports to imports. As long as this ratio stays constant, the competitiveness on the world market is not affected—either positively nor negatively.

The aim of the simulation is to recreate similar patterns as in the real world data but without referring to it—simply out of assumptions on how the agents behave. Therefore, the agents in the simulation get a third property beyond the export and import values: Each round, they choose a strategy that affects their values and therefore also the important relative values of the other agents.

I defined three strategies for the model:

- Research: The state supports research and development in the field of PV. This has a positive effect on exports and imports, because it fosters the market for PV-devices and provides competitive advantage for the domestic industry.
- Domestic market subsidies: The state subsidizes the domestic market for PV-devices. This has a strong positive effect on imports and a positive effect on exports, because the development of the domestic market again leads to competitive advantages.
- World market subsidies: The state supports domestic companies on the world market. This leads to more exports and also gradually increases the imports, because the national industry has a positive effect on the domestic market.

Of course, these strategies are not made up out of thin air but are my educated guess after studying the literature on the market of solar cells. But for the simulation it does not matter where these strategies come from but only what will evolve out of them.

The most accessible way to create one's own ABM is to use a spread-sheet software such as Microsoft Excel.[9] Spread-sheet simulation has been a common way to construct models since the 1990s (Grafton and Permaloff 1995).

The columns are used to define the variables and the rows contain the values and their development over time. The columns are specified as "Country" (defining the agent), "Year," "Import," and "Export" (the state's values in the actual year), "Strategy" (the strategy the state uses in the actual year), and two columns for every strategy containing the values by which the state's values will be changed in case the strategy is picked. The simulation can now be simply implemented by adding a function in the cells of the Import and Export values. This function should look like this:

$$C_i = IF\left(E_i = \text{'Research'};\ F_i;\ \text{IF}(E_i = \text{'Domestic Market'};\ H_i; J_i)\right) + C_h$$

where C_i is the cell in which the state's import or export value for the actual year shall be calculated, E_i is the cell in which the actual strategy is defined, F_i, H_i, and J_i are the cells in which the effects of the strategies are defined and C_h is the cell that contains last year's value for the relevant state and value. Also, the function is called "IF" in Excel, it is a nested "IF ELSE"-function: The first term in brackets is the condition. The value after the first semicolon is taken if the condition is true and the value after the next semicolon is the "else"-value. In this case this value is again conditioned.

In most cases Excel will not be the choice when it comes to building ABM. Instead, platforms such as Repast Symphony might be used. These powerful tools are often complicated to use because basic understanding of computer programming is required. But if you want to make high quality simulations, these efforts should definitely be taken.

From looking at the real world data, I had the impression that the US were following a constant strategy while China seemed to change strategy in 2000 followed by a German strategy change in 2003. Therefore, I defined the US strategy as "Research" for the whole period, the Chinese strategy as "Domestic Market" until 2000 and then as "World Market", and the German strategy as "Research" and later "Domestic Market."

In a last step, the effects of the strategies had to be defined. I chose a linear dynamic for "Research" with high starting values and progressive dynamic with the factor 2 for "Domestic Market" and "World Market."

ABM consists of agents affecting the properties of other agents by their behavior. The level of complexity is rising if the behavior of the agents has an effect on the behavior of other agents so that there is re-action. Complexity is increasing again, if not just the properties of agents but also the rules of their behavior are affected by the behavior of other agents. It is often a good starting point to implement these effects "by hand" (e.g., the changing of the strategy in the example).

This creates a dataset that can be treated exactly as the real world OECD data with the results shown in Figure 31.9, 31.10, and 31.11, all of which are highly comparable to their real world pendants. Especially the simulated import distribution is hard to discern from the real world figure. One main deviation can be found in the German development in the 1990s. While the simulation predicts a moderate increase followed by a moderate decline before the strategy change in 2003, the real world data seems to indicate a moderate decline in exports and imports followed by an increase. This might hint at a wrong selection of the first strategy for Germany. For example, Hilpert argues for a mixed strategy of research and export to developing countries, referring to the 1980s (Hilpert 1991b: 94–98), but mixed strategies cannot be integrated in this simple model.

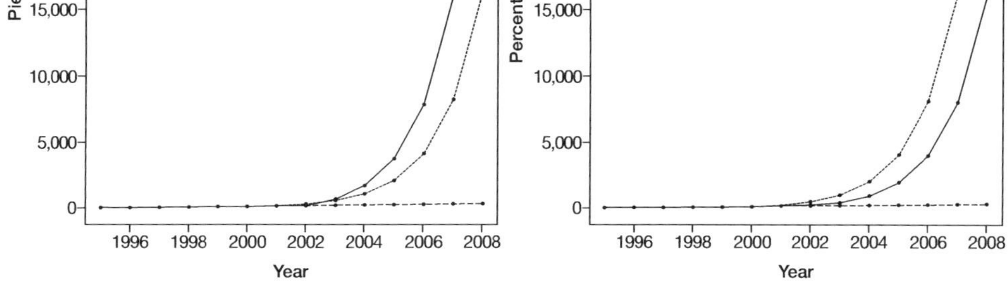

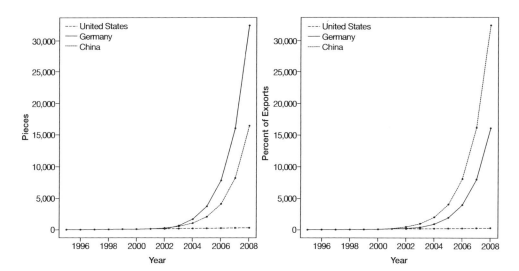

Figure 31.9 Simulated imports and exports.
Source: Own calculation.

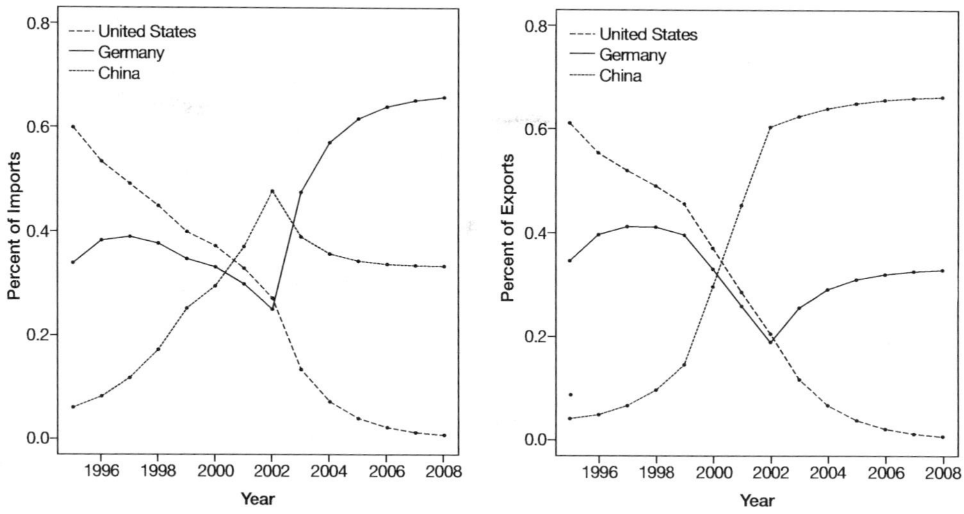

Figure 31.10 Simulated shares of imports and exports.
Source: Own calculation.

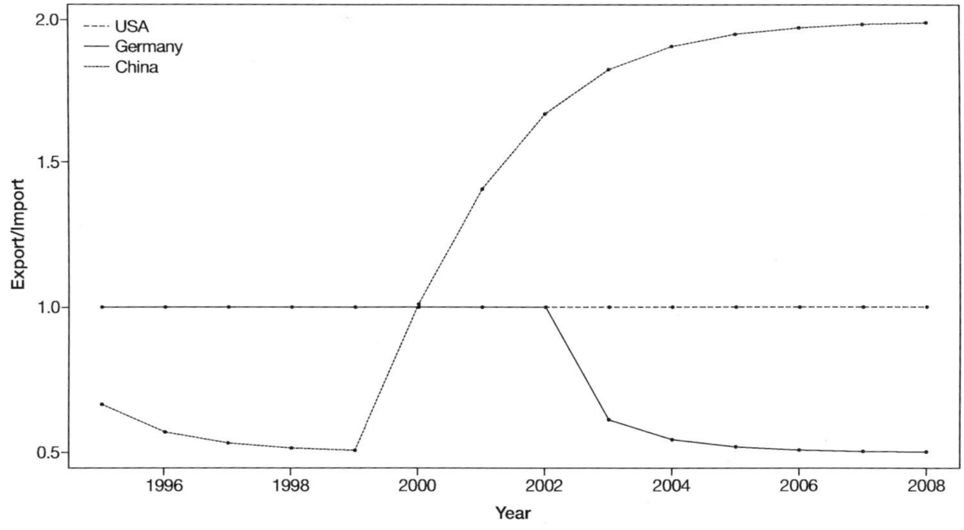

Figure 31.11 Simulated export/import relations.
Source: Own calculation.

Of course, all details are missing. For example there was a decrease in imports and exports in 2008—probably as a result of the financial crisis—that cannot be re-created by the simple rules.

To present a model that fits well to the data on which the model was developed is often not very convincing. As with quantitative models, it is good practice to divide the data into two sets before the model is built: one to create and fit the model, one to test it later.

In ABM the understanding of an agent is strongly influenced by object oriented programming. Often, different classes of agents are defined, so that an agent might have nothing to do with a real world entity that is "acting" in any way. E.g., the environment might be defined as an agent, or the simulation has a "watcher" included that is just an entity in the simulation gathering the values of certain variables—defined as an agent as well.

Outlook

One way of further research would be to optimize the models. It would be easy to find values that fit even better or to add rules that make the virtual picture even more realistic.

More demanding—and also more interesting—is again the way back to the real world. The central assumption of the last model is that research changes from a superior strategy to a relatively weak strategy in comparison to the other strategies. Is this plausible? If there had been a change in strategies, this must have become visible in real world policies. Is there empirical evidence for such an assumption? In the simulation China is the winner because of the superior use of strategies. Why do the USA and Germany not adopt the same strategy? Or more generally: What kinds of strategies are available and how do states decide which to pick? The last questions especially offer a strong link to research on regional knowledge and development (see Hilpert 2006), because from a political science perspective it is obvious that strategies are only available if they fit with the regional and institutional background. ABM simulations especially can add important aspects to the analysis of such "path dependencies" because they can show how continuous patterns derive from simple heuristics.

These questions—again—demonstrate the strength of the simulation approach. It is not a way to prove causal explanations[10] but it is an aid to intuition. And of course, this is the basic weakness, as well:

> One issue is common to all modeling techniques: a model has to serve a purpose; a general-purpose model cannot work. The model has to be built at the right level of description, with just the right amount of detail to serve its purpose; this remains an art more than a science.
>
> *(Bonabeau 2002: 7287)*

Notes

1 Eppstein even goes a step further and describes agent based models as "generic" in differentiation to deductive or inductive approaches (Eppstein 1999).
2 Johnson provides a broad discussion of the strength and weaknesses of simulations versus statistical methods in political science (Johnson 1999).
3 Any software for statistical proposes—including Microsoft Excel—offers standard deviation and mean as predefined functions.
4 A good explanation of these formulas can be found in Stockburger's "Introductory Statistics" at www.psychstat.missouristate.edu/introbook/sbk15.htm.
5 Taken seriously, this assumption would mean that at least the relative proportion of the budget share that is dedicated to PV would stay constant.
6 The recent work of de la Tour et al. offers a great explanation: They show that China is very innovative in the field of silicon production (De la Tour et al. 2011). This is one reason why the OECD patent statistics are not valid for the Chinese innovation capacity.
7 The term "simple heuristics" refers to the work of Simon (1983), Gigerenzer (2008), and Todd (2001). The theory of bounded rationality has been very productive in simulation approaches (Manson 2006; Rosenfeld and Kraus 2010).

8 It should be noted that there are complex ABM in the field of electricity markets (Wang et al. 2009) and for national solar power markets (Roloff et al. 2009).
9 Most accessible does not mean most preferable. For complex models special software tools such as Repast Symphony are of great help (Druckenmiller et al. 2004; Macal and North 2010).
10 Because of the division of virtual and real worlds, a positive proof is not possible. But there are many excellent examples of simulation falsifying theorems, e.g., Klahr's early work on the paradox of voting (Klahr 1966) or Lin's work on party competition (Lin 2008).

References

Axelrod, R., 2003: Advancing the Art of Simulation in the Social Sciences. *Japanese Journal for Management Information System* 12, pp. 1–19.

Behnke, J., 2009: Simulation. In: Schnapp, K.-U., Behnke, N. and Behnke, J. (Eds.): *Datenwelten—Datenerhebung und Datenbestände in der Politikwissenschaft*. Baden-Baden: Nomos, pp. 174–195.

Bonabeau, E., 2002: Agent-based modeling: methods and techniques for simulating human systems. *PNAS* 99, pp. 7280–7287.

De la Tour, A., Glachant, M. and Ménière, Y., 2011: Innovation and international technology transfer: the case of the Chinese photovoltaic industry. *Energy Policy* 39, pp. 761–770.

Druckenmiller, D., Acar, W. and Troutt, M., 2004: Agent-based Modeling and Simulation of Strategic Scenarios with Repast 2.0. Paper submitted to Swarmfest 2004. Kent: Graduate School of Management, Kent University.

Eppstein, J.M., 1999: Agent-based computational models and generative social Science. *Complexity* 4, pp. 41–60.

Gelman, A. and Hill, J., 2007: *Data Analysis Using Regression and Multilevel/Hierarchical Models*. New York: Cambridge University Press.

Gigerenzer, G., 2008: *Rationality for Mortals. Evolution and cognition*. Oxford: Oxford University Press.

Grafton, C. and Permaloff, A., 1995: Computer modeling using spreadsheets and related software. *PS: Political Science and Politics* 28, pp. 500–504.

Hilpert, U., 1991a: The state, science and techno-industrial innovation. In: Hilpert, U. (Ed.): *State Policies and Techno-Industrial Innovation*. New York: Routledge, pp. 3–39.

Hilpert, U., 1991b: Economic adjustment by techno-industrial innovation and the role of the state. In: Hilpert, U. (Ed.): *State Policies and Techno-Industrial Innovation*. New York: Routledge, pp. 85–106.

Hilpert, U., 2006: Knowledge in the region: development based on tradition, culture and change. *European Planning Studies* 15, pp. 581–599.

Johnson, P.E., 1999: Simulation modeling in political science. *American Behavioral Scientist* 42, pp. 1509–1530.

Klahr, D., 1966: A computer simulation of the paradox of voting. *American Political Science Review* 60, pp. 384–390.

Lin, J.-S., 2008: Learning and party competition. *Swiss Political Science Review* 14, pp. 131–55.

Macal, C.M. and North, M.J., 2010: Tutorial on agent-based modelling and simulation. *Journal of Simulation* 4, pp. 151–162.

Manson, S.M., 2006: Bounded rationality in agent-based models: experiments with evolutionary programs. *International Journal of Geographical Information Science* 20, pp. 991–1012.

OECD, 2015. Available online at: http://stats.oecd.org/Index.aspx/App_Themes/OECD/img/logo/Controls/Controls/Index.aspx?DataSetCode=ICTGRP# (accessed June 09, 2015).

Roloff, N., Lehr, U. und Krewitt, W., 2009: Modelling the Effects of Technology-Push and Demand-Pull Policies on Technological Change in the Energy Sector. Available online at: www.aaee.at/2009-IAEE/uploads/fullpaper_iaee09/P_178_Roloff_Nils_27-Aug-2009,%2015:50.pdf (accessed August 18, 2012).

Rosenfeld, A. and Kraus, S., 2010: Modeling agents based on aspiration adaptation theory. *Autonomous Agents and Multi-Agent Systems* 24, pp. 221–254.

Simon, H.A., 1983: *Models of Bounded Rationality*. Cambridge, MA: MIT Press.

Simon, H.A., 2008: *The Sciences of the Artificial*. Cambridge, MA: MIT Press.

Todd, P.M., 2001: Fast and frugal heuristics for environmentally bounded minds. In: Gigerenzer, G. and Selten, R. (Eds.): *Bounded Rationality: The adaptive toolbox*. Cambridge, MA: MIT Press, pp. 51–70.

Wang, J., Botterud, A., Conzelmann, G. and Koritarov, V.S., 2009: Multi-agent system for short and long-term power market simulations. *International Journal of Innovations in Energy Systems and Power* 4, pp. 36–43.

PART 8

Conclusions

32

CONCLUSIONS

New phenomena and advanced analysis – exploring variations for a deeper understanding of a rich diversity of technologies and innovations

Ulrich Hilpert

This handbook has turned the key to open some of the doors that expose the relationship between politics and technology, and that help to understand some of the conditions of new technology development, of innovation, and of technology problem solving through policies in divergent governmental systems and involving different political interests. This is a fairly young area of the social and political sciences and requires research. It is clearly not an area that remains within the boundaries of individual disciplines, but requires mutual learning. It demonstrates that academia and its disciplines are permanently developing as they seek to understand new phenomena such as modern high-technology and its relationship to society, economy and ecology – and, that political science, as an interdisciplinary approach, can make its contribution while exchanging ideas and findings with neighbouring disciplines. As governments and political interventions pursue particular processes of economic and social development, new technologies become fundamentally important, and research on the relationship between politics and technology may help our understanding of whether there are opportunities productively to influence socio-economic developments that respect divergent interests and the condition of the ecosystem. Thus, the relationship between the political system and technologies is more than a mere matter of influence alone: it refers directly to the efficacy of proactive government policies – which are reflective social, cultural, geographic and political situations – when solving economic and social problems that can impact fundamentally on conditions of life and social welfare.

These relationships can also be viewed the other way round, because new technologies and high-technology industries create opportunities for divergent policies that reflect the needs of different interests. In many places and situations, new interests emerge once the opportunities of new technologies and innovations become known or can be applied. Thus, *metropolises* are of particular interest, since scientific breakthroughs, new technologies and the most advanced processes of innovation concentrate at these locations. Already, the recent economic and financial crisis demonstrates variations in coping with such challenges. Metropolises (and the enterprises based in them) that engage in high-technology manufacturing and services clearly performed better and have lower levels of unemployment than other locations – in particular in comparison to locations dominated by finance and realty services. This needs additional research and indicates that the current state of knowledge is not yet sufficient to explain these processes, nor the role of metropolises in *divergent governmental systems*. In particular, there is not sufficient understanding of their *socio-economic, cultural and historical situations* and opportunities. More systematic research is needed that uses these territorial concentrations to understand the transfer of knowledge, personnel and competences in *collaborative networks* across continents, or even between continents. Here it is clear that political systems and government policies play a fundamental role for such developments – but, there are *differences between democratic systems and authoritarian countries*, and further divergences across societies and cultures.

Such open questions engage a wide range of *research, and they also indicate a need for research to identify and explain a systematic, long term relationship* rather than just an issue of current, and perhaps passing interest. They may help build a better understanding of the process of new technology development and innovation, which is obviously closely – though differently – related to political systems and policies. While there is almost always a direct or indirect relationship between political decisions and the supply of funds, or the organisation of particular contexts based on the policies involved, it is still an open question, how these interrelate. Further research on different innovatory contexts will widen our knowledge and contribute to such an understanding. In addition, and in relation to that body of knowledge, there is a need for a deeper understanding of the *relationship between different situations and the contexts in which they emerge*. This forms the arena of political intervention and impact. Analysing individual situations in the light of their opportunities and limitations will provide additional systematic understanding of both the process of techno-industrial innovation and the role of government.

Such phenomena need to be identified and to become the subject of further interdisciplinary research that is based on the existing findings and is complemented by a view that includes the *embeddedness of regional or metropolitan development* within a trans-national or continental context. Metropolises are constantly increasing in their importance for new technologies and concerning processes of innovation proximity need to be reconsidered as they have at least the potential to become a virtual dimension. Short travel times between distant metropolises and close relationships, because of previous collaborations or exchange of researchers, academics and knowledge workers, indicate a changing situation for future processes; while trans-national or continental networks have been built between locations of outstanding technological and scientific competences. Paying particular reference to the dominance of Islands of Innovation (which concentrate about two thirds of all capabilities and collaborations), the increasing importance of metropolises indicates their role as dynamic centres of future high-technology development. This implicitly raises the question of continentalisation, and the relationship between such systems. In addition, the concentration of Islands of Innovation, which help to build collaborative networks, are mostly based in metropolises. This raises the question of whether there is a 'metropolisation' of such processes – because these networks are increasingly formed linking such outstanding locations. Understanding such concentration of innovative development will help us to understand the direction of collaborations towards trans-national or continental systems of innovation. Additionally it will help us to understand how new Islands of Innovation in metropolises emerge and may link with the collaborative systems of innovation. This emergence and collaboration may relate to complementary situations, because of divergent competences, and it may pose the question of whether there is more competition among the locations, or whether there will be more opportunities because of the growing number of metropolises and their growing bodies of knowledge.

Although there is, of course, competition and a *global race in innovation and new technologies*, there is a global body of knowledge and a clear advantage in collaboration. The international division of labour is changing. This can be seen when new technologies and academic research are considered. Mutual advantages in collaboration provide opportunities that cannot be realised without networks and the exchange of knowledge and collaboration to make new findings. Different Islands of Innovation, newly emerging innovative metropolises, and contributions from different countries add more than pure knowledge. Traditions in academic research and industrial applications, divergent scientific cultures and applications of technology all vary, and thus there is divergent tacit knowledge that creates variations in research and technology. Divergent techno-industrial and sociocultural constellations at the different Islands of Innovation and metropolises in countries with different cultures and political systems all contribute to a *global body of knowledge that is shared by all contributors*. Exchange and collaboration builds synergy among potential competitors for the mutual benefit of those ready to contribute and to exploit this knowledge in collaboration. Continental and trans-continental networks might inhibit this potential and, thus, provide the subject of research to understand the changes in the international division of labour when it comes to new technologies. The *identification of networks in new technologies* and a better knowledge of the situation of the Islands of Innovation and metropolises involved will help us to understand the particular opportunities of countries and regions that relate to their specific contributions that relate to the origin of knowledge and its application. A deeper understanding of these contributions and of networks will help to identify new and changing tendencies in the international division of labour concerning knowledge-based and research-intensive technological products.

The importance of both regional or metropolitan concentrations of high-technology potential and of political decisions about government policies, indicate a direct relationship with international processes concerning new technologies. Governmental structures that are flexible with regard to regional or metropolitan situations, as well as having significant funds for research and development provided, will perform differently from those that are highly centralised, bureaucratic and insufficiently funded. Thus, *regions, metropolises and technologies need to be considered in the light of the governmental systems* and their budgetary opportunities, in order to explore a better understanding of the divergent international performances of countries. Tradition, history and culture combine with existing capabilities of governmental systems to form a particular situation that can be identified through the different networks of collaboration, exchange and trade. Although these situations show strong stability over time, they do change because of both the continuing development of new technologies and the opportunities for new locations to emerge and contribute to these networks. The continuity of Islands of Innovation is an ongoing, dynamic process that on the one hand privileges existing strong locations when continuing their engagement in innovation processes, but on the other hand allows new participants to be included.

In any case, there is a relationship between policies and governmental systems that provides fundamentally for such opportunities in divergent ways and concerning different elements of innovation. The existing situation at a location, and the close contact of policy makers with it, indicates the importance of particular decisions about the modernisation of industries and the application of new technologies. Such continuation and change also clearly relate to university trained and highly skilled blue collar labour – as a basis for new and innovative enterprises, or to make use of the technological opportunities of existing industries. In addition, highly specialised and capable services can help such socio-economic development to flourish. The variety of situations in countries, regions and metropolises, in conjunction with the divergences of technologies and industries, of course provides a rich variation that requires a *systematic view concerning their similarities and divergences*, as this will help to integrate the rich body of existing and future knowledge of cases into a systematic relationship. There is strong need to explore and understand these varieties, which will help us to understand opportunities of political decision and support.

Public funding of academic research and particular technology programmes is considered to be in the interest of an entire country and its society. Innovation based on new technologies may provide attractive jobs and opportunities for university trained and highly skilled labour. Traditional industries may continue based on new technologies. Finally, such technologies may also help to protect the natural environment and to provide the energy required by society. But, in contrast to such public interests and public funding, there is private exploitation of new scientific findings that are fundamental to new technologies as highly attractive and marketable products. While liberal Western democracies make a distinct differentiation between private life and public affairs, here it is the opposite, when *public funding provides for private exploitation and private profits*. It is an open question, whether private exploitation will provide sufficient public benefits, through growth of enterprises and attractive job opportunities. In addition, it raises the question whether such privatisation of profits vs a socialisation of costs is acceptable in the different Western countries or whether this is to be understood in relationship to other political decisions on taxation, labour market policies, social welfare etc. Thus, it needs to be asked to what extent such privatisation is a systematic approach and an *appropriate path to generate public benefits – or are there dominant ideologies and interest groups* able to gain inequitable benefits from the socio-economic effects of new technologies and innovative industries.

Societies vary and so do their ideas about both the distribution of benefits and about opportunities for participation based on university education and the skills of blue collar workers. Some countries, as in continental Europe, consider education should be widely provided for free at universities. Gifted individuals may have the chance to enjoy university education. Income and family background may not matter, or at least matter less. While there are differences among countries and national models of financing, and university education may vary in its content and quality, in general they all agree that more and higher educated and skilled personnel is demanded by constantly growing high-technology industries and innovative enterprises. While some countries may produce more graduates than appropriate jobs, others can attract graduates in a brain drain and use immigration to supply the extra labour they require. Star scientists may migrate to 'magnets' of science or Islands of Innovation where they find attractive incomes and the best research opportunities. Cultures, languages and life opportunities may play a fundamental role, and will provide more advantages for some countries than others. Thus it is the question of *providing education and skills to a constantly growing number of people that may make societies more innovative* than others – by providing the human capital demanded. Providing such highly needed skills is closely dependent upon governmental education and training policies.

But, this kind of human capital is based on the education of brains that may not have been taken into consideration before. Education and education policies are frequently associated with the question of who will participate in these opportunities. Societies vary in their participation rates in education, and thus they *vary by the extent of their untapped talent and the unexploited opportunities provided by capable individuals* who have not passed through higher education. An under-representation of women in some disciplines and in universities in general indicates both the problem and the opportunities. Similarly, minorities in general are under-represented in higher education of Western countries. Countries may demonstrate different levels of participation in higher education and advanced skills. But, still there is a general phenomenon of uneven opportunities and this raises the interesting and open question of whether *innovative societies are associated with a different attitude towards women and minorities* as resources of potentially highly educated human capital. More socially open educational systems of high quality may find themselves in a different situation and may perform differently when it comes to new technologies and innovative industries.

This transforms a question of equal opportunities into a matter of innovative societies and the role of political decisions and government policies for new technologies and innovative industries – and it needs a different perspective on these problems and situations. While in the past it was a question of democratic participation, it now becomes a fundamental question of advanced socio-economic development based on high-technology. Now, the issue clearly reaches out much further than just science and industry, but non-economic processes indicate their socio-economic importance and they relate to areas that are not technology and research policies, but clearly indicate their relationship to such developments and are fundamental to such processes.

The identification of such phenomena in specific situations and contexts will contribute further to our knowledge about new technologies and innovation. Since this knowledge will relate to the entire process it will suggest a wider impact than just on the economy and science. While, for a long time, the Western liberal democracies of Europe and the US were the leading countries in scientific research, new technologies and innovative industries, today this traditional geographic interrelationship is not as certain anymore. In science and technological application *countries with non-democratic or authoritarian systems have established strong competences and capabilities*. Although freedom of thought was always considered to be fundamental for flourishing scientific research and the application of new technologies, it might not be that certain anymore. Thus, it is an open question *whether innovation and technologies need liberal democratic systems* and appropriate policies. Some countries (e.g. Korea), of course, do suggest that there is a change in culture and political freedom associated with processes of techno-industrial innovation. Nevertheless, it remains as an open question whether there are more creative ideas when there is more freedom of thought. While successful industrialisation and modern mass production is also realised in authoritarian and non-democratic systems, in Western societies the freedom of the liberal arts and social sciences is associated with a political and social development that underpins the existing situations of highly innovative development and technological breakthroughs.

Clearly, there is a diversity of technologies, processes of techno-industrial innovation, political situations and political systems that need attention and an explanation, which also takes into consideration the relationships of regional development embedded in continental or trans-continental networks of collaboration and exchange, emerging roles of metropolises in different governmental systems, and government policies reflecting in the light of divergent cultures and societies. The increasing and deepening interrelationships in the development of new technologies and the innovative application of contributions from many locations and countries (based on divergent areas of creativity) require an identification of the variables associated with explanations both of the basis of their expertise and their contribution to new technologies that expand national or even continental capabilities. In the end, identifying and explaining this diversity and how it is integrated in the entire process of research and development requires understanding of the process as a system – and understanding of the role of policies and politics in different political systems that enable a national or even a metropolitan contribution and participation in new technologies and innovation. Such diversity might be as rich as the *diversity of political systems and interests* that are associated with different societies, cultures, industries and histories. They may vary in their technologies but they may help understanding of the relationship involved and the *role of political decisions to support new technologies*, and they may also help us to understand why these relationships may take different expressions.

Thus, the different areas that await further academic exploration and explanation need to widen the knowledge about the diversity and the systematic relationships that permit such processes, but they need to consider the whole situation. Contexts and individual processes may be explored and put into an explanation that then leads to further questions and research on areas not yet anticipated. But it is clear that the relationship between new technologies and political decisions immediately reaches out across different academic disciplines that can benefit from contributing to a better picture of this highly complex process. Understanding individual regions, metropolises and countries in the light of societies, cultures and continental or trans-continental systems of collaboration may indicate the *varieties of techno-industrial opportunities that are enabled through policies that reflect divergent politics in different political systems*. The integration of fields of research in different projects, and investigation from different viewpoints, help to link the broad fields of new technologies, innovation and political intervention. Understanding regions or metropolises as part of both the national situation and the collaborative system of innovations permits the mutual use of such findings to learn about regions and about transnational or transcontinental collaboration processes. Finally, embedding the regions into such a context brings divergent cultures and societies into the interpretation of such processes.

The analysis of this rich diversity demands *specific methods* and *the identification of the opportunities for political intervention*. Clearly, strategies and successful policies at one location may not have the same effects at a different location. Since contexts differ, the variables at work in them need to be identified clearly and this will require many studies. The rich variety of innovatory contexts requires comparative research and the further development of methods that suit the divergent situations being studied, and that take advantage of an interdisciplinary body of knowledge. While some indicators are already well employed and some tendencies have emerged in different political systems, a widening body of research into areas not yet investigated will need methods that allow for comparison and the identification of new variables and indicators. Thus, future research includes a constant improvement of the methods that can be employed in comparative research.

While such research helps to establish a better and wider understanding, it needs to be taken into consideration that new technologies and innovation are processes of development that reach fruition at certain moments in time and space and reflect particular opportunities. As certain situations may change with regard to both opportunities and context, they may not be ready for replication elsewhere at a different time, or in divergent social, cultural and political situations. Although it is quite impressive that some policy instruments are employed in divergent political systems, and by different political ideologies, the development of new technologies is clearly a relationship between political decisions that aim at initiating such processes and the opportunities that exist. There are, of course, windows of opportunity that are open only to those who qualify and they close rather quickly once an innovatory system is established that clearly privileges the locations and countries that participate in the network from the very beginning. New players enter with new findings, new technologies or new applications – but the existing situation, which has formed on the basis of a window of opportunity, will not be changed fundamentally. Since windows of opportunity change and technologies are characterised by aging, time matters a lot for understanding technologies and innovation, and also for understanding the role of political decisions and support. Once such a relationship is understood in the light of a certain point in time and development, it will help in making an advanced comparison, and in understanding how governments can influence technology development, areas of expertise and opportunities to make such processes faster – thus, time becomes an important subject of research and provides a method of scientific investigation.

The area of politics and technology allows for contributions based on modern political science in collaboration with other social sciences. New technologies, as a field of political science with an interdisciplinary orientation, can provide views and findings that match those of other disciplines and take advantage of the exchange of ideas and findings. It is, of course, more than a mere documentation of interests and bargaining – it is related to opportunities for political intervention and the inducement of development. Political programmes in different situations and systems play an important role in the highly divergent opportunities for technological development and for locations in different countries. Further research will need a close collaboration with other disciplines to identify the opportunities of political programmes and the role of interests in such programmes in different systems. Even more, it may explain about the opportunities for intervention to support processes that are fundamental for future socio-economic developments that are based on new technologies and innovation. While investigating these important phenomena *modern political science* can use the relationship of political decisions with new technologies and innovation for more systematic research and to make an important contribution to knowledge and policy making. It will help to develop a *deeper understanding of opportunities and diversities of development based on new technologies and appropriate public policies*.

INDEX